THE INSIDER
2000

Gary Gillette and Stuart Shea
with Doug White and Peter Palmer

Organizational Reports by Jim Keller
and Joe Barbieri, Howe Sportsdata

Total Sports
New York

Copyright © 2000 by Total Sports, Inc.
All rights reserved. No part of this book may be reproduced or transmitted in any form or by any means, electronic or mechanical, including photocopying, recording, or by any information storage and retrieval system, without the permission of the publisher.

For information about permission to reproduce selections from this book, please write to:
Permissions
Total Sports, Inc.
100 Enterprise Drive
Kingston, NY
12401
Total Sports™ is a trademark of Total Sports, Inc.

Interior design: Erin Monty

ISSN 1523-4428
ISBN 1-892129-15-9

First Edition 2000
Printed in United States of America
10 9 8 7 6 5 4 3 2 1

Book produced by Balliett & Fitzgerald, Inc.

ACKNOWLEDGEMENTS

Several good people played major behind-the-scenes roles in the publishing of *The Insider*. Special thanks to John Thorn and Jed Thorn at Total Sports, to Tom Dyja at Balliett and Fitzgerald, and to Paul White at *Baseball Weekly*.

David W. Smith, President of Retrosheet, was more than gracious, as always, in sharing his research on Candlestick Park, Dodger Stadium, Sandy Koufax, and Greg Maddux.

Many Total Sports baseball stringers contributed opinions and analysis on their team, making *The Insider* better for their help. Alphabetical thanks to Bob Biermann, Jeff Campbell, Rich Carletti, Barb Davis, Michael Duca, Joe Elinich, Larry Epke, Bob Gale, Kevin Hennessy, Brigg Hewitt, Dic Humphrey, John Matthew IV, Fred Percival, Jim Planamento, Mal Romanin, Denis Repp, Frank Schetski, Tom Shea, Randy Shedelbower, Dale Stevens, Wes Tervo, Ted Turocy, Hank Widmer, and Jim Wohlenhaus.

Finally, our all-too-often-unspoken gratitude to Vicki Gillette, Cecilia Garibay, and Anita White. They really should get co-bylines, even though they didn't write a word.

CONTENTS

Introduction 4
Essays 7
   The Retrosheet Story: Restoring Baseball's Past 8
   Sandy Versus the Surgeon 14
   Darryl, We Hardly Knew Ye 18
   They Don't Make Wonders of the World Like They Used to 19
   Chasing Henry 22
Team Reports 24
Projections 280

AMERICAN LEAGUE

AL Wild Card Race	24
Eastern Division	**26**
Baltimore Orioles	28
Boston Red Sox	36
New York Yankees	44
Tampa Bay Devil Rays	52
Toronto Blue Jays	60
Central Division	**68**
Chicago White Sox	70
Cleveland Indians	78
Detroit Tigers	86
Kansas City Royals	94
Minnesota Twins	102
Western Division	**110**
Anaheim Angels	112
Oakland Athletics	120
Seattle Mariners	128
Texas Rangers	136

NATIONAL LEAGUE

NL Wild Card Race	144
Eastern Division	**146**
Atlanta Braves	148
Florida Marlins	156
Montreal Expos	164
New York Mets	172
Philadelphia Phillies	180
Central Division	**188**
Chicago Cubs	190
Cincinnati Reds	198
Houston Astros	206
Milwaukee Brewers	214
Pittsburgh Pirates	222
St. Louis Cardinals	230
Western Division	**238**
Arizona Diamondbacks	240
Colorado Rockies	248
Los Angeles Dodgers	256
San Diego Padres	264
San Francisco Giants	272

INTRODUCTION

Welcome to *The Baseball Weekly Insider 2000*, Total Sports' spring baseball annual. We've worked very hard on *The Insider*, and we hope that the book shows the results of that hard work as well as our passion for the game.

GAME REPORTS. The opening section of the book contains five general essays on a variety of topics.

TEAM REPORTS. Each team chapter consists of six parts: an introductory page summarizing the 1999 season, an essay, several sidebars, an organization report, capsule scouting reports on four top prospects, and a depth chart as of the winter meetings in December. Most changes that occurred after mid-December won't be reflected in the book, but you can find updates on *The Insider*'s Web site during spring training.

DIVISIONAL and WILD CARD RACES. Each League and Division is introduced with a chart plotting the number of each team's wins against weeks of the season, giving a new way of looking at the year and the title races.

TEAM SUMMARY PAGES. The top of the page shows information about the team management as well as details of the team's '99 record, along with a set of statistics that give an overview of the '99 season. Management information includes career records for each team's manager at the end of 1999 as well as its 2000 skipper, if different. Similar career records for GMs and owners are also shown. The only difference is that these records are compiled from the start of their first season with the current team.

Twelve breakdowns of each team's 1999 record follow. The pre-season consensus projection line shows the average finish predicted for that team by nationally published sources before the 1999 season, three of which need some explaining. "Comebacks" are games in which a team wins (or loses) after trailing (or leading) by as many runs as there are innings left in the game. The same standard applies in reverse for blowing leads ("comeback" losses). This sliding scale was set up to avoid having a team get credit for a cheap comeback by overcoming a two-run deficit in the fourth inning. "Blowouts" are games that are won or lost by five or more runs. Despite conventional wisdom, blowouts are a far better indicator of a team's overall strength than its record in close games. "Nail-biters" are games that are won by one or two runs. While contending teams generally have good records in close games, these contests are frequently decided by one chance bounce of the ball rather than skill. Mediocre teams can have excellent records in close games and thereby become contenders, but look for a serious fall-off the following year.

The final section on the page, "Numbers Don't Lie," plots the team's league ranking in nine categories, its opponents' ranking, and the league average.

ESSAYS AND SIDEBARS. Throughout each team chapter, various sidebars discuss different aspects of the 1999 season.

ORGANIZATION REPORTS. Each team report includes a review of that team's organization prepared by Jim Keller and the staff of Howe Sportsdata. Howe is the official statistician for all minor-leagues, and Jim is the foremost expert writing on the minor-leagues today. His analysis of top prospects has been featured for years in *Baseball Weekly* as well as other national publications. Four top prospects for each team are also featured separately in "Under the Microscope."

For updated information about these and other prospects in each organization, check out *The Insider*'s web site during spring training and early in the 2000 season.

DEPTH CHARTS. These are graphical analyses of the status of each position in that organization as of mid-December. The legend printed at the bottom of each chart explains the information included.

Players are shown at their primary positions, with major-leaguers at the top and minor-leaguers underneath. The incumbent from the 1999 season or the projected regular for 2000 at each position is in boldface, with reserves below. Because of off-season player moves and because many veteran players had not yet signed with a team for 2000 as of December, there are not necessarily big-league incumbents at each position on some teams. Ages as of July 1, 2000, are printed after player names, as well as how they bat or throw.

Minor leaguers are shown in order by their level: a prospect who spent most of the '99 season at Triple-A would be listed above someone at Double-A, who would be above someone at Advanced Class A, etc. Therefore, the order in which minor-leaguers are shown does not necessarily reflect what kind of prospects they are.

Additional information is shown for all players who did not establish themselves in the major-leagues last year. The prospect rating system distinguishes between the best prospects and fringe prospects; the minor-league level, the draft round, and draft year are also shown. All minor-leaguers who were in Triple-A (3A), Double-A (2A), or Advanced Class A (A+) in 1999 and who are considered realistic prospects are listed, as well as selected prospects below Advanced Class A (A-). First-round draft picks from the past three years still active in the minors are always listed, regardless of their level or prospect status.

2000 PROJECTIONS. At the end of the book, you'll find comprehensive player projections for the 2000 season made by Pete Palmer, renowned baseball analyst and co-editor of *Total Baseball*, the official encyclopedia of Major League Baseball. Projections are not predictions, of course, but Pete has spent hundreds of hours refining his system.

We're confident that these projections will be the most accurate ones available. They take into account age, career averages, recent performance, position, and injuries. If a player has not seen substantial playing time in the majors, they also use his recent performance in the high minors (i.e., Triple-A and Double-A). If a player has no significant big-league time, the projections are made using solely his minor-league performance. Ballpark effects have been factored into minor-league performance to account for the large differences between parks in the minors. Projections are shown for all players who had significant playing time in the majors or high minors last year.

UPDATES. To stay up-to-date throughout the spring, be sure to check out *The Insider*'s web site, www.totalbaseballweekly.com, for additional topical articles, updated rosters and projections, injury information, roster analysis, etc.

ESSAYS

THE INSIDER

RETROSHEET: RESTORING BASEBALL'S PAST

While you're sleeping, baseball history is being restored—during the season, after the season, every day, and every night.

During the 19th century, it was often said that the sun never set on the British Empire. That statement could now be true, in a 20th century virtual way, of Retrosheet. Scores of Retro volunteers work in dozens of locations around the world, day and night, to restore lost statistics and never-before-seen records from the grand and glorious past of our national game.

Have you ever wondered where the columns and columns of "new" information in baseball encyclopedias have come from in the past 20 years? If information—such as hit by a pitch or runners caught stealing—hadn't been compiled previously, it was done by someone like master researcher and statistician Pete Palmer, by members of the Society for American Baseball Research (SABR), or by members of Retrosheet.

For example, complete pitch-by-pitch and play-by-play information now exists for the Brooklyn Dodgers of the 1950s. Today, most of Sandy Koufax's career can be examined, pitch by unhittable pitch. Due to Retrosheet's efforts, we know more about Babe Ruth's career than we did previously. In addition, some errors in official statistics have been (and more certainly will be) corrected thanks to the diligence of Retrosheet volunteers.

So, exactly what is Retrosheet?

Retrosheet is a volunteer organization of baseball fans who collect, interpret, computerize, and proof accounts of games from throughout major-league baseball history, from the 1870s through the early 1980s. (Retrosheet has no need to collect the games from 1984 to the present, as those games are available from *Total Sports*. *Total Sports* purchased the Baseball Workshop in 1997, and the Workshop had complete records of all games from 1984 forward.)

David W. Smith, an unassuming biology professor at the University of Delaware, personifies Retrosheet's heart and soul. In the late 1980s, Smith thought of doing for all of baseball history what Project Scoresheet was then doing for current games.

The basement of Smith's home, just a pop fly from the University of Delaware campus in downtown Newark, Del., is a treasure trove of baseball research. Thousands of detailed scoresheets occupy filing cabinets, awaiting the time and attention of a Retrosheet volunteer who will convert the handwritten score sheets into a computer file.

These score sheets must first be translated into a standard scoring system—you'd be surprised how many different ways there are to score baseball games, as well as how many idiosyncratic notations there are on different people's score sheets. Then they are entered into a standardized computer format using software specially written for this purpose. A box score is then generated and proofread against box scores from newspapers or from *The Sporting News*.

Once scores for all games from one year have been individually entered and proofed, the final step in this laborious process is to compile statistics for the season. These stats are then proofread against official league stats for that year to resolve any discrepancies between the two sets of figures. During the proofing process, errors in the official stats are frequently discovered—which shouldn't be surprising, considering that official baseball stats were entered by hand and kept on paper until well into the 1970s, when they were computerized.

Smith and his legion of volunteers have already committed to digital form more than 50,000 games—including every game from 1980 through 1983, plus almost all games from the 1970s. They're working on many other seasons as well.

Most of the recent (i.e., 1970s–1980s) scoresheets in the Retro archive were obtained with the cooperation of the major-league teams themselves. In the early 1990s, Smith persuaded most teams to allow him to copy whatever scorebooks they had in their files from seasons predating 1984. Unfortunately, while a few teams had archives going back to the early 1960s or the late 1950s, most team scorebooks for years prior to the 1970s were long gone. These scorebooks were typically kept by the teams' public relations directors, who often kept the books when they retired. Tragically, many of these irreplaceable records were simply thrown away after collecting dust for years, especially when teams changed cities or moved to new ballparks.

Historical research is not always straightforward

Because baseball keeps such a wealth of records, and because baseball statistics are publicly invoked as often as profane oaths in a bar full of drunken sailors, you might reasonably think that most of this work would be unnecessary. But surprisingly, more than a few teams didn't even have basic box scores for their own games for many seasons.

Why not just trek off to Cooperstown to fill in the gaps? Unfortunately, that can't be done. Although the National Baseball Library at the Hall of Fame in Cooperstown has tons of valuable archival records, it does not collect actual game scoresheets. For the vast majority of games in baseball history, the Hall has a box score and detailed individual player statistics, but no records of what actually happened, play-by-play, in the game.

What about the official scorers at every game? Don't they send their scoresheets to the league or to Cooperstown? In a word, no. Official scorers are required to send an official report to the league, and that report ends up in Cooperstown's collection, but it is essentially a gigantic, complete box score. It doesn't contain play-by-play information. So, while it is the basis for computing official league stats, it can't be used to reconstruct the game events or to do the kind of sophisticated situational analysis of players, teams, or seasons that baseball fans have come to expect in the late 20th century.

If Smith and his baseball army are ever to achieve their dream of finding scoresheets for all games, they'll have to figure out how to resurrect the 1940s and 1950s. You would think that it should be easy to find detailed accounts for games in those two decades when baseball was still king, but exactly the opposite is true.

Games from the 19th and early 20th century are far easier to find—albeit not so easy to copy. Back then, many daily newspapers would print complete play-by-plays of the hometown nine's games. Typically, an afternoon paper would print a play-by-play account of the game along with a story as late-breaking news, including both in an edition sold to the workers who were heading home at the end of the day shift. In a pre-television era, this was like a paper-and-ink version of ESPN's *Baseball Tonight*.

Since all games were played in the daytime prior to 1935, contests from the early part of the century are much easier to track down. But space restrictions brought upon by rationed paper supplies during World War II—plus the advent of night baseball—prompted most newspapers to stop printing complete play-by-plays in the 1940s. A few papers carried on this tradition into the 1950s, and one Chicago paper even continued it through 1964.

Even with many papers printing play-by-plays, there is still that second stage of data collection to be done. To many, it would be tedious work to sit in a library for hours at a stretch, locating and photocopying game accounts from microfilm reels of newspapers long defunct. Nevertheless, it is being done, and microfilmed collections of urban daily newspapers aren't deteriorating or in danger of being thrown out. This is where baseball research really happens—and this is where you come in.

How you can help

While Retrosheet has done great work, computerizing almost 60,000 of the more than 115,000 big-league games from 1901 to 1983, the hunt for records of many older games—especially from the 1940s and 1950s—is ongoing.

Every game from 1980 to the present is accounted for, but scoresheets from the 1940s through the early 1970s—especially those of the Boston and Milwaukee Braves, Pittsburgh Pirates, Cincinnati Reds, Chicago Cubs, New York Giants, Philadelphia and Kansas City Athletics, and St. Louis Browns—are scarce.

If you went to ball games in those days and scored them from the stands, please contact Retrosheet to see if they need copies of your scorecards. If you used to sit next to a static-filled AM radio, keeping track of the exploits of your heroes on the diamond miles away, your scoresheets may be valuable to others. If you have audio tapes in any format, or videotapes of any games prior to 1980, please make a list of your collection and send it to Retrosheet. No game—even between the lowly St. Louis Browns and the Washington Senators—is unimportant.

Extending the circle is critical as well. If you have a baseball nut in the family tree, or if there is a former sportswriter among your relatives, your friends, or your parents' friends, please ask if they have any dusty old scorecards or scorebooks lying around. If they do, please let Dave Smith know. He will gladly make arrangements to borrow or copy these scorecards or notebooks at Retrosheet's expense, and return them safely to their owners if they can't be donated to the cause.

How to contact the good folks at Retrosheet

Even if you don't have old scorebooks, you can still help. Retrosheet can always use more volunteers to proofread box scores and league stats, and to track down old game accounts from newspaper microfilm. If this kind of baseball detective work intrigues you, post an e-mail at the Retrosheet Web site, www.retrosheet.org, or write to Retrosheet, care of Dave Smith, at 20 Sunset Road, Neward, DE 19711. So far, hundreds of volunteers have made significant contributions to the collective effort in various ways.

An example of the real-world difficulties encountered by Retrosheet is that the organization has a few thousand unprocessed newspaper accounts on hand for games from the 1950s and earlier. Many of these present a separate problem, namely that there are no box scores to go along with them. Without a box score, it is almost impossible to enter one of these newspaper accounts into the computer, since fielders are referred to by name, not by position. For example, "a fly ball to [Babe] Ruth" in a newspaper account might be scored as "7" or "9", depending on which park the Yankees were playing in. (New York typically played Ruth in right field at home and in either left or right on the road, depending on the ballpark. As the Babe slowed down, he was normally positioned in the less spacious corner of the outfield.)

This problem can be solved by consulting the box score for that game from *The Sporting News* or *The New York Times*. Of course, obtaining copies of thousands of such box scores is no trivial matter in itself, and volunteers are needed to help copy them from microfilm before these games can be archived and proofed.

You can find out more about Retrosheet, and review its impressive body of work, by checking out the group's Web site. Retrosheet.org is packed with details and interesting facts about baseball history that have been uncovered by the organization's volunteers. It also has complete play-by-play records from several seasons, available for free.

Historical oddities from Retrosheet research

For the amusement of baseball fans who are fascinated by the game's long and quirky legacy, herewith is a list of Dave Smith's favorite odd plays and historical nuggets that have been dug out by various Retrosheet volunteers over the last few years. While they are certainly entertaining, the true value of Retrosheet's work is in completing accounts for games and seasons that can be used by historians to fill in lost portions of the game's past.

• **THE ODDEST STRIKEOUT?** How about a strikeout with the batter being retired 7-6-7? At Minnesota, on April 25, 1970, Tigers pitcher Earl Wilson struck out to end the seventh inning—or so it appeared (to everyone except Detroit third base coach Grover Resinger, that is). Grover saw that Twins catcher Paul Ratliff had trapped the pitch in the dirt and had not tagged Wilson, rolling the ball to the mound. Resinger told Wilson to run, as most of the Twins entered their dugout. Earl, who was a big pitcher and certainly no gazelle, made it to first easily and promptly headed for second. Since no one had interfered with him, he started for third. By this time, left fielder Brant Alyea, trotting in from his position, heard Resinger shouting at Wilson. Alyea hustled to the mound but had trouble picking up the ball. Wilson headed for home, where Twins players Leo Cardenas and Ratliff had returned to action. Alyea picked up the ball and threw to Cardenas. Wilson turned back to third but was tagged out by Alyea for a K-7-6-7. Rookie catcher Ratliff was charged with an error. After the game, Detroit catcher Bill Freehan said, "If Alyea had been hustling, Earl might have made it [home]. Tell him [Alyea] to start coming in and off the field a little quicker." On the play, Wilson pulled a hamstring running the bases and had to leave the game.

• **A HOWARD JOHNSON:** In a game at Washington in 1970, Sam McDowell of the Indians issued five intentional walks to the Senators, three of them to Frank Howard—and two of those occuring when Howard led off an inning! The fourth time Frank came to bat, McDowell went to play first base, returning to the mound in the following inning. (Alvin Dark was the overly enthusiastic Cleveland manager.) McDowell has noted in recent public speeches that Howard always hit him effectively.

• **TURKEY HAWK?** On September 20, 1963, in the first game of a Kansas City at New York twin bill, Ken "Hawk" Harrelson of the Athletics was the victim of the hidden ball trick at second base in the 11th inning. Pedro Gonzalez was the second baseman who fooled him. Hawk, now on Chicago's WGN White Sox broadcasts, would probably like to forget about his faux pas.

• **AFTER YOU, PLEASE:** In the early part of the century, there was a long-forgotten custom of allowing "courtesy runners"—that is, a pinch-runner who temporarily replaced a man on base, with the replaced player allowed to return to the field for the next inning. Retrosheet has found that the practice occurred as late as 1949, when the Indians were twice allowed to use such runners. The use of courtesy runners was formally outlawed in 1950.

• **IS THIS WHY SANDY QUIT EARLY?** On May 28, 1960, Sandy Koufax threw 210 pitches in a game at Wrigley Field. This was not the only occurrence of Koufax throwing more than 200 pitches. In the 14th inning, he was allowed to bat with a runner on first base; he botched a sacrifice attempt by running into the catcher. He was then knocked out of the game in the bottom of the inning and took the loss. Given Koufax's deserved reputation as a terrible hitter, the fact that it was the 14th inning, and his high pitch count, why on earth did manager Walter Alston let him bat?

• **NEWKLEAR BAT:** Don Newcombe had a great year for the Dodgers in 1955, both on the mound and at the plate. In addition to winning 20 games, he batted .359 and slugged .632. On May 26 in Pittsburgh, Roy Face came in to pitch for the Pirates in the ninth inning of the 3–2 game. Newk responded with a triple, then proceeded to steal home. Amazing.

•**MORE NEWK:** The Brooklyn-Philadelphia game of August 20, 1955, shows the way pitcher usage has changed in recent years. Trailing 3–2 with two out in the ninth, Dodger manager Walter Alston called on pitcher Newcombe, who was the Dodgers' best pinch-hitter that year. The Phillies countered by bringing in Hall of Fame starter Robin Roberts, who had pitched a complete game the night before. Although Newk batted .381 that year as a pinch-hitter, this time he grounded out to Roberts to end the game.

•**MANAGING TO WIN?** On April 25, 1959, Solly Hemus, the St. Louis Cardinals' player-manager, started himself at third base, moving All-Star third sacker Ken Boyer to shortstop. Hemus singled in the first inning off Don Drysdale. In the second, against Danny McDevitt, Hemus used Ray Jablonski as a pinch-hitter for himself, and Jabbo hit a home run. Great managing!

SANDY VERSUS THE SURGEON

One of the benefits of the kind of research that Retrosheet has been doing is the extra insight we can gain into the great players of the past. This comparison between two great pitchers is an updated version of a 1999 research paper presented by David Smith, based on the information Retrosheet has uncovered and developed for Sandy Koufax's career.

Koufax pitched for only 12 years, of which five are so strikingly brilliant as to have earned him a spot in baseball's pantheon despite his generally unimpressive career totals. In the last five years of his career, Koufax was often referred to as "dominating" and "overpowering." These words have also been applied to Greg Maddux in the seven years that he has pitched for the Braves.

But Kofufax and Maddux are dissimilar in many ways: Besides the obvious lefty/righty difference, their styles also differ greatly. Koufax was the archetype of the power pitcher; Maddux is renowned for his extraordinary control. They played in very different eras in terms of the strike zone, the introduction of artificial turf, and the use of relief pitchers, to name just a few factors.

Here are the basic numbers for Koufax's last five seasons and for Maddux's last seven years:

Koufax

Year	GS	CG	W	L	ShO	IP	H	SO	BB	ERA
1962	26	11	14	7	2	184.1	134	216	57	2.54
1963	40	20	25	5	11	311	214	306	58	1.88
1964	28	15	19	5	7	223	154	223	53	1.74
1965	41	27	26	8	8	335.2	216	382	71	2.04
1966	41	27	27	9	5	323	241	317	77	1.73
Total	176	100	111	34	33	1377	959	1444	316	1.95

Maddux

Year	GS	CG	W	L	ShO	IP	H	SO	BB	ERA
1993	36	8	20	10	1	267	228	197	52	2.36
1994	25	10	16	6	3	202	150	156	31	1.56
1995	28	10	19	2	3	209.2	147	181	23	1.63
1996	35	5	15	11	1	245	225	172	28	2.72
1997	33	5	19	4	2	232.2	200	177	20	2.20
1998	34	9	18	9	5	251	201	204	45	2.22
1999	33	4	19	9	0	219.1	258	136	37	3.57
Total	224	51	126	51	15	1626.2	1509	1223	236	2.34

There are huge differences in games started, complete games, and innings pitched, partly because the 1994 strike reduced the opportunities for Maddux for that year and the start of the next. Koufax also had two shortened seasons due to injuries (finger in 1962, elbow in 1964), plus five relief appearances in this period, totaling eight innings and three saves. The composite ERA each pitcher compiled is similar, although one must consider the level of offense in the two eras.

Those basic numbers can be massaged a bit to obtain some additional measurements. The following table gives composite hits plus walks per nine innings, strikeouts per nine innings, walks per nine innings, and strikeout-to-walk ratio.

	H+BB/9 IP	SO/9 IP	BB/9 IP	SO/BB
Koufax	8.33	9.44	2.07	4.57
Maddux (thru 1998)	8.63	6.95	1.27	5.46
Maddux (thru 1999)	9.10	6.77	1.31	5.18

The most striking differences, as expected, are that Koufax struck out many more batters and Maddux walked far fewer. However, Koufax also allowed considerably fewer hits. The ratio of base runners each allowed per nine innings was pretty similar until 1999, with the advantage to Koufax.

Great performances in different eras

Of course, there were substantial differences in offense between the 1960s and the 1990s. One simple measure is the league ERA for each season:

Year	NL ERA
1962	3.94
1963	3.29
1964	3.54
1965	3.54
1966	3.61
1993	4.04
1994	4.21
1995	4.18
1996	4.21
1997	4.20
1998	4.23
1999	4.57

The NL average for each period:
1962-1966 NL ERA = 3.59
1993-1998 NL ERA = 4.18
1993-1999 NL ERA = 4.23

That is, Koufax had an ERA that was 1.64 better than the league average, while Maddux was 1.89 runs better, a very impressive achievement. Through 1998, Maddux was an incredible 2.03 runs better than the NL average.

Home, sweet home

To compare the two pitchers, you must consider the ballparks in which they played.

It is important to note that park effect is compares performance in a given park to that in all other parks in the league. That is, it is a relative measure, not an absolute one. Therefore, a given park may be a hitters' park or a pitchers' park, even with the same level of offense, depending on how it compares to other parks in the league.

The eras analyzed for Koufax and Maddux both saw some significant park changes. The Mets moved from the Polo Grounds to Shea Stadium in 1964, the Astros (née Colt .45s) from Colt Stadium to the Astrodome in 1965, the Rockies from Mile High Stadium to Coors Field in 1995, and the Braves from Atlanta-Fulton County Stadium to Turner Field in 1997. There were many other changes to existing parks, including alterations in distances, fence heights, and the amount of foul territory, most of which are hard to pin down. Local weather also has a profound effect on the game, so an especially hot or cool summer can change the way a park plays relative to the league.

The park effect of Dodger Stadium and of the two Atlanta stadiums for these years are shown below. Increases in scoring compared to the league average are positive numbers, decreases in scoring are negative numbers. It is clear that Koufax pitched in a much friendlier environment at home than Maddux did.

PARK	YEAR	PARK EFFECT
Dodger Stadium	1962	-18.0%
Dodger Stadium	1963	-14.7%
Dodger Stadium	1964	-20.5%
Dodger Stadium	1965	-24.4%
Dodger Stadium	1966	-14.2%
Fulton County	1993	-1.3%
Fulton County	1994	-6.5%
Fulton County	1995	+8.6%
Fulton County	1996	+6.8%
Turner Field	1997	-3.1%
Turner Field	1998	+3.2%
Turner Field	1999	-12.7%

Another way to check the effect of a pitcher's home park is to look at his record at home and on the road. The following table gives these numbers for opponents' batting average, on-base average, and slugging average, as well as ERA. (OPS is on-base plus slugging.)

Koufax

Year	Site	BA	OBA	SA	OPS	ERA
1962	Home	.184	.237	.268	.505	1.84
	Road	.212	.288	.315	.603	3.53
1963	Home	.163	.203	.208	.411	1.36
	Road	.211	.254	.326	.580	2.39
1964	Home	.179	.210	.245	.455	0.85
	Road	.206	.276	.309	.585	2.91
1965	Home	.152	.196	.224	.420	1.38
	Road	.205	.256	.331	.587	2.72
1966	Home	.202	.255	.279	.534	1.52
	Road	.207	.249	.308	.557	1.90

Maddux

Year	Site	BA	OBA	SA	OPS	ERA
1993	Home	.216	.265	.284	.549	2.19
	Road	.245	.279	.345	.624	2.51
1994	Home	.199	.222	.247	.469	1.76
	Road	.214	.264	.270	.534	1.37
1995	Home	.218	.245	.288	.533	2.23
	Road	.178	.205	.231	.436	1.12
1996	Home	.223	.243	.330	.573	2.44
	Road	.263	.290	.346	.636	3.09
1997	Home	.244	.266	.314	.580	2.18
	Road	.225	.243	.307	.550	2.24
1998	Home	.222	.257	.318	.569	2.02
	Road	.217	.265	.274	.539	2.51
1999	Home	.262	.290	.270	.560	2.86
	Road	.339	.371	.451	.822	4.71

These numbers show that Koufax did much better in Dodger Stadium, with only his last year showing anything like comparable performances at home and away. On the other hand, the home park effect on Maddux has been quite variable, with his performance being better on the road in some years and better at home in others.

The philosophy of pitcher usage has changed dramatically in the past three decades, with starters no longer expected to pitch complete games. The raw numbers for Koufax and Maddux seem to bear this out, since Sandy completed 56.8 percent of his starts, while Greg finished just 24.6 percent of his. However, looking at the average number of innings pitched per start changes that perception: Koufax pitched an average of 7.78 innings in his 176 starts, while Maddux went 7.26 innings in his 224 starts, a difference of just over half an inning. Therefore, even though Greg did not complete many of his starts, he did pitch into the eighth inning regularly. The phenomenon of the one-inning closer is presumably at play here.

One final note: Even though it might seem counterintuitive, the overall percentage of strikes thrown for both pitchers was surprisingly similar (within two percentage points), given their radically different styles, for those games for which Retrosheet had pitch-by-pitch data.

The envelope, please

What makes these two superstar pitchers great? At least part of the enduring legend of Sandy Koufax is his being a dominating strikeout pitcher who overpowered his opponents. On the other hand, Greg Maddux's name conjures up none of this imagery; very few of his opponents speak of being overpowered. The analogy most often drawn is that Maddux is a surgeon on the mound, precisely evaluating his opponent and then surgically exploiting their weaknesses with his precise control and mixture of pitches.

After considering the evidence, the basic question must be addressed: Which of these two great pitchers was better? When Koufax's and Maddux's performances are normalized per nine innings, with appropriate adjustments for the different eras and their home parks, it seems that the performance of Greg Maddux over the last seven years has been superior.

However, when one considers that Sandy Koufax was performing at an extremely high level for nearly 20 percent more innings per year over his last five years (275.4 for Koufax, 232.4 for Maddux), then the overall value to his team might be comparable.

DARRYL, WE HARDLY KNEW YE

Making a successful comeback in 1998 after years in the baseball wilderness, Darryl Strawberry started 1999 as an important member of the defending world champions. That might have been enough for most of us, but it was obviously not exciting enough for Mr. Strawberry. After yet another brush with the law, yet another suspension, yet another grievance hearing, and yet another comeback, "the Straw that stirs his own drink" finally made it back into the Yankees' lineup late in the season.

Who knows what the year 2000 will bring to the Yankees' enigmatic outfielder? While it would be foolhardy to try to predict what twists and turns Strawberry's life and career will take this year, it is interesting to take a look at what might have been—if Darryl hadn't thrown away the better part of six years of his baseball life.

Strawberry's last full season before his precipitous decline was also his first in Los Angeles after eight productive seasons with the Mets. He hit .265 that year, with 28 homers and 99 runs batted in, as the Dodgers fell one game short of the Braves after a thrilling pennant race. Expert statistician Pete Palmer projected what Strawberry's career might have looked like after '91, had he not encountered numerous off-the-field problems.

Sobering, isn't it?

YEAR	BA	G	AB	R	H	2B	3B	HR	RBI	BB	SO	SB	SA	OBA
1992	.260	136	490	81	128	20	3	29	93	68	112	11	.490	.351
1993	.262	130	467	77	122	19	3	27	89	65	106	10	.489	.352
1994	.259	123	444	73	115	18	3	25	84	62	101	9	.484	.350
1995	.257	116	420	68	108	17	3	24	79	58	94	9	.481	.348
1996	.256	109	393	63	101	16	3	22	73	54	88	8	.478	.347
1997	.255	101	364	58	93	15	3	20	68	50	81	7	.476	.346
1998	.254	92	333	53	85	14	3	18	62	45	74	7	.473	.345
1999	.254	83	299	47	76	12	3	16	55	40	66	6	.472	.344
2000	.253	72	261	41	66	11	2	14	48	35	57	5	.469	.343
2001	.252	60	217	34	55	9	2	12	40	29	47	4	.469	.342
2002	.252	48	173	27	43	7	2	9	32	23	37	3	.467	.342
Totals	.260	2318	8269	1370	2151	367	64	496	1555	1184	1948	280	.499	.354

THEY DON'T MAKE WONDERS OF THE WORLD LIKE THEY USED TO

Though it didn't evoke one scintilla of the nostalgia that the closing of Tiger Stadium did, Houston's farewell to the Astrodome in 1999 was a notable event in baseball history. Not remotely for the reasons that are given, though.

The very first tall tale told about the Astrodome was a short one: labeling it as the "Eighth Wonder of the World." True, the Astrodome was different, and in the realm of sports it was unique when it was built. But really, who could have had the hubris to call it the "Eighth Wonder of the World"?

For those who have forgotten their grade-school lessons in classical history, here is a list of the so-called Seven Wonders of the Ancient World. The list varies somewhat depending on the time it was compiled and by whom, but this selection from around 500 A.D. is representative:

The Great Pyramids in Egypt, the only ancient wonder still standing intact today; The Hanging Gardens of Babylon in Mesopotamia; the statue of Zeus at Olympia in Greece; the Mausoleum at Halicarnassus in Asia Minor; the Temple of Artemis at Ephesus in Asia Minor; The Colossus of Rhodes; and the Pharos of Alexandria, Egypt.

A few sample details show the monumental nature of these wonders. The Great Pyramid at Giza is about 450 feet tall and has lasted for 44 centuries. The Hanging Gardens on the banks of the Euphrates River were so magnificent that they were said to have awed the hard-bitten and well-traveled combat veterans of Alexander the Great's army. The statue of Zeus is thought to have been 40 feet tall, made of gold and ivory, and decorated with precious stones. It lasted between 900 and 1,000 years. The tomb built for King Mausolus of Caria was so impressive that his name has been applied to every other monumental necropolis built in memoriam thereafter. The Temple of Artemis was constructed in honor of the goddess of nature; it took 120 years to complete. The Colossus of Rhodes was a bronze statue, thought to have been 105 feet tall, guarding that Aegean island's harbor. It was destroyed by an earthquake after barely a half-century. The Pharos of Alexandria was a lighthouse made of marble and is thought to have been 400 feet tall.

Does the Astrodome even remotely qualify for being appended to this list? It was big enough all right—an 18-story building would easily fit under the dome. From a distance, it looks like an ugly alien mothership has landed on the late 20th-century Texas prairie (i.e., in the middle of the acres of pavement and with long ribbons of concrete freeways leading away from it).

True to local tradition, where—according to the natives—everything in Texas is bigger and better than anywhere else, Houston put the best possible face on the end of the 35-year "tradition" of baseball at the Astrodome. Now that the Astros have left the building, the sole remaining tenant of any importance is the annual Houston Livestock Show and Rodeo, which seems entirely fitting given the amount of BS that has been shoveled in the Astrodome's name.

Right from the start, the Astrodome proved to be a venue completely unsuitable for baseball. Unfortunately, with so much money and so much ego invested in the building, the game was radically altered to accommodate the stadium, instead of vice versa. The geniuses who built the Eighth Wonder didn't have the common sense to ask the ballplayers if they could see fly balls under the translucent panels of the dome roof, nor did they do a realistic test to see if they could successfully grow grass indoors.

To appease the players, who couldn't follow the flight of the ball, part of the dome's roof was painted to block out the sunlight. This, of course, caused the grass to die, and shortly thereafter resulted in the invention of Astroturf. Both the dome and the turf dramatically altered the way baseball would be played.

Despite its checkered debut, the Astrodome spawned a generation of imitators who combined to radically change the game. At the time, of course, it was thought that the change was for the better. Now, however, virtually everyone regards these gigantic concrete muffins as white elephants that helped speed the decline of the national pastime in the 1970s and 1980s.

The Astrodome eventually begat the Kingdome in Seattle, the Metrodome in Minneapolis, Olympic Stadium in Montreal, and, finally, Tropicana Field in St. Petersburg. Tropicana was built in 1990 in a vain attempt to seduce major-league Baseball into relocating an existing team or granting an expansion franchise, but it didn't get a big-league tenant till 1998.

In the intervening time, sentiment against domed ballparks became so negative that the domed stadium in St. Pete became the first to eschew the word *dome* in its name. (Olympic Stadium didn't use the word either, but it wasn't domed when it was built. The Big Owe's original roof was supposed to be retractable, but it never worked properly.) Even so, the use of the pastoral term field to describe a concrete dome with plastic artificial turf is almost as much of a stretch as calling the Astrodome the Eighth Wonder of the World. In recognition of its already obsolete state, almost $200 million was spent to renovate Tropicana Field before it was acceptable for the Devil Rays.

The direct effects of the Astrodome are easy to see. However, one of the indirect legacies of the Astrodome was to eventually help empty the pockets of taxpayers three decades later. How? Because the Astrodome was such a magnificent failure for baseball, teams in both hot and cold climates now insist on moveable or retractable roofs on their new pleasure palaces. While the design and cost of these engineering marvels vary, estimates for the additional expense for operable domes are generally in the $50 million to 100 million range.

Since most teams have made deals that fix their costs, this additional expense has been effectively born by the public. Starting with Toronto's SkyDome (which opened in midseason 1989), cities, counties, states, and their taxpayers have spent hundreds of millions of extra dollars to make sure that pampered baseball fans could be sheltered from inclement weather when needed, yet continue to enjoy good weather by opening up the stadium to the outdoors.

By the start of the 2001 season, one sixth of all major-league games will be played in ballparks with movable roofs, and more of these sophisticated behemoths will surely be built to replace existing parks. Bank One Ballpark in Phoenix, Safeco Field in Seattle, Enron Field in Houston, and Miller Park in Milwaukee will have joined the trendsetting SkyDome—which the Blue Jays, ironically, threatened to leave recently in a dispute with their landlord. Whether the baseball public will feel as warm and fuzzy about these new high-tech marvels as it does about open-air retro parks like Camden Yards remains to be seen.

Nevertheless, the age of the fixed-domed stadium is quickly drawing to a close. Olympic Stadium is now definitely scheduled for replacement in 2002. The Twins threaten almost daily to leave Minnesota, if only the good burghers of some other metropolis would kindly build them a new ballpark. If it weren't so sad, it would be almost comic how desperate the Twins' ownership is to be relieved of the burden of a stadium that was viewed as an economic godsend merely a decade ago.

Unfortunately, the last remaining legacy of the Astrodome, Tropicana Field, will be plaguing baseball for years to come. Unless, that is, the Devil Rays end up relocating because of poor attendance. If they do, it will certainly be partly because of their home park—a soulless imitation of the great white elephant in Houston that started it all back in 1965.

CHASING HENRY

The worldwide attention given to the great home run race of 1998 made a powerful argument that baseball's single-season home run record was the most important record in major professional sports. The only other record of comparable magnitude is the mark set by the great Hank Aaron with his 755 career home runs. In light of the last two years, that record is now viewed as very vulnerable.

While Aaron's career achievement must be viewed as more substantial than Maris' one-year peak, the inherent drama of finally breaking a career record is understandably less than that of shattering a single-season mark. After all, by the time a great athlete gets near an all-time record, it is typically only a matter of time until he succeeds—unless he suffers a terrible, unexpected injury. In a short season, though, any minor setback is a serious threat to a record-setting performance.

Until 1999, everyone—including Aaron—had assumed that Ken Griffey Jr. had by far the best chance of anyone to reach Aaron's heights. After all, Junior had it all: superstar performance, excellent athleticism, good health, and a favorable ballpark for home run hitting. At 29, he could expect to play for another 10 years or so, giving him enough time to overcome an off year or two, or a major injury.

Now, however, things look much different. Griffey didn't exactly struggle in '99, and his AL-best 48 homers didn't take him out of the race. But in a season in which Mark McGwire and Sammy Sosa again bashed 60-plus round-trippers, and in which 10 other players (besides Griffey, McGwire, and Sosa) knocked 40 or more out of the park, Junior's star shines a bit less brightly. Combine that with the fact that Safeco Field is certain to be a lot less helpful to sluggers than the Kingdome, plus the uncertainty about where he will end up playing, and Griffey's future looks less rosy.

In contrast, after another year of good health and unbelievably prolific moonshots, McGwire has muscled his way into the all-time home run picture. Big Mac's 65 pushed him well past the magic 500 mark, and it also upped the projection for the rest of his career into Aaron country.

Pete Palmer, co-editor of *Total Baseball*, projected the balance of Griffey's and McGwire's careers after the 1999 season. His projections take into account each player's age, his past performance, and his injury history. Here's how Palmer views the future of these two great players:

Griffey

YEAR	BA	G	AB	R	H	2B	3B	HR	RBI	BB	SO	SB	SA	OBA
2000	.281	154	593	115	166	27	3	48	131	80	107	20	.581	.370
2001	.276	148	569	109	157	25	3	45	124	76	101	19	.571	.366
2002	.273	140	539	102	147	23	3	42	116	72	94	18	.563	.363
2003	.269	132	508	95	137	22	3	39	108	67	88	17	.556	.358
2004	.266	124	475	88	127	20	3	36	100	62	81	16	.550	.356
2005	.264	115	440	81	116	18	3	33	92	57	74	15	.545	.353
2006	.261	105	404	73	105	17	3	30	83	52	67	13	.540	.349
2007	.258	95	365	65	94	15	3	27	74	46	60	12	.535	.346
2008	.256	84	322	57	82	13	2	24	65	40	53	10	.530	.342
2009	.253	71	274	48	69	11	2	20	55	34	45	9	.527	.339
2010	.251	58	221	39	56	9	2	16	44	27	36	7	.522	.337
Totals	.284	2761	10542	1935	2998	520	60	758	2144	1360	1790	323	.561	.369

McGwire

YEAR	BA	G	AB	R	H	2B	3B	HR	RBI	BB	SO	SB	SA	OBA
2000	.272	151	511	110	139	21	1	62	135	129	139	1	.676	.419
2001	.267	145	490	105	131	19	1	59	128	123	130	1	.665	.415
2002	.260	138	467	97	122	18	1	55	119	113	121	1	.648	.405
2003	.255	128	434	88	111	16	1	50	108	103	110	1	.635	.399
2004	.251	116	394	78	99	14	1	44	96	92	98	1	.622	.393
2005	.246	103	349	68	86	12	1	38	84	80	85	1	.610	.388
Totals	.263	2313	7757	1519	2038	313	12	772	1824	1724	1924	14	.603	.398

Palmer's system degrades performance gradually but does not predict rare but catastrophic events like major injuries. Such uncommon events cannot truly be predicted, though their overall effects in a player's career are reflected in his seasonal numbers and in his career totals.

The reason that McGwire's career has such an unusually strong finish is that he has hit a record number of homers at ages 34 and 35. Based on those performances, the projection for the twilight of his career is unique. Of course, at his age, the chance of a career-ending injury is substantially greater.

The upshot is that two active players now have realistic chances of mounting an assault on Henry Aaron's Olympian heights. Baseball fans—as well as major-league Baseball itself—should feel fortunate to witness these two potential home run kings battle it out over the next several years.

⟨24⟩

AL WILD CARD

WINS	
110	
100	
90	
80	
70	
60	
50	
40	
30	
20	
10	
0	

WEEK 4/5 | 4/12 | 4/19 | 4/26 | 5/3 | 5/10 | 5/17 | 5/24 | 5/31 | 6/7 | 6/14 | 6/2

▶ THE INSIDER 2000

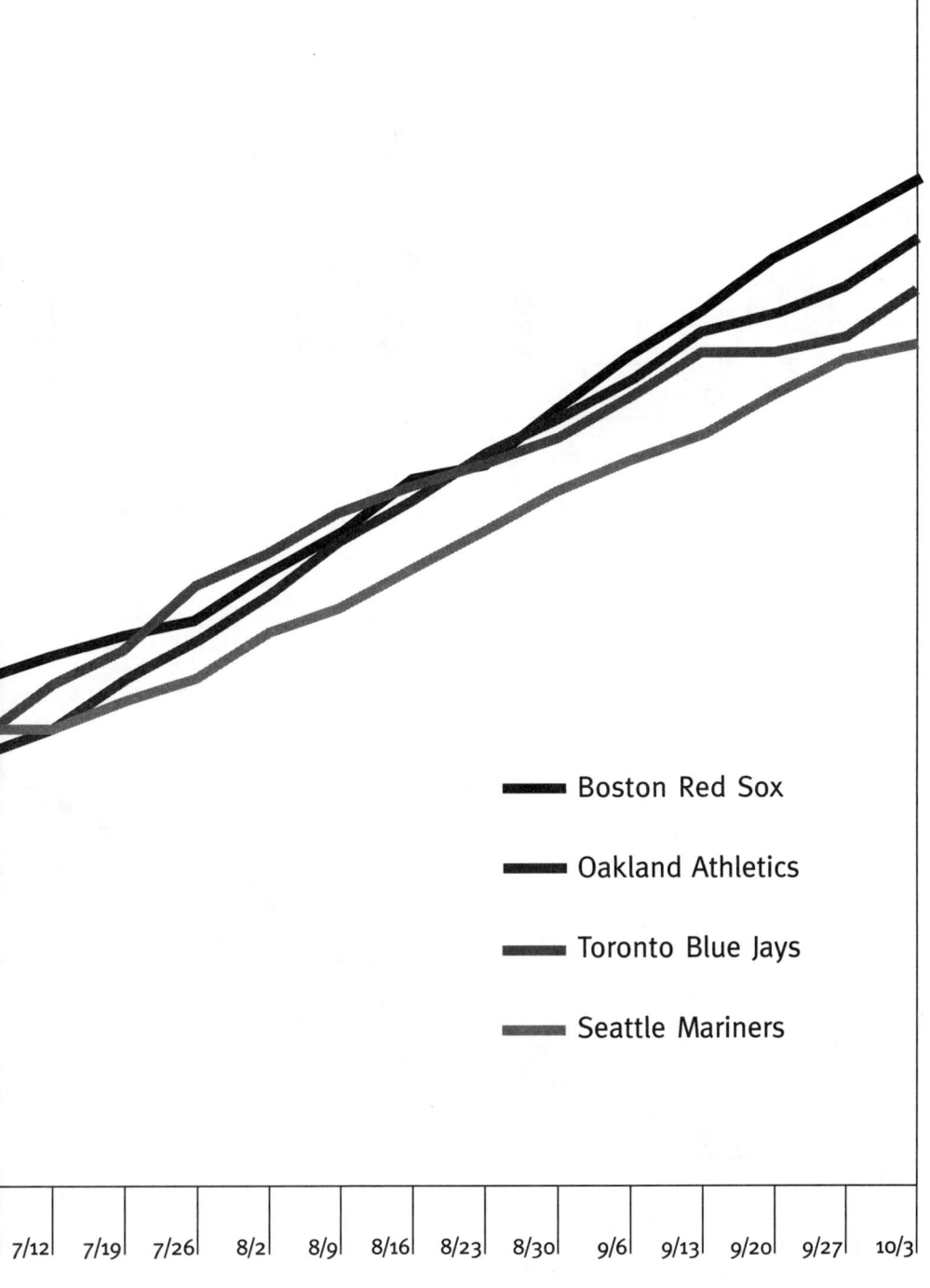

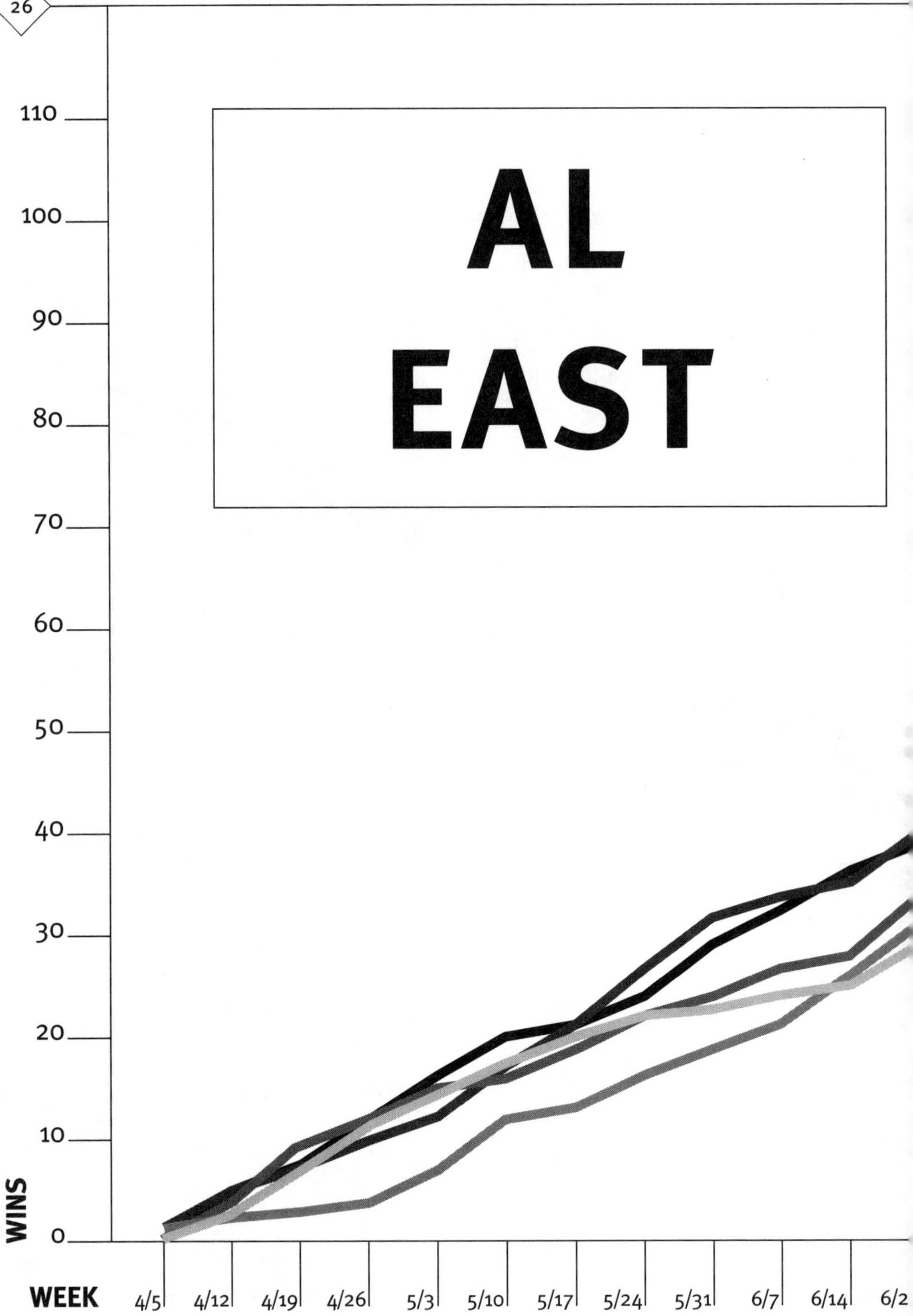

AL EAST

(Chart: Wins vs Week, 4/5 through 6/2)

▶ THE INSIDER 2000

New York Yankees

Boston Red Sox

Toronto Blue Jays

Baltimore Orioles

Tampa Bay Devil Rays

7/12 7/19 7/26 8/2 8/9 8/16 8/23 8/30 9/6 9/13 9/20 9/27 10/3

BALTIMORE ORIOLES

MANAGEMENT
		CAREER RECORD
Manager	Ray Miller [fired]	266–297 / .472
G.M.	Frank Wren [resigned]	78–84 / .481
President/CEO	Peter Angelos	562–504 / .527

1999 RECORD
Won–Lost	Pct.	Finish/G.B. (Division)	Finish/G.B. (Wild Card)
78–84	.481	4/20 (E)	5/16

PRESEASON CONSENSUS PROJECTION
2 (2.40)

1ST HALF	2ND HALF	HOME	ROAD	INTRADIVISION	INTERLEAGUE
32–44	46–40	41–40	37–44	15–34	11–7

COMEBACKS	BLOWOUTS	NAIL-BITERS	GRASS	TURF	SEPT.–OCT.
8–12	26–24	36–38	70–71	8–13	20–11

NUMBERS DON'T LIE

	TEAM (RANK)	OPPONENTS (RANK)	LEAGUE AVG.
Runs/Game	5.25 (8)	5.03 (3)	5.18
Batting Avg.	.279 (6)	.269 (4)	.274
On-Base Avg.	.353 (5)	.349 (8)	.347
Slugging Avg.	.447 (7)	.439 (6)	.439
Strikeouts	890 (2)	983 (6)	998
Home Runs	203 (7)	198 (10)	188
Stolen Bases	107 (9)	93 (4)	104
ERA	4.77 (4)		4.87
Errors	89 (1)		114

▶ THE INSIDER 2000

ANGEL(O)S IN THE OLD FOLKS' HOME

The Orioles were nightmarishly bad, almost from Opening Day, last season. The team lost 10 of its first 13 games and was already 6½ games out in the AL East on April 20. A week later, the O's were eight games out of first place, and things never got any better. The first-glance explanation seemed to be that Baltimore was an old team—one of the oldest in baseball history—with a lineup dominated by players well into the twilight of their careers. The superannuated Birds, who should have been retired to baseball's old folks' home, performed like worn-out studs overdue for a dose of Viagra.

Unlike in 1998, nobody expected the Orioles to do much in 1999. The club brought in ferocious slugger Albert Belle to play right field, grossly overrated Will Clark to play first base, and strong-armed Charles Johnson to catch, but, essentially, the rest of the team that finished 35 games back of New York was the same as in '98. The result in the standings was the same also, as Baltimore won one game less than it had the season before. The Orioles finished *only* 20 games back in the standings, but that 15-game difference was due to the Yankees' winning 16 fewer games than in '98.

Were the 1999 Orioles destined to fail because of their age? Was the team simply too old to compete with younger clubs?

Not by New York standards. Both the Yankees and the Mets were older teams (albeit only slightly) than the Orioles were, but that didn't stop the Yankees from winning the World Series and the Mets from advancing to the NLCS.

The 1999 Orioles were the 25th-oldest team in 20th-century major-league history—but the Yankees had the 21st-oldest team and the Mets had the 10th-oldest, and both were significantly better than the Orioles. In fact, of the 25 oldest teams, six have finished first and another six finished within 5 games of first place. That means nearly half of those clubs won titles or finished within striking distance.

If it's not a kiss of death to be an old team, what exactly were the differences among the Orioles, the Yankees, and the Mets? Baltimore allowed the third-fewest runs in the league last year, so the team didn't fail because of pitching and defense. Mike Mussina was superb, Scott Erickson recovered from a miserable first half with a very strong finish, Juan Guzman was good before being traded, and promising 23-year-old Sidney Ponson was above par.

MOMENT OF TRUTH

The Orioles were long out of the pennant race on July 22, but they faced a critical decision about their roster when second baseman Delino DeShields came off the disabled list. Jerry Hairston had been playing well since taking over a month earlier when DeShields got hurt. However, instead of giving the 23-year-old Hairston an extended chance to show what he could do, they shipped him back to the minors and went back to the older and relatively unproductive DeShields. That move typified the attitude of the organization for the past several seasons: very little faith in young players.

BIGGEST SURPRISE

It's hard to believe that manager Ray Miller made it through the entire season before getting canned. Miller didn't have the best team in the world to manage, but the $75 million payroll put tremendous pressure on him to give owner Peter Angelos a winner. The vultures came out for Miller when the O's fell behind early (they were eight games back and in last place on May 9), but Angelos shocked everybody by not pulling the trigger until after the season.

BIGGEST DISAPPOINTMENT

Will Clark was a decent hitter when he was in the lineup, but, unfortunately, that was only about half the time. Clark played in only 77 games and had 251 at-bats for the season, missing a month early in the season because of a broken thumb and missing the last seven weeks of the season with a bad left elbow. Baltimore really should have seen it coming, considering the last time Clark played in more than 123 games was in 1998—when he was about to become a free agent.

Clearly the blame falls on the offense, which finished in the middle of the pack in runs. The youngest starter the O's had in 1999 was then-27-year-old catcher Charles Johnson. However, the rest of the starting eight averaged almost 34 years of age: Cal Ripken was 38, Brady Anderson and Will Clark were 35, B. J. Surhoff was 34, Mike Bordick was 33, Albert Belle was 32, and Delino DeShields was 30. The Yankees and the Mets, on the other hand, both had key players who were far younger than that. Derek Jeter was 25 last season, Bernie Williams was 30, Edgardo Alfonzo was 25, and Roger Cedeno was 24.

Clark, DeShields, and Ripken all spent a significant amount of time on the DL, but even had they been healthy the entire season, they alone wouldn't have made any difference. Ripken hit .340 last year, but he certainly wouldn't have maintained that level of production playing 162 games instead of 86. Why did Baltimore's front office decide to go with essentially the same players last year who had collapsed in 1998?

The Orioles were already an old team in 1997 when they won the AL East. Even though old teams can and do win, the problem the club didn't understand is that many old teams crash and burn within a season or two of winning if they don't overhaul their rosters.

Philadelphia had the sixth-oldest team in history in 1983 when the Phillies lost the World Series to Baltimore; the "Wheeze Kids" finished fourth in 1984 and fifth in '85. Oakland won the AL West in 1992, its fourth division title in five seasons, then slipped to last in the next two full seasons (1993 and '95).

The California Angels of the early 1980s fielded some of the oldest teams in baseball history, but the franchise stayed successful over a five-year span because it phased out some of the veterans and brought in different players.

The 1982 Angels were the oldest in history, but managed to win the AL West. The 1983 team was the second-oldest ever and finished fifth, but the '84 team rebounded to finish second despite being the 11th-oldest. The Angels finished second again in '85 and won the division again in '86, but there were precious few players left on that team compared with the lineup five years earlier: Only three regular players and no starting pitchers remained from the earlier club.

The same is true of the Tiger's teams in the late 1980s. Detroit won the AL East in 1987 (losing the ALCS to the younger Twins) and finished a game behind Boston in '88 with the fifth-oldest team of all time. The Tigers then fell about as far as a team could, landing squarely in the cellar of the AL East in

1989, 30 games behind Toronto. The club overhauled the roster and did much better the next two seasons, finishing third in 1990 and second in '91. That season the Tigers had only three regular players and three of the top 10 pitchers who were with the team two years earlier.

Unfortunately for the O's, things won't get much better this year. Clark, DeShields, Ripken, Surhoff, and Anderson all have guaranteed contracts for 2000; Johnson and Bordick don't, but they will either go to arbitration or sign new deals. So unless management is willing to make some major deals or eat some contracts, the team will probably look very similar to the 1999 version.

Everything points to another disaster if the team tries to play another year with the same players. New manager Mike Hargrove has grown used to playing in the fall—five straight postseason appearances with the Indians—but he'll have October off this year.

THE STREAK REDUX

Cal Ripken played a record 2,632 consecutive games, all the while saying that The Streak wasn't affecting his offensive performance. In a perfect world, Ripken could have his cake and eat it, too. That's not the case in baseball, and with The Streak a year past, it's painfully obvious that Ripken would have been a much better hitter for much of the 1990s if he'd have taken some time off.

Ripken has hit .300 only twice since 1991; not coincidentally, in both of those years he played less than a full season. He hit .315 in 1994, but played in only 112 games because of the players' strike that wiped out the last six weeks of the season. Last year, Ripken played in only 86 games due to a back injury that forced him onto the DL twice. Not so strangely, the result was a career-best .340 and a career-high slugging percentage of .584.

Iron Man Cal was an above-average player every year from his rookie season of 1982 through 1991, the year he won his second AL MVP award. He hit at least 21 home runs per year during that time, belting 25 or more 7 of the 10 seasons, but his career definitely peaked in 1991. After that, he experienced a dramatic drop in production and became a below-average player, one who was hurting his team. Excepting 1994, Ripken never hit above .278 from 1992 through '98, and he hit 20 homers only twice from '92 through '99 (including prorating the strike years).

SECRET WEAPON

Rookie Jerry Hairston played an inspired second base when regular Delino DeShields went down with a hamstring injury. Hairston, whose grandfather and father both were major-leaguers, brought some welcome youthful exuberance to an otherwise ancient Baltimore lineup. He not only hustled, but also did a lot of other things very well. He hit for a higher average with more power than DeShields and ran the bases better as well. Hairston also showed plus range while playing flawless defense, committing no errors in 50 games in the field.

ACHILLES HEEL

Of the Orioles' many problems that need fixing, their bullpen is the worst. Baltimore used 14 different relievers in 1999, with none having any real success. Closer Mike Timlin saved 27 games, but he also blew 9 saves and lost 9 games. And Timlin was the best of the bunch; he was the only reliever with more than 13 appearances to log an ERA of less than 4.34. The bullpen was cluttered with never-wases and has-beens.

ENOUGH ALREADY

The merry-go-round in the Baltimore front office needs to stop if the franchise is going to return to contention anytime soon. The team will have its third general manager in three years in 2000, not to mention its third manager in the past four years. All of this, of course, is directly attributable to owner Peter Angelos' super-sized ego and constant meddling. Angelos should take a lesson from his counterpart in New York, George Steinbrenner. The Yankess were hugely successful in the second half of the 1990s partly because their owner greatly reduced his direct interference in day-to-day management. That, of course, was largely due to hiring strong people (particularly manager Joe Torre and former GM Bob Watson, who hasn't gotten the credit he deserves) who could stand up to the boss.

The most telling evidence of all is Cal's dramatically worse second-half performance record. From 1995 through '98, Ripken hit .293 and slugged .472 in June, but he fell all the way to .281/.421 in August and .235/.397 in September. It's clear that he was getting more and more tired as each season progressed, despite his wearisome denials. Last year Ripken hit .365 and slugged .556 in September after spending all of August resting while on the DL.

One of the hidden costs of protecting the Ripken legend is that the Orioles haven't acquired a good reserve third baseman. Last year's substitutes (Jeff Reboulet, Ryan Minor, and Willis Otanez) were truly awful, hurting the team as much as Cal helped when he was in the lineup. It's plain that Ripken won't be able to contribute the way he used to if he plays every day, and that Baltimore needs to face reality and secure a quality alternative at the hot corner.

Because of Ripken's immense popularity, both in Baltimore and everywhere else, the Orioles are under tremendous pressure to play him as much as he's able. However, it's clearly in the best interests of the club if Ripken finishes his career as a part-time or platoon player. Cal doesn't show a pronounced left/right split in his hitting, but the Birds might have to settle for a true platoon player to share time with him.

BEST CASE

The Orioles have good pitching but need to get good years from their aging hitters if they hope to move up in the competitive American League East. The fate of this year's team clearly lies with Cal Ripken, Brady Anderson, and Will Clark. If those three can show a last fling of greatness, Baltimore will have a shot at hanging around the fringes of playoff contention. It's too much to expect that the club will actually make the postseason in 2000, but after the past two years, finishing within striking distance of .500 will be a success—whether that satisfies Peter Angelos or not.

WORST CASE

Baltimore has finished poorly the past two seasons and hasn't done much to make anybody think that 2000 will be different. Albert Belle and Charles Johnson are the only Bird hitters in their prime, and only Belle is truly gifted offensively. The rest of the hitters are frightfully old and well past their prime. The biggest move the club made at December's winter meetings was to bring back designated hitter Harold Baines. While Baines is popular and has been a decent hitter even late in his career, he's not going to bring home a pennant. While the Orioles can't be much worse than they were in 1998 and '99, there's not much reason to expect improvement either.

UNDER THE MICROSCOPE

JERRY HAIRSTON: A solid all-around player with good bloodlines, Hairston does everything well but nothing spectacularly. He projects to be a run-of-the-mill second baseman who will hit for average and for occasional power, but he may end up as a utility player.

CALVIN PICKERING: The 1998 Eastern League MVP (.309, 31 HR, 114 RBI) struggled early in '99 with nagging shoulder problems. The 6'6" left-handed swinger recovered to belt 10 home runs in July. "Pick" is an outstanding pure hitter with an opposite-field stroke and an understanding of the strike zone, but he's had troubles against left-handers and is still extremely raw defensively.

MATT RILEY: Undoubtedly one of the best southpaw pitchers in the minor-leagues, Riley still needs some polish. The 20-year-old dominated at the Class A and Double-A levels and certainly has the stuff to be a frontline pitcher, but he's only thrown 260 innings in the minor-leagues. He fanned 325 batters and allowed just 189 hits in that span, but don't look for him at the Birds' spring training.

B. J. RYAN: Ryan has had a great deal of success—especially against fellow left-handers—in his brief two-year career. The 1998 17th-round pick also has been effective against right-handers. Ryan throws in the 89–92 mph range with a deceptive delivery and a very good breaking ball. He should fit into the Baltimore bullpen on a full-time basis this season.

BALTIMORE

TOP PROSPECTS

The Baltimore Orioles had a another disastrous season in 1999. Despite having one of the highest payrolls in the game, the Birds failed to play .500 baseball for the second straight season, and its minor-league affiliates had the third-worst winning percentage (.453) of any organization.

On the bright side, RHP **SIDNEY PONSON** established himself as a front-of-the-rotation pitcher; the organization got a chance to audition several of its top prospects; and it received six additional first-round picks in 1999 for the losses of Roberto Alomar, Eric Davis, and Rafael Palmeiro to free agency.

The strength of the Baltimore farm system lies in a core of young, talented position players and LHP **MATT RILEY**.

2B **JERRY HAIRSTON** showed that he has the ability to play second base on an everyday basis. 1B **CALVIN PICKERING**, who won Double-A Eastern League MVP honors with a monster season in 1998, struggled with shoulder injuries all season, surfaced at the big-league level for the second straight September and is expected to be an everyday contributor in the near future. Much-hyped 3B **RYAN MINOR** has not shown that he can hit advanced minor-league pitching consistently, let alone major-league pitching. OF **EUGENE KINGSALE** isn't likely to be an everyday player. C **JAYSON WERTH**, a 1997 first-rounder who ended the season in Double-A, is one of the most talented backstops in the game, but he has yet to demonstrate his skills on a consistent basis.

Baltimore also has a trio of 20-year-old outfield talents with multiple skills: **LUIS MATOS**, **DARNELL MCDONALD**, and **NTEMA NDUNGIDI**.

Few pitchers can match the progress of Riley in his first two years of pro ball. Selected for the HOWE SPORTSDATA All-Prospect Team in 1999, the 20-year-old has dominated every level he's pitched with a fastball and sharp curveball.

The upper-level pitching depth from a few years ago has just about disappeared. Solid prospects RHP **JULIO MORENO, BRIAN FALKENBORG, DARIN BLOOD**, and **ALVIE SHEPHERD**, '95 first-rounder who was released in '99, have had their careers stalled by arm injuries. LHP **B. J. RYAN**, acquired from the Reds in the Juan Guzman deal, has thrived in his first two years of pro ball and has a tremendous upside as a setup man. RHP **GABE MOLINA** has had success all the way up the ladder and has a chance to be a serviceable reliever for the big club.

The organization has hopes for RHP **JACOBO SEQUEA**, a power arm also acquired in the Guzman deal, and RHP **JOHN STEPHENS**, the 1999 minor-league strikeout leader, but Stephens is not overpowering and will struggle to reach those totals at a higher level.

Baltimore had seven of the first 50 selections in the 1999 draft, selecting four pitchers, two outfielders, and a shortstop: RHP **MIKE PARADIS**, OF **KEITH REED**, OF **LARRY BIGBIE**, and SS **BRIAN ROBERTS**.

CF
*BRADY ANDERSON 36
? #Eugene Kingsale ML 23 93/ND
↑ Luis Matos 2A 21 96/10H

LF
*B.J. SURHOFF 35
RICH AMARAL 38
? #Roberto Rivera 2A 23 94/ND
○ *Ntema Ndungidi A+ 21 97/1H

RF
ALBERT BELLE 33
? Wady Almonte 2A 25 93/ND
↑ Darnell McDonald A+ 21 97/1H

SS
MIKE BORDICK 34
? Jesse Garcia ML 26 93/26C
○ Eddy Martinez A+ 22 94/ND
○ Maikell Diaz A- 21 95/ND
○ #Brian Roberts A- 22 99/1C

2B
*DELINO DESHIELDS 31
↑ Jerry Hairston ML 24 97/11C
? Carlos Casimiro 2A 23 94/ND
? #Eddy Garabito A+ 21 96/ND

3B
CAL RIPKEN 39
? Ryan Minor ML 26 96/33C
? Richard Paz 2A 22 93/ND
? *Ivanon Coffie 2A 23 95/ND

1B
*WILL CLARK 36
JEFF CONINE 34
? Franky Figueroa A+ 23 96/5H
○ *Rick Elder A- 20 98/1H

SP/RP

RELIEVERS
MIKE TIMLIN 34
*CHUCK McELROY 32
*DOUG JOHNS 32
MIKE TROMBLEY 33
AL REYES 29
○ Gabe Molina ML 25 96/21C
? Ryan Kohlmeier 2A 23 96/14C
? Derek Brown A+ 23 94/40H
○ *B.J. Ryan ML 24 98/17C
? *Radhames Dykhoff 3A 25 93/ND
? *Jeff Wilson A+ 24 97/29C

C
CHARLES JOHNSON 28
MIKE FIGGA 29
? Tommy Davis ML 27 94/2C
? #Chip Alley 2A 23 95/2H
↑ Jayson Werth 2A 21 97/1H

DH
*HAROLD BAINES 41
↑ *Calvin Pickering ML 23 95/35H

STARTERS
MIKE MUSSINA 31
SCOTT ERICKSON 32
SIDNEY PONSON 23
JASON JOHNSON 26
★ *Matt Riley ML 20 97/3C
? Brian Falkenborg 2A 22 96/2H
? Josh Towers 2A 23 96/15C
? Richard Bauer A+ 23 97/5C
? Sean Douglass A+ 21 97/2H
↑ Jacobo Sequea A- 18 97/ND
○ John Stephens A- 20 96/ND
○ Steve Bechler A- 20 98/3H
○ Mike Paradis A- 22 99/1C
? *John Parrish 2A 22 96/25H
↓ *Richard Stahl DP 19 99/1H

MAJOR LEAGUERS IN ALL CAPS
Minor leaguers in upper-and-lower case

BEFORE A PLAYER'S NAME:
* left-handed hitter/pitcher
# switch-hitter
?=prospect status (see explanation)

AFTER A PLAYER'S NAME:
Level at which he spent most of 1999 season; age as of July 1, 2000; year he was drafted; round drafted (ND= non-drafted amateur free agent); drafted out of high school (H) or college (C)

EXPLANATION OF PROSPECT RATINGS

★ Potential big-league star

↑ Projected regular player in majors (for pitchers: rotation starter or closer)

○ Projected platoon or utility player in majors (pitcher: setup or middle relief)

? Possible big-league reserve or long reliever

↓ High draft pick or "tools" player who hasn't performed to expectations

BALTIMORE

BOSTON RED SOX

Management
Manager	Jimy Williams
G.M.	Dan Duquette
President/CEO	JRY Corp./John Harrington

Career Record
545–463 / .541
670–561 / .544
489–418 / .539

1999 Record
Won–Lost	Pct.	Finish/G.B. (Division)	Finish/G.B. (Wild Card)
94–68	.580	2/4 (E)	1

Preseason Consensus Projection
4 (3.55)

1st Half	2nd Half	Home	Road	Intradivision	Interleague
45–32	49–36	49–32	45–36	28–21	6–12

Comebacks	Blowouts	Nail-Biters	Grass	Turf	Sept.–Oct.
8–9	34–20	36–28	83–57	11–11	20–10

NUMBERS DON'T LIE

	Team (Rank)	Opponents (Rank)	League Avg.
Runs/Game	5.16 (9)	4.43 (1)	5.18
Batting Avg.	.278 (7)	.253 (1)	.274
On-Base Avg.	.350 (7)	.315 (1)	.347
Slugging Avg.	.448 (6)	.398 (1)	.439
Strikeouts	929 (3)	1131 (1)	998
Home Runs	176 (9)	160 (2)	188
Stolen Bases	67 (14)	159 (14)	104
ERA	4.00 (1)		4.87
Errors	127 (12)		114

▶ THE INSIDER 2000

NOMAR AND PEDRO DON'T NEED NO MO HELP

While the underdog Red Sox ultimately failed once more to make it to the October Classic, the team and its oft-criticized GM, Dan Duquette, had a pretty good year in 1999. Duquette survived a storm of controversy over the departure of fan hero Mo Vaughn to watch his team go head-to-head against the hated Yankees for the AL pennant.

The 1999 Red Sox were a team unlike most others Boston has fielded in recent years. Instead of a team loaded with name players, instead of a lineup of aging stars whose batting numbers look good only after Fenway's inflation, instead of a staff of overrated veteran hurlers whose reputations far exceeded their remaining stuff, the Bosox were carried on the backs of two true superstars—Nomar Garciaparra and Pedro Martinez.

The rest of Boston's roster in '99 was made up of a bunch of modestly talented but hungry ballplayers who could do a few things right—most important, not lose the games that Pedro and Nomar had already won. Whereas the 1998 Red Sox had virtually all of their talent concentrated in four players (Garciaparra, Vaughn, Martinez, and closer Tom Gordon), last year's team concentrated its talent into half that number of bodies.

Most championship teams get six to eight wins above average from their two best players. Using *Total Baseball*'s rating system, the '99 Sox got 12.2 from Martinez and Garciaparra. Since Boston finished at 94–68, that meant that everyone else on the team contributed a net of less than one win! Of the remaining Bosox, only Bret Saberhagen (3.2 wins above average) had a really impressive season.

One of the ways the Sox made up for the lack of their big bopper was the team's solid defense—not normally a hallmark of Boston teams—especially on the left side of the infield. In the outfield, Troy O'Leary and Trot Nixon in the corners and Damon Buford in center were adequate, and Darren Lewis displayed plus range in both center and right.

Without Mo, the Sox hit "only" 176 homers, ranking them ninth in the AL, even though it was the 10th-highest score in Boston history. (The 1996 and '98 teams were ranked second and third, respectively; the '97 team was eighth. The '95 team also would have hit more homers if adjusted for the games missed due to the strike.) Rookies Brian Daubach and Nixon, along with veterans O'Leary (who led the team with a career-high 28

MOMENT OF TRUTH

On July 30 the Red Sox were crushed by the Yankees, 13–3, a loss that allowed Toronto to move past Boston into second place in the AL East. With two more games left with New York and three against Cleveland immediately afterward, plenty of Boston fans expected another collapse. The Sox didn't fold, however, taking the next two games against the Yankees and winning 18 games in August. By the beginning of September, Boston was five games ahead of Toronto and had solidified its position as the AL wild-card leader.

BIGGEST SURPRISE

It's not often that a club is happy finishing below the middle of the league in offense, but the Red Sox had to be pleased by what their batters accomplished in 1999, even though they finished ninth in both runs and homers. Though losing Mo Vaughn was supposed to be a fatal blow for the team, several players stepped up to the plate with first baseman–DH Brian Daubach and catcher Jason Varitek leading the way. Daubach hit .294 with 21 homers and 73 RBIs in only 381 at-bats. Varitek's 20 home runs, 39 doubles, and 76 RBIs were far beyond expectations.

BIGGEST DISAPPOINTMENT

John Valentin was expected to pick up some of the slack left by Vaughn's departure, but the 32-year-old endured his worst season as a full-time player. Valentin's batting average failed to bounce back to the .300 neighborhood, where it had been from 1994 to 1997, and his .398 slugging percentage was one of the worst among AL third basemen and 74 points below his previous average.

round-trippers), Mike Stanley, and surprising Jason Varitek more than made up for Vaughn's lost power.

Not just unheralded, but also completely unknown, career minor-leaguer Brian Daubach slugged .526 with an on-base percentage of .360, better than Vaughn in '99. While Daubach and his platoon partner Mike Stanley weren't in contention for a Gold Glove (or even a bronze glove) at first, neither was the injury-hobbled Vaughn. Overall for Boston first basemen: .280 batting average, .369 on-base percentage, and .502 slugging with 31 homers and 102 RBI. For Vaughn in 139 games at first and DH in Anaheim: .281, .358, and .506, with 33 homers and 108 RBI.

Who would have guessed before the season that Boston could have almost replaced Vaughn with those two guys?

PEDRO THE MAGNIFICENT

Pedro Martinez had an outstanding season. The numbers speak for themselves—23–4, 2.07 ERA, 313 strikeouts, and only 206 total base runners allowed in 213.1 innings. Martinez is easily the best pitcher in the game right now and was light-years ahead of any other hurler in 1999, including Randy Johnson.

Martinez posted an ERA of 2.07, the third-lowest in the AL in the 1990s. Roger Clemens posted an ERA of 1.93 in 1990 and 2.05 in '97, and while the Rocket clearly was the best pitcher in the league during those years, he wasn't as far ahead of the pack as Martinez was in 1999. Four other pitchers were within a run of Clemens in both those seasons, David Cone was 1.37 runs per game behind Martinez last year, and only seven others were within 2 runs per game.

It's hard to imagine one player being so much better than everybody else in the league. Martinez not only surpassed any other AL pitcher in every major category, but the second-best pitchers weren't even close.

The unanimous AL Cy Young award winner's ERA was 40 percent lower than David Cone's. Opponents hit for an average 10 percent less against Martinez than against Cone. Pedro allowed 22 percent fewer runners per nine innings than Eric Milton, and his opponents' on-base average was 17 percent less than Milton's. Martinez struck out 56 percent more batters per 9 innings than Chuck Finley. Finally, the slugging average of Pedro's opponents was 23 percent less than Cone's.

In the NL, Cy Young winner Randy Johnson's ERA was 7.5 percent better than Kevin Millwood's, and Johnson's strikeout total was 65 percent higher than Kevin Brown's. Johnson didn't lead in any of the other categories that Martinez did. In base runners, opponents' on-base average, and opponents' batting average, Millwood was the NL's best; Johnson was second. In opponents' slugging, Mike Hampton was ahead of Johnson.

Martinez acheived his stellar performance despite pitching in Fenway. While the Fens is no longer a paradise for home-run hitters, it's still a good hitters' park: Nearly 7 percent more runs were scored in Boston's home games last year than in away games. Pedro went an amazing 13–2 at home with a 2.22 ERA. And on the road, 10–2 and 1.88.

Martinez was truly awesome, but many were surprised to learn that he had one of the best seasons any pitcher has had in since the advent of the American League in 1901. Fans who grew up in the 1960s and '70s are conditioned to expect the top pitchers in each league to have ERAs well below 3.00. And Roger Clemens was nearly as dominating in 1997 as Martinez was in '99.

The fact is that Pedro Martinez in '99 had the fifth-best single season of any pitcher in the 20th century. He finished with 8.1 adjusted pitching wins, the *Total Baseball* ranking that compares a pitcher's ERA and innings to the league average and adjusts for his home park.

The 10 best pitchers in a season since 1900 are: Walter Johnson, who was 9.8 wins above average in 1912; Johnson again, with 9.3 in 1913; Lefty Grove, 9.0 in 1931; Cy Young, 8.5 in 1901; Martinez; Christy Mathewson, 8.0 in 1905; Pete Alexander, 7.8 in 1915; Clemens, 7.6 in 1997; Dolf Luque, 7.5 in 1923; and Bob Gibson, 7.5 in 1968. These great performances include Gibson's remarkable '68 campaign, when he posted a 1.12 ERA, and Johnson's back-to-back 1912–13 seasons, when he won 69 and lost only 19.

Martinez in 1999 was in pretty rare company. Every retired pitcher on the list above is in the Hall of Fame except Luque. Young (511), Johnson (417), Alexander (373), and Mathewson (373) are the four winningest pitchers in major-league history. Grove won 300; Gibson, 251. The Hall of Famers need no introduction, but Luque deserves a short one.

Luque was a right-handed Cuban pitcher who pitched for 20 years and won 194 games between 1914 and 1935, mostly with the Reds. He had two great seasons with Cincinnati in '23 and '25, leading the NL in wins and percentage (.771) in 1923 and leading the league in ERA both years (1.93 in 1923, more than two runs below the NL average; 2.63 in 1925, more than 1.5 runs below the league average).

SECRET WEAPON

Knuckleballer Tim Wakefield had made only 13 relief appearances in his big-league career prior to the 1999 season. Then came his remarkable conversion into an emergency closer after Tom Gordon went down with an arm injury. It was a move that few would have thought of, much less had the courage to try, but Jimy Williams' decision to bring Wakefield out of the pen paid huge dividends for the Red Sox. Wakefield's 15 saves (in 18 opportunities) tied him with Derek Lowe, who succeeded him as closer the last two months.

ACHILLES HEEL

The Sox struggled to find consistent starting pitching behind Martinez. With Wakefield in the bullpen and Bret Saberhagen pitching only half the season because of injuries, Boston had to give too many starts to pitchers who shouldn't have been in the rotation. Mark Portugal was awful (5.51 ERA), rookie Brian Rose was mediocre (4.87), and Pat Rapp (4.12) had as many bad days as good ones. The Red Sox were so desperate that they gave rookie Jin Ho Cho seven starts (5.72).

ENOUGH ALREADY

The "Curse of the Bambino" story is a great one, detailing how owner Harry Frazee sold Babe Ruth to the Yankees for cash to help him finance a Broadway play, *No No Nanette*, thus putting a curse on the Red Sox that prevents the team from winning the World Series. It's common knowledge that The Curse is what made Bill Buckner boot that easy grounder in 1986; it also made the Yankees' Bucky Dent hit that infamous home run in 1978. However, after 1,375,299,102 retellings, it's now time to retire the story as the Red Sox enter their second century of baseball.

Most of these pitchers led their leagues in wins, ERA and strikeouts—the so-called pitching Triple Crown. The only exceptions were in 1912, when Smokey Joe Wood of the Red Sox led the AL in wins instead of Johnson; in 1923, when Dazzy Vance of Brooklyn led the NL in strikeouts instead of Luque; and in 1968, when Juan Marichal led the NL in wins instead of Gibson.

Of course, Pedro Martinez also meant the world to his team. The Red Sox were little more than a .500 team when Martinez didn't get the decision, going 71–64 in such games. By comparison, Grove was 31–4 for the A's in 1931; the rest of the staff went 76–41. Mathewson was 31–9 for the 1905 Giants, while their other pitchers were 74–39. The '68 Cardinals were 75–56 when Gibson didn't get the decision.

Martinez was so good in 1999 that he may never be able to repeat that brilliance. That's not to say he won't be dominating or won't win the Cy Young award again; but of all the great pitchers who managed to reach this level, only the legendary Walter Johnson managed to have two of the top 10 single-season performances of all time.

At 28, Martinez has seven full seasons in the majors under his belt, and he's been disabled only once in his career (for 15 days, immediately after the 1999 All-Star break). However, if there's anybody in the game today who's capable of being that good again, it's Pedro.

BEST CASE

Assuming Pedro Martinez and Nomar Garciaparra stay healthy, Boston again has a chance to compete with their archrivals from the Bronx. It's not likely that Carl Everett will be any better than he was in 1999, but he is still an upgrade in the outfield. The Sox fully expect that Ramon Martinez will be able to return and pitch a full season, thus strengthening the rotation. Both Jason Varitek and Brian Daubach had surprising seasons in 1999, which they are capable of repeating. If Boston can find a closer (and Derek Lowe certainly has the stuff), Pedro and Nomar have the ability to carry the club deep into October.

WORST CASE

Any doom-and-gloom scenario begins with Pedro Martinez or Nomar Garciaparra missing significant time due to injury. If anything happens to either player, it'll be panic time in Beantown. Even if the two megastars are healthy and productive, there are still some things to worry about. John Valentin needs to regain his footing after an awful year, and there are gaping holes in the bullpen. Tom Gordon will miss the entire season after elbow surgery, and Rod Beck's arm is just about worn out. The Sox got away with using Tim Wakefield to close games in the second half of last season, but few expect the versatile knuckleballer to save 40 games.

UNDER THE MICROSCOPE

JIN HO CHO: Cho, who looked dominant in the minors in '98, was 9–3 with 3.45 ERA at Pawtucket in '99, and commands a slider, change-up, and curve to supplement a low-90s fastball. His downfall at the major-league level has been leaving too many pitches in the heart of the strike zone. He is a long shot to make the starting rotation before 2001.

TOMOKAZU OHKA: Ohka, a Japanese import in his first year in the States, has good breaking stuff, a low-90s fastball, and decent command. He was literally unbeatable in the minors but, like Cho, needs to work on better placement to get major-leaguers out consistently.

DERNELL STENSON: Stenson has breathtaking power and good patience at the plate but has to make drastic improvements defensively to take over the first-base job. Despite a strong arm, Stenson was moved to first base in '99 due to questionable range in the outfield. He piled up errors there, including four in one game, and if his problems aren't rectified, Stenson could be destined for a platoon or a DH role.

MICHAEL COLEMAN: Attitude problems plagued him in 1998, but Coleman rebounded strongly in '99 under the guidance of Pawtucket manager Gary Jones. Coleman homered 30 times and stole 14 bases while playing a solid center field. But because of his past indiscretions, susceptibility to off-speed pitches, and defensive lapses, the Red Sox do not appear willing to give Coleman an opportunity to win a job with the club.

BOSTON

TOP PROSPECTS

The Boston Red Sox made good use of their organizational resources to supplement their big-name talents and march into the playoffs in 1999. The previous year's farm graduate OF **TROT NIXON** made valuable contributions on an everyday basis. When a need arose early in the season, RHPs **JUAN PENA, BRIAN ROSE,** and **JIN HO CHO** came through with several quality starts. When John Valentin went down twice with knee problems, 3B **WILTON VERAS** was summoned from Double-A and more than held his own. In addition, Dan Duquette and Jimy Williams gave minor-league veteran 1B **BRIAN DAUBACH** a chance, and he was under consideration for AL Rookie of the Year.

The Red Sox also dipped into the farm system and traded 3B **COLE LINIAK**, LHP **ROBERT RAMSAY**, and LHP **MIKE MAROTH** to bring in the likes of Rod Beck, Butch Huskey, and Bryce Florie for the stretch drive. Though deals over the past few seasons have thinned out some of the talent in the organization, the Red Sox still have some pitching depth and a few skilled position players on the horizon.

RHP **TOMOKAZU OHKA,** who won all 15 of his minor-league decisions, heads the list of pitching prospects. He went 8–0 in the Double-A Eastern League and 7–0 at Triple-A, but struggled when promoted to the big leagues for a few starts early in the season. Cho and fellow Korean RHPs **SUNNY KIM** and **SEUNG JUN SONG** complete a young, strong stable of Pacific Rim finds. RHP **JUSTIN DUCHSCHERER** broke through with good seasons at the Class A level, but injuries stalled the progress of 1997 first-rounder LHP **JOHN CURTICE,** hard-throwing closer RHP **JEFF TAGLIENTI,** and LHP **BRIAN BARKLEY**. Pena, who won both of his starts in Boston, was also sidetracked with arm problems.

However, Triple-A 2B **JIM CHAMBLEE** and Double-A 2B **DAVID ECKSTEIN** have consistently performed well throughout the minor-leagues and are nearly ready. C **STEVE LOMASNEY,** who belted 20 homers between Class A and Double-A, has emerged as the best of Boston's crop of backstops.

1B **DERNELL STENSON,** one of the organization's best hitters entering 1999, held his own offensively as the youngest player in the Triple-A International League, but struggled terribly with his defense. Stenson made the switch from the outfield and led all minor-league outfielders with 34 errors in only 121 games. OF **MICHAEL COLEMAN,** once considered the organization's center fielder of the future, had a solid Triple-A repeat season but was not given a look in the majors until very late September.

▶ THE INSIDER 2000

LF
*TROY O'LEARY 30
JERMAINE ALLENSWORTH 28
? Virgil Chevalier 2A 26 94/NDH

CF
#CARL EVERETT 30
DARREN LEWIS 32
○ Michael Coleman 3A 24 94/18H
? Rontrez Johnson A+ 23 95/16H
? Tonayne Brown A- 22 98/36C
↓ Julio Guerrero A- 19 98/NDC
↓ Rick Asadoorian DP 19 99/1H

RF
*TROT NIXON 26
? Mark Fischer A+ 24 97/1C

SS
NOMAR GARCIAPARRA 26
MANNY ALEXANDER 29
○ Donnie Sadler ML 25 94/11H
? #Aaron Capista A+ 21 97/2H
? Alejandro Ahumada A- 21 96/NDH

2B
#JOSE OFFERMAN 31
JEFF FRYE 33
○ Jim Chamblee 3A 25 95/12C
○ David Eckstein 2A 25 97/19C
○ #Angel Santos A- 20 97/4C

3B
JOHN VALENTIN 33
○ Wilton Veras ML 22 95/ND

1B
MIKE STANLEY 37
*BRIAN DAUBACH 28
↑ *Dernell Stenson 3A 22 96/3H

SP/RP

RELIEVERS
DEREK LOWE 27
TOM GORDON 32
ROD BECK 31
JOHN WASDIN 27
BRYCE FLORIE 30
*RHEAL CORMIER 33
? Rafael Betancourt 2A 25 93/ND
○ Jeff Taglienti 2A 24 97/7C

C
#JASON VARITEK 28
*SCOTT HATTEBERG 30
↑ Steve Lomasney 2A 22 95/5C
○ Shea Hillenbrand 2A 24 96/10C

DH
BUTCH HUSKEY 28

STARTERS
PEDRO MARTINEZ 28
BRET SABERHAGEN 36
BRIAN ROSE 24
RAMON MARTINEZ 32
TIM WAKEFIELD 33
JEFF FASSERO 37
○ Jin Ho Cho ML 24 98/NDC
↑ Juan Pena ML 23 95/27C
↑ Tomokazu Ohka ML 24 98/ND
? Jason Sekany 3A 24 96/2C
○ Sun Kim 2A 22 97/ND
? Paxton Crawford 2A 22 95/9H
? Josh Garrett A+ 22 96/1H
? Justin Duchscherer A+ 22 96/8H
↑ Seung Jun Song A- 20 99/ND
↓ Brad Baker A- 19 99/1H
? *Brian Barkley 3A 24 94/5H
↓ *John Curtice A- 20 97/1H

MAJOR LEAGUERS IN ALL CAPS
Minor leaguers in upper-and-lower case

BEFORE A PLAYER'S NAME:
* left-handed hitter/pitcher
# switch-hitter
?=prospect status (see explanation)

AFTER A PLAYER'S NAME:
Level at which he spent most of 1999 season; age as of July 1, 2000; year he was drafted; round drafted (ND= non-drafted amateur free agent); drafted out of high school (H) or college (C)

EXPLANATION OF PROSPECT RATINGS

★ Potential big-league star

↑ Projected regular player in majors (for pitchers: rotation starter or closer)

○ Projected platoon or utility player in majors (pitcher: setup or middle relief)

? Possible big-league reserve or long reliever

↓ High draft pick or "tools" player who hasn't performed to expectations

BOSTON

NEW YORK YANKEES

Management
Manager	Joe Torre
G.M.	Brian Cashman
President/CEO	George Steinbrenner

Career Record
1273–1236 / .507
212–112 / .654
2343–1900 / .552

1999 Record
Won–Lost	Pct.	Finish/G.B. (Division)	Finish/G.B. (Wild Card)
98–64	.605	1 (E)	

Preseason Consensus Projection
1 (1.00)

1st Half	2nd Half	Home	Road	Intradivision	Interleague
46–29	52–35	48–33	50–31	31–18	9–9

Comebacks	Blowouts	Nail-Biters	Grass	Turf	Sept.–Oct.
9–3	31–19	35–26	83–58	15–6	17–14

NUMBERS DON'T LIE

	Team (Rank)	Opponents (Rank)	League Avg.
Runs/Game	5.56 (3)	4.51 (2)	5.18
Batting Avg.	.282 (4)	.255 (2)	.274
On-Base Avg.	.366 (2)	.329 (2)	.347
Slugging Avg.	.453 (5)	.400 (2)	.439
Strikeouts	978 (6)	1111 (3)	998
Home Runs	193 (8)	158 (1)	188
Stolen Bases	104 (10)	131 (13)	104
ERA	4.16 (2)		4.87
Errors	111 (7)		114

▶ THE INSIDER 2000

A STELLAR TEAM WITH FEW SUPERSTARS

One of the many attributes that has made Joe Torre's Yankees so attractive to baseball fans is how well they fit the team concept. The Yanks feature good pitching, superior hitting, and plus defense at almost every position. The team has a few superstars—it would be very hard to be this good without some—but what has made it extraordinary is the quality and depth throughout the rotation, the bullpen, and the lineup. Because the Yanks have virtually no weaknesses to be exploited, they represent the archetype of a solid team.

The 1996–99 Yankees, three-time World Champions, certainly have proved themselves to be the team of the 1990s and one the best teams of all time. But how do the individual players stack up? In other words, where do today's players rate among their historic pinstriped brethren?

Catcher Jorge Posada is a fine two-way player, but he is several levels below the greatest catchers in the history of the Yankees. Surely Yogi Berra, Bill Dickey, Elston Howard, and Thurman Munson were head, shoulders, and face masks above Posada—and that covers about 60 years. Posada's mentor, Joe Girardi, wouldn't even register on this scale.

The Yanks have had many excellent first basemen in their history: Lou Gehrig, Don Mattingly, and Chris Chambliss. Bill Skowron could also hit. People forget that Wally Pipp, Gehrig's predecessor, was a damn fine player. Tino Martinez, the current first sacker, fits into the middle of this continuum. Never a dominant player in any category, Martinez is a good, consistent offensive and defensive performer, but nowhere near the heart of his team like Gehrig and Mattingly.

Second baseman Chuck Knoblauch hasn't performed up to his early-career level since coming to New York. Struggling offensively in 1998 and defensively in '99, he is still an above-average player but no longer one of the best at his position. Tony Lazzeri, Joe Gordon, Willie Randolph, and even Bobby Richardson are tough competition.

Derek Jeter is already New York's best shortstop ever. The franchise has had good shortstops, such as Kid Elberfeld, Roger Peckinpaugh, Phil Rizzuto, Frank Crosetti, and Tony Kubek, but the Yanks have lacked a top-notch player at the position for decades. Remember that the club went through five different starting shortstops in as many seasons (Alvaro Espinoza, Andy

MOMENT OF TRUTH

Because of New York's postseason dominance, many will quickly forget that the Yankees weren't nearly as powerful in the regular season of 1999 as in their dream season. In fact, the Yankees were a second-place club over a two-week stretch in late May and early June. New York trailed Boston by 2 ½ games on May 25 after a 5–2 loss to the Red Sox, but the Yankees beat Boston 8–3 and 4–1 the next two days. That started a stretch of eight wins in 10 games, and although the Yankees didn't take over first place for good until June 9, their rebound was a signal that they were playing better and weren't going to panic at the first sign of trouble.

BIGGEST SURPRISE

David Cone had an outstanding season for a 36-year-old pitcher with a history of injuries, especially after he appeared to be finished in 1996. Cone would have been a serious contender for the Cy Young award except for a pitching demigod named Pedro Martinez. Although Cone tired in the last six weeks of the season, he began the year by going 7–2, establishing himself as the staff ace while many of the team's other starters were struggling. The wily veteran was very good in the postseason as well, dominating the Braves in the second game of the World Series.

BIGGEST DISAPPOINTMENT

Roger Clemens certainly wasn't horrible in 1999, but he didn't come close to matching the stellar performance of his previous two seasons, in Toronto. Expected to be the ace of an already outstanding staff, the Rocket missed nearly a month early in the season with a strained hamstring, and didn't win consecutive starts after June 29; he lost eight of his last 14 decisions.

Stankiewicz, Spike Owen, Mike Gallego, and Tony Fernandez) before Jeter came along.

The Yankees, like most other clubs in the early and mid-20th century, used glovemen and basically singles hitters such as Joe Dugan, Red Rolfe, Andy Carey, and Clete Boyer at third (notable exception: Frank "Home Run" Baker). Scott Brosius is in many ways quite comparable to Clete Boyer; both are slow but steady players with some pop in their bats and fine gloves. Brosius isn't as good as Graig Nettles, though.

The 1998–99 Yankees had only one legitimately weak position, left field, with Ricky Ledee, Shane Spencer, and Chad Curtis sharing time there in '99. The only one with a chance to be a plus player is Ledee, and his star doesn't shine as brightly as it once did. While the Yankees haven't been blessed with many star left fielders—the club's greatest ever are Dave Winfield, George Selkirk, Gene Woodling, and Roy White—Ledee isn't yet a threat to any of his forebears.

In most other franchises, center fielder Bernie Williams would be thought of as an all-time great. The Yankees, however, have some mighty big shoes to fill at that position—would anyone argue that Williams is better than Mickey Mantle or Joe DiMaggio? Although he is better than Earle Combs, Bobby Murcer, and Mickey Rivers. Williams will need several more great seasons even to be considered in the same company as the Mick or Joltin' Joe. But that's no insult to Bernie.

In right field, the world champs feature a hardscrabble, emotional, oft-injured, clutch-hitting fan favorite. He's not Babe Ruth, nor even Reggie Jackson, but Paul O'Neill is a terrific player and comparable to Bob Meusel. O'Neill certainly ranks ahead of Hank Bauer and Lou Piniella, his former manager in Cincinnati. O'Neill is most like Roger Maris; though Paul has never had two MVP seasons, as Maris did, he already has had a longer and more consistent career. Their lifetime slugging averages are but one point apart (.475 for O'Neill, .476 for Maris); O'Neill has higher batting and on-base averages, but didn't play in the pitching-dominated 1960s; both were regarded as good defensively.

What about pitching? Back in the late 1920s, the Yankees had a fearsome foursome in Waite Hoyt, Herb Pennock, Bob Shawkey, and Urban Shocker. Before he came to the Bronx, Roger Clemens was a far greater pitcher than any of them, and David Cone, Orlando Hernandez, and Andy Pettitte stack up pretty well with the rotation of the original "Murderers' Row."

Over the years, New York has featured many excellent

starters, such as Whitey Ford, Ron Guidry, Lefty Gomez, Mel Stottlemyre, Vic Raschi, Allie Reynolds, Red Ruffing, Hoyt, Pennock, Shawkey, Carl Mays, and Al Downing. Cone ranks in the top echelon of this accomplished list, but it's too early in their careers to evaluate Pettitte and Hernandez.

Closer Mariano Rivera has to rank near the top of the club's all-time relief list. Johnny Murphy and Joe Page were great out of the bullpen in the 1930s and '40s, respectively, and Righetti was outstanding after a fine career as a starter. Rivera is the game's dominant short man and ranks right up there with Cy Young award winner Sparky Lyle and Rich Gossage, two of the greatest relievers of all time.

The Yankees, unquestionably the greatest franchise ever in American professional sports, have had more than their share of immortals. Looking at the current roster, it's sobering to see how few of the players rank with the franchise's all-time best. What they do well, despite not having many superstars, is play together. Rarely do they make fundamental mistakes. They understand their roles and are blessed to play for a manager who knows how to keep everyone involved. The times have changed in baseball — the age of the old-time steamroller dynasty, where teams used 16 players while nine guys sat around and shined their belt buckles on the bench, is gone. What the Yankees have is a team composed of good-to-excellent performers at every position, supported by a strong bench, a productive farm system, and an owner willing and able to spend money to acquire or retain deserving players.

WAIT A MINUTE

The Yankees had the AL's second-best ERA in 1999, notching an impressive 4.13 mark that was higher only than Boston's. However, a close look reveals that the Yankees' much-heralded pitching staff isn't quite as good as it looks.

First of all, the Yankees play in what was in 1999 the best pitchers' park in the American League (Seattle's new Safeco Field, opened at midseason, was nearly as inhibiting to hitters as Yankee Stadium). In 1999 intraleague regular-season contests, only 642 runs were scored in games at Yankee Stadium. In games the club played on the road, 790 runs were tallied. That's an 18.7 percent difference.

David Cone's 1.90 ERA at home was the best in the AL, while Roger Clemens' 3.56 mark was sixth-best in the league. Andy

SECRET WEAPON

Some of the credit for New York's success in 1999 should go to Don Zimmer, who filled in as interim manager while Joe Torre was getting treatment for prostate cancer. Zimmer, the Yankees' bench coach who has extensive managerial experience with the Padres, Red Sox, Rangers, and Cubs, kept the team focused during Torre's absence. Zimmer prevented things from falling apart, which was all the Yanks needed to stay on course for their third world championship in the past four years.

ACHILLES HEEL

If there is a weakness on New York's team, it's out in left field. Ricky Ledee, Shane Spencer, and Chad Curtis all played at least 46 games in left, but none ever got hot enough to earn a full-time job. Yankee left fielders hit a combined .234 with only 19 homers and 63 RBIs, well below the AL average for left fielders. Ledee may have some upside, but he struck out 73 times in 250 at-bats. Spencer, the Wunderkind of late 1998, did better in one month in '98 than he did in all of '99, and Curtis simply isn't good enough to

ENOUGH ALREADY

Chuck Knoblauch didn't have a very good year in the field in 1999, but his defensive struggles were blown way out of proportion during the postseason. Every throw he made was replayed several times, and the media even went so far as to film him making throws during infield practice. Yes, 26 errors is high for a second baseman, especially one who won a Gold Glove in 1997, but Jay Bell committed 22 errors at second for Arizona, and his defense didn't get dissected nearly as minutely as Knoblauch's did.

Pettitte had a 5.24 ERA in his road games, and Hideki Irabu struggled to a 5.11 mark away from the Bronx. The staff's ERA at home was 3.45, but on the road, it was 4.85, nearly 1.5 runs higher.

This isn't to say that the Yankees don't have good pitchers. But while their pitching has been overrated the past few years, while their offense has been far better than the raw stats show. The Bombers scored about an extra run per game on the road last year than at home. Their legitimately great hitters, Williams and Jeter, were good everywhere, but some of the more mundane talents really suffered at Yankee Stadium.

Scott Brosius hit just .237 with four homers in home games; Chad Curtis, .225 with no homers. Joe Girardi's on-base plus slugging was a measly .584. At Yankee Stadium, Tino Martinez batted .227 with seven home runs. Jorge Posada hit four homers with a .220 average. All were much better on the road, and, in fact, Martinez was an All-Star hitter when he was out of the Bronx.

ON THE FAST TRACK TO 161 ST. AND RIVER AVE.

As if they needed more help... the Yankees have plenty of good prospects. Pitcher Ed Yarnall, first baseman Nick Johnson, and shortstop Alfonso Soriano are knocking—hard—on the door. Which Yankees will be sent packing to make room for them?

Yarnall, 24, is almost certain to be in the rotation even if David Cone returns. If Cone comes back, Hideki Irabu will probably be dealt. Tino Martinez, signed through 2000, is 32. If Johnson plays well at Triple-A this year, first base will be his in 2001. Chili Davis's retirement clears the way for more at-bats for Ricky Ledee and Darryl Strawberry.

Chuck Knoblauch, inked through 2001, may not get a new deal unless he plays better this season. Despite his improved offensive production in 1999, he could be traded if the Yanks were willing to pay a chunk of his salary. He hasn't played up to his ability in New York and has displayed a questionable attitude and an occasional lack of focus.

Soriano could well be moved to second base this year in an attempt to make him Jeter's long-term double-play partner, especially since the organization has no legitimate prospects at second base. There has also been talk of his eventually playing third base (reasonable) as well as center field (unlikely even if management makes a blockbuster deal for Bernie Williams).

BEST CASE

It's not difficult to imagine the Yankees as 2000 champs. Even with the losses of Joe Girardi, Chili Davis, and Chad Curtis, the lineup and bench are well stocked with qualified role players. Most of the club's top performers are still young, and for the few possible trouble spots (third base, first base), help is on the way from the minors. New York's pitching remains strong, and both Roger Clemens and Andy Pettitte are due for bounce-back seasons. New York has talent, youngsters, money, and history, and that's about as good as it gets in baseball today.

WORST CASE

Ruling out freak injuries, the biggest threats to the Yankees are age and its fallout. Pitchers Clemens and David Cone are old enough now that their workloads have had to be reduced (Cone can no longer pitch every fourth day); Paul O'Neill is strong but can't go on forever. Darryl Strawberry is a truly unknown quantity. Will the club be able to stay aggressive and let veterans (Brosius? Martinez? Knoblauch? the relievers?) depart when they are no longer effective? New York's history has been one of breaking in key young players even when the club was on top. They can't afford to let go of that aggressiveness.

UNDER THE MICROSCOPE

ALFONSO SORIANO: A natural shortstop with an awesome offensive package, Soriano will force the front office to make a tough decision soon. The 21-year-old won't replace Derek Jeter, but Chuck Knoblauch and Scott Brosius are signed through 2001, and Soriano has started working at both spots.

NICK JOHNSON: Some have questioned his over-the-fence power, but the 21-year-old posted a minor-league-leading on-base percentage of .525 and a Double-A Eastern League–best .345 batting average in 1999. The power will come when he gets stronger and learns how to pull the ball more often. Johnson will definitely be ready to take over first base when Tino Martinez's contract expires after this season.

ED YARNALL: Yarnall established himself as one of the top southpaws in the game when he started the 1998 campaign 7–0 with a 0.39 ERA in his first seven Double-A starts. He was selected the Most Valuable Pitcher in the International League in '99. He's ready for a starting role should one surface this spring.

RYAN BRADLEY: Bradley blazed through the minor-leagues in 1998, having had success as both a starter and a closer. In '99 Bradley struggled with command of his mid-90s fastball and splitter, allowing 73 walks, 23 wild pitches, and 28 homers in 145 innings. This season will probably go a long way in determining if Bradley is indeed a prospect or just another power arm who lacks control.

NEW YORK

TOP PROSPECTS

The Yankees' farm system is arguably the most talented in the game. The system may lack overall depth, especially in hitters, but no organization can match its potential impact players.

Both 1B **NICK JOHNSON** and SS **ALFONSO SORIANO** were selected for the HOWE SPORTSDATA All-Prospect Team and should be all-stars for years to come. 3B **DREW HENSON** put up big numbers in the Class A Florida State League, despite starting the year with only 10 professional games under his belt due to his quarterback commitment at the University of Michigan. Scouts salivate over Class A OF **JACKSON MELIAN**, though he has yet to put up the numbers his ability suggests. Seventeen-year-old OF **WILY PENA** is the next impact talent on the way, but he's still too far away for an accurate project. Both Henson and Pena were selected for HOWE SPORTSDATA's All-Teen Team in 1999.

The Yankees also have several other solid position prospects who should have productive big-league careers. SS **D'ANGELO JIMENEZ** raised his stock with an outstanding Triple-A campaign, hitting for average and power while playing a very good shortstop. However, with Jeter and Soriano around, the 21-year-old Jimenez may become trade bait. Double-A 3B **DONNY LEON** emerged as a legitimate power-hitting prospect, slugging 21 homers in a pitcher-friendly home park, but his defense needs an upgrade. Young OF **JUAN RIVERA** is another potential big leaguer. He has the ability to hit and hit for power and should only improve with experience.

New York has some decent pitching depth but it has few front-of-the-rotation pitchers. LHP **ED YARNALL** is one of the top left-handed prospects in the game, winning 26 games at the minor-league level the past two years, and he just needs an opening to join the starting rotation. RHP **RYAN BRADLEY** entered '99 as the top pitcher in the organization, but he struggled terribly with his command at Triple-A. Second-round 1998 pick LHP **RANDY KEISLER** has moved quickly and throws uncommonly hard for a southpaw. The club also used upstart RHP **GERALDO PADUA** to acquire Jim Leyritz from the Padres.

As in most organizations, injuries and inconsistencies stunted the progress of several promising youngsters: RHPs **LUIS DE LOS SANTOS, TODD NOEL, ZACH DAY,** and **RICARDO ARAMBOLES**.

The Yankees have had a fruitful system for much of this decade. They have invested heavily in the foreign market and have stressed winning at the minor-league level. The Yankees' minor-league affiliates, along with those of the Athletics, Mets, and Indians have posted a winning record in each season this decade.

CF
#BERNIE WILLIAMS 31
? #Donzell McDonald 2A 25 95/22C
○ Jackson Melian A+ 20 96/ND

LF
***RICKY LEDEE 26**
SHANE SPENCER 28
? *Richard Brown 2A 23 95/2H
? Jeremy Morris 2A 25 97/8C

RF
***PAUL O'NEILL 37**
○ Juan Rivera A+ 21 96/ND
↓ *Andy Brown A- 20 98/1H
↑ Wily Pena A- 18 98/ND

SS
DEREK JETER 26
↑ #D'Angelo Jimenez ML 22 94/ND
★ Alfonso Soriano ML 22 98/ND
? Erick Almonte A+ 22 96/ND

2B
CHUCK KNOBLAUCH 31
? #Rod Smith 2A 24 94/2H
? *Nick Leach A+ 22 96/5H

3B
SCOTT BROSIUS 33
CLAY BELLINGER 31
○ #Donny Leon 2A 24 95/NDH
↑ Drew Henson A+ 20 98/3H

1B
***TINO MARTINEZ 32**
★ *Nick Johnson 2A 21 96/3H

SP/RP

RELIEVERS
MARIANO RIVERA 30
JASON GRIMSLEY 32
RAMIRO MENDOZA 28
*MIKE STANTON 33
JEFF NELSON 33
*ALLEN WATSON 29
? Todd Erdos ML 26 92/9H
? Jay Tessmer ML 28 95/19C
? Ben Ford 3A 24 94/20C
○ Craig Dingman 2A 26 93/36C
? Craig Lewis A+ 23 97/NDC

C
#JORGE POSADA 28
JIM LEYRITZ 36
○ Victor Valencia 2A 23 93/ND

DH
***DARRYL STRAWBERRY 38**

STARTERS
ORLANDO HERNANDEZ 34
ROGER CLEMENS 37
DAVID CONE 37
*ANDY PETTITTE 28
↑ *Ed Yarnall ML 24 96/3C
? Cam Spence 3A 25 95/12C
○ Jake Westbrook 2A 22 96/1H
? Luis DelosSantos 3A 22 95/ND
○ Ryan Bradley 3A 24 97/1C
○ Jason Beverlin 2A 26 94/4C
? Brian Reith A+ 22 96/6H
? Brandon Knight 3A 24 95/14C
↓ Todd Noel A+ 21 96/1H
? Brian Rogers A+ 23 98/5C
↓ Ricardo Aramboles A- 18 96/ND
↓ David Walling A- 21 99/1C
? *Randy Flores 2A 24 97/9C
○ *Randy Keisler 2A 24 98/2C

MAJOR LEAGUERS IN ALL CAPS
minor leaguers in upper-and-lower case

BEFORE A PLAYER'S NAME:
* left-handed hitter/pitcher
# switch-hitter
?=prospect status (see explanation)

AFTER A PLAYER'S NAME:
Level at which he spent most of 1999 season; age as of July 1, 2000; year he was drafted; round drafted (ND= non-drafted amateur free agent); drafted out of high school (H) or college (C)

EXPLANATION OF PROSPECT RATINGS

★ Potential big-league star

↑ Projected regular player in majors (for pitchers: rotation starter or closer)

○ Projected platoon or utility player in majors (pitcher: setup or middle relief)

? Possible big-league reserve or long reliever

↓ High draft pick or "tools" player who hasn't performed to expectations

NEW YORK

TAMPA BAY DEVIL RAYS

MANAGEMENT
Manager	Larry Rothschild	
G.M.	Chuck LaMar	
President/CEO	Vincent Naimoli	

CAREER RECORD
132–192 / .407
132–192 / .407
132–192 / .407

1999 RECORD

Won–Lost	Pct.	Finish/G.B. (Division)	Finish/G.B. (Wild Card)
69–93	.426	5/29 (E)	9/25

PRESEASON CONSENSUS PROJECTION
5 (5.00)

1ST HALF	2ND HALF	HOME	ROAD	INTRADIVISION	INTERLEAGUE
33–44	36–49	33–48	36–45	25–25	4–14

COMEBACKS	BLOWOUTS	NAIL-BITERS	GRASS	TURF	SEPT.–OCT.
5–6	15–29	37–39	29–35	40–58	10–20

NUMBERS DON'T LIE

	TEAM (RANK)	OPPONENTS (RANK)	LEAGUE AVG.
Runs/Game	4.77 (11)	5.64 (13)	5.18
Batting Avg.	.274 (9)	.286 (11)	.274
On-Base Avg.	.343 (10)	.370 (14)	.347
Slugging Avg.	.411 (12)	.447 (7)	.439
Strikeouts	1042 (9)	1055 (4)	998
Home Runs	145 (13)	172 (4)	188
Stolen Bases	73 (11)	101 (5)	104
ERA	5.06 (10)		4.87
Errors	135 (13)		114

▶ THE INSIDER 2000

RAYS OF HOPE?

In only two years, the Devil Rays have already slipped under the waves. They're old, slow, injury-riddled, unexciting to watch, thin in legitimate prospects, playing in an ugly stadium, and lacking in personality. Worse yet, they've already been deserted by most of their hometown fans.

The second-year franchise's attendance fell so sharply in 1999 (down by more than 30 percent) that commissioner Bud Selig met with Tampa Bay's management to voice his "concern." In contrast, fellow '98 expansion franchise Arizona lost a little more than 16 percent from its first-year attendance, and it started from a much higher base—3.6 million for the D-backs, 2.5 million for the D-Rays. (Of course, if low attendance is cause enough for the commissioner's office to get involved, perhaps the commish should investigate the Milwaukee Brewers.)

Attendance at Tropicana Field was barely above the American League average in 1998 (2.5 million to 2.3 million). Last year the crowds in St. Pete were barely three-quarters of the league average. If the team gets off to a bad start in 2000, it could well be drawing half the crowd of the typical AL team.

In reality, all the Devil Rays' lack of box-office success shows is that most fans will not pay to see a loser that isn't fun to watch and doesn't have a realistic chance to improve. The people of Tampa–St. Petersburg, who waited so patiently for so long for major-league baseball, deserve a lot better than what they've gotten so far.

INTO TOMORROW

Late in the disappointing 1999 season, reports circulated that Tampa Bay would undertake an all-out push for an Arizona-style championship in 2000. The push never materialized, largely due to two factors: the Devil Rays' lack of enough existing quality players to trade, and a weak class of free agents. Even if the money were available, it would have been virtually impossible to make the necessary signings to lift the club into contention.

The Rays had an awful team, constructed through a terrible expansion draft and an overreliance on fading stars. General manager Chuck LaMar, in his first couple of seasons, made very few significant trades. Perhaps LaMar became leery of big deals because his first major trade—sending expansion draft pickup Bob Abreu to the Phillies for veteran Kevin Stocker—was such

MOMENT OF TRUTH

Tampa Bay general manager Chuck LaMar received a new five-year contract in January 1998, just a couple of months before the Devil Rays played their first game. "We couldn't be more pleased with what Chuck has accomplished," said owner Vince Naimoli (quoted in the 1999 *Devil Rays' Information Guide*). Presumably that deal was a reward for putting a team on the field in the few years since the city was awarded an expansion franchise.

Less than two years later, in September 1999, the Arizona Diamondbacks, also members of the '98 expansion round, were on their way to winning a division title, while the Devil Rays were foundering at the bottom of the AL East. LaMar still had more than three years left on his current contract, but that didn't stop Naimoli from giving him a contract extension, this time for two more years (through the 2004 season). The team that Chuck built was horrible and there was little hope for improvement, so essentially LaMar was rewarded for doing nothing.

TAMPA BAY DEVIL RAYS

BIGGEST SURPRISE

The surprise wasn't that Jose Canseco hit plenty of home runs over the Tropicana Field fences. After all, he hit 46 in 1998 with Toronto and had 397 for his career. What was amazing was that Canseco was able to come back as quickly as he did after having had back surgery on July 11. The optimistic prognosis was that he might return to play some games in September but he was activated just 34 days later, on August 20. That's a remarkable comeback from any kind of major surgery, much less surgery that ends the careers of many athletes. For that reason alone, it doesn't really matter that he hit only two home runs the rest of the season.

BIGGEST DISAPPOINTMENT

It's not Rolando Arrojo's fault that he had shoulder problems and was on the disabled list for nearly two months, but it was a big disappointment that he went 7–12 with a 5.18 ERA in the 24 starts he did make. Expectations for Arrojo were high after his impressive major-league debut in 1998, yet he never came close to duplicating that success.

a stinker. This unwillingness to deal hurt the Rays in '99, when they wouldn't trade Fred McGriff or Jose Canseco, even though both were coveted by other teams down the stretch.

While it is understandable that the Devil Rays wanted to have at least two major-league hitters in the lineup, the truth is that neither McGriff nor Canseco will be around by the time the Rays get to be any good. Their actual value as players to a non-contending team that is building for the future is much, much lower than their trade value. Furthermore, dumping the salaries of such veterans would also allow the club to save some money and pursue more quality players in the next couple of seasons.

Since the Rays didn't have many other good players, LaMar decided he would try to trade hurler Rolando Arrojo to obtain some of the players he needed to build a competitive club. But Arrojo, the club's only good starting pitcher in 1998, suffered from inflammation in his pitching shoulder early in the '99 season. When able to pitch, he wasn't particularly effective until later in the year. So, while Arrojo's very low salary and ineligibility for arbitration until 2001 were attractive to other clubs, his age—31—and arm problems weren't.

LEFT OUTFIELD

The Devil Rays' biggest weakness in 1999 was an outfield of almost comic ineptitude. Many would blame the problems on Quinton McCracken's knee injury, which ended his season after just 40 games and forced other players into the lineup. But the fact is that "The Q" isn't all that good even when he's healthy. Even with McCracken in the lineup, the Rays still would have been awful because they had no power, little speed, and subpar range in the pasture.

Speedy center fielder Randy Winn, who was barely adequate as a rookie in 1998, wasn't even close last year. The Rays need to get a real leadoff hitter, and fast, if they expect to improve. They would have been better off giving the job to veteran Dave Martinez (.361 OBA) or Terrell Lowery, who had success when batting in the first slot (.400 OBA in 71 AB).

Dave Martinez, very effective as a fourth or fifth outfielder, was forced into everyday duty in '99 and turned in a performance just south of mediocre. Meanwhile, the presence in the lineup of too many immobile sluggers such as Fred McGriff, Jose Canseco, and Herb Perry, forced the slothlike Paul Sorrento into left field for 57 games. Finally, Jose Guillen, liberated from his purgatory in Pittsburgh, was awful in right.

The only saving grace in the Tampa Bay outfield was Bubba Trammell, excellent in a part-time role. He finished third in the club in homers and doubles in only 283 at-bats, and he walked more than he struck out. While it's unlikely that Trammell would be nearly this productive if he played every day, this team has little alternative but to give him that chance.

Because the Rays don't have much outfield talent in the high minors, it appears that McCracken, Martinez, Trammell, Guillen, and maybe Winn will patrol the outfield again this year. The Devil Rays better pray that their first-round pick in the 1999 draft, high school super prospect Josh Hamilton, develops into the slugging outfielder they expect—and soon.

BOGGED DOWN

The biggest story for the Rays in 1999 was that Wade Boggs collected his 3,000th hit in a Tampa Bay uniform. Unfortunately, his presence did the club far more harm than good.

At the end of his career, Boggs did only one thing well: get on base (.377 OBA). Sure, he managed to eke out a .301 batting average in his final season, but for a third baseman with abominable range, no power, and no speed, that wasn't nearly good enough. The 292 at-bats he used up could have been given usefully to one of several other players who might actually help the Devil Rays in the future. With Boggs just hanging on to reach the milestone, and second-year player Robert Smith unsure about his future, stuck in a platoon role, and hitting badly, the Rays had a chance to make a real decision.

They could have taken the plunge and given the job to Smith outright. They could have given it to Herb Perry or even Aaron Ledesma. They could have promoted longtime Triple-A standout Scott McClain, at least until a real solution could be found. But manager Larry Rothschild did none of those things.

Instead, Smith went down to Triple-A, not returning until September. Perry and Ledesma got some at-bats. With nothing but time to build, and nothing but opportunity to see if his kids could play, management simply did nothing but wait for Wade to hit 3,000. Whatever boost Boggs presence might have given the team's declining attendance, the club it was surely lost in the overall sense of despair into which the Devil Rays have sunk.

SECRET WEAPON

Roberto Hernandez saved 43 games in 47 chances in 1999, but his outstanding season was accomplished in virtual anonymity because the Devil Rays were so bad. Hernandez was signed as an expensive free agent for the D-Rays' inaugural season because management felt it would devastate their young players to suffer late-inning losses in games they had "already won." A top-flight closer, Hernandez will continue to pitch outstandingly in relative obscurity until Tampa Bay trades him for prospects.

ACHILLES HEEL

Tampa Bay plays in one of the best hitting parks in baseball, but that just accentuates how little production the Devil Rays have gotten from their outfield. The 12 players who played in Tampa Bay's outfield in 1999 hit just 37 home runs; many teams got at least that many from one outfielder. The top offender was Dave Martinez, who hit only six home runs in 143 games and 514 at-bats while posting a slugging average 52 points below the league mark and more than 100 points worse than the average AL right fielder.

TAMPA BAY

ENOUGH ALREADY

Wade Boggs got his 3,000th hit on August 7 by batting a solo home run, a line drive that cleared the fence in right field by only a few feet. That meant that Boggs was the first player to get his 3,000th hit on a home run and, predictably, way too much was made of that random fact. What does it matter whether sluggers Hank Aaron, Willie Mays, and Eddie Murray (as well as 18 other players, including Tony Gwynn) got their milestone hit on a single, a double, or a triple? It's one of those statistical oddities that the media love to beat to death without the slightest reflection on its insignificance.

THE STARTING GATE

The Tampa Bay Devil Rays' 1999 pitching story can be expressed in four painful sentences:

1. Bobby Witt, who could've been had last winter for a song by any club in baseball, led the club in starts.

2. One of the team's hottest pitching prospects by year's end was 35-year-old reliever Jim Morris, who had been plucked from a tryout camp.

3. Wilson Alvarez was the staff leader with nine wins.

4. Thirtysomething Dave Eiland, who has pitched for 11 consecutive years in Triple-A, made 15 starts.

Injuries to Arrojo, Tony Saunders, Jim Mecir, and Rick Gorecki destroyed the staff last year, leading to call-ups of prospects Mickey Callaway (not ready) and Dan Wheeler (might be ready).

Despite all the Devil Rays' problems, however, there is some real potential to look forward to in the pitching department at the Orangedome. Rookie Ryan Rupe, who has the ability to develop into a star, was perhaps the club's top starting pitcher by season's end. He, Alvarez, Saunders, and Wheeler could form the basis of what might be a very good rotation. The bullpen's not too bad, either, especially if Mecir and Albie Lopez come back strong and if the team keeps closer Roberto Hernandez.

It wasn't the pitching that kept the Rays in the basement in 1999, and it could well be the club's only strength this year. Management needs to do something to improve the team's weak offense, especially in the outfield, if it hopes to be respectable anytime soon—especially if it hopes to win back its fans.

BEST CASE

Tampa Bay made a big push for offense after the '99 season, grabbing high-profile sluggers Greg Vaughn and Vinny Castilla. Should the key members of the club's power core stay off the DL, the Rays ought to score far more runs than they have in either of their first two seasons. And if both Kevin Stocker and Quinton McCracken stay healthy the defense should be better, too. While the club hasn't moved toward shoring up its mound staff, youngster Ryan Rupe could be good enough to move into the No. 1 spot by mid-season.

WORST CASE

Despite a needed infusion of power, the D-Rays' offense may not be that much better in 2000. Tampa's biggest problem—poor team on-base average—was not addressed by the club's December moves. With nobody on base to start the attack, Vaughn, Castilla, Fred McGriff, and Jose Canseco could each end up hitting 35 homers and driving in 80 runs. Throw in a starting staff thin on proven talent, and the Rays could be doomed to another miserable campaign.

UNDER THE MICROSCOPE

AUBREY HUFF: The 22-year-old third baseman has hit well in each of his minor-league stops since being a fifth-round pick in '98, and is an above-average fielder with a good arm. Huff will likely begin 2000 at Triple-A, but as Bobby Smith struggles, Huff could land an opportunity in the majors before the All-Star break.
STEVE COX: Cox put up gaudy numbers at Triple-A, proving he's more than ready to take the next step. Having shaken his identity as an injury-plagued player, Cox has three years of Triple-A experience under his belt, and he's only 25. If the Devil Rays don't re-sign Fred McGriff, Cox will certainly get a crack at the position.
JIM MORRIS: The 35-year-old Morris made headlines with his improbable rise to the majors in 1999. Drafted by the Milwaukee Brewers in 1983, Morris spent seven years in professional ball before leaving the game due to arm problems. With a fastball clocked at close to 100 mph, Morris caught on with the Rays following a tryout. He may be able to work in a setup role in 2000. He is not likely to last beyond that, however.
DAN WHEELER: Wheeler, a 21-year-old right-hander, worked his way through the Rays' system and made a few encouraging appearances at the big-league level toward the end of 1999. He has good command and a fastball that tops out in the mid-90s. Wheeler will be given every chance to make the rotation out of spring training in 2000.

TAMPA BAY DEVIL RAYS

TOP PROSPECTS

The Devil Rays looked much more like an expansion team in their second year of existence than their counterparts the Diamondbacks did in 1999. The minor-league affiliates, however, produced a winning percentage of .508. It was the second-best organizational winning percentage for a second-year expansion franchise (behind Houston in 1963).

The Orlando Rays in the Double-A Southern League and Hudson Valley Renegades in the short-season Class A New York–Penn League were league champions, making the Devil Rays the first franchise to ever produce two titles within its first two years. Triple-A Durham, beaten by Charlotte in the International League finals, nearly gave them three.

Despite all the minor-league success, Tampa Bay still needs a few more drafts to fully stock its farm system. For now, a decent collection of arms serves as its strength. RHP **RYAN RUPE**, selected in the fifth round of the 1998 draft, was impressive in his first season and needed little minor-league work in '99 before becoming the first organizational product to make the majors. Both RHPs **MICKEY CALLAWAY** and **DAN WHEELER**, drafted by the Rays in '96, earned starts with the big club later in the season.

RHP **MATT WHITE** and LHP **BOBBY SEAY**, both loophole free agents signed after being first-round picks of other teams in 1996, have been brought along slowly but are the Rays' most valued assets. First-round 1997 pick RHP **JASON STANDRIDGE**, a hard thrower, had a breakthrough year in '99 after struggling in his first two seasons. He pitched a no-hitter on June 28 and was promoted to advanced Class A soon afterward.

In 1999, Tampa Bay selected OF **JOSH HAMILTON** in the first overall pick, and he immediately became the top positional prospect in the organization. Hamilton, who received a signing bonus of $3.65 million, has all the tools and displayed them in two short-season leagues. 3B **AUBREY HUFF**, selected in the fifth round in '98, was a great hitter at the University of Miami and has continued to impress with the bat in his first two seasons of professional ball. He closed the '99 regular season with a 28-game hitting streak and hit safely in his first four playoff games with Orlando. OF **KENNY KELLY**, also the starting quarterback for the University of Miami, is a gifted athlete with tremendous upside if he chooses to go the baseball route.

Farther down, the Devil Rays have a pair of teenage shortstops showing promise. Eighteen-year-old **RAMON SOLER**, who spent the entire season at lower-level Class A, and 17-year-old **JORGE CANTU** have demonstrated strong potential. Both are understandably raw but have already put up numbers indicative of bright futures. 3B **ANDREW BEINBRINK**, selected in the seventh round in '99, received recognition for his efforts in his debut season. With a .339 average, 11 homers, and 51 RBI, he was selected as HOWE SPORTSDATA's Star of Stars for statistical excellence in the New York–Penn League.

1B **STEVE COX**, the Triple-A International League's MVP (.341, 25 HR, 127 RBI) in 1999, returned to the form that made him a top prospect with the A's a few years ago.

LF
GREG VAUGHN 34
BUBBA TRAMMELL 28
#QUINTON MCCRACKEN 29
? Danny Clyburn ML 26 92/2H

CF
#**RANDY WINN** 26
○ *Alex Sanchez 3A 23 96/5C
? *Carlos Mendoza 3A 25 93/ND
↑ Kenny Kelly A+ 21 97/2C
↑ *Josh Hamilton A- 19 99/1H

RF
GERALD WILLIAMS 34
*DAVE MARTINEZ 35
JOSE GUILLEN 24
↓ Paul Wilder* A- 22 96/1H

SS
#**KEVIN STOCKER** 30
#DAVID LAMB 25
○ Eddy DelosSantos 2A 22 96/ND
↑ #Ramon Soler A- 18 97/ND

2B
MIGUEL CAIRO 26
TONY GRAFFANINO 28
? Dustin Carr 2A 25 97/22C
○ *Adonis Harrison 2A 23 94/24C

3B
VINNY CASTILLA 32
BOBBY SMITH 26
↑ #Aubrey Huff 2A 23 98/5C
○ Jared Sandberg A+ 22 96/16H

1B
*****FRED MCGRIFF** 36
○ *Steve Cox ML 25 92/5H
○ *Josh Pressley A- 20 98/4H

SP/RP

RELIEVERS
ROBERTO HERNANDEZ 35
RICK WHITE 31
ALBIE LOPEZ 28
ESTEBAN YAN 26
*MIKE DUVALL 25
? John Daniels 3A 26 93/16C
? Eddy Reyes 2A 24 97/7C
↑ Matt White A+ 21 96/NDH
? *Trever Enders 2A 25 96/NDC

STARTERS
WILSON ALVAREZ 30
RYAN RUPE 25
DAVE EILAND 33
CHAD OGEA 29
○ Dan Wheeler ML 22 96/34C
? Pablo Ortega 3A 23 95/ND
○ Travis Harper 2A 24 97/3C
↑ Jason Standridge A+ 21 97/1H
? Ed Kofler A- 22 96/3H
↑ *Bobby Seay 2A 22 96/NDH
↓ Chris Reitsma A+ 22 96/1C
? *Cedrick Bowers 2A 22 96/4H
○ *Todd Belitz 2A 24 97/4C

C
JOHN FLAHERTY 32
MIKE DIFELICE 31
? Toby Hall 2A 24 97/9C

DH
JOSE CANSECO 35

MAJOR LEAGUERS IN ALL CAPS
Minor leaguers in upper-and-lower case

BEFORE A PLAYER'S NAME:
* lefthanded hitter/pitcher
# switch-hitter
?=prospect status (see explanation)

AFTER A PLAYER'S NAME:
Level at which he spent most of 1999 season; age as of July 1, 2000; year he was drafted; round drafted (ND= non-drafted amateur free agent); drafted out of high school (H) or college (C)

EXPLANATION OF PROSPECT RATINGS

★ Potential big-league star

↑ Projected regular player in majors (for pitchers: rotation starter or closer)

○ Projected platoon or utility player in majors (pitcher: setup or middle relief)

? Possible big-league reserve or long reliever

↓ High draft pick or "tools" player who hasn't performed to expectations

TAMPA BAY

TORONTO BLUE JAYS

Management
Manager	Jim Fregosi	
G.M.	Gord Ash	
President/CEO	Interbrew S.A.	

Career Record
945–1016 / .482
378–394 / .490
322–326 / .497

1999 Record
Won–Lost	Pct.	Finish/G.B. (Division)	Finish/G.B. (Wild Card)
84–78	.519	3/14 (E)	3/10

Preseason Consensus Projection
3 (3.05)

1st Half	2nd Half	Home	Road	Intradivision	Interleague
39–41	45–37	40–41	44–37	24–25	9–9

Comebacks	Blowouts	Nail–Biters	Grass	Turf	Sept.–Oct.
11–10	28–21	30–31	33–26	51–52	14–14

NUMBERS DON'T LIE

	Team (Rank)		Opponents (Rank)		League Avg.
Runs/Game	5.45	(5)	5.32	(9)	5.18
Batting Avg.	.280	(5)	.280	(8)	.274
On-Base Avg.	.352	(6)	.349	(10)	.347
Slugging Avg.	.457	(3)	.451	(10)	.439
Strikeouts	1077	(11)	1009	(5)	998
Home Runs	212	(4)	191	(7)	188
Stolen Bases	119	(4)	124	(12)	104
ERA	4.93	(8)			4.87
Errors	106	(3)			114

▶ THE INSIDER 2000

CLEMEN-CY

The Jays were terrible early—and late—in the 1999 season, but they surprised people by vaulting into contention with a hot summer. The open question is whether their inconsistent play indicates an improving team on the way up or a team that is about to slide backward.

Last year, after an early eight-game win streak, the Jays seemingly buried themselves with a poor stretch during which they lost 32 of 47 games. From that point Toronto played excellent ball and, improbably, climbed back into the playoff hunt. Then the team fell apart again in August and sank to what was viewed by many as an unsatisfying 84–78 mark.

The Jays have first-rate talent at only two positions: first base and right field. They have average performers up the middle and a tolerable leadoff hitter–left fielder in Shannon Stewart, who can be expected to improve somewhat. Unfortunately, the Jays' first baseman is a slugger in the prime of his career, up for a rich new contract at the end of this season; their right fielder has all the raw talent one could hope for, but his dedication to the game has been a question mark.

Carlos Delgado and Raul Mondesi are the kind of players a contending team is built around. Both Delgado and budding star Shawn Green rejected long-term deals, necessitating the trade for Mondesi and leaving Delgado's future in Toronto up in the air. The Jays did well to get some value in return for Green before he became a free agent, though a comparison of Mondesi's and Green's age and recent production isn't favorable for the Jays. Thus the team's current core players are far from reliable fixtures as the franchise heads into the new millennium.

RUFFLED FEATHERS

The recurring turmoil in the Toronto clubhouse in recent years may have substantially hindered the team's progress. Green never got along with former manager Cito Gaston, known for his lack of patience with youngsters, and Shawn blossomed into one of the league's best hitters only after Gaston was fired in 1997. Oddly enough, Toronto rehired Gaston—who retains managerial ambitions—to be the Jays' hitting coach for 2000.

There are plenty of Jays still around who played for Gaston. In particular, Cito and David Wells were often at odds when Gaston was manager. Of course, the team's clubhouse problems don't all

MOMENT OF TRUTH

On August 13 the Blue Jays began a six-game home stand with a half-game lead in the AL wild-card race and some hope of still catching the Yankees. But Toronto pitchers allowed 53 runs during that home stand, losing all six games to Oakland and Seattle. That sent the Blue Jays into a tailspin from which they never recovered. Toronto won only four more games the rest of August and never got close to Boston in the wild-card standings after that.

BIGGEST SURPRISE

The surprise wasn't that Tony Batista played as well as he did after the Blue Jays got him from the Diamondbacks in mid-June. The real surprise was that Arizona just gave him away. Batista, just 24 at the time, hit 18 home runs and 16 doubles in only 293 at-bats with Arizona in 1998, and exploded in '99 with the Jays. He set a club record by hitting 26 home runs as a shortstop and, counting the five long balls he hit with Arizona before the trade, he finished the year with an impressive total of 31. Batista has a bright future ahead of him, to say the least.

BIGGEST DISAPPOINTMENT

When the Blue Jays traded for Joey Hamilton and then signed him to a lucrative contract extension before the 1999 season, the club thought it had acquired a key piece to the contender puzzle. Hamilton, one of San Diego's top starting pitchers for four years, was expected to solidify the Jays' rotation. Instead, he was a complete bust, hurt often and ineffective when he did pitch. He made only 18 starts and finished with the worst ERA among Toronto's regular starters.

relate to Gaston. Late in 1998 it was disclosed that the Jays manager at the time, Tim Johnson, had fabricated stories about serving in Vietnam to inspire his players. His pitching coach, Mel Queen (no friend of Johnson's anyway), used that opportunity to openly rip his boss.

Johnson, who obviously had problems ranging beyond when to hit-and-run, earned his ticket out of town. He clearly should have been dumped at the end of the '98 season; bringing in a new manager during spring training was hard on everyone involved. GM Gord Ash was responsible for letting Johnson twist in the wind way too long, which meant that Tim Fregosi didn't have the luxury of getting to know his team during spring training and shaping it to his liking.

Always predisposed toward veterans, Fregosi didn't make much room for rookies in 1999, with a couple of exceptions. He played Homer Bush at second base, and he put some of the Jays' young pitchers in the rotation primarily because of veteran Joey Hamilton's injury.

The starting rotation had its problems. Kelvim Escobar experienced growing pains, and Hamilton missed much of the season. But David Wells went 17–10, Pat Hentgen was acceptable, and 24-year-old Chris Carpenter showed he belonged in a big-league rotation. The bullpen was fine, as outstanding rookie closer Billy Koch was complemented by a deep middle-relief corps of John Frascatore, Paul Quantrill, Graeme Lloyd, and Paul Spoljaric.

Though he employed many veteran players, Fregosi didn't have much of a bench. Craig Grebeck was hurt much of the year, and the Jays were especially weak in the outfield, where has-beens such as Jacob Brumfield were employed. When Jose Cruz Jr., again disappointed, the Jays had no one left to step in. Behind the plate, Fregosi kept catcher Kevin Brown at Triple-A while running the miserable Mike Matheny—who wasn't good enough to play for Milwaukee—out there 57 times.

But it was the inability to find a productive DH that really killed the offense. After making a gutsy decision to let Jose Canseco walk after 1998, Toronto hoped that a platoon of veterans would do the job. They didn't, and the Jays used 18 different players at DH, more than any other AL team. The most frequent designated "hitter" was Willie Greene, who hit only .204 with 12 homers in 226 at-bats overall. As bad as Greene was, most of the other DHs—Dave Hollins, Geronimo Berroa, Brian McRae, and Kevin Witt—were even worse. The only success was David Segui, acquired in a stretch-drive deal with Seattle.

HALLADAY ON ICE

Despite riding into town claiming that he had no set managerial style, Fregosi is clearly a veterans' manager. His years with the Phillies, Angels, and White Sox provide ample evidence of this, and he continued to go with it in Toronto.

Fregosi cut young third baseman Tom Evans late in spring training to hold on to Berroa, then wound up short at the position when his veterans didn't work out. He kept using Tony Fernandez, who was well below average at third base due to a bad knee, instead of giving youngsters such as Evans or Willis Otanez a real chance to play.

This is too bad, because the Jays have a productive minor-league system and when Fregosi did give a young player a chance, he was richly rewarded. After Robert Person was traded, leaving no experienced pitcher who could step into the short-relief role, Koch showed convincingly that he could close in the majors. Roy Halladay and Carpenter made strides. Bush played well, and Otanez showed some sock.

Perhaps the hardest thing to understand was the way Fregosi used rookie righty Halladay. The lanky 22-year-old began the season in the bullpen, then started from mid-April to late May, surrendering 11 runs in one appearance. In his last three May starts he was very effective, but Fregosi shifted him between the rotation and bullpen for the next couple of weeks. In his starts on June 19 and 24, he pitched 13 innings while allowing no runs on five hits.

Not good enough, apparently. Halladay didn't start again until August 13. Fregosi may have disliked watching Halladay struggle with his command, but the evidence from last year showed that the more innings the youngster pitched, the better his control was.

GOOD NEWS UP THE MIDDLE

Tony Batista came to Toronto on June 12 in a trade with Arizona for Dan Plesac. Batista hit the tar out of the ball for the rest of the season, finishing with 26 homers, third on the team despite playing in just 98 games, and filled in well at shortstop after Alex Gonzalez went down with a season-ending shoulder injury. Batista is very important to this team because he can play both shortstop and third base, and he gives the Jays badly needed punch.

SECRET WEAPON

Billy Koch's baseball future looked bleak in 1997 when, only three games into his professional career, the first-round draft choice required reconstructive elbow surgery. But Koch turned out to be Toronto's best story of the year after being called up in early May. A starter in the minors, he quickly became Toronto's closer and posted big numbers, especially for a rookie fireman. With pitches that regularly reached 100 mph, Koch finished with 31 saves while solidifying the entire bullpen.

ACHILLES HEEL

There was a perception in Toronto that pitching was the weak link during the last two months of the season, but the majority of the blame for the team's late-season collapse should be laid on the offense. The Blue Jays scored one less run per game in the second half of the season than in the first, and the designated hitters were bad all year. Although Toronto tried everybody from Tony Fernandez to retread Dave Hollins in the DH role, the entire corps hit only .242 with 22 home runs and 74 RBI.

TORONTO BLUE JAYS

ENOUGH ALREADY

The idea that the Blue Jays had a disappointing season because they failed to make the playoffs is a foolish one, as the team had to trade its best player in the off-season and still managed to play over its head for most of the year. The Jays were too harshly criticized by the local media when the team faded late in the year, yet these same media were among the biggest bandwagon-jumpers in town early on. The fact is that Toronto finished with a record that was just about right for its ability.

But to some members of the press, it was as if Batista never existed. "His swing is a slump waiting to happen," harped one national columnist. Well then, where's the slump? Batista has had two good, productive seasons. He's an extremely valuable player with his more-than-acceptable defense—especially in turning the double play—and his big bat.

Perhaps the general lack of respect for Batista, who at age 25 was already with his third team, comes from a prejudice against anyone in the game who does things too differently. Batista has the most open stance in baseball: He takes his stance well back in the batter's box, with his body literally facing the pitcher. As the pitch is delivered, he moves into a more conventional posture, but this technique allows him to effectively spray pitches to all fields with power.

TV analysts love breaking down his swing, talking about his "weaknesses." Of course, due to his stance, Batista has problems with good breaking balls away from the plate. But what hitter, regardless of his stance, doesn't have problems with good breaking balls? Sammy Sosa does. Mark McGwire does. Ken Griffey does.

No one would teach youngsters a batting stance like Tony Batista's, but that doesn't mean he can't hit. Batista has come up with a technique that works for him; he should be applauded, not sniped at—and the Jays should be congratulated for a hell of a smart trade.

Meanwhile, Batista's double-play partner, rookie Homer Bush, got nothing but accolades. Bush hit .320, stole 32 bases, and played a very good second base. He cut down on his swing, reduced his strikeouts, and hit the ball the other way, sometimes for doubles. Fair enough, but a closer look reveals some weaknesses in Bush's game.

For starters, Bush is not a legitimate top-of-the-order hitter despite his batting average and speed. He walked just 22 times, leading to a mediocre .353 on-base average, and scored only 69 runs despite hitting second for most of the year.

In some ways, Bush resembles 1980s Toronto second sacker Damaso Garcia, who also was a high-average, low-walk, little-power player. Bush is a better defender than Garcia, but the two are similar offensively. Like Garcia, Bush didn't come up early enough to promise a long career: Due to injuries and mediocre performance in the minors, he didn't get his shot until he was 26. He had a fine year in 1995, but it was likely his peak.

BEST CASE

Signing Carlos Delgado to a long-term contract should do wonders for the disposition of Toronto's players and fans. If the Jays hope to contend, Delgado must have a monster year. Raul Mondesi is a good player, and playing in Toronto half the time instead of Dodger Stadium should boost his numbers. Mix in outfielder Shannon Stewart and shortstop Tony Batista, and you have the makings of a competitive club. The starting staff isn't half bad, either. Any scenario that has Toronto winning more games than it loses starts with David Wells as the staff ace. Joey Hamilton, horrendous in 1999, is due to rebound. Plus, Chris Carpenter, Kelvim Escobar, and Roy Halladay—all 25 or younger—appear ready to become mainstays in the rotation.

WORST CASE

Should Mondesi pout the way he did in Los Angeles, the Blue Jays will be in trouble. Toronto needs him to be not only productive on the field but also a positive force in the clubhouse. With youngsters expected to play key roles, the last thing the Jays need is for one veteran player to bring down everyone else. (This situation will be a test for Jim Fregosi.) The young pitchers, especially, are going to have a hard enough time getting AL hitters out without any added distractions.

UNDER THE MICROSCOPE

VERNON WELLS: Wells sped through the system in '99 after spending all of 1998 in the lower-level Class A South Atlantic League and earning HOWE SPORTSDATA All-Teen honors. In the heat of Toronto's playoff race, the 20-year-old proved he has all the tools. He should play every day in the Blue Jays' outfield this year.
BRENT ABERNATHY: Abernathy, a second-round pick in the 1996 draft, is a spark plug at the top of the order. He makes good contact and, when on base, is a pest for opposing pitchers. Abernathy's defense is unspectacular but very solid. The 22-year-old's all-around skills could be witnessed at the major-league level by the end of the 2000 season.
CLAYTON ANDREWS: Andrews, the Blue Jays' third-round pick in 1996, won the Class A South Atlantic League's ERA title in 1998 and skipped advanced Class A to make a strong showing at Double-A in '99. The 21-year-old posted 19 consecutive scoreless innings at one point and went 10–8, 3.93 ERA before being sampled at Triple-A. It will be difficult for him to crack Toronto's rotation in the near future, but he could be valuable in a relief role before he gets the call to enter the rotation.
GARY GLOVER: Glover struggled mightily in his first crack at Double-A in 1998 and was demoted to Class A after going 0–5, 6.75 ERA in just 37 innings. The 23-year-old and his live fastball looked much better in '99, as he posted his first winning season as a pro. His command will dictate future success.

TOP PROSPECTS

The Toronto Blue Jays' stocked farm system spilled into the big-league club as the organization made a push for the postseason in 1999. RHP **ROY HALLADAY**, following an impressive finale to the 1998 season, fared well this season in time split between starting and relieving. Halladay was the Jays' first-round pick in 1995. RHP **BILLY KOCH**, a first-round pick in 1996, took over the closer role by the second month of the season and performed admirably. OF **VERNON WELLS**, the fifth overall choice in the 1997 draft, was a standout in three minor-league levels before playing regularly in center field for Toronto down the stretch.

In addition to the wave of solid players to come off the farm in 1999, there remains plenty of depth, namely at middle infield. After a strong showing in 1998, 2B **BRENT ABERNATHY** rebounded from a disappointing Arizona Fall League performance to put together a well-rounded 1999 season in the Double-A Southern League. Not only does he possess the qualifications of a good leadoff hitter, but Abernathy has also proven to be a capable fielder. Farther down, speedster 2B **JORGE NUNEZ**, SS **FELIPE LOPEZ**, and SS **CESAR IZTURIS** have shown great promise. On the corners, 3B **JOE LAWRENCE**, a supplemental first-round pick in 1996, battled injuries in 1999 but has plus tools. 1B **KEVIN WITT**, the 28th overall pick in the 1994 draft, put up good power numbers for the second season in a row at Triple-A, and unheralded 1B **TIM GILES** led the Southern League RBI. 1B **JAY GIBBONS** followed up his Triple Crown Pioneer League season with 25 homers and 108 RBIs at Class A, but his fielding is adequate at best.

Pitching depth is also evident in the progress of RHP **JOHN SNEED**, RHP **GARY GLOVER**, and LHP **CLAYTON ANDREWS**. Sneed, who owns a 36–6 record through three professional seasons, is 6'6" and throws hard. Glover, whose stuff was better than his 19–47, 5.10 ERA numbers entering 1999, proved it by posting a 12-win season between Double-A and Triple-A. Andrews, the best lefty in the system, is not overpowering but has good command of three pitches. RHP **PASCUAL COCO** emerged with a good fastball and wins in 10 consecutive starts at Class A.

The organization is weakest in its lack of quality outfielders and catchers. In the event of an injury to Shannon Stewart, Wells, or Jose Cruz at the major-league level, the Blue Jays have little to choose from. OF **ANTHONY SANDERS**, the most exciting player in the organization two years ago, has struggled with the bat at Triple-A the past two years and strikes out too often. OF **ANDY THOMPSON**, a converted third baseman, opened eyes with his power numbers in '99, but lacks polish in the outfield. C **BOBBY CRIPPS**, who broke through with a tremendous power display at Class A in 1998, was sidelined for much of '99 with injuries.

LF
SHANNON STEWART 26

CF
#JOSE CRUZ JR. 26
? Anthony Sanders ML 26 92/7H
★ Vernon Wells ML 21 97/1H
↓ Alexis Rios A- 19 99/1H

RF
RAUL MONDESI 29
○ Andy Thompson 3A 24 94/23H

SS
TONY BATISTA 26
ALEX GONZALEZ 27
? Fausto Solano 3A 26 91/ND
↑ Cesar Izturis# A+ 20 96/ND
↑ Felipe Lopez# A- 20 98/1H

2B
HOMER BUSH 27
CRAIG GREBECK 35
↑ Brent Abernathy 2A 22 96/2H
○ Mike Young A+ 23 97/5C
? Jamie Goudie A- 21 97/9H

3B
? Casey Blake ML 26 96/7C
? Rudy Gomez 2A 25 96/10C
○ Joe Lawrence 2A 23 96/1H
↓ Josephang Bernhardt A- 19 96/ND

SP/RP

1B
***CARLOS DELGADO 28**
WILLIS OTANEZ 27
○ Kevin Witt ML 24 94/1H
? Luis Lopez 3A 26 95/ND
? *Tim Giles 2A 24 96/20C
? *Greg Morrison A+ 24 94/71C
? *Jay Gibbons A+ 23 98/14C

RELIEVERS
BILLY KOCH 25
*PEDRO BORBON 32
*LANCE PAINTER 32
JOHN FRASCATORE 30
? Peter Munro ML 25 93/6C
? Bob File A+ 23 98/19C
? *John Bale 3A 26 96/5C
? *Clint Lawrence A+ 23 95/NDC

C
***DARRIN FLETCHER 33**
MIKE MATHENY 29
ALBERTO CASTILLO 30
? *Bobby Cripps 2A 23 95/40H

DH
***WILLIE GREENE 28**

STARTERS
*DAVID WELLS 37
CHRIS CARPENTER 25
JOEY HAMILTON 29
KELVIM ESCOBAR 24
ROY HALLADAY 23
? Jay Yennaco 3A 24 95/3H
○ Gary Glover 3A 24 94/15H
? John Sneed 2A 24 97/22H
? Matt DeWitt 2A 22 95/10H
? Leo Estrella A+ 25 93/ND
○ Pascual Coco A+ 22 94/ND
? Scott Cassidy A- 24 98/NDC
○ *Clayton Andrews 3A 22 96/3H

MAJOR LEAGUERS IN ALL CAPS
Minor leaguers in upper-and-lower case
BEFORE A PLAYER'S NAME:
* lefthanded hitter/pitcher
# switch-hitter
?=prospect status (see explanation)

AFTER A PLAYER'S NAME:
Level at which he spent most of 1999 season; age as of July 1, 2000; year he was drafted; round drafted (ND= non-drafted amateur free agent); drafted out of high school (H) or college (C)

EXPLANATION OF PROSPECT RATINGS

★ Potential big-league star

↑ Projected regular player in majors (for pitchers: rotation starter or closer)

○ Projected platoon or utility player in majors (pitcher: setup or middle relief)

? Possible big-league reserve or long reliever

↓ High draft pick or "tools" player who hasn't performed to expectations

TORONTO

AL CENTRAL

WINS vs **WEEK** (4/5, 4/12, 4/19, 4/26, 5/3, 5/10, 5/17, 5/24, 5/31, 6/7, 6/14, 6/2)

▶ THE INSIDER 2000

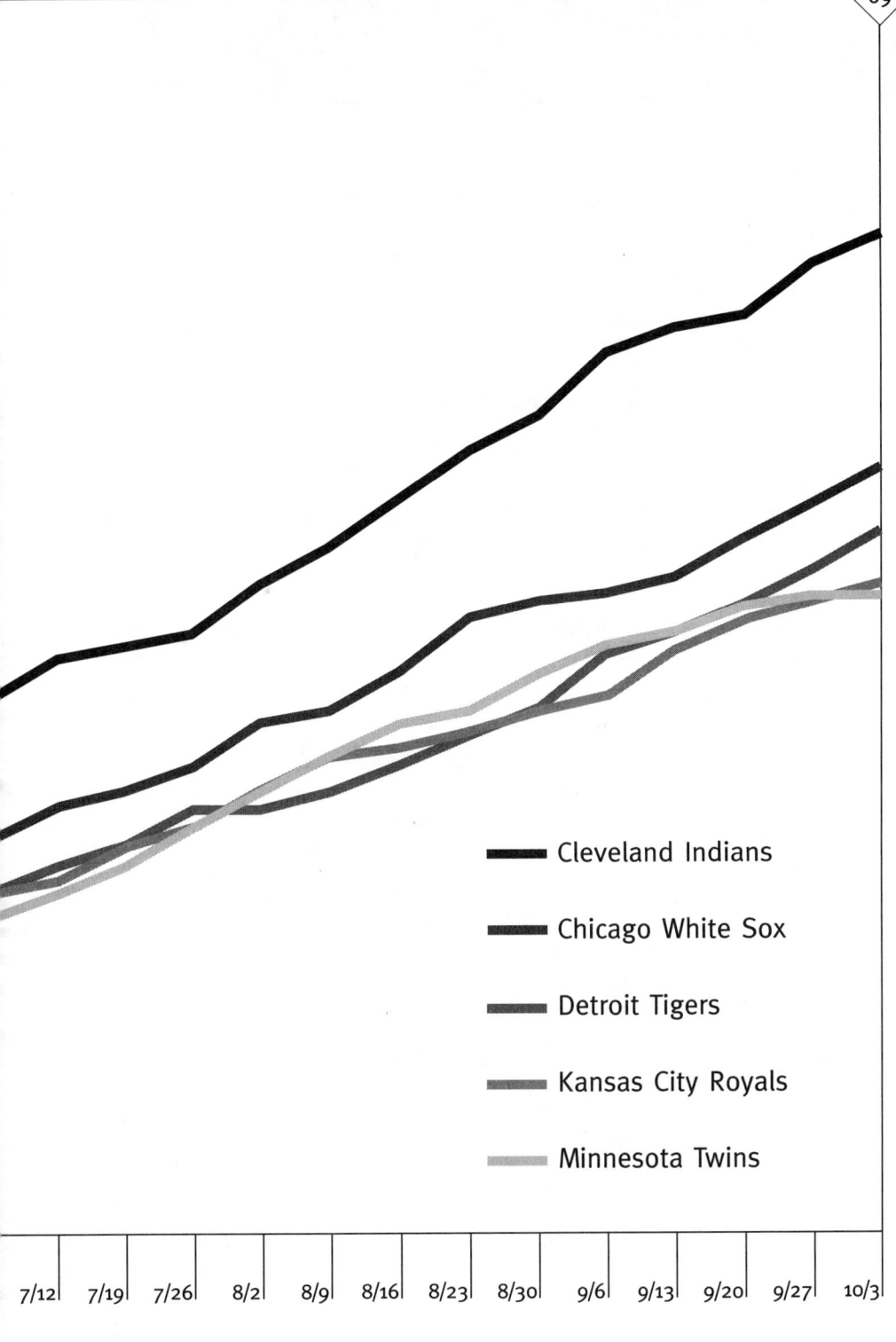

CHICAGO WHITE SOX

Management
Manager	Jerry Manuel
G.M.	Ron Schueler
President/CEO	Jerry Reinsdorf

Career Record
155–168 / .480
722–667 / .520
1504–1447 / .510

1999 Record
Won–Lost	Pct.	Finish/G.B. (Division)	Finish/G.B. (Wild Card)
75–86	.466	2/21.5 (C)	6/18.5

Preseason Consensus Projection
3 (2.95)

1st Half	2nd Half	Home	Road	Intradivision	Interleague
37–38	38–48	38–42	37–44	24–23	9–9

Comebacks	Blowouts	Nail-Biters	Grass	Turf	Sept.–Oct.
11–11	27–29	30–37	62–80	13–6	13–15

NUMBERS DON'T LIE

	Team (Rank)		Opponents (Rank)		League Avg.
Runs/Game	4.80	(10)	5.37	(10)	5.18
Batting Avg.	.277	(8)	.282	(9)	.274
On-Base Avg.	.337	(11)	.353	(11)	.347
Slugging Avg.	.429	(11)	.447	(8)	.439
Strikeouts	810	(1)	968	(10)	998
Home Runs	162	(10)	210	(14)	188
Stolen Bases	110	(7)	102	(6)	104
ERA	4.92	(7)			4.87
Errors	136	(14)			114

▶ THE INSIDER 2000

FRANKLY SPEAKING

Until 1998, Frank Thomas looked like he was in the middle of one of the most productive offensive careers ever. He won back-to-back MVP awards, led the AL in on-base three times, paced the loop in slugging once, and had never hit less than .300.

But Thomas no longer displays the explosive swing that was his trademark. Despite hitting .305 last year with a .414 OBA, he now looks tentative at the plate—when he doesn't look lost. Those numbers would be good for most players, but they are conspicuously inadequate for a player of Thomas's ability, stature, and salary.

Compounding his offensive struggles, Thomas—like many big but immobile sluggers of the past—has had ongoing defensive problems. This resulted in his distinct unwillingness to play first base, to the extent that it became an openly divisive issue with his teammates and his manager.

What happened to Thomas? A bone spur and tendinitis in his right foot may have contributed to his offensive slide, but the physical maladies certainly don't totally explain his decline. The rest can be attributed to his unwillingness or inability to adjust to a change in the way AL pitchers are approaching him.

To push Thomas back and reclaim the outer half of the plate, opposing pitchers have started consistently busting him inside. Challenging him to adjust, they have refused to let him extend his powerful arms as he used to. When he does, he can drive pitches that are over the plate or on the outside corner up the gaps or over the right-center field fence. Rather than stick with his strength, Thomas has reacted by backing away from the plate, meaning that he now has to dive into the pitch to reach outside offerings. Even worse, changing his stance has not allowed him to pull most inside pitches for power.

Since it's unlikely he will be able to change into a dead-pull hitter who could feast on his current steady diet of inside pitches, his best bet would seem to be a return to his previous plan of attack. The Big Hurt used to take inside pitches that he couldn't pull (because they were too fast or too close to his hands) and attack pitches over the middle or outside part of the plate, lashing them up the middle or to the opposite field. While he wasn't trying to hit home runs most of the time, his awesome strength and bat speed resulted in plenty of four-baggers.

September surgery should have fixed Thomas's foot problem. Whether his contentious attitude will improve, and whether he can regain his once-fearsome form, is another question.

MOMENT OF TRUTH

Coming into a three-game set at Comiskey Park on May 17 against Cleveland, the upstart Sox had the AL's best ERA. Unfortunately, the Indians' sluggers didn't appear to have read the stat sheets. They swept the series by scores of 13–9, 13–0, and 13–7, hitting two grand slams. The brutalized Sox never threatened Cleveland after that. To be fair, no one except the ghost of Bill Veeck really expected them to be able to compete with the Indians, but the Indians made it clear very early in the season that they were light-years ahead of everyone else in the AL Central.

BIGGEST SURPRISE

One thing that went right for the Sox last year was the emergence of several young outfielders. While Magglio Ordonez, Carlos Lee, and Chris Singleton all posted subpar on-base averages, they all showed surprising power. Ordonez led the club in homers and RBI, Singleton hit .300 with 17 homers, and Lee showed that, at age 23, he could hit big-league stuff with authority.

BIGGEST DISAPPOINTMENT

The continuing downward slide of franchise player Frank Thomas was as bewildering as it was frustrating for everyone involved—the coaches, the management, the fans and, especially, Thomas himself. Big Frank made a bad situation worse by not carrying out his business with the best of attitudes. By the end of the season, Comiskey patrons were heartily booing "The Big Hurt"—something that was unthinkable two short years ago.

PATIENCE IS A VIRTUE

The biggest factors in the Sox' 1999 offensive collapse were the poor season of Frank Thomas, the loss of Albert Belle, and, most important, a lineup full of impatient hitters. Chicago finished next-to-last in the AL in walks, and despite a good .278 batting average, its .337 on-base average was well below the league's. The team's power also declined dramatically, dipping from a franchise-record 198 homers in 1998 to just 162 (10th in the AL) last season.

With poor plate discipline throughout the lineup, the Sox rarely had enough runners on base at any time to sustain long rallies or come back from large deficits. With hackers like Caruso, Singleton, Carlos Lee, Brook Fordyce, and Magglio Ordonez added to the mix, the Sox weren't going to hit many three-run homers.

Jerry Manuel talked all season about how important it was for the team to have high on-base average at the top of the order. So why did Mike Caruso lead off so often, and why did Chris Singleton spend so much of the year near the top of the lineup? Even though he has enough power to hit farther down in the order, Ray Durham would have been a far better choice to lead off for the team. In fact, Durham may have been the only realistic option, but he spent most of the season batting second.

CAN THE KIDS PLAY?

Chicago's 1999 marketing campaign centered on the franchise's cost-cutting—er, rebuilding—effort. "The Kids Can Play," the corporate line read. For the first few months, the kids did a good job. But they fell apart dramatically after the All-Star break. While an overall tendency to swing at any pitch within two feet of the plate doomed the offense, the starting pitching was largely to blame for the second-half collapse.

Mike Sirotka was the only member of the rotation with an ERA lower than league average. Jim Parque was hurt and pitched poorly. Jaime Navarro just got worse and worse. James Baldwin had serious control problems. John Snyder, diagnosed in September with bone spurs in his elbow, started off well but slid downhill.

Exacerbating the pitching problems was the young team's extraordinarily poor defense. Many of the "kids" are fundamentally poor defensive players. Lee was mediocre in left field, Singleton didn't have much of a feel for center, Caruso was again miserable at short, Mark Johnson didn't win points for his game calling, and neither Konerko nor Norton are going to win many cheers for their gloves. With few of those guys contributing much offensively, the entire package was hardly encouraging.

The mound staff was a little better: Starters Sirotka, Parque, and Baldwin have talent; Jesus Pena, Bobby Howry, Keith Foulke, and Sean Lowe were all effective out of the pen. But Navarro has one more year left on what has turned out to be an absolutely disastrous four-year contract; and one-time potential closer Bill Simas has lost his fastball and is close to falling out of the league.

To have a realistic hope of playing competitive ball in 2000, the Sox will also have to upgrade what was a terrible bench. Their '99 reserve corps was packed with youngsters who wanted to be regulars rather than with veteran contributors who could fill in when needed. The decisions to go with Craig Wilson and Liu Rodriguez as utility men worked out very poorly.

Which of the current Sox will improve in 2000? Konerko still has growth left in him. Manuel deserves credit for sticking with the promising slugger through his early-season slump. Lee has both obvious talent and obvious weaknesses. Backup catcher Johnson, who has some offensive gifts, is already being pushed by prospect Josh Paul. The Sox can expect Singleton to decline after his surprising rookie year, but they already have Brian Simmons ready and McKay Christensen on the way.

Without a dominant Frank Thomas, the Sox are desperately in need of impact players. Magglio Ordonez has developed into a good hitter, but he doesn't scare anyone.

WEIGHTY DECISIONS

Right-handed reliever Carlos Castillo weighed close to 300 pounds at the end of the 1998 season. He lost 40 pounds at a Duke University nutrition program that winter and came to spring training in '99 at a svelte (for him) 250. However, when he made his way up to Chicago last September for yet another cup of coffee—and, one can be sure, a danish or two—Carlos looked as if he had spent the entire season eating his way through the Pacific Coast League. Playing for an organization that has plenty of opportunity for a talented reliever, Castillo is eating himself out of baseball.

The Sox aren't blameless here. Castillo, who obviously has

SECRET WEAPON

The Sox didn't have many weapons in 1999, and few of them were unknown to their opponents. First baseman Paul Konerko, who had flopped when given limited opportunities in Los Angeles and Cincinnati in '98, started the season poorly but improved steadily as the year went on. After hitting just .203 in April, the right-handed slugger improved to a robust .420 with seven homers in July. Productive against both lefties and righties, the 23-year-old Konerko finished second on the team in homers and paced the club in slugging average.

ACHILLES HEEL

The 1999 White Sox suffered through the kinds of problems that most young teams call their own: impatient hitters, inconsistent pitchers, and, perhaps worst of all, poor defense. Chicago led the AL in errors with 136, 22 more than the league average. Third baseman Greg Norton and shortstop Mike Caruso's combined total of 51 miscues was the ugliest sign of the club's porous defense, but it did not have an above-average glove at any position.

ENOUGH ALREADY

It's almost impossible to imagine that Jaime Navarro could have pitched worse in 1999 than he did in '98, but he did. Despite getting good offensive support from his mates, Navarro continued to struggle with his control both on and off the hill. As badly as he pitched, his clubhouse tirades—against umpires, teammates, and fans—were even uglier than his stats. It seemed that no one was immune from Jaime's wrath except Jaime.

either physical or psychological problems in controlling his weight, was thrust into the limelight long before he was ready. After pitching very well in Class A in 1996, he was immediately promoted to the big club for 1997. At that time he weighed 240 pounds and was just about to turn 22. Two seasons later, he had bloated unacceptably, was an unhappy camper in the clubhouse, was struggling with his command, and had earned a ticket back to Triple-A.

Unfortunately, Castillo's experience wasn't atypical. Chicago has aggressively promoted young players in recent years. Mike Caruso, acquired from the Giants, was elevated to starting shortstop in 1998 after spending the previous season in the California League—with disastrous results. Last season, seven players who had ended the previous year in Class A (or hadn't even played pro ball) made their big-league debuts for the White Sox. Two of them—pitchers Kip Wells and Aaron Myette—are projected as possible starters for the big club as early as this season.

Few players make the jump to the majors with little or no experience in the high minors. If they do, it's usually because they're rare talents or because they're being used in a protected role—for example as a left-handed spot reliever (like Scott Radinsky for the Sox in 1990) or as a reserve who is under little pressure.

The difficult experiences of rookies McKay Christiansen, Liu Rodriguez, Pat Daneker, Josh Paul, and Jason Dellaero in 1999, plus the earlier examples of Castillo and Caruso, should sound a cautionary note. If the Chicago brain trust hears that note, it won't expect too much of Wells and Myette right away.

Fat chance.

BEST CASE

Chicago's young players have high ceilings for growth. Many of the young Sox are of potential All-Star-quality, and second baseman Ray Durham is a major talent. There are several young arms on the way and ready to contribute, and the Sox lineup is already young at nearly every position. Almost everyone in baseball assumes that Frank Thomas will shake off his midcareer blues and return to peak levels; a big season from The Big Hurt would give the Sox offense a huge, much-needed kick in the rump.

WORST CASE

The problem with young players is that they're young. There is no way to know if Singleton will improve his on-base ability, or whether he'll be so bad against smart pitchers that he'll fall out of the league. Will Lee maintain his power pace, or will his problems with breaking pitches force him back to the minors? Can pitchers Kip Wells and Aaron Myette remain healthy and work with confidence in Chicago? And, finally, what if Frank Thomas can't come back? While Paul Konerko and Magglio Ordonez are decent players, the chances of their leading a team into the postseason are slim to none.

UNDER THE MICROSCOPE

KIP WELLS: The White Sox first-round pick in 1998 handled each minor-league stop with ease and was in Chicago's rotation for a good part of the second half of the season. Wells combines his low-to-mid-90s fastball and reliable breaking ball with a very strong work ethic and good composure. He can become a front-line major-league starter in 2000.

JON GARLAND: Garland's nasty sinking fastball is already being compared to that of Los Angeles ace Kevin Brown. The 20-year-old probably needs another full year in the minors, but will become a quality second or third starter in the White Sox rotation in 2001 or 2002.

AARON ROWAND: Rowand, Chicago's 35th overall pick in the 1998 draft has exhibited a good bat and a powerful outfield arm in his two seasons of professional ball. The 22-year-old is the best everyday hopeful below the Double-A level and could become a solid run producer for the big club in a couple of years.

JASON DELLAERO: The best asset of Jason Dellaero's game is his tremendous arm at shortstop. The White Sox's first-round pick in 1997 has cut down on his errors and has picked up his offensive production within the past year. He batted .268 after a promotion from Class A Winston-Salem to Double-A Birmingham. Unless the switch-hitter gets a better grasp of the strike zone and cuts down on his strikeouts, he'll have a hard time earning an everyday job in the majors.

CHICAGO

TOP PROSPECTS

Without a wealth of experienced talent at the major-league level last season, the White Sox looked to their minor-league system to provide, if nothing else, some promise for the future.

The emergence of OF **CARLOS LEE**, a converted third baseman, and RHP **KIP WELLS** gave the organization something to look forward to in the years to come. Lee, a .304 career minor-league hitter, spent the majority of the season with the big club, hitting for a good average and decent power. Wells, the club's first-round pick in the 1998 draft, was given the ball in the majors just a few months after making his professional debut. The 22-year-old Wells made some encouraging starts for the White Sox and, with a live fastball and a great work ethic, looks to be their ace of the future.

Several other youngsters got a chance to display their skills at various points in the season. C **MARK JOHNSON**, 1B **JEFF LIEFER**, and OF **MCKAY CHRISTENSEN** all started the season with the club. 2B **LIU RODRIGUEZ**, '97 first-round pick SS **JASON DELLAERO**, C **JOSH PAUL**, and OF **BRIAN SIMMONS** saw some time in the field later in the season, while RHP **AARON MYETTE** and RHP **PAT DANEKER** made some appearances on the mound.

Johnson was given a chance at the major-league level but did not impress. Paul is better defensively than Johnson but lacks offensive punch. Simmons and Christensen are capable defensive center fielders, but both are marginal offensively. Liefer has hitting potential but is a liability in the field, and Rodriguez is a utility infielder at best. The highly regarded Dellaero has had problems at the plate in his young career.

The strength of the organization is by far its pitching, and it was made even deeper by the selection of five pitchers in the first two rounds of the 1999 draft.

Wells has the makings of a staff ace. Myette, who was given a few starts with the big club, has a low-to-mid-90s fastball with stamina and a good-looking breaking pitch. RHP **JON GARLAND**, a first-round pick of the Cubs who was acquired in the deal for Matt Karchner last year, has a tremendous sinking fastball and is very mature for a 20-year-old. He was selected for the HOWE SPORTSDATA All-Teen Team. Another right-hander with a chance is Daneker, who doesn't throw hard but gets the job done with good sinker and slider deliveries along with an advanced understanding of pitching. RHP **JOSH FOGG**, a third-round pick in the 1998 draft, is also highly regarded, though he struggled after being promoted to Double-A in '99.

Additionally, closer prospect RHP **LORENZO BARCELO** made a successful return from elbow surgery. His heavy fastball has been clocked in the mid-90s, and the movement on his curveball has actually improved since the injury.

The White Sox are not nearly as deep beyond the pitching staff, however. Other than Lee, all the players who debuted in the big leagues last season are marginal prospects at best. Farther down, OF **AARON ROWAND**, a supplemental first-round pick in the 1998 draft, belted 24 home runs in the advanced Class A Carolina League and looks to have the brightest future of all the everyday players in the system. The 22-year-old is a capable right fielder with a very strong arm as well. 3B **JOE CREDE**, who fell just short of winning the Triple Crown in the Class A Carolina League in '98, had his progress stalled at Double-A by an injury.

LF
CARLOS LEE 24
#BRIAN SIMMONS 26
○ Jeff Inglin 3A 24 96/16C
○ *Brett Caradonna A+ 21 97/1H
○ Mario Valenzuela A- 23 96/ND

CF
***CHRIS SINGLETON 27**
○ *McKay Christensen ML 24 94/1H
↑ #Brian Simmons ML 26 95/2C
○ *Terrell Merriman A- 22 98/34C

RF
MAGGLIO ORDONEZ 26
↑ Aaron Rowand A+ 22 98/1C

SS
***MIKE CARUSO 23**
○ #Jason Dellaero ML 23 97/1C
○ #Danny Sandoval A- 21 96/ND

2B
#RAY DURHAM 28
? #Liu Rodriguez ML 23 95/ND

3B
#GREG NORTON 27
  CRAIG WILSON 29
○ Joe Crede 2A 22 96/5H
? *Jimmy Terrell A+ 22 96/3H

1B
PAUL KONERKO 24
○ *Jeff Liefer ML 25 95/1C
? Eric Battersby A- 24 98/27C

SP/RP

RELIEVERS
BOBBY HOWRY 26
BILL SIMAS 28
KEITH FOULKE 27
SEAN LOWE 29
CARLOS CASTILLO 25
*BRYAN WARD 28
*JESUS PENA 25
*SCOTT EYRE 28
DAVID LUNDQUIST 27
? Chadwick Bradford ML 25 96/13C

C
BROOK FORDYCE 30
*MARK JOHNSON 24
○ Josh Paul ML 25 96/2C

DH
FRANK THOMAS 32

STARTERS
JAMES BALDWIN 28
*MIKE SIROTKA 29
*JIM PARQUE 24
JAMIE NAVARRO 32
JOHN SNYDER 25
↑ Aaron Myette ML 22 97/1C
○ Pat Daneker ML 24 97/5C
↑ Kip Wells ML 23 98/1C
○ Kevin Beirne 3A 26 95/11C
↑ Jon Garland 2A 20 97/1H
? Jason Lakman 2A 23 95/7H
○ Lorenzo Barcelo 2A 22 94/ND
? Carlos Chantres 2A 24 94/12H
? Josh Fogg 2A 23 98/3C
? Brian Scott A+ 24 97/6C
? Hansel Izquierdo A+ 23 95/7H
○ Juan Figueroa A+ 21 95/ND
↓ Jason Stumm A- 19 99/H
? *Ken Vining 2A 25 96/4C
○ *Mark Buehrle A- 21 98/38C

MAJOR LEAGUERS IN ALL CAPS
Minor leaguers in upper-and-lower case

BEFORE A PLAYER'S NAME:
* lefthanded hitter/pitcher
# switch-hitter
?=prospect status (see explanation)

AFTER A PLAYER'S NAME:
Level at which he spent most of 1999 season; age as of July 1, 2000; year he was drafted; round drafted (ND= non-drafted amateur free agent); drafted out of high school (H) or college (C)

EXPLANATION OF PROSPECT RATINGS

★ Potential big-league star

↑ Projected regular player in majors (for pitchers: rotation starter or closer)

○ Projected platoon or utility player in majors (pitcher: setup or middle relief)

? Possible big-league reserve or long reliever

↓ High draft pick or "tools" player who hasn't performed to expectations

CHICAGO

CLEVELAND INDIANS

MANAGEMENT
Manager	Mike Hargrove [fired]	
G.M.	John Hart	
President/CEO	Richard Jacobs	

CAREER RECORD
721–591 / .550
689–538 / .562
1035–1002 / .508

1999 RECORD

Won–Lost	Pct.	Finish/G.B. (Division)	Finish/G.B. (Wild Card)
97–65	.599	1 (C)	

PRESEASON CONSENSUS PROJECTION
1 (1.00)

1ST HALF	2ND HALF	HOME	ROAD	INTRADIVISION	INTERLEAGUE
50–26	47–39	47–34	50–31	33–16	9–9

COMEBACKS	BLOWOUTS	NAIL-BITERS	GRASS	TURF	SEPT.–OCT.
17–8	34–20	38–33	82–56	15–9	16–15

NUMBERS DON'T LIE

	TEAM	(RANK)	OPPONENTS	(RANK)	LEAGUE AVG.
Runs/Game	6.23	(1)	5.31	(8)	5.18
Batting Avg.	.289	(2)	.268	(3)	.274
On-Base Avg.	.373	(1)	.346	(6)	.347
Slugging Avg.	.467	(2)	.438	(5)	.439
Strikeouts	1099	(13)	1120	(2)	998
Home Runs	209	(6	197	(9)	188
Stolen Bases	147	(1)	118	(11)	104
ERA	4.91	(6)			4.87
Errors	106	(3)			114

▶ THE INSIDER 2000

FROM MISTAKE BY THE LAKE TO MODEL AT THE JAKE

After their bitter disappointment in the 1999 postseason, and with all the resultant hand-wringing about why the Indians have failed to win in October, it's instructive to take a quick look backward at just how far the franchise came in the 1990s.

For decades, the Cleveland Indians were one of the laughingstocks of baseball. They failed to win a title for 40 years after 1954, and between 1969 and 1993, they had just four winning seasons, never once finishing above fourth place. From 1969 to 1985, the Tribe drew a million fans to Cleveland Stadium just four times, and in 1985, the turnstiles clicked but 655,181 times—an average of just 8,190 fans per home date.

The Indians finally began to improve in the mid-1980s, trading for good young players and drafting talent for their farm system. However, despite a roster featuring Joe Carter, Cory Snyder, Tony Bernazard, and others, they weren't ready to win. When Dick Jacobs bought the team in 1986, he ended a 40-year period in which the Indians had not had an owner stick around for more than six years. Spending money where it needed to be spent and working to rebuild the trust of the fans, Jacobs saw his work come to fruition a few years later.

After falling back into the lower reaches of the AL East, the Indians began to see daylight in 1992, manager Mike Hargrove's first full year at the helm. They were beginning to build a solid infrastructure.

In 1992, Cleveland improved 19 games to 76-86 and sparked some interest in the fans again. Homegrown players (including Albert Belle, Steve Olin, Charles Nagy) and players acquired in savvy trades (Carlos Baerga, Kenny Lofton, Sandy Alomar) were key performers. More good youngsters, like Jim Thome and Manny Ramirez, began to work their way into the equation in 1993.

Then, after a 76–86 season in their final year in Cleveland Stadium, the Indians finally blossomed into contenders in 1994. Finishing one game back in the AL Central, Cleveland drew nearly two million fans to the new Jacobs Field in 51 home games in the strike-truncated season. From then on, it was a quick progression to the World Series and sellouts every day at the Jake.

How did the Indians manage to build a good club? Part of it was making good trades. In addition to grabbing Baerga, Lofton, and Alomar in sweet deals, the Tribe picked up short-

MOMENT OF TRUTH

The third game of the 1999 AL Division Series against Boston is not a game Cleveland is likely to forget. It wasn't just that the Indians were beaten by the Red Sox and wound up losing the series, it was the way it happened that made it so hard to take. The Indians came into the game feeling cocky and expecting to cruise to an ALCS showdown with the Yankees, but the Red Sox scored 15 runs in the first four innings and set numerous playoff records in this 23-7 butt-whipping. The Indians never recovered and dropped the next two games, including the deciding game in Cleveland. The third game, in effect, started a chain reaction that saw manager Mike Hargrove fired a few days after the Division Series was over; the team was sold by the first week of November (although it had been on the market for months). That one game may have completely changed baseball in Cleveland.

BIGGEST SURPRISE

Cleveland looked to be in big trouble when Sandy Alomar Jr. went down with a knee injury only six weeks into the season. Backup receiver Einar Diaz had only 56 major-league at-bats in parts of three seasons; but despite his lack of experience, Diaz stepped in and provided a stable presence in the lineup. He didn't hit for much power, but he did do many things well. He hit for average, handled the pitching staff reasonably well, threw out 35 percent of base stealers, and stole 11 bases in 15 attempts.

BIGGEST DISAPPOINTMENT

Third baseman Travis Fryman's injuries put the Indians in a pinch. Back and knee problems put Fryman on the disabled list twice during the season and limited him to only 85 games. He wound up missing most of the second half of the season, and his absence turned third base into a revolving door. Carlos Baerga and Tyler Houston failed in brief stints there, forcing the Indians to go with soft-hitting Enrique Wilson at a position that requires power.

stop Omar Vizquel for Felix Fermin and Reggie Jefferson in December 1993. Jose Mesa was liberated from Baltimore in 1992 for forgotten outfielder Kyle Washington. A few—but only a few—veteran free agents also came to the club. Most of the talent was acquired not with raw dollars, but with sound baseball judgment.

The Indians also developed a pool of their own talent after a good series of drafts in the late '80s and early '90s. The result has been a steady pipeline of quality position players plus a few solid pitchers.

Once they had the talent and the new ballpark on the horizon, the Indians knew that they had to find a way to keep their core players together in order to keep the fans loyal. So they took a big chance and put into effect a long-term plan in which they signed their top young players to lucrative multiyear deals. By doing so, Cleveland became a model franchise for rebuilding clubs.

One other part of the equation was that the Indians had the courage to dump veteran players that other clubs might have held on to. Although the decisions to let go of popular and productive players like Belle, Baerga, Paul Sorrento, Tony Pena, and Orel Hershiser were criticized when they were made, the wisdom of Cleveland's management was proven many times over.

HALL-OF-FAME COMPANY

In 1999, Cleveland slugger Manny Ramirez drove in 165 runs, the 11th-highest total in baseball history and the most in one season since 1938. It was an incredible personal performance for Ramirez, who became just the 10th player to drive in that many in a season. What do the other nine players have in common?

For starters, they're all in the Hall of Fame. Hack Wilson, Lou Gehrig, Hank Greenberg, Jimmie Foxx, Babe Ruth, Chuck Klein, Joe DiMaggio, Sam Thompson, and Al Simmons are the other players with 165 or more RBIs in a season, and all of them have plaques in Cooperstown.

Looking at the careers of these nine Hall of Famers, most were among the best hitters of their respective eras. They also played on high-scoring and, for the most part, winning teams. No surprise here, as it would be hard for a team to have as productive a hitter and not be pretty good.

Of the 16 times one of these players has driven in 165 or more runs, his club has finished first or second in the league in scoring every time but once. The only exception is the 1930 Phillies, who finished fourth in the NL in runs while Chuck Klein was driving in 170. Thirteen of these 16 teams won the pennant or finished second. Only the 1930 Yankees, who were third in the American League, the 1895 Phillies, third in the NL, and the 1930 Phillies, last in the NL, failed to finish first or second.

Most of the highest-RBI seasons came in the late 1920s and early '30s during baseball's Ruthian offensive explosion. Count out Ramirez (1999) and Sam Thompson (1887 and 1895), and nine of the other 13 highest single-season totals came between 1927 and '35. The greatest individual run-producing year was 1930, when Wilson had 190 for the Cubs, Klein had 170 for the Phillies, and Simmons had 165 for the Athletics.

In the 22 years from 1920 to '41, Ruth was first in RBIs, Gehrig second, Foxx third, Simmons fifth, and Greenberg 15th. DiMaggio was third in RBIs from 1942 through '60 despite playing half his career before the war, including his big year, in 1937. Overall, Ruth is second on the all-time list, Gehrig third, Foxx sixth, and Simmons 14th. DiMaggio is 32nd all-time, and certainly would have moved up on the list had he not retired early because of injuries. Thompson also was a dominating run producer in his time, finishing in the top five in the National League in RBIs eight times from 1886 through 1895, and winning the RBI title in his two big years.

Wilson and Klein were great over a few seasons, but didn't have the longevity of the other six. Wilson had five outstanding seasons, leading the NL in home runs four times and RBIs twice from 1926 to '30, but a drinking problem forced him out of baseball by 1935. Klein was awesome from 1929 to '33, when he took advantage of the 280-foot right field fence in Philadelphia's Baker Bowl. He led the NL in runs three times, homers four times, and slugging three times with the Phillies, but was no better than mediocre after he was traded to the Cubs in 1934.

THE GAME'S BEST UNDERSTUDY

In his first nine years in the majors (1988–96), Mike Jackson pitched in 623 games, all but seven in relief. His career ERA stood at 3.33, 22 percent better than average for his league and his home parks. Jackson logged an ERA of 3.73 or less each season but one, including ERAs of less than 3.25 seven times.

SECRET WEAPON

Richie Sexson put up some pretty impressive numbers in the minor-leagues, but it's doubtful that many expected the 24-year-old to hit 31 home runs in his first full season with the Indians—especially while playing three positions and filling in as part-time DH. Sexson hit 31 homers in 1997 in Triple-A and a combined 32 in '98, in Buffalo and Cleveland, but it was a pleasant surprise that he finished third in homers and RBIs on a club that already had plenty of lumber.

ACHILLES HEEL

Cleveland's startimg rotation of Bartolo Colon, Charles Nagy, and Dave Burba combined to go 50–25 but only Colon really had a good year, and even he wasn't dominating. Burba had serious control problems and allowed 30 home runs, and Nagy allowed a lot of hits, runs, and everything else. It got even uglier in the last two spots in the rotation as Jaret Wright, Dwight Gooden, and Tom Candiotti were brutalized. The fact that Candiotti got 13 starts after being released by Oakland shows just how desperate Cleveland was for starting pitching.

ENOUGH ALREADY

Wil Cordero, who has had more chances to redeem himself than a 747 full of over-the-hill junk-balling southpaws, picked up another paycheck for doing very little. He split his limited time on the active roster between DH and left field, which he played like a true DH. It wouldn't be so bad if it weren't for all the people in baseball who fall all over themselves praising Cordero's impressive skills while proclaiming what a great guy he is. The fact is that Cordero has had exactly one good season in his seven and a half years in the big leagues—in 1994 with Montreal—and that was a long time ago.

Opposing hitters were batting only .217 against him, and he had fanned 721 in his 810 innings of work.

By the mid-1990s, Jackson had established himself as one of the best setup pitchers in baseball, and there were plenty of observers who felt he should be finishing games. So why wasn't he given a chance to be a full-time closer earlier in his career?

The answer is that Jackson was simply a victim of circumstances. In his rookie year with Philadelphia in 1987, Steve Bedrosian led the NL with 40 saves. Jackson was traded to the Mariners prior to 1988, and even though the club didn't have an established closer, the club was unwilling to give the job to a second-year pitcher. Jackson saved four games that year, but Mike Schooler led the club with 15 and held the job for the next two years, saving 33 in '89 and 30 in '90. Jackson got his first chance to close games in '91 when he, Schooler, and Bill Swift split the job. Swift led Seattle with 17 saves, Jackson had 14, and Schooler had seven.

Jackson and Swift were traded to San Francisco prior to the '92 season, but the Giants already had Jeff Brantley and Rod Beck in the bullpen. Those two combined for 24 of San Francisco's 30 saves that year, then Beck won the job outright and saved 72 games over 1993 and '94. Three stints on the DL from 1993–94 didn't help Jackson's situation.

After signing with Cincinnati as a free agent for 1995, Jackson yet again was stuck behind Brantley, whom the Reds had acquired the year before. Unlucky Mike spent the first two months of '95 on the disabled list, then spent the second half setting up Brantley.

Peripatetic Mike was back in Seattle in 1996, but the Mariners had Norm Charlton by then. Jackson, then 32, signed with Cleveland for '97, where he finally got his first real opportunity to be a closer. He began the year setting up Jose Mesa, but Mesa faltered badly during the summer. Jackson took advantage of the opportunity by saving a career-high 15 games, and went on to save 40 games in 1998 and 39 in '99.

BEST CASE

The Indians would have been the class of the American League Central even without bolstering their pitching staff with veteran lefty Chuck Finley, who will fit in nicely behind Bartolo Colon in the rotation. Better pitching will go a long way toward improving Cleveland's chances in a short postseason series. Finley's signing leaves only one hole in the rotation, and the Tribe has enough arms to try and find a number three. Jaret Wright is the pitcher most likely to emerge in 2000.

WORST CASE

Anything short of a World Series appearance will disappoint Cleveland. The Indians are in no danger of missing the playoffs, but another first-round exit is possible, especially if things don't go just right. Kenny Lofton will miss as much as half the season while recovering from shoulder surgery, and nobody knows if he'll be 100 percent when he returns. Cleveland also really needs Sandy Alomar back in the lineup. But starting pitching is the club's big worry—Finley has been reliable, but he is 37. Dave Burba has also tossed a great many innings over the past few years.

UNDER THE MICROSCOPE

RUSSELL BRANYAN: Will Branyan be the player who has averaged a home run every 13 at-bats or the player who, in two separate slumps last season, went a combined 3-for-98 with 58 strikeouts? Only a midseason promotion prevented Branyan from eclipsing the all-time minor-league record of 220 strikeouts. This season will determine the 23-year-old's future.

WILLIE MARTINEZ: After two mediocre seasons at Double-A, the 21-year-old Martinez's star has fallen. His fastball tops out in the low-90 mph range, but he hasn't been able to command his secondary pitches. The Indians have been tinkering with his mechanics the past two years as well.

JACOB CRUZ: Cruz was on the verge of winning a full-time spot on the Cleveland roster by batting .330 in 88 at-bats before he tore ligaments in his thumb. Acquired from the Giants in the Jose Mesa deal last season, Cruz is a pure hitter with decent power, as well as a capable corner outfielder. He gives the club an alternative to David Justice.

TIM DREW: Drew did not impress in his first two years, but the 1997 first-round pick led the Class A Carolina League with 13 wins last season. He won his last five starts and allowed only 8 runs in 39 innings. He is not overpowering, but he keeps the ball down and in the park. With the pitching ranks thinning out, Drew is now the top young gun in the system.

CLEVELAND

TOP PROSPECTS

The Cleveland Indians organization has been one of the most productive in the past decade, winning at the major-league level and developing talent in the minors. The organization was one of only four to post a winning record at the minor-league level every season during that period.

That said, it appears that the talent base is beginning to level off. C **EINAR DIAZ** filled in admirably for Sandy Alomar, and OFs **JACOB CRUZ** (originally drafted by the Giants) and **ALEX RAMIREZ** came through when called upon, but the well of impact talents developed over the years is running dry.

Cleveland's top batting and pitching prospects both struggled in '99. 3B **RUSSELL BRANYAN**, the top slugging prospect in the game, had a terrible season. He made more headlines for his unbelievable slumps and strikeout totals than for his prodigious home runs. RHP **WILLIE MARTINEZ**, tabbed for years as the next Bartolo Colon–type talent in the organization, completed his second straight mediocre campaign in Double-A.

After Branyan, 19-year-old SS **MAICER ISTURIZ** could be the only legitimate infield hopeful. Cruz has the ability to play every day in the outfield, but it may not be in Cleveland. The free-swinging Ramirez is also a talent, but his lack of plate discipline hurts his potential. Slugging OF **SCOTT MORGAN** would have probably gotten a chance in the bigs by now with any other club, but he's stuck behind several others.

With Martinez not progressing as hoped, 1997 first-round pick RHP **TIM DREW** has become the top pitcher in the organization. He combined power, poise, and command in a 21-year-old body. LHP **C. C. SABATHIA**, a 6'7" intimidating presence, has received rave reviews from the organization but missed more than half of '99 with arm problems. He has the highest ceiling of any pitcher in the organization. RHP **ROB PUGMIRE** also had a nice season and opened some eyes. Two starters-turned-closers, RHPs **JARED CAMP** and **JARROD MAYS**, had success in their new roles and showed some serious heat.

A few upper-level hurlers pitched for Cleveland this season (David Riske, Jason Rakers, Jim Brower, Sean DePaula), but all are marginal prospects. RHP **PAUL RIGDON** had a breakthrough season, going 7–0, 0.90 ERA at Double-A before a promotion, but he is not overpowering. RHPs **J. D. BRAMMER**, **FRANKIE SANDERS**, **JAMIE BROWN**, and **ALBERTO GARZA** all struggled.

LF
*DAVID JUSTICE 34
↑ *Jacob Cruz ML 27 94/1C
○ Scott Morgan 3A 26 95/7C
? *Dan McKinley 2A 24 97/1C
? *Jason Fitzgerald A+ 24 97/1C

CF
*KENNY LOFTON 33
*DAVE ROBERTS 28
JOLBERT CABRERA 27
? *David Miller 3A 26 95/1C
? *Jon Hamilton A+ 22 97/5C

RF
MANNY RAMIREZ 28
○ Alex Ramirez ML 25 91/ND
? *Chad Whitaker 2A 23 95/3H
? *Jesus Hernandez A- 23 94/ND

SS
#OMAR VIZQUEL 33
#ENRIQUE WILSON 24
○ John McDonald ML 25 96/12C
? Luis Gonzalez A+ 21 96/ND
○ #Zach Sorensen A+ 23 98/2C
↑ #Maicer Isturiz A- 19 98/ND

2B
#ROBERTO ALOMAR 32
○ Marcos Scutaro 3A 24 94/ND
○ *Scott Pratt A+ 23 98/3C
? #Jose Olmeda A+ 22 95/2H

3B
TRAVIS FRYMAN 31
*TYLER HOUSTON 29
○ *Russ Branyan ML 24 94/7H
? Mike Edwards A+ 23 95/9H

1B
*JIM THOME 29
? Danny Peoples 2A 25 96/1C

SP/RP

RELIEVERS
PAUL SHUEY 29
*RICARDO RINCON 30
STEVE REED 34
STEVE KARSAY 28
SEAN DEPAULA 26
○ Dave Riske ML 23 96/56C
? Jim Brower ML 27 94/6C
? J.D. Brammer 2A 25 96/4C
? Jarrod Mays A+ 25 96/3C

C
SANDY ALOMAR JR. 34
EINAR DIAZ 27
? Edgar Cruz A+ 21 97/2H

DH
RICHIE SEXSON 25

STARTERS
BARTOLO COLON 25
*CHUCK FINLEY 37
CHARLES NAGY 33
DAVE BURBA 33
JARET WRIGHT 24
*MARK LANGSTON 39
SCOTT KAMIENIECKI 36
DANYS BAEZ 25
? Jason Rakers ML 27 95/25C
○ Willie Martinez 3A 22 95/ND
? Jamie Brown 3A 23 96/21C
? Paul Rigdon 3A 24 96/6C
? Alberto Garza 2A 23 95/44C
? Mark Turnbow 2A 21 97/7H
↑ Tim Drew A+ 21 97/1H
○ Rob Pugmire A+ 21 97/3H
? *Mike Bacsik 2A 22 96/18H
? *Josh Santos A+ 23 98/4C
↓ *C.C. Sabathia A+ 19 98/1H

MAJOR LEAGUERS IN ALL CAPS
Minor leaguers in upper-and-lower case
BEFORE A PLAYER'S NAME:
* left-handed hitter/pitcher
# switch-hitter
?=prospect status (see explanation)

AFTER A PLAYER'S NAME:
Level at which he spent most of 1999 season; age as of July 1, 2000; year he was drafted; round drafted (ND= non-drafted amateur free agent); drafted out of high school (H) or college (C)

EXPLANATION OF PROSPECT RATINGS

★ Potential big-league star

↑ Projected regular player in majors (for pitchers: rotation starter or closer)

○ Projected platoon or utility player in majors (pitcher: setup or middle relief)

? Possible big-league reserve or long reliever

↓ High draft pick or "tools" player who hasn't performed to expectations

CLEVELAND

DETROIT TIGERS

Management
		Career Record
Manager	Larry Parrish	82–104 / .441
G.M.	Randy Smith	444–626 / .415
President/CEO	Michael Ilitch	464–604 / .434

1999 Record
Won–Lost	Pct.	Finish/G.B. (Division)	Finish/G.B. (Wild Card)
69–92	.429	3/27.5 (C)	8/24.5

Preseason Consensus Projection
2 (2.20)

1st Half	2nd Half	Home	Road	Intradivision	Interleague
33–45	36–47	38–43	31–49	23–25	8–10

Comebacks	Blowouts	Nail-Biters	Grass	Turf	Sept.–Oct.
6–8	22–38	38–35	57–76	12–16	16–14

NUMBERS DON'T LIE

	Team (Rank)	Opponents (Rank)	League Avg.
Runs/Game	4.64 (12)	5.48 (11)	5.18
Batting Avg.	.261 (12)	.276 (7)	.274
On-Base Avg.	.326 (13)	.349 (9)	.347
Slugging Avg.	.443 (9)	.451 (9)	.439
Strikeouts	1049 (10)	976 (9)	998
Home Runs	212 (4)	209 (13)	188
Stolen Bases	108 (8)	81 (3)	104
ERA	5.22 (12)		4.87
Errors	106 (3)		114

▶ THE INSIDER 2000

YOU CAN TAKE IT TO THE BANK

Four years ago, Randy Smith rode into Detroit on a white steed, ready to tear apart a moribund organization and rebuild it from scratch. One of his first acts was to hire Buddy Bell as Detroit's manager, replacing Sparky Anderson, who was a legend in his own time.

Three years ago, Detroit lost 109 games while suffering through the worst year in team history. After the season, Smith consummated a nine-player trade with Houston, the largest trade made by Detroit in 39 years.

Two years ago, the young and hungry Tigers improved by 26 games as Smith's rebuilding plan took hold. Randy was named Executive of the Year by *Baseball America* as dramatic improvements in the Detroit farm system resulted in its being named Organization of the Year.

One year ago, the Tigers crashed back into the basement as key young players disappointed and several of Smith's veteran acquisitions flopped. Buddy Bell paid for the backslide with his job.

By late 1999, the hoopla surrounding the final days of Tiger Stadium couldn't obscure the fact that Smith's job was now in jeopardy. People who had lionized him two short years before were whispering that he needed to be fired so that the team could become a legitimate contender in its new ballpark-bank, Comerica Park. Instead of Smith being guillotined, though, it was Larry Parrish's head that rolled, as Randy jumped at the chance to hire Phil Garner, a prototypical NL player and manager.

How did things change so radically in just 24 months? Has Randy Smith risen to the level of his incompetence? Was he as good as everyone thought in his first few years in Detroit, or merely lucky enough to take over a team that was so far down that improvement was inevitable?

THE PETER PRINCIPLE

"Groomed to be a baseball executive from an early age," trumpeted a glowing profile of the Tigers' hot young GM in a prominent 1998 spring baseball annual. That was certainly true. What was also true was that Smith was born and bred in the National League, which has apparently influenced his judgment to the detriment of the Tigers.

The once-huge differences between the American League

MOMENT OF TRUTH

At the All-Star break, the Tigers were 36–52, more than 20 games out of first. To reinforce the point that the season was irretrievably lost, they began the second half being swept in Houston in three close games. However, they then started showing unexpected signs of life, winning two of three from Cincy, sweeping a two-game series from Kansas City, and taking two of three weekend games from Boston during their 1984 World Championship team reunion.

Perhaps because the fans could see the remaining games at the ballpark dwindling, or perhaps because the team was playing better, attendance picked up. For a brief time, the Tigers' home games felt like the 1980s, when the city still cared about the team—rather than the '90s, when the team plodded through endless slugfests in front of mostly empty seats. These good feelings were short-lived, though, as the Tigers were swept by the Indians in Cleveland to start a nine-game losing streak.

BIGGEST SURPRISE

Luis Polonia spent 1997–98 as one of the best players in the Mexican League, but it was generally assumed that his big-league career was over. The Tigers signed him to be an extra bat off the bench, but he was much more valuable than that. In a platoon role as designated hitter and part-time left fielder, he hit for average with surprising line drive power—especially for a 34-year-old who hadn't seen big-league pitching in two years.

BIGGEST DISAPPOINTMENT

Tony Clark was supposed to anchor the club's offense, but in the first half of the season when the team was struggling badly, he was missing in action. His batting average was horrible (.219 on June 11), and his power numbers weren't any better. He had only 13 doubles and eight home runs at the All-Star break, nowhere close to the production the team was counting on. Clark's final numbers looked decent, but that was because he exploded late in the season when the Tigers were so far behind Cleveland that the games didn't matter.

and the National League have narrowed in recent years, partly unintentionally and partly by design. Even as commissioner Bud Selig tries to mold the national pastime into a corporate monolith called Major League Baseball, some distinctions between the AL and the NL remain. One critical distinction lingers in the minds of many of the game's senior executives—a value judgment about the way the game is played in the two leagues.

That long-held judgment manifests itself in patronizing descriptions of AL games, AL managers, and AL players. In this NL-centric worldview, NL teams play "real" baseball, where pitching, speed, and defense are still important. AL teams merely bludgeon each other to death in dreary four-hour slugfests where gutless pitchers, afraid to challenge hitters with their fastball, nibble at the corners until someone hits a three-run homer. NL players have to play both ways; many AL players, especially the big power hitters, are designated hitters—or might as well be, given how slow they are and how unimportant their defense is.

The ultimate expression of this superior attitude is that many players are dismissed as distinctly "AL players": immobile giants who couldn't survive in the Senior (Superior) League. A prime example of how that smug judgment can be taken too far is that Frank Thomas was considered by many scouts in 1989 to be unable to play in the NL because he was an immobile slugger. While that may be true now, as Thomas has fallen on (relatively) hard times in the past two seasons, it certainly wasn't true from 1990 to '97 when The Big Hurt was terrorizing pitchers and would have been a godsend to the NL teams that didn't have Jeff Bagwell in their lineup. Moreover, this NL prejudice conveniently ignores dozens of defensively challenged NL sluggers who have had long careers in the senior leagues.

Randy Smith apparently subscribes that view. One of the consistent themes of Smith's many player moves in Detroit is an attempt to acquire NL-type players: players who hit for average, have some speed, and are good athletes. If they were free-swingers who didn't get on base often, that was acceptable. If their batting averages weren't complemented by power, that was okay as well.

In essence, Smith spent four years trying to make the Tigers into a speedy, NL-style team instead of a powerful AL-style team. For a while it worked, but that was mostly because Smith cleaned out the deadwood during his honeymoon as GM, which was virtually certain to result in improvement. His bias culminated in the past two years in the inexplicable acquisitions of washed-up singles hitters Bip Roberts and Gregg Jefferies to fill DH roles—the symbolic final nails in Detroit's coffin.

▶ THE INSIDER 2000

WHEELING AND DEALING

Since Randy Smith took over in November 1995, he made 46 trades through the Juan Gonzalez deal. That's an average of almost one trade per month, including the 23 trades he made in 1996 alone! Smith came to Detroit after spending two and a half years as GM of the San Diego Padres. Since then, he has made seven trades with his former club, including four during the year after he left. Smith's father, Tal, is the longtime president of the Houston Astros; that connection has produced four trades, including seven-player and nine-player deals. Of the 46 trades Smith has made while in Detroit, 27 have been with NL clubs.

To put in perspective just how dramatically different the Smith regime has been, consider that it took the team nine years to make the previous 46 trades before Smith took over. Consider also that Smith has made more trades in four years than the Tigers made in the first half of the 20th century (43 trades total from 1901 to '51). That comparison ignores the drastic changes in the game since 1951, but it does show nicely how relentlessly Smith has made personnel moves.

The blockbuster November deal with Texas signaled that perhaps Smith finally understood that he had to build an AL team, not an NL team, if he was going to prosper in Detroit. On the other hand, raw power wasn't Detroit's big problem last year—getting on base for the power hitters was, and Gonzo (career .343 on base average) isn't the solution to that problem. The free-swinging Tigers were fourth in the league in homers in '99 but a miserable next-to-last in on-base (ditto their '98 OBA), which is precisely why Detroit scored fewer runs than anyone but Anaheim (which ranked, not coincidentally, last in OBA).

ROLLING THE DICE

Detroit could afford to send Francisco Cordero to Texas because the Tigers' Matt Anderson, another righty closer prospect with extreme heat. Oft-injured Justin Thompson might not be missed, as he probably won't be a big winner in the future unless he recovers his lost stuff. Giving up southpaw prospect Alan Webb will likely hurt in a year or two when the team is looking for another starting pitcher to shore up its rotation.

For Comerica Park's inaugural season, Detroit is relying on a starting staff with many question marks. Brian Moehler, 31, must prove that hitters haven't permanently caught on to his tricks. Dave Mlicki, 32, was adequate but hardly inspiring; now

SECRET WEAPON

The Tigers' unsung catching duo, Brad Ausmus and Bill Haselman, both contributed a bit at the plate, but it was their defense that was outstanding. Ausmus threw out 37 percent of enemy base stealers (league average was 32 percent) while committing only two errors in 127 games. Haselman threw out 31 percent of base stealers while making only one miscue in 39 games. Of course, cutting down the running game isn't nearly as important in Detroit as it is in most other places.

ACHILLES HEEL

The Bengals' weakness: lack of plate discipline up and down the lineup. Their .326 team OBA was 13th in the AL, ahead of only Anaheim and well below the league norm of .347. Likewise, their team batting average was .261, 12th in the AL and 14 points below league average. The impatient Detroit hitters proved once again that major-league pitchers know enough to not give batters anything good to hit if the hitters consistently swing at bad pitches.

ENOUGH ALREADY

Actually, in Detroit's case, it was "Can't Get Enough Already." The closing of Tiger Stadium found the Motor City landscape completely awash in sepia-toned sentiment. Nothing wrong with nostalgia, but the outpouring of affection for the ancient ballpark served as a trenchant reminder of just how far the Detroit franchise, once considered a model for others to emulate, had fallen in the late 1980s and the '90s.

the beneficiary of a long-term deal, he needs to be both durable and consistent. Talented Jeff Weaver might make the necessary adjustments to succeed in the majors at 23, or he might spend most of 2000 in Triple-A. Ditto Dave Borkowski.

Trading young Gabe Kapler puts the pressure on Smith to find a good defensive replacement for him in center. This is especially true since replacing Bobby Higginson in right with Gonzalez would be another defensive downgrade that would hurt the Bengals' pitchers, who badly need outfielders who can run down deep flyballs in Detroit, where everyone swings for the fences.

Trading for Gonzalez was a huge gamble for the Tigers, even aside from all the young talent it cost. First, there was no guarantee that they could sign him to a long-term deal. Even if they could, the amount of money required to satisfy Gonzalez' grossly overblown estimate of his own value could hamstring the team for years. It is one thing for a team owner to consider breaking the bank for a multidimensional superstar like Ken Griffey or Alex Rodriguez. It is another thing entirely to commit that kind of money to a slow slugger who is a defensive liability.

Detroit made this kind of strategic mistake once before, and it crippled the club for years. In January 1993, new owner Mike Ilitch faced a Hobson's choice: He could either let popular slugger Cecil Fielder walk, incurring the wrath of the Tigers' dwindling fan base, or he could ante up to show he wasn't going to starve the club like Tom Monaghan had. Ilitch understandably chose to re-sign Fielder, who hauled in almost as much money as Barry Bonds had just received from the Giants.

The aftermath was predictable. Bonds won his third MVP trophy in his first year on the left coast as the Giants won 103 games. Barry has been an All-Star each year until the injury-marred 1999, and he remains one of the best players in the game today. The one-dimensional Fielder quickly faded, becoming a huge albatross as well as a symbol of the franchise's slide into decrepitude.

Mortgaging the future to have Gonzalez in 2000 is dicey, especially since Gonzalez isn't the solution to the team's recent problems. The big question, then, as Detroit is poised to start its second century of AL baseball, is whether Randy Smith will grasp the salient facts of life in the AL before it's too late for the franchise.

BEST CASE

Randy Smith regains his genius laurels as Detroit celebrates the opening of Comerica Park with a wild card berth and the team plays its first meaningful October games in more than a decade. MVP candidate Juan Gonzalez bashes 40 or 50 homers and drives in 125-plus runs, leading the Tigers back into contention in their new playground. Solid seasons from infielders Clark, Easley, and Palmer, and comebacks from outfielders Higginson and Encarnacion form a fearsome lineup. Matt Anderson harnesses his 100-mph heater and develops into a dominating closer, anchoring a solid bullpen. Detroit's big bats make up for a mediocre rotation anchored by veteran Dave Mlicki and sophomore Jeff Weaver.

WORST CASE

An unhappy Gonzalez doesn't get the megabucks long-term deal he expects, has a good—but not great—year on the field, and is a disruptive force in the clubhouse. If the outfield fails to improve and the starting rotation struggles, the inaugural season at the new park might be a rough one. Unless Mlicki, Weaver, Moehler, Borkowski, or some combination of the four can step up and succeed consistently, the summer of 2000 could be Randy Smith's swan song in Motown.

UNDER THE MICROSCOPE

ROBERT FICK: A shoulder problem kept Fick out most of last season, but he returned in time to hit the last home run in Tiger Stadium history—a grand slam. Fick won MVP honors in the Class A Midwest League in '97 before hitting .318 with 114 RBIs in '98 at Double-A. The left-handed swinger hit a combined 97 doubles over the two seasons. Can Fick hold up on an everyday basis behind the plate? The Tigers will have to wait until this season to find the answer.

ERIC MUNSON: The Tigers need Munson, their '99 first-round pick, to move quickly. An advanced hitter with power potential, the USC product could fill a power void from the left side at Comerica Park in the near future, perhaps 2001. A collegiate catcher, Munson would prefer to remain one, but he may lack the defensive tools.

DAVID BORKOWSKI: The 23-year-old gained valuable experience as a starter and as a reliever. He has won big at the minor-league level, displaying a lively arm and sinking fastball, and he should get an opportunity in either role this season on this subpar pitching staff.

ADAM PETTYJOHN: The 1998 second-round draft pick pitched well at both Class A and Double-A levels in 1999, winning 14 times. With his good slider and two fastballs, Pettyjohn should contribute at the major-league level but won't be ready this season.

DETROIT

TOP PROSPECTS

After an outstanding 1997 season in which the major-league club won a surprising 79 games and Detroit earned HOWE SPORTSDATA's Organization of the Year award, the past two seasons have been disastrous for the parent club and General Manager Randy Smith.

Smith was the toast of the town two years ago, but there was speculation last season that he might be fired. Smith has done a tremendous job rebuilding a dormant farm system, boasting as much talent as any club the past three years, but unrealistic expectations set by the fans after the '97 season have not been met. Trying to re-energize the major league club, Smith used OF **GABE KAPLER**, RHP **FRANCISCO CORDERO**, and LHP **ALAN WEBB**, three of the top young players in the system, to lure Juan Gonzalez from Texas. Cordero rebounded from an injury-filled '98 to return to form and make the HOWE SPORTSDATA All-Prospect Team. Kapler was a member of that team in 1998. Webb, the youngest pitcher in the Southern League, had a bright first half before slumping in the second half.

Detroit believes it has the position players to compete but must upgrade its pitching. Many of the highly touted pitchers have not lived up to early expectations, at least not yet. 1996 first-round pick RHP **SETH GREISINGER** went down early last season with elbow problems. First-round 1997 pick RHP **MATT ANDERSON** had all kinds of command problems and was shipped back to the minor-leagues. Japanese import RHP **MASADA KIDA** did not perform as advertised.

At the minor-league level, RHP **MATT DREWS** and RHP **MIKE DRUMRIGHT**, two former first-rounders whom the organization counted on to anchor the rotation, have combined for a 17–62 record and an ERA over 7.00 the past two years. The Tigers gave up on Drumright, shipping him to the Marlins in a minor-league deal on July 31. RHP **WILLIS ROBERTS**, another high-octane arm, posted a 6.26 ERA.

The trade of Cordero and Webb seriously cuts into the organization's young pitching depth. First-round 1998 pick RHP **JEFF WEAVER** had an outstanding first half. RHP **DAVE BORKOWSKI**, a big winner at the minor-league level, received some valuable big-league experience. RHP **VICTOR SANTOS** has a chance, as do RHP **SHANE LOUX**, RHP **NATE CORNEJO**, and LHP **ADAM PETTYJOHN** farther down, but each is still years away.

Behind the plate the organization has a quality hitter in C **ROB FICK**, added another big stick in the '99 draft with 1B-C **ERIC MUNSON**, and got a big season from C **JAVIER CARDONA**, but the everyday ranks are thinning out. There really isn't a legitimate prospect in the entire infield, and the outfield doesn't have much to offer either. OF **CHRIS WAKELAND** has a potent bat, but his defense needs an upgrade and he is already 25. OF **RICHARD GOMEZ** is a fine hitter and has great speed and a chance to add power, but he is several years away from the big leagues.

LF
JUAN ENCARNACION 24
*BOBBY HIGGINSON 29
○ *Chris Wakeland 2A 26 96/15C
↑ Richard Gomez A- 22 96/NDH

CF
***KARIM GARCIA 24**
? Rodney Lindsey 2A 24 94/39H
? Kurt Airoso 2A 25 96/29C

RF
JUAN GONZALEZ 30

SS
DEIVI CRUZ 24
? Luis Garcia ML 25 93/ND
? Derek Mitchell 2A 25 95/32C

2B
DAMION EASLEY 30
? #Jose Macias ML 26 92/ND
? Pedro Santana 2A 23 94/ND

3B
DEAN PALMER 31
? Gabe Alvarez ML 26 95/2C
? Rob Sasser 2A 25 93/10H
? Matt Boone A- 20 97/3H

1B
#TONY CLARK 28
○ *Robert Fick ML 26 96/5C
↑ *Eric Munson A+ 22 99/1

SP/RP

RELIEVERS
TODD JONES 32
DOUG BROCAIL 33
MASAO KIDA 31
MATT ANDERSON 23
DANNY PATTERSON 29
ERIK HILJUS 27
NELSON CRUZ 27
? Willis Roberts ML 25 92/ND
? Brandon Reed 3A 25 93/45H
? *Alberto Blanco 2A 24 92/ND

C
BRAD AUSMUS 31
#GREG ZAUN 29
○ Javier Cardona 2A 24 94/23C
○ Brandon Inge A- 23 98/2C

DH
#GREGG JEFFERIES 32
*LUIS POLONIA 35
GABE ALVAREZ 26

STARTERS
BRIAN MOEHLER 28
DAVE MLICKI 32
JEFF WEAVER 23
WILLIE BLAIR 34
*C.J. NITKOWSKI 27
○ David Borkowski ML 23 95/11H
? Matt Drews 3A 25 93/1H
○ Victor Santos 2A 23 95/NDH
? Shane Loux A+ 20 97/2H
○ Nate Cornejo A- 20 98/2H
? *Matt Miller 2A 25 96/2C
? *David Darwin 2A 26 96/26C
? Mark Johnson 2A 25 96/1C
○ *Adam Pettyjohn 2A 23 98/2C
○ *Mike Maroth 2A 22 98/3C

MAJOR LEAGUERS IN ALL CAPS
Minor leaguers in upper-and-lower case

BEFORE A PLAYER'S NAME:
* left-handed hitter/pitcher
\# switch-hitter
?=prospect status (see explanation)

AFTER A PLAYER'S NAME:
Level at which he spent most of 1999 season; age as of July 1, 2000; year he was drafted; round drafted (ND= non-drafted amateur free agent); drafted out of high school (H) or college (C)

EXPLANATION OF PROSPECT RATINGS

★ Potential big-league star

↑ Projected regular player in majors (for pitchers: rotation starter or closer)

○ Projected platoon or utility player in majors (pitcher: setup or middle relief)

? Possible big-league reserve or long reliever

↓ High draft pick or "tools" player who hasn't performed to expectations

DETROIT

KANSAS CITY ROYALS

MANAGEMENT
		CAREER RECORD
Manager	Tony Muser	167–234 / .416
G.M.	Herk Robinson	650–739 / .468
President/CEO	Greater K.C. Community Foundation	412–491 / .456

1999 RECORD
Won–Lost	Pct.	Finish/G.B. (Division)	Finish/G.B. (Wild Card)
64–97	.398	4/32.5 (C)	10/29.5

PRESEASON CONSENSUS PROJECTION
4 (4.25)

1st Half	2nd Half	Home	Road	Intradivision	Interleague
32–44	32–53	33–47	31–50	20–28	6–12

Comebacks	Blowouts	Nail-Biters	Grass	Turf	Sept.–Oct.
8–19	25–24	21–46	55–83	9–14	13–16

NUMBERS DON'T LIE

	Team (Rank)	Opponents (Rank)	League Avg.
Runs/Game	5.32 (6)	5.72 (14)	5.18
Batting Avg.	.282 (3)	.288 (14)	.274
On-Base Avg.	.348 (8)	.365 (12)	.347
Slugging Avg.	.433 (10)	.454 (11)	.439
Strikeouts	932 (4)	831 (14)	998
Home Runs	151 (12)	202 (11)	188
Stolen Bases	127 (3)	111 (10)	104
ERA	5.35 (14)		4.87
Errors	125 (11)		114

▶ THE INSIDER 2000

RENAISSANCE FOR THE ROYALS?

Despite a very tough year during which they lost 97 games and posted their worst-ever winning percentage (.398), the Royals sported several fine young talents—including a five-tool center fielder who exploded onto the scene to become one of the game's top young players.

Carlos Beltran's emergence meant the world to the Royals in 1999, for it gave the fans some reason to hope that the future will be brighter. But the same scenario took place 30 years ago. In 1970 the Royals also lost 97 games, but they were laying the foundation for their successful future in only their second season. One of the key decisions they made that year was to hand over center field to Amos Otis, a skilled but unproven youngster acquired from the Mets.

The Royals' decision to go with young and unproven talent was the main factor in their rise to prominence in the 1970s. Now, after several years of trying to plug holes with on-the-decline veterans and one-dimensional fill-ins, the Bip Roberts era appears to be over. The talent express, letting out a lusty whistle, has finally pulled into Kansas City. Whether the Royals can shape such excellent raw material into a winning club may be the most interesting question in baseball today.

In the 1970s the Royals developed Frank White, George Brett, Al Cowens, Dennis Leonard, Dan Quisenberry, and Willie Wilson, among others, out of their farm system. They traded for John Mayberry, Fred Patek, Hal McRae, and others. While there probably are no George Bretts in their system or on their roster now, Beltran is a legitimate star in the making. Carlos Febles has a good chance to be as great a second baseman as White and is almost certain to contribute more offensively. It is not yet clear how good Dee Brown will be, but saying he could be better than Al Cowens isn't unreasonable.

The current Royals have shown an important parallel to their successful clubs of the 1970s: the ability to draft, sign, and produce first-class talent. For some reason, the Royals just don't get much credit for their player development, but of the current club, Beltran, Damon, Sweeney, Febles, Randa, Fasano, Giambi, Rosado, and Pichardo have all come from the farm (as did Michael Tucker, who was dealt for Jermaine Dye). Others, such as Dee Brown, Dan Reichert, and Mark Quinn, are on the way. The pitching produced by the system hasn't been that strong,

MOMENT OF TRUTH

Perhaps the Royals set themselves up for a fall by being too good too early. Kansas City went 22–9 in spring training games, the best spring record in the majors, and was 22–20 in the regular season through May 23, but the rest of the season was a disaster. In the end, the Royals probably finished about where they should have, given the players on their roster. Still, things were looking good until rookie Carlos Febles had to miss nearly a week in the early part of June with a shoulder strain. The club had nobody to replace him offensively or defensively, and his absence seemed to take the life out of the entire team. K.C. lost every game Febles missed and wound up losing nine straight and 17 of their next 21 to fall well out of contention.

BIGGEST SURPRISE

Jermaine Dye went from being a huge disappointment to the best hitter on his team in a single season. Dye struggled badly for a few years after he was traded from Atlanta to the Royals, bouncing back and forth between Kansas City and Triple A Omaha trying to find his batting stroke. In 1999 he finally broke through, easily eclipsing his previous career-best numbers. He showed remarkable improvement in plate discipline, drawing 58 walks—18 more than his previous career total—in 769 at-bats.

BIGGEST DISAPPOINTMENT

Veteran reliever Jeff Montgomery managed to hang around long enough to get 300 saves, at the cost of being one of the worst closers in baseball last season. Montgomery won only a single game to go with his 12 saves, losing four and blowing seven saves. The Royals were counting on Montgomery to stabilize their bullpen and provide support for their young pitchers, but Monty was a complete bust. He quietly retired soon after the end of the season.

---

nor was it in the 1970s. The great Royal teams had deep staffs of able-bodied and skilled pitchers but few stars.

Another way the Royals built their clubs in the 1970s was through sharp trading. Some of the current Royals acquired in deals include Dye, Suppan, Witasick, Stein, and Rigby. Herk Robinson isn't known for having a good trading record, though he's done better of late. Of course, it isn't that easy to *steal* talent anymore. Philosophies have changed in baseball in the 1990s; since the infamous Jeff Bagwell deal, clubs are more disposed to hold on to their very best prospects. Instead, what happens is that clubs such as Kansas City are forced into trading players such as Kevin Appier for a handful of lesser prospects. The Royals appear to have gotten all that they could for Appier, who has thrown a lot of good innings and whose health always will be a concern.

THERE IS A FORM IN VOID

In some ways the Royals' 1999 season was a crushing disappointment. Only Minnesota had a worse overall record, and the Royals' staff ERA of 5.35 was the worst in the majors. The bullpen was terrible—as was the bench—the club's longtime rotation anchor was traded in midseason, and a bid for new ownership was scuttled by Major League Baseball.

What looks like bleakness in the short term is very, very promising in the big picture, however. Last season was the end of the old era in K.C. and the start of a new one. With Terry Pendleton retiring after 1998 as other vets such as Hal Morris, Jeff Conine, Shane Mack, Tim Belcher, and Pat Rapp were being shown the door, there was boundless opportunity for young players to grab jobs in 1999.

Mike Sweeney, finally allowed to play every day at first base when Jeff King called it quits early in May, blossomed into a dangerous hitter at age 25. Febles showed good defensive skills and made important offensive contributions. Beltran won the AL Rookie of the Year award, hitting for average and power and throwing out 16 base runners.

Combining these performances with fine showings from veterans Johnny Damon (age 25), Jermaine Dye (25), and third sacker Joe Randa (29), the Royals finished a surprising seventh in the AL in runs. Things could have been even better had the Royals gotten even mediocre production from behind the plate, at shortstop, or at DH. In some cases, however, young players (DH

Jeremy Giambi, first baseman Larry Sutton) couldn't carry the load; in others, weak sticks such as Chad Kreuter and Rey Sanchez dragged the offense down.

Pitching was an entirely different story. Kevin Appier's trade was yet another sign that the Royals would be a different club in the 21st century, but the improvement was not so painless as it was with the offense. Jose Rosado, Jeff Suppan, and Jay Witasick (who dealt with growing pains but showed fine stuff) might form the core of a solid rotation this year. The rest of a rebuilt rotation could come from quality young arms such as Dan Reichert, Blake Stein, and Chris Fussell. Even in '99, the Royals' starters' ERA was better than six other AL clubs despite the burden of breaking in many young arms.

Going into the '99 season with 37-year-old Jeff Montgomery as the closer was a risky proposition, and when the cagey vet's shoulder (and, by extension, his slider) finally broke down beyond repair, the Royals starters were left without any help. It would not be an exaggeration to say that for much of the season Kansas City did not have a single consistently effective pitcher in the bullpen. Montgomery's postseason retirement was the final sign that the past was buried—and given that the Royals haven't made the postseason since 1985, it's high time.

DAYS OF FUTURE PAST

What can the Royals realistically expect for 2000? Of the club's productive hitters, at least one and probably two will decline somewhat. However, the club's problem areas on offense can easily be improved. It's not hard to find a productive DH, and rookie Mark Quinn (who had an outstanding September trial) should fit somewhere. Upgrades at catcher and shortstop shouldn't be difficult. Sal Fasano could finally get a chance of a full season behind the dish, and Mendy Lopez is still a fine fielder with some promise in his bat. There's no reason to assume that the Royals' hitters won't continue to produce at a similar rate.

The pitching is, obviously, a crapshoot. Having to build a bullpen out of Scott Service, Orber Moreno, Mac Suzuki, Brad Rigby, Chad Durbin, Lance Carter, and Jose Santiago might seem daunting, but all of those guys have fine arms. The Royals are bound to have better results in relief than they did in '99.

Manager Tony Muser showed himself unafraid to use youngsters, especially in key spots, last season. He is a pitching-

SECRET WEAPON

Lots of teams lusted after former Boston prospect Jeff Suppan at one time or another, but the Royals were able to acquire him for nothing. The expansion Diamondbacks gave up on him after only 13 starts in 1998, and Kansas City quickly jumped at the opportunity to purchase him without having to give up any players. The 24-year-old improved tremendously in 1999, and if the Royals show some patience, they could reap the rewards for years to come.

ACHILLES HEEL

During the 1999 season, Kansas City had 12 pitchers who appeared in at least 10 games in relief. Jose Santiago was the only one who showed any consistency. Santiago (3–4, 3.42) was the only reliever with more than 10 innings whose ERA was less than 4.00; Alvin Morman and Terry Mathews were the only other two to come in under 5.00. Jeff Montgomery obviously was on his last legs, but he wasn't the only one who pitched well below expectations. The bullpen as a whole blew 30 saves and logged an ERA of 5.77, making it one of the worst relief corps in modern history.

ENOUGH ALREADY

Just sell Miles Prentice the bloody team! What right did Major League Baseball have to deny him and his investment group ownership? MLB claimed it was worried because Prentice's group had more than 40 investors with less than majority interest, but the real reason was clearly that it wanted the team to sell for more than the $75 million Prentice was willing to pay. No car dealership holds out expecting some fool to pay a Cadillac price for an economy car, so why expect someone to overpay for a depressed, small-market team that's been for sale for years? If the Royals are left twisting in the wind while waiting for a $100 million bid, the long-term damage to the franchise and to the game itself will be far greater than any short-term gain in the sale price.

and-defense manager, going last year with Kreuter and Sanchez largely for defensive reasons. Shifting Johnny Damon to left and leaving Jermaine Dye in right full-time gave the club an outstanding defensive outfield. One-dimensional hitters such as Sutton and Joe Vitiello didn't play much.

Perhaps spooked by Muser's lousy bullpen, his pitchers threw 11 complete games, fourth in the league, despite having 11 different starters during the season. Muser also played the traditional "little" game of teams without a lot of power (the Royals were 12th in the AL in home runs), frequently calling for the hit-and-run. K.C. ended up third in the AL in steals and second in sac bunts.

Muser also showed a tendency to use veterans off the bench. Despite having several young players well qualified to fill a utility infield position (Mendy Lopez, Felix Martinez), he instead tried Scott Leius, Ray Holbert, and Steve Scarsone in addition to holdover Jed Hansen. Other Royals reserves included well-traveled vets Scott Pose and Tim Spehr. This was hardly an inspiring group, but none of them shoved the youngsters onto the pine—which is probably the most important and welcome development of all.

On July 5, 1999, George Brett was inducted into the Hall of Fame in Cooperstown. The enshrinement of the greatest Royals player of them all certainly served as a poignant reminder of the great baseball played in Kansas City in the past. Perhaps it was a harbinger of better times ahead as well.

BEST CASE

While it's tough to project too far into the future, you can see the germinating seeds of a winning club in Kansas City. The rebuilding Royals boast good young players at most positions, and some promising arms. If the Royals' bullpen is improved by the acquisitions of Tyler Green and Jerry Spradlin, if rotation starters Jeff Suppan and Jose Rosado continue to develop, and if someone—anyone—can step into some relatively easy-to-fill shoes at DH, Kansas City could easily move up a spot or two in the standings.

WORST CASE

Obviously the Royals need good performances from their young position players, such as Beltran, Febles, Dye, Sweeney, Fasano, and Damon. However, pitching (terrible last year, especially the pen) is the big question surrounding this team. Will key youngsters like Blake Stein, Brad Rigby, Jamie Walker, Dan Reichert, and Orber Moreno take the next step and become key contributors to a winning young club? If not, the Royals will be in trouble again. The last thing KC needs is to sail down the Ricky Bones river, just trying to stay afloat by grabbing any piece of deadwood it sees.

UNDER THE MICROSCOPE

DAN REICHERT: The '97 first-rounder missed substantial time in '98 because of diabetes and was shut down last season with a broken bone in his elbow. Reichert had an outstanding 9-2, 3.71 ERA in the hitter-friendly Pacific Coast League and was leading it with 123 strikeouts when promoted. He has a quality arm and good stuff, but the time lost will hurt his chances this spring.

ORBER MORENO: Moreno completed his meteoric rise to the big leagues when he was called up in late May after posting a 2.03 ERA and fanning 31 batters in 27 innings at Triple A. After a few scoreless outings, Moreno injured his shoulder and was sidelined the remainder of the season. If he stays healthy, the 22-year-old he should ascend to the closer role in the near future.

MARK QUINN: By winning his second straight batting championship and having an outstanding September with the Royals, the 25-year-old Quinn convinced the organization that he was indeed a big-league prospect. Although defense is a concern, Quinn could provide an alternative to arbitration-eligible Johnny Damon.

DEE BROWN: Much like Carlos Beltran in 1998, Brown returned to Class A ball in '99, dominated at two levels, and ended the season in the major leagues. It's unlikely he will follow Beltran to the majors this season because he's not as polished defensively or as experienced, but Brown soon should be an offensive force.

KANSAS CITY

TOP PROSPECTS

1999 was a season of mixed feedback for the Royals. They left Florida with a spring training–best 22–9 record and played .500 ball for five weeks before finishing with the worst winning percentage in club history, .398. The bullpen became the first in major-league history to finish with more blown saves (30) than saves (29), but several youngsters in the organization impressed.

Of the four 1998 farm graduates, OF **CARLOS BELTRAN** and 2B **CARLOS FEBLES** played well on a daily basis, 1B **JEREMY GIAMBI** showed promise offensively, and OF **MARK QUINN** hit .341 with five homers in 44 September at-bats. These players combined with past grads Mike Sweeney, Joe Randa, Jermaine Dye, and Johnny Damon to score a franchise record 856 runs. On the minor-league front, the Royals finished with the third-best winning percentage for the fifth time in the past six years they had finished in the top 10. The Triple A Omaha club slugged a Pacific Coast League record 231 homers, although Quinn was the only real prospect to play there.

Unfortunately, none of the organization's top pitching prospects could come through at the major-league level. Injuries shut down the two most promising, RHP **DAN REICHERT** and RHP **ORBER MORENO**, and nobody else could fill the void. The Royals brought in three marginal prospects from outside the organization: Jay Witasick, Chris Fussell, and Mac Suzuki. They combined for a 9–20 record and an ERA of about 6.00.

The strength of the organization is decent young pitching. Reichert and Moreno have a chance to be productive big leaguers. First-round 1998 pick RHP **JEFF AUSTIN** and RHP **CHAD DURBIN** are two finesse pitchers with a chance, although many were not that impressed with the Stanford-bred Austin. Twenty-year-old RHP **JUNIOR GUERRERO**, a power pitcher, emerged last season much like Moreno did in '98. RHP **ROBBIE MORRISON** has a chance to help out of the bullpen in the future.

LHP **CHRIS GEORGE** emerged as the top southpaw in the system, but LHP **SCOTT MULLEN** has a chance despite his Triple A problems last season. In addition, the Royals added six more young arms in the first two rounds of the draft, gaining additional picks for the losses of Jose Offerman and Dean Palmer.

With Beltran and Febles established in the big leagues and Quinn and Giambi on the verge, the organization is thinning out. OF **DEE BROWN** had a monster season, batting .331 with 25 homers and 30 steals over two levels, although he was just 2-for-25 at the big-league level. OF **GEOFF TOMLINSON** is a bona fide prospect, but he's still very inexperienced. C **PAUL PHILLIPS** has moved quickly since being drafted in '98 and converting from the outfield, but he has little pop. 3Bs **KIT PELLOW** and **SEAN MCNALLY**, both 26, combined for 71 homers, but neither is a legitimate prospect. Oft-maligned SS **FELIX MARTINEZ** and 2B **JED HANSEN** were waived this fall and picked up by other clubs.

LF
*JOHNNY DAMON 26
*SCOTT POSE 33
↑ Mark Quinn ML 26 95/11C
↑ *Dee Brown ML 22 96/1H

CF
#CARLOS BELTRAN 23
*TODD DUNWOODY 25
○ *Goef Tomlinson 2A 23 97/4C
? *Mike Curry A+ 23 98/6C
? Jose Tavares A- 23 93/ND

RF
JERMAINE DYE 26

SS
REY SANCHEZ 32
RAY HOLBERT 29
#FELIX MARTINEZ 26
? Alejandro Prieto 2A 24 92/ND
? #Steve Medrano A+ 22 95/5H
? Mendy Lopez ML 25 92/ND

2B
CARLOS FEBLES 24
? Tony Medrano 3A 25 93/2H
? Willy Ruiz A- 21 95/ND

3B
JOE RANDA 30
JEFF REBOULET 36
? Kit Pellow 3A 26 96/22C

1B
MIKE SWEENEY 26
? Jose Amado 2A 25 93/ND

SP/RP

RELIEVERS
SCOTT SERVICE 33
*ALVIN MORMAN 31
BRAD RIGBY 27
DEREK WALLACE 28
*TIM BYRDAK 26
JERRY SPALDLIN 33
? Ken Ray ML 25 93/18H
↑ Orber Moreno ML 23 93/ND
? Jeff D'Amico 3A 25 93/2H
? Kris Wilson 3A 23 97/9C
○ Robbie Morrison 2A 23 98/2C
? Edwin Gonzalez A+ 22 95/ND
? Sonny Sonnier A+ 23 98/NDC

C
BRIAN JOHNSON 32
SAL FASANO 28
○ Paul Phillips 2A 23 98/9C

DH
*JEREMY GIAMBI 25

STARTERS
*JOSE ROSADO 25
JEFF SUPPAN 25
JAY WITASICK 27
BLAKE STEIN 26
TYLER GREEN 30
MAC SUZUKI 25
? Dan Murray ML 26 95/10C
? Chris Fussell ML 24 94/9H
↑ Dan Reichert ML 23 97/1C
○ Chad Durbin ML 22 96/3H
? Kiko Calera 2A 25 96/27C
○ Jeff Austin 2A 23 98/1C
↑ Junior Guerrero A+ 20 96/ND
↓ Matt Burch A- 23 98/1C
↓ Kyle Snyder A- 22 99/1C
○ *Scott Mullen 3A 25 96/7C
? *Jason Gooding 3A 25 97/5C
↑ *Chris George A+ 20 98/1H
? *Jeremy Affeldt A- 21 97/3H

MAJOR LEAGUERS IN ALL CAPS
Minor leaguers in upper-and-lower case

BEFORE A PLAYER'S NAME:
* left-handed hitter/pitcher
# switch-hitter
?= prospect status (see explanation)

AFTER A PLAYER'S NAME:
Level at which he spent most of 1999 season; age as of July 1, 2000; year he was drafted; round drafted (ND= non-drafted amateur free agent); drafted out of high school (H) or college (C)

EXPLANATION OF PROSPECT RATINGS

★ Potential big-league star

↑ Projected regular player in majors (for pitchers: rotation starter or closer)

○ Projected platoon or utility player in majors (pitcher: setup or middle relief)

? Possible big-league reserve or long reliever

↓ High draft pick or "tools" player who hasn't performed to expectations

KANSAS CITY

MINNESOTA TWINS

MANAGEMENT
Manager	Tom Kelly	
G.M.	Terry Ryan	
President/CEO	Carl Pohlad	

CAREER RECORD
986–1074 / .479
335–455 / .424
1122–1239 / .475

1999 RECORD

Won–Lost	Pct.	Finish/G.B. (Division)	Finish/G.B. (Wild Card)
63–97	.394	5/33 (C)	11/30

PRESEASON CONSENSUS PROJECTION
5 (4.60)

1ST HALF	2ND HALF	HOME	ROAD	INTRADIVISION	INTERLEAGUE
29–47	34–50	31–50	32–47	20–28	10–7

COMEBACKS	BLOWOUTS	NAIL-BITERS	GRASS	TURF	SEPT.–OCT.
9–10	21–37	25–42	27–39	36–58	7–23

NUMBERS DON'T LIE

	TEAM (RANK)		OPPONENTS (RANK)		LEAGUE AVG.
Runs/Game	4.26	(14)	5.25	(6)	5.18
Batting Avg.	.264	(11)	.283	(10)	.274
On-Base Avg.	.328	(12)	.341	(3)	.347
Slugging Avg.	.384	(14)	.464	(14)	.439
Strikeouts	978	(6)	927	(12)	998
Home Runs	105	(14)	208	(12)	188
Stolen Bases	118	(5)	73	(2)	104
ERA	5.03	(9)			4.87
Errors	92	(2)			114

▶ THE INSIDER 2000

BLEEDING TO DEATH

The Minnesota Twins will start the 2000 season without a single championship-quality position player. In fact, they don't even have a single position player who played well in 1999. The best of last season's Twins players—infielders Ron Coomer, Corey Koskie, and Todd Walker, and outfielder Chad Allen—would be no better than fill-ins on many good teams.

Koskie had a nice rookie season as a hitter, but he's unlikely to become a top-flight regular. While outfielders Allen, Torii Hunter, and Jacque Jones have some tools and can play the field, none of them boasts a good minor-league hitting profile. And none of the Twins' young players are likely to develop into stars. At best, some of them will be decent everyday players.

The Twins' veterans weren't so hot in '99, either. Marty Cordova had yet another disappointing season and elected free agency after being outrighted in October. Matt Lawton, who was hitting fairly well early on, took a Dennys Reyes fastball in the face on June 8 and hit just two homers the rest of the way. Infielder Brent Gates was able to get more than 300 at-bats despite contributing little. Ron Coomer led the team in homers—with 16. And Todd Walker, for whom the desperate Twins had such high hopes a couple of years ago, took a step backward instead of improving with experience.

It was clear from the way manager Tom Kelly employed Walker last season that he has little faith in the infielder whom the Twins thought would be a star they could build around. Kelly regularly bemoaned the fact that he had to play some players who seemed happy being mediocre, but that they were the best he had, so he had no choice. Walker was certainly was one of those slackers in Kelly's eyes, and Kelly's disdain was evident in how often he used Gates against tough lefties or DH Walker rather than play him at second. At 27, Walker still has a lot of value; if Kelly doesn't want to play him every day, trading him would be advisable before another season like '99 destroys that value.

BAD ATTITUDE, BAD MANAGEMENT, OR BOTH?

The Twins have given no indication that they're going to spend any money on free agents until and unless the team gets a new stadium. Therefore, it's a little ridiculous to keep

MOMENT OF TRUTH

The Twins were hoping they'd finally turned the corner in July, the franchise's first winning month in three seasons. But reality set in soon after, when both the pitching and the offense went into the tank. Minnesota began August with a four-game losing streak, and things rapidly deteriorated. The Twinkies won more than two consecutive games only twice in the last two months of the season and finished right where they were expected to be—with the worst record in baseball.

MINNESOTA TWINS

BIGGEST SURPRISE

Joe Mays made the jump all the way from Double-A to Minnesota at the start of the season and had a very respectable rookie year at age 23. Like most young, promising pitchers, Mays made enough mistakes to inflate his ERA but he had plenty of positive outings, too. He shut out the Cubs in Wrigley Field right after the All-Star break, had a streak of 29 scoreless innings, and avoided a prolonged slump until late in the season. Since he still doesn't have enough experience above Class A, it will take a little more time before Mays becomes a consistent winner. Nevertheless, he did give the organization much to look forward to.

BIGGEST DISAPPOINTMENT

Marty Cordova, AL Rookie of the Year in 1995, continued his downward spiral. He was so bad by the end of the year that the Twins tried to trade him, but they found no takers. Immediately after the season, the club out-righted him to Triple-A, knowing he'd elect free agency and they'd be rid of him.

---

thinking of the team as being in a rebuilding mode, as the organization wants fans to believe. The reality is the team has been stripped of most of its useful players, and any good players who do develop in the next few years will likely be traded as well if there's no new ballpark on the horizon. Minnesota is still several years away from the point where it can actually be rebuilt into a contender.

The only Twins position player who is young, has top-flight talent, and possesses a good minor-league résumé is 24-year-old first sacker David Ortiz, who rakes with big-time power, will take walks, and can hit for average. He has already proven that in the major-leagues.

But where was David Ortiz in 1999? At Triple-A Salt Lake, hitting .315 with 79 walks, 30 home runs, and a PCL-leading 110 RBI. First base in Minneapolis was manned by 25-year-old Doug Mientkiewicz, who in 118 games batted .229 with two home runs. Mientkiewicz's résumé included a fine season at Double-A in 1999, which came after a poor one at the same level. If he can recover from his debacle last season, he might have a career as a big-league reserve.

So why were the Twins ready to give a critical offensive spot to a guy who took two years to figure out Double-A pitching, who doesn't have the power needed from a first baseman, and, as a bonus, is also two years older than Ortiz? Mientkiewicz was a mediocre hitter with a good glove—a classic overachiever who became a prospect after '98. His lackluster '97 performance was excused due to a broken bone in his foot that went undetected for two years.

The Twins felt Ortiz had a poor attitude that, along with a poor spring-training performance, made it easy for them to ship him out. Far better teams than the Twins would have made room for someone with David Ortiz's talent. It's a testament to Tom Kelly's hardheadedness that he would saddle his team with a fatal lack of offense while the organization's best power hitter was crushing Triple-A pitching.

It's certainly understandable that Kelly wouldn't want to have a player with a problem attitude on his team, but doesn't the manager owe it to the players and the fans to put the best possible team on the field? The best managers in the game find ways to get to guys with questionable attitudes and make them productive players. Witness the Astros' ability to get the most out of Carl Everett and Jose Lima, or the job Dusty Baker has done with guys like Jeff Kent and Charlie Hayes.

Ortiz's attitude apparently didn't improve at Salt Lake City, where manager Phil Roof publicly spoke out against the slugging first baseman. One question: Would a talented player with potential and what should be boundless opportunity be happy down in Triple-A while someone hitting for neither power nor average plays ahead of him in the majors?

Not often will you find good organizations suffering through these types of problems. However, mismanaged organizations tend to fritter away the little talent they do have. In 1999, the Twins wasted an entire year of David Ortiz's career while simultaneously hurting themselves.

To cap it all off, Ortiz was awful in a brief September look-see in Minnesota, going 1-for-20 while fanning 12 times. Such small samples shouldn't cloud a team's long-term vision, but they do all too frequently. Even after that horrid performance, Ortiz's major-league career averages (.268 BA, .358 OBA, .421 SA) are respectable enough given the improvement expected of a player his age as he matures and gains big-league experience.

Baseball is full of instances where a handful of misleading late-season at-bats overcame a team's better judgment. The White Sox wasted 252 at-bats on a non-prospect—28-year-old utility infielder Craig Wilson—who hit .238 with four homers in '99, because he lucked into a .468 average with three homers in 13 games in September 1998. The first sentence in the Sox's 1999 media guide bio of Wilson read, "His .468 average (22–47) is the highest in major-league history among players with a minimum of 50 plate appearances."

In 1996, the immortal Rudy Pemberton hit .512 with nine extra-base hits in 41 September at-bats for Boston at age 26. To be fair, Pemberton had beaten up on Triple-A pitching in Pawtucket that summer, but you can be sure that his lucky 41 at-bats had more to do with his starting '97 as the Red Sox' regular right fielder. Rudy's bio in the 1997 Red Sox media guide included this statement in boldface: "[O]nly player in M.L. history to hit over .500 with at least 30 AB." Not surprisingly, Pemberton was playing in Japan well before the 1997 season was over after hitting .238 with four extra-base hits in 63 at-bats for the BoSox.

Willie Mays started his career 0-for-22. David Ortiz is surely no Willie Mays, but he ain't no Doug Mientkiewicz, either. If Ortiz is lucky, he'll be traded to another club where the manager wants guys with real talent rather than hustling players of limited potential who are just happy to be in the Show.

SECRET WEAPON

Javier Valentin might have earned himself a starting spot in 2000 even if Terry Steinbach hadn't retired after the '99 season. He didn't hit as well as Steinbach, but he threw out 46 percent of runners trying to steal, a far higher percentage than his counterpart. Valentin has plenty of work to do—he hit only .219 against right-handed pitchers—but it's reasonable to assume that the 24-year-old switch-hitter will improve enough to be a respectable hitter.

ACHILLES HEEL

It's not hard to figure out that Minnesota's biggest weakness is its lack of power, yet just how pathetic the offense has become is horrifying. Ron Coomer led the Twins in 1999 with just 16 homers—only one Minnesota player since 1995 has hit more than 16 home runs in a season. Matt Lawton hit 21 homers as a sophomore in 1998, but you have to go all the way back to the Kirby Puckett era to find a time when the Twins had an offense with more sock than their current anemic attack.

MINNESOTA TWINS

ENOUGH ALREADY

When the Twins hired former Mets GM Joe McIlvaine as an assistant to GM Terry Ryan, they certainly didn't expect him to grab headlines. However, he at least provided some comic relief on April 12 when he was arrested for nude sunbathing on Jensen Beach in Florida. McIlvaine's explanation was that he thought he was on a private beach.

HOPEFUL SIGNS

As bad as the Twins are, they have some pitching talent to be proud of. Brad Radke, 27, is a genuine staff ace due to his durability and skill. Eric Milton, 24—of the September no-hitter against the Anaheim Anemic Angels—would be a 15-game winner on a good team. Joe Mays, who began the year in the bullpen, worked his way into the rotation and showed he belonged there.

The enigma—again—was LaTroy Hawkins, who signed a long-term deal in the spring but then went out and had another frustrating season. After giving up eight runs in his first start of the year, he got worse, posting a 1-6 record after seven appearances. He improved somewhat as the season went on, yet ended with a 10-14 record and a league-worst 6.66 ERA.

That said, Hawkins took his turns, ate up innings, and refused to give up on himself after his terrible spring. The Twins can spare the time for the 27-year-old Hawkins to improve, and they shouldn't give up on him either.

Minnesota's bullpen also showed promise. Even with Hector Carrasco out for half the year with a circulation problem, Minnesota had quality lefties in Eddie Guardado and Travis Miller, plus a fine contingency closer in Mike Trombley, who took over late-inning duty after Rick Aguilera and his salary were sent packing to Chicago. However, the chances that Trombley will be back are low; he could very well go free agent, leaving the Twins with few options.

BEST CASE

There is literally no hope for the Twins to make the playoffs this year, next year, or the year after that. Now, with this bad news out of the way, let's focus on a more realistic goal: a .500 record. There is some talent on this club (and some players who should be better than they are), and a few judicious veteran acquisitions could take some pressure off the kids. Minnesota owner Carl Pohlad now says that he is not selling the team, and if that's true, he has some obligation to make the Twins competitive for the sake of the long-suffering fans of the frozen north.

WORST CASE

The worst case? Another year of submediocrity. Manager Tom Kelly is beginning to exude hopelessness through his pores. After well over a decade of running this club, he may be running out of gas. Kelly's strength has allegedly always been an ability to get the most out of kids, but in the last few years, he has publicly feuded with and even scolded David McCarty, Todd Walker, Denny Hocking, David Ortiz, and others. Is Kelly burned out from managing without the tools to compete? It would be hard to blame him. It may be time, both for the organization and for Kelly, to make a change.

UNDER THE MICROSCOPE

MATT LECROY: Last season LeCroy clubbed 30 homers between Class A and Triple-A and he hit .288 in his two pro seasons. While his defensive value lags, the 24-year-old works hard behind the plate and should improve. He has a good chance to make the big club in 2000.

MICHAEL CUDDYER: Cuddyer has made the smooth transition from shortstop to third base while maintaining a high productivity level at the plate. The 20-year-old followed up a debut season with a franchise-record 81 RBI in the lower-level Class A Midwest League and solid numbers (.298, 16 HR, 82 RBI) against older competition at advanced Class A. Cuddyer should move into the starting lineup on a full-time basis in 2001.

JASON RYAN: Acquired by the Twins in the Rick Aguilera deal in May 1999, Ryan was given a crack at the big leagues after stints in Double and Triple-A. The 6'3" Ryan showed good movement on his pitches during his call-up and should be in the rotation this season. He almost quit the game two years ago and has not posted great numbers in any of his past four years in the minors, however; the Twins shouldn't be overly optimistic about a change in the majors.

RYAN MILLS: Mills was given a $2 million signing bonus and rewarded the Twins with a 3–10, 8.87 ERA showing in Class A. Shoulder woes from 1998 may have had something to do with his 87 walks and 20 wild pitches in 95 innings. He needs to have a solid, injury-free 2000 season to regain prospect status.

MINNESOTA

TOP PROSPECTS

The Minnesota Twins suffered through another dismal season in 1999. With one of the smallest payrolls in the game, the Twins trotted out only a few experienced veterans, opening the door for many players who were in Double and Triple-A in '98. 3B **COREY KOSKIE** and OF **CHAD ALLEN** held their own with the bat, and SS **CHRISTIAN GUZMAN** and OF **TORII HUNTER** impressed with the glove, but will likely prove marginal everyday players at best. Though OF **JACQUES JONES**, 24, was perhaps the most well-rounded of the bunch, hitting well and covering a lot of ground in center field, his low walk totals may keep him from being a top-of-the-order hitter. 1B **DOUG MIENTKIEWICZ** was also given a job out of spring training but struggled.

In the rotation, RHP **JOE MAYS** put together a dominant midseason stretch and finished with a respectable 4.37 ERA. Fellow righties **MIKE LINCOLN**, **JASON RYAN**, and **DAN PERKINS** also saw time, presenting the Twins with some options when rounding out the rotation for 2000.

Despite the widespread infiltration of minor leaguers onto the big-league roster, the Twins still have a solid supply of positional players on the farm. C **MATT LECROY**, a supplemental first-round pick in 1997, put up impressive power numbers for the second straight year. With Terry Steinbach now retired, LeCroy and C **A. J. PIERZYNSKI** will battle to make the team out of spring training. SS **LUIS RIVAS**, the youngest player in the Double-A Eastern League in '99, is a junior version of Guzman with a little more pop and upside. 1B **DAVID ORTIZ** led the Triple-A Pacific Coast League with 110 RBIs but has not won over Tom Kelly with his attitude. His future was futher put in jeopardy by an 0-for-20 performance in his September call-up.

Farther down, 1997 first-round pick 3B **MICHAEL CUDDYER**, a converted shortstop, has the offensive upside indicative of a franchise-type player. OF **MICHAEL RESTOVICH**, selected in the second round in '97, is a pure hitter with power potential and has emerged as the best outfield prospect in the organization. The Twins chose OF **B. J. GARBE** with their first-round pick in 1999, and he handled himself well in his debut.

While the organization has not produced many quality big leaguers recently, pitching has been a problem for most of the past two decades. Aside from Ryan and RHP **KYLE LOHSE**, both acquired in the trade that sent Rick Aguilera to the Cubs, the Twins have not received much encouragement from the pitchers. Injuries and struggles summed up the organization's staff in '99. RHP **MATT KINNEY**, who performed well at times in Double-A, sat out almost the entire second half or the season with a shoulder injury. LHP **RYAN MILLS**, the organization's first-round pick in '98, had a disastrous showing in Class A in his first full professional season. LHP **BRAD THOMAS**, RHP **JASON BELL**, and reliever RHP **BRENT STENTZ**, who led the minors with 43 saves in 1998, all struggled after promising performances the previous season. LHP **JOE THOMAS**, a 15-game winner in '98, missed all of last season with surgery on his pitching shoulder.

LF
CHAD ALLEN 25
? #Rafael Alvarez 3A 23 94/ND
? Marc Lewis 2A 25 94/25C
? #Ramon Borrego A+ 22 95/ND

CF
TORII HUNTER 24
*JACQUE JONES 25
? *Anthony Felston 2A 25 96/34C
? John Barnes 2A 24 96/4C
○ Cesar Bolivar A+ 21 96/ND
? #Bobby Kielty A- 23 98/NDC
? Brian McMillin A- 23 98/31C
↓ B.J. Garbe A- 19 99/1H

RF
***MATT LAWTON 28**
? Brian Buchanan 3A 26 94/1C
↑ Mike Restovich A- 21 97/2H

SS
#CRISTIAN GUZMAN 22
? Mike Moriarty 3A 26 95/7C
↑ Luis Rivas 2A 20 95/ND

2B
***TODD WALKER 27**
#DENNY HOCKING 30
? #Cleatus Davidson ML 23 94/2H
○ Dan Cey 3A 24 96/3C
? *Mike Ryan A+ 22 96/5H
○ #Luis Rodriguez A- 20 97/ND

3B
***COREY KOSKIE 27**
↑ Michael Cuddyer A+ 21 97/1H

1B
***DOUG MIENTKIEWICZ 26**
↑ *David Ortiz ML 24 92/ND
? Steve Hacker 3A 25 95/14C
○ *Tommy Peterman 2A 25 96/11C

SP/RP

RELIEVERS
BOB WELLS 33
*EDDIE GUARDADO 29
HECTOR CARRASCO 30
DAN PERKINS 25
SEAN BERGMAN 30
*TRAVIS MILLER 27
*BENJ SAMPSON 25
? *Mark Redman ML 26 95/1C
? *J.C. Romero ML 24 97/21C
? Brent Stentz 3A 24 94/33C
○ Daniel Mota 2A 24 94/ND
○ Saul Rivera A- 22 98/9C
? *Alan Mahaffey 3A 26 95/16C

C
#JAVIER VALENTIN 24
○ *A.J. Pierzynski ML 23 94/3H
? *Jeff Smith 3A 26 95/20C
↑ Matt LeCroy 3A 24 97/1C
? Chad Moeller 2A 25 96/7H
↓ #Rob Bowen A- 19 99/2H

STARTERS
BRAD RADKE 27
*ERIC MILTON 24
LATROY HAWKINS 27
MIKE LINCOLN 25
JOE MAYS 24
↑ Jason Ryan ML 24 94/9H
? Scott Randall 3A 24 95/11C
○ Matt Kinney 2A 23 95/6H
? Jack Cressend 2A 25 96/NDC
○ Kyle Lohse 2A 21 96/29C
○ Juan Rincon A- 21 96/ND
↓ Marcus Sents A- 19 98/2H
? *Brad Thomas A+ 22 95/ND
↓ *Ryan Mills A+ 22 98/1C
○ *Brent Hoard A- 23 98/3C
○ *Johan Santana A- 21 95/11C
? Kenny Pumphrey 2A 23 94/4H

DH
RON COOMER 33

MAJOR LEAGUERS IN ALL CAPS
minor leaguers in upper-and-lower case

BEFORE A PLAYER'S NAME:
* left-handed hitter/pitcher
# switch-hitter
?=prospect status (see explanation)

AFTER A PLAYER'S NAME:
Level at which he spent most of 1999 season; age as of July 1, 2000; year he was drafted; round drafted (ND= non-drafted amateur free agent); drafted out of high school (H) or college (C)

EXPLANATION OF PROSPECT RATINGS

★ Potential big-league star

↑ Projected regular player in majors (for pitchers: rotation starter or closer)

○ Projected platoon or utility player in majors (pitcher: setup or middle relief)

? Possible big-league reserve or long reliever

↓ High draft pick or "tools" player who hasn't performed to expectations

MINNESOTA

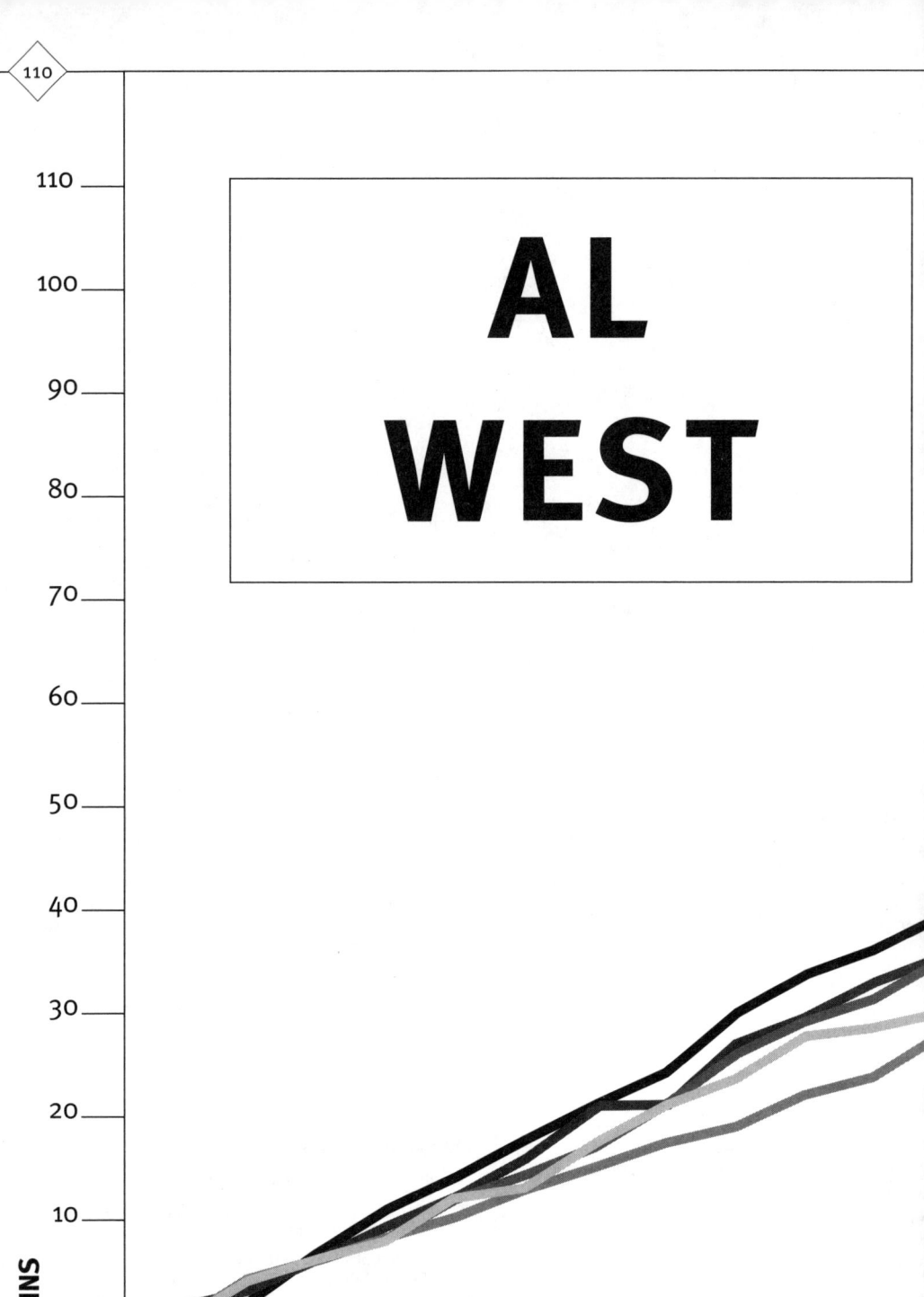

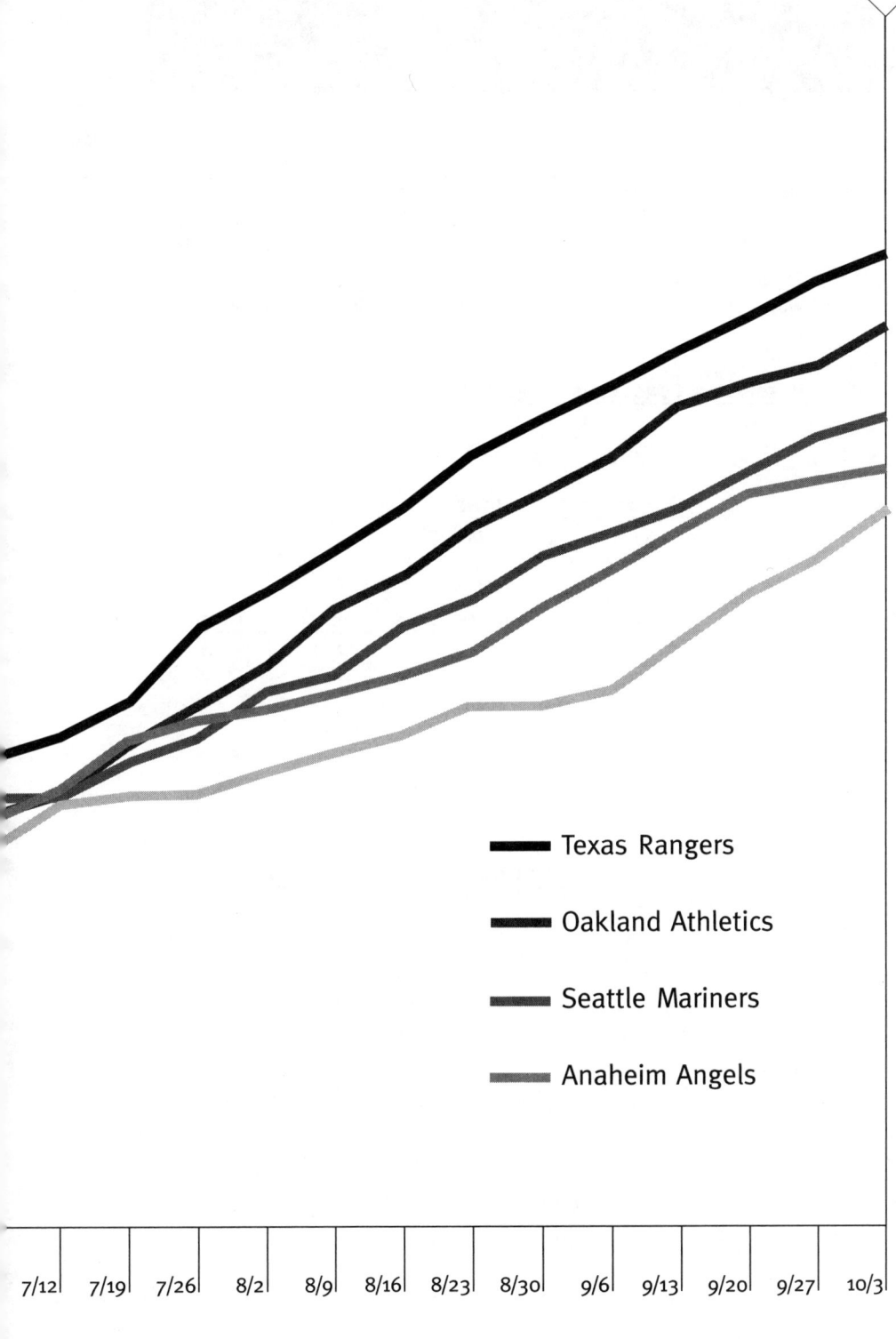

ANAHEIM ANGELS

Management
		Career Record
Manager	Joe Maddon	19–10 / .655
G.M.	Bill Bavasi [resigned]	434–473 / .479
President/CEO	Disney	239–247 / .492

1999 Record
Won-Lost	Pct.	Finish/G.B. (Division)	Finish/G.B. (Wild Card)
70–92	.432	4–25W	7–24

Preseason Consensus Projection
3 (3.20)

1st Half	2nd Half	Home	Road	Intradivision	Interleague
35–42	35–50	37–44	33–48	20–16	6–12

Comebacks	Blowouts	Nail-Biters	Grass	Turf	Sept-Oct
11–11	18–35	34–36	62–81	8–111	9–12

NUMBERS DON'T LIE

	Team (Rank)	Opponents (Rank)	League Avg.
Runs/Game	4.39 (13)	5.10 (4)	5.18
Batting Avg.	.256 (14)	.269 (5)	.274
On-Base Avg.	.322 (14)	.346 (5)	.347
Slugging Avg.	.395 (13)	.427 (3).	439
Strikeouts	1022 (8)	877 (13)	998
Home Runs	158 (11)	177 (5)	188
Stolen Bases	71 (12)	103 (7)	104
ERA	4.79 (5)		4.87
Errors	106 (3)		114

▶ THE INSIDER 2000

THE NOT-SO-WONDERFUL WORLD OF DISNEY

The idea that the Angels could have been contenders in 1999 was dreamy and far-fetched. It was a vain Hollywood fantasy lodged in the collective minds of the Angels and their management, all based upon the assumption that adding one player—a high-profile slugging first baseman named Mo Vaughn—would make the difference.

Mo Vaughn is indeed a good hitter, but he can't play second base or catcher or provide quality starting pitching, the three things that bedeviled the Angels in 1998 and didn't get solved in 1999. Injuries helped destroy the club's season, as nearly every key player on the club went down at one point or another; but even had the entire club been healthy, they wouldn't have been good enough to win.

After the great crash of '99, it's no secret that the Angels are a truly bad team. Catching is a huge problem. They have power at the corners in Mo Vaughn and Troy Glaus. Second base is a black hole, and shortstop Gary DiSarcina is a good defender but an atrocious hitter. Their best outfielders (Tim Salmon and Jim Edmonds) are injury-prone. Left fielder Garret Anderson is woefully overrated. Once-promising Darin Erstad, now 27, is coming off a disastrous campaign in which he looked nothing like a big-league hitter. The starting pitching is bad, except for Chuck Finley, and the bullpen is mediocre.

Unfortunately, the Anaheim farm system is largely devoid of quality position players. Two outfielders acquired in last summer's deal that sent Omar Olivares and Randy Velarde to Oakland could help out. Jeff DaVanon has the ability to be a decent fourth or fifth outfielder; Nathan Haynes, a tools player with a good upside, is several years away.

For pitchers, the Angels have some young arms with promise. Seth Etherton and Brian Cooper are control pitchers with average fastballs, but the best arm in the organization belongs to Ramon Ortiz. A fireballing 24-year-old right-hander with a biting slider, Ortiz will almost certainly be in Anaheim's rotation this season. His readiness to assume a key role is vital to the team's improvement.

MOMENT OF TRUTH

The writing was on the wall early in Southern California. When Mo Vaughn fell into the first-base dugout on Opening Day chasing a foul pop, his ankle and Anaheim's chances both went "pop." The twisted ankle Vaughn suffered on that play dogged him all year. Even though he was able to play on it much of the season, it clearly affected his performance—and the club never recovered from the resultant loss of offense. By June, Vaughn had hit rock bottom; when the team needed him to carry them offensively because of other key injuries, he simply wasn't physically capable of doing it.

ANAHEIM ANGELS

BIGGEST SURPRISE

It was fortunate for the Angels that the season-long display of pettiness and bickering didn't corrupt their young phenom Troy Glaus. Glaus was the third overall pick in the 1997 draft, but there probably weren't too many who expected him to be this good at early age 22. Although he struggled at times, he was probably Anaheim's most consistent player in '99. He showed decent range, a strong arm, and an ability to come in on softly hit balls. Glaus also was fun to watch, as he played the game with an obvious joy that was missing from many of his teammates.

BIGGEST DISAPPOINTMENT

A solid starter for nearly a decade, Ken Hill completely lost it last season. Hill has never been a big-time strikeout pitcher, but fanning 76 while walking exactly that many is a bad sign. Hill had an outstanding year with Texas in '96, but the last two seasons in Anaheim make it appear that his career is winding down—and that the team was foolish to re-sign him to a three-year deal after '97.

HOW DID IT GET THIS BAD?

It's not for lack of front-line talent. While the Angels don't have a deep farm system, they have drafted a key player most years in the past decade. In 1988, Edmonds was drafted. The next season, Anaheim took Salmon. From the 1990 draft came Anderson and Troy Percival. The 1993 draft produced Todd Greene. A year later it was Jason Dickson. In 1995, Erstad was drafted. Two years later, it was Troy Glaus.

The Angels just haven't been able to build successfully around their young talent, and their perpetual love affair with supposedly proven veterans has been a major factor in their failure to win. In 1999, a continuing overreliance on burned-out veteran pitchers and a related fear of trying out unproven prospects combined for lethal results.

Because of the Angels' pitching shortfall (caused by numerous injuries to the starting rotation and the trade of Olivares), a first-rate opportunity existed to discover if prospects like Geoff Edsell, Scott Schoeneweis, or Lou Pote could pitch. Instead of giving the future a chance, however, Anaheim assigned seven starts to career scrub Mike Fyrhie, who was as awful as one could have expected.

As the year rolled to its ugly finish, a few of the youngsters (Ortiz, Cooper, and Jarrod Washburn) were given some starts. The three of them combined with workhorse southpaw Finley to form the core of a promising rotation. Perhaps now the Angels have seen the worst and are ready to commit to youth.

IT'S NOT MY FAULT LINE

Focusing on Anaheim's 1999 pitching injuries shows that the club has been the victim both of bad luck and bad judgment. Wing ailments certainly cramped the Halos' hurlers, as Dickson, Mike James, and Pep Harris missed the entire season with injuries. The careers of all three are in jeopardy.

Two of them, Harris and James, have had the "double whammy"—concurrent elbow and shoulder injuries. James already had experienced elbow problems in 1997, and in May '98 tore a flexor muscle in his forearm, necessitating surgery. He hasn't pitched since and was released in September. Harris began 1998 on the DL with a sore shoulder. A few months later, he ripped up his elbow pitching in winter ball. Dickson, who had a fine rookie season in 1997 and a poor sophomore campaign in

1998, came up with a damaged shoulder last spring and missed the whole year to undergo surgery.

Another injury, this one farther in the past, also continues to hobble the club. Closer Troy Percival has never really recovered from a 1997 shoulder problem. In his first two years in the AL (1995–96), he was perhaps the most dominant reliever in the game. Since the injury, he doesn't throw as hard or as effectively, and now is just another veteran closer. By the end of September his shoulder had broken down and he couldn't pitch at all.

Those injuries were as unpredictable as they were unwelcome. The only thing you could reasonably fault the Angels for in those cases was being victims of bad luck. Nevertheless, they did take two risky gambles with pitchers whose baggage included lengthy injury histories—with awful results. Those pitchers, Jack McDowell and Ken Hill, have been unhealthy and unproductive since being signed. What a shock.

McDowell was clearly on the way down when the Angels inked him in March 1998, and his problems just continued. Black Jack, a workhorse with the White Sox years ago, was miserable the handful of times he was actually healthy enough to take the ball for Anaheim. McDowell was a shell of the pitcher he was from 1988 through '95, when Anaheim picked him up. He retired in August after being released by the team.

Hill, who was an outstanding pitcher in the NL years ago, was acquired from the Rangers in July 1997. He had missed more than three weeks that year with a bad elbow, but put together a dozen decent starts for the Angels down the stretch. As a result, the club inked him to a lucrative three-year deal.

Since then, Hill has been neither healthy nor effective, a drain on the team's finances as well as on their pitching staff. His 4.77 ERA actually was below the AL average last season, but allowing 129 hits and 76 walks in 128 innings doesn't quite cut it, especially for a highly paid vet working in one of the league's best parks for pitchers.

EVERBODY JUST SHUT UP AND PLAY BALL

Saddest of all, the club's attitude in 1999 stank, despite the presence of such noted veteran "character guys" as Vaughn, Erstad, and Salmon. (Perhaps character doesn't lead to winning but rather comes from the experience of doing so.) By the summer, the clubhouse was openly divided, and players were regu-

SECRET WEAPON

Veteran lefty reliever Mike Magnante had his best season last year and proved to be a valuable setup pitcher for Troy Percival. Magnante cut down on his walks and allowed only two home runs all season, which was impressive considering he appeared in 53 games and threw nearly 70 innings. He was one of the few acquisitions Anaheim made for 1999 that actually worked. In fact, he might have been too good to stick around for 2000, as many teams were looking for a left-handed reliever with those kinds of numbers.

ACHILLES HEEL

The attitude of Anaheim's players in 1999 was as bad as it could get. The team quit on manager Terry Collins early in the season, and the extremely nasty atmosphere meant that when the players weren't trying to get Collins fired, they were battling among themselves. The team fought itself long and hard in the clubhouse, but was meek and mild on the field. No one knows how much better things might have been had the players used the energy wasted on internecine warfare on the field instead.

ENOUGH ALREADY

Anaheim's executives had apparently deluded themselves into thinking the club was "a pitcher or two away from being a contender." Or that's what management wanted the fans to believe as the Angels entered each of the past three seasons thinking they were ready to play with the big boys. The Disney brain trust must have begun the season figuring that since Texas and Seattle didn't have much pitching, the Angels could get by without any as well. In reality, the Angels were two or three pitchers, a second baseman, and a catcher away from being contenders. Until management realizes that tinkering with the team by bringing in one or two free agents isn't a solution, they will continue to be a second-division club.

larly sniping at each other. Most notably at odds were Erstad (who didn't do a thing right all year) and Anderson (known as a malcontent and nonhustler).

Manager Terry Collins, a high-strung sort even in good times, again lost the respect of his players, a pattern that doomed him during his tenure in Houston. In September he left the organization, dissolving into tears of frustration during his resignation press conference. Collins punched his own ticket out of Disneyland: He had his chance and couldn't motivate the young—or the older—players to do their jobs.

It's clear that this organization needs to completely clean house, and everybody from the front office to the players and the manager must shoulder their portion of the blame for the mess this franchise has become. It was a step forward into a better future when GM Bill Bavasi left after the season; he brought nothing home with all the money he spent in the six years he was at the helm. The director of player development, Jeff Parker, also resigned after the season ended.

The 1999 Angels were badly constructed and badly run, and a completely new management team—one that expects to win and knows how it's done—is the only appropriate approach. The question is whether the Angels have the intestinal fortitude to gut baseball's worst club and start over. The future belongs to Ortiz, Glaus, Haynes, and other young players, supported by a returning nucleus of only the best of the club's veterans.

It's time to dump the deadwood, stop relying on creaky vets such as Ken Hill and Tim Belcher, and start over.

It's time to make deals that, if nothing else, will shatter the complacency and bad attitudes that have plagued this franchise—even if it means dumping overrated players such as Anderson and DiSarcina for nothing—and rebuild.

For real this time.

BEST CASE

The Mouse That Snored through 1999 ought to be better this year if the big boys (Tim Salmon, Troy Percival, Mo Vaughn, Jim Edmonds) can stay off the disabled list. The other keys to the club's success are rookie pitcher Ramon Ortiz and third baseman Troy Glaus. Both have the ability to be star players in the majors, and with the Halos coming off one of their worst seasons ever, this is the time for them to jump to the forefront. The two youngsters can't bring Anaheim back to contention by themselves, but things will be much better if Ortiz and Glaus pan out.

WORST CASE

The loss of Chuck Finley via free agency stripped away both the team's best pitcher and, according to comments by some of his teammates, the soul of the club. The Angels were the crabbiest, most dispirited bunch of players in the big leagues in 1999, and there is little to suggest that this lack of spunk has been rectified. Even more important, the starting pitching is thin, GM Bill Stoneman has already gotten off to a rocky start, Darin Erstad must again prove that he can play in the majors, and there is still one outfielder too many in the equation. Finally, the Angels can simply not survive without upgrades at shortstop, second base, and catcher.

UNDER THE MICROSCOPE

RAMON ORTIZ: The 23-year-old Ortiz, compared to Pedro Martinez because of his size, has a fastball routinely clocked in the low to mid-90s to go with a nasty, late-breaking slider and a very good change-up. Though inexperienced, he has the stuff to be a quality starter and will be given that chance this spring.

SETH ETHERTON: While not overpowering, Etherton has the command of three pitches necessary to compensate. The 23-year-old struck out 13 hitters in a game twice at Double-A with a fastball that tops out in the low 90s, and above-average curve and change-up offerings. He's probably not ready for the big leagues yet, but he should be able to earn a spot in the rotation in the near future.

LARRY BARNES: Entering the 1999 season, Barnes lacked the power necessary to be considered a legitimate first-base prospect. The 25-year-old then hit 20 home runs—his most since belting 27 in 1996—in Double-A last season. He'll need to maintain that level to get a look at the major-league but he'll be no more than a platoon player or a defensive replacement.

NATHAN HAYNES: After growing up an A's fan and chasing his dream of playing in an Oakland uniform, the 19-year-old was traded by the A's to Anaheim. Undaunted, Haynes played very well at the Class A level. He displayed a quick bat and good range in center field, and has time to develop power.

ANAHEIM

TOP PROSPECTS

In addition to Anaheim's miserable season at the big-league level, only one of the Angels' full-season minor-league affiliates posted a winning record. While the big club's performance was considered disappointing, the less-than-stellar output of the farm system has become predictable over the years.

After producing big-name talents such as Tim Salmon, Jim Edmonds, Darin Erstad, Garrett Anderson, and Troy Percival earlier in the decade, the system has all but run dry since. Troy Glaus was HOWE SPORTSDATA's Player of the Year in 1998 and began '99 as Anaheim's everyday third baseman. In his wake, the organization has a few pitchers with the ability to contribute at the major-league level, but little else that can help in the near future.

The core of pitching depth comes from a trio of right-handers: **RAMON ORTIZ, SETH ETHERTON,** and **BRIAN COOPER**. Ortiz, a hard-throwing native of the Dominican Republic, led the minors in strikeouts in 1997 but missed all but seven starts in '98 with an injured elbow. The 23-year-old returned to form in '99, winning 14 games and striking out 150 batters between Double and Triple-A before getting the call to the majors. Etherton, Anaheim's first-round pick in 1998 out of USC, put up solid numbers in Double-A (10–10, 3.27 ERA, 153 SO) before being summoned for four starts at the Triple-A level. Cooper, who pitched six complete games at Double-A, went 2–1, 3.77 ERA at Triple-A Edmonton before getting a taste of the majors.

Farther down, RHP **SCOT SHIELDS**, who entered the season strictly as a reliever, began starting at advanced Class A Lake Elsinore and went 4–1 with a 2.08 ERA before being promoted to Double-A. Shields is a fiery competitor who throws effectively from different arm angles. RHP **ELVIN NINA**, acquired from the A's in the deal that sent Omar Olivares to Oakland, has a deceptive fastball, and RHP **STEVE GREEN** posted four shutouts at Class A. The best lefthander in the organization is **DOUG BRIDGES**, who led the minors with 18 victories between two Class A levels in 1999.

OF **NATHAN HAYNES** (also acquired in the trade with Oakland) immediately became the top position prospect in the organization. Haynes has terrific speed and decent defensive skills but is still very inexperienced. OF **JEFF DAVANON**, the third player received in the deal for Olivares, enjoyed a breakout year in 1999 and was rewarded with a trip to the big club. He doesn't appear likely to serve regularly in the outfield anytime soon, however. OF **DARREN BLAKLEY**, moved from center field to left upon Hayne's arrival, has good tools, but his work ethic is a question mark. OF **ELPIDIO GUZMAN**, who, like Haynes, is 20 years old, has shown promise but is still two or three years away.

The system doesn't have another legitimate hitting prospect. 1B **LARRY BARNES**, who hit 20 homers and drove in 100 runs at Double-A, opened eyes with a good year, but he does not look to be a reliable producer at the major-league level. Elsewhere around the infield, 2B **TRENT DURRINGTON** and SS **NELSON CASTRO** are both speedy with little pop. Durrington has a great work ethic but struggled in a call-up to the big leagues. Despite good defensive tools, Castro's inconsistency has stunted his progress. The Angels have some numbers at catcher, led by **BEN MOLINA**, but none look to be a long-term solution at that position.

CF
*GARRET ANDERSON 28
 *JIM EDMONDS 30
 ○ #Norm Hutchins 3A 24 94/2H
 ↑ *Nathan Haynes 2A 20 97/1H
 ? Juan Tolentino 2A 24 94/ND
 ? #Darren Blakely A+ 23 98/5C
 ↑ *Elpidio Guzman A- 21 95/ND

LF
*DARIN ERSTAD 26
 *ORLANDO PALMEIRO 31
 ? Mike Colangelo ML 23 97/21C

RF
TIM SALMON 31
 ○ #Jerry DaVanon ML 26 95/26C
 ? *Nate Murphy 2A 25 96/16C
 ? Jeb Dougherty A+ 24 97/25C

SS
GARY DISARCINA 32
 ? Chuck Abbott 2A 25 96/2C
 ? Brian Oliver A- 23 98/4C

2B
ANDY SHEETS 28
 ? Trent Durrington ML 24 93/ND
 ? Keith Luuloa 3A 25 93/33C
 ? E. J. t'Hoen 3A 24 95/32C

3B
TROY GLAUS 23

1B
*MO VAUGHN 32
 ? *Larry Barnes 2A 25 95/NDC

SP/RP

RELIEVERS
TROY PERCIVAL 30
MARK PETKOVSEK 34
SHIGETOSHI HASEGAWA 31
*MIKE HOLTZ 27
MIKE FYRHIE 30
 ○ Scot Shields 2A 24 97/38C
 ? Renney Duarte A+ 21 96/ND

STARTERS
KEN HILL 34
TIM BELCHER 38
JASON DICKSON 27
*JARROD WASHBURN 25
 ○ Brian Cooper ML 25 95/4C
 ↑ Ramon Ortiz ML 24 95/ND
 ○ Seth Etherton 3A 23 98/1C
 ? Matt Wise 2A 24 97/6C
 ○ Steve Green 2A 22 97/10C
 ○ Elvin Nina 2A 24 97/17C
 ? Derrick Turnbow A- 22 97/5H
 ↓ Brandon Emanuel A+ 24 98/2C
 ? *Doug Bridges A+ 24 98/98C
 ○ *Jeff Hundley A- 23 98/7C

C
#MATT WALBECK 30
 #BRET HEMPHILL 28
 STEVE DECKER 34
 ○ Ben Molina ML 25 93/ND
 ? Jason Dewey 2A 23 96/26C
 ? Steve Hagins A+ 25 97/NDC
 ? Jason Hill A- 23 98/8C

DH
TODD GREENE 29

MAJOR LEAGUERS IN ALL CAPS
minor leaguers in upper-and-lower case

BEFORE A PLAYER'S NAME:
* left-handed hitter/pitcher
# switch-hitter
=prospect status (see explanation)

AFTER A PLAYER'S NAME:
Level at which he spent most of 1999 season; age as of July 1, 2000; year he was drafted; round drafted ND= non-drafted amateur free agent); drafted out of high school (H) or college (C)

EXPLANATION OF PROSPECT RATINGS

★ Potential big-league star

↑ Projected regular player in majors (for pitchers: rotation starter or closer)

○ Projected platoon or utility player in majors (pitcher: setup or middle relief)

? Possible big-league reserve or long reliever

↓ High draft pick or "tools" player who hasn't performed to expectations

ANAHEIM

OAKLAND ATHLETICS

Management
		Career Record
Manager	Art Howe	696–762 / .477
G.M.	Billy Beane	161–163 / .497
President/CEO	Steve Schott/Ken Hofman	304–344 / .469

1999 Record
Won–Lost	Pct.	Finish/G.B. (Division)	Finish/G.B. (Wild Card)
87–75	.537	2/8 (W)	2/7

Preseason Consensus Projection
4 (3.90)

1st Half	2nd Half	Home	Road	Intradivision	Interleague
37–40	50–35	52–29	35–46	15–21	12–6

Comebacks	Blowouts	Nail-Biters	Grass	Turf	Sept.–Oct.
9–12	24–24	36–26	75–67	12–8	15–15

NUMBERS DON'T LIE

	Team (Rank)	Opponents (Rank)	League Avg.
Runs/Game	5.51 (4)	5.22 (5)	5.18
Batting Avg.	.259 (13)	.274 (6)	.274
On-Base Avg.	.355 (4)	.344 (4)	.347
Slugging Avg.	.446 (8)	.429 (4)	.439
Strikeouts	1129 (14)	967 (11)	998
Home Runs	235 (2)	160 (2)	188
Stolen Bases	70 (13)	110 (9)	104
ERA	4.76 (3)		4.87
Errors	122 (10)		114

▶ THE INSIDER 2000

NO BIG MACS, BUT LOTS OF BEANE'S BABIES

General manager Billy Beane deserves much of the credit for building the Athletics from a last-place team in 1997 to surprise postseason contenders in 1999. Beane has been involved in the development of the current Oakland team, either directly or indirectly, for the past 10 seasons, starting in 1990, when he became one of the club's major-league scouts.

Beane, a former first-round draft pick of the Mets, managed only 301 at-bats in his major-league career, which ended in 1989 after his only season as a player for Oakland. He became the Athletics' assistant GM in 1993 under Sandy Alderson, who had run the club since 1983.

At the end of the year Jason Giambi was the only player on Oakland's roster who hadn't been acquired since Beane moved into the front office in 1993. Beane also has had plenty of input on drafting players such as Ben Grieve and Eric Chavez, and signing others such as Miguel Tejada as undrafted amateur free agents.

Beane's biggest contribution has come since he became GM in October 1997, especially in the last year. He signed low-rent free agents such as John Jaha and Tony Phillips, both of whom were important players in '99. He wasn't afraid to make big mid-season trades that seemed controversial but wound up being great moves.

Because Oakland was above .500, in second place in the AL West, and still in contention for the wild card in late July, Beane got a lot of flak for shopping veteran Kenny Rogers around before the trading deadline. Beane sent the malcontented southpaw to the Mets on July 23, then followed up by dealing closer Billy Taylor to the Mets for Greg McMichael and Jason Isringhausen. But dumping Rogers' salary allowed Beane to acquire starting pitchers Omar Olivares and Kevin Appier (as well as second baseman Randy Velarde) without exceeding the club's budget, and Isringhausen proved to be far more effective than Taylor in his brief tryout as a closer at the end of the season.

So far, Beane hasn't been afraid to admit to his mistakes, as he did after signing Tom Candiotti to a two-year deal with an option for a third before the 1998 season. Candiotti had a poor year in '98, but the Athletics had hoped he would be able to get his knuckleball working and at least eat up innings. That didn't happen. Candiotti pitched badly in 11 starts and was released on

MOMENT OF TRUTH

Oakland had stayed on the fringe of the AL wild-card race all season but was expected to fall back in mid-August when the Athletics were to play 14 of 20 games on the road, including eight against the Yankees and Red Sox. Early in that stretch the A's lost the opener of a four-game series in Boston as Brian Daubach hit a two-out, three-run double in the bottom of the ninth. That was expected to be the end of the dream season for Oakland, but the Athletics came back the next night to spank Boston, 12–1, wound up splitting the series, and played well enough to stay in the running until the final week of the regular season.

BIGGEST SURPRISE

Tim Hudson blossomed in 1999. After going 10–9 with a 4.54 ERA at Double-A Huntsville in '98, Hudson was undefeated at Triple-A Vancouver and quickly became the ace of Oakland's rotation after his June call-up. His best pitch is his change-up, but he also uses his slider, a two-seam fastball, and a four-seam fastball to get hitters out. He'll likely finish his climb to the top if, as expected, he's named Oakland's Opening Day starter.

BIGGEST DISAPPOINTMENT

The unhappy attitude of veteran Kenny Rogers was a constant thorn in the side of the younger Oakland players who truly cared about helping their club win. It was no secret that Rogers wanted out of Oakland, and he ensured that he'd be traded by not performing nearly as well as he did in 1998. All was not lost, however, as the A's clubhouse became a much happier place after his departure, and the payroll room freed up by dumping Rogers' contract allowed the team to trade for Kevin Appier. Unfortunately, Appier pitched even worse than Rogers did.

June 16. The decision cost the salary-conscious Athletics a significant amount of money, but it demonstrated in a small way that things had changed.

For two years, Beane has made the right moves and earned a reputation as one of the best and brightest general managers in the game. Of course, climbing out of the basement is the easiest part of building a contender—there's only one way to go from the bottom, and any improvement is welcomed with praise.

ISRINGHAUSEN RINGS THE BULLPEN BELL

If Jason Isringhausen can pitch for a full season the way he did in the last two months of 1999, Beane will have yet another feather in his cap.

Isringhausen was one of the top pitching prospects in all of baseball while coming up through the Mets' organization in the early 1990s. He was 9–2 with a 2.81 ERA in 14 starts in 1995, which further enhanced expectations for the young right-hander. But he suffered a rash of injuries, missing most of 1997 and all of '98 recovering from three separate surgeries—to remove bone chips from his right elbow, repair a tear in his right shoulder, and, finally, totally reconstruct his elbow.

Even though he finally regained his velocity, the Mets gave up on him by 1999, trading him to Oakland for Billy Taylor after Isringhausen went 1–3 with a 6.41 ERA in 13 games. Deciding that his powerful—yet fragile—arm would be better suited to short outings, the A's made Isringhausen a closer, and he finished 1999 by saving eight games in as many chances. The Athletics don't have many other options to close games in 2000, so Isringhausen will get a chance to show what he can do over a full season. He's still only 27 and has thrown only 172 innings in the past three seasons; so if he doesn't suffer any setbacks with his arm, he could be closing games for Oakland for years to come.

A TRIO OF POTENTIAL STARS

With Ben Grieve, Miguel Tejada, and Eric Chavez, the Athletics hope to have the core group of future stars that will allow them to build a contending team for the next decade. The key question is whether these three players will become the perennial All-Stars the club is counting on.

▶ THE INSIDER 2000

It's still too early to be certain, but the Athletics are hopeful. Tejada is only 24, but has played every day the last two seasons and last year showed signs that he might become the next outstanding shortstop in the AL. Miguel showed plus range in the field while boosting his batting average by 18 points, upping his on-base by 27 points and his slugging by 43 points.

Grieve got off to an incredibly slow start in 1999, hitting a dreadful .133 through his first 33 games. After May 19, however, he recovered to hit .303 with 25 homers and 75 RBIs. His turnaround left Oakland very encouraged about the 2000 season. Grieve's batting and slugging averages both dropped 23 points in '99, though he hit 10 more homers than he did in '98.

Overall, the 1998 AL Rookie of the Year's first two seasons compare favorably with Colorado's Larry Walker, the NL MVP in 1997. Through two full seasons (327 games), Grieve has hit .281 with 49 homers and 199 RBIs with .376 on-base and .469 slugging averages. Walker hit .262 with 35 homers and 119 RBI with a .335 on-base and .433 slugging in 290 games in Montreal in 1989–91.

There have been five other outfielders who won Rookie of the Year honors in the 1990s: David Justice (1990 NL, age 24), Tim Salmon (1993 AL, age 24), Raul Mondesi (1994 NL, age 23), Marty Cordova (1995 AL, age 25), and Todd Hollandsworth (1996 NL, age 23). So far, Grieve fits in comfortably: He's clearly better than the two subsequent disappointments—Cordova and Hollandsworth—about the same as Mondesi, but not as good as Justice and Salmon.

The Triple Crown numbers with on-base and slugging averages through the first two full seasons for these outfielders: Justice (252 games: .276 BA / 50 HR / 168 RBI, .371 OBA, .510 SA), Salmon (265 games: .276 / 56 / 171, .374, .512), Mondesi (293 games: .294 / 46 / 154, .329, .504), Cordova (282 games: .294 / 40 / 195, .362, .482), and Hollandsworth (296 games: .269/ 21 / 103, .322, .409). Moises Alou finished second in NL rookie voting in 1992 at age 25, but he hit .282 with only 27 homers and 141 RBIs with a .332 OBA and .467 SA in 267 games after his first two full years.

At 24, Grieve has not yet shown that he will develop into the franchise-quality player many had projected. Ben slumped to an extremely weak .156 with a .240 OBA and only three homers in 109 at-bats versus lefties in 1999. Since he doesn't have speed and isn't going to win any Gold Gloves in the pasture, he needs to dramatically improve his batting against left-handers if he wants to become a major force in the lineup.

SECRET WEAPON

Overshadowed by the sophomore struggles of '98 Rookie of the Year Ben Grieve and by the resurgence of John Jaha, Matt Stairs turned in another fine season without much fanfare, moving from DH to right field to accommodate Jaha. Stairs played his first full season in the outfield, reaching career highs in runs (94) and homers (38) while driving in more than 100 runs for the second consecutive year. Oakland's future is clearly tied to younger players such Grieve and Eric Chavez, but that shouldn't obscure the valuable contributions Stairs has made.

ACHILLES HEEL

Oakland's middle and setup relievers were the weak links on the team. Billy Taylor and Jason Isringhausen performed well as closers, but right-handers Greg McMichael and Tim Worrell were spotty throughout the season, as was situational lefty Buddy Groom. A good indication of how bad a season the bullpen had was the fact that soft-tossing journeyman Doug Jones was given a chance to regain his former glory with a brief and unsuccessful tryout as closer.

OAKLAND ATHLETICS

ENOUGH ALREADY

The 1999 season should eliminate any further talk about Art Howe not being able to take talented young players and mold them into contenders. Most pundits expected Howe to be one of the first managers fired last season, but his fourth year in Oakland produced a career high in wins instead. Howe was forced by circumstance to be a speed-and-defense manager in Houston, but he has adapted well to GM Billy Beane's philosophy of stressing power and on-base average—the trademarks of the championship Oakland teams of the late 1980s. Not coincidentally, the Athletics have improved 22 games since 1997.

Chavez is two years younger than both Grieve and Tejada. Chavez had a somewhat disappointing year, but he was only 21, and his numbers were dragged down by foot problems late in the season. Even so, he was much better in the second half, hitting .275 with six homers in only 142 at-bats after the All-Star break. Chavez hit 33 home runs in the high minors in 1998 at 20, and has the potential to become a true impact hitter as he becomes stronger and gets more experience. To do so, however, he also needs to solve his problems against left-handers (.192 BA with no homers in 52 big-league at-bats).

ACT II

Oakland's offense finished second in the AL in homers and third in on-base average in 1999 due largely to the disciplined power hitting of veterans Jason Giambi (33 HR, .422 OBA), Tony Phillips (15 HR in 406 AB, .362 OBA), Matt Stairs (38 HR, .366 OBA), and John Jaha (35 HR, .414 OBA). While 37-year-old Randy Velarde (16 HR in 631 AB, .390 OBA) is ready to replace Phillips, the Athletics need the 29-year-old Giambi, the 32-year-old Stairs, and the 34-year-old Jaha to avoid injuries and reprise their performances.

Rookie pitching sensation Tim Hudson heads a staff full of inconsistent thirtysomething vets who will have to hold up until the club's top pitching prospects can step in. Omar Olivares, 32, was the best of the lot in '99, yet he walked 81 and struck out only 85 while allowing 217 hits in 205.2 innings. Gil Heredia's comeback at 33 shouldn't obscure a very mediocre performance. Kevin Appier, 32, needs to remain healthy while improving on his disappointing 5.17 ERA. Mike Oquist, 32, is always flirting with disaster. The bullpen, filled out by righties Doug Jones and T. J. Mathews, is serviceable if Isringhausen is really as good as he looked last September.

Now that he's raised expectations for his young and talented team, Billy Beane will have to follow it up with a more difficult performance in Act II. Succeeding will no longer be surprising, and failing will no longer be expected. Competing head-to-head with teams with far larger budgets is not easy, and Oakland has little margin for failure if key veterans slump or if key young players fail to improve.

BEST CASE

Often the toughest thing for a young club to do is repeat a surprising season, but the Athletics have reason to be optimistic about 2000. They were competitive last year without a good showing from Ben Grieve, survived Kenny Rogers' pouting, and stayed in the wild-card hunt until the final two weeks. The A's have essentially the same roster they finished last season with, and since the club didn't have a bunch of players with career years in 1999, there's no reason why they can't be in the hunt again.

WORST CASE

There's no guarantee that Oakland will be able to match last season's success. Tim Hudson is already the ace of the staff, but the rest of the rotation's projected starters are in their 30s. The club still is relying on young position players, who may or may not develop. Grieve, after an outstanding rookie season, was a huge disappointment in 1999. How he responds this year will be crucial to his future—and the same can be said of catcher A. J. Hinch and infielders Miguel Tejada and Eric Chavez. If they continue to progress, they have the potential to put the Athletics over the top. If they don't, the club will again be sitting come October.

UNDER THE MICROSCOPE

TERRENCE LONG: With a void in center field, the Athletics hoped that Long, acquired from the Mets in the Kenny Rogers deal, steps up in the very near future. A highly touted "five-tool" talent, Long has yet to live up to those expectations. He made progress with the bat in the past two years, but doesn't appear to have what it takes to be the answer in center field.

ADAM PIATT: Piatt hit .345 with 39 homers and 135 RBI to go along with 48 doubles and 93 walks in the Texas League. He played much of his season in a hitter's park in a hitter's league, but the 23-year-old was a Class A Northwest League All-Star in '97 and led the Class A California League in RBI, so he's proven himself as a hitter and a run producer. Piatt could move to fisrt base or to the outfield. Either way, his bat will carry him to the big leagues.

MARK MULDER: He doesn't throw as hard as advertised, topping out in the low 90s, but he does have good secondary pitches and control. He tossed 17 consecutive scoreless innings during the PCL playoffs and Triple-A World Series. He doesn't have the look of a staff leader.

BARRY ZITO: Zito has been placed on the fast track. He was 6–1, 3.16 ERA with 97 strikeouts in 68 innings after being selected in the first round last summer. He started 1999 in Class A and ended it in the Triple-A World Series. His fastball may dip to 90 mph, but he has a great curveball.

OAKLAND

TOP PROSPECTS

Without having the benefit of deep financial resources, the Athletics are on the verge of becoming serious contenders after seven years of being a second-division club. Despite competing at the major-league level with a $22 million salary—fifth lowest in the game—and having one of the smallest player development budgets, the farm system has supplied several quality players to the big-league club the past few years.

On top of that, Oakland's affiliates finished with a .573 winning percentage, the best in baseball. Oakland was selected by HOWE SPORTSDATA as its Organization of the Year for 1999.

Unlike many clubs, the majority of the Athletics are homegrown: A. J. Hinch, Ramon Hernandez, Jason Giambi, Scott Spiezio, Miguel Tejada, Eric Chavez, Ben Grieve, Ryan Christenson, and Jason McDonald. Hinch, Tejada, Chavez, and Grieve are past All-Prospect Team selections.

The organization didn't have any players on the All-Prospect Team this season, but 3B **ADAM PIATT** won the first Triple Crown in the Double-A Texas League since 1927, and the organization is still well stocked all around the diamond.

In recent years the organization has started to address its one glaring weakness—pitching. It has concentrated on college pitchers in the draft, and RHP **TIM HUDSON** is the first to break through. The organization has high expectations for LHP **MARK MULDER**—the second player selected in the '98 draft—RHP **BRETT LAXTON**, RHP **CHAD HARVILLE**, and LHP **BARRY ZITO** in the near future and several others, especially RHP **JESUS COLOME**, farther down the road. Colome was selected for the HOWE SPORTSDATA All-Teen Team.

Despite all the young hitting stars who have reached the major-leagues in recent years, the Athletics still have a pretty deep crop of position players. Hernandez and C **MIGUEL OLIVO** are young hopefuls behind the plate, 1B **JASON HART** is a solid prospect, 2B **ESTEBAN GERMAN** is an exciting talent, and SS **JOSUE ESPADA** and SS **JOSE ORTIZ** have a chance. Piatt is a major-league hitter in waiting; but will it be at first base, third base, left field, or DH?

There's an opening in center field, and the Athletics hope recently acquired OF **TERRENCE LONG** will be the long-term solution. OF **MARIO ENCARNACION** is also an everyday hopeful. OF **ERIC BYRNES**, an exceptionally hard worker with every tool except over-the-fence power, is another player to watch.

LF
*BEN GRIEVE 24
? *Roberto Vaz 3A 25 97/7C
↑ Eric Byrnes 2A 23 98/8C

CF
*RICH BECKER 28
RYAN CHRISTENSON 26
#JASON MCDONALD 28
○ *Terrence Long ML 24 94/1H
○ Gary Thomas A+ 20 97/23H
? Rusty Keith A+ 22 98/15C

RF
*MATT STAIRS 32
○ Mario Encarnacion 3A 22 94/ND
○ Ryan Ludwick A+ 21 99/2C

SS
MIGUEL TEJADA 24
FRANK MENECHINO 29
○ Josue Espada 3A 24 96/2C
○ Jose Ortiz 3A 23 94/ND

2B
RANDY VELARDE 37
#SCOTT SPIEZIO 27
○ Esteban German A+ 21 96/ND
? Oscar Salazar A+ 22 94/ND

3B
*ERIC CHAVEZ 22
OLMEDO SAENZ 29
↑ Adam Piatt 3A 24 97/8C
? Gary Schneidmiller A+ 20 98/6H

1B
*JASON GIAMBI 29
? T. R. Marcinczyk 2A 26 96/28C
○ Jason Hart A+ 22 98/5C
? *Todd Mensik A+ 25 96/12C

SP/RP

RELIEVERS
JASON ISRINGHAUSEN 27
DOUG JONES 43
T. J. MATHEWS 30
*TIM KUBINSKI 28
MIKE MAGNANTE 35
○ Chad Harville ML 23 97/2C
○ Luis Vizcaino ML 23 94/ND
? Andrew Kimball 2A 24 97/5C
? Jon Adkins A+ 22 98/9C
? *Benito Baez 3A 23 93/ND
? *Juan Pena A+ 21 96/ND

C
A. J. HINCH 26
↑ Ramon Hernandez ML 24 94/ND
? Danny Ardoin 3A 25 95/5C
? Miguel Olivo A+ 21 96/ND

DH
JOHN JAHA 34

STARTERS
KEVIN APPIER 32
TIM HUDSON 24
GIL HEREDIA 34
ARIEL PRIETO 30
○ Brett Laxton ML 26 96/24C
? Kevin Gregg 3A 22 96/15H
? Chris Enochs 2A 24 97/1C
○ Denny Wagner 2A 23 97/1C
? Julian Leyva 2A 22 96/5H
↑ Jesus Colome A+ 20 96/ND
↑ *Mark Mulder 3A 22 98/1C
↑ *Barry Zito 3A 22 99/1C
○ *Eric Dubose 2A 24 97/1C

MAJOR LEAGUERS IN ALL CAPS
Minor leaguers in upper-and-lower case

BEFORE A PLAYER'S NAME:
* left-handed hitter/pitcher
# switch-hitter
?=prospect status (see explanation)

AFTER A PLAYER'S NAME:
Level at which he spent most of 1999 season; age as of July 1, 2000; year he was drafted; round drafted (ND= non-drafted amateur free agent); drafted out of high school (H) or college (C)

EXPLANATION OF PROSPECT RATINGS

★ Potential big-league star

↑ Projected regular player in majors (for pitchers: rotation starter or closer)

○ Projected platoon or utility player in majors (pitcher: setup or middle relief)

? Possible big-league reserve or long reliever

↓ High draft pick or "tools" player who hasn't performed to expectations

OAKLAND ATHLETICS

SEATTLE MARINERS

MANAGEMENT
Manager	Lou Piniella
G.M.	Woody Woodward [retired]
President/CEO	Baseball Club of Seattle

CAREER RECORD
1019–949 / .518
926–949 / .494
540–525 / .507

1999 RECORD
Won–Lost	Pct.	Finish/G.B. (Division)	Finish/G.B. (Wild Card)
79–83	.488	3/16 (W)	4/15

PRESEASON CONSENSUS PROJECTION
2 (2.80)

1ST HALF	2ND HALF	HOME	ROAD	INTRADIVISION	INTERLEAGUE
39–38	40–45	43–38	36–45	17–20	7–11

COMEBACKS	BLOWOUTS	NAIL-BITERS	GRASS	TURF	SEPT.–OCT.
11–15	25–36	28–27	49–59	30–24	13–17

NUMBERS DON'T LIE

	TEAM (RANK)	OPPONENTS (RANK)	LEAGUE AVG.
Runs/Game	5.30 (7)	5.59 (12)	5.18
Batting Avg.	.269 (10)	.287 (13)	.274
On-Base Avg.	.343 (9)	.368 (13)	.347
Slugging Avg.	.455 (4)	.454 (12)	.439
Strikeouts	1095 (12)	980 (7)	998
Home Runs	244 (1)	191 (7)	188
Stolen Bases	130 (2)	107 (8)	104
ERA	5.25 (13)		4.87
Errors	113 (8)		114

▶ THE INSIDER 2000

UNSAFE(CO) AT HOME

Another disappointing season in the Emerald City has the Seattle franchise poised on the edge of the precipice. Overshadowing the opening of gorgeous new Safeco Field, several potential disasters loom for a ball club that has done very little right in its 23-year history.

Far bigger news than the new ballpark was the dread announcement that megastar Ken Griffey Jr., had asked for a trade; the team will be hard-pressed to get "full value" for a player who can become a free agent after 2000 and who will expect a bank-breaking contract.

If the prospect of losing their marquee player, the best in team history, wasn't bad enough, rumors swirled late in the year that the M's might trade their other franchise player, Alex Rodriguez, as well. If Seattle ends up without both Junior and A-Rod, the club that won division titles in 1995 and '97 might seem like it's back where it started, as an expansion team.

Even for an expansion team, the Mariners' record has been undistinguished. Seattle finished no higher than fourth in its first 17 years of existence, finishing last or next to last in the AL West 11 times. In the mid-1990s, however, the long-slumbering Mariners turned things around, winning the hearts of fans in the Pacific Northwest when Rodriguez arrived and Griffey matured into a devastating power hitter. After finishing third in 1994 (only two games out at the time of the strike), Seattle finally won the division in '95 in one of the most exciting pennant races in history.

With the gray concrete Kingdome packed to its ugly rafters with screaming fans, the Mariners beat the Angels in a single-game playoff for the '95 AL West title, then defeated the Yankees in a barn burner of a Division Series before finally succumbing to Cleveland in six games in the ALCS. The M's finished second to Texas in '96, then won the division again in '97 as the team enjoyed a 75 percent increase in per-game attendance from 1995. Much of that goodwill has now been dissipated as the team fell to lackluster third-place finishes in each of the past two campaigns.

MISSED OPPORTUNITIES

Despite the presence of two franchise players in the same lineup since 1996, Seattle has never made it to the World

MOMENT OF TRUTH

The Mariners' move into brand-spanking new Safeco Field after the All-Star break was supposed to symbolize the beginning of a new era in Seattle baseball. Instead, it generated substantial controversy. The hitters didn't like the dimensions of the new ballpark, there was plenty of media coverage about the huge cost overruns in building the park, and the team wasn't any more successful than it had been in the Kingdome. The Mariners were 42–45 in the first half of the season, but only marginally better, at 37–38, after making the move to Safeco.

SEATTLE MARINERS

BIGGEST SURPRISE

Seattle has made some questionable trades in recent years, but the August 1998 deal that got David Bell for Joey Cora proved to be an excellent swap. Bell came into his own in 1999, more than doubling his '98 home run total, and providing much-needed stability at a position that has given the team trouble for years. The Cardinals and the Indians had both given up on Buddy's son, but David and the Mariners perfectly fit.

BIGGEST DISAPPOINTMENT

The Mariners went into 1999 counting on Jeff Fassero to provide stability and leadership on a young pitching staff. Instead, Fassero provided nothing of the sort; he finally was dumped on Texas on August 27 for a weak-hitting outfielder with no real major-league future. Fassero averaged more than 14 wins per season in the previous four years, but he went 4–14 with Seattle, allowing seven runs per game and 34 homers in 27 starts for the M's. He was the only weak link in a rotation that surprised most everybody and otherwise performed quite admirably.

Series. Many believe the core of the problem is that management has spent too much on its offense and not enough on its pitching staff. Actually, the club would have been in much better shape five years ago—and might still be one of the top teams in the league—had it not made some very poor personnel decisions just as it was emerging as a contender.

The 1995 Mariners were a very powerful and exciting team. Even with Griffey missing half the season with a broken wrist, Seattle scored the second-most runs in baseball that season. Tino Martinez, Edgar Martinez, and Jay Buhner all had monster seasons at the plate, and the pitching staff was very respectable, finishing with the fifth-best ERA in the AL. One thing that really hurt that club was its middle infield. Alex Rodriguez was only 19 years old at the time and shuttled between Seattle and Triple-A Tacoma, while Joey Cora and Luis Sojo manned second and short, respectively.

The Mariners would have been a far superior club if they hadn't traded Omar Vizquel to Cleveland in 1994 for Felix Fermin and Reggie Jefferson. Everyone knows now what Vizquel means to Cleveland, and he was just beginning to develop as a hitter when Seattle dumped him in a classic, shortsighted move to save salary. If the Mariners had kept Vizquel, he could have been moved to second base, solving one of the infield problems, or A-Rod easily could have been moved to third, solving a perennial problem.

The Vizquel trade was probably the worst deal that retired GM Woody Woodward made in 11 years running the Mariners, but there were plenty of others that had people in the front offices of other teams scratching their heads. How much blame should Woodward take for Seattle's failures? The Mariners, like the Astros, had a core of two superstar players who could do it all, but they were never able to assemble the proper supporting cast.

In hindsight, Woodward had the players—especially the pitchers—who really could have made a difference, but he gave them all away. Before the '92 season he traded Dave Burba and Mike Jackson, both of whom were still productive seven years later, for Kevin Mitchell, a problem player who spent only a season in Seattle. He had Mike Hampton, arguably the best pitcher in the NL last year, but traded him after the 1993 season for Eric Anthony, another power hitter who, like Mitchell, spent only a single unproductive year in Seattle.

The list of odorous bartering over the years is fairly remarkable. While some of the deals can be excused by financial exigencies, many of them represent just plain misjudgment of talent. Woodward traded Shawn Estes for Salomon Torres in 1995. He dealt Derek Lowe and Jason Varitek to Boston in July 1997 for Heathcliff Slocumb, who wasn't even pitching well at the time. He swapped Sterling Hitchcock to San Diego after 1996 for Scott Sanders, who didn't last even four months in Seattle. Woody made a good deal with Houston to excise carcinogenic Randy Johnson late in the '98 season. However, by waiting so long to pull the trigger, he and Randy—in a macabre dance—completely destroyed the M's chances that year.

WELCOME, PAT—TO AN IMPOSSIBLE SITUATION

Woodward has been succeeded by Pat Gillick, who built Toronto into a powerhouse in the late 1980s. Gillick did not have much time to get settled in, though, as Griffey asked to be traded shortly after he took over. Speculation was that the Braves and the Yankees would be interested in Griffey, thus driving up the asking price, but neither team seemed to grab the bait. The Reds were the team that wanted Griffey the most: Junior grew up in Cincinnati while his father played on the Big Red Machine teams of the 1970s. Senior still coaches there and is viewed as the heir apparent to manager Jack McKeon.

The Reds would be a perfect fit for Griffey. If Cincinnati were the winner of the Junior sweepstakes, the entire city would go ga-ga. Such a megadeal would make what already is one of the best baseball markets in the country even stronger—and, more important, send a message to the rest of baseball that small-market teams can still hope to see veteran superstars in their lineups.

Griffey's acquisition would mean much to a franchise that has seen more than its share of turmoil in the past decade. From the Pete Rose scandal in 1989 to former owner Marge Schott's two suspensions, Reds fans have had to fight through many dispiriting moments. Junior would be an indirect link between the current squad and the glory days of the Big Red Machine and would give Cincinnati its first marquee player in a long, long time.

Of course, Gillick properly announced that he wouldn't give Griffey away just to accommodate Junior's desire to play elsewhere. There's no reason to be low-balled into taking a lesser offer just to trade a player before he becomes a free agent, even

SECRET WEAPON

It's hard to imagine a pitcher with a record of 59–25 over the past four seasons going virtually unnoticed, but that's what has happened with Jamie Moyer. Moyer keeps on winning—at least 13 games in each of the past four years—and every year he is ignored or written off. He's not a young gun anymore and was never overpowering, but the 37-year-old stays successful by not walking many hitters and letting his defense help him. One of these years he's going to lose it, but that's what was said two, three, and four years ago.

ACHILLES HEEL

Seattle's bullpen was a complete disaster in 1999. The relief corps posted an ERA of almost 6.00, highest in the league. Seattle used 27 pitchers in relief, but there were precious few good ones. Jose Mesa saved 33 games but finished with an ERA of almost 5.00 while allowing 40 walks and 84 hits in 68.2 innings. It got worse from there, as only two relievers who appeared in 10 games or more finished with an ERA of less than 4.00.

ENOUGH ALREADY

Even before the Mariners moved into their new palace, a bitter dispute arose with the Washington State Public Facilities District about who should pay for the approximately $100 million in cost overruns on Safeco Field. The Mariners claimed that there was a surplus of $60 million raised by the taxes levied to build the park and that this surplus should be applied to the overruns. The PFD claimed that the Mariners were obligated by their lease and other agreements to pay for all overages. Now, $60 million is one hell of a lot of money, but what is the long-term value of the goodwill the team will lose by permanently alienating tens of thousands—if not hundreds of thousands—of fans, who see the team as breaking its promise with the local citizenry?

though many teams have done so in the past. The common opinion is that when a top player leaves as a free agent, his former club gets nothing in return, but that's not true. If Seattle doesn't trade Griffey and he signs with another team after the 2000 season, the Mariners will get two draft choices as compensation, including a first-rounder, and the same would be true if Rodriguez walks.

M-N-A

After years of being owned by Nintendo—but not being *run* by Nintendo, according to the charade set up by Major-League Baseball—the Mariners finally reorganized top management as their two-headed crisis loomed. Howard Lincoln replaced John Ellis as chair and chief executive officer; Lincoln is the retired chairman of Nintendo of America. Presumably he has the ownership's confidence to make the enormous commitment required to retain Rodriguez, Griffey, or both.

Lincoln said that he planned to move the Mariners' payroll into a higher-rent neighborhood, which is welcome news for Seattle fans. Unfortunately, it could be a year too late. If the team can't persuade A-Rod or Junior to re-up, even the shrewdest negotiating probably won't result in a contender this year. Regardless of that reality, though, management will be under tremendous pressure to assemble a team that will impress season ticket holders, even if rebuilding would be preferable in the long run.

The ironic element in this megabucks tragicomedy is that—at long last—the Mariners may very well have the makings of a fine starting staff in Freddy Garcia, 23, John Halama, 28, and Gil Meche, 21. Combine these three arms with a solid veteran (perhaps a returning Jamie Moyer) and top prospect Ryan Anderson, and the Mariners could have a good chance in their weak division. If they are serious about contending, however, they must re-sign Edgar Martinez, without whose productive bat a Griffey-less and Buhner-less offense would be weak.

Then, of course, there's the annual disaster called the Seattle bullpen. But the relief corps won't matter one whit if the lineup is stripped of impact hitters and the rotation doesn't jell.

BEST CASE

In a perfect world, the Mariners choose to hold on to Ken Griffey for at least one more season and resist the urge to trade Alex Rodriguez. Griffey puts aside his personal feelings, hits 55 homers, and helps lead a very good offense and a promising pitching staff to the playoffs. That's definitely not out of the question, as there isn't a dominant team in the AL West now that Texas has dramatically altered its roster. Seattle, having added free agent first baseman John Olerud, certainly is capable of playing with the rest of the teams in the division—especially if young pitchers Freddy Garcia, Gil Meche, and John Halama are for real.

WORST CASE

The Griffey trade talks rapidly turned into a fiasco and a public relations nightmare for the Mariners. By mid-December Griffey had told the M's that he'd only approve a trade to Cincinnati, but the club couldn't work out a deal, and talks ended. Nobody has suggested that Griffey would give less than his best if he played the 2000 season in Seattle, but if he begins the year there all of the attention will be focused on him. That could make it harder for him to do his job, and if the Mariners stumble, GM Pat Gillick might be blamed for not making the trade while he had the chance. And an unhappy Griffey probably means an unhappy Rodriguez.

UNDER THE MICROSCOPE

RYAN ANDERSON: One of the best pitching prospects in baseball, Anderson has the size and stuff to become an impact player in the major leagues. He throws in the upper 90s and has yet to completely fill out his 6-foot-10 frame. Anderson needs another full season in the minors to become more polished and poised.

GIL MECHE: Meche fit nicely into the Mariners' rotation in the latter part of 1999. After starting the season alongside Anderson at Double-A, Meche proved he was ready for the next step and did not disappoint. The 21-year-old locates a low-to-mid-90s fastball very well and has mixed in an improved change-up. If he can master the curveball, he will become a front-line starter.

CARLOS GUILLEN: Guillen was dubbed the Mariners' second baseman of the future upon being acquired in the deal that sent Randy Johnson to Houston in '98. The 24-year-old had injury problems that resurfaced in April, when he went down with a torn ACL. The Mariners then acquired David Bell, who emerged as the club's second baseman for the long haul. As a result, Guillen—assuming he can stay healthy—may be moved to third base or shortstop. Otherwise, he may be trade bait.

RYAN CHRISTIANSON: Christianson became the Mariners' top catching prospect when he was selected in the first round of the 1999 draft. He has good power to all fields and was the first non-pitcher to be the Mariners' initial choice in the draft since Jose Cruz Jr. in '95.

SEATTLE

TOP PROSPECTS

The main problem that has plagued the Mariners the past few years has been a lack of front-line pitching. Randy Johnson had clearly been their ace, but with his contract up at the end of the 1998 season, he was dealt to the Astros at the trading deadline. While the pitching staff wasn't the same after Johnson departed, the rookie pitchers received in the deal made serious contributions in '99. RHP **FREDDY GARCIA** won 17 games and finished ninth in the league in ERA. LHP **JOHN HALAMA** was also in the top 10 in ERA until the final week of the season. The huge success of the duo more than made up for the loss of the supposed key to the deal, 2B **CARLOS GUILLEN**, who suffered a season-ending injury in April. Homegrown RHP **GIL MECHE**, the first-round pick in '96, was called up at midseason and showed that he belonged on the major-league staff. With a young, talented core of starters and a more pitcher-friendly home ballpark, the Mariners could become known as much for their pitching as for their offensive prowess.

Despite the success of the youngsters at the major-league level, the best still may be yet to come. LHP **RYAN ANDERSON**, who has been the jewel of the farm system since being drafted in the first round in 1997, is still working his way through the ranks. The 6'10" Anderson struggled a bit in the Double-A Eastern League, but did end up leading the loop with 162 strikeouts. RHP **JOEL PINEIRO** had bouts of inconsistency, but like Anderson and Meche, was one of the youngest players in the Eastern League. The Mariners also picked up LHP **ROBERT RAMSAY** from the Red Sox in the Butch Huskey deal, and Ramsey should be serviceable in a relief role.

The pitching depth carries into the lower levels as well. RHP **CHRIS MEARS** followed up a 1998 season in which he was the Mariners' Pitcher of the Year with another solid campaign. The 21-year-old won 13 games between two Class A levels and pitched well in the PanAm Games. RHP **JEFF HEAVERLO**, a supplemental first-round pick in the '99 draft, impressed in his debut and could come quickly. Nineteen-year-old RHP **RAFAEL SORIANO**, a converted outfielder, demonstrated a live fastball in the short-season Northwest League and is someone to keep an eye on.

Beyond the wealth of pitching talent, however, the Mariners' farm is barren. Aside from a pair of 23-year-old second basemen in **ADONIS HARRISON** and **JERMAINE CLARK**, there are no position players with a legitimate chance of making the majors in the next couple years. Teenagers OF **ALEX FERNANDEZ**, OF **CHRIS SNELLING**, and C **RYAN CHRISTIANSON** look to have bright futures, but will need to stand the test of time.

CF
*KEN GRIFFEY JR. 30
? Harvey Hargrove A+ 24 97/6C

LF
BRIAN HUNTER 29
? *Shane Monahan ML 25 95/2C
? *Joe Mathis 3A 25 93/27H
? Mike Marchiano A+ 25 97/20C

RF
JAY BUHNER 35
*RAUL IBANEZ 28
CHARLES GIPSON 27
○ *Jake Weber 2A 24 98/6C
? Chad Alexander 3A 26 95/3C
↑ *Alex Fernandez A+ 19 98/ND

SS
ALEX RODRIGUEZ 24
RAFAEL BOURNIGAL 34
? #Giomar Guevara ML 27 90/ND
○ *Ramon Vazquez 2A 23 95/27C

2B
#CARLOS GUILLEN 24
DAVID BELL 27
○ *Jermaine Clark A+ 23 97/5C

3B
RUSS DAVIS 30
? Jason Regan 2A 24 96/51C
○ Bo Robinson A- 24 98/28C

SP/RP

1B
*JOHN OLERUD 31
*RYAN JACKSON 28
? Peanut Williams A+ 22 96/6H

RELIEVERS
JOSE MESA 34
JOSE PANIAGUA 26
TOM DAVEY 26
PAUL ABBOTT 32
TODD WILLIAMS 29
*STEVE SINCLAIR 28
○ Aaron Scheffer ML 24 93/NDH
? Patrick Dunham 2A 24 97/3C
? Jeff Farnsworth A+ 24 96/2C
? Justin Kaye A+ 24 95/19H
○ Enmanuel Ulloa A- 21 97/21H
↓ *Matt Thornton A- 23 98/1C
○ *Damaso Marte ML 25 92/ND
○ *Jordan Zimmerman ML 25 94/32C

C
DAN WILSON 31
*TOM LAMPKIN 36
↑ Carlos Maldonado A- 21 95/ND
↑ Ryan Christianson A- 19 99/1H

DH
EDGAR MARTINEZ 37

STARTERS
FREDDY GARCIA 23
*JAMIE MOYER 37
*JOHN HALAMA 28
KEN CLOUDE 25
FRANK RODRIGUEZ 27
↑ Gil Meche ML 22 96/1H
○ Dennis Stark ML 25 96/4C
○ Brett Hinchliffe ML 25 92/16H
○ *Robert Ramsay ML 26 96/7C
○ *Sean Spencer ML 25 96/40C
↑ *Ryan Anderson 2A 20 97/1H
↑ Joel Pineiro 2A 21 97/12C
? Greg Wooten A+ 26 95/3C
○ Brandon Parker A+ 24 97/2C
○ Chris Mears A+ 22 96/5H
○ Josue Matos A- 22 96/27
↑ Jeff Heaverlo A- 22 99/1

MAJOR LEAGUERS IN ALL CAPS
Minor leaguers in upper-and-lower case

BEFORE A PLAYER'S NAME:
* left-handed hitter/pitcher
# switch-hitter
?=prospect status (see explanation)

AFTER A PLAYER'S NAME:
Level at which he spent most of 1999 season; age as of July 1, 2000; year he was drafted; round drafted (ND= non-drafted amateur free agent); drafted out of high school (H) or college (C)

EXPLANATION OF PROSPECT RATINGS

★ Potential big-league star

↑ Projected regular player in majors (for pitchers: rotation starter or closer)

○ Projected platoon or utility player in majors (pitcher: setup or middle relief)

? Possible big-league reserve or long reliever

↓ High draft pick or "tools" player who hasn't performed to expectations

SEATTLE MARINERS

TEXAS RANGERS

Management
Manager	Johnny Oates	
G.M.	Doug Melvin	
President/CEO	Tom Hicks	

Career Record
715–638 / .528
424–368 / .535
183–141 / .565

1999 Record
Won–Lost	Pct.	Finish/G.B. (Division)	Finish/G.B. (Wild Card)
95–67	.586	1 (W)	

Preseason Consensus Projection
1 (1.70)

1st Half	2nd Half	Home	Road	Intradivision	Interleague
45–33	50–34	51–30	44–37	21–16	10–8

Comebacks	Blowouts	Nail-Biters	Grass	Turf	Sept.–Oct.
10–9	41–20	35–26	74–64	21–31	6–13

NUMBERS DON'T LIE

	Team (Rank)		Opponents (Rank)		League Avg.
Runs/Game	5.83	(2)	5.30	(7)	5.18
Batting Avg.	.293	(1)	.286	(12)	.274
On-Base Avg.	.361	(3)	.346	(7)	.347
Slugging Avg.	.479	(1)	.459	(13)	.439
Strikeouts	937	(5)	979	(8)	998
Home Runs	230	(3)	186	(6)	188
Stolen Bases	111	(6)	47	(1)	104
ERA	5.07	(11)			4.87
Errors	119	(9)			114

▶ THE INSIDER 2000

DEEP IN THE HEART OF (MEDIOCRITY IN) TEXAS

The Rangers' postseason annihilation by the Yankees left a cloud hanging over what otherwise was the best year in the franchise's modest history. The blockbuster Juan Gonzalez trade may well be the first move in a dramatic reconfiguration of the Rangers. The team got younger, cheaper, and *better* defensively by unloading the temperamental two-time AL MVP.

If Justin Thompson's elbow holds up and if Gabe Kapler develops as a hitter, the deal will be a good one. If Francisco Cordero harnesses his blazing fastball and Alan Webb matures into a serviceable big-league pitcher, it will be a *great* deal. If Ruben Mateo lives up to his billing, no one in Texas will care where Juan Gonzalez is playing.

The Rangers' postseason failures were linked to two factors: a lack of plate discipline up and down the lineup, and mediocre starting pitching that depended on lots of run support. What Texas has demonstrated is that a team configured like that has almost no chance of advancing to the World Series even if it makes the postseason year after year.

Aggressive hitting is fine during the regular season when batters face lots of mediocre or worse pitchers, but it doesn't work when a team is facing smart veteran pitchers with good control. Orlando Hernandez, David Cone, et al., won't bother to give hitters a pitch to hit if they swing at marginal strikes and get themselves out.

Conversely, the won-lost record of any decent and durable starting pitcher whose team scores six runs per game for him—think Aaron Sele here—will look pretty good. But when you advance to the next level, the other team is scoring six runs per game or better as well, and the relative weaknesses of pitchers like Sele and Rick Helling are exposed.

UNDERAPPRECIATED SUPERSTAR, OR DURABLE BUT HARDLY BRILLIANT?

In the 1990s, Rafael Palmeiro was second among all major-league players in hits (Mark Grace was first). Palmeiro also posted the third-highest home-run and RBI totals over the past six seasons. He had his best season in 1999, when he posted

MOMENT OF TRUTH

The Rangers won a team record 95 games in 1999 and were generally thought to be the best Texas team ever. Four players drove in at least 100 runs, six players hit 20 or more homers, and numerous team offensive records were set. All of that feeling of accomplishment was whisked away, though, in a three-game sweep by the Yankees in the AL Division Series—a defeat that may have altered the course of the franchise for the future. Texas scored only one run in the Series, after scoring only one in a New York sweep the year before, and now many player changes appear imminent. Management once thought this would be a contending team that it would keep together for a few years, but in the aftermath of the crushing defeat, the talk switched to salary cutbacks and retrenchment.

BIGGEST SURPRISE

Jeff Zimmerman had to beg and plead to get a minor-league contract, but the result was a storybook season in 1999. Zimmerman did have some credentials, as he was the Rangers' minor-league Pitcher of the Year in 1998, and many thought he should have made the team in spring training. As it was, he spent only a week in the minors before getting his first taste the big leagues. The 26-year-old native of British Columbia was impressive from the start, going 8–0 with an 0.86 ERA through mid-July and earning a spot on the AL All-Star team.

BIGGEST DISAPPOINTMENT

The Rangers signed veteran pitcher Mark Clark to a lucrative free-agent contract a year ago to provide much-needed help in the starting rotation, but elbow problems severely limited his effectiveness. He made only 15 starts before landing on the disabled list on June 20. Clark had gone 3–7 while allowing nearly a run per inning and wound up missing the rest of the season— the team was in no hurry to stick him back in the rotation in the middle of a pennant race.

career highs in the big offensive categories (.324 BA, 47 HR, .630 SA). That year, he finished fourth in the AL MVP voting.

In recent years, Palmeiro has been depicted as an unsung superstar. As nice as that sounds, it isn't true. Palmeiro has had a fine career, and he's been remarkably durable and consistent in the 1990s, but he's not a top-tier superstar. He's never had a season in which he was the best player in his league, and sometimes he hasn't even been the best player on his club. He's led the AL in any offensive category only three times in 11 years—191 hits in 1990, 49 doubles in '91, and 124 runs in '93—but has not been the best at anything in the past six seasons.

His numbers, especially his home run totals, look good for the past six years, but much of that is due to baseball's overall offensive explosion. From 1971 through '77, no AL player hit more than 39 home runs in one season; Palmeiro has hit at least that many in four of the past five seasons—yet he never led the league. In this five-year span, Rafael has hit at least 38 homers every year; however, 1999 was the only year that even placed him in the top three in the league. Only in one other year (1995) did it even put him in the top five.

On the other hand, Palmeiro has been a much better player over the past six years than Will Clark, whose career has been linked with Palmeiro's since the two sluggers were teammates and All-Americans at Mississippi State from 1983 to 1985.

THINGS CHANGE

Palmeiro became a free agent for the first time after the 1993 season. He left Texas for Baltimore even though he wanted to stay put, because the Rangers didn't want to pay as much as the Birds. The Rangers didn't think they'd lose anything at that position because they signed Clark as a free agent from San Francisco.

Clark had been carving out quite a reputation for the Giants, leading the NL in RBI in 1988, in runs in 1989, and in slugging in 1991. Will "The Thrill" was the NLCS MVP in 1989, setting a record with 13 hits as he led the Giants to their first World Series in 27 years. One year older than Palmeiro, Clark was having banner years (five consecutive NL All-Star selections) while his counterpart was trying to find his way, first with the Cubs and then with the Rangers.

While Clark was head-and-shoulders above Palmeiro as a player when the two were in their 20s, their fortunes have been reversed in the past six years. Choosing Clark hurt the Rangers badly in the five years Palmeiro was in Baltimore, as Palmeiro hit

.292 with 182 home runs and 553 RBI, while Clark hit .308 with 77 homers and 397 RBI. But that doesn't tell the whole story.

A good example of the difference between the two first basemen was the 1996 season. The Rangers won the AL West with Clark in the lineup, but Palmeiro had a much better season, and Texas would have stood a much better chance against the Yankees in the postseason. Clark hit .284 with only 13 homers in '96, while Palmeiro was hitting 39 homers for Baltimore. According to *Total Baseball*'s Total Player Rating, Palmeiro was more than three wins better than Clark—a substantial difference. Considering that the three games Texas lost in the Division Series were by a total of four runs, having Palmeiro in the lineup easily could have made the difference against New York. Will had only two singles in four games in the '96 postseason, scoring one run and driving in none. Rafael had seven hits in nine games (including three homers), scoring eight runs and driving home six.

In 1999, of course, the prodigal son returned home, and the Rangers won their division while the Orioles endured a long, frustrating summer. Late in the season, one Texas player said that Will Clark was actually the Rangers' 1999 MVP—because his departure made the team so much better.

I-ROD IN THE PANTHEON?

Now that Ivan Rodriguez has won a Most Valuable Player award, he is in truly select company with other great catchers. Hall of Famer Bill Dickey was a 10-time All-Star, but he never won the MVP award in his 17-year career. Neither did Gary Carter or Carlton Fisk, players who will be enshrined in Cooperstown before long. Gabby Hartnett won one MVP award in his 20-year career.

Rodriguez has put up some impressive numbers in his first nine seasons in the major-leagues. He's hit .300 with 144 homers and 621 RBI, and has been selected for the All-Star game every year except his rookie season, though his unwillingness to take pitches keeps him from being a great hitter. He's universally recognized as the best all-around catcher in the game, and talk about him entering the Hall one day has begun.

Johnny Bench, Yogi Berra, Roy Campanella, Carter, Mickey Cochrane, Dickey, Fisk, and Hartnett are the greatest catchers in major-league history. It's a pretty short list, partially due to the physical demands of the position. How does Rodriguez compare with these Hall of Famers?

Like Bench, Rodriguez debuted at 19 and played his first

SECRET WEAPON

Over the course of the season, Mike Venafro became a fine left-handed complement to fellow rookie Jeff Zimmerman. Venafro, a four-year player at James Madison, features a sidearm motion that is extremely tough on left-handed hitters, who batted only .193 against him. He spent the first three weeks in the minors but still wound up pitching in 65 games, which tied him with Zimmerman for most appearances by AL rookies. He developed nicely, and by the end of the year, was being entrusted with tough situations in the late innings.

ACHILLES HEEL

The Rangers simply haven't found a way to beat the Yankees. Texas was only 4–8 against the Bronx Bombers in the regular season, setting the stage for another ignominious exit from postseason play. To many shell-shocked Rangers' fans it now seems as if every break, close call, and freak play naturally goes the Yankees' way—and that the only way their team can make it to the late-October Classic is if the Yankees don't make the postseason.

TEXAS RANGERS

ENOUGH ALREADY

About the only answer manager Johnny Oates had for the team's failures was that his players were "trying to do too much." Oates used that excuse for swinging at bad pitches, for fielding errors, and for everything else that lost games. However, if this was the season-long problem Oates made it out to be, he needs to shoulder some of the blame for its continuation. He could have tried to try to break his players of such bad habits, but instead chose to simply keep harping about the problem to the media rather than deal with it in the clubhouse and in the dugout.

full season at 20. Berra debuted at 21 and became a regular at 23. Carter made the Show at 20 and was a regular at 21. Cochrane played regularly at 22, in his first season. Dickey was a regular at 22, in his second year. Fisk made his debut at 21 and became a regular at 23. Hartnett debuted at 21 but didn't play in 140 games until he was 29. Campy is a special case: He first played in the majors at 26, but had previously played nine years in the Negro Leagues (starting at age 15!) and clearly could have played big-league ball a lot earlier.

Bench won his first of two NL MVP awards in his third season, in 1970; Berra won the first of his three AL awards in his fifth season, in 1951. Campanella won three MVP awards in 10 years before an auto accident paralyzed him; like Bench, he hit in a yo-yo pattern of huge seasons followed by off years. Through their first nine seasons, Bench, Berra, and Campanella were substantially better than Cochrane, Dickey, Fisk, and Rodriguez offensively. Bench, Berra, and Campy were more powerful hitters, blasting many more home runs and driving in many more runs.

Like Bench, Rodriguez is acknowledged to be a truly great defensive catcher. Opposing managers have become so afraid of his ability to throw out base stealers that opposing teams literally stop running. In 1999 Rodriguez threw out 54 percent of runners trying to steal, which was easily the best percentage in baseball and astonishingly better than the league average of 32 percent. Pudge has thrown out a staggering 47 percent of runners over his nine-year career.

Bench was a regular catcher for 14 seasons, although he had only one really good year after his ninth. Berra caught regularly for 10 seasons and was a part-time catcher for four more, which helped lengthen his career. Cochrane burned out after 11 seasons behind the plate, playing only 71 games combined in his last two years before a nearly fatal beaning ended his career. Dickey declined rapidly after his 11th year as a full-time backstop. Fisk played for 24 seasons, but missed a lot of games early in his career and rarely caught more than 130 games in a season. He had a longer career than the others, but he was never as good.

It's common for a ballplayer to have a career year at age 27, as Ivan did in 1999. That stellar season may partly have been due to his not playing winter ball for the first time since 1992. Rodriguez now has a realistic chance to vault into the highest reaches of baseball's catching pantheon if he can continue to play at this level for another three or four seasons. However, he's clearly fighting the odds, as history shows.

BEST CASE

The Rangers will be a vastly different team in 2000, but still could contend for a spot in the playoffs. Of course, the team still has reigning MVP Ivan Rodriguez. And by trading Juan Gonzalez to Detroit, Texas was able to address part of its pitching problem and find a spot for top prospect Ruben Mateo. The 24-year-old Gabe Kapler, one of the players Texas got from Detroit, had decent power numbers last year and could thrive in the hitter-happy Ballpark at Arlington. At worst, Ruben Mateo should perform about as well in center field as Tom Goodwin, and has the potential to be much, much better. He could even wind up better than the temperamental Juan Gonzalez, which would be a huge plus for the team.

WORST CASE

The pitching staff isn't particularly strong, although the loss of the overvalued Aaron Sele won't hurt the club as much as some might think. Texas will have to rely on a group of young—and as yet unproven—position players in the upcoming season. The pressure will be on, especially for the players involved in the Gonzalez trade. If Kapler and Justin Thompson fail to deliver, there will be enough headaches to go around. Should the Rangers fail to make the playoffs, management will be second-guessed for trading Gonzalez, and there will be a great deal of scrutiny placed on manager Johnny Oates and GM Doug Melvin.

UNDER THE MICROSCOPE

RUBEN MATEO: Mateo received an earlier-than-anticipated call to the majors when Tom Goodwin went down with an injury. While Mateo didn't set the world on fire, his considerable talents surfaced before a broken wrist ended his season. The 21-year-old should take over on an everyday basis this spring.

MIKE LAMB: The 23-year-old batted .302 with 35 doubles and 93 RBI at Class A Charlotte in 1998. Last season, the left-handed swinger hit .324 with 51 doubles and 21 homers and walked nearly as many times as he struck out. Lamb may get a shot this spring to start what should be a long career in the major-leagues.

DAN KOLB: The hard-throwing Kolb has had moderate success since his electrifying 1996 season, when he posted a 2.82 ERA and fanned 162 batters over three levels. With an ideal pitcher's frame at 6'4" and 195 pounds, and a low-90s sinking fastball, Kolb has a chance to develop into the starting pitcher the organization needs. However, his lack of consistency hasn't done much to inspire confidence in his long-term potential.

FRANCISCO CORDERO: Dubbed the "closer of the future" in 1997, Cordero was virtually forgotten after an elbow injury curtailed his '98 season. But he returned to form last season with 27 saves and a 1.38 ERA at Double-A. The 22-year-old has the heat and slider to contribute as a big-league setup pitcher this season, and should be ready to challenge for a closer's job in a year or two.

TEXAS

TOP PROSPECTS

After coming aboard in 1995, Doug Melvin has rebuilt a farm system that was totally barren. In 1998, Texas affiliates combined to experience their first winning season since 1992, ranking eighth with a .526 percentage. That turnaround, combined with solid hitting prospects and the makings of some pitching depth, earned the Rangers HOWE SPORTSDATA's 1998 Organization of the Year award.

In 1999, the big club received help from RHP **JEFF ZIMMERMAN** and LHP **MIKE VENAFRO**. Outstanding OF **RUBEN MATEO** and SS **KELLY DRANSFELDT** got their feet wet, with Mateo enjoying much more success than Dransfeldt. The minor-league affiliates finished with the fourth-best record (.541), and four clubs made the playoffs. 3B **MIKE LAMB** became the heir apparent to Todd Zeile, and 2B **JASON ROMANO** and 3B **JASON GRABOWSKI** established themselves as big-league prospects. In addition, the Rangers added even more minor-league depth when they acquired RHP **FRANCISCO CORDERO** and LHP **ALAN WEBB**, the two best pitchers in the Tigers' organization, in the deal for Juan Gonzalez. Cordero rebounded from an injury-filled '98 to make the HOWE SPORTSDATA All-Prospect Team. Webb, the youngest pitcher in the Double-A Southern League, had a bright first half before slumping in the second half. OF **GABE KAPLER**, another young outfielder the Rangers acquired, was a 1998 All-Prospect Team member.

Mateo is poised to become the Rangers' next all-star player. After a breakout 1998 season in which he hit .289 with 27 homers, Dransfeldt struggled mightily at the Triple-A and major-league levels last season. Lamb, a sleeper prior to this season, is a hitting machine and an adequate defender; Romano—called a "baseball rat" due to his tireless efforts to improve—can hit, run, and field, earning a spot on the All-Teen team last season; Grabowski, a converted catcher, has a quick bat and command of the strike zone. He hit three homers in an exhibition against the big club, then had a big Double-A playoff subbing for the promoted Lamb.

1B **SHAWN GALLAGHER** and 1B **CARLOS PENA**, the Rangers' first-round pick in 1998, are decent prospects but still a few years away. C **CESAR KING** had his second straight sub-par season after earning back-to-back nods on the All-Teen team. The organization needs him to improve both his hitting and his work ethic.

Zimmerman established himself as one of the best relievers in baseball, but the Rangers need others to step up and help, especially in the starting rotation. RHP **DAN KOLB** and RHP **RYAN GLYNN** had shots last season but did not come through. Kolb and Glynn are both young and will receive other chances, but LHP **MATT PERISHO**, LHP **COREY LEE**, and LHP **DOUG DAVIS** may also get shots in the near future, though all are marginal prospects. LHP **JUAN MORENO**, who throws uncommonly hard for a southpaw, had a very good season at Double-A, and LHP **ANDY PRATT** used a great change-up to pile up 100 strikeouts in 72 innings at Class A before going down with arm problems.

The Rangers further boosted their mound depth by selecting pitchers with their first three picks. Two of those, RHP **COLBY LEWIS** and RHP **NICK REGILIO**, combined for 11 wins, a 1.82 ERA, and 142 strikeouts in 115 innings.

▶ THE INSIDER 2000

LF
*RUSTY GREER 31
CHAD CURTIS 31
? Cliff Brumbaugh 3A 26 95/13C

CF
★ Ruben Mateo ML 22 95/ND
? #Scarborough Green ML 26 92/10C

RF
GABE KAPLER 24
? Mike Zywica 3A 25 96/24C
? Juan Piniella 2A 22 96/7H

SS
ROYCE CLAYTON 30
○ Kelly Dransfeldt ML 25 96/4C
? Juan Bautista 2A 25 92/ND

2B
#LUIS ALICEA 34
? *Tom Sergio 2A 25 97/11C
↑ Jason Romano A+ 21 97/1H

3B
*FRANK CATALANOTTO 26
↑ *Mike Lamb 3A 24 97/7C
○ *Jason Grabowski 2A 24 97/2C

1B
*LEE STEVENS 32
○ Shawn Gallagher 2A 23 95/5H
○ *Carlos Pena A+ 22 98/1C

SP/RP

RELIEVERS
JOHN WETTELAND 33
JEFF ZIMMERMAN 27
*MIKE VENAFRO 26
TIM CRABTREE 30
*MIKE MUNOZ 34
↑ Francisco Cordero ML 22 94/ND
? Jonathan Johnson ML 25 95/1C
? *Matt Perisho ML 25 93/3H
? R.A. Dickey 3A 25 96/1C
? *Juan Moreno 2A 25 93/ND

STARTERS
RICK HELLING 29
MARK CLARK 32
ESTEBAN LOAIZA 28
*JUSTIN THOMPSON 27
○ Dan Kolb ML 25 95/6
? Ryan Glynn ML 25 95/4C
? Brian Sikorski 3A 25 95/4C
? Ted Silva 2A 25 95/21C
↑ *Alan Webb 2A 20 97/4H
↓ Joaquin Benoit A+ 20 96/ND
↓ Colby Lewis A- 20 99/1C
○ *Corey Lee ML 25 96/1C
? *Doug Davis ML 24 96/10C
? *Trey Poland 2A 25 97/5C
? *Andy Pratt A- 20 98/9H

C
IVAN RODRIGUEZ 28
BILL HASELMAN 34
○ Cesar King 2A 22 94/ND

DH
*RAFAEL PALMEIRO 35
MIKE SIMMS 33

MAJOR LEAGUERS IN ALL CAPS
Minor leaguers in upper-and-lower case

BEFORE A PLAYER'S NAME:
* left-handed hitter/pitcher
# switch-hitter
?=prospect status (see explanation)

AFTER A PLAYER'S NAME:
Level at which he spent most of 1999 season; age as of July 1, 2000; year he was drafted; round drafted (ND= non-drafted amateur free agent); drafted out of high school (H) or college (C)

EXPLANATION OF PROSPECT RATINGS

★ Potential big-league star

↑ Projected regular player in majors (for pitchers: rotation starter or closer)

○ Projected platoon or utility player in majors (pitcher: setup or middle relief)

? Possible big-league reserve or long reliever

↓ High draft pick or "tools" player who hasn't performed to expectations

TEXAS

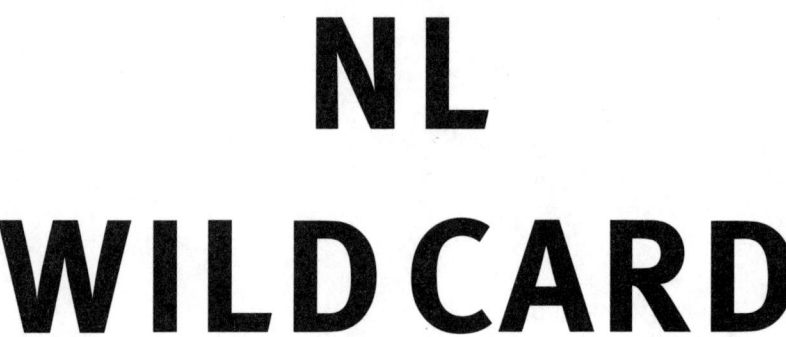

▶ THE INSIDER 2000

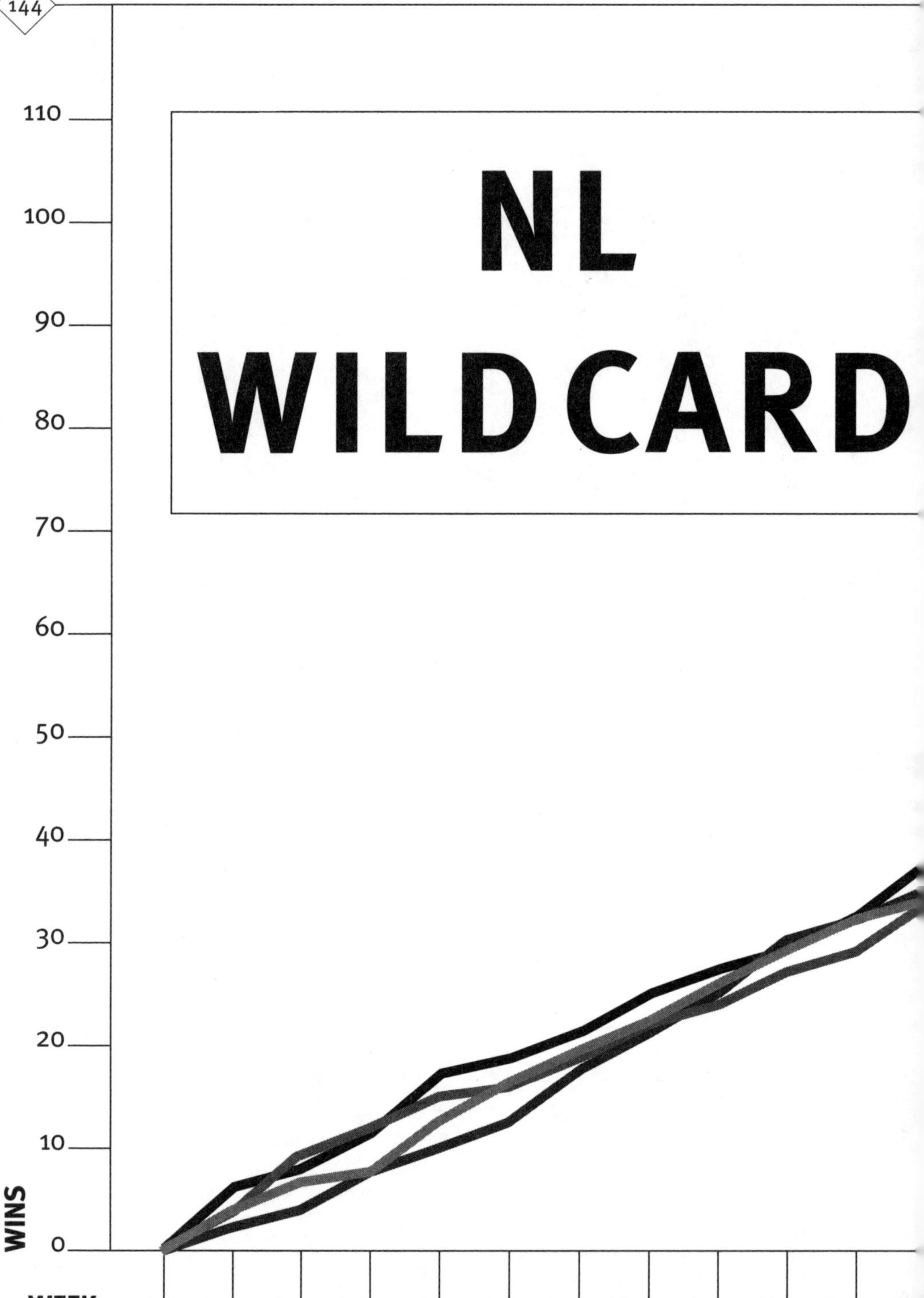

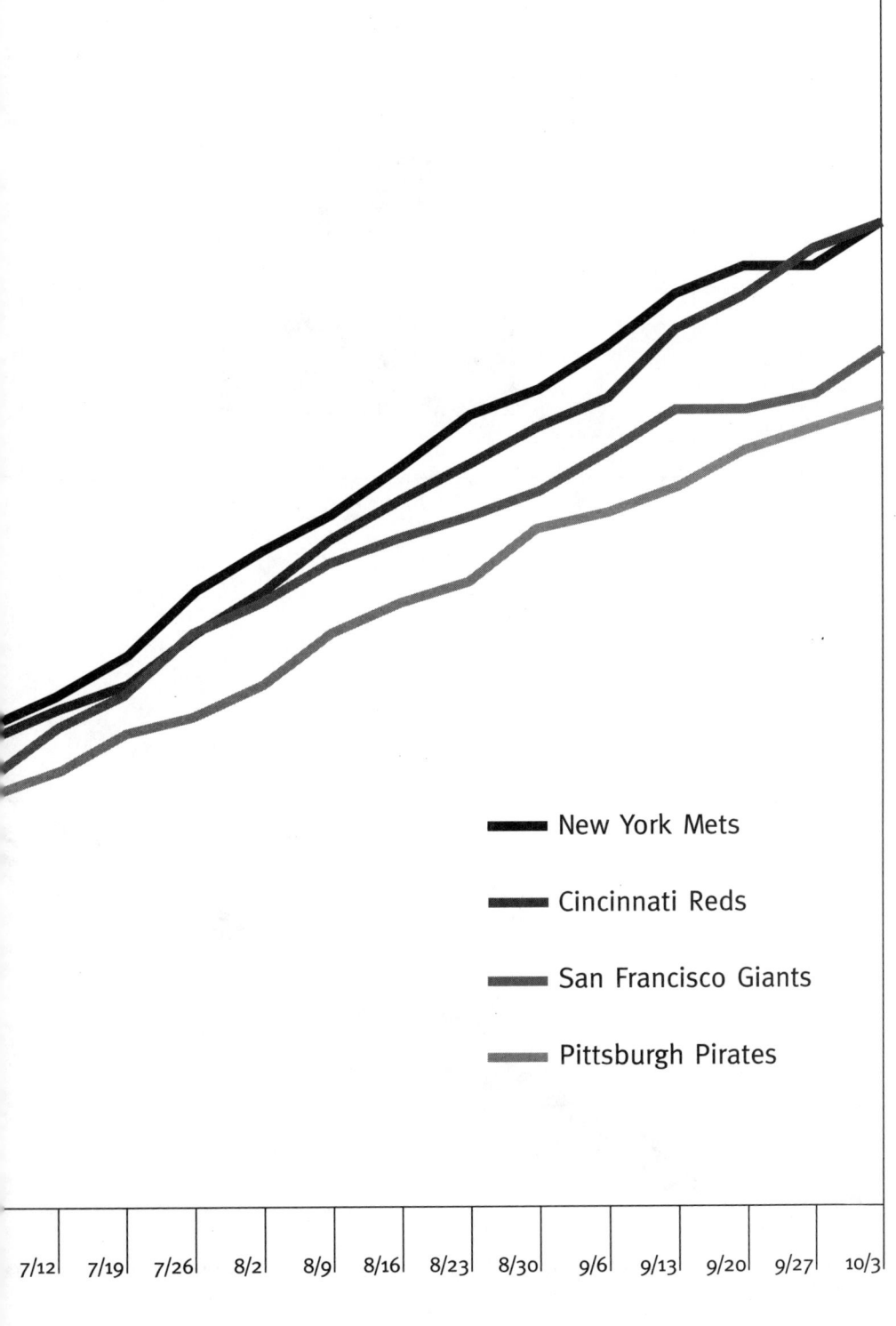

NL EAST

WINS — 110, 100, 90, 80, 70, 60, 50, 40, 30, 20, 10, 0

WEEK — 4/5, 4/12, 4/19, 4/26, 5/3, 5/10, 5/17, 5/24, 5/31, 6/7, 6/14, 6/2

▶ THE INSIDER 2000

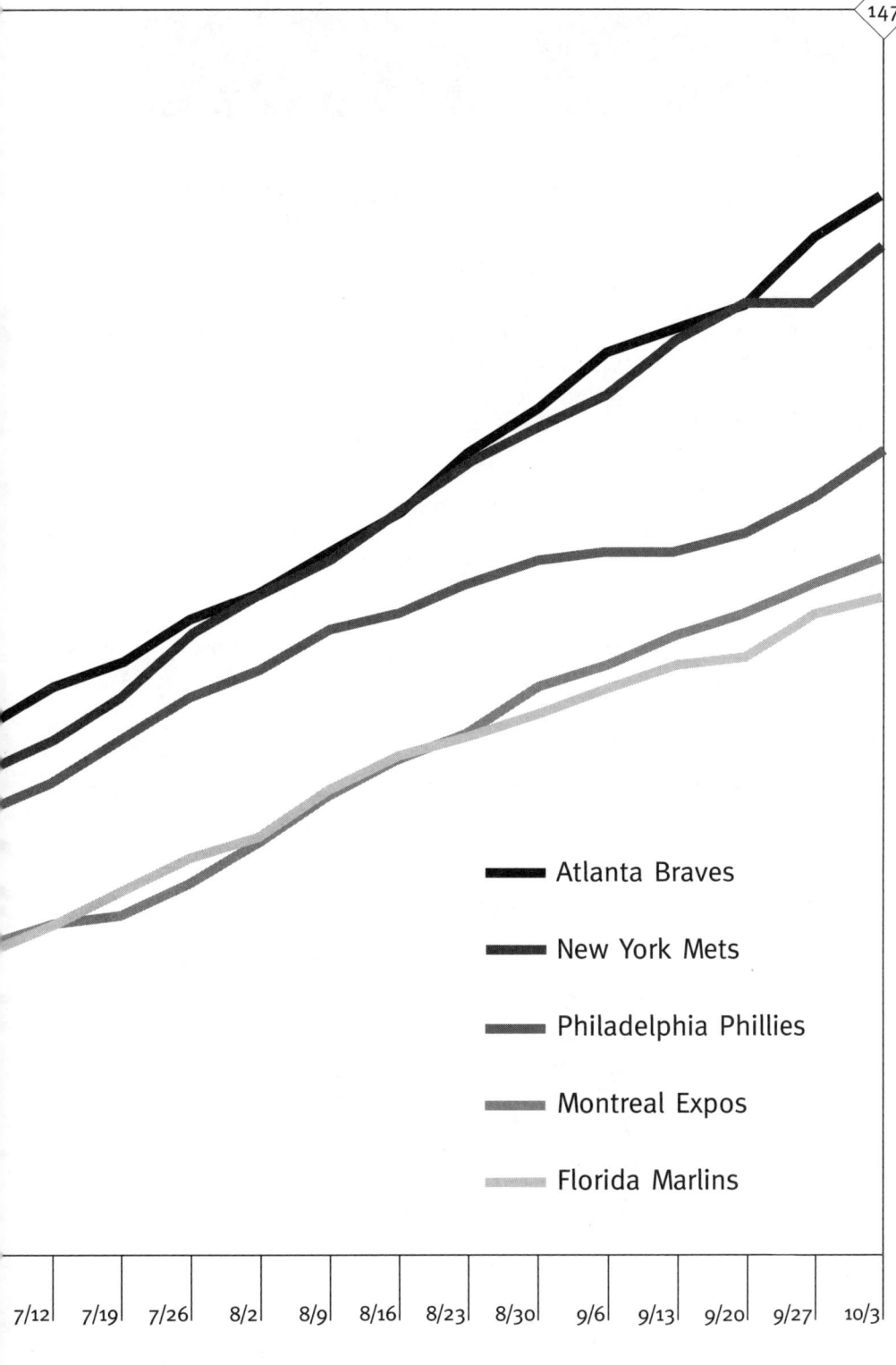

ATLANTA BRAVES

Management
Manager	Bobby Cox
G.M.	John Schuerholz
President/CEO	Ted Turner

Career Record
1521–1204 / .558
1614–1234 / .567
1903–1854 / .507

1999 Record
Won–Lost	Pct.	Finish/G.B. (Division)	Finish/G.B. (Wild Card)
103–59	.636	1 (E)	

Preseason Consensus Projection
1 (1.00)

1st Half	2nd Half	Home	Road	Intradivision	Interleague
47–31	56–28	56–25	47–34	40–20	9–9

Comebacks	Blowouts	Nail-Biters	Grass	Turf	Sept.–Oct.
11–9	27–14	46–26	88–48	15–11	19–9

NUMBERS DON'T LIE

	Team (Rank)		Opponents (Rank)		League Avg.
Runs/Game	5.19	(7)	4.08	(1)	5.00
Batting Avg.	.266	(9)	.251	(3)	.268
On-Base Avg.	.341	(8)	.314	(1)	.342
Slugging Avg.	.436	(4)	.377	(1)	.429
Strikeouts	962	(3)	1197	(3)	1072
Home Runs	197	(4)	142	(2)	181
Stolen Bases	148	(6)	108	(7)	122
ERA	3.65	(1)			4.57
Errors	111	(7)			120

▶ THE INSIDER 2000

A LITTLE PANIC IS A GOOD THING

In 1999, as in years past, the Atlanta Braves went through the regular season with style, panache, and self-control. Even when first baseman Andres Galarraga, catcher Javy Lopez, and closer Kerry Ligtenberg went down with injuries, the Braves stayed calm, didn't panic, and made it through an unexpectedly tight pennant race. They won the NL East for the eighth straight time (excluding 1994), advanced through two tough postseason series, and proceeded to the World Series—where they had their heads handed to them by a clearly superior Yankee club.

The Braves—the most consistently dominant club of the decade—have just one World Series title to show for their efforts during that time. Atlanta's policies of smart trading, reliance on talent from their minor-league clubs, prudent free-agent signings, and sound fiscal management have made it a model organization. In 1999, however, the club's stoic stance in the face of adversity combined with habitual success to blind the Braves' management to some very real on-field weaknesses. By the time they barely scraped by the Mets in a too-close NLCS, there was little doubt that they'd be cut to pieces by the Yankees. That's exactly what happened.

First of all, the club's bench was quite weak even before the injuries to Galarraga and Lopez. Brian Hunter, Randall Simon, Keith Lockhart, Ozzie Guillen, Eddie Perez, and Otis Nixon are hardly names that strike fear into an opposing club. While manager Bobby Cox has always preferred a veteran bench, the supernumerary quality of this reserve corps was almost surreal. When injuries opened up holes at first and behind the plate, a weak bench got even weaker as Hunter's and Perez's roles expanded.

Before the season, Atlanta had signed Brian Jordan to play right field, an excellent move that paid big dividends. During the year, though, Atlanta's acquisitions were more on the order of those made by a club on a tight budget. Howard Battle? Freddy Garcia? Greg Myers? Jorge Fabregas? Moreover, once they went out and got Jose Hernandez, a legitimate bat, they put him back on the bench by the NLCS.

The fallout from Galarraga's illness exposed two players—Gerald Williams and Ryan Klesko—as major weaknesses. Williams, a career platoon player who has always hit lefthanders well, was thrust into everyday duty when Galarraga went down, and became the full-time leadoff hitter when Walt Weiss failed miserably (.193 BA, .287 OBA in the leadoff slot).

MOMENT OF TRUTH

Only Bobby Cox really knows what he was thinking when he started Ozzie Guillen and Greg Myers in the second game of the World Series. Atlanta had played the Yankees tough in the first game and lost a heartbreaker, so why make such a sudden change? And why play weak hitters when it was the offense that needed a boost? The move smacked of desperation, and when it didn't work, the Braves found themselves down 2–0 in the Series—and another disappointing late October was only a couple of games away.

BIGGEST SURPRISE

John Rocker had a good season in 1998, although he was used primarily as a left-handed relief specialist and often faced only one or two hitters in an outing. But he was effective last season against all hitters, especially in the second half. The fireballing southpaw saved 21 games after the All-Star break and was a dominating force down the stretch. For the season, lefty hitters batted just .140 against him, righties .191. Without him, the Braves might not have made it to the postseason for the eighth straight year.

BIGGEST DISAPPOINTMENT

Already viewed as the best defensive centerfielder in the NL and possessing outstanding athletic ability, Andruw Jones was expected to emerge as one of the best players in the league. Instead, the 22-year-old took a step back in several areas offensively and irritated some teammates with what was perceived as a lack of hustle and an unwillingness to work hard to improve.

Williams was a terrible leadoff hitter for a championship club. He was a poor base stealer (19 SB / 11 CS) who didn't hit for high average or walk often enough (.335 OBA). He finished fifth on the team in runs despite hitting first for a good portion of the season. Klesko, another platoon player, is a monster against righthanders (.324 BA, .402 OBA, .583 SA) but can't hit a southpaw to save his life. A career .221 hitter against lefties coming into 1999, he was even worse than usual, batting .102 with one extra-base hit in 49 at-bats. In addition, he's almost as bad defensively at first base as he is in left field—which is really saying something.

The fact that Atlanta management has been so good at identifying the team's problems and addressing them in the past made it particulary striking that the Braves apparently didn't realize that good opponents would exploit these weaknesses.

There had been good everyday players available on the trade market during the spring and summer. For the Braves to have picked up one or two of them wouldn't have been difficult. While not mortgaging the future to win today is a laudable goal, the Braves have plenty of good prospects, and they needed to do something to buff up their lineup and bench. But they didn't, and they paid the consequences.

Atlanta GM John Schuerholz has admirably kept the Braves on a steady course over the past decade; but if anyone in the Braves' executive suite wants to win the World Series as badly as the Yankees do, it's hard to see.

RUSHING 'EM?

Once again the Braves made young pitchers a big part of their success in 1999. Two impressive rookies were Kevin McGlinchy, a nonroster invitee who spent the season as a reliable righthanded reliever, and Odalis Perez, who made 17 starts.

Neither pitcher had even a full year's experience above Single A before landing in the majors. They joined John Rocker, Kevin Millwood, and Kerry Ligtenberg in that distinction; those three had assumed major roles in '98 with less than a full year of experience in the high minors.

All these pitchers have helped Atlanta, but not without some cost. Perez, with just 39 starts under his belt (21 at Double-A, none at Triple-A) in four pro seasons, ripped up his left elbow midway through 1999 and underwent "Tommy John" ligament replacement surgery last fall. Meanwhile, Ligtenberg missed all of last season after pitching 73 games (75 innings) in '98 and tearing the medial collateral ligament in his elbow in spring '99.

There is cause for concern with Millwood as well. He had never pitched more than 150 innings in any minor-league season from 1993 to 1996. In 1997 he tossed 173 innings. Coming to the majors in 1998 after just 20 high-minors starts, he threw 174 innings. Last season he tossed 228 frames, finishing eighth in the league in that category (as well as second in the league in ERA), and then pitched another fistful of games in the playoffs. Come the World Series, Millwood was spent.

The Braves had not previously pushed their pitching prospects this aggressively. John Smoltz made 44 starts above Class A before joining the Braves. Tom Glavine made 49 starts in the high minors, and Jason Schmidt made 43 before coming up. Terrell Wade had 56 starts in Double and Triple-A before reaching Atlanta.

Remember Mike Cather, whom the Braves dug out of independent ball back in 1996? After a year at Double-A, he vaulted to the majors in '97, pitching a combined 70 games and 101 innings. The next season he suffered a side injury that affected his motion, an injury from which he has never recovered. He was released last fall.

There is no definite connection between number of innings pitched and pitcher injuries, but exposing young pitchers to dramatically increased workloads often seems to result in injuries. The Braves have, for many years, been able to keep their pitchers uncannily healthy. Perhaps a return to their more careful handling of hurlers would be in order, before anyone else goes down.

SEÑOR AVERAGE

Infielder Jose Hernandez, who began the season with the last-place Cubs and ended it sitting on the bench with first-place Atlanta, was close to an average offensive performer in 1999, though he did have more power than most other shortstops:

Jose: 266 BA, .339 OBA, and .425 SA;

NL averages for SS: 267 BA, .333 OBA, .385 SA.

For an average performer, Hernandez is an interesting player. Back in 1992 it looked like Hernandez would be a Triple-A infielder at best. Stuck in the Rangers' farm system, he wasn't hitting and was waived. The Indians claimed him, then sent him to the Cubs in 1993 for Heathcliff Slocumb.

Hernandez made the majors the next season after hitting well at Double-A. He was a spare infielder in 1994–95. After the Cubs let go of Shawon Dunston following 1995, Rey Sanchez

SECRET WEAPON

Bret Boone and Denny Neagle were the big names in the trade following the 1998 season, but it was Mike Remlinger who had the best season of anyone involved in the deal. He ended the year as the primary setup pitcher for closer John Rocker. His 10 wins were a career high, more even than in 1997 and '98, when he was a part-time starter for the Reds. He so impressed Atlanta that the club signed him to a two-year contract—the first multiyear deal of his career—during the postseason.

ACHILLES HEEL

The Braves thought they had solved their ongoing shortstop problem two years ago by signing Walt Weiss, but it's now clear that his years in Colorado had inflated his value. Weiss's solid defense made him adequate in his first year in Atlanta, but he wasn't close to being respectable last season. With no other options, Atlanta traded for Chicago's Jose Hernandez late in the year, but the team was uncomfortable with his defense and turned back to Weiss in the postseason.

ENOUGH ALREADY

Former starting pitcher and ESPN television analyst Rick Sutcliffe continued a long baseball tradition of excusing preferential treatment for star players during the Division Series broadcasts. With all the moral authority that he could muster, Sutcliffe pontificated about how Atlanta pitchers such as Tom Glavine had earned the right to expect that outside pitches be called strikes. Despite whatever Sutcliffe thinks, it would be a refreshing change to see everyone playing on a level field.

got the starting shortstop job, with Hernandez again coming off the bench.

Then he began to hit. Hernandez learned to pull the ball and, although he continued to strike out often, he developed legitimate power. Since then, he's improved at the plate and his glove has been adequate or better, yet he's never gotten a chance to play every day.

Why the Cubs went through Dunston again (in 1997), Sanchez, Jeff Blauser, Manny Alexander, Felix Fermin, and last year, Jose Nieves without simply installing Hernandez at short is bizarre. To get his bat in the lineup, Jim Riggleman would play him at second, at third, and even in center field (a misadventure that cost the Cubs runs). Even after hitting 23 doubles and 23 homers in '98, Hernandez had to fight off Blauser and Alexander last spring to nail down everyday duty.

After another solid offensive season, Hernandez went to the Braves for the stretch drive. He never was able to persuade Bobby Cox that he was clearly better than Walt Weiss, though, so Jose didn't play much in the postseason. Despite Weiss's spectacular play in the Division Series that killed Houston's chances, his range was much worse than that of Hernandez in '99.

While Hernandez isn't a star even if he hits 25 homers, he is a solid player at a key defensive position who should be an incumbent, not just someone fighting for a job. He deserves a lot more respect than he's gotten. At 30, he probably has several more seasons like 1999 in him. Atlanta was looking to upgrade at short in the off-season, but the Braves have won for years with a lot worse than Hernandez at shortstop.

BEST CASE

The Braves have, literally, all the top-flight talent they need to win every year. If everyone is healthy, there's no reason for Atlanta to stop short of the World Series again—especially if Andres Galarraga can come back and solidify the heart of the lineup. However, in order to get past the great teams, the Braves have to play to annihilate, not just squeak by. The Yankees, for instance, don't have a mediocre bench; they have a great one.

WORST CASE

Relying on mediocre players like Walt Weiss, Ryan Klesko, and Gerald Williams to fill key roles last year didn't work out. If Atlanta can't acquire more impact players, it could be a tougher time for the club to win the NL East than anyone would expect. Bobby Cox, never viewed as a great in-game manager, works best when he can concentrate on his pitchers, not his hitters. Without a top-flight leadoff man, Cox may have to work too hard to manufacture runs—a gambit that works against his club's natural tilt toward power.

UNDER THE MICROSCOPE

JASON MARQUIS: The 21-year-old battled back from a subpar 1998 season to reemerge as one of the Braves' best pitchers on the farm. He was practically untouchable in a repeat stint at advanced Class A and was impressive in his first six Double-A starts before injury problems.

BRUCE CHEN: The 22-year-old was expected to step into the rotation out of spring training in '99, but he struggled and was moved to the bullpen. Chen still could be the pitcher the Braves thought he would become, possessing a combination of great control and three solid pitches. At this stage, however, continued problems could leave Chen tradable.

MARCUS GILES: The 1998 MVP of the lower-level Class A South Atlantic League dominated in similar fashion in '99, claiming the advanced Class A Carolina League MVP. While the 21-year-old won the batting title by 20 points. The 5'8", 180-pounder has been underrated since being a 53rd-round pick in the '96 draft, but if Giles continues to stand out at every level, he will force the Braves to clear the way for him at second base.

RAFAEL FURCAL: The 19-year-old Furcal didn't break stride after setting the Appalachian League record with 60 stolen bases in 1998. He swiped 96 bases between two Class A levels in '99, most in the minors in 12 years. He also shined in his first season at shortstop. The switch-hitting Furcal has all the tools of an ideal leadoff hitter but he still has to prove himself at the higher levels of the minors, so his presence won't be felt in the majors until probably 2002.

ATLANTA

TOP PROSPECTS

Throughout the '90s, the Atlanta Braves have flashed an abundance of pitching depth, which has made them the most successful team of the decade. They managed to replace their closer in two consecutive seasons without having to make a trade.

The same cannot be said for the positional-player base, as the wealth of pitching was needed to lure key players up the middle. Prior to the start of the 1999 season, pitching depth allowed the Braves to deal Denny Neagle and RHP **ROB BELL**, a top prospect, to the Reds in exchange for Bret Boone, filling a glaring hole at second base. The depth also facilitated the trade of LHP **MICAH BOWIE** and RHP **RUBEN QUEVADA** to the Cubs for Terry Mulholland and Jose Hernandez.

Even with the deals draining some of the pitching talent, the Braves appear well stocked heading into the new millennium. Although the coming-out party for LHP **BRUCE CHEN** was postponed, RHP **KEVIN McGLINCHY** stepped forward and proved he belonged in the big leagues. Twenty-one-year-old LHP **ODALIS PEREZ** struggled at times but displayed the stuff that will make him a force once he fully matures. Perez has a nasty curveball in addition to a mid-90s fastball. RHP **JASON MARQUIS** rebounded from a 2-12 record in '98 to dominate in advanced Class A before getting the call to Double-A. Marquis, who battled injuries in the Southern League, has a moving fastball that tops out in the mid-90s when he's healthy.

RHP **LUIS RIVERA**, a hard thrower, leads the lower-level pitching with tremendous upside. Rivera, who had sporadic back problems in 1998, averaged 10.88 strikeouts per nine innings in the '99 regular season and fanned 23 over 12 scoreless frames in the post-season. Once this 21-year-old learns to effectively use his supplementary pitches, he could be a staff ace in waiting. RHPs **SCOTT SOBKOWIAK** and **WINSTON ABREU** emerged as promising pitching talents with strong arms and good numbers at Class A. Sobkowiak ranked third in the advanced Class A Carolina League in ERA and second in strikeouts, while Abreu went 7–2, 1.69 ERA in lower-level Class A before joining Sobkowiak at Myrtle Beach. LHP **JIMMY OSTING**, Abreu's staffmate the first three months of the season, set a Macon franchise record with 14 wins. Nineteen-year-old LHP **JONG BONG**, a native of Korea, also looked impressive at times in the Class A South Atlantic League.

2B **MARCUS GILES** heads the list—very short compared to the pitching list—of everyday players with a chance. Giles (younger brother of Pittsburgh's Brian) followed up an MVP campaign in the South Atlantic League in '98 with another MVP in the advanced Class A Carolina League in '99, earning a spot on the HOWE SPORTSDATA All-Prospect Team. Though he doesn't possess a prototypical star's physique, Marcus's numbers cannot be ignored. Nineteen-year-old SS **RAFAEL FURCAL** stole 96 bases last season and has solid all-around tools. 3B **TROY CAMERON**, drafted as a shortstop, cut his errors down but failed to prove he could hit consistently in a repeat season at lower-level Class A.

The Braves still have high hopes for talented OF **GEORGE LOMBARD**, who emerged as a top minor-league prospect in 1998 but struggled terribly at Triple-A last season, batting .206 while battling hamstring problems.

LF
*REGGIE SANDERS 32
- ○ *George Lombard ML 24 94/2H
- ? *Adam Johnson 3A 24 96/55C
- ? Jeff Spencer A+ 23 95/ND

CF
ANDRUW JONES 23
- ○ #Tyrone Pendergrass 2A 23 95/NDC
- ? Junior Brignac A+ 22 96/3H

RF
BRIAN JORDAN 33
- ? Jason Ross A+ 26 96/13C
- ○ *Ryan Langerhans A- 20 98/3H

SS
#WALT WEISS 36
- *OZZIE GUILLEN 36
- ○ Mark DeRosa ML 25 96/7C
- ↑ #Rafael Furcal A+ 19 96/ND

2B
#QUILVIO VERAS 29
- *KEITH LOCKHART 35
- ? Glenn Williams 2A 22 93/ND
- ↑ Marcus Giles A+ 22 96/50C
- ○ Travis Wilson A- 22 96/NDH

3B
#CHIPPER JONES 28
- HOWARD BATTLE 28
- ? Mike Hessman A+ 22 96/15H
- ○ #Troy Cameron A- 21 97/1H
- ○ Asdrubal Oropeza A- 19 96/ND

1B
ANDRES GALARRAGA 39
- *WALLY JOYNER 38
- *RANDALL SIMON 25
- BRIAN HUNTER 32
- ? Wes Helms 2A 24 94/10H
- ○ Ryan Lehr A+ 21 97/8H
- ? *A.J. Zapp A- 22 96/1H

SP/RP

C
JAVY LOPEZ 29
- EDDIE PEREZ 32
- *JORGE FABREGAS 30
- ? Fernando Lunar 2A 23 94/ND

RELIEVERS
- *JOHN ROCKER 25
- *MIKE REMLINGER 34
- *TERRY MULHOLLAND 37
- KEVIN McGLINCHY 23
- KERRY LIGTENBERG 29
- ? Dave Cortes ML 26 96/ND
- ? Joe Nelson 3A 25 96/4C
- ? Ismael Villegas 3A 23 95/5H
- ? Jacob Shumate 2A 24 94/1H
- ? Adrian Manzano 2A 21 96/ND
- ? Delvis Pacheco A+ 22 94/ND
- ↑ Luis Rivera A+ 22 95/ND

STARTERS
- GREG MADDUX 34
- JOHN SMOLTZ 33
- *TOM GLAVINE 34
- KEVIN MILLWOOD 25
- *ODALIS PEREZ 22
- ○ *Darrin Ebert ML 23 94/18H
- ↑ *Bruce Chen ML 23 93/ND
- ↑ Jason Marquis 2A 21 96/1H
- ○ Winston Abreu A+ 23 93/ND
- ? Derrick Lewis A+ 24 97/20C
- ○ Scott Sobkowiak A+ 22 98/7C
- ? *Damian Moss 2A 23 93/ND
- ? *Jimmy Osting A- 23 95/4H
- ↑ *Jung Bong A- 19 97/ND

MAJOR LEAGUERS IN ALL CAPS
Minor leaguers in upper-and-lower case

BEFORE A PLAYER'S NAME:
* left-handed hitter/pitcher
# switch-hitter
?=prospect status (see explanation)

AFTER A PLAYER'S NAME:
Level at which he spent most of 1999 season; age as of July 1, 2000; year he was drafted; round drafted (ND= non-drafted amateur free agent); drafted out of high school (H) or college (C)

EXPLANATION OF PROSPECT RATINGS.

★ Potential big-league star

↑ Projected regular player in majors (for pitchers: rotation starter or closer)

○ Projected platoon or utility player in majors (pitcher: setup or middle relief)

? Possible big-league reserve or long reliever

↓ High draft pick or "tools" player who hasn't performed to expectations

ATLANTA

FLORIDA MARLINS

Management
Manager	John Boles
G.M.	Dave Dombrowski
President/CEO	John Henry

Career Record
104–133 / .439
628–753 / .455
64–98 / .395

1999 Record
Won–Lost	Pct.	Finish/G.B. (Division)	Finish/G.B. (Wild Card)
64–98	.395	5/39 (E)	13/32.5

Preseason Consensus Projection
5 (4.90)

1st Half	2nd Half	Home	Road	Intradivision	Interleague
27–51	37–47	35–45	29–53	24–36	11–7

Comebacks	Blowouts	Nail-Biters	Grass	Turf	Sept.–Oct.
11–10	14–32	34–43	52–80	12–18	11–19

NUMBERS DON'T LIE

	Team (Rank)	Opponents (Rank)	League Avg.
Runs/Game	4.27 (16)	5.26 (12)	5.00
Batting Avg.	.263 (12)	.281 (13)	.268
On-Base Avg.	.325 (15)	.359 (15)	.342
Slugging Avg.	.395 (15)	.441 (12)	.429
Strikeouts	1145 (12)	943 (16)	1072
Home Runs	128 (16)	171 (7)	181
Stolen Bases	92 (12)	94 (2)	122
ERA	4.90 (12)		4.57
Errors	127 (9)		120

▶ THE INSIDER 2000

MARLIN FISHING

The best that can be said about the 1999 Marlins is that they didn't lose 108 games again (they lost only 98), that they continued stockpiling minor-league prospects via trades for their veterans, and that their young players got valuable big-league experience. Otherwise, the team was simply treading water, waiting for new owner John Henry to put together a viable plan for a baseball-only ballpark that would ensure the team's future.

Of course, prospects are not the established major leaguers that fans come out to see—and Miami fans didn't have much to root for in '99. As catcher, strong-armed sophomore Mike Redmond hit .302 with a .381 on-base percentage, but had absolutely no power; Jorge Fabregas was virtually an automatic out. At first, Derrek Lee flopped miserably; at 24, he could make a comeback but probably isn't going to be a top hitter. Kevin Millar, 28, was a creditable stand-in for Lee but isn't regular material. At second, Luis Castillo hit .302 with a fine .384 on-base percentage, though with no power. Shortstop Alex Gonzalez, 23, had a promising but schizoid season. At third, Mike Lowell, 26, came back from cancer in '99; he should hit better by gaining strength and experience. In left field, Cliff Floyd again showed his power bat, but spent half the year on the DL. Center fielder Preston Wilson was very impressive; right fielder Mark Kotsay wasn't, though he's only 24 and could improve.

The Marlins' starting staff has plenty of promise and lots to prove in 2000. Alex Fernandez needs to show he can handle a full-season workload. Ryan Dempster (age 24), Brian Meadows (24), and Vladimir Nunez (25) need to use their '99 experience to improve their performance. A. J. Burnett needs to prove his seven starts (3.48 ERA) weren't a fluke. The '99 relief corps was a mess and may well be again this year. Fortunately, the Florida system is deep in good, young arms.

THE EXPANSION DRAFT: MANY ARE CHOSEN, BUT FEW SUCCEED

On November 17, 1992, the fledgling Florida Marlins and Colorado Rockies participated in an expansion draft to stock their rosters for big-league action. At the time, most believed that the Marlins had done a good job, drafting highly

MOMENT OF TRUTH

The Marlins upset many fans when they traded closer Matt Mantei to Arizona on "Matt Mantei Pin Night." After the deal, Mantei saved 22 games in 25 chances for Arizona, while Antonio Alfonseca stepped up and saved 21 games in 25 chances for Florida. It's true the bullpen would be stronger with Alfonseca in a setup role, but the club has many young arms it can groom for that job. Those players the Marlins got from the Diamondbacks for Mantei should play major roles in the next year or two. Vladimir Nunez was decent in 12 starts for the Marlins and still has a lot of upside. Brad Penny is a top prospect who pitched well in the Arizona Fall League and could make the starting rotation out of spring training this year.

BIGGEST SURPRISE

Alex Fernandez bounced back after missing the entire 1998 season to pitch well in '99. Expectations weren't high for Fernandez, who had major reconstructive surgery on his right shoulder. But he showed his career wasn't finished. Even though he didn't have the old zip on his fastball, he pitched well enough to keep the Marlins in the game most of the time. He went on the DL twice, first with a groin pull and then with a sore shoulder that ended his year early. The Marlins believe he'll have no setbacks during the 2000 season.

BIGGEST DISAPPOINTMENT

Shortstop Alex Gonzalez had an outstanding first half of the season but nearly disappeared after the All-Star break. Gonzalez hit .291 with 19 doubles, nine homers, and 39 RBI in the first half, but became moody as the season wore on and his production fell off. His lack of hustle irritated manager John Boles, who benched the youngster twice in the second half. The Marlins desperately need Gonzalez to become their starter, so they're hoping that the 23-year-old got the message.

---

regarded players lauded by scouts for their tools, while the Rockies had chosen a bunch of older guys, some who were good and some who were stiffs.

USA TODAY Baseball Weekly put the contrasting drafts in perspective in its November 19, 1992 issue:

"The two expansion franchises were on such separate wavelengths that Marlins officials contend that they never lost a particular player they wanted directly to the Rockies."

"We knew right then [during the expansion draft] that things were going to work out far better than we expected," said Marlins GM Dave Dombrowski on draft day. The *Baseball Weekly* article stressed that the Rockies went for "experience" while the Marlins went for "prospects."

A funny thing happened on the way to fame and fortune for Dombrowski. Despite a World Series title for Florida in 1997, the Marlins' young talent bombed, and the Rockies' talent blossomed.

Certainly some of Colorado's selections were failures (e.g., first-round choices Kevin Reimer, Jerald Clark, and Alex Cole); but, at the same time, the Rockies also snagged Andy Ashby, Eric Young, Charlie Hayes, Joe Girardi, and Darren Holmes. Despite failures of high-profile picks such as David Nied and Jayhawk Owens, the Rocks drafted several excellent big leaguers. Colorado selected Vinny Castilla in the second round and chose Brad Ausmus, Armando Reynoso, Steve Reed, and Curt Leskanic in the third.

Meanwhile, the Marlins went for young outfielders. Remember how the first-round picks of Nigel Wilson, Darrell Whitmore, Chuck Carr, and Jesus Tavarez and second-rounder Carl Everett were supposed to be astute? Of all those highly regarded youngsters, only Everett turned into a good player—but only after the Marlins and the Mets had given up on him.

In fact, Florida's draft turned out to be more of a disaster than a bright beginning. The only quality players the Marlins got in the draft were pitchers John Johnstone, Jim Corsi, Pat Rapp, and Trevor Hoffman, and outfielders Jeff Conine and Everett. Other picks, such as outfielder Monty Fariss, catcher Steve Decker, and pitchers Kip Yaughn, Scott Chiamparino, Ryan Bowen, and Jack Armstrong, bombed. The Marlins also took veteran closer Bryan Harvey, who had just one good year before he blew out his elbow.

The Marlins' picks did not play up to expectations, but how do they look compared to those other other expansion clubs? Expansion picks can't be rated just by how they did in their first year; plenty of picks, both kids and veterans, had one good year before fading. Trying to measure long-term value, "quality" players are defined as having two or more years left of above-average regular play in the majors.

For example, "Coco" Laboy, a 30-year-old rookie, hit 18 homers for the Expos in 1969, then faded quickly. Not a "quality" player. Dick Donovan won the ERA title for the 1961 Senators, then won 20 in '62 for Cleveland. He counts. Gil Hodges doesn't, despite his previous great years, because he was finished a year after being drafted by the Mets. Eddie Yost, a 1961 Angels pick, also doesn't count: It's not what a player did before being drafted, it's what he did afterward.

The Seattle Mariners and the Toronto Blue Jays began play in 1977. The only real values the Mariners got were pitcher Glenn Abbott, second baseman Julio Cruz, reserve infielders Steve Braun and Bill Stein, and outfielders Ruppert Jones and Dave Collins. Most of Seattle's players made literally no impact in the big leagues.

The Blue Jays went for youth in 1977, selecting pitchers Jerry Garvin, Jim Clancy, and Pete Vuckovich; catcher Ernie Whitt; infielders Bob Bailor and Garth Iorg; and outfielder Otto Velez. Three of them (Clancy, Whitt, and Iorg) were still around when the Jays became contenders in the 1980s. Vuckovich won the AL Cy Young award in Milwaukee in 1982.

In 1969 the Kansas City Royals and the Seattle Pilots were hatched. Kansas City, a franchise that subsequently developed a proud tradition of producing excellent young players, snagged a fair amount of talent in their draft, including pitchers Jim Rooker, Dick Drago, Al Fitzmorris, and Tom Burgmeier; catchers Ellie Rodriguez and Fran Healy; infielders Bob Oliver and Paul Schaal; and outfielder Pat Kelly. They also picked up veteran reliever Moe Drabowsky, who still had some good seasons left in him.

Even the Pilots, a terrible team that remained bad after moving to Milwaukee, netted plenty of major leaguers. Pitchers Marty Pattin, Mike Marshall, Diego Segui, Jack Aker, and Skip Lockwood; first baseman Don Mincher; and outfielders Tommy Harper, Tommy Davis, and Lou Piniella were drafted by Seattle. Piniella and Marshall became stars after leaving Milwaukee.

In 1969 the National League also welcomed the Montreal Expos and San Diego Padres—two clubs that were horrid for years. The Expos didn't harvest much young talent at all, going mostly for established veterans. Their long-term picks were pitchers Bill Stoneman, Jack Billingham, Ernie McAnally, and Carl Morton, and outfielders Manny Mota and Jay Alou.

San Diego went mostly for kids, augmenting veteran hurler

SECRET WEAPON

Heading into spring training, Preston Wilson was ticketed for Triple-A, but his play toward the end of the Grapefruit League season won him a spot on the Marlins as a reserve outfielder. Once Todd Dunwoody showed he still hadn't learned how to hit big-league pitching, Wilson got his chance and never looked back. He showed good power and decent speed; while he still needs to improve his defense, he was more than good enough to take Dunwoody's job permanently.

ACHILLES HEEL

Other than Alfonseca and Braden Looper, there weren't many bright spots in Florida's bullpen. Left-handers Vic Darensbourg and Jesus Sanchez were considered two of the biggest failures. Neither was able to consistently get out lefty batters, and Darensbourg, especially, was worthless against righties, who hit .413 against him. Their woes put even more pressure on an already young and inexperienced pen, who couldn't handle the strain. Right-hander Brian Edmondson blew six saves, and youngsters Rafael Medina and Hector Almonte struggled to find any consistency.

ENOUGH ALREADY

When John Henry was in the process of buying the Marlins, he said that he would pay out of his own pocket, if necessary, to get a new, baseball-only ballpark for the team. Henry knew that former owner Wayne Huizenga's blunt and brutal threats in his campaign to get a publicly funded park had alienated a majority of South Florida's baseball fans and taxpayers. Now that he owns the team, Henry is out there pitching for—you guessed it—public financing for a new park. As a sweetener, Henry magnanimously announced in early November that he was willing to return to the community 90 percent of the putative profits generated by any taxpayer-subsidized park. Henry told the *Miami Herald* that he was "still developing the profit-sharing concept and, for that reason, he hasn't formally presented it." Memo to Mr. Henry: If you're serious, get specific. If not, stop floating trial balloons and polluting the debate about the propriety of public financing.

Dave Giusti with young pitchers Dick Selma, Clay Kirby, Steve Arlin, and Dave Roberts; first baseman Nate Colbert; and outfielders Cito Gaston, Jerry Morales, and Ollie Brown. For an expansion draft, that was a high yield.

In the NL in 1962, the Houston Colt .45s took pitchers Dick Farrell, Ken Johnson, and Jim Umbricht; infielders Joe Amalfitano, Bob Aspromonte, and Eddie Bressoud; and outfielder Al Spangler. There was depth but not much impact talent. Most of the players the Colts chose were veterans who had at best one good year left, or else prospects who had failed elsewhere and who also failed for Houston.

The New York Mets, in a disastrous draft, focused mostly on veterans, then suffered grievously on the field for that choice. The first player they chose was Hobie Landrith. A few of their picks, such as pitchers Bob Miller, Al Jackson, and Roger Craig; catcher Chris Cannizzaro; infielder Felix Mantilla; and outfielder Jim Hickman, had good years.

There are two critical points to consider when looking at expansion drafts across the years. First, the quality of players available in expansion drafts has increased over the years. The rules have changed significantly since the early days of expansion. Back then, the players available were truly the dregs of most clubs' systems.

The current availability of talent is the main reason why the Marlins' draft looks so bad in hindsight. They had the opportunity to scout everyone and had the resources to build a contending team—but they couldn't. The Rockies, on the other hand, got plenty of talent and were successful initially. That they could not mold that talent into a good team in the long run is another matter.

BEST CASE

Florida's lineup is inexperienced almost everywhere; when Cliff Floyd is the senior member, itís a young team. The talent is there. However, this organization has had to make so many salary-related deals that establishing any sort of consistent approach has been impossible.

Opportunity exists for these talented youngsters to grab jobs and become All Stars, but this season, even a .500 record seems like pie-in-the-sky. However, if Mark Kotsay and Mike Lowell can break out, and Preston Wilson, A.J. Burnett, and Braden Looper contribute the way the Marlins believe they can, this will be an interesting team.

WORST CASE

The current Marlins club has some fine kids, but few impact players (although Burnett and Wilson are encouraging). The high-profile prospects expected to blossom must make their moves this year or be left behind. The front office has made some strange, hard-to-fathom deals in the off-season, acquiring Brant Brown and Dan Miceli for Bruce Aven and Brian Meadows. While continuing to sort out the talent, the Fish could drop 100 games.

UNDER THE MICROSCOPE

A. J. BURNETT: The 23-year-old's fearless style and impressive assortment of pitches paved the way for a breakout year in '98, but he stumbled at Double-A in '99. More frequent use of his sharp breaking ball and change-up, in addition to better movement on the fastball, should land Burnett with the big club this spring.

BRAD PENNY: Penny followed a dominant Class A performance in 1998 with struggles at Double-A in '99. He was 2–7, 4.80 ERA in 17 Texas League starts prior to being obtained from Arizona. Penny battled shoulder tendinitis early but appeared healthy by the time he joined the Marlins organization, pitching well in five of six starts. The 21-year-old has a low-to-mid-90s fastball and good curve and change-up offerings. He will need another full year in the minors, however.

JULIO RAMIREZ: Billed as having five-tool capabilities, Ramirez impressed mostly with his speed and defense in the Double-A Eastern League. He led the circuit with 64 stolen bases and tied for second with 14 outfield assists. The 22-year-old's BB/SO and ground ball/fly ball ratios need to improve for him to become a productive leadoff hitter.

PABLO OZUNA: After posting astounding numbers at lower-level Class A in 1998, Ozuna skipped advanced Class A in '99. While the 21-year-old held his own with the bat, he owned a paltry .315 on-base average and did not show the arm and range of a potential major-league shortstop.

FLORIDA

TOP PROSPECTS

Since winning the 1997 World Series, the Marlins have gone through a drastic overhaul of personnel, both on and off the field. The translation has been a hapless product at the major-league level but a tremendous amount of highly touted talent on its way up. The organization has more first-round picks scattered throughout the system than any other, and has been able to inject plenty of its youngsters into the majors due to the lack of veterans. Doors were opened for SS **ALEX GONZALEZ**, OF **PRESTON WILSON**, OF **KEVIN MILLAR**, 2B **LUIS CASTILLO**, 3B **MIKE LOWELL**, and RHP **BRADEN LOOPER** to make lasting impressions at the big-league level. Despite another season with many more losses than wins, the Marlins' youth, both in the majors and below, has given hope for a competitive team within the next few years.

The biggest surplus as a result of the budget-awareness trading has been in the area of pitching. RHPs **VLADIMIR NUNEZ**, **BRAD PENNY**, **JASON GRILLI**, and **NATE BUMP** headline the list of quality hurlers acquired in 1999 alone. Nunez impressed the big club, while Penny was involved in a combined no-hitter in his first start in the minors. Grilli and Bump, both first-round picks of the Giants, didn't put up good numbers in '99 but are regarded as having great potential.

In 1998, RHP **A. J. BURNETT**, acquired in the Al Leiter deal, emerged as a dominant pitcher at the Class A level. Though he had trouble with location at Double-A in '99, Burnett enjoyed success in his stint with the major-league club and remains one of their best pitching prospects. LHP **GEOFF GOETZ**, received from New York for Mike Piazza, and RHP **JOE FONTENOT**, traded by San Francisco for Robb Nen, both are former first-round picks who battled shoulder problems in '99 but should rebound. Further down, LHP **SCOTT COMER**, picked up in the deal that sent Dennis Cook to the Mets, ranked second with a 2.35 ERA in the advanced Class A Florida State League.

The Marlins also have talented, homegrown arms in stock. LHP **MICHAEL TEJERA**, a sixth-round pick in 1995, was a standout in Double-A, posting the best ERA in Portland's franchise history at 2.62. The 22-year-old former member of the Cuban Junior National Team is more of a crafty lefty than anything else, however. RHP **WES ANDERSON** stepped forward as the best right-hander at the lower levels of the minors. The 20-year-old Anderson, selected in the 14th round in '97, has gone 14-7, 2.63 ERA with 200 strikeouts in his first 202 professional innings. RHP **JOSH BECKETT**, selected second overall in the '99 draft, signed too late and will begin his pro career in 2000.

The Marlins also have put together a solid supply of position players in the farm system. In addition to the array of first-year major-leaguers in '99, C **RAMON CASTRO**, 2B **AMAURY GARCIA**, SS **PABLO OZUNA**, and OF **JULIO RAMIREZ** are all highly regarded and are not too far away. Castro, acquired from the Astros in '98, has good offensive skills and a strong arm behind the plate. Garcia has good speed, some power, and improving defense. Ozuna, acquired along with Looper in the Edgar Renteria deal with St. Louis, has raw talent but drew just 15 walks in 538 plate appearances in '99. Ramirez, who is still developing his five-tool potential, may turn out to be the best of the bunch.

CF
PRESTON WILSON 25
*TODD DUNWOODY 25
↑ Julio Ramirez ML 22 94/ND
↑ Chip Ambres A- 20 98/1H

LF
CLIFF FLOYD 27
BRUCE AVEN 28
? #Fletcher Bates 2A 26 93/5H

RF
MARK KOTSAY 24
DANNY BAUTISTA 28
? *Jaime Jones 3A 23 95/1H
? *Brett Roneberg A- 21 96/ND

SS
ALEX GONZALEZ 23
↑ Pablo Ozuna 2A 21 96/ND
? #Derek Wathan A- 23 98/2C

2B
#LUIS CASTILLO 24
DAVE BERG 29
○ Amaury Garcia ML 25 92/ND
? Raul Franco 3A 24 93/NDC
? *Matt Erickson 2A 24 97/7C
○ #Cesar Crespo A+ 21 97/3H
? Jesus Medrano A- 21 97/11H

3B
MIKE LOWELL 26
#CHRIS CLAPINSKI 28
○ Joe Funaro 2A 27 95/21C
○ Jose Santo A- 22 95/ND

1B
KEVIN MILLAR 28
DERREK LEE 24
? *Nate Rolison 2A 23 95/2H
? *Ross Gload A+ 24 97/13C

SP/RP

RELIEVERS
ANTONIO ALFONSECA 28
DAN MICELI 29
BRADEN LOOPER 25
*JESUS SANCHEZ 25
BRIAN EDMONDSON 27
*VIC DARENSBOURG 29
○ Hector Almonte ML 24 93/NDH
? Nelson Lara A- 21 94/ND
○ *Armando Almanza ML 27 93/21C

C
MIKE REDMOND 29
○ Ramon Castro ML 24 94/1H
? Matt Treanor A- 24 94/4H
○ Jeff Bailey A- 21 97/2H

STARTERS
RYAN DEMPSTER 23
ALEX FERNANDEZ 30
VLADIMIR NUNEZ 25
REID CORNELIUS 30
↑ A.J. Burnett ML 23 95/8C
○ Jason Grilli 3A 23 97/1C
? Joe Fontenot 3A 23 95/1H
○ Nate Bump 2A 23 98/1C
↑ Brad Penny 2A 22 96/5H
? Bobby Rodgers 2A 25 95/17C
○ Gary Knotts 2A 23 95/11C
↑ Wes Anderson A- 20 97/14H
↓ Josh Beckett DP 19 99/1H
○ *Michael Tejera ML 23 95/6H
? *Ryan Moskau A+ 22 98/6C
○ *Scott Comer A+ 23 96/10H
↓ *Geoff Goetz A- 21 97/1H

MAJOR LEAGUERS IN ALL CAPS
Minor leaguers in upper-and-lower case

BEFORE A PLAYER'S NAME:
* left-handed hitter/pitcher
# switch-hitter
?=prospect status (see explanation)

AFTER A PLAYER'S NAME:
Level at which he spent most of 1999 season; age as of July 1, 2000; year he was drafted; round drafted (ND= non-drafted amateur free agent); drafted out of high school (H) or college (C)

EXPLANATION OF PROSPECT RATINGS

★ Potential big-league star

↑ Projected regular player in majors (for pitchers: rotation starter or closer)

○ Projected platoon or utility player in majors (pitcher: setup or middle reliever)

? Possible big-league reserve or long reliever

↓ High draft pick or "tools" player who hasn't performed to expectations

FLORIDA

MONTREAL EXPOS

MANAGEMENT
Manager	Felipe Alou
G.M.	Jim Beattie
President/CEO	Claude Brochu

CAREER RECORD
603–590 / .505
299–349 / .461
620–610 / .504

1999 RECORD
Won–Lost	Pct.	Finish/G.B. (Division)	Finish/G.B. (Wild Card)
68–94	.420	4/35 (E)	11/28.5

PRESEASON CONSENSUS PROJECTION
4 (3.90)

1ST HALF	2ND HALF	HOME	ROAD	INTRADIVISION	INTERLEAGUE
30–44	38–50	35–46	33–48	23–36	8–10

COMEBACKS	BLOWOUTS	NAIL-BITERS	GRASS	TURF	SEPT.–OCT.
10–9	17–36	34–36	23–34	45–60	12–18

NUMBERS DON'T LIE

	TEAM (RANK)	OPPONENTS (RANK)	LEAGUE AVG.
Runs/Game	4.43 (14)	5.27 (13)	5.00
Batting Avg.	.265 (11)	.270 (11)	.268
On-Base Avg.	.323 (16)	.342 (8)	.342
Slugging Avg.	.427 (8)	.418 (6)	.429
Strikeouts	939 (2)	1043 (10)	1072
Home Runs	163 (13)	152 (3)	181
Stolen Bases	70 (14)	157 (14)	122
ERA	4.69 (9)		4.57
Errors	160 (16)		120

▶ THE INSIDER 2000

YOUPPI! LES EXPOS SONT LA!

Thirty years after their debut season ended—after 30 months of controversy, doubt, and recrimination—the Montreal Expos found out that they had a future again. In November 1999, major-league Baseball approved a plan for restructuring Montreal's ownership group, recapitalizing the team and putting into motion a viable plan to build a new downtown ballpark. While details remained to be finalized, Labatt Park was finally a constructive reality; it should open in April 2002.

In a move that was both symbolic and substantive, Stephen Bronfman was appointed as co-chair of the ownership committee. He is the son of Charles Bronfman, who was instrumental in originally bringing the team to Quebec in 1969 and owned it through 1991.

The '99 Expos finished 35 games behind Atlanta, well south of .500. The season was ruined by bad play, bad attendance, and bad feelings about the franchise's future. Montreal also lost its vice president for baseball operations, Bill Stoneman, who became Anaheim's GM after the season ended. However, GM Jim Beattie and manager Felipe Alou remain, faced with the challenge of building yet another contender on smart scouting, player development, and astute trades. This time, at least, they should have a reasonable budget to work with.

BINGING AND PURGING

In the 1990s, the Expos twice built contending teams, only to completely tear them apart for financial reasons. Montreal finished last in the NL East in 1991, but it improved to post the best record in baseball in the strike-shortened 1994 season. After purging the roster of most players for salary reasons, Montreal fell to last again in 1995, then finished second the following season—only to clear the roster of high-priced players for the second time.

Montreal built the 1994 team mostly through its farm system. The majority of players were either drafted by the club or signed as non-drafted free agents in their teens. This was not only true of Latin players like Mel Rojas and Wil Cordero, but also true of Canadian Larry Walker, signed in 1984 before Canadians became subject to the amateur draft.

The key 1994 players acquired via the draft were Marquis Grissom, a third-round pick in 1988; Cliff Floyd, a first-rounder

MOMENT OF TRUTH

The Expos committed two errors in each of their first three games of the season, and that set the bleak tone for the rest of the year. Vladimir Guerrero made 19 errors in right field, including nine in April; Rondell White made 11 in left and center, and six other players made at least nine miscues during the season. Montreal booted 160 plays on the season, easily the worst in the majors. The porous defense put even more pressure on Montreal's young and beleaguered pitching staff, which had enough trouble rising to the challenge without sloppy support.

BIGGEST SURPRISE

Jose Vidro took advantage of a second chance and had an impressive season. Vidro began 1998 as Montreal's starting second baseman, but severe offensive troubles sent him back to the minors; he wound up hitting only .220. He exploded in '99, boosting his average 84 points while slugging .476, taking the starting second base job away from Wilton Guerrero. The switch hitter tore up right-handed pitchers (.315 BA, 48 extra-base hits in 394 at-bats), and his 45 doubles were 14 more than he'd ever hit in seven previous professional seasons.

BIGGEST DISAPPOINTMENT

Dustin Hermanson's first-half struggles caught nearly everyone by surprise. Hermanson won 22 games in his first two years in Montreal, and his 3.13 ERA in 1998 convinced many he could be the Expos' new ace. Things didn't turn out that way, as the 26-year-old won only three games in the first half, losing 14 by the seasons end. The converted reliever did turn it around in the second half, winning six and posting a 2.95 ERA, but the damage was already done.

in 1991; and Kirk Rueter, a low-round pick in 1991. Mike Lansing was purchased from an independent minor-league club. Most of the rest were obtained in trades. Montreal obtained Moises Alou from the Pirates in a multiplayer deal for Zane Smith in 1990; got Ken Hill in a 1991 trade with St. Louis for Andres Galarraga; traded Willie Greene and Dave Martinez for John Wetteland after 1991; dealt Delino DeShields to Los Angeles for 22-year-old Pedro Martinez after 1993 season; and got catcher Darrin Fletcher, third baseman Sean Berry, and pitcher Butch Henry in other minor deals. Jeff Fassero was signed as a minor-league free agent in 1991.

The DeShields trade, in particular, showed how astute Montreal management was. While driven by salary considerations, the Expos traded a player viewed universally as a rising young star at a key position for a pitcher who was then a middle reliever. DeShields completely tanked in L.A. while Martinez instantly became a star.

By 1996, the only key players left from two years earlier were Fletcher, Lansing, Alou, Martinez, Fassero, and Rojas. The Expos were able to make a run at Atlanta that year mostly because their scouting department was so damn good. F.P. Santangelo, Shane Andrews, Mark Grudzielanek, and Rondell White all were drafted between 1989 and 1991, and Ugueth Urbina was signed as a non-drafted free agent. Popular slugger Henry Rodriguez and other valuable players like David Segui, Rheal Cormier, Omar Daal, and Dave Veres were acquired via sharp trading.

Afterward, Montreal purged most of its best players from the '96 squad; only Urbina and White remain with the club. However, the bounty from those trades and draft picks has built the foundation of what the club hopes will become its next contender.

The Expos obtained pitching prospect Ted Lilly and outfield prospect Peter Bergeron, along with Wilton Guerrero, from the Dodgers for Mark Grudzielanek and Carlos Perez. They acquired top pitching prospects Tony Armas Jr. and Carl Pavano in the trade with Boston for Pedro Martinez. Montreal also traded Cliff Floyd to Florida for Dustin Hermanson; dumped Jeff Juden on Cleveland for Steve Kline; sent Jeff Fassero to Seattle for Chris Widger, Trey Moore, and Matt Wagner; and got first base prospect Fernando Seguignol from the Yankees for John Wetteland in one of its least productive deals.

RISKS ARE PART OF THE GAME

There's little doubt that Montreal would be a contender now if it had been able to keep Pedro Martinez, Moises Alou, and Larry Walker. Even retaining two of the three probably would have kept them competitive. Those superstars left the Expos and continued their excellence elsewhere, though that's not been the case for most of the players the club has let go for budgetary reasons in the 1990s.

Marquis Grissom was one of the top center fielders in the league with Montreal. He had a couple of decent years with Atlanta, but then declined to mediocrity in Cleveland and worse in Milwaukee. Cliff Floyd is a good player, but he's been out of the lineup with injuries as much as he's been in it during his three seasons with the Marlins. Wil Cordero, an All-Star in 1994 who was then viewed as a franchise player, had plenty of trouble both on and off the field in Boston; he has never played anywhere near his potential. Mark Grudzielanek has been a disappointment in Los Angeles. Sean Berry was productive in Houston but bombed in Milwaukee last year.

Does this mean the Expos were justified in letting all of those players go? Of course not. What it does illustrate is that signing expensive free agents is quite risky. Unfortunately for struggling franchises, taking some risks is mandatory or a team ends up in a seemingly endless rebuilding cycle, playing in an empty stadium. Worse, that kind of atmosphere can impel many players to demand more money to stick around, and some will leave town as soon as possible regardless of the money offered. A team like Montreal has frequently made the right choice by not re-signing a player like Grissom to a fat, multi-year contract. But other players, like Martinez and Walker, are essentially irreplaceable and require taking a risk to keep the team in contention.

ERECTING THE SCAFFOLDING AGAIN

Because many of the club's best prospects haven't seen much—if any—action in the majors, it's too early to tell if Montreal is poised to contend again in the near future. Much depends on whether the club's current crop of young arms can develop into quality major-league pitchers. Armas, Lilly, and Jeremy Powell are all highly regarded and have the potential to be very good. If

SECRET WEAPON

Michael Barrett provided versatility seldom seen from a rookie. Barrett shuttled between catcher and third base most of the season, but didn't let the lack of a regular position hurt his batting and was equally good offensively at each position. His versatility was no more obvious than in the last home game of the season when he started at catcher and finished the game playing shortstop! Barrett also improved at the plate after the All-Star break, hitting .312 in the second half.

ACHILLES HEEL

The Expos suffered through 1998 with many rookie starters, so the club figured there would be much improvement in '99. That improvement never came for the pitching staff. Dustin Hermanson slumped badly, Carl Pavano's ERA jumped nearly a run and a half, and only Javier Vazquez and Miguel Batista posted winning records as starters. Dan Smith won his major-league debut, giving up three hits and one run over seven innings against the Red Sox, but came back to earth quickly, losing his next five decisions and finishing with a 6.02 ERA.

MONTREAL EXPOS

> **ENOUGH ALREADY**
>
> It seemed that every time a contender lost to the Expos, the reflexive comment was that the Expos were a "tough young team." (e.g., John Rocker on June 30). In reality, the '99 Expos weren't a tough team at all, they were one of the worst teams in the major leagues, with a horrible defense to boot. Teams that lost to these Expos usually played badly and didn't pitch around Vladimir Guerrero. To John Rocker and all those others who cut the Expos way too much slack: Stop making excuses and just admit you were bad.

even two of the three become consistent winners, many of Montreal's problems will be solved.

The team already has one bona fide superstar and marquee player in Vladimir Guerrero. A franchise player at age 24, Vlad is signed through 2003, ensuring that the Expos will have time to develop some complementary players. Along with White, he could form the core of a decent offense, but he can't carry the team to October by himself.

Montreal's offense needs improvement at several positions, especially at the infield corners. Brad Fullmer, 25, didn't improve in '99 and must contribute more at a power position. Michael Barrett, 23, whom the Expos need to install permanently at either catcher or third base, is highly regarded. If he can become an impact player as he gains experience, the future looks a lot brighter. Bergeron, 22, has the potential to develop into a quality leadoff hitter and should add some power as he matures. Milton Bradley, also 22, is developing some power in the high minors and shouldn't be more than a year away from moving into Montreal's outfield.

Montreal has justifiably taken a lot of heat in the 1990s, from both fans and the media, for letting every good player it developed go when he came due for a substantial salary via arbitration or free agency. That changed somewhat in the late '90s when the club signed White, Urbina, and Guerrero to long-term deals; but, by then, it was too late to diffuse the pervasive doom-and-gloom atmosphere.

The next two years will tell if these youngsters are going to develop into the players that can put *Les Expos* back in the pennant chase. The club probably isn't going to go out and sign any big-name free agents for a year or two, but with new ownership and a new ballpark on the horizon, holding on to most of the players the franchise develops seems more than a reasonable expectation.

New ownership, smart management, and a new home won't necessarily turn potential into performance. But a new era in Montreal baseball has now dawned, with the promise that the binge-and-purge days of the '90s will be left behind.

BEST CASE

New owner Jeffrey Loria's purchase of the team bodes well for the future. How much, if any, improvement the Expos make this season depends on the club's trio of young arms. Hurlers Antonio Armas, Ted Lilly, and Jeremy Powell have impressive minor-league résumés, but this season will be their first real test in the bigs. Montreal has a lot riding on those three arms, as well as on the bat and glove of center fielder Peter Bergeron. If the kids contribute in a meaningful way, the Expos could be the surprise team in the league. It's too much to expect the team to approach .500, but a 10- or 12-game improvement isn't out of the question.

WORST CASE

The Expos will be in a world of hurt if their pitching doesn't improve. Vladimir Guerrero, Rondell White, and Michael Barrett can carry the team only so far, and it's not fair to ask them to outscore the opposition every night. Montreal desperately needs Carl Pavano and Dustin Hermanson to pitch to their abilities. Hermanson, especially, was awful the first half of last season. It will be hard enough for the young pitchers to stay focused if the rest of the starting staff isn't providing any support. As bad as the Expos were last year, it won't take much for them to slip past Florida and into the cellar of the NL East.

UNDER THE MICROSCOPE

PETER BERGERON: Bergeron has all the tools to be a solid contributor with the big club starting in 2000. With good speed and a strong arm, the 22-year-old can make all the plays in center field and has the makings of an ideal leadoff guy. He is an accomplished bunter, knows how to work the count in his favor, and can steal a base.

MILTON BRADLEY: The 21-year-old switch-hitter, who played the entire season at Double-A, hit above .300 from both sides in 1999 and brought his overall career average to .299. After a full season at Triple-A this year, he should make his mark in the Expos' outfield in 2001.

ANTONIO ARMAS: The 21-year-old Armas followed up a stellar 1998 campaign in advanced Class A with similar results at the Double-A level in '99. The son of former major-leaguer Tony Armas, Antonio has two great pitches in a sinking fastball that hits the mid-90s and a late-breaking slider. He may need another full year in the minors.

TED LILLY: With parts of two seasons at the Triple-A level under his belt, the 24-year-old Lilly is ready to make the jump to the big leagues. Lilly has a good moving fastball, but his best pitch is the curve. He was roughed up a bit in his brief stint in the majors in '99 and underwent minor arthroscopic surgery on his pitching shoulder in the off-season. If Lilly returns to full strength as expected, he could become a reliable starter for the Expos this season.

MONTREAL

TOP PROSPECTS

With one of the smallest payrolls in baseball during the '90s, the Expos have had one of the best farm systems in the game but have been forced to trade it or lose it to free agency. The result has been an abundance of highly regarded minor-leaguers and additional draft picks.

The system is now stocked with quality pitchers and some multidimensional position players at every level of the minor leagues. Entering the new millennium with a new majority owner and a higher payroll, the franchise will have a much better chance of retaining its talent as it matures into a competitive major-league product.

The upper crust of the pitching depth, which can be expected to surface in the majors within the next year or two, includes RHP **ANTONIO ARMAS**, and LHP **TED LILLY**. Armas, acquired from the Red Sox along with Carl Pavano in the Pedro Martinez deal, ranked third in the Double-A Eastern League with a 2.89 ERA last season before getting his feet wet in the majors. Lilly, the best lefty in the system, struggled with his control during his brief major-league tenure but has the stuff of a quality starter. Not far behind is RHP **T.J. TUCKER**, one of several products of the '97 draft showing promise with the Expos. Tucker, selected 47th overall, was nothing short of dominant in the advanced Class A Florida State League in '99. The 21-year-old did not give up a run in his first $24\frac{2}{3}$ innings and was 5–1 with a 1.23 ERA when promoted to Double-A. Tucker proceeded to give up a total of five runs in his first seven starts at Harrisburg before hitting the wall. LHP **MATT BLANK**, an 11th-round pick, followed up an impressive '98 season with 15 victories and a 3.14 ERA between the Florida State and Eastern Leagues in '99. RHPs **DONNIE BRIDGES**, **BRYAN HEBSON**, **SHANE ARTHURS**, and **MARK MAGNUM**, and LHP **RYAN BECKS**—all taken within the first eight rounds of the '97 draft—have shown some promise in the lower levels of the minors.

In the outfield, **PETER BERGERON** looks to be nearly ready for the big leagues, while **MILTON BRADLEY** may be a year away. Bergeron, acquired from Los Angeles in the deal for Mark Grudzielanek, could take over as both the everyday center fielder and leadoff batter. Bradley, who won the Eastern League championship for Harrisburg with a ninth-inning grand slam, handled Double-A pitching very well in '99 and has good tools. OF **BRAD WILKERSON**, a supplemental first-round pick in '98, spent his first full professional campaign at Double-A and tied the Harrisburg record for walks drawn in a season with 88.

Although the Expos are a bit thin around the infield, there are still a handful of players who have a chance. 3B **ANDY TRACY**, who posted tremendous power numbers in the Eastern League, and 3B **JOSE FERNANDEZ** may be given a crack at the hot corner out of spring training. The key variable is whether the Expos would rather use **MICHAEL BARRETT** there or as a full-time catcher. The organization also has a backstop with solid all-around skills in **BRIAN SCHNEIDER**, who impressed at the Double-A level in '99. The best prospect up the middle is SS **TOMAS DELAROSA**, who is a gifted and reliable fielder with excellent speed. 1B **FERNANDO SEGUIGNOL** is a 6'5" switch-hitter with great power and a good feel for first base, but he may not hit consistently enough to play every day.

▶ THE INSIDER 2000

LF
RONDELL WHITE 28
JAMES MOUTON 31

CF
MANNY MARTINEZ 29
↑ *Peter Bergeron ML 22 96/4H
○ #Milton Bradley 2A 22 96/2H

RF
VLADIMIR GUERRERO 24
○ *Brad Wilkerson 2A 23 98/1C

SS
ORLANDO CABRERA 25
#GEOFF BLUM 27
○ Tomas DelaRosa 2A 22 95/ND
? #Albenis Machado A- 21 96/ND
○ #Josh McKinley A- 20 98/1H

2B
#JOSE VIDRO 25
#WILTON GUERRERO 25
MIKE MORDECAI 32
? Trace Coquillette ML 26 93/10C
? #Henry Mateo A+ 23 95/2H
? Tootie Myers A- 21 97/1H

3B
MIKE BARRETT 23
? *Andy Tracy 2A 26 96/16C
○ *Scott Hodges A- 21 97/1H

SP/RP

1B
***BRAD FULLMER 25**
*RYAN MCGUIRE 28
○ #Fernando Seguignol ML 25 93/ND
? *Jon Tucker 2A 23 95/8H
? *Talmadge Nunnari 2A 25 97/9C
? Thomas Pittman A- 20 97/1H

RELIEVERS
UGUETH URBINA 26
ANTHONY TELFORD 34
*GRAEME LLOYD 33
MIGUEL BATISTA 29
*STEVE KLINE 27
GUILLERMO MOTA 26
? Christian Parker 3A 24 96/4C
? John Nicholson A+ 22 96/2H

C
CHRIS WIDGER 29
ROBERT MACHADO 27
○ *Brian Schneider 2A 23 95/5H
○ Bob Henley A- 27 91/26C
? Yojanny Valera 3A 23 93/ND

STARTERS
DUSTIN HERMANSON 27
MIKE THURMAN 26
JAVIER VASQUEZ 23
CARL PAVANO 24
HIDEKI IRABU 31
↑ Antonio Armas ML 22 94/ND
↑ Jeremy Powell ML 24 94/4H
↑ *Ted Lilly ML 24 96/23C
? Mike Johnson ML 24 93/17C
? Keith Evans 3A 24 96/8C
○ T.J. Tucker 2A 21 97/1H
? *Brent Billingsley ML 25 96/5C
○ Donnie Bridges A+ 21 97/1H
○ Bryan Hebson A+ 24 97/1C
○ Shane Arthurs A- 20 97/1H
↑ Mark Mangum A- 21 97/1H
? *Matt Blank 2A 24 97/11C
↓ *Josh Girdley A- 19 99/1H

MAJOR LEAGUERS IN ALL CAPS
Minor leaguers in upper-and-lower case

BEFORE A PLAYER'S NAME:
* left-handed hitter/pitcher
\# switch-hitter
?=prospect status (see explanation)

AFTER A PLAYER'S NAME:
Level at which he spent most of 1999 season; age as of July 1, 2000; year he was drafted; round drafted (ND= non-drafted amateur free agent); drafted out of high school (H) or college (C)

EXPLANATION OF PROSPECT RATINGS

★ Potential big-league star

↑ Projected regular player in majors (for pitchers: rotation starter or closer)

○ Projected platoon or utility player in majors (pitcher: setup or middle relief)

? Possible big-league reserve or long reliever

↓ High draft pick or "tools" player who hasn't performed to expectations

MONTREAL

NEW YORK METS

Management
Manager	Bobby Valentine
G.M.	Steve Phillips
President/CEO	Fred Wilpon/Nelson Doubleday

Career Record
866–838 / .508
185–140 / .569
1046–991 / .514

1999 Record
Won–Lost	Pct.	Finish/G.B. (Division)	Finish/G.B. (Wild Card)
97–66	.595	0/6.5 (E)	1

Preseason Consensus Projection
2 (2.00)

1st Half	2nd Half	Home	Road	Intradivision	Interleague
44–34	53–32	49–32	48–34	31–27	12–6

Comebacks	Blowouts	Nail-Biters	Grass	Turf	Sept.–Oct.
10–3	31–15	42–29	79–56	18–10	17–13

NUMBERS DON'T LIE

	Team (Rank)		Opponents (Rank)		League Avg.
Runs/Game	5.23	(5)	4.36	(4)	5.00
Batting Avg.	.279	(2)	.252	(4)	.268
On-Base Avg.	.363	(1)	.331	(5)	.342
Slugging Avg.	.434	(5)	.418	(5)	.429
Strikeouts	994	(4)	1172	(4)	1072
Home Runs	181	(9)	167	(6)	181
Stolen Bases	150	(5)	134	(11)	122
ERA	4.27	(5)			4.57
Errors	68	(1)			120

▶ THE INSIDER 2000

SHOWING THEIR METTLE

The 1999 Mets, despite having "just" the fifth-best offense in the league and "just" the fifth-best ERA, swooped into the NL postseason, knocked off NL West champion Arizona, and played the Braves to the hilt in an NLCS far more exciting than most would have predicted.

One amazin' thing about the Mets is how most players on the team exceeded already high expectations. First baseman John Olerud finished fifth in the league in on-base percentage at .427. Both Mike Piazza and Robin Ventura knocked in 120 runs. Edgardo Alfonzo made the shift to second base superbly and had an outstanding year at bat. Rickey Henderson jump-started the whole team with an excellent season, arguably his best in a decade. Old man Orel Hershiser, 40, wasn't that good, but his presence in the rotation kept a tattered staff from falling apart when Opening Day starter Bobby Jones went down with a sore shoulder.

Then there were the unexpected pleasures: an 8–0 season from Pat Mahomes in middle relief; a big season from former Dodger burnout Roger Cedeno; Octavio Dotel's emergence as a big-league pitcher; a good stretch run from Kenny Rogers; and surprising contributions from a strong bench that included catcher Todd Pratt, outfielder Benny Agbayani, infielder Luis Lopez, and infielder-outfielder Matt Franco.

An integral component of the *Sturm und Drang* of the NL East race and the wild-card chase was the manager. Bobby Valentine, more than any other current big-league skipper, has made himself the focus of attention on his club—not an easy thing to do on a team with personalities as big Bobby Bonilla, Kenny Rogers, Rickey Henderson, Mike Piazza, John Franco, and Turk Wendell.

Say what you will about his vanity, arrogance, and frankly wobbly sense of propriety—many already have. The fact is that Bobby V. did a good job keeping the lid on his volatile veteran team in 1999. Valentine set up his lineup to score runs: The Mets led the league with a .363 on-base average. Roger Cedeno and Rickey Henderson stole bases plentifully and effectively. In the late innings, Valentine had two top-quality closers of completely different types as well as several good situational relievers.

There were problems, of course, or the Mets wouldn't have made the season so interesting. Most of them arose from lack of arm and foot speed.

What killed the Mets' offense was an inability to stay out of

MOMENT OF TRUTH

The Mets entered the last three games of the regular season about as low as a team could be. They had just lost their fifth game to Atlanta in a week and had seen a four-game lead over Cincinnati in the wild-card standings turn into a two-game deficit. Remembering how the Mets lost their last five games in 1998 to miss out on the postseason, New Yorkers quickly coined the phrase "Ya gotta bereave" to describe the Mets' fall. But things quickly turned around. New York won a hard-fought 11-inning game against Pittsburgh on October 1. That started a string of seven wins in eight games, including the single-game playoff in Cincinnati and the Division Series win over Arizona. The streak brought the team back from the dead with enough momentum to nearly make it to the World Series.

BIGGEST SURPRISE

Roger Cedeno was a highly regarded prospect with Los Angeles, but he struggled to be consistent and never won the confidence of L.A.'s management. But the speedy Cedeno flourished in the Big Apple and provided everything the Mets could have wished for. His .314 batting average was 41 points higher than his previous big-league mark, he had an on-base average close to .400, he stole a Mets single-season record 66 bases, and he played well defensively, committing only three errors while playing all three outfield positions.

BIGGEST DISAPPOINTMENT

Benny Agbayani got a lot of attention after his home-run binge in mid-May and early June. He exploded onto the scene at Shea, hitting 10 homers in his first 75 at-bats, but his offense tailed off dramatically after that. Overall, his numbers look decent— .286 batting average with 14 home runs and 42 RBIs in 276 at-bats—but he hit only three homers after the All-Star break. He stole six bases but was caught four times, and he showed below-average range in the outfield.

the double play. New York rolled into 149 twin disasters, most in the NL. With multiple slow players in the heart of the lineup (Alfonso, Olerud, Piazza, and Ventura), plenty of Met runners were turned into pumpkins before they could round the bases. Rey Ordonez damaged the offense with his inability to do very basic things at bat. As the NLCS showed, he's not a very good bunter, and with an on-base average 23 points below league average and only 27 extra-base hits in 520 at-bats, Ordonez can't afford to be grounding into 16 double plays.

What else hurt the Mets? Poor starting pitching. Playing half of their games in an excellent pitchers' park, the Mets didn't have a single full-time starter with an ERA less than 4.23. None of the full-time starters except Leiter was a particularly hard thrower, and Leiter often couldn't find the strike zone. The lack of a rotation anchor was showed down the stretch, as Rogers assumed the role of big guy when others failed.

HOLD ON JUST A MINUTE

National magazines fell all over each other last summer proclaiming the Mets' infield of Olerud, Alfonzo, Ordonez, and Ventura was one of the best ever—less than half a season into their tenure together. No doubt the Mets' quartet was a fine infield, but could they really be the best? Cleveland fans might argue that Jim Thome, Roberto Alomar, Omar Vizquel, and Travis Fryman were as good, if not better. Across town, the Yankees could lay claim as well.

In baseball's long history, there have been many great infields. How do the Mets stack up? How were they preceived while playing, and how do they look through the lens of history?

The fabled Big Red Machine infield of the mid-1970s is our pick for the best ever. Perez, Morgan, Concepcion, and Rose only played together as an infield for two years (1975–76), but they rate well above most, if not all, of the other groups here. All four were above-average hitters in their prime, with all but Concepcion well above average. Hall of Famer Morgan was one of the best players ever at his peak, Rose was a dynamic offensive force, Perez was an excellent power hitter, and Concepcion is vastly underrated both offensively and defensively. Dan Driessen played third base before Rose moved there and first base after Perez left, and was good enough to help the club continue to win.

Speaking of defense, Morgan won Gold Gloves from 1973 through '77, and Concepcion won them from '74 through '77. Morgan, Concepcion, Rose, and Perez all were All-Stars in 1975

▶ THE INSIDER 2000

and '76. All four are honored in "The 400 Greatest" section of *Total Baseball*, the official encyclopedia of Major-League Baseball.

The Philadelphia A's infield of 1911–14 is an all-time classic. Collins and Baker are Hall of Famers, McInnis was a good hitter, and all were fine glovemen. In the bad-infield and tattered baseball days when fielding average was still meaningful, McInnis led his position in fielding in 1913–14, Collins in 1914, and both Barry and Baker in 1911. Collins was the AL MVP in 1914. This group played for World Champions in 1911 and 1913 and won the AL pennant in 1914.

It would be hard to argue that the poetic Cubs' 1906–10 infield composed of three Hall of Famers—Tinker, Evers, and Chance—and Steinfeldt wasn't the best defensive infield ever. Chance, the best hitter of the four, was an excellent first baseman by both reputation and record, and probably would have won the MVP in 1906 if there had been such an award. Evers was an excellent offensive player with defensive value, and Tinker (one of the top-fielding shortstops ever) and Steinfeldt both led the league in fielding three times. The Cubs dynasty captured NL pennants in 1906 and 1910 and won the World Series in 1907 and 1908.

The prosaic Cubs infield of the late 1960s and 1970 wasn't bad either. Santo, Kessinger, and Beckert all won Gold Gloves, and all four, with Banks were All-Stars at some point from 1965 through 1970. The foursome was the NL's starting infield in the 1969 midsummer classic. Santo was a marvelous two-way player who deserves to be in the Hall of Fame and while both Beckert and Kessinger were marginal offensive players by today's standards, their offense was acceptable in the late 1960s and they were considered the ideal double-play combination.

Boston had a great infield from 1948 through 1951. Goodman was an excellent contact hitter, and second sacker Bobby Doerr is in the Hall of Fame for both his glove and his bat. Vern Stephens was a power-hitting machine who led the AL in runs batted in three times. Third baseman Johnny Pesky, a shortstop before Stephens arrived, was a terrific fielder who was on base all the time. When Walt Dropo took over for Goodman in 1950, Dropo tied Stephens for the AL lead in RBIs.

With Hodges providing defense and power at first, Hall of Famer Robinson a complete player at second and NL MVP in 1949, Pee Wee Reese carving out a Hall of Fame career at short, and Billy Cox providing good glovework and some line-drive pop at the hot corner, Brooklyn won its only World Series in 1955 and also won the pennant in 1949, 1952, 1953, and 1956.

SECRET WEAPON

In his six seasons with the Twins and Red Sox, Pat Mahomes never had an ERA of less than 4.73, and his combined ERA for 1995–97 was well over 7.00. He spent the end of 1997 and all of '98 pitching in Japan after the Red Sox gave up on him. Mahomes evidently learned something in the Far East, because he was terrific with the Mets in 1999. Opponents hit a paltry .198 against him as he posted a fine 3.68 ERA, proving very valuable as a bridge between the starters and Cook, Wendell, and Benitez.

ACHILLES HEEL

Bobby Valentine acts like he has a plan, even when he's doing the wacky things. A sampler of his antics last year: He returned to the dugout in a disguise after being ejected from a game: he ripped his players publicly and he practically begged to be fired if the Mets didn't make the postseason. It's possible that New York won last year more because the veteran players were able to shrug off all the distractions than because Valentine was a shrewd skipper.

NEW YORK

ENOUGH ALREADY

Only Bobby Bonilla could fail to understand why a guy hitting well below .200 doesn't get to play every day. Bonilla got off to a slow start in 1999, then began sulking the minute he was benched. With Roger Cedeno and Robin Ventura having great years in right field and third base, respectively, there quickly became no place for Bonilla to play. Instead of accepting a role as a bench player, the 36-year-old whined and moped and complained. If he weren't making nearly $6 million (with a guaranteed contract through 2000), he would have been dumped when he refused to pinch-hit during a game.

When Jim Gilliam came up in 1953, moving Robinson to the outfield and to third base, the Dodgers had an even better offense than previously.

For consistency and longevity, there isn't much question that the Dodgers infield that played together from 1974 through 1981 wins the prize. It was a very good offensive infield, and all of them were multiple All-Stars. Defensively, they weren't exceptional: Neither Russell nor Cey (thanks to Mike Schmidt) ever took Gold Gloves, with Lopes winning only one and Garvey winning four during that span. Their Dodgers won NL pennants in 1974 (when Garvey won the MVP), '77, and '78.

The Cardinals had great infields in the 1960s. All four of their infielders were All-Stars in 1963 (White, Javier, Groat, and Boyer). By 1967, Hall of Famer Cepeda, the NL MVP that year, had replaced White, who won Gold Gloves from 1963 through '65. Boyer, the 1964 NL MVP, had been replaced by Shannon, a good two-way player, and Maxvill, a premier fielder, had stepped in for Groat. St. Louis won the World Series in 1964 and '67 and the NL pennant in '68. Boyer won a Gold Glove in 1963, Maxvill in '68.

The 1980s Redbirds' infield was legendary primarily for its defense, and it led the team to a world championship in 1982. Smith and Hernandez both won Gold Gloves in 1982–83, although Smith was a poor hitter at that point and neither Herr nor Oberkfell were much above average. By 1985, when the Cards won the NL pennant, Jack Clark had replaced Hernandez, and Pendleton had replaced Oberkfell. With Herr having a great season and Smith having matured into an excellent offensive shortstop, it was a more versatile infield. Although not yet eligible, Smith will surely make the Hall of Fame.

As good as the Mets' infield was in 1999, it can't yet rate with the all-time greats. They need to put together at least another season at their current levels to rank with the Big Red Machine, the $100,000 Infield, the Boys of Summer, or the "trio of bear cubs . . . fleeter than birds."

BEST CASE

Getting rid of bench-riding, mouth-shooting Bobby Bonilla was a long-overdue strategy, and the Mets should be commended for biting the bullet on his fat salary. Last year, the Mets had a balanced club, and Bobby Valentine used his lineup and bullpen well. The starting rotation ought to be at least a little better this year with Bobby Jones back to health, and the bullpen and bench are two of the strongest in the game. Finally, the Mets have some true stars; Mike Piazza, Edgardo Alfonzo, and Robin Ventura are as good as most anybody's top guns.

WORST CASE

Trying to replace John Olerud at first base with Todd Zeile isn't going to help the Mets. Olerud, an unsung hero due to his great on-base ability, is far better than his journeyman supplement. Otherwise, the Mets aren't that different from the club that won in 1999, except that they're a bit older. The pitching staff needs at least one more starter. The big question will be whether closer Armando Benitez, shortstop Rey Ordonez, and catcher Mike Piazza will come through. Confidence problems, poor hitting, and injuries are real risks to these three critical players.

UNDER THE MICROSCOPE

JORGE TOCA: Toca, a Cuban defector who signed for $1.4 million, looks much older than his listed 24. But he is an outstanding hitter with the best power in the organization. More comfortable at first base, Toca held up surprisingly well in left field, but it looks like he'll have a small window of opportunity with New York.

JAY PAYTON: In his six-year career, Payton—who won batting titles in each of his first two seasons—has batted 1,500 times and had six stints on the disabled list. Payton hit .382 in 170 at-bats at Triple-A last season but has been dogged by injuries. He has the bat to contribute but may be better suited for an American League club.

GRANT ROBERTS: Roberts dominated pro ball in his first two years before undergoing elbow surgery following the '97 season. His arm is back to full strength, registering a fastball that tops out at 95 mph and a breaking pitch that has potential, but his performance the last two years was inconsistent. However, Roberts is still young and has the ability to be a starter for the Mets in the next couple of years.

ERIC CAMMACK: Cammack is a bulldog with a fastball clocking in the low 90s and a nasty slider. A relative sleeper, the 24-year-old caught the organization's eye last season by fanning 100 batters over 65 innings after whiffing 102 batters in 68 innings the previous year. In his three-year career Cammack has allowed 83 hits in 164 innings.

NEW YORK METS

TOP PROSPECTS

In 1998 the Mets traded away much of their future (Preston Wilson, A. J. Burnett, Ed Yarnall, Geoff Goetz, Cesar Crespo, Jesus Sanchez) to acquire Al Leiter and Mike Piazza. Last season the Mets shipped out OF **TERRENCE LONG**, their top remaining upper-level position prospect, to Oakland in the deal to acquire Kenny Rogers.

The New York farm system, already relatively thin entering '98, is practically barren now. It also doesn't help that OF **ALEX ESCOBAR**, a '98 member of the HOWE SPORTSDATA All-Prospect Team, was limited to 11 at-bats because of two different injuries. OF **JUAN LEBRON**, a former first-round pick of the Royals who was acquired over the winter for Joe Randa, was out all season after undergoing shoulder surgery. LHP **JIM DOUGHERTY**, who had gone 21–3 in his first two years, was out all season with shoulder surgery, and RHP **JAE WONG SEO** missed the majority of his second straight season because of elbow problems. OF **JAY PAYTON**, who played well at Triple-A when healthy, batted just 170 times due to injuries, which have interrupted his career the past four years.

The major-league club did get a boost last season from minor-league veteran OF **BENNY AGBAYANI** and RHP **OCTAVIO DOTEL**, who entered the season as the system's top prospect. Also, Cuban defector 1B-OF **JORGE TOCA** came on board last winter and showed he's a big-league hitter, but finding a position for him may be a problem.

On the field, Escobar likely represents the only everyday prospect in the system, and he has been hurt more than he's been healthy. 2B **TY WIGGINTON** did have a breakthrough year at Class A, hitting for average and power, but his defense is too short at this stage. 2B **MO BRUCE**, making the conversion from the hot corner, is a pretty good hitter, but strikeouts, defense, and health are concerns. 3B **MIKE KINKADE**, who received some time with the big club, is a solid hitter but unreliable defensively.

OF **JASON TYNER**, a '98 first-round pick, has shown an ability to get on base and roam center field. More than 25 percent of his hits were of the infield variety, and he walked more than he struck out, but he has not homered since high school. OF **BRIAN COLE**, who had 63 extra-base hits and 50 steals at Class A, is a multitalented player worth watching.

The mound crop is equally thin after Dotel. RHP **GRANT ROBERTS** is highly regarded and has good stuff, but he's still feeling his way back after elbow surgery two years ago. Double-A closer RHP **ERIC CAMMACK** has an above-average arm and had a terrific '99 campaign. Twenty-year-old RHP **DICKY GONZALEZ** emerged as a legitimate prospect this season, adding velocity to his already fantastic command. RHP **PAT STRANGE**, a '98 second-rounder, had a fine season at Class A.

Without a first-round pick in 1999, the Mets hope that Tyner will be able to turn around the dismal showings of New York's first-round picks. Since 1985, when the club tabbed Gregg Jeffries in the first round, it hasn't had a first-rounder other than Paul Wilson or Chris Donnels make it to the majors with New York. Jeromy Burnitz, a top pick in 1990, has been successful the past three years with the Brewers, and Preston Wilson had a solid rookie year with the Marlins.

CF
*DARRYL HAMILTON 35
○ *Jason Tyner 3A 23 98/1C
? Allen Dina 2A 26 98/NDC
↓ Alex Escobar A+ 21 95/NDC
○ Brian Cole A- 21 98/18C

LF
BENNY AGBAYANI 28
*JON NUNNALLY 28
MELVIN MORA 28
○ Jay Payton ML 27 94/1C
? Juan Moreno A+ 24 93/ND

RF
DEREK BELL 31
? Robert Stratton A- 22 96/1H
○ Brian Jenkins A- 21 97/5H
↓ Juan LeBron DP 23 95/1H

SS
REY ORDONEZ 27
? Jersen Perez A+ 24 96/22C

2B
EDGARDO ALFONZO 26
? Mo Bruce 2A 25 95/NDC
? Ty Wigginton A+ 22 98/17C

3B
*ROBIN VENTURA 32
? Mike Kinkade ML 27 95/9C
? Junior Zamora 2A 24 93/ND

1B
TODD ZEILE 34
*MATT FRANCO 30
○ Jorge Toca ML 25 98/ND
? *Bryon Gainey 2A 24 94/3H
? Earl Snyder A- 24 98/36C

SP/RP

RELIEVERS
ARMANDO BENITEZ 27
*JOHN FRANCO 39
*DENNIS COOK 37
TURK WENDELL 33
PAT MAHOMES 29
○ Eric Cammack 3A 24 97/13C

STARTERS
*MIKE HAMPTON 27
*AL LEITER 34
RICK REED 34
BOBBY JONES 30
*BILL PULSIPHER 26
○ Grant Roberts 3A 22 95/11H
○ Dicky Gonzalez 3A 21 96/16H
? Brett Herbison 2A 23 95/2H
? Kenny Pumphrey 2A 23 94/4H
? Tyler Walker 2A 24 97/2C
○ Pat Strange A- 19 98/2H
? *Yon German A+ 22 94/ND

C
MIKE PIAZZA 31
TODD PRATT 33
VANCE WILSON 27

MAJOR LEAGUERS IN ALL CAPS
Minor leaguers in upper-and-lower case

BEFORE A PLAYER'S NAME:
* left-handed hitter/pitcher
# switch-hitter
?=prospect status (see explanation)

AFTER A PLAYER'S NAME:
Level at which he spent most of 1999 season; age as of July 1, 2000; year he was drafted; round drafted (ND= non-drafted amateur free agent); drafted out of high school (H) or college (C)

EXPLANATION OF PROSPECT RATINGS

★ Potential big-league star

↑ Projected regular player in majors (for pitchers: rotation starter or closer)

○ Projected platoon or utility player in majors (pitcher: setup or middle relief)

? Possible big-league reserve or long reliever

↓ High draft pick or "tools" player who hasn't performed to expectations

NEW YORK

PHILADELPHIA PHILLIES

Management
Manager	Terry Francona
G.M.	Ed Wade
President/CEO	Dave Montgomery

Career Record
220–266 / .453
152–172 / .469
152–172 / .469

1999 Record
Won–Lost	Pct.	Finish/G.B. (Division)	Finish/G.B. (Wild Card)
77-85	.475	3/26 (E)	5/19.5

Preseason Consensus Projection
3 (3.20)

1st Half	2nd Half	Home	Road	Intradivision	Interleague
40-36	37-49	41-40	36-45	31-28	11-7

Comebacks	Blowouts	Nail-Biters	Grass	Turf	Sept.–Oct.
15-10	26-28	35-38	27-35	50-50	10-21

NUMBERS DON'T LIE

	Team (Rank)	Opponents (Rank)	League Avg.
Runs/Game	5.19 (6)	5.22 (11)	5.00
Batting Avg.	.275 (4)	.269 (10)	.268
On-Base Avg.	.351 (5)	.347 (12)	.342
Slugging Avg.	.431 (7)	.447 (13)	.429
Strikeouts	1081 (9)	1030 (12)	1072
Home Runs	161 (14)	212 (13)	181
Stolen Bases	125 (9)	94 (2)	122
ERA	4.93 (13)		4.57
Errors	100 (2)		120

▶ THE INSIDER 2000

WAIT TILL NEXT CENTURY

What can you say when a team has lost the affection of its fans to such an extent that only 23,892 even care enough to show up for Fan Appreciation Day? Not much, especially when the general despair among those who did show up was characterized by a banner reading "Wait Till Next Century."

Since the aptly named "Wheeze Kids" of the early 1980s grabbed their canes and hobbled off the field after their second NL pennant in '83, the fans in Philadelphia haven't had much to shout about. One exhilarating roller-coaster ride to the pennant (1993), two winning seasons (1993 and '86), and one hell of a lot of bad baseball.

The 1997–98 Phillies quickly climbed from atrocious to decent. Unfortunately, that was no guarantee they could get to the next level—contending. The 1999 team was in contention for a wild-card berth until early August (which is not saying much, given that most teams that are above .500 are in the wild-card hunt until September), then completely and utterly collapsed.

STOP WHINING AND KEEP PLAYING

Staff ace and self-designated know-it-all Curt Schilling blasted team management at the end of July for not being committed to winning. Schilling was just articulating the prevailing philosophy in the 1990s: If the team plays well enough to be within sight of a playoff berth early in the second half, management is obligated to make short-term trades to shore up any weaknesses.

Trading for veterans with big salaries or making risky deals for players who are in the walk year of their contracts has become an annual midsummer rite in baseball. But why should that be so? Why should the fans—and, more important, the players—blithely assume that management can and will make such risky and expensive deals?

In many cases, such midseason, just-above-.500 teams aren't really contenders: They were simply lucky enough not to fall too far behind in the first half. In that case, making a short-term deal that might hurt the team in the long term isn't smart at all.

Frankly, it has gotten to the point now that the expectation that management will deliver a player *ex machina* in these circumstances just gives the players an excuse to avoid responsibility if they don't play well. After all, if they're still in contention

MOMENT OF TRUTH

The two players the team relied on—Curt Schilling and Scott Rolen—were shut down for the season about the same time the team's slide began, and no one was able to take their places. Schilling made only two starts after the All-Star break due to continuing problems with his pitching shoulder, while Rolen suffered a strained back muscle sliding feet first—which he almost never does. Whatever wind Philadelphia had in its sails at that point died, and the team drifted listlessly in the doldrums for the rest of the season.

PHILADELPHIA

BIGGEST SURPRISE

The Phils were 13 games over .500 until August 7. That was the weekend Gene Mauch, star of the 1964 NL pennant race tragedy, came to town for Philadelphia's "Greatest Moments of the Century" celebration. Apparently the veteran manager was accompanied by the specter of '64, as the bottom dropped out of the Phillies' season after that. Philadelphia went 6–16 the rest of August.

BIGGEST DISAPPOINTMENT

Once again the Phils were unable to pull off a deal before the trading deadline to help the team stay in the wild-card hunt. The team apparently leaked the news that they were in serious negotiations with the Yankees to trade for Andy Pettitte, but there was good reason to believe that the Yanks had no intention of making a deal with them. While other teams made trades to strengthen their rosters for the stretch run, Philadelphia GM Ed Wade held his chin up high and said something like: "We're staying the course.... We're not going to panic.... We did our best.... Sure we're disappointed.... Yadda, yadda, yadda."

---

in late July, they might very well have what it takes to compete. Whether the team makes it to the postseason or not, it's not the players' job to run the club.

Players are paid to give it everything they have on the field, not to second-guess management. If they don't like the way a club is run, veterans can leave via free agency. In many cases, they can force a trade. Maybe, instead, the players should stop whining and do a gut check.

In response to Schilling's sharp criticism, GM Ed Wade fired back in an e-mail to the team's beat writers that was printed in the *Philadelphia Daily News*. Saying that it was "wrong to say we have not been committed to improving the team," Wade explained management's position. "[W]e set out on a course of building with our young guys, and that plan has been validated. Yes, the challenge is to move to the next level, but that doesn't mean we haven't been committed to improving.

"Earlier this month, Curt was quoted saying, 'It's up to ownership to get good players.' What message does that send to his teammates, the guys he shares the clubhouse with and the guys who play behind him? We've been trying to upgrade our rotation since the end of last season and we will continue to try," he said. "We haven't turned down any trade for starting pitchers because of dollars."

BUILDING, REBUILDING, OR JUST TREADING WATER?

The November trade with San Diego for Andy Ashby might have been a signal that the Philadelphia management is willing to change the way it does business. For years the excuse was a supposedly bad lease; recently it's been the lack of a new ballpark. Unfortunately, due to political infighting and neighborhood resistance to building a new park downtown, the Phillies are almost certainly going to end up building next door to Veterans Stadium. That's more of a lost opportunity for the city than for the team, with one crucial exception: The delay in picking a site means that the team won't move into its new ballpark until at least Opening Day 2003.

Owner Bill Giles didn't seem too concerned about the delay, but the loss of revenue could easily impact negatively on the team's ability to sign or re-sign a key player in the next couple of seasons. Including Ashby.

Though he pitched better on the road than at home in '99, Ashby, like most moundsmen in the Friars' club at Qualcomm, benefited substantially from his home park. Nevertheless, Ashby's acquisition gives the Phils the raw material for a solid rotation, something they haven't seen since their glory days in 1993–94. Schilling and Ashby will anchor a staff that could be very effective when Randy Wolf, Paul Byrd, and Robert Person are added.

Of course, they're many question marks attached to that rosy scenario. First, there's no guarantee that Schilling will be 100 percent healthy. Second, Wolf could continue to struggle for another year or more before he learns how to pitch effectively in the majors. Third, Byrd's 5.61 ERA after the All-Star break could easily mean the league has caught up to him, or that he can't stand the strain of 30 to 35 starts. Fourth, Person is an enigma, one of those players with obvious talent that hasn't translated into performance, and there's certainly no guarantee that he won't backslide this year. Fifth, Ashby has not yet been signed to a long-term deal.

ROLL OUT THE BURRELL

Pat Burrell, Philadelphia's first-round pick in 1998, punished Double-A pitching last year and projects as a middle-of-the-order power threat. Pat "The Bat" should be a fixture in the cleanup slot in Philadelphia very soon if nothing goes awry. While the team would like Burrell to play left field, it's much more likely that he'll have to be put at first base, where the Phillies' brain trust is in love with overrated first baseman Rico Brogna. Rico's superb glove doesn't make up for his below-average bat at a power position.

The J D Drew debacle now looms larger over the team's chances to become truly competitive. It seems especially tragic because Drew could have made the team's already productive lineup into a championship-caliber offense, or he could have been used as the centerpiece of a deal to get the Phils some much-needed pitching.

While Drew certainly isn't yet a big-league star, the 23-year-old showed good power and excellent base-stealing ability last year. Combine that with average range in center field and he's a short step away from being a productive regular, and only two steps away from being a star. Eric Valent, the power-hitting outfielder selected by the Phillies with their compensation pick for not signing Drew, had a pretty good year in the Florida State League in '99, but he's several years away from the Show.

SECRET WEAPON

The Phillies' big asset in '99 was a corps of terrific bench players—Kevin Jordan, Alex Arias, Rob Ducey, and Kevin Sefcik. Jordan (.285 BA) and Arias (.303 BA, .373 OBA) played every day at third and short, respectively, for much of the season when regulars Scott Rolen and Desi Relaford went down. KJ also filled in at first and second in addition to learning how to play the hot corner. Ducey and Sefcik were the team's top pinch hitters; both played all three outfield positions, and ex-infielder Sefcik also played 15 games at second base.

ACHILLES HEEL

Can you spell r-e-l-i-e-f? None of the pitchers in the Phillies' bullpen could. Former first-round pick Wayne Gomes, 26, failed to mature into a dominant closer, mostly due to continuing lack of control (56 BB in 74 IP). Although he's still young enough to improve, it looks like he'd be best used in middle relief. Elderly rookie Steve Montgomery, with his fifth organization at age 28, turned in a decent season, but the rest of the pen was full of flotsam and jetsam.

ATTENTION KMART SHOPPERS

ENOUGH ALREADY

How many times do fans want to hear that this team is "coming along"? As usual, there was lots of talk and precious little action at the highest levels in 1999 in terms of solving the Phillies' chronic problems. GM Ed Wade announced at the end of the season that the largely anonymous partners who own the team were going to loosen their purse strings so he could go out and compete in the free-agent market for a change. In what was a definite shift in strategy, Wade said they'd be willing to trade some of their prospects, and they did just that in November by including '96 first-round pick Adam Eaton in the Andy Ashby deal. Without more dramatic changes like that, this team seems doomed to perpetual mediocrity, which would truly be a shame given that it has a core of young stars to build around.

The problem that Philadelphia faces is that it has some of the important components of a championship club, but the organization hasn't demonstrated the commitment to fill out the rest of a championship team.

The Phillies have a bona fide superstar at third base in Scott Rolen. They have a budding superstar in right fielder Bobby Abreu. They have a staff ace in Curt Schilling, assuming that his 1999 arm problems do not recur. They have a surprisingly powerful two-way catcher in Mike Lieberthal, who plays with many injuries that would disable most other players. They have a decent leadoff hitter in center fielder Doug Glanville.

Think for a moment about where these key performers came from. Rolen was a second-round pick, the sparkling jewel of scouting director Mike Arbuckle's regime who quickly developed into a star. Abreu and Glanville were acquired via trade, the former swiped from a clueless expansion team and the latter acquired partly to save money on Mickey Morandini's salary. Schilling himself was pilfered years ago from a team that thought it was swapping talented but troubled hard-throwing youngsters. Lieberthal is a former first-round pick left over from the previous scouting director.

Notwithstanding these successes, it's not enough. The failure of the Philadelphia farm system to produce enough talent in the 1990s left the team constantly on the lookout for opportunities to hornswoggle other teams out of promising players. In the long lulls between deals of the Schilling-Abreu magnitude, management was constantly rummaging through baseball's bargain basement (waivers, Rule 5 draft, teams offering cut-rate deals to unload underachieving veterans), trying desperately to find another diamond in the rough.

At some point the Phillies have to stop doing all their shopping at blue-light specials. They need to stop cruising the interstates looking for ballplayers at fire-sale prices and pay the going rate for first-class talent. At some point Philadelphia general managers have to stop pointing defensively to the good trades they've made and start pointing proudly to the team's winning record. At some point the management has to give the fans something to cheer about. Until then it's going to be more of the same old story of disappointment salted with occasional streaks of false hope.

BEST CASE

The Phillies might finally graduate to real contender status in 2000. If Schilling can return early in the season from his shoulder surgery, and if free-agent acquisition Mike Jackson can close games with efficiency, Philadelphia should be a solid contender for the wild card. If everything else goes right and the team gets productive years from Rolen, Abreu, Lieberthal, and Glanville, they could even challenge the big kids for the NL East title. To do that, though, the team needs Ashby to anchor the rotation and Wolf and Person to fulfill their promise. GM Ed Wade received a contract extension as a Christmas present, so it's time for him to prove that he can put the pieces of the build-a-contender puzzle together.

WORST CASE

The Phillies find out, as so many other overly patient teams have, that slowly adding pieces of the puzzle doesn't vault them into contention. As they are gradually making improvements, other players can easily backslide due to age, injury, or other factors. Every member of the rotation carries a big question mark except for Ashby; and if Schilling struggles to recover from his shoulder injury, the team is probably doomed to another mediocre year. If Burrell isn't ready for prime time yet, or if any of the team's other big guns (Rolen, Abreu, Lieberthal) slump, it'll be "wait till next year" again at the corner of Broad and Pattison.

UNDER THE MICROSCOPE

PAT BURRELL: With a .320 average, 29 homers, and 83 walks, Burrell showed the awesome presence he can have in a lineup. A collegiate third baseman, the 22-year-old moved over to first after turning pro. He was moved to left field late last season when the Phillies decided that Rico Brogna would remain their first baseman. Left field is the only opening, and Burrell may not have the mobility to play there.
JIMMY ROLLINS: Rollins has smooth hands, good range, and a strong arm. The 5'8" switch-hitter makes consistent contact, and can steal a base. The 20-year-old is still a year or so away from the big time.
ADAM EATON: The 21-year-old took a three-level trip through the minor leagues in 1999. Eaton was most impressive at Double-A, where he pitched a no-hitter (despite taking the loss) in his first start and went 5–4, 2.92 ERA in 12 appearances. A 1996 first-round pick equipped with a 92–93 mph moving fastball, Eaton should become a quality major-league starter, but it's too early to expect that this season.
BRAD BAISLEY: With the stagnation of many of the Phillies' top pitchers, the development of Baisley became that much more important. His success in '99 was at the lowest level of full-season ball, but the 20-year-old showed the live fastball, the breaking ball, and the command of a much more experienced hurler. He could give the organization a big boost with another productive season in 2000.

PHILADELPHIA

TOP PROSPECTS

For the second straight season the Phillies played winning baseball well past the All-Star break before collapsing because of injuries and lack of pitching depth. If 1B-OF **PAT BURRELL** can take over left field next season as hoped, the Phillies will have a solid player at every position with the possible exception of shortstop. That leaves the organization with the same old problem: pitching.

The Phillies had RHP **CARLTON LOEWER** step up in 1998 and LHP **RANDY WOLF** contribute last season, but they simply need more help to become serious contenders. Many highly regarded prospects were injured or faltered in '99 (**DAVE COGGIN, ROB BURGER, RYAN BRANNAN, KRIS STEVENS, BRETT BLACK, MARK RUTHERFORD**), and there doesn't seem to be much help on the immediate horizon. This lack of production caused general manager Ed Wade to clean house in the player development department last season.

Towering RHP **BRAD BAISLEY**, a '98 second-round pick, also moved forward, going 10–7, 2.26 ERA with a no-hitter of his own in Class A, displaying a 90 mph fastball and a good hook. There is not much help in between, however. RHP **CLIFF POLITTE**, who began the '98 season in the Cardinals' starting rotation, and RHP **EVAN THOMAS** have a chance.

Coggin has had shoulder problems much of the past two years and has not been able to live up to expectations. Burger lost 18 straight Double-A decisions and his confidence over the past two years after a promising '97 campaign at Class A. Brannan has been a major disappointment since earning HOWE SPORTSDATA All-Prospect Team honors in '97. The Phillies had hoped he'd be their closer by now, but he's stumbled badly enough to be put into the rotation to work things out. Stevens, who pitched in Double-A at age 20 in '98, missed last season because of knee surgery. Additionally, RHP **BRETT BLACK**, who saved 34 games and fanned 88 batters in 66 innings in '98, posted a 5.16 ERA and three saves last season, while Rutherford posted a 6.85 ERA before going down with arm problems.

The Phillies hoped Burrell would become an impact hitter when they drafted him with the first overall pick, and he hasn't disappointed. The organization had similar hopes for C **BOBBY ESTALLELA**, but he has stagnated over the past two years and is almost a forgotten man now with the development of Mike Lieberthal. The Phillies need 2B **MARLON ANDERSON** to improve both offensively and defensively from his rookie season. If either he or Desi Relaford doesn't improve, SS **JIMMY ROLLINS** may soon get a shot at either middle infield spot. OF **REGGIE TAYLOR** has started to transfer his gifted athletic ability to the baseball diamond, but his lack of patience will prevent him from being a starting player. OF **ERIC VALENT**, an excellent hitting prospect, and OF **JASON MICHAELS** are a pair of Class A performers with a chance to progress.

LF
RON GANT 35
*ROB DUCEY 35

CF
DOUG GLANVILLE 29
WENDELL MAGEE JR. 27
? *Reggie Taylor 2A 23 95/1H
○ Jason Michaels A+ 24 98/4C

RF
***BOBBY ABREU 26**
? *David Francia 2A 25 96/8C
↑ *Eric Valent A+ 23 98/1C
? Jorge Padilla A- 20 98/3H

SS
ALEX ARIAS 32
#DESI RELAFORD 26
○ #Jim Rollins 3A 21 96/2H
? #Nick Punto A+ 22 98/21C

2B
***MARLON ANDERSON 26**
KEVIN SEFCIK 29

3B
SCOTT ROLEN 25
KEVIN JORDAN 30
? Rusty McNamara 2A 25 97/21C
? Carlos Duncan A- 23 94/ND

1B
***RICO BROGNA 30**
★ Pat Burrell 3A 23 98/1C
? Nate Espy A- 22 98/18C

SP/RP

C
MIKE LIEBERTHAL 28
GARY BENNETT 28
TOM PRINCE 35
? #Johnny Estrada A+ 24 97/17C

RELIEVERS
MIKE JACKSON 35
JEFF BRANYLEY 36
WAYNE GOMES 27
CARLOS REYES 31
AMAURY TELEMACO 26
*SCOTT ALDRED 32
STEVE SCHRENK 31
○ Cliff Politte ML 26 95/54C
? Evan Thomas 2A 26 96/10C
? Ryan Brannan 2A 25 96/4C

STARTERS
CURT SCHILLING 33
ANDY ASHBY 32
PAUL BYRD 29
ROBERT PERSON 30
*RANDY WOLF 23
CHRIS BROCK 30
? *Anthony Shumaker ML 27 95/23C
↓ Dave Coggin 2A 23 95/1H
? Geoff Geary A+ 23 98/15C
↑ Brad Baisley A- 20 98/2H
? Carlos Silva A- 21 96/ND
↓ Brett Myers A- 19 99/1
? *Jason Brester 2A 23 95/2H
? *Adam Walker A+ 24 97/27C
? *Greg Kubes A- 23 98/14C
↓ *Kris Stevens DP 22 96/3H

MAJOR-LEAGUERS IN ALL CAPS
Minor-leaguers in upper-and-lower case

BEFORE A PLAYER'S NAME:
* left-handed hitter/pitcher
# switch-hitter
?=Player's prospect status (see explanation)

AFTER A PLAYER'S NAME:
Level at which he spent most of 1999 season; age as of July 1, 2000; year he was drafted; round drafted (ND= non-drafted amateur free agent); drafted out of high school (H) or college (C)

EXPLANATION OF PROSPECT RATINGS

★ Potential big-league star

↑ Projected regular player in majors (for pitchers: rotation starter or closer)

○ Projected platoon or utility player in majors (pitcher: setup or middle relief)

? Possible big-league reserve or long reliever

↓ High draft pick or "tools" player who hasn't performed to expectations

PHILADELPHIA

NL CENTRAL

(Chart: Wins vs Week, 4/5 through 6/21)

THE INSIDER 2000

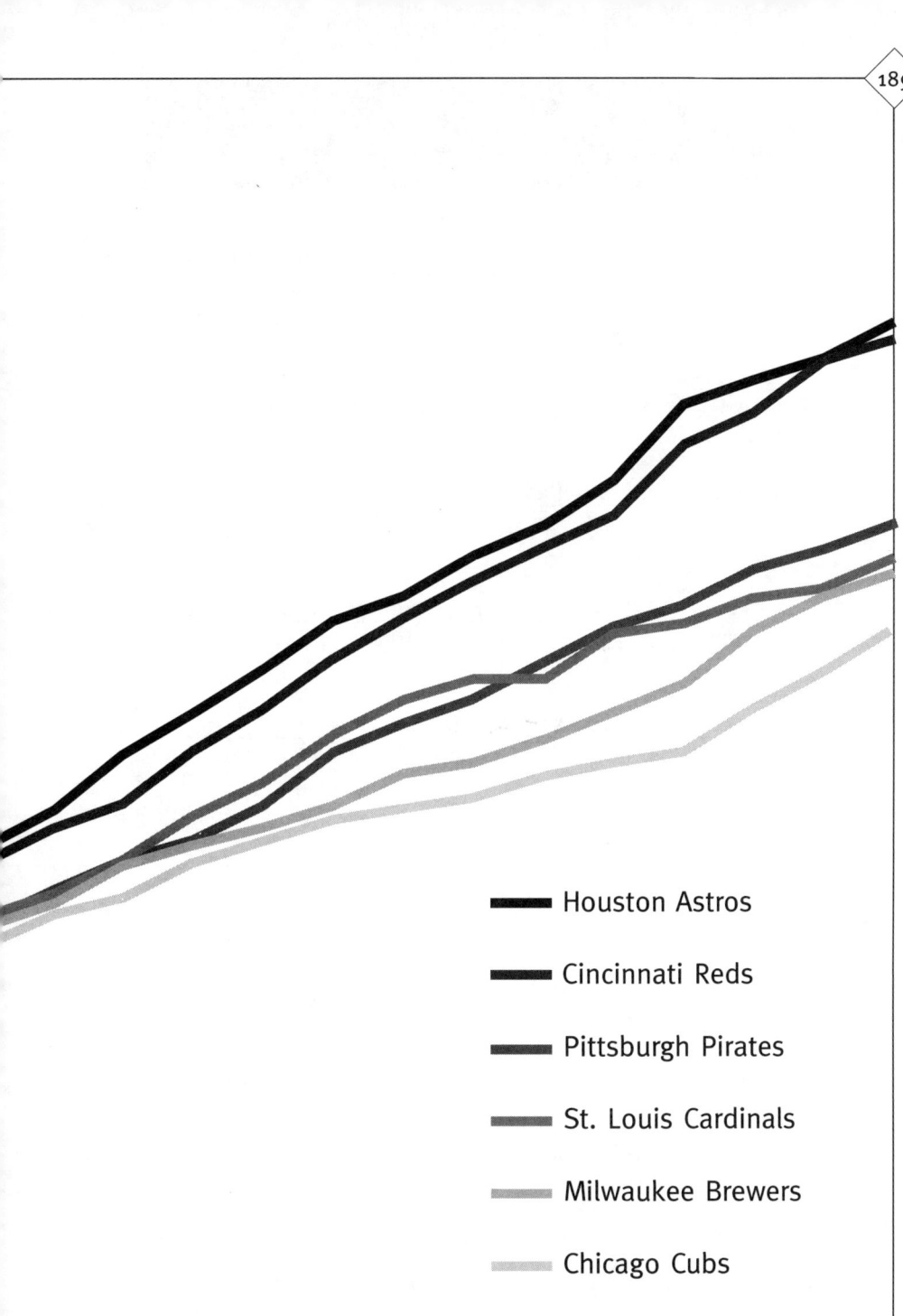

CHICAGO CUBS

Management
		Career Record
Manager	Jim Riggleman [fired]	486–598 / .448
G.M.	Ed Lynch	374–419 / .472
President/CEO	Tribune Co.	1410–1536 / .479

1999 Record
Won–Lost	Pct.	Finish/G.B. (Division)	Finish/G.B. (Wild Card)
67–95	.414	6/30 (C)	12/29.5

Preseason Consensus Projection
3 (3.00)

1st Half	2nd Half	Home	Road	Intradivision	Interleague
37–37	30–58	34–47	33–48	28–34	6–9

Comebacks	Blowouts	Nail-Biters	Grass	Turf	Sept.–Oct.
14–13	17–38	36–35	58–76	9–19	13–18

NUMBERS DON'T LIE

	Team (Rank)		Opponents (Rank)		League Avg.
Runs/Game	4.61	(13)	5.68	(15)	5.00
Batting Avg.	.257	(15)	.286	(15)	.268
On-Base Avg.	.329	(14)	.346	(11)	.342
Slugging Avg.	.420	(13)	.467	(15)	.429
Strikeouts	1170	(14)	980	(15)	1072
Home Runs	189	(6)	221	(15)	181
Stolen Bases	60	(16)	100	(6)	122
ERA	5.27	(15)			4.57
Errors	139	(14)			120

▶ THE INSIDER 2000

A SUMMER OF DISCONTENT

The 1999 Cubs were doomed almost from the start. With several veterans coming off unmatchable seasons, the pressure was on the big guns—Sosa, Grace, and Rodriguez—to produce. As good as that trio was, the Big Three couldn't carry an old and slow team with a low on-base average and mediocre power that was, in some cases, uninterested in playing.

Case in point: outfielder Lance Johnson, who was a critical part of the team. Unfortunately, the season turned on a Johnson mistake, and it haunted the club the rest of the way. On June 9, Johnson—inserted as a pinch runner with the Cubs trailing 8–7 at Arizona—shook off instructions to stay close to the bag and was picked off to end the game. At the time the Cubs were 32–23; from then on, the team was a pathetic 35–72.

In that June game, Lance suffered an abdominal strain that shelved him for most of the rest of the season. Many close to the team felt that Johnson was less than diligent in his recovery, and he and then manager Jim Riggleman clashed more than once. Johnson's attitude seemed to rub off on some of the other veteran players, many of whom quit on the manager. Underperforming utility player Tyler Houston, was unloaded shortly after ripping his skipper in the newspapers. It is no coincidence that the Cubs released Johnson on October 6, just after the season ended.

Riggleman wanted a veteran club, possibly to avoid having to deal with the kind of rookie mistakes that can doom a team in a pennant race. Unfortunately, history tells us that going with supposedly proven veterans (who may have nothing left to prove) isn't necessarily a safe alternative. Riggleman's conservative personnel strategy didn't win the Cubs many games and probably cost him his job.

MOMENT OF TRUTH

From June 11–13 the Cubs hosted the White Sox in another installment of their Windy City rivalry. Coming off a series of surprising late-inning victories and riding high and confident in second place in the NL Central at 32–24, the Cubs expected to sweep their crosstown brethren and continue their winning ways. Instead, the Bruins were themselves swept by scores of 5–3, 8–2, and 6–4 by their upstart visitors and never again looked anything like a contending club. As their performance unraveled on the field, the club began to lose confidence and never regained its stride.

GAETT-UILLOTINED

One of the keys to the Cubs' improbable wild-card ride in 1998 was the late-season acquisition of veteran third baseman Gary Gaetti. After a mediocre half season with the Cardinals, Gaetti was dumped on August 14 before inking with Chicago a few days later.

Entrusted with a starting position in the playoff hunt, a reenergized Gaetti put together a hot streak typical of several previous career-saving bursts (see 1986, 1993, 1995), hitting .320 in 37 games with eight homers. So the Cubs decided to re-sign the 40-year-old Gaetti to be their everyday third baseman in 1999.

BIGGEST SURPRISE

The Cubs had precious few positive surprises in 1999. The biggest was that Sammy Sosa—to his credit—didn't fall off much from his outstanding '98. He still struck out a lot, and his batting average dropped from .308 to .288, but he continued to hit with monstrous power and took 78 walks. Outside of Sammy-world, when rookie starter Kyle Farnsworth returned in September from a demotion to Triple-A he pitched more effectively and strung together several fine appearances. He likely won himself a rotation job for 2000.

BIGGEST DISAPPOINTMENT

The spring training loss of 1998 rookie sensation Kerry Wood threw a pall over the team that barely lifted all year. Wood's absence put extra pressure on everyone else on the staff, and none of the other starters could take up the slack. Unfortunately, rough-hewn, no-BS rookie pitching coach Marty DeMerritt couldn't get the staff back on track once their midseason struggles began, and he eventually paid with his job.

Gaetti's resultant failure was hardly surprising. Had the Cubs finished lower in the standings in '98, they almost certainly would not have kept him; plenty of veteran players put on one last burst before they retire. The Cubs either believed that Gaetti's level of play in those 37 games was real or, more cynically, knew that they could hardly be blamed for keeping Gaetti if he played badly. More important, they would look smart if he succeeded. That kind of cover-your-rear management is seen all the time on second-division clubs.

Gaetti wasn't just bad; he was atrocious, clearly one of the worst everyday players in the majors. In desperation, the Cubs tried everyone possible at third base—Tyler Houston and Jose Hernandez were run out there before being traded, and Manny Alexander and Jeff Blauser saw action at the hot corner a few times—but held on to the aged Gaetti all year.

Even though the hardworking and affable Gaetti stunk all season, he remained a popular figure with the Wrigley faithful—perhaps for having hit the wild-card playoff game-winning homer, perhaps for his hustle, perhaps because he doesn't look all that different from most of the bleacherites.

Gaetti wasn't the only old soldier who faded away when the bell rang in 1999. Second baseman Mickey Morandini had a brutal season, even though he never stopped hustling. Catcher Benito Santiago, who had disappointed several other teams over the past few seasons, did nothing to arrest his steady decline. Blauser had another miserable year.

Even though the Cubs jettisoned or benched many of their veterans by September, Gaetti was still playing even after rookie Cole Liniak and newly signed Shane Andrews had joined the club. Why? So Gary could reach a personal goal: playing 2,500 games at third base.

Such a concern with individual statistics, streaks, and milestones during a time when young players could be evaluated was inexcusable. To his credit, Riggleman refused to blame GM Ed Lynch entirely for going with the veterans who let the team down, saying that both he and Lynch had input concerning the club's composition.

CHICAGO FUTURES EXCHANGE

By the end of the year the Cubs had young players seeing action at several key spots. Up the middle, shortstop Jose Nieves and second baseman Chad Meyers were receiving an extended audition. Nieves, a weak hitter who had shown some signs of developing power in the high minors, turned out to be a solid shortstop. Jose has a good arm and an ability to go deep into the hole that has been unseen in Wrigley since the heyday of Shawon Dunston. Meyers, an on-base machine in the minors, showed good speed but little power, though he displayed far better defensive tools than had been advertised.

Outfielders Bo Porter and Roosevelt Brown also got auditions. Neither impressed much during their demitasses of cappuccino, but neither one had much left to prove at Triple-A Iowa. Catcher Jose Molina, a classic catch-and-throw receiver with a very strong arm but a terrible set of offensive skills, moved ahead of Sandy Martinez on the organizational chart and may have captured a bench job for 2000.

Unfortunately, all five of the above "young" players will be 24 or older this season, and none is projected to be future star. The Cubs will be lucky if any of them turns out to be a good, everyday player. Meyers might be best used as an Eric Owens-style "designated irritant." Nieves might be a regular, but looks more like an old-style Mike Bordick or Rey Sanchez defense-and-singles player.

The best prospect in the system is 1998 first-round pick Corey Patterson, who hits for average and power, runs well, and plays a quality center field. There is a very slight chance that Patterson could jump from Single A ball to the majors this season, even though such a move would probably be to his detriment. Patterson showed a lack of patience at Class A Lansing that, unless addressed, will be cruelly exploited by higher-level pitchers.

FROM THE OUTLAND TO THE PENTLAND

Sammy Sosa's blossoming into a world-class slugger came only with major improvement in his discipline as a hitter. Prior to '98 he was a free swinger who tried to pull every pitch within a statute mile of home plate. Sosa still strikes out plenty often, but he has now become far more willing to take outside pitches the

SECRET WEAPON

If the Cubs had a secret weapon in 1999, it certainly was a secret even to them. Perhaps the most underrated performer the club boasted was part-time outfielder Glenallen Hill, who had an outstanding season in a platoon role. Oddly, Hill remained with the club even as other teams were clamoring for his bat around the trading deadline.

ACHILLES HEEL

While the starting pitching did not perform up to expectations—the staff ERA of 5.27 was second worst in the league—the Cubs' offense was equally, if not more, disappointing. Despite big seasons from Sosa, first sacker Mark Grace, and left fielder Henry Rodriguez, only three NL teams—San Diego, Florida, and Montreal—scored fewer runs than the toothless Cubs, who still play in one of the game's best hitters' parks. While Cub pitchers allowed 221 homers, worst in the league for any team not one mile high and 23 more than the old NL record, Chicago hitters finished just sixth in long-balls even with Sosa's performance.

ENOUGH ALREADY

The media's and fans' fascination with Sosa's home-run totals obscured the rest of the Cubs' 1999 picture—especially late in the season, when the team wasn't playing well. While it is understandable that the good news about Sosa got more ink and airtime than the bad news about the rest of the club, a more balanced assessment of the team would have been helpful. While it wasn't Sammy's fault that the media were in his face all year, his rather transparent "I'm not trying to hit home runs; I'm just trying to swing the bat and help the team" routine got tiresome very quickly.

other way—he's so strong that he can hit some of those for home runs anyway—and hold up on bad breaking pitches thrown low and outside.

Largely anonymous outside of Chicago, hitting coach Jeff Pentland deservedly received a great deal of credit for Sosa's improvement at the plate. Jeff spent 20 years toiling in college baseball as assistant coach, assistant athletic director, and hitting coach at various schools. He then spent almost five years as a scout and minor-league coach for the Marlins before he made it to the Show as hitting coach in Florida.

That role in Sosa's success was not the only reason Pentland survived the purge of the Cubs' coaching staff when Jim Riggleman was fired. Jeff was also credited with helping Henry Rodriguez iron out his swing against lefthanders.

A perfect example of the hitting coach's importance to the Cubs could be seen on the day veteran third baseman Shane Andrews reported to Chicago. Shane was found in the cage at Wrigley with Pentland, working to recover the power swing that got him to the majors in the first place. While it's too early to tell for sure, the early results were encouraging: Andrews hit .254 in 19 games with the Cubs while whacking 5 homers, compared to .181 with 11 homers in 98 games in Montreal.

It's really difficult to tell exactly how good a hitting coach is—especially if he's not a self-promoter or so controversial that he draws attention, like Walt Hriniak did. However, Pentland has clearly been a positive factor on the Cubs since he was hired in midseason '97, partly by getting into the heads of some players who were formerly believed to be uncoachable.

BEST CASE

A flurry of December transactions addressed what were some of the team's major 1999 problem areas: a low team on-base percentage, thin starting pitching, and poor catching. Veteran deadwood has been cleared away, some legitimate prospects are on the way, and, perhaps most importantly, the hiring of manager Don Baylor shows a commitment to ridding the organization of complacency. Key's to Chicago hope's are new second baseman Eric Young and pitcher Ismael Valdes, young shortstop Jose Nieves, and third baseman Shane Andrews, who appeared rejuvenated in a late-season trial. Now, if Kerry Wood can come back . . .

WORST CASE

Chicago depended on three star-quality players for its offense in 1999, and paid the price when the remainder of the lineup failed. Even now, after acquiring some decent players, the Cubs are still weak up the middle; there will be little offense generated by anyone behind the plate, in center field, or at shortstop. If Andrews doesn't come through at the hot corner, it'll be just another trouble spot for a superficially good but actually sub-average "attack." Combine that with a starting staff long on questions and a bullpen that can kindly be called paper-thin, and Baylor could face a very long season—especially from fans and media already on his bandwagon.

UNDER THE MICROSCOPE

CHAD MEYERS: The 185-pound 24-year-old does whatever it takes to get on base. He bunts well, always hustles, and has compiled more walks than strikeouts, a .302 average, and 115 stolen bases over the past three seasons. But Meyers didn't display the on-base ability in his two-month trial last year, and there are still doubts about his defense.
ROOSEVELT BROWN: Last year the 24-year-old hit 22 homers in just 268 Triple-A at-bats after beginning the campaign in Double-A. With an open spot in the Cubs' outfield, Brown's offense makes him a leading candidate. His defensive skills are average at best, so his production at the plate will likely determine his major-league tenure.
MIKE MEYERS: Meyers has opened eyes ever since being selected in the 26th round of the 1997 draft. The 22-year-old has posted a 24–9, 2.18 ERA mark through three professional seasons with 10.28 K/IP. He has a great breaking ball and a chance to crack the roster out of spring training.
RUBEN QUEVEDO: The best acquisition from Atlanta in the deal that involved Terry Mulholland and Jose Hernandez, Quevedo gives the Cubs a quality starter in waiting. The 21-year-old's low-90s fastball sneaks up on batters thanks to a fluid delivery and a loose arm. Quevedo also has decent curve and change-up offerings, giving him three solid pitches. The Venezuela native will get a chance out of spring training and should settle into the starting rotation nicely.

CHICAGO C U B S

TOP PROSPECTS

The Cubs set a club record by using 25 different pitchers to compensate for the loss of injured Kerry Wood in 1999. **KYLE FARNSWORTH**, who split '98 between Double-A and Triple-A, had some impressive starts with the big club but looked awful at times, too. LHP **MICAH BOWIE**, a highly regarded pitcher in the Braves' system, was roughed up badly in just about all of his starts after coming over in a trade. Others, rookies and veterans alike, all struggled, especially in the second half of the season.

While there are no pitchers in the system who compare to Wood, some minor-league arms may be ready to offer assistance this season. RHP **MIKE MEYERS**, who allowed just 89 hits while striking out 173 in 140 innings split between advanced Class A and Double-A, enjoyed a tremendous breakthrough season and could come along quickly this year. RHP **RUBEN QUEVEDO** turned his '99 season at Triple-A around following the trade that brought him and Bowie to the Cubs. Quevedo—who was 6–5, 5.37 ERA before and 3-1, 3.45 ERA after—is young with good stuff and could make the rotation out of spring training. LHP **SCOTT DOWNS**, who closed the season 8–1, 1.35 ERA at Double-A, and LHP **PHILLIP NORTON** will also be given opportunities for roster spots in 2000.

The two highest-regarded pitchers in the organization, RHP **CARLOS ZAMBRANO** and RHP **BEN CHRISTENSEN**, have yet to be tested above Class A. Zambrano more than held his own as an 18-year-old in the Midwest League, going 13–7, 4.17 ERA, and displaying a fastball reaching the mid-90s. Christensen, the Cubs' controversial first-round pick in 1999, is expected to throw in the mid-90s as well, despite lingering in the low 90s after signing. The Cubs also have high hopes for LHP **JOEY NATION**, the third hurler acquired from Atlanta in the trade.

The best position prospect in the system and one of the best in the game, OF **COREY PATTERSON**, has yet to play above Class A but is expected to make his presence felt as early as 2001. Patterson, the third overall pick in the 1998 draft, impressed in all areas in his debut season. He hit for average and power, displayed blazing speed on the bases and in center field, and showed a maturity beyond his 20 years. OF **JAISEN RANDOLPH**, who played a level higher than Patterson at the same age, has good speed and can play the outfield well but lacks the offensive upside of Patterson. The best outfielder in the higher levels of the minors in '99 was OF **ROOSEVELT BROWN**, who will be given a crack at filling the open spot in the Cubs' outfield this year.

The acquisition of 3B **COLE LINIAK** from Boston for Rod Beck added to a solid crop of infielders in the system. While Liniak could be ready to take over at the hot corner this year, **ERIC HINSKE** and **DAVID KELTON** will make pushes for that job in the seasons to follow. 2B **CHAD MEYERS** and SS **JOSE NIEVES** got their feet wet at the big-league level in '99 and are leading candidates to stick in 2000. Meyers, who has all the tools of a solid leadoff man, will need to shore up his defense, however, to ward off a move to the outfield. At first base, **JULIO ZULETA** has earned a spot on the 40-man roster with solid numbers in two straight seasons, and **HEE CHOI**, a native of Korea, passed his first season with flying colors. C **JEFF GOLDBACH**, who spent the entire '99 season at lower-level Class A, impressed with his power bat and strong arm and could be on the fast track.

▶ THE INSIDER 2000

CF
DAMON BUFORD 30
○ Jaisen Randolph A+ 21 97/5H
★ *Corey Patterson A- 20 98/1H

LF
***HENRY RODRIGUEZ 32**
GLENALLEN HILL 35
↑ *Roosevelt Brown ML 24 93/20H
? Scott Vieira 2A 26 95/28C
○ Franklin German A- 20 97/ND
○ Tydus Meadows A- 22 98/27C
? *Scott Sollmann 2A 25 96/7C

RF
SAMMY SOSA 31
*ROOSEVELT BROWN 24
? Marty Gazarek 3A 27 94/12C

SS
○ Jose Nieves ML 25 92/ND
○ Franklin Font 2A 22 95/ND
? *Jason Smith A+ 22 96/23C
? #Augie Ojeda 3A 25 96/13C

2B
ERIC YOUNG 33
↑ Chad Meyers ML 24 96/5C
○ Dennis Abreu A+ 22 94/ND
○ Tony Schrager A- 23 98/6C

3B
SHANE ANDREWS 28
○ Cole Liniak ML 23 95/7H
↑ *Eric Hinske 3A 22 98/17C
? Ron Walker 2A 24 97/8C
○ David Kelton A- 20 98/2H

1B
***MARK GRACE 36**
? Julio Zuleta 2A 25 92/ND
↑ *Hee Choi A- 21 99/ND

SP/RP

RELIEVERS
RICK AGUILERA 38
*FELIX HEREDIA 24
RODNEY MYERS 31
*MARK GUTHRIE 34
MATT KARCHNER 33
○ Steve Rain ML 25 93/11H
? Richie Barker ML 27 94/37C
? *Jon Cannon A+ 25 96/7C
? *Ray King ML 26 95/8C

C
JOE GIRARDI 35
***JEFF REED 37**
JOSE MOLINA 25
? Pat Cline 3A 25 93/6H
? Brad King 2A 25 96/17C
? Brad Ramsey A+ 23 96/39C
↑ Jeff Goldbach A- 20 98/2H

STARTERS
KEVIN TAPANI 36
JON LIEBER 30
KYLE FARNSWORTH 24
ISMAEL VALDES 26
SCOTT SANDERS 31
*ANDREW LORRAINE 27
KERRY WOOD 23
↑ Ruben Quevedo 3A 21 95/ND
? Elvin Hernandez 2A 22 93/ND
○ Chris Gissell 2A 22 96/4H
○ Jeff Yoder 2A 24 95/3H
↑ Mike Meyers 2A 22 97/26C
↓ Ben Christensen A+ 22 99/1C
↑ Carlos Zambrano A- 19 97/ND
? Matt Bruback A- 21 97/47C
? Michael Wuertz A- 21 97/11H
○ *Joey Nation A+ 21 97/2H
? *Ricardo Palma A- 20 96/ND
○ *Phillip Norton 3A 24 96/10C
○ *Micah Bowie ML 25 93/8H
○ *Brian McNichol ML 26 95/2C

MAJOR LEAGUERS IN ALL CAPS
Minor leaguers in upper-and-lower case

BEFORE A PLAYER'S NAME:
* left-handed hitter/pitcher
# switch-hitter
?=prospect status (see explanation)

AFTER A PLAYER'S NAME:
Level at which he spent most of 1999 season; age as of July 1, 2000; year he was drafted; round drafted (ND= non-drafted amateur free agent); drafted out of high school (H) or college (C)

EXPLANATION OF PROSPECT RATINGS

★ Potential big-league star

↑ Projected regular player in majors (for pitchers: rotation starter or closer)

○ Projected platoon or utility player in majors (pitcher: setup or middle relief)

? Possible big-league reserve or long reliever

↓ High draft pick or "tools" player who hasn't performed to expectations

CHICAGO

CINCINNATI REDS

Management
		Career Record
Manager	Jack McKeon	685–656 / .511
G.M.	Jim Bowden	554–515 / .518
President/CEO	Marge Schott [Carl Lindner]	249–238 / .511

1999 Record
Won–Lost	Pct.	Finish/G.B. (Division)	Finish/G.B. (Wild Card)
96–67	.589	2/1.5 (C)	2/1

Preseason Consensus Projection
4 (3.60)

1st Half	2nd Half	Home	Road	Intradivision	Interleague
43–31	53–36	45–37	51–30	38–25	7–8

Comebacks	Blowouts	Nail-Biters	Grass	Turf	Sept.–Oct.
13–12	24–14	45–37	36–20	60–47	20–12

NUMBERS DON'T LIE

	Team (Rank)		Opponents (Rank)		League Avg.
Runs/Game	5.31	(4)	4.36	(4)	5.00
Batting Avg.	.272	(6)	.241	(1)	.268
On-Base Avg.	.341	(9)	.324	(3)	.342
Slugging Avg.	.451	(3)	.411	(4)	.429
Strikeouts	1125	(10)	1081	(6)	1072
Home Runs	209	(3)	190	(9)	181
Stolen Bases	164	(4)	124	(9)	122
ERA	3.99	(4)			4.57
Errors	105	(4)			120

▶ THE INSIDER 2000

SURPRISING SYNERGY

The Reds delighted their fans with a Cinderella season in 1999, but it's still a long way to 2003 and the opening of their new ballpark. Cincinnati didn't spend the entire winter of 1998–99 looking for a way to become a contender in the NL Central, but now that it has happened, general manager Jim Bowden and his staff have many more tough decisions than they did a year ago. Construction on Corporate Sponsor Field hasn't started yet, so can the Reds realistically expect to compete until their new home finally is finished?

CASEY AT THE BAT AND POKEY-MON

Clearly the Reds view the right side of their infield as the players most likely to remain in the starting lineup come Opening Day 2003. Both Sean Casey and Pokey Reese exceeded even the wildest expectations with their play in '99, and the Reds should sign both to multiyear contracts. That alone would do wonders for the team's public image by immediately demonstrating that managment is willing to do what it takes to become a consistent contender.

Casey and Reese were perfect complements in many ways, the proverbial yin and yang of winning baseball games. While Casey was killing National League pitching in the first half of the season, Reese was stealing seemingly as many hits from opposing batters with his defense.

Reese played shortstop while coming up through Cincinnati's minor-league system and, though he played adequately in 24 starts at third base in 1998, there were serious questions about his ability to play the keystone position. Pokey ended all speculation early in the season with an amazing defensive display that produced one highlight clip after another. Bret Boone won a Gold Glove in 1998 in Cincinnati, but there wasn't any doubt among observers that Reese was the better defensive second baseman. Reese won his first Gold Glove in 1999; it won't be long before he's universally acknowledged as being the best at his position in the NL.

Bowden shocked most of the baseball world when he announced that Casey would be the next Fred McGriff or Jim Thome. Considering that Jack McKeon's son was the scout who signed Casey, maybe the world shouldn't have been shocked at Bowden's comment. At the time the Reds acquired Casey from

MOMENT OF TRUTH

Former Reds manager Ray Knight—doing commentary for ESPN during the playoffs—couldn't have been more correct when he said about Cincinnati: "Get me out of there and great things happen." With Knight running things like a preteen on a sugar high, there is little doubt the Reds would have self-destructed in spring training. But with a calm Jack McKeon at the helm, the young players on the roster were able to mature into a strong, cohesive unit and provide fitting complements to the veterans. McKeon's 50 years in baseball helped him push all the right buttons and led to him getting much of the credit for the team's success.

BIGGEST SURPRISE

Despite the Reds' sub-.500 record at home for the entire first half of the season, attendance was up nearly 15 percent in Cincinnati last year, and radio call-in show lines were overloaded with nothing but positive comments. And in a final tribute, more than 54,000 tickets were gobbled up in fewer than seven hours for the one-game wild-card playoff against the Mets—a game nobody knew was going to be played until five pre-dawn hours before the tickets went on sale.

BIGGEST DISAPPOINTMENT

Brett Tomko won 11 games in each of his first two seasons with the Reds, so expectations for him were high heading into 1999. Tomko never got things going, however, and clashed with manager Jack McKeon and pitching coach Don Gullett often during the season. Less than one month into the season Tomako made management mad enough to send him packing for Triple-A, and he never reconciled with McKeon or Gullett once he was recalled. He had some good outings, but he wasn't close to being the No. 1 or 2 starter.

Cleveland, there were plenty of baseball people who thought he would wind up being a glorified version of Hal Morris: a .300-hitting first baseman with little power.

Casey is a big player: He's listed as 6' 4" and 215 pounds, although he's certainly heavier than that. He didn't do much to discourage the Hal Morris—clone line of thinking in 1998, his first year with the Reds. Granted, he spent much of the first half recovering from being hit in the face with a thrown ball during batting practice, and he had a better second half. Overall, however, he hit only seven homers in 302 at-bats and didn't show much ability to pull the ball.

That changed last year, when Casey began turning on inside pitches. He was still lining outside pitches to left for hits, but he began pulling inside pitches with authority early in the season. Another positive sign was the way Casey fought through an extended second-half slump, changing his approach to counter adjustments made by NL pitchers.

Neither Casey nor Reese gave any indications last year that they would do anything but get better in the next few seasons. It didn't take Casey long to hit seven home runs in 1999, and while he's not likely to ever hit 50 homers, he should hit for more power as he gets older, a little stronger, and more experienced.

Reese won't ever hit for that kind of power, but he also has shown signs of making the necessary adjustments. He's cut down on his swing dramatically since his minor-league days, which has boosted his average to an acceptable level and erased a huge question mark. Given his defense, that's good enough. If he can add some more walks or more extra-base hits to his portfolio, he'll be terrific.

YOUNG GUNS

Most of the best young players the Reds have are in their bullpen. The fact that the bullpen was one of the biggest reasons for the team's success in '99 leads to plenty of optimism, especially for the near future. Cincinnati's top four relief pitchers were all youngsters: Danny Graves, Scott Williamson, Scott Sullivan, and Dennys Reyes were all 28 or younger at the start of the season.

Sullivan, who will be 29 on Opening Day, is the old man of the bullpen, and he's also the most experienced. He's been the workhorse of the pen, throwing more than 100 innings each of the past three seasons (counting his 29 Triple-A innings in 1997). That might be a cause for concern, but Sullivan throws sidearm (which is much easier on a pitcher's arm), gets his innings in bunches (averaging about 1.5 innings per appearance), and hasn't shown any signs of arm problems in the past three seasons. Graves also threw more than 100 innings last year, and Williamson would have as well if he hadn't missed two weeks in September with a cut on his finger and a mild case of shoulder tendinitis.

Williamson has the brightest future of any Reds pitcher. He is just 24 and gained valuable experience in his rookie season. The tendinitis he suffered was very mild, but it showed him he needs to be diligent with his arm-strengthening exercises. He's a strikeout pitcher with a power arm and could wind up being a dominating closer. He started the season in long relief but quickly began sharing the closing duties with Graves, pitching well enough to land on the NL All-Star team.

GREG VAUGHN: 40 HOMERS AND LITTLE ELSE

Greg Vaughn didn't have a very good year in 1999. It might be hard to believe that a guy who hit 45 homers and was the first Reds hitter to drive in more than 100 runs in a decade had a bad year, but it's true. Heading into a home stand on August 30, Vaughn was hitting only .230 with 29 homers and 80 RBI, which is unacceptable from a cleanup hitter in the late 1990s.

Vaughn often looked terrible at the plate up to the last month of the season. He was swinging at breaking pitches six inches outside, and it didn't take opposing teams long to figure out they'd rather face Vaughn than Casey. The Reds would be well advised to let some other team make a big-bucks mistake on a 34-year-old outfielder who has had only a handful of truly good years.

The trade for Dante Bichette is a strong indication that Vaughn's days in Cincinnati are numbered. Even if the Reds had not gone after Bichette, they easily could have moved Dmitri Young back to left field and platooned Michael Tucker and Jeffrey Hammonds in right. Young won't hit 40 homers, but he would hit for a much higher average than Vaughn, hit a lot more doubles, play as good or better defense, and might be worth more to the team in the long run. He will certainly be more cost-effective for a team that can't afford to overspend.

The Reds added D. T. Cromer to their 40-man roster shortly after the season ended, which is a good indication they think he could be a decent hitter. Cromer, 28, had an outstanding year at Triple-A Indianapolis in 1999, finishing in the top four in the

SECRET WEAPON

Dmitri Young has done so much with his bat the past two years, but sometimes it seems as if the Reds don't even notice his offensive success. An early-season slump put Young on the bench until July, but he was Cincinnati's best hitter the second half of the season. Sean Casey fought several slumps the second half of the season, and Greg Vaughn's bat was virtually comatose until September, but Young kept swinging away and maintained a torrid pace when the Reds needed his bat the most.

ACHILLES HEEL

One can't help but wonder how different things might have been had the Reds not wasted 29 starts on Steve Avery and Jason Bere, who were awful in all but a few of them. It was somewhat understandable that Bere was given 10 starts to try to get things straightened out before being yanked out of the rotation, considering how well he pitched at the end of the 1998 season, but Avery was another story. Avery hadn't been a viable starter for several years, and had no business even being on the Opening Day roster.

CINCINNATI

ENOUGH ALREADY

Whenever Greg Vaughn's name was mentioned through the majority of last season, his "valuable clubhouse leadership" was invariably the first thing talked about by television and radio analysts. The reality is, however, that Sean Casey quickly became the most important Reds player both on and off the field. He was the leader of a clubhouse near-revolt when there was talk of sending Steve Parris back to Triple-A because Parris was one of the few players with options remaining. Casey's pleading with Reds executives led to Mark Sweeney—a former teammate in San Diego and a close friend to Vaughn—being the one shipped to Indianapolis. That should have been the first indication of exactly where the clubhouse leadership rested.

International League in home runs (30), RBI (107), slugging (.563), hits (166), and extra-base hits (71). While Cromer is probably too old to become a star, he has shown the ability to punish minor-league pitching and could wind up being a valuable big-league hitter for a couple of years.

In many ways Cromer has had a career similar to that of Roberto Petagine, who spent 1998 in the Reds' farm system. Petagine was a better prospect: He started beating up on minor-league pitching in 1992, when he was a 21-year-old playing at Double-A in the Houston system and never stopped. Roberto never got a real chance in the majors with the Astros, the Padres, the Mets, or the Reds, getting just 307 at-bats in 193 games spread over parts of five seasons. Petagine spent last year playing every day in Japan; he smacked more than 40 homers, led his league in several offensive categories, and may have finally earned a long-overdue shot in the bigs.

THE SMELL OF THE GRASS

Team captain Barry Larkin made the strong suggestion at the All-Star break to install a grass field at Cinergy for 2000, since the NFL Bengals will no longer be playing there. Cinergy is known in the majors and in the NFL for having one of the most unforgiving turfs in pro sports; Larkin, like many aging veterans, feels playing on grass could keep him healthier and extend his career. Late in the 1999 season, management made the decision to spend the money.

But, a scheduling conflict has the Reds playing a home game in 2000 on the same day that the Bengals play an exhibition game in their brand-new stadium next door. Therefore, the Bengals' executives prohibited changing Cinergy's field to grass (their lease gives them veto power over changes in the old ballpark until August) unless the Reds agree to move the baseball game to another date. The Bengals, one of the worst NFL teams of the 1990s, have prevented the Reds from making improvements to Cinergy Field in the past, so it's not likely they will give in unless they get what they want.

It will be a big blow to the Reds if they aren't able to change from turf to grass for another season. Grass is far more popular with the players as well as with the fans, and it would be another sign to the public that the team has left behind the penny-pinching days of the past. Even if the Reds have to cave in to the Bengals' demands, it would be worth it in the long run to play 81 fewer games on plastic.

BEST CASE

The talent is there for the Reds to make the playoffs this year, even with Ken Griffey spending the season in Seattle. The only change to the lineup is replacing Greg Vaughn with Dante Bichette. If Dante can hit even reasonably well outside of Coors Field, Cincinnati's offense should be good enough; Sean Casey, Pokey Reese, Aaron Boone, and Dmitri Young should be at least as productive as they were last year. By not getting Griffey, the Reds kept their pitching staff intact as well. Cincinnati had the best bullpen in the National League last year, and Scott Sullivan and Scott Williamson pitching the seventh and eighth innings made up for a sometimes shaky rotation.

WORST CASE

Denny Neagle, Steve Parris, and Scott Williamson all missed time last season with various arm injuries, and the only reason Pete Harnisch didn't was because of sheer grit and determination. All are expected to be ready for the start of the season, yet questions remain. The Reds wanted Harnisch to have shoulder surgery after the '99 season to repair a frayed muscle, but he elected to try to strengthen the shoulder instead. Even though Neagle was dominating last August and September, can his shoulder last a full season? Needless to say, Cincy can't make a run at the playoffs with too many key pitchers out of action.

UNDER THE MICROSCOPE

TRAVIS DAWKINS: This 20-year-old played at Class A, Double-A, the majors, and for Team USA in the Pan American games, impressing with his outstanding defensive skills, stolen-base ability, and improved bat. Dawkins hit .300 at two levels with 17 doubles, 10 homers, and 53 stolen bases last season.

JASON LARUE: This 25-year-old backstop has established himself as one of the best-hitting catchers in the minor leagues, recording a .311 career average, a Double-A batting title in '98, and a whopping 93 doubles over the 1997 and '98 seasons. He handled the Cincinnati staff well enough in 1999 to have a roster spot set aside for him for this season.

ROB BELL: Reluctantly included by Atlanta in the Bret Boone deal, Bell became one of the Reds' top pitching prospects the day he was acquired. Likened to a young John Smoltz, the 21-year-old Bell has good size (6'5", 225 pounds) and throws a devastating curveball to go with an average fastball and change-up. Bell could surface in the big leagues sometime this season.

JOHN RIEDLING: A starter turned reliever, the 24-year-old Riedling may have found his niche in the bullpen. With a fastball in the low-90s range, the 5'11", 190-pounder posted a 2.57 ERA over 77 innings. Finishing at Triple-A, Riedling allowed 19 hits and a 1.54 ERA in 35 innings. He's still a fringe prospect but has a chance to relocate to Cincinnati sometime this season.

CINCINNATI R E

TOP PROSPECTS

1999 was a dream season for the Cincinnati Reds. They came within one game of reaching the playoffs, and many young players—some developed by the organization (Aaron Boone, Pokey Reese, Scott Sullivan, Scott Williamson) and some acquired from outside in trades for veterans (Sean Casey, Danny Graves, Dennis Reyes, Ron Villone)—emerged as quality major leaguers.

Heading into 2000, the Reds' farm system has several young outfield prospects, a few quality infield prospects, and a solid catcher, but few mound hopefuls. SS **TRAVIS "GOOKIE" DAWKINS** emerged last season as the top position prospect in the organization. 3B **BRANDON LARSON**, a 1997 first-round pick whose first two years ended with leg injuries, was healthy all season and batted .294 with 25 homers. SS-2B **ANTONIO PEREZ**, 18, batted .288 in a full-season league and is already considered the fastest player in the organization.

With the departure of Brian Johnson, C **JASON LARUE** will take over as the backup catcher, having shown a productive bat at the minor-league level in 1997–98 and continued defensive progress at the major-league level last season.

While the Reds have several talented outfielders, none is ready to step in at the big-league level. OF **MIKE FRANK** spent the entire 1999 season at Triple-A. He has leveled off after blistering 1997 and '98 campaigns. OF **BRADY CLARK** won the Double-A Southern League MVP award (.326, 17 HR, 75 RBI, 25 SB) and has plus tools, but he is already 26. The organization is excited about four young outfielders who played mostly at the lower Class A levels last season: **ALEJANDRO DIAZ, BEN BROUSSARD, AUSTIN KEARNS,** and **ADAM DUNN.** Diaz is a high-priced foreign talent with power and speed, and the other three were all high draft picks. Kearns and Dunn are noted for a complete arsenal of skills, while Broussard, drafted in 1999, is known as a basher. He blasted 24 homers in 292 at-bats while hitting .332 at three levels.

The Reds shouldn't count on much pitching help from the minor leagues this season. RHP **ROB BELL**, acquired from the Braves in the Denny Neagle deal, is one who could help, but he's coming off shoulder problems. The organization got a combined 34 wins from RHP **JOHN RIEDLING**, RHP **PHIL MERRELL**, and RHP **DAVE THERNAU** in 1999, but only Riedling is considered even a fringe prospect. Former big leaguers LHP **JIM CROWELL** and RHP **SCOTT WINCHESTER** continued their arm rehabs last season, and the organization traded away talented LHP **B. J. RYAN** and 17-year-old RHP **JACOBO SEQUEA** to acquire Jose Guzman from Baltimore.

CF
MIKE CAMERON 27
*KERRY ROBINSON 26
KIMERA BARTEE 27
○ *Mike Frank 3A 25 97/7C
○ Alejandro Diaz 2A 21 99/ND

LF
DANTE BICHETTE 36
PAT WATKINS 27
? Darron Ingram 2A 24 94/12H
? Andy Burress 2A 22 95/6H
○ *Ben Broussard 2A 23 99/2C
↑ *Adam Dunn A- 20 98/2H

RF
#DMITRI YOUNG 26
*MICHAEL TUCKER 29
○ Brady Clark 2A 27 96/NDC
↑ Austin Kearns A- 20 98/1H

SS
BARRY LARKIN 36
↑ Travis Dawkins ML 21 97/2H
? #Wilmy Caceras A- 21 97/ND
↑ Antonio Perez A- 18 98/ND

2B
POKEY REESE 27
CHRIS STYNES 27
? Jason Williams 3A 26 96/16C

3B
AARON BOONE 27
MARK LEWIS 30
CHRIS SEXTON 28
○ Brandon Larson 2A 24 97/1C

1B
***SEAN CASEY 25**
*HAL MORRIS 35
*MARK SWEENEY 30
*D.T. CROMER 29
↓ Ron Wright 2A 24 94/7H

SP/RP

RELIEVERS
DANNY GRAVES 26
SCOTT WILLIAMSON 24
SCOTT SULLIVAN 29
*GABE WHITE 28
*DENNYS REYES 23
*HEATH MURRAY 27
RICK GREENE 29
KEITH GLAUBER 28
? John Riedling 3A 24 94/22H
? Jose Acevedo A- 22 97/ND
? Pedro Minaya A- 22 93/ND

C
***EDDIE TAUBENSEE 31**
○ Jason LaRue ML 26 95/5C
○ Corky Miller 2A 24 98/NDH
? *Bobby Cripps 2A 23 95/40H

STARTERS
PETE HARNISCH 33
*DENNY NEAGLE 31
BRETT TOMKO 27
STEVE PARRIS 32
*RON VILLONE 30
? Phil Merrell 3A 22 96/4H
? Dave Thernau 3A 24 98/9C
↑ Rob Bell 2A 23 95/3H
? *Eddie Priest 3A 26 94/9C
? *Justin Atchley 3A 26 95/12C
↓ Ty Howington DP 22 99/1H
? *Jim Crowell 2A 26 95/NDC
? *Brett Haring 2A 25 97/NDC
? *Adrian Burnside A+ 23 95/ND

MAJOR LEAGUERS IN ALL CAPS
Minor leaguers in upper-and-lower case

BEFORE A PLAYER'S NAME:
* left-handed hitter/pitcher
# switch-hitter
?=prospect status (see explanation)

AFTER A PLAYER'S NAME:
Level at which he spent most of 1999 season; age as of July 1, 2000; year he was drafted; round drafted (ND= non-drafted amateur free agent); drafted out of high school (H) or college (C)

EXPLANATION OF PROSPECT RATINGS

★ Potential big-league star

↑ Projected regular player in majors (for pitchers: rotation starter or closer)

○ Projected platoon or utility player in majors (pitcher: setup or middle relief)

? Possible big-league reserve or long reliever

↓ High draft pick or "tools" player who hasn't performed to expectations

CINCINNATI

HOUSTON ASTROS

Management
Manager	Larry Dierker
G.M.	Gerry Hunsicker
President/CEO	Drayton McLane Jr.

Career Record
270–189 / .588
365–283 / .563
592–477 / ..554

1999 Record
Won–Lost	Pct.	Finish/G.B. (Division)	Finish/G.B. (Wild Card)
97–65	.599	1 (C)	

Preseason Consensus Projection
1 (1.20)

1st Half	2nd Half	Home	Road	Intradivision	Interleague
45–32	52–33	50–32	47–33	31–31	12–3

Comebacks	Blowouts	Nail-Biters	Grass	Turf	Sept.–Oct.
12–2	35–14	30–31	34–23	63–42	18–10

NUMBERS DON'T LIE

	Team (Rank)	Opponents (Rank)	League Avg.
Runs/Game	5.08 (8)	4.17 (2)	5.00
Batting Avg.	.267 (8)	.266 (9)	.268
On-Base Avg.	.355 (3)	.326 (4)	.342
Slugging Avg.	.420 (11)	.397 (2)	.429
Strikeouts	1138 (11)	1204 (1)	1072
Home Runs	168 (11)	128 (1)	181
Stolen Bases	166 (3)	94 (2)	122
ERA	3.84 (3)		4.57
Errors	106 (6)		120

▶ THE INSIDER 2000

LOOK OUT, CLEVELAND!

The Houston Astros are perfectly positioned to become the National League's version of the Cleveland Indians. Whereas Cleveland and Atlanta were the rags-to-riches stories of the '90s, Houston could very well be the success story of the next decade.

Until Atlanta's Walt Weiss made his unbelievable play in the 10th inning of game three of the Division Series—effectively ending the Astros' season—it was a successful final year in the Astrodome. The team drew 2,706,017 fans, setting a franchise record by a comfortable margin, partly because the Astros were in first place from April 30 through the end of June. They had the best record in the league in early June when they were stunned by manager Larry Dierker's life-threatening seizure during a game on June 13.

Despite the distraction and the inevitable disruption, interim manager Matt Galante managed to keep the team from nosediving. During the 27 games Dierker missed, the Astros went 13–14 and retained a tenuous hold on first place even as four more regulars went down with injuries. Dierker's much-quicker-than-expected return to the dugout after the All-Star break was, of course, a huge emotional lift for the team and the fans.

Until the last week of the season the increasingly banged-up Astros kept ahead of the upstart Cincinnati Reds, except for one week in mid-August when the two teams shared first place for six days. On September 26, though, an 11–3 drubbing by Milwaukee dropped Houston into a tie for first with Cincinnati on the eve of a two-game series between the two clubs. Jose Lima lost 4–1 in the first game before a franchise record 54,037 fans at the Dome, giving the Cincy a one-game lead. Mike Hampton saved the Astros the next day, shutting down the Reds, 4–1, to restore the deadlock.

In the final weekend of the season Houston triumphed in a bizarre, seesawing, three-way race with Cincinnati and New York for two postseason spots: the NL Central title and the wild-card championship. The Astros started the postseason by beating the Braves in Atlanta, but they ultimately lost a heartbreaking series to the eventual NL pennant winners.

Despite the familiar taste of defeat after the team's third straight exit in the NL Division Series, everyone connected with the Astros should look on the bright side. In a dramatic turnaround that no one would have predicted a few years ago, Houston has managed to do something that even Cleveland—along with Atlanta, the model franchises of the past decade—couldn't.

MOMENT OF TRUTH

Houston was riding high with the best record in the National League when manager Larry Dierker suffered a seizure during a game against San Diego on June 13. Houston won their first game without Dierker, but then lost nine of the next 14, including a four-game sweep that let the Reds back in the race and gave the Cincinnati upstarts a feeling that they could compete with the two-time defending NL Central champs. Although the Astros led the division for most of the second half of the season, and never fell too far behind the Reds, they couldn't shake the Reds until the last three games of the season.

BIGGEST SURPRISE

Based on his performance in 1997 and '98, it could have been expected that Carl Everett would have a good year in 1999, but even the most ardent fans could not have predicted how well he'd play. The former first-round draft choice set career highs in virtually every offensive category. His .325 average was 29 points better than he'd hit before, his .398 OBA was 66 points above his career average, and he scored 14 more runs, stole 13 more bases, and hit 10 more home runs than he had in any other season. He helped solidify Houston's offense with Moises Alou out all year and Ken Caminiti on the DL for half the season.

BIGGEST DISAPPOINTMENT

Third base had been something of a revolving door for the Astros in the four seasons since they traded Ken Caminiti to the Padres, so the team was understandably overjoyed when it got the popular player back as a free agent prior to 1999. The good feelings didn't last long, however, as Caminiti quickly suffered a leg injury that caused him to miss the middle three months of the season.

(The Astros circumstances more closely parallel the Indians of the early 1990s than those of the Braves.) Unlike the Indians (which limped out of the Mistake by the Lake in sixth place in 1993 toward their bright future in the Jake), the Astros built a contending club and won the hearts of their fans while they were still in their old ballpark.

Also unlike Cleveland, Houston has a great manager to guide them into the future. Larry Dierker is one of only six managers in major-league history to win a division title in his first season, and one of only four skippers to win a division title in each of his first three years. He took a club that had finished a disappointing second in a weak division for three consecutive years under Terry Collins and turned it into a winner. Larry finished third in NL Manager of the Year voting in 1997 and '99 and won the award in '98.

Like Cleveland in 1993, Houston has a couple of superstar hitters (though Bagwell and Biggio are in their 30s while Albert Belle was 26 and Manny Ramirez had just made his debut at 21). Unlike Cleveland, Houston has a deep and solid starting rotation as well as a brilliant closer. Like Cleveland, Houston has a productive farm system, though the Astros' organization is deeper in pitching and not as rich in hitting talent as the Indians' system.

In their 38-year history, the Astros have never played in the World Series. As Cleveland was in 1994, Houston is a team on the verge of breaking into the top ranks of perennial contenders, and baseball fans will soon be watching October Classic games broadcast from Enron Field.

SECOND-CHANCE CITY

Much of Houston's success in the past three years has been due to getting real value from players other teams have cast off. A talent-deprived team can rarely make itself into a contender by astute trading and cash acquisitions (e.g., Philadelphia and Milwaukee), but a team with superior core talent can frequently acquire surplus talent cheaply to cover its holes and fill in for injuries.

Last year Houston suffered from 14 disabling injuries, including injuries to all regulars in the lineup except Bagwell and Biggio, though Biggio was playing through foot problems. Billy Spiers and Tim Bogar again contributed significantly to the NL Central champions, Billy with his bat and versatility (he played every position except pitcher and catcher), and Bogar with his glove. Stan Javier and Matt Mieske also helped out, especially late in the season when Richard Hidalgo was out with injuries and Derek Bell had played himself out of regular duty.

The biggest prizes reeled in on the cheap by GM Gerry Hunsicker, of course, have been outfielder Carl Everett and pitcher Jose Lima. Lima was probably the least important part of the nine-player deal Houston made with Detroit in 1996, given that he was a failed prospect with an 8–16 record and a 6.24 ERA in parts of three seasons with the Tigers. Everett was acquired for John Hudek, a 30-year-old reliever then recovering from career-threatening arm problems.

Everett, considered one of the prize draft picks Florida made in the 1992 expansion draft, played himself out of New York after three disappointing seasons in the Mets' outfield (career .245 BA and .319 OBA through '97). In '98 Everett hit .296 with a .356 on-base percentage in Houston; in '99 his career year made him a mainstay of the Astros' lineup as he hit .325 with superb .398 on-base and .571 slugging averages. With Moises Alou out for the whole season, the Astros wouldn't have won the division without Everett. Moreover, as a switch-hitter with far more power from the left side, his 21 homers versus righties was an important counterweight to Houston's mostly right-handed lineup.

As it turned out, Lima needed both a second and a third chance in Houston: He went 1–6 with a 5.28 ERA in relief in his first season with the Astros. But Larry Dierker and pitching coach Vern Ruhle kept working with the supercompetitive Lima, helping him develop a decent sinker and a serviceable slider to mix with his four-seam fastball which wasn't good enough to throw by hitters who were looking for it. Lima turned into a big winner due to his exceptional control and his mixture of pitches, not his raw stuff.

The Houston brain trust saw a huge payoff for their work with Lima in 1998–99 (37 wins and 18 losses). The 27-year-old Lima, combined with homegrown starters Shane Reynolds (32), Mike Hampton (27), and the very promising Scott Elarton (24), now form a rotation that most teams besides Atlanta and the Yankees are jealous of.

Baseball's Mahatma, Branch Rickey, is often quoted as having said, "Luck is the residue of design." Larry Dierker's design for Jose Lima certainly paid off.

BILLY THE KID

Flamethrowing closer Billy Wagner had one of the truly great relief seasons of all time in 1999. How good was he?

SECRET WEAPON

Houston's catching platoon of Tony Eusebio and Paul Bako doesn't get the recognition it deserves. They provide a lot of value, especially defensively, at a critical position. They handled the pitching staff well, combined to throw out 35 percent of runners attempting to steal, and contributed a bit on offense. Things could have been a lot worse after Mitch Meluskey went down for the season with a shoulder injury in late April.

ACHILLES HEEL

There is no doubt that Craig Biggio and Jeff Bagwell are Houston's best players, but their complete lack of post-season production is the biggest reason the Astros have been eliminated from the Division Series in each of the past three years. Biggio, the team's leadoff hitter and offensive sparkplug, is a combined 5-for-42 in Division Series losses to the Braves, Padres, and Braves again. Bagwell hasn't fared any better, managing just five hits in 39 at-bats. Neither has more than two hits in any of the series, so it's not hard to see why Houston has won only one of its past 10 postseason games.

HOUSTON ASTROS

ENOUGH ALREADY

Derek Bell shot his mouth off all season, complaining mostly about playing time, and ruined the good thing he had going. It's one thing to whine if you're hitting the cover off the ball, but Bell's numbers didn't justify him getting more at-bats than he did. Bell has had his moments, but he's never been a consistent hitter, either for average or power, and his play in the outfield has sometimes been suspect. The club wasn't happy with his performance either on or off the field in 1999, so his days in Houston will be over if the club can find anyone to take his contract.

In 66 appearances Wagner saved 39 games and won four more, losing only one game and blowing only three saves. He posted a 1.57 ERA, allowing an incredible 35 hits in 74.2 innings. Enemy hitters managed only a meek .135 batting average and a .208 on-base average against Wagner. What's more, he did all of this with excellent control, allowing only 22 unintentional walks. From August 13 till the end of the regular season, Wagner was literally untouchable (as opposed to virtually untouchable the rest of the year). He saved 11 games in 21 appearances, striking out 38 while allowing only 5 hits and no runs in 23 innings.

Depending exclusively on his fastball, Wagner generates seemingly impossible velocity from his 5'11", 180-pound frame. If hitters get a glimpse of it rushing by at 98–100 miles per hour, they can rarely get their bat on it. If they hit it, they can rarely hit it squarely: Billy allowed only five homers in '99. Lefty power hitters, of course, have even more problems because they never see Wagner's high heat in their down-and-in hot zone, where they generate most of their power. In five years and 253 innings, only one left-handed hitter has taken him out of the yard.

Wagner has saved 101 games in the three-plus years he's been a closer. At 28, he could easily clinch a place as one of the greatest lefty relievers in history over the next couple of years. If he remains injury-free (he suffered a slight strain in his pitching elbow in late September, but it wasn't believed to be serious) and can master his curve or develop a change-up as his fastball drops in velocity—both big ifs—he's got a chance to become one of the greatest relievers ever.

BEST CASE

The Astros have again positioned themselves to make a serious run in the postseason and will again be the favorite in the NL Central this spring. The club traded Carl Everett to Boston but expects that Moises Alou will be back after missing all of last year. Houston also desperately wants to find a way to get top prospect Daryle Ward into the lineup. (Good-bye, Derek Bell?) Houston has a solid lineup and easily the best starting rotation in the division, meaning the first year in their new ballpark should mean a return trip to the postseason.

WORST CASE

In mid-December GM Gerry Hunsicker made waves by saying the Astros might trade Mike Hampton rather than see him walk as a free agent after this season. Houston wanted to sign Hampton to a contract extension, but the talented lefty said he wanted to see how much money he could get on the open market. It's surely debatable whether it's better to trade a player in that situation or to keep him and take draft choices as compensation, now that Hampton is with the Mets, the Astros may see their string of division titles end.

UNDER THE MICROSCOPE

LANCE BERKMAN: Berkman underwent arthroscopic knee surgery one month into the 1999 season and missed some valuable development time prior to his call-up to Houston. The switch-hitter batted .323 in 226 Triple-A at-bats and .237 in 93 big-league at-bats. Berkman will have an opportunity to win a corner outfield job this spring if he can show that his defense has progressed enough.
JULIO LUGO: Lugo made significant progress in his repeat season in Double-A, batting .319 with 10 homers and 25 stolen bases. Still just 23, he has five-plus tools, can bunt, and has extra-base power. With the Astros in search of a shortstop, Lugo could put his name in for 2001.
WADE MILLER: Miller was off to a great start in '98 at Double-A before a finger injury shut him down in May. He returned to full strength last season and went 11–9, 4.38 ERA at Triple-A, reestablishing himself as a legitimate prospect. Miller's fastball tops out at 94 mph, with good command and sinking action. There probably will not be a spot in the rotation for the 24-year-old this season, but he could stick as a middle reliever.
TONY MCKNIGHT: McKnight went 9–9, 2.75 ERA at Double-A. He's big and strong at 6'5", 220 pounds, and he dominated righties with his low-90s fastball, effective curve, and change. He's stuck behind Miller and one of the best starting rotations in the game, but he does provide the Astros with insurance or trade bait.

HOUSTON

TOP PROSPECTS

Despite a smaller budget than most organizations and a reputation for poor drafts in the '90s, the Astros have a solid minor-league system that has produced many quality players. They won their third straight division title last season and got contributions from several graduates of their farm system. RHP **SCOTT ELARTON** did a magnificent job in middle relief before being moved to the starting rotation at mid season. Despite minor shoulder surgery over the winter, he should be okay and a fixture in the starting rotation for some time. Despite defensive questions, 1B **DARYLE WARD** showed that his thunderous bat will be difficult to keep out of the lineup this season. 3B **RUSS JOHNSON** proved a dependable utility player and OF **LANCE BERKMAN**, the top hitting prospect in the organization, provided a glimpse into the future when myriad injuries forced the Astros to bring him up earlier than expected. Houston had hopes for C **MITCH MELUSKEY**, but a shoulder injury felled him early in the season. Still, the organization is counting on him to play a significant role in 2000.

The Astros traded away several prospects (Ramon Castro, Oscar Henriquez, Mark Johnson, Manny Barrios, Freddy Garcia, John Halama, Carlos Guillen) in 1998 to bring in Jay Powell, Moises Alou, and Randy Johnson. Although they made no such moves last season, those trades depleted much of the overall depth the organization had accumulated. With Ward, Johnson, Meluskey, and perhaps Berkman set to play in the major-leagues this season, pitching has become the strength of the organization. RHP **WADE MILLER**, who missed most of the '98 season with a finger injury, rebounded last season and is capable of winning 15 games in the near future. RHP **TONY MCKNIGHT**, a 1995 first-round pick, had a breakthrough season at Double-A and is now considered a legitimate prospect. Fifteen-game winner LHP **WILFREDO RODRIGUEZ** was the top pitching prospect in the Class A Florida State League and has a big upside. Another southpaw to watch is fellow 15-game winner LHP **JEROMIE ROBERTSON**, who pitched at Double-A and broke the Jackson franchise record for innings pitched. RHP **ERIC IRELAND** had his second consecutive solid season at Class A. Though he doesn't possess an overpowering fastball, Ireland is a workhorse and has command and location, as he demonstrated with a nine-inning perfect game in the Florida State League.

Berkman and Ward will be offensive forces if they can find a spot to play; however, there isn't anybody else with a chance to contribute in the near future. 1B **AARON MCNEAL** slugged 38 homers at Class A but he's several levels away; SS-2B **CARLOS HERNANDEZ** has the makings of a fine utility infielder but lacks the offense to play every day. SS **JULIO LUGO** is the most talented of the upper-level prospects, but he spent his second straight season at Double-A. 3B **CHRIS TRUBY** clubbed 28 homers at Double-A and is excellent defensively, but he's 25 years old. Both Lugo and Truby were blocked from Triple-A by Hernandez and 3B **CARLOS VILLALOBOS**, but will probably move past them on the depth chart.

While they have not graded out well in the amateur draft, the Astros reaped huge dividends by being the first organization to mine Venezuela, signing Bobby Abreu, Richard Hidalgo, Carlos Guillen, Carlos Hernandez, Freddy Garcia, and Wilfredo Rodriguez, among others. Since Gerry Hunsicker took over general manager duties in '96, Houston has refocused its development efforts, pouring money into scouting and instruction and not relying as heavily on the Latin connection.

▶ THE INSIDER 2000

LF
MOISES ALOU 33
MATT MIESKE 32
★ #Lance Berkman ML 24 97/1C

CF
RICHARD HIDALGO 24
#GLEN BARKER 29

RF
#**ROGER CEDENO** 25
? Eric Cole 2A 24 95/20C

SS
TIM BOGAR 33
○ Adam Everett 2A 23 98/1C
○ Carlos Hernandez ML 24 92/ND
○ Julio Lugo 2A 24 94/43C

2B
CRAIG BIGGIO 34
? Jhonny Perez 2A 23 93/ND

3B
#**KEN CAMINITI** 37
RUSS JOHNSON 27
*BILL SPIERS 34
○ Chris Truby 2A 26 92/NDH

1B
JEFF BAGWELL 32
↑ *Daryle Ward ML 25 94/15C
○ Aaron McNeal A- 22 95/27C

SP/RP

RELIEVERS
*BILLY WAGNER 28
JAY POWELL 28
*TREVER MILLER 27
DOUG HENRY 36
JOSE CABRERA
? Tim Redding A- 22 97/20C
? *Tony Mounce 3A 25 94/7H

C
TONY EUSEBIO 33
*PAUL BAKO 28
#MITCH MELUSKEY 26
? #Mike Rose 2A 23 95/5H
? John Buck A- 19 98/7H

STARTERS
JOSE LIMA 27
SHANE REYNOLDS 32
SCOTT ELARTON 24
OCTAVIO DOTEL 24
CHRIS HOLT 28
↑ Wade Miller ML 23 96/20C
↑ Tony McKnight 2A 23 95/1H
○ Eric Ireland 2A 23 95/2H
? Tom Shearn A+ 22 96/29H
↓ Brad Lidge A+ 23 98/1C
○ Roy Oswalt A- 22 96/23C
↓ Mike Nannini A- 19 98/1H
↑ *Jeromie Robertson 2A 23 95/24H
? *Bryan Braswell 2A 25 96/4C
↑ *Wilfredo Rodriguez A+ 21 95/ND
? *Greg Miller A- 20 97/5H

MAJOR LEAGUERS IN ALL CAPS
Minor leaguers in upper-and-lower case

BEFORE A PLAYER'S NAME:
* left-handed hitter/pitcher
# switch-hitter
*=prospect status (see explanation)

AFTER A PLAYER'S NAME:
Level at which he spent most of 1999 season; age as of July 1, 2000; year he was drafted; round drafted ND= non-drafted amateur free agent); drafted out of high school (H) or college (C)

EXPLANATION OF PROSPECT RATINGS

★ Potential big-league star

↑ Projected regular player in majors (for pitchers: rotation starter or closer)

○ Projected platoon or utility player in majors (pitcher: setup or middle relief)

? Possible big-league reserve or long reliever

↓ High draft pick or "tools" player who hasn't performed to expectations

HOUSTON

MILWAUKEE BREWERS

Management
		Career Record
Manager	Jim Lefebvre	417–442 / .485
G.M.	Sal Bando [Dean Taylor]	585–644 / .476
President/CEO	Wendy Selig-Prieb	74–87 / .460

1999 Record
Won–Lost	Pct.	Finish/G.B. (Division)	Finish/G.B. (Wild Card)
74-87	.460	5/22.5 (C)	8/22

Preseason Consensus Projection
6 (5.55)

1st Half	2nd Half	Home	Road	Intradivision	Interleague
35–41	39–46	32–48	42–39	32–30	8–6

Comebacks	Blowouts	Nail-Biters	Grass	Turf	Sept.–Oct.
12–11	19–28	41–42	58–75	16–12	17–13

NUMBERS DON'T LIE

	Team (Rank)		Opponents (Rank)		League Avg.
Runs/Game	5.06	(9)	5.50	(14)	5.00
Batting Avg.	.273	(5)	.284	(14)	.268
On-Base Avg.	.353	(4)	.356	(14)	.342
Slugging Avg.	.426	(9)	.456	(14)	.429
Strikeouts	1065	(8)	987	(14)	1072
Home Runs	165	(12)	213	(14)	181
Stolen Bases	81	(13)	177	(16)	122
ERA	5.08	(14)			4.57
Errors	127	(9)			120

▶ THE INSIDER 2000

TRIPLE WITCHING HOUR

You really have to feel for the Milwaukee Brewers. With a chance to make a clean break from the past and move into brand-new Miller Park, the 2000 season was viewed as salvation for the struggling franchise. Commissioner Bud Selig finally excused himself, putting his daughter Wendy Selig-Prieb in charge, and the team brought in some interesting players as it geared up for the final year in old County Stadium. Thus 1999 seemed like the end of a disappointing era for Milwaukee.

At midseason, everything was going well: The Brew Crew was just two games under .500, Jeromy Burnitz was hitting the tar out of the ball, and unexpected pitching hero Hideo Nomo had resurrected his career. The final year in County Stadium was shaping up to be as memorable as anyone could have hoped.

On July 14, tragedy struck during construction of Miller Park. A crane lifting a 400-ton section of the new park's roof fell, killing three ironworkers and wrecking a large part of the park. The structural damage caused the grand opening to be postponed until spring 2001, meaning a huge loss in projected revenues to the ball club this year (some estimates were as high as $45 million).

Despite this terrible setback, the Brewers did not crawl into a hole and die. Perhaps it even accelerated their gut rehab plans, as Selig-Prieb dumped GM Sal Bando and manager Phil Garner in August. Former Braves' assistant GM Dean Taylor was named to run the team a month later; on November 4, Davey Lopes was named the new skipper. The Brewers also rolled out new uniforms and a new logo for 2000.

Taylor is one of the new breed of GMs, trained in economics and sports management rather than baseball. He openly admits to not being skilled in the evaluation of talent. His approach, therefore, is to bring in people who know talent and to supervise them. Early returns were encouraging; new VP of player personnel Dave Wilder, brought in from the Cubs, is well regarded, and most people in the game felt it was high time that Lopes, a smart player respected for his leadership ability, got a chance to run a club.

Unfortunately for the new brain trust, the talent they inherited is distinctly middle-of-the-pack. The farm system has a few pitching prospects but is otherwise very thin. Clearly the Brewers will have to do more with less, at least for another year until new stadium revenues kick in.

The question is whether the struggling Brewers can survive the triple whammy of their miserable 1999 season, their lackluster tradition, and the Miller Park tragedy.

MOMENT OF TRUTH

Things were looking up in Milwaukee on the morning of July 14. The team was playing decent ball, hanging around the .500 mark, and Jeromy Burnitz had just finished putting on a show in the Home Run Derby contest before the All-Star game. On that fateful afternoon, however, a crane used in the construction of Miller Park broke loose and brought part of the retractable roof, as well as hopes for the team's future, crashing down. The new park won't be ready for at least another year, and the club's plan for making the team a contender might take even longer. The horrible accident ruined what was supposed to be a happy farewell to County Stadium, and the gloom and doom it spawned might have led directly to manager Phil Garner's firing.

BIGGEST SURPRISE

When an announcement was made in the County Stadium press box during an April 29 game with the Dodgers that the Brewers had signed Hideo Nomo, laughter rang out from the sportswriters from both Milwaukee and Los Angeles. But Nomo, the ex-Dodger star who had been released by both the Mets and the Cubs in the previous month, wound up with the last laugh. Hideo regained some velocity and control and finished leading the team in wins. Nomo is not back to where he was in his first two years in Los Angeles, but he was plenty good enough to revive his career and shut his critics up.

BIGGEST DISAPPOINTMENT

Third baseman Sean Berry had played exactly three games in his career at first base, so there was plenty of head scratching when the Brewers made him their starting first baseman for '99. Berry has never had the kind of power needed from that position; even allowing for that, his performance in Brewtown lacked. Sean hit only .175 against left-handers and managed to clout only two home runs, both coming in the first two months of the season.

COLLAPSE AFTER THE CRASH

At the All-Star break, Milwaukee was 42–44, 7.5 games out of first. Afterward, the team went 32–43 and plummeted to 22.5 games out. Things hit rock bottom in August, when they lost 21 of 29 games, including an unbelievable streak of 13 games in which no Brewers' player hit a homer. The fans were so angry that they were even booing former favorites like Jeff Cirillo. Only a strong September and October (17–13) saved the team from complete hopelessness, but by then it was far too late.

For many years the Brewers have struggled to score runs, lacking both power and high-average hitters. In 1999, however, Milwaukee's offense did a decent job—even playing half their games in a park somewhat hostile to hitters.

The Brewers ranked ninth in the league in runs, but could have and should have been better; their on-base average was fourth in the NL, at .353. They stole bases effectively, hit doubles, and did not ground into many double plays. Power was a weakness, and the Brew Crew led the loop in runners left on base.

The offense would have been adequate if the Milwaukee pitching had been good at all. It wasn't. The Brewers' staff was an ugly mess, racking up a 5.07 ERA, which was better only than the Cubs and the Rockies. Most of the problems centered on the back end of the starting rotation. Among Rafael Roque, Bill Pulsipher, and Cal Eldred, the Brewers started 55 games with pitchers with starting ERAs of 6.00 or higher.

As bad as this was, the future of Milwaukee's rotation looks far better than it did a year ago, even though the departure of Hideo Nomo hurts. None of the above disasters should see a major role in 2000, and the holdovers—Scott Karl, Kyle Peterson, and Steve Woodard—are all quality pitchers. Since none of them is a power pitcher, they will need good defensive support to succeed.

As for the rest of the rotation, Milwaukee has some options. The signing of Jason Bere was a low-cost gamble that could work out. A few prospects, including Horacio Estrada, Allen Levrault, and Brian Passini, also could develop. Trading out-of-favor middle infielders Jose Valentin or Fernando Vina would work nicely, since it wouldn't open up any new holes.

It's clear that the intense Lopes won't lose with a grin. He quickly said that he planned to shake up the Brewers' oft-complacent clubhouse. With a few quality players in place (Burnitz, Cirillo, Jenkins, Belliard, Wickman) and a lot more question marks (Rocky Coppinger, Jeff DiAmico, Bere, Vina, Valentin), Lopes will have to get the maximum production from his talent.

In particular, Lopes will need to jump-start Marquis Grissom, whose offense has been disappointing. Worse, his speed has declined and his range is now average at best. Heis signed through 2002; Lopes needs to find out if he has anything left in the tank.

So there will be one more season in drafty, lovable, friendly old County Stadium: one more year to see a vanishing breed of pre-mall, old-fashioned, family-run baseball. The team is not going to be great, but enjoy the experience while you can—it'll be gone before you know it.

THE BOO CREW

The Milwaukee Brewers don't exactly have a proud tradition. Other than a five-year stretch from 1978 through 1982, the Brewers have finished higher than fourth only five times since the bankrupt Seattle Pilots franchise moved to Milwaukee in 1970.

The Brewers finished fourth in 1970, then finished fifth or sixth until 1978. That year the club finished third and began to assemble the players who would make up its 1982 pennant winner. In 1978 Paul Molitor was a rookie, Gorman Thomas played his first full season, and Ben Oglivie was in his first year with the Brewers. Those three teamed with Robin Yount and Cecil Cooper to form the nucleus of the 1981–82 team.

Since that magical season, the Brewers have fallen on hard times. The Brewers won 87 games in 1983 but finished fifth in a tough AL East that had Baltimore, Detroit, and New York all winning more than 90 games. Yount went from a unanimous MVP selection in '82 to just a good player as he hit 12 fewer homers and drove in 34 fewer runs. Molitor scored 41 fewer runs as his batting average fell by 32 points, Oglivie suffered through injuries (200 fewer at-bats, 21 fewer home runs, 36 fewer RBIs), and Thomas was traded to Cleveland in June. The pitching staff didn't suffer as much, but Rollie Fingers missed the whole season with an arm injury and Don Sutton, acquired late in '82, went 8–13. The team finished last in 1984 and has had only four winning seasons since.

Milwaukee appeared to finally turn the corner in 1992, when the Brewers hired Sal Bando as general manager, and Bando

SECRET WEAPON

Geoff Jenkins quietly emerged as a quality player in his second season with the Brewers. The former first-round draft pick was among the team leaders in most offensive categories even though he didn't get the recognition garnered by Jeromy Burnitz, Jeff Cirillo, or Dave Nilsson. Jenkins finished second on the Brewers in batting and slugging average in his sophomore year while displaying plus range in left field.

ACHILLES HEEL

It's never a good sign when an unknown and untested pitcher such as Rafael Roque is your Opening Day starter. While the Brewers found a hidden gem in Hideo Nomo for a year, the rest of the starting rotation was in perpetual chaos. Scott Karl once had promise, but now is no better than a fourth or fifth starter. Jason Bere and Bill Pulsipher proved they're not the pitchers they used to be, and Cal Eldred apparently will continue to throw belt-high fastballs until opposing hitters prove they can't hit them out of the ballpark.

ENOUGH ALREADY

The Cincinnati Reds and low-budget Oakland Athletics have put the heat on organizations like the Milwaukee Brewers. By being competitive with payrolls of about $35 million, the Reds and the A's have shown that if you manage your money wisely, you can play good baseball and at least have a chance of making the playoffs. The Brewers, who spent half of their payroll on good but nowhere near outstanding players such as Cal Eldred, Dave Nilsson, and Marquis Grissom, are being forced to learn fiscal responsibility—and learn it quickly. Because of the disappointment in recent seasons, the new Brewers' regime will be under the gun to turn the franchise around immediately, new park or no new park.

hired Phil Garner to manage. That tandem produced instant success, winning a surprising 92 games and finishing second in the AL East. Milwaukee had the best pitching in the AL in 1992, with a starting staff of Bill Wegman, Jaime Navarro, Chris Bosio, Ricky Bones, and Cal Eldred. That optimism didn't last very long, however, as Milwaukee finished last in '93 and has had a losing record every season since.

Milwaukee's starting pitching should take most of the blame for the team's collapse in 1993. Things fell apart that year, especially among the top three starters. Bill Wegman won 13 games with a 3.20 ERA in '92 but was 4–14 with a 4.48 ERA in '93. Jaime Navarro went from 17–11, 3.33 in '92 to 11–12, 5.33 in '93. Cal Eldred went from 11–2, 1.79 in a half-season to 16–16, 4.01.

Milwaukee went from fifth in the league in runs in '92 to ninth in '93 and 13th in '94. The club has finished no higher than seventh in runs since 1992 and has managed to finish that high only twice. In the past three seasons the club has been 13th, 10th, and ninth offensively.

As bad as the hitting has been recently, the pitching has been even worse. In fact, Milwaukee's pitching has been downright brutal since 1992. The only exception was in '97, when the team allowed the fourth-fewest runs in the AL (but finished third in the Central division because their offense was next to last in the league). Other than that, the staff consistently has been in the bottom half of the league, finishing eighth or worse five times in the past seven seasons.

BEST CASE

The Brewers, perpetual overachievers (or underachievers, depending on your viewpoint), have a no-BS manager this year in Davey Lopes, who won't allow the kind of loafing and complacency that this franchise has suffered from in previous years. The club's already-talented youngsters, such as Ronnie Belliard, Geoff Jenkins, Valerio de los Santos, and Kyle Peterson, will continue their development with an entirely different type of manager and coaching staff than the Brewers have had in the recent past. If nothing else, Milwaukee should be better fundamentally and more exciting to watch.

WORST CASE

Unfortunately, Lopes won't have much talent to work with in 2000. The collapse of Miller Park took care of that. The salary-motivated December dumping of Jeff Cirillo and Scott Karl (and make no mistake, the deal wasn't made in order to obtain Henry Blanco, Jamey Wright, or Jimmy Haynes) rips apart an already-frayed offense and removes southpaw innings from a fragile starting rotation. The Brewers say that the Miller Park disaster cost them tens of millions of dollars, which in turn makes it harder for the club to spend money on players.

UNDER THE MICROSCOPE

KYLE PETERSON: The 24-year-old began '99 at Triple-A and pitched well enough to be given a chance in the big leagues by midseason. Peterson has an unorthodox, across-the-body delivery and doesn't have the stuff to overpower hitters, but he knows how to mix his fastball, curve, and change-up effectively. He'll be a quality starter for years if his delivery doesn't cause arm trouble.

ALLEN LEVRAULT: The hard-throwing Levrault also has a quality change-up and the mentality to succeed. The 22-year-old works quickly, he mixes in an occasional slider but mainly throws the hard stuff. Levrault will likely begin 2000 at the Triple-A level. If he can learn to effectively mix his pitches there, the call to the big leagues will soon follow.

KEVIN BARKER: With 74 homers and 305 RBIs over his past three seasons in the minors, Barker could be the answer to the Brewers' lack of a productive first baseman. The 24-year-old is a solid hitter with decent power and adequate defense. The Brewers will probably try to upgrade at this position, but Barker could provide punch.

CHAD GREEN: Drafted for his speed and leadoff potential, Green has yet to become the player the Brewers envisioned. The 24-year-old draws too few walks and strikes out far too often to do the job at the top of the order. Green has good gap power, but his desire to smack line drives all over the park causes him to lose track of what he should be trying to accomplish.

MILWAUKEE

TOP PROSPECTS

The Brewers spent another season out of contention, prompting an overhaul in the front office. The organization will begin the new millennium with a new general manager, assistant general manager, and farm director, among others. There is also some hope for new life on the field with the emergence of 2B **RONNIE BELLIARD** and RHP **KYLE PETERSON**.

Belliard, who stepped in for '98 all-star Fernando Vina, impressed with pop in his bat and solid defense. Peterson pitched well enough to guarantee himself a spot in next season's rotation. Also, 1B **KEVIN BARKER**, who has maintained solid numbers in the minors, hinted at being a good producer at the big-league level with 23 RBIs in just 117 at-bats.

Overall, the farm system is not blessed with an abundance of talent. There are some pitchers scattered throughout but practically nothing in the way of position players with a legitimate chance. RHP **ALLEN LEVRAULT** could be given a shot out of spring training due to a lack of arms at the major-league level. Levrault, a starter with a closer's mentality, pitched well at Double-A but struggled at Triple-A. He combines a good moving fastball with strong curve and change-up offerings. RHP **JOSE GARCIA**, who was one of the better pitchers in the advanced Class A California League in 1998, missed all of '99 with an elbow injury suffered in spring training. Garcia has good stuff but has had trouble with getting behind in the count.

The Brewers are excited about a few young pitchers they have signed. With the 10th overall pick in the '99 draft, the Brewers selected RHP **BEN SHEETS** out of Northeast Louisiana University with the hope that he can fly through the system and help in the majors soon. Sheets pitched as high as the advanced Class A level last year. RHP **NICK NEUGEBAUER**, a second-round pick in 1998, posted 125 strikeouts in 81 innings and a batting average of .178—the lowest among minor-league starters—during his debut season. 1998 first-round pick RHP **J. M. GOLD** had difficulty pitching at the same level as Neugebauer, however. RHP **JOSE MIESES** won nine straight starts in the short-season Pioneer League.

Heading the thin list of position players is OF **CHAD GREEN**, a first-round pick in the 1996 draft. Green's physical attributes make him a good leadoff-type player, but he has not made enough consistent contact or drawn enough walks to realize his potential.

OF **SCOTT KRAUSE** put up solid numbers at Triple-A for the second straight season, but he's 26 years old and lacks that one real plus tool that could get him to the show. OF **BUCKY JACOBSEN**, who emerged in '98 with 27 homers at the lower Class-A level, was overmatched at Double-A and advanced Class A, batting .222 with 8 homers, and he did not take well with a switch to first base. Twenty-five-year-old OF **SCOTT SOLLMAN** batted .334 with 49 steals over two levels but has absolutely no power. Way down, the Brewers have hope for 19-year-old OF **CRISTIAN GUERRERO**, a tools guy already showing power and speed.

Around the infield, SS **SANTIAGO PEREZ**, who had an outstanding season at hitter-friendly El Paso in '98, leveled off at the plate last season at Triple-A. He has a good glove but doesn't project to be a major-league starter. 3B **SCOTT KIRBY** had a very strong season at two Class A levels to emerge as a fringe prospect at the hot corner.

CF
MARQUIS GRISSOM 33
○ #Chad Green 2A 25 96/1C
? *Ramy Beatriz A+ 21 96/ND

LF
***GEOFF JENKINS 25**
ALEX OCHOA 28
LYLE MOUTON 31
? Bucky Jacobsen 2A 24 97/7C
? Alvin Morrow A- 22 97/2H

RF
***JEROMY BURNITZ 31**
? Scott Krause 3A 26 94/10C

SS
#JOSE VALENTIN 30
LOU COLLIER 26
○ #Santiago Perez 3A 24 93/ND
? Chris Rowan A+ 21 97/14H

2B
RON BELLIARD 25
? #Mickey Lopez 3A 26 95/13C
? *Jeff Pickler 2A 24 98/11C

3B
JOSE HERNANDEZ 30
? Scott Kirby A+ 22 95/30C
? Jeff Deardorff A+ 21 97/3H

1B
SEAN BERRY 34
MARK LORETTA 28
○ *Kevin Barker ML 24 96/3C

SP/RP

RELIEVERS
BOB WICKMAN 31
*RAFAEL ROQUE 26
ROCKY COPPINGER 26
CURTIS LESKANIC 32
JUAN ACEVEDO 30
DAVID WEATHERS 30
*VALERIO DE LOS SANTOS 24
CHAD FOX 29

C
HENRY BLANCO 28
#BRIAN BANKS 29
CHARLIE GREENE 29
ROBINSON CANCEL 24
? #Brian Moon A+ 22 96/48C

STARTERS
STEVE WOODWARD 25
JASON BERE 29
CAL ELDRED 32
JAMEY WRIGHT 25
JIMMY HANES 27
KYLE PETERSON 24
○ Allen Levrault 3A 22 96/13C
? Doug Johnston 2A 22 96/9H
? Al Hawkins 2A 22 96/15H
? Paul Stewart A+ 21 96/6H
↑ Ben Sheets A+ 21 99/1C
○ J.M. Gold A- 20 98/1H
○ Nick Neugebauer A- 19 98/2H
↓ Jose Garcia DP 22 96/2H
? *Horacio Estrada ML 24 92/ND

MAJOR LEAGUERS IN ALL CAPS
Minor leaguers in upper-and-lower case

BEFORE A PLAYER'S NAME:
* left-handed hitter/pitcher
# switch-hitter
°=Player's prospect status (see explanation)

AFTER A PLAYER'S NAME:
Level at which he spent most of 1999 season; age as of July 1, 2000; year he was drafted; round drafted (ND= non-drafted amateur free agent); drafted out of high school (H) or college (C)

EXPLANATION OF PROSPECT RATINGS

★ Potential big-league star

↑ Projected regular player in majors (for pitchers: rotation starter or closer)

○ Projected platoon or utility player in majors (pitcher: setup or middle relief)

? Possible big-league reserve or long reliever

↓ High draft pick or "tools" player who hasn't performed to expectations

MILWAUKEE

PITTSBURGH PIRATES

Management
Manager	Gene Lamont	
G.M.	Cam Bonifay	
President/CEO	Kevin McClatchy	

Career Record
484–469 / .508
410–495 / .453
299–348 / .462

1999 Record
Won–Lost	Pct.	Finish/G.B. (Division)	Finish/G.B. (Wild Card)
78–83	.484	3/18.5 (C)	4/18

Preseason Consensus Projection
5 (5.10)

1st Half	2nd Half	Home	Road	Intradivision	Interleague
39–37	39–46	45–36	33–47	30–32	7–8

Comebacks	Blowouts	Nail-Biters	Grass	Turf	Sept.–Oct.
7–6	22–24	33–36	24–34	54–49	12–16

NUMBERS DON'T LIE

	Team (Rank)	Opponents (Rank)	League Avg.
Runs/Game	4.81 (12)	4.86 (7)	5.00
Batting Avg.	.259 (14)	.263 (6)	.268
On-Base Avg.	.334 (12)	.343 (9)	.342
Slugging Avg.	.419 (14)	.420 (7)	.429
Strikeouts	1197 (15)	1083 (5)	1072
Home Runs	171 (10)	160 (4)	181
Stolen Bases	112 (10)	99 (5)	122
ERA	4.35 (6)		4.57
Errors	147 (15)		120

▶ THE INSIDER 2000

MODEST ACCOMPLISHMENTS

The Pirates' 1999 season could have ended with Jason Kendall's gruesome leg injury on July 4. From then on, the Bucs got nothing out of the several catchers they employed, and they certainly missed Kendall's productive bat, his remarkable base running (for a catcher), and his on-field intensity.

But the season didn't end: The Pirates didn't collapse. They hung around the .500 mark the rest of the way, stumbling only in the season's last few games, when their list of wounded grew to include Brian Giles, Al Martin, and Ed Sprague. That may have been a modest accomplishment, but it was still an accomplishment.

So what kept the Bucs afloat? It certainly wasn't aging receiver Joe Oliver, brought over from the Devil Rays' Triple-A club in a surprising deal for outfielder Jose Guillen (who was so far out of favor with Pittsburgh management that he was in a cave in the hillside behind the doghouses). It wasn't the contribution of free-agent infielders Pat Meares or Mike Benjamin or pitcher Pete Schourek, all of whom played poorly when not injured. Nor was it outfielder Brant Brown, who disappointed after being acquired in the trade for pitcher Jon Lieber.

While most of the deals Pittsburgh made to improve the club for 1999 didn't work out well, two did pan out. The biggest one came in November '98, when the Indians inexplicably accepted left-handed reliever Ricardo Rincon straight up for outfielder Brian Giles, then only 27. Cleveland had turned down many other offers for Giles in the preceding years, including a deal that would have brought in Curt Schilling but was vetoed by Cleveland when Philly insisted on getting Giles as part of the package.

The acquisition of Giles completely changed the character of the Pirates' lineup, giving them a real power threat after several years of a popgun attack. Giles, the club's first big-time power hitter since Barry Bonds, hit 39 homers—eighth-best in the NL—in only 141 games. It was the highest total by any Pirates player since Willie Stargell bashed 44 in 1973. Giles's acquisition had an ancillary benefit as well, as he successfully made the transition to center field despite having played mostly left field in Cleveland. That allowed the Bucs to get Al Martin's bat in the lineup alongside Giles's. Giles's range in center was somewhat below par, but completely acceptable given his hitting. Martin hit 24 homers and slugged .506, both career highs.

Manager Gene Lamont deserved credit for several in-season decisions that helped the team. When Pat Meares came up lame,

MOMENT OF TRUTH

The Pirates sent an interesting message to fans and players in the organization when they traded Jose Guillen to Tampa Bay for aging catcher Joe Oliver. Clearly management had grown tired of what it perceived to be a lazy attitude on Guillen's part, but it raised more than a few eyebrows that the club basically gave him away. Trading Guillen might have sent a message to the other prospects in the system that they need to work hard if they're going to get a shot. On the other hand, it doesn't bode well for the club's long-term success if it gives up so easily on other young players.

PITTSBURGH PIRATES

BIGGEST SURPRISE

Todd Ritchie hadn't posted an ERA below 4.15 at any level since 1993, and he had never won more than 11 games in his professional career. Yet he was Pittsburgh's best pitcher in '99. Ritchie was solid all season, with much of his improvement being credited to his improved control. It's unlikely that he'll be able to duplicate last year's performance, but he finally lived up to expectations as he resurrected his career.

BIGGEST DISAPPOINTMENT

Abraham Nunez clearly was the biggest failure for the Pirates last year. He didn't merely have a bad year—he had an *incredibly* bad year. Nunez had only eight extra-base hits (all doubles) in 259 at-bats, which made his slugging average a pitiful .251, although he showed good range in the field and stole nine bases in 10 attempts. That, combined with his awful performance at the end of 1998 (seven errors in 23 games—including three in a single inning—and a .225 batting average), made the Pittsburgh brass wonder seriously if he has what it takes to be a major-leaguer.

Lamont quickly installed Warren Morris as the regular second baseman. Providing solid offense and steady defense, the 25-year-old Morris established himself as a big leaguer and finished third in the NL Rookie of the Year voting.

Meanwhile, pitcher Todd Ritchie—a minor-league free agent who previously had seen some action in the Twins' bullpen—worked his way into the starting rotation and surprised everyone. The sinkerballing Ritchie ended up a big winner at 14–9, though he's probably best suited to be a No. 3 or 4 starter in the majors.

Lamont also installed former Phillies and Royals washout Mike Williams as the team's closer early in April when Rich Loiselle couldn't regain his velocity. As a starter, Williams had been a disaster in the majors; his only good big-league season prior to coming to the Bucs was in 1995, when he was used mostly in middle relief.

However, with a newfound mastery of his slider, Williams saved 23 games for the Pirates in '99 after posting a 1.94 ERA in 51 innings for the Bucs in '98 as a junk-time reliever. He wasn't great—he had a 4.31 ERA and allowed 10 of 21 inherited runners to score—but he established himself as a respectable big-league pitcher while whiffing 76 in his 58 frames. Williams was hit hard in the last two months, though, and would be better used in setup or middle relief.

ON THE BENSON BURNER

Assuming that erstwhile rotation anchor Francisco Cordova, who had shoulder problems early in the season, can pitch as well as he did in the second half, Ritchie should round out a promising starting staff of Cordova, Kris Benson, and Jason Schmidt. Despite some disappointment that the 27-year-old Schmidt hasn't blossomed into a star, the Bucs were confident enough in his future to turn down trade offers for him in the off-season.

Nobody ever doubted that Kris Benson had some of the best stuff in the minors. The big question facing the first pick in the 1996 draft was whether he could harness that stuff and be a productive major-league pitcher.

The question was answered fairly quickly in '99. After a rocky April, Benson used an outstanding curve and a good fastball to pulverize right-handed hitters. He had some trouble with lefties, but Benson showed that at age 24 he is ready to become a first-class big-league starter and very possibly the kind of ace who can lead a team to a pennant.

The Pirates will certainly be looking forward to getting Kendall back this season. While he may not regain 100 percent of his speed, Jason should still be a dynamic two-way player and an important team leader. The difference between the Pirates of 2000 and those of 1998–99 is that there are more quality players in the Bucs' flannels awaiting his return.

Assuming that Morris and Benson don't have major sophomore slumps, Pittsburgh has reason for optimism, given the other youngsters who can make a difference in 2000 and beyond. The Bucs have several potential impact players waiting for their chance, and they have other players who have the potential to become regulars or valuable role players on a contending team.

Chad Hermansen, a 1995 first-round pick, has now played two full seasons at Triple-A and shown good power. Defense has been the big problem: He's been moved from shortstop to second base to left field, but he played center late last summer for the Pirates. Even if he is below average in the field, adding Hermansen to an outfield of Giles and a combination of Brant, Adrian, and Emil Brown wouldn't hurt the team given Al Martin's statuesque range in left. Brant Brown was a disaster last year, but he should rebound. Adrian Brown showed decent leadoff skills (.364 OBA) in a part-time role. Emil Brown has some power and some speed to contribute.

Pittsburgh hoped that Aramis Ramirez would be ready for the majors in 1998, but Ramirez was only 20 and had fewer than 50 games above Class A when he was called up. His lack of experience showed, and the team decided to give him a full season at Triple-A in '99 rather than risk having him fail in the majors. If Sprague is re-signed for 2000, he will have to fend off the 22-year-old top prospect, who is champing at the bit after a stellar season in Nashville.

As for pitching, the Pirates have searched for a quality southpaw starter since Denny Neagle's departure. The search bore no fruit in 1999, as Pete Schourek didn't work out and Chris Peters backslid. It would not surprise anyone if the Pirates gave Scott Sauerbeck a shot. Chosen from deep in the Mets' system as a Rule 5 pick in '98, Sauerbeck worked in middle relief as a rookie for Pittsburgh and fared well. His role could expand.

Jimmy Anderson is the Pirates' best hope for a lefty starter this year. An overachiever, he was impressive in 13 late-season games (four starts) for the Bucs. Paul Ah Yat, another overachiever, and Mike Gonzalez are other left-handed possibilities, along with right-handers Bronson Arroyo and Javier Martinez. All may need more Triple-A time, however. Long shot Mike Garcia—a 55th-round pick of the Tigers in 1989—is a righty

SECRET WEAPON

Pittsburgh acquired Scott Sauerbeck in the 1998 Rule 5 draft; the 27-year-old southpaw ended up as one of the team's top relievers by the end of the season. He didn't see much early action (common for Rule 5 players) but pitched well, slowly earning Gene Lamont's confidence as he matured into a solid setup pitcher.

ACHILLES HEEL

The Pirates relied far too much on middle-market free-agent veterans such as Ed Sprague and Mike Benjamin when younger players in the organization deserved more of a chance to play. Aramis Ramirez wasn't very good in 1998, and it almost seemed as if Pittsburgh was punishing him by making him play the whole season in Triple-A. Ramirez put up good numbers at Nashville, but not good enough to earn a promotion until rosters were expanded in September. Aramis might have been rushed to the big leagues in '98, but his first half of the season in the minors should have earned him another shot. Playing Sprague at third every day isn't going to help the team when PNC Park opens.

PITTSBURGH PIRATES

ENOUGH ALREADY

Jason Kendall was Pittsburgh's best player and clearly the heart and soul of the team, but the organization's overall attitude after his season-ending injury was a bit over the top. Having all the players write "Kid" on their caps and hanging his uniform in the dugout during games like he was a Hall of Famer were excessive. Sure, Kendall suffered a nasty injury that effectively eliminated any chance of the team hanging in the wild-card race, but we're not talking about Clemente here.

who might contribute. He certainly has paid his dues, working first in the Northern League, then spending two years in Mexico and three in Taiwan.

"A MAN, A PLAN, A BALLPARK . . . PNC-AMA"

Pittsburgh rebounded from a miserable 1998 to finish at 79–83, the same record it posted during the club's great leap forward in '97. In '99, GM Cam Bonifay's team avoided possible disaster and made some progress toward its goal of having a contending club when it moves into new PNC Park in 2001.

If the organization's top prospects (Ramirez, Hermansen, J. J. Davis) develop as expected into solid regulars or stars, and if none of the team's core players falls off a cliff, the Pirates have a realistic chance of being able to play with the big boys in 2001 and beyond. However, there's little room for error or key disappointments—such is the plight of the financially disadvantaged in major-league baseball these days.

Bonifay affirmed after the season, the third in his five-year plan, that he believed the team was on track. However, next year is critical: The tone for the opening of the new ballpark will be set by how much the 2000 team appeals to those Steel City fans who haven't cared about baseball in almost a decade.

BEST CASE

If is a big word. IF Jason Kendall comes back with his speed intact . . . IF Al Martin's improvement is real . . . IF Kris Benson doesn't backslide as Jason Schmidt has . . . IF Aramis Ramirez, Adrian and Emil Brown, and Chad Hermansen are ready . . . IF Brian Giles and Warren Morris are for real, THEN the Pirates could well move into contention. With a little bit of help in the pitching department (Jose Silva may become the closer this year, and Francisco Cordova should be healthy the whole season), the growth the Bucs started two years ago can be continued.

WORST CASE

The Bucs continue to tinker with the makeup of their club, adding a Bruce Aven here, a Wil Cordero there . . . and that's the real problem. This club doesn't need tinkering; it needs a real direction. In dealing Jose Guillen for nothing, losing Ron Wright on waivers, and wavering on Hermansen's future, it seems that Pittsburgh is slowly giving up on its recent crop of prospects. This would be premature. After all, several of their best players have been farm-developed (Morris, Kendall, Benson), and the Pirates are a lot better playing .480 ball with Hermansen in the lineup than they are playing .520 ball with Dale Sveum getting 300 at-bats.

UNDER THE MICROSCOPE

ARAMIS RAMIREZ: One of the top hitting prospects in the game, Ramirez returned to Triple-A last season and hit .328 with more walks than strikeouts. But he didn't fare well in his September at-bats with Pittsburgh, and he made 42 errors at the hot corner, raising questions about his fielding. Third base has been put aside for the 21-year-old, but he'll need to prove he belongs this spring.

CHAD HERMANSEN: Only 22, Hermansen already has two years and 60 homers at the Triple-A level. He has all the tools to become a perennial All-Star, having improved his outfield defense and down on his strikeouts, but he could be more selective and he has an uppercut that could be exploited at the major-league level.

JIMMY ANDERSON: After blazing through the lower levels and stumbling at Triple-A in 1997–98, Anderson may finally be ready to make the last jump. Leading the Pacific Coast League with 11 wins when promoted to Pittsburgh in July, Anderson afforded himself nicely in two stints with the club. The 23-year-old, whose best pitch is his sinker, stopped nibbling last season and learned to trust his stuff.

JAVIER MARTINEZ: A Rule 5 pick from Chicago after the 1997 season, Martinez impressed the Pirates with a fastball clocked at 98 mph. Pittsburgh kept him around all of '98 and returned him to the minor-leagues to continue honing the skills that could make him a future closer.

PITTSBURGH

TOP PROSPECTS

The Pirates, entering their fourth year of Cam Bonifay's five-year rebuilding plan, suffered their seventh straight losing season in 1999. Over the past four years, however, they have built a deep farm system—aided by good drafts, trades of veteran players, and scouting in Latin America.

Prior to 1999, the Pirates were aggressively promoting their top prospects, but they changed that philosophy after several of those players had trouble adapting to the big leagues. That meant several players were left in the minors until September. Still, the major-league club received help from RHP **KRIS BENSON**, who had scuffled the past two years after being the first overall pick in the 1996 draft, and 2B **WARREN MORRIS** (acquired from the Rangers in '98) displayed a power bat and played a steady second base.

The Pirates have a solid base to build a contending club, especially since the payroll is being upped $10 million to $32 million, but they still need a few more position players and several pitchers.

Two openings exist this spring for two of the most highly touted prospects in the entire minor-leagues, OF **CHAD HERMANSEN** and 3B **ARAMIS RAMIREZ**, both left in the minor-leagues until September. Both could be dangerous hitters but still have questions to answer. OF **EMIL BROWN** also has the potential to play every day, and farther down, OF **KORY DEHAAN** opened eyes, and OF **J. J. DAVIS**—the top pick in 1997—started to live up to expectations.

The Pirates have another emerging talent in C-3B **RICO WASHINGTON**. An outstanding "pure" hitter who hit .325 with 20 homers over two Class A levels, the 21-year-old is trying to learn how to catch. The organization also acquired 20-year-old C **HUMBERTO COTA** from the Devil Rays in the Jose Guillen trade. Once considered by some the first baseman of the future, 1B **RON WRIGHT** was waived this fall and picked up by Cincinnati after three years of back problems.

Other than LHP **JIMMY ANDERSON**, the Bucs don't seem to have any other immediate pitching help on the horizon. RHPs **JASON PHILLIPS**, **JAVIER MARTINEZ**, and **JOSE PETT**, and LHP **KEVIN PICKFORD** missed virtually the entire season with injuries. Phillips and Pett left the organization as six-year free agents after the season.

The organization got strong performances from RHP **BRONSON ARROYO** and LHP **PAUL AH YAT**, who combined for 27 wins and ended the season at Triple-A. LHP **MIKE GONZALEZ**, a hard-throwing southpaw, won 12 games between two levels and fanned better than a batter per inning. LHPs **JOHN GRABOW** and **DAVE WILLIAMS** showed promise in the lower Class A leagues, and 1999 first-round pick RHP **BOBBY BRADLEY** had a solid debut.

LF
*AL MARTIN 32
WILL CORDERO 28
BRUCE AVEN 28
? Garrett Long 2A 23 95/2H
? *Derrick Lankford A+ 25 97/42C
? Jovanny Sosa A- 20 97/ND

CF
*BRIAN GILES 29
↑ Chad Hermansen ML 22 95/1H
? *Tike Redman 2A 23 96/5C
? *Freddy May A+ 24 95/9H

RF
#ADRIAN BROWN 26
○ Emil Brown ML 25 94/6C
? *Alex Hernandez 2A 23 95/4H
↑ J. J. Davis A- 21 97/1H

SS
#ABRAHAM NUNEZ 24
MIKE BENJAMIN 34
? Victor Gutierrez A+ 22 95/ND

2B
*WARREN MORRIS 26

3B
↑ Aramis Ramirez ML 22 95/ND
? Kevin Haverbusch 2A 24 97/20C

1B
KEVIN YOUNG 31
? *Eddy Furniss A+ 24 98/4C
? *Carlos Rivera A- 22 96/10H

SP/RP

RELIEVERS
MIKE WILLIAMS 31
*SCOTT SAUERBECK 28
JOSE SILVA 26
*JASON CHRISTIANSEN 30
MARC WILKINS 29
○ *Jimmy Anderson ML 24 94/9H
↓ Javier Martinez 2A 23 94/3H
? Alex Pena 2A 22 95/ND
↓ *Clint Johnston A- 22 98/1C

STARTERS
JASON SCHMIDT 27
KRIS BENSON 25
FRANCISCO CORDOVA 28
TODD RITCHIE 28
*CHRIS PETERS 28
○ Bronson Arroyo 3A 23 95/3H
↓ Bobby Bradley A- 19 99/1H
○ *Paul Ah Yat 3A 25 96/21C
○ *Mike Gonzalez 2A 22 97/30C
? *Sam McConnell 2A 24 97/11C
? *Brian O'Connor 2A 23 95/11H
○ *John Grabow A- 21 97/3H
○ *David Williams A- 21 98/17C
↓ *Kevin Pickford DP 25 93/2H

C
JASON KENDALL 26
KEITH OSIK 31
○ Yamid Haad ML 22 94/ND
? Craig Wilson 2A 23 95/2H
? #Jason Evans A+ 22 96/4H
↑ *Rico Washington A+ 22 97/10H
○ Humberto Cota A- 21 95/ND

MAJOR LEAGUERS IN ALL CAPS
Minor leaguers in upper-and-lower case

BEFORE A PLAYER'S NAME:
* left-handed hitter/pitcher
# switch-hitter
?= prospect status (see explanation)

AFTER A PLAYER'S NAME:
Level at which he spent most of 1999 season; age as of July 1, 2000; year he was drafted; round drafted (ND= non-drafted amateur free agent); drafted out of high school (H) or college (C)

EXPLANATION OF PROSPECT RATINGS.

★ Potential big-league star

↑ Projected regular player in majors (for pitchers: rotation starter or closer)

○ Projected platoon or utility player in majors (pitcher: setup or middle relief)

? Possible big-league reserve or long reliever

↓ High draft pick or "tools" player who hasn't performed to expectations

PITTSBURGH

ST. LOUIS CARDINALS

Management
Manager	Tony La Russa
G.M.	Walt Jocketty
President/CEO	William O. DeWitt Jr.

Career Record
1639–1511 / .520
381–409 / .482
319–328 / .493

1999 Record
Won–Lost	Pct.	Finish/G.B. (Division)	Finish/G.B. (Wild Card)
75–86	.466	4/21.5 (C)	7/21

Preseason Consensus Projection
2 (2.55)

1st Half	2nd Half	Home	Road	Intradivision	Interleague
37–40	38–46	38–42	37–44	27–34	7–8

Comebacks	Blowouts	Nail-Biters	Grass	Turf	Sept.–Oct.
13–16	17–11	39–47	64–70	11–16	11–17

NUMBERS DON'T LIE

	Team (Rank)	Opponents (Rank)	League Avg.
Runs/Game	5.02 (10)	5.20 (10)	5.00
Batting Avg.	.262 (13)	.273 (12)	.268
On-Base Avg.	.338 (11)	.355 (13)	.342
Slugging Avg.	.426 (10)	.427 (10)	.429
Strikeouts	1202 (16)	1025 (13)	1072
Home Runs	194 (5)	161 (5)	181
Stolen Bases	134 (8)	80 (1)	122
ERA	4.76 (11)		4.57
Errors	132 (12)		120

▶ THE INSIDER 2000

LA RUSSA AND LA BAMBA

Despite the presence of two of the biggest names in baseball, the 1999 Cardinals struggled through a miserable season, finishing fourth in the NL Central. Tony La Russa's reputation as a managerial genius couldn't compensate for the fact that this was a team built on fragile pitching and underproductive hitting—and two huge talents: one who continued to awe everyone, and one who didn't rise to everyone's lofty expectations.

After coming within a single game of the World Series in 1996—La Russa's first year in St. Louis—this was the third straight disappointing season for the Cardinals. Moreover, with otherworldly slugger Mark McGwire continuing his assault on home-run records, it was especially difficult to watch the team struggle.

As part of the rebuilding process, GM Walt Jocketty inked his manager to a contract extension after the season, squelching rumors that La Russa and the Redbirds would part ways. La Russa, smarting from criticism that he's a showboat manager whose veritable blizzards of tactical moves aren't doing his team any good, indirectly acknowledged some responsibility for his team's poor play. Tony promised to work his players hard in spring training this year to prevent the kinds of fundamental mistakes characteristic of bad teams. The obvious question was why an astute veteran manager would have allowed such a problem to take root in the first place.

Showing the fans that management didn't plan on taking years to overhaul the club, Jocketty made trades for veteran hurlers to stabilize the pitching staff. While these couldn't exactly be called future-is-now deals, trading Manny Aybar (who still has a big upside at age 25) plus serviceable pitchers Rick Croushore and Jose Jimenez to Colorado was admittedly risky. The Hentgen deal was low-risk, as the Cards took advantage of the Blue Jays' salary purge and didn't have to part with any important players.

The starters St. Louis acquired, veterans Hentgen and Darryl Kile, both 31, have struggled the past two years—Hentgen with arm problems in Toronto, and Kile with altitude and attitude problems in Colorado. Hentgen lowered his ERA almost two runs after the All-Star break, indicating he may be completely healthy and ready to return to his pre-1998 form.

Kile is a more problematic pitcher: While everyone was willing to make allowances for the huge problems he had pitching in Denver, the reality is that he didn't pitch well anywhere else,

MOMENT OF TRUTH

The Cardinals might not have made it to October anyway, but Matt Morris's injury in spring training lowered expectations to "Let's see how many homers McGwire can hit for an encore." The Cards were counting on Morris to come back strong from shoulder problems that limited him to only one start in the second half of 1998, but Morris blew out his elbow in March, and Cardinals fans took that as the end of their chances to contend.

ST. LOUIS CARDINALS

BIGGEST SURPRISE

Fernando Tatis was the one young St. Louis player who performed up to his abilities. Tatis had an outstanding season, especially for a 24-year-old, and established himself as the second-best power hitter on the team. Though less than a year older than J. D. Drew, Tatis is much farther along in his development. He won't catch anybody by surprise now, but his emergence makes the Cards' future a lot brighter, especially if Drew and Ray Lankford hit for more power than they did in '99.

BIGGEST DISAPPOINTMENT

Expectations were immensely high for J. D. Drew, who tore through four leagues in 1998, but the controversial top prospect had a subpar year. Drew, who arrived with as much hype as any player in recent memory, spent nearly a month on the DL with a bad leg, then performed so poorly he was shipped back to Triple A for a while after he was healthy. He swung at many bad pitches, resulting in a .242 batting average that detracted from decent power numbers and a respectable 19 stolen bases.

either. His road ERA in '99 was 5.89; in '98, it was better (4.26), though nowhere near star quality. Throughout his career, Kile has always had the talent to dominate, but his inability to apply that talent productively was viewed as the problem. In nine years in the majors he's had two All-Star seasons to go with years of frustration. Pitching coach Pat Duncan will clearly have his work cut out for him.

New reliever Dave Veres, 33, will probably win the closer job, with Juan Acevedo returning to the rotation and erstwhile closers Ricky Bottalico and Heathcliff Slocumb handling setup duty. Veres closed full-time in '99 for the first time in his six-year career, saving 31 of 39 games, with only a single blown save outside of Denver. However, he was hit hard in the last two months of the season, and his awful September–October performance (10.1 IP, 15 H, 10 BB, 3 SO) could indicate he was simply tired or could indicate something more serious.

The overhauled Redbird starting staff has lots of promise for a large improvement in 2000. After Hentgen, Kile, and Acevedo, La Russa has Kent Bottenfield (very overrated in '99 but still a good fourth starter) and late-season surprise Garrett Stephenson to choose from, plus possible comebacks from Alan Benes and Matt Morris. If St. Louis re-signs free agent Darren Oliver or signs free agent Andy Benes, the staff depth will be even more impressive. And none of this includes the enormous potential of Rick Ankiel.

Thus, the Cardinals' pitching (10th in the NL) should improve markedly in 2000. For the team to return to contention, though, the team offense (also 10th) will need to improve as well. McGwire provides a rock-solid anchor for the lineup, and Fernando Tatis provides even more power. After that, there's plenty of room for improvement.

The catching position was a black hole offensively in '99, and Alberto Castillo, the better of St. Louis's two receivers, was traded for Hentgen. At 26, there's reason to believe Eli Marrero, who is fine defensively, has the ability to improve dramatically on his hitting. Eli surprised everyone by coming back so quickly from cancer treatment last season, and it's quite possible that his terrible '99 hitting was largely due to his not having fully recovered his strength. Since there's no catching prospect in the high levels of the farm system, Jocketty will have to find a veteran receiver to platoon or offer an alternative if Marrero doesn't improve.

At second base, overachiever Joe McEwing won the hearts of the fans but isn't capable of playing regularly. If St. Louis were convinced that 24-year-old prospect Adam Kennedy could handle the keystone position defensively, he'd be handed the job. Kennedy can hit for average with decent line-drive power and speed. If the Cardinals can't trade for a veteran solution, Kennedy will get his chance by default.

At shortstop, Edgar Renteria, 24, showed better offense and worse defense (especially his 26 errors) than expected. His offensive improvement should continue and in time his defensive problems should diminish.

In the outfield, all three regulars the team was counting on in '99 failed. Eric Davis played in only 58 games and hit only five homers before shoulder surgery at the end of June ended his season. Ray Lankford had a decent season but missed 40 games and hit only 15 homers, not the kind of performance the team needs from a star who hit 31 homers in both '97 and '98. Lankford will probably rebound in 2000, but another Davis comeback is a big question mark at 38. J. D. Drew struggled with injury, inexperience, and inconsistency. Thomas Howard and Darren Bragg provide capable backup, but neither can fill the shoes of one of the regulars.

Overall, the potential for the team's offensive improvement in 2000 is great, but the margin for error (e.g., a serious injury to McGwire or Lankford) is much less than for the pitching.

HYPE AND (MAYBE) GLORY

Rick Ankiel and J. D. Drew have been touted as two of the best prospects to come along this decade. Are they really that good? As a dominant college hitter with all five tools, some scouts compared Drew to Barry Bonds. J. D. has shown at times that his ability is everything the Cardinals had hoped for, but he now needs to prove that his yearlong delay in signing with a big-league organization didn't permanently damaged his development. At 24 he needs to demonstrate that he will develop into an impact player soon, not that he will end up merely as just another good young outfielder.

There are good reasons for optimism. Drew has only 188 games of nonindependent league professional experience, barely more than a single season to learn his trade. Even while struggling to hit for average in the majors, he has shown remarkable discipline for a young hitter (54 walks in 471 plate appearances). He has demonstrated substantial power that should improve with experience as he learns which pitches he should try to hit

SECRET WEAPON

Rookie second sacker Joe McEwing came out of nowhere in the spring to hit well the first month. He also became a fan favorite with his aggressive play, positive attitude, and an obvious love for playing the game. While McEwing, 27, certainly shouldn't be viewed as a solution to the Cards' problems at second base, he could wind up having a decent big-league career as a utility player, much like Rex Hudler, another maximum-effort fan favorite.

ACHILLES HEEL

It was a mistake for the Cardinals to count on 30-year-old Donovan Osborne to return from injuries. He has been able to pitch only a single full season since 1993 because of an assortment of arm problems. Depending on the fragile lefty to make anything more than a handful of starts set the team up for a critical pitching shortage, compounded by with the other injuries suffered by St. Louis hurlers.

ENOUGH ALREADY

The Tony La Russa Show is beginning to wear thin in the Gateway to the West. La Russa did nothing to discourage the impression that he regards himself as a certified genius, continuing to engage in his pattern of endless lefty-righty matchups and double switches as the team endured another disappointing season. La Russa's myriad position and pitching changes, which seemed more frequent in nationally televised games where he could demonstrate to the entire country just how smart he is, wouldn't be so irritating if the Cardinals were winning—or if there were some purpose to them. However, it often seemed as if La Russa was making changes just to amuse himself.

---

for power and which he should slash for line drives. Unlike many left-handed hitters, he hasn't been intimidated by southpaws. In fact, he actually hit better against lefties than righties last year, though that pattern is almost certain not to hold up in the long run. Drew's mediocre showing in '99 was likely due to the fact that he was hobbled by leg problems.

Despite being universally judged as having top-of-the-draft talent, Ankiel was drafted in the second round in '97 because his predraft bonus demands scared away other teams. The Cardinals took the risk on the high school lefthander, eventually signing him for $2.5 million—a record bonus at the time for any drafted player, never mind a late-second-round pick.

Making his pro debut in '98, Ankiel started his career with a record 17.2-inning hitless streak. He hasn't looked back since. He made his big-league debut at age 19 and has yet to taste failure professionally. His minor-league record in 1998–99 would be astonishing for a polished college pitcher three years older, so looking at his record to date takes one's breath away when factoring in that it was compiled as a teenager against players typically three to 10 years older than he.

Unless he struggles in spring training, Ankiel will start 2000 in the Cardinals' rotation. He has all the markers of a great pitcher in the making—youth, velocity, breaking ball, change-up, command, and poise. But there's no guarantee he won't get cuffed around by major-league hitters this year, and he could easily spend much of the season in Triple A, gaining more experience.

One of the things that has historically characterized the Cardinals is their willingness to trust their own judgment and not worry about what others will say or think. Drafting and signing Drew and Ankiel were classic Cardinal moves—reasonably risky but with a high potential reward.

If Ankiel and Drew both develop into stars in the next year or two while McGwire and the rest of the current team is still together, St. Louis will be looking at a return to the World Series.

BEST CASE

The Cardinals need help to move up in what looks to be an extremely competitive National League Central. Several off-season deals brought in starting pitching and help at second base, which were two real problems in 1999. While both the starting rotation and the bullpen should be better, the odds of St. Louis finishing ahead of the other teams in the division remain slim. But with hitters such as Big Mac, Fernando Tatis, and Ray Lankford, the club has the potential to finish second and beat out the other wild-card contenders. Rookie hurler Rick Ankiel could be a big player in any Redbirds surge.

WORST CASE

St. Louis took a lot of risks in the off-season, trading for veteran pitchers who have been less than outstanding over the past couple of seasons. The Cardinals are depending on Pat Hentgen and Darryl Kile to provide stability to a pitching staff plagued by injuries the past several years. If they can't measure up, or if young slugger J. D. Drew fails to improve, the Cards could be in for another fourth-place finish, or worse.

UNDER THE MICROSCOPE

RICK ANKIEL: Ankiel dominated the minor leagues in his first two years of pro baseball, going 25-9, 2.50 ERA in 52 starts with 416 strikeouts in 299 innings. He led the minors with 222 strikeouts in 1998 and was leading with 194 strikeouts last season when called up to St. Louis. The 20-year-old could become one of the best pitchers in the game.

CHAD HUTCHINSON: Hutchinson tossed aside a promising NFL career for a $3.4 million crack at pro baseball. Despite a losing record and command problems, Hutchinson fared well in his first full season. He consistently throws his fastball in the 93–94 mph range and has a nasty slider.

ADAM KENNEDY: Kennedy is an outstanding offensive talent who makes consistent contact, hits for extra bases, and runs well. His defense, however, does not come close to matching what he can do with the bat. Serious questions about his range, ability to turn the double play, and overall defense will have to be answered this spring if he is to take advantage of the opening at second base.

LUTHER HACKMAN: Hackman was highly regarded until going 4-22 with an ERA over 6.00 in 1997–98. He made some changes in his delivery last season, increasing his velocity to the 95-mph range. He also throws a hard slider, but his command and off-speed pitches need work if he is to contribute at the major-league level.

ST. LOUIS

TOP PROSPECTS

For the second time in three years the Cardinals finished a disappointing 11 games under .500. The farmhands expected to make big contributions early in the season, OF **J. D. DREW**, C **ELI MARRERO**, RHP **JOSE JIMENEZ**, and RHP **MANNY AYBAR** struggled. St. Louis did get more positive results from several players not expected to contribute much, at least in 1999: 2B-OF **JOE MCEWING**, 2B-SS **PLACIDO POLANCO**, LHP **RICK ANKIEL**, and 2B **ADAM KENNEDY**.

It's no secret that the Cardinals have concentrated on selecting college pitchers in the June draft. 1999 was no different, with 23 of their 42 picks being college pitchers. St. Louis has selected pitchers with their first pick in 12 of the past 18 drafts, and all 12 hurlers were collegians. Several of these developed into quality big leaguers, although some have succumbed to injuries (Andy Benes, Matt Morris, Donovan Osborne).

The Cardinals tried everything they could to slow down the progress of Ankiel, HOWE SPORTSDATA's Teenager of the Year the past two seasons and its Player of the Year in 1999, but they couldn't find any more reasons to keep him in the minor leagues. If Ankiel can avoid the arm problems that have spoiled several other careers, his stuff and makeup will make him one of the best pitchers in the game. Right behind Ankiel is RHP **CHAD HUTCHINSON**, a hard thrower with a great slider but limited experience. He also could be a staff ace.

Unfortunately, despite the concentration in this area, St. Louis has little pitching after Ankiel and Hutchinson, and its position players don't offer much depth either.

Middle infield has been the best-stocked position the past couple of years, but the Cardinals admit that they may have over hyped those players. Kennedy is a big-league hitter, but there are serious doubts about his defense. SS **BRENT BUTLER**, who moved to second and third base during the season, didn't have the offensive season hoped, and was shipped to Colorado in the Darryl Kile trade. SS **JASON WOOLF** again missed a great deal of time due to injuries. SS **JACK WILSON**, the least hyped of the group, had his second straight outstanding season, impressing at two Class A levels while batting .319. At the major-league level, McEwing and Polanco gave the organization more than it could have expected, but neither is a front-line player.

The organization has little depth throughout the rest of the lineup. C **GABE JOHNSON**, the system's best behind the plate, hit less than .200 in short-season ball. There isn't a first-base prospect, and both hot-corner prospects, **CHRIS HAAS** and **JOSE LEON**, combined for a .231 average and 269 strikeouts at the two highest levels. In the outfield, Drew will have to earn a spot this spring because of his performance last season, while **LUIS SATURRIA** struggled at Double A.

LF
*RAY LANKFORD 33
? David Kim A+ 24 97/18C

CF
*J.D. DREW 24
↓ Tim Lemon A- 19 98/2H

RF
ERIC DAVIS 38
CRAIG PAQUETTE 31
? Jason Lariviere 3A 26 95/44C
? Luis Saturria 2A 23 94/ND
? Bill Ortega 2A 24 97/ND
? Andy Bevins A+ 24 97/36C

SS
EDGAR RENTERIA 24
? Luis Ordaz ML 24 93/ND
? #Jason Woolf 2A 23 95/2H
○ Jack Wilson A+ 22 98/9C

2B
*FERNANDO VINA 31
JOE MCEWING 27
PLACIDO POLANCO 24
↑ *Adam Kennedy ML 24 97/1C
? *Stubby Clapp 3A 27 96/36C

3B
FERNANDO TATIS 25
? *Chris Haas 3A 23 95/1H
? Jose Leon 2A 23 94/22H

1B
MARK MCGWIRE 36
EDUARDO PEREZ 30

SP/RP

RELIEVERS
DAVE VERES 33
RICKY BOTTALICO 30
JUAN ACEVEDO 30
*PAUL SPOLJARIC 29
HEATHCLIFF SLOCUMB 34
MARK THOMPSON 29

C
ELI MARRERO 26
#MARCUS JENSEN 27
? Gabe Johnson A- 20 98/3H

STARTERS
PAT HENTGEN 31
DARRYL KILE 31
ALAN BENES 28
KENT BOTTENFIELD 31
GARRETT STEPHENSON 28
MATT MORRIS 25
★ *Rich Ankiel ML 20 97/2H
★ Chad Hutchinson 3A 23 98/2C
? Jason Karnuth 2A 24 97/8C
? Britt Reames A+ 26 95/17C
? Luther Hackman ML 25 94/6H
? Steve Stemle A- 23 98/5C
↓ Chance Caple A- 21 99/1
? *Kris Detmers 3A 26 93/22C
? *Robert Smith A+ 20 98/4C

MAJOR LEAGUERS IN ALL CAPS
Minor leaguers in upper-and-lower case

BEFORE A PLAYER'S NAME:
* left-handed hitter/pitcher
# switch-hitter
*=prospect status (see explanation)

AFTER A PLAYER'S NAME:
Level at which he spent most of 1999 season; age as of July 1, 2000; year he was drafted; round drafted (ND= Non-drafted amateur free agent); drafted out of high school (H) or college (C)

EXPLANATION OF PROSPECT RATINGS

★ Potential big-league star

↑ Projected regular player in majors (for pitchers: rotation starter or closer)

○ Projected platoon or utility player in majors (pitcher: setup or middle relief)

? Possible big-league reserve or long reliever

↓ High draft pick or "tools" player who hasn't performed to expectations

ST. LOUIS

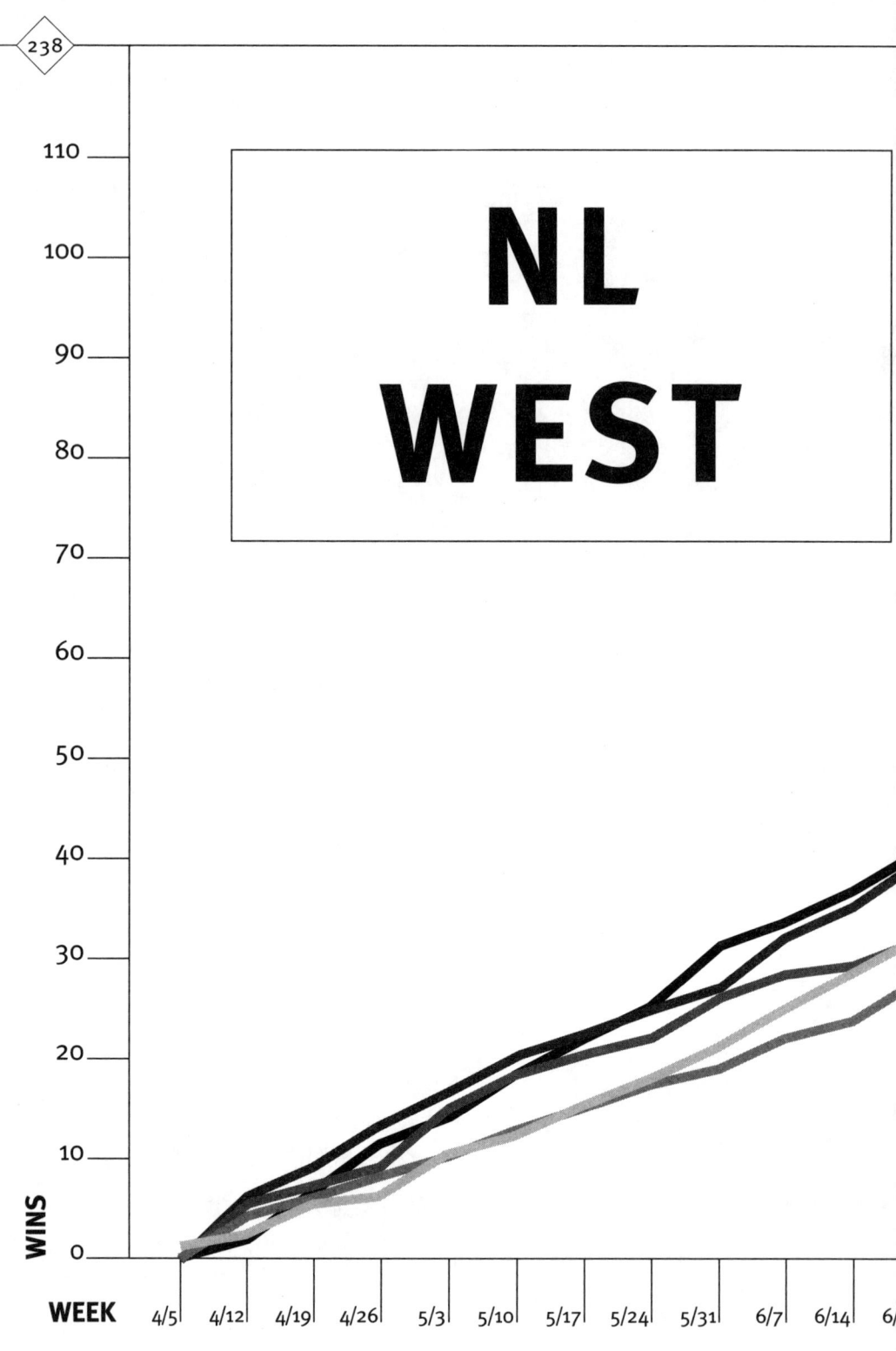

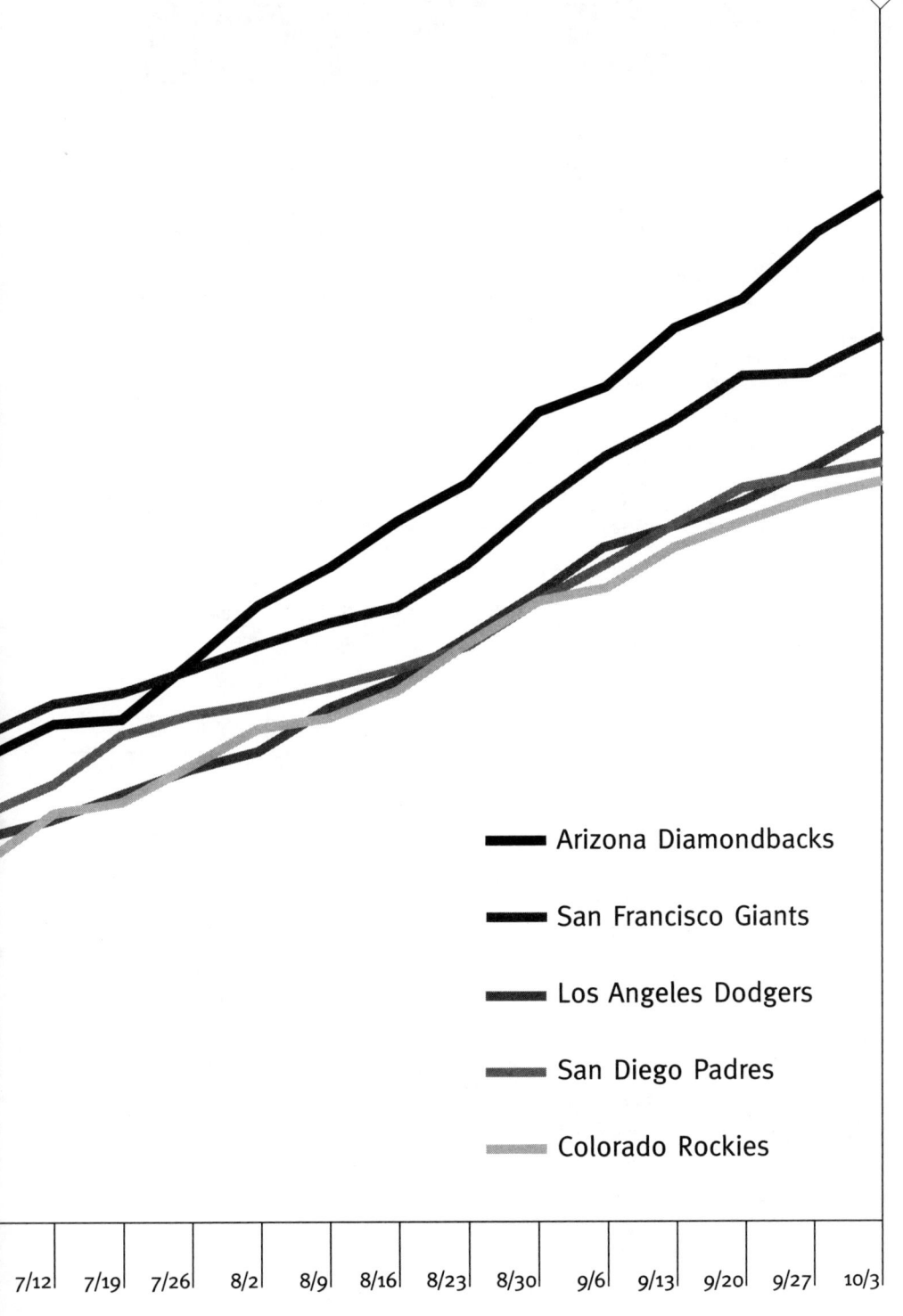

ARIZONA DIAMONDBACKS

MANAGEMENT

Manager	Buck Showalter	
G.M.	Joe Garagiola Jr.	
President/CEO	Jerry Colangelo	

CAREER RECORD

478–427 / .528
165–159 / .509
165–159 / .509

1999 RECORD

Won–Lost	Pct.	Finish/G.B. (Division)	Finish/G.B. (Wild Card)
100–62	.617	1 (W)	

PRESEASON CONSENSUS PROJECTION

4 (3.20)

1ST HALF	2ND HALF	HOME	ROAD	INTRADIVISION	INTERLEAGUE
43–35	57–27	52–29	48–33	26–12	7–8

COMEBACKS	BLOWOUTS	NAIL-BITERS	GRASS	TURF	SEPT.–OCT.
11–14	30–11	48–37	89–51	11–11	21–8

NUMBERS DON'T LIE

	TEAM	(RANK)	OPPONENTS	(RANK)	LEAGUE AVG.
Runs/Game	5.60	(1)	4.17	(3)	5.00
Batting Avg.	.277	(3)	.249	(2)	.268
On-Base Avg.	.347	(7)	.320	(2)	.342
Slugging Avg.	.459	(2)	.402	(3)	.429
Strikeouts	1045	(7)	1198	(2)	1072
Home Runs	216	(2)	176	(8)	181
Stolen Bases	137	(7)	138	(12)	122
ERA	3.77	(2)			4.57
Errors	104	(3)			120

▶ THE INSIDER 2000

A MAN—AND A TEAM—WITH A PLAN

In just their second season, the Arizona Diamondbacks won 100 games, finishing first in the NL West by 14 games. They're by far the most quickly competitive club in expansion history, and their championship wasn't an accident: Arizona did everything right in 1999.

The Diamondbacks finished first in the NL in runs and second in ERA, sporting several outstanding players and pitchers. They had the depth to survive slumps, trades, and injuries, partly because they made plenty of daring deals—including a critical midseason move to secure closer Matt Mantei from the Marlins.

The deal to get Mantei, which gave the club the strong closer it needed to pull away from the rest of the division, symbolized the Diamondbacks' season. It was a year in which a team, largely brought together just before the season, coalesced into a strong unit and played outstanding ball. While the D-backs got burned trading Tony Batista and John Frascatore for Dan Plesac, and might regret the Mantei deal somewhere down the line (they sent Brad Penney and Vlad Nunez to Florida), they clearly struck paydirt by obtaining Luis Gonzalez for Karim Garcia and Tony Womack for essentially nothing.

Another large portion of the Diamondbacks joined the team via the free-agent route. Jay Bell, Andy Benes, Steve Finley, Randy Johnson, Todd Stottlemyre, and Greg Swindell all signed as free agents. All except Bell and Benes were imported after Arizona's first year.

The credit clearly belongs to Arizona's management for building the powerhouse team. Managing general partner Jerry Colangelo had the foresight to see what might happen if the team suffered through another year in the basement—witness the precipitous 25 percent attendance decline and the pervading atmosphere of despair in Tampa Bay in '99—plus the concomitant courage to spend beaucoup bucks to upgrade the team. General manager Joe Garagiola Jr., manager Buck Showalter, and senior VP Roland Hemond had the guts to tacitly admit their first year was a complete failure. The Diamondbacks thus implemented their new strategy: Obtain the necessary veteran talent to become a winner, even if it was costly.

The franchise certainly hadn't been proud of its inaugural campaign, finishing 1998 at 65–97 with poor players at most positions. But simply going out and throwing money at expen-

MOMENT OF TRUTH

On July 9, the Diamondbacks were 47–40, sixth in the National League, and 2½ games behind San Francisco in the NL West. Gregg Olson, the team's closer, had 11 saves but also had blown six and had an ERA of 4.71. On that day, Arizona executives addressed what they felt was the team's biggest weakness and made a trade with the Marlins for Matt Mantei. Mantei reported to Arizona immediately, saving the D-backs' win over Oakland on July 10, and proved to be the spark the team was looking for. Just three weeks after the trade Arizona had vaulted to a 60–47 record, 3½ games ahead of the Giants. Mantei went on to save 22 games for the Diamondbacks and clearly was a key to the team's second half.

BIGGEST SURPRISE

When Jay Bell played in Pittsburgh, he hit second in the order most of the time and frequently was asked to move runners along with sacrifice bunts. In his seven years with the Pirates he averaged fewer than 11 homers per season. After leaving the Steel City, Bell clouted 21 homers in 1997 with Kansas City, then slugged 20 with Arizona in '98. No one figured he'd belt 38 last season in Arizona. Bell still hit second; however, once he started hitting for big power early in the season (he hit seven homers in April and eight more in May), any thoughts of bunting quickly disappeared.

BIGGEST DISAPPOINTMENT

Travis Lee was so bad last season that the once-untouchable cornerstone of the franchise was reduced to pinch-hitting duty. Lee never found his rhythm all year and, although a sprained left ankle sent him to the disabled list in mid-August, he had already lost his starting job to rookie Erubiel Durazo. By the time he came back it was too late.

sive veterans doesn't necessarily work (e.g., the Orioles, the Dallas Green–era Mets, the A's); it takes the ability to choose the right mix of players and personalities to achieve success.

Arizona's initial strategy was a bomb. Little of the team's 1999 personnel came from the expansion draft of November 1997. Of the 35 players drafted by the club, only pitchers Brian Anderson and Omar Daal and catchers Damian Miller and Kelly Stinnett played key roles last year. Just eight of them were even on the '99 team. While two years is usually too early to write off a new organization's expansion draft, this one's easy to judge.

It's clear that Colangelo will continue to spend the money it takes to win if he believes that winning will keep his club a box-office draw. The D-Backs finished fifth last season among NL clubs in attendance (behind Colorado, Atlanta, St. Louis, and Los Angeles) despite a 16 percent drop from their first year. Coming off their exciting year, the defending NL West champs should draw better in 2000.

Will the club continue to play well? It will certainly remain a division contender this year even if the Dodgers and Giants improve, as is likely. There is tremendous talent on the Arizona roster, but it's a tall order to win 100 games every season. It's likely that some, if not all, of the D-backs' 1999 hitting stars—Finley (35), Williams (34), Bell (34), Gonzalez (32), and Erubiel Durazo (26)—will decline somewhat. This is not a young club, and there is little position-playing help in the high minors

The pitching is a better bet to retain its level of productivity, especially if Todd Stottlemyre remains healthy. There is some mound help in the high minors, such as Byung Kim, Nick Bierbrodt, and John Patterson. A very deep and skilled bullpen was an underrated contributor to the Diamondbacks' 1999 success, and the key pitchers should all be back in 2000.

One critical thing to remember is that if the Diamondbacks stagger, they'll probably have the wherewithal to make important deals to improve. Again.

EXCEEDING THEIR PEERS

It's no surprise that the Diamondbacks are the only expansion team that has won more games than it has lost in its first few years of existence. Arizona, in fact, is the only expansion team that has approached being a .500 ball club.

No expansion team has ever had a winning record its first season. The 1961 Angels and the 1969 Royals came the closest, winning 70 and 69 games, respectively. The Diamondbacks and the 1962 Angels (86–76) are the only expansion teams to have a winning second season, and only the 1971 Royals and the 1995 Rockies had winning third seasons. The legendarily inept 1962 Mets easily had the worst season, of all expansion teams in their inaugural season when the hapless New Yorkers went 40–120.

None of the 12 expansion teams in the past three decades, not counting Arizona and Tampa Bay, had combined winning records in their first three year; the Marlins World Series title more a fluke than anything else. The Devil Rays won't finish with one either, sitting at 60 games under .500 headed into 2000. Colorado, which made the postseason in 1995 as a wild-card team, came the closest, but the Rockies still were 29 games below .500 from 1993 to 1995. Arizona needs to win only 78 games in 2000 to finish at .500 over its first three seasons.

The woebegone Mets of 1962–64 easily had the worst three-year record, going 144–340, a .298 won-lost percentage. Second worst were the Blue Jays of 1977–79, which had a winning percentage of only .343. The Devil Rays have played .407 ball in the past two years and can avoid finishing among the very worst expansion teams by winning 65 games in their third season.

Decades ago, when losing teams could still break even if they kept their expenses down, taking five or more years to gain respectability was both expected and survivable. In the what-have-you-done-for-me-lately 1990s, not giving the fans something to cheer for could quickly be fatal. The muddling management in St. Petersburg is currently in the midst of just such a crisis; it has essentially already been put on the corporate DL by Major League Baseball. The decisive actions of Arizona ownership avoided a similar crisis in Phoenix.

THE GOAL OF A LEADOFF HITTER IS ELEMENTAL

It's awfully hard for a player with a puny .370 slugging average and a subpar (especially for a leadoff hitter) .332 on-base average to score 111 runs. Fortunately for the Diamondbacks, Tony Womack had two things going for him in 1999: tremendous speed, and teammates who could hit for power.

For most of 1999, Womack (originally a minor-league shortstop converted to second base), played out of position in Arizona. Forced off second by Jay Bell, Womack spent the season

SECRET WEAPON

Erubiel Durazo is the Diamondbacks' Cinderella story. The 25-year-old wasn't signed by a major-league organization after playing two years of junior college ball, but he had two good seasons in the Mexican League in 1997 and '98 and signed with the Diamondbacks as a free agent. He started 1999 in Double A and tore up both the Texas League (.403, 14 home runs) and the Pacific Coast League (.417, 10 homers), earning a quick promotion to the majors. He got a chance to start because of Travis Lee's continuing struggles, and never stopped pounding the ball.

ACHILLES HEEL

The Diamondbacks had quality bats at every position except catcher. Kelly Stinnett and Damian Miller were barely adequate defensively, combining to throw out only a quarter of potential base stealers. They split time almost equally during the season because neither hit well enough to play every day. Miller hit .270 and Stinnett hit just .232.

ENOUGH ALREADY

Randy Johnson had a brilliant season in 1999, as his shiny new Cy Young award attests. He also lost quite a few close games, which means that his 17–9 record could easily have been 20–6 or better. Randy's mates supported him with 5.09 runs per game, substantially below the 5.6 runs per game that they averaged overall. The worst stretch was a series of five starts from June 25 to July 15 in which the Big Ugly allowed only five earned runs in 40 innings, surrendered only 25 hits and 12 walks, and whiffed 62—yet lost four games while winning not a one because Arizona scored only two runs in those five games. The media went out of their collective minds, hyperventilating for weeks about Johnson's bad luck, beating a decomposed horse way past its demise as if they personally owned shares in Big Unit, Inc.

trying to learn right field on the fly. He also played 18 games at short, where the D-backs would like him to play this year. Tony doesn't have a particularly good glove anywhere on the field, which puts a heavy burden on his offense to justify his spot in the regular lineup.

In '99 Womack had his most impressive season statistically. While he's not much of a hitter—his .277 average was the lowest of his career—he did take a career-high 52 walks and swiped a league-best and career-high 72 bases. The main difference between scoring 85 runs, as he had for Pittsburgh in both 1997 and '98, and tallying 111 for the Diamondbacks, is that Womack hit in front of four players (Bell, Gonzalez, Williams, and Finley) who combined to clout 146 doubles, 22 triples, and 133 homers.

Had the Diamondbacks had a really good hitter at the top of their order in 1999, he would have scored far more than 111 runs. Shouldn't the number one batter of the league's best offense at least rank in the league's top 10? Womack didn't, finishing behind teammates Bell (132) and Gonzalez (112) in 11th place.

Womack is, at best, a mediocre leadoff choice. While he does supplement his poor on-base skills with frequent and successful base stealing, there is just no substitute for getting on base—after all, the only alternative is making an out. Defenders of Womack-style leadoff hitters, who are far less common than a decade ago, argue that such a hitter's ability to get to second on his own is a mitigating factor. This is true, but if you were going to lead off someone with a .332 OBA, wouldn't you rather have one who can get to second with extra-base power rather than his legs?

It is also true that it's easier to single and steal second than lace a double down the line or up the gap. But the easiest way to get on base is to be disciplined at the plate and take what the pitcher gives you. By laying off marginal pitches and waiting for a good pitch, a batter either walks down to first or gets a better pitch to hit. A runner on first will score on any triple or home run and, if he's speedy, on most doubles.

BEST CASE

With a few star-quality players and a couple of good prospects, the Diamondbacks should be favorites to repeat in the NL West, which isn't that strong of a division to start with. While none of their big guns are particularly young, most of them (with the exceptions of Steve Finley and Luis Gonzalez) are extremely consistent, day-in, day-out hitters. The pitching staff may even be stronger this year than last; Andy Benes shouldn't really be missed. Buck Showalter is in his heaven with a consistent, veteran club that does not make silly mistakes, and he'll have the resources he needs to get the job done should any of his players suddenly fail.

WORST CASE

The long-term prospects are not so bright. Trading pitching prospects Vlad Nunez and John Penny was terrible from an organizational standpoint, even though Matt Mantei came over in the deal. As befits a still-young franchise, the farm system is not deep, although the D-Backs aren't afraid to use it. Barring injuries (and Matt Williams has been healthy for a while), the Arizona lineup should be dependable enough for another year or two, at which point the club will either restock with veterans or try the kids—and there aren't many kids. The one thing that could drag this club down quickly is if the older guys get too old together.

UNDER THE MICROSCOPE

JOHN PATTERSON: The 22-year-old Patterson did not enjoy the same success in the higher levels of the minor leagues in '99 as he did the previous year, but his numbers were affected by hitter-friendly parks. The 6'6", 200-pound righty has an above-average fastball that clocks in the mid-90s, but his best offering is a devastating curveball. He'll need another full season in the minors to work on his change-up.

BYUNG-HYUN KIM: The ace on the Korean national team, Kim has an assortment of above-average pitches that could make him into one of the better setup men in the game. The 21-year-old has a sidearm delivery that generates nasty movement on two different types of sliders. He can also reach the low 90s with his moving fastball.

ERUBIEL DURAZO: Durazo, signed out of the Mexican League prior to the 1999 season, was easily the biggest surprise of the organization last season. The left-handed hitter became the first player since 1961 to hit over .400 in the minor leagues.

DANNY KLASSEN: Klassen, plucked from the Milwaukee Brewers in the expansion draft, has had some success with the bat in each of his last three minor-league seasons. In 1998 the organization tried to get him some work as a second baseman, but now the Diamondbacks are back in the market for an everyday shortstop. Klassen has a strong arm, but his unreliable glove work and inconsistent bat make the club wary of taking a chance on him.

ARIZONA DIAMONDBACKS

TOP PROSPECTS

1999 was a great season for the Diamondbacks, an expansion team in its second season. Arizona reached the playoffs thanks mainly to pricey free-agent signings, but the young farm system did provide help when called on. 1B **ERUBIEL DURAZO**, who had played strictly in the Mexican League until last year, fit right into Arizona's explosive lineup, forcing Travis Lee off first base. Also, RHPs **VLADIMIR NUNEZ** and **BRAD PENNY**, two highly regarded arms in the system, were used to pry Matt Mantei away from Florida and address the need for a reliable closer. 2B **BELVANI MARTINEZ** fetched veteran pinch-hitter Lenny Harris.

With the dealing of two of its top pitchers, the strength of the organization now lies with its position players. The outfield is well stocked from top to bottom starting with a pair of major league-ready players in **ROB RYAN** and **JASON CONTI**. Ryan, who got a taste of the majors last season, is mainly an offensive threat, while Conti does a little bit of everything. At the advanced Class A level, both **JACK CUST** and **ABRAHAM NUNEZ** are good-looking prospects. Cust led the California League in homers, slugging (.651), and on-base percentage (.450). Nunez, a member of HOWE SPORTSDATA's All-Teen Team, has one of the strongest outfield arms in all of professional baseball and already has a good combination of power and discipline at the plate.

The Diamondbacks seem set at first base for some time, but 1B **LYLE OVERBAY**, an 18th-round pick in the 1999 draft, set a short-season Class A record with 101 RBIs. 2B **EDWIN DIAZ**, selected from the Rangers in the expansion draft, has lingered on the verge of being a major leaguer but has a less-than-stellar BB/K ratio. On-base percentage is one of the strong points of 21-year-old 2B **JACKIE REXRODE**'s game, but his defense isn't as good as Diaz's. 2B **CARLOS URQUIOLA** won the lower-level Class A Midwest League batting title last season and has great speed. C **ROD BARAJAS**, who played well at Double A, has above-average skills both offensively and defensively, giving him a chance.

The left side of the infield includes SS **DANNY KLASSEN**, who has a strong arm and a decent bat but has not been able to put it all together to make the jump to the majors. SS **ALEX CINTRON**, who spent the entire season at advanced-level Class A, is solid defensively but lacks offensive punch. Infielder **HANLEY FRIAS**, who has split each of the past three seasons between the majors and Triple A, wears the label of backup or defensive replacement.

Headlining the pitchers are RHPs **JOHN PATTERSON** and **BYUNG-HYUN KIM** and LHP **NICK BIERBRODT**. Patterson, who won the advanced Class A California League ERA title in '98, struggled at the higher levels in '99 but has an excellent fastball/curve combination. Kim, a former member of the Korean national team, has an impressive array of pitches with nasty movement. Bierbrodt, the organization's first amateur draft pick, isn't overpowering but has a great feel for pitching. He had some strong starts at Double A in '99 but had troubles adjusting at the Triple A level. RHP **BEN NORRIS**, a 13th-round pick in '96, emerged with decent numbers in time split between Class A High Desert and Double A El Paso, two of the best hitters' parks in the minor leagues.

LF
*LUIS GONZALEZ 32
? *Garry Maddox 2A 25 96/NDC
↑ *Jack Cust A+ 21 97/1H

CF
*STEVE FINLEY 35
○ *Jason Conti 3A 25 96/32C
? Adam Neubart 2A 22 98/43C

RF
*TONY WOMACK 30
BERNARD GILKEY 33
*DAVID DELLUCCI 26
? *Rob Ryan ML 27 96/26C
↓ Jhensy Sandoval 2A 21 96/ND
? Jamie Sykes A- 25 97/11C

SS
*ANDY FOX 29
#HANLEY FRIAS 26
○ Danny Klassen ML 24 93/2H
? LUIS ORDAZ ML 24 93/ND
? #Alex Cintron A+ 21 97/36C
○ Corey Myers A- 20 99/1H

2B
JAY BELL 34
? Edwin Diaz ML 25 93/2C
? *Jackie Rexrode 2A 21 96/17H
? Junior Spivey 2A 25 96/36C
○ *Carlos Urquiola A- 20 96/ND

3B
MATT WILLIAMS 34
*LENNY HARRIS 35

1B
↑ *Erubiel Durazo ML 26 97/ND
*TRAVIS LEE 25
GREG COLBRUNN 30

SP/RP

RELIEVERS
MATT MANTEI 26
RUSS SPRINGER 31
DARREN HOLMES 34
BOBBY CHOUINARD 28
BRAD CLONTZ 29
*GREG SWINDELL 35
ERIK SABEL 25
↑ Byung-Hyun Kim ML 21 99/ND
? *Jeff Kubenka ML 25 96/38C
○ Jeremy Ward 3A 22 99/2C
? Martin Sanchez 2A 23 93/ND
? Russell Jacob 2A 25 93/26H
? Jason Martines A+ 24 97/24C
○ Jason Royer A- 21 97/2H
? *Chris Cernates A+ 21 98/15C

C
KELLY STINNETT 30
DAMIAN MILLER 30
○ Rod Barajas ML 24 96/NDC
? *Mark Osborne A+ 22 96/3H
○ #J. D. Closser A- 20 98/5H

STARTERS
*RANDY JOHNSON 36
*OMAR DAAL 28
TODD STOTTLEMYRE 35
ARMANDO REYNOSO 34
*BRIAN ANDERSON 28
? Vicente Padilla ML 22 98/NDH
↑ John Patterson 3A 22 96/NDH
? Nelson Figueroa 3A 26 95/30C
? Andrew Good A- 20 98/8H
↓ Casey Daigle DP 19 99/1H
↑ *Nick Bierbrodt 3A 22 96/1H
? *Steven Randolph 3A 26 95/18C
○ *Ben Norris 2A 22 96/13H

MAJOR LEAGUERS IN ALL CAPS
Minor leaguers in upper-and-lower case

BEFORE A PLAYER'S NAME:
* left-handed hitter/pitcher
# switch-hitter
=prospect status (see explanation)

AFTER A PLAYER'S NAME:
level at which he spent most of 1999 season; age as of July 1, 2000; year he was drafted; round drafted (ND= non-drafted amateur free agent); drafted out of high school (H) or college (C)

EXPLANATION OF PROSPECT RATINGS

★ Potential big-league star

↑ Projected regular player in majors (for pitchers: rotation starter or closer)

○ Projected platoon or utility player in majors (pitcher: setup or middle relief)

? Possible big-league reserve or long reliever

↓ High draft pick or "tools" player who hasn't performed to expectations

ARIZONA DIAMONDBACKS

COLORADO ROCKIES

MANAGEMENT
Manager — Jim Leyland [resigned]
G.M. — Bob Gebhard [Dan O'Dowd]
President/CEO — Jerry McMorris

CAREER RECORD
1069–1131 / .486
511–559 / .478
511–559 / .478

1999 RECORD

Won–Lost	Pct.	Finish/G.B. (Division)	Finish/G.B. (Wild Card)
72–90	.444	5/28 (W)	10/24.5

PRESEASON CONSENSUS PROJECTION
3 (3.00)

1st Half	2nd Half	Home	Road	Intradivision	Interleague
34–40	38–50	39–42	33–48	15–24	4–8

Comebacks	Blowouts	Nail-Biters	Grass	Turf	Sept.–Oct.
8–12	18–32	34–34	63–77	9–13	12–16

NUMBERS DON'T LIE

	Team (Rank)	Opponents (Rank)	League Avg.
Runs/Game	5.59 (2)	6.35 (16)	5.00
Batting Avg.	.288 (1)	.301 (16)	.268
On-Base Avg.	.348 (6)	.384 (16)	.342
Slugging Avg.	.472 (1)	.499 (16)	.429
Strikeouts	863 (1)	1032 (11)	1072
Home Runs	223 (1)	237 (16)	181
Stolen Bases	70 (14)	163 (15)	122
ERA	6.03 (16)		4.57
Errors	118 (8)		120

▶ THE INSIDER 2000

THE LEY OF THE LAND

After a stunningly successful debut in their first three years (1993–95), the 1999 Rockies slid below mediocrity into their first-ever last-place finish. The resultant turmoil cost the franchise's original general manager his job and caused the team's veteran manager to announce he would forgo the last two years—as well as the $4 million—remaining on his lucrative contract.

After a disappointing 1998, manager Don Baylor took the fall and Jim Leyland was brought in. Leyland has a great reputation and is considered to be one of the smartest skippers in the game. He was successful in Pittsburgh—when he had good players. With Barry Bonds, Bobby Bonilla, and Doug Drabek in the lineup, the Pirates won three straight NL East titles from 1990–1992, twice coming heartbreakingly close to the World Series. When those stars left for greener pastures, Pittsburgh finished fifth three times in the next four years.

Leyland then spent two years in Florida, winning the World Series when he had the players (1997) and losing 108 games when he didn't (1998). The polite form of an old baseball aphorism is applicable here: You can't make chicken salad out of chicken feathers. It doesn't matter who manages the club, the Rockies aren't going to win until they get better players. It's that simple.

What went wrong with a franchise that just a few years ago was hailed as a model for new clubs to emulate? A heaping portion of the blame for the Rockies' recent demise can be traced to the same foundation on which they built their early success. Colorado's original team was built on short-term expansion draft picks such as Charlie Hayes, who impressed early but then faded. Of the three dozen players drafted seven years ago, only two (Vinny Castilla and Curtis Leskanic) played for the Rockies in '99. The Rocks' brain trust started with a distinct leaning toward veterans, and they initially succeeded (and later died) with that bias.

Attendance at Coors Field declined to 42,976 per game in '99, an average that most other teams would kill for, but it was more than 10 percent less than in 1996–97. And when a team depends on packing its ballpark to earn the revenue it needs to compete with the big media markets such as New York and Los Angeles, any downward trend is worrisome.

MOMENT OF TRUTH

On June 14 the Rockies were in third place, seven games behind the Diamondbacks at the start of a nine-game home stand that gave them a chance to get back in the NL West race. They won the first two games against the Giants, but were slaughtered, 15–2, in the last game of the series. Colorado then won four of its next five games to improve to a game over .500, 4½ games out of first. That was the end of all hope, however, as the Rockies lost the last game of the home stand to the Cubs, then proceeded to lose their next eight games on the road.

BIGGEST SURPRISE

Dave Veres a top-notch closer? It sounds ridiculous, but it wasn't far from the truth. Veres saved 31 games last season for a team that won only 72, and while a 5.14 ERA looks poor on the surface, it's not bad for a Colorado pitcher. He lost eight games and blew eight saves, but that's going to happen when you come in with runners on base and a broken-bat fly ball has the potential to go 425 feet. Away from his home park, Veres had a 2.52 ERA in 35.2 innings, allowing only 34 hits while fanning 38 and saving 20 games in 21 opportunities.

BIGGEST DISAPPOINTMENT

Darryl Kile didn't have a very good year in 1998, but he wasn't horrible. In 1999, he pitched even worse. He didn't win consecutive starts all season, and he was absolutely awful from mid-June to early August, when he went 2–8. The Rockies were so fed up with his pitching that they tried to trade him in July but found no takers. They had to wait until November to move Kile to St. Louis.

THE NEXT LARRY WALKER— OR NEXT DANTE BICHETTE?

Colorado first baseman Todd Helton, 26, is generally viewed as a rising young star after a little more than two years in the majors. Some baseball people even think of him as a franchise player. After all, he hits for average (.320 in '99), for power (35 homers, .587 slugging), and gets on base (.395 OBA). In 159 games he scored 114 runs and drove 113 home. What's not to like?

What's not to like about Helton is that he hasn't yet demonstrated he can be an impact hitter when he's not cosseted by friendly Coors Field. At lesser altitudes, Helton was quite ordinary for a first baseman (.252 BA, .324 OBA, .447 SA). Take a gander at the average production NL teams got from their first basemen last season (.288 BA, .375 OBA, .487 SA, 99 R, 33 HR, 104 RBI) and Todd doesn't look like such a hotshot anymore.

In his supposedly impressive rookie season in '98, Helton was only 12 percent better than the average hitter when his park, the level of league offense, and his position were taken into account. He was a tad better than that last year (14 percent), but certainly nothing to write to Cooperstown about.

There's no way to evaluate the true talent of Rockies' batters without keeping in mind the magnitude of the benefit Coors Field bestows on them. Dante Bichette hit 86 points higher in his career in Coors, with huge jumps of 87 points in his on-base average and 219 points in his slugging average at home. Larry Walker has a 116-point spread in his batting average, 89 points in his on-base percentage, and 215 points in his slugging average between Coors and elsewhere since he signed with Colorado.

Unless Todd accelerates his learning curve, he's going to be a lot more like Dante Bichette—a grossly overrated player who was barely above par as a hitter—than Larry Walker. Walker is an excellent hitter who takes full advantage of Coors to have great seasons. Todd Helton certainly isn't the problem in Denver. However, at this modest level of production, he isn't the solution, either.

LIFE IN A LAUNCHING PAD

Many baseball executives, writers, and fans think that harping on players' road performances is unfair nitpicking. After all, they play half their games at home and only a half-dozen or so in any other park. If they're taking advantage of their primary residence, that's both expected and desirable, right?

Wrong. As the Cubs have proven for decades, and as the Rockies are confirming, having a team that is grotesquely skewed by its home park doesn't normally result in a champion. Moreover, it frequently results in a loser. Plenty of research has been done over the years to show that the more extreme a team's home circumstances are, the worse that team plays on the road. The trade-off isn't an even one in such unusual circumstances: The benefit clubs get from taking advantage of extreme home fields is more than outweighed by the extra games they lose when playing in "normal" venues.

What are the best hitters' parks of all time? (Prior to Coors Field, that is, because the effect of Coors Field is unlike anything the venerable game has seen since ballparks graduated from being semipermanent wooden structures that regularly burned down.) Measuring the effect of a ballpark on the game is more complex than just adding up all the runs scored by the home team. The only fair way is to total the scoring by both the home and visiting teams (i.e., the rest of the league) in a park, then compare that with the total scoring of that team and its opponents in away games. This method removes the inherent bias of the talent level of that team and gives a true measure of a park's effect—which simply looking at the totals of one team does not.

It won't come as much of a surprise to find out that in the five seasons Coors Field has been open, it has captured the four highest spots on the all-time list of hitters' parks. With the exception of 1997, when Coors inflated runs by *only* 30 percent, the jewel of the Rockies has boosted scoring by at least 50 percent every year, with the highest figure ever being 64 percent, in '96. Needless to say, this is unlike anything seen in baseball outside of Colorado in the 20th century.

Mile High Stadium, where the Rockies played their first two years, was a terrific hitters' park as well. Its inaugural season of 1993 ranks sixth on the hit parade by increasing scoring 45 percent. The only non-Denver ballpark to break into this exclusive "bandbox" club is Fenway Park, which goosed scoring by 46 percent in 1955.

BREAKING UP THE ROCKS

Salient facts about the 1999 Rockies that explain why the team finished 72-90: More homers were hit at Coors Field (303) in '99 than in any other park in a single season in big-league history.

SECRET WEAPON

Pedro Astacio had an outstanding season in 1999. He finished 17–11 with a 5.04 ERA, but his overall numbers were inflated by pitching half the time in Coors Field. Astacio was excellent on the road, finishing 12–6 with a 3.60 ERA away from Denver. He overpowered the Reds twice in Cincinnati in the three weeks after the All-Star break. The Reds were playing as well as any team in baseball during that time, but Astacio allowed only eight hits and three runs in 17 innings over those two games.

ACHILLES HEEL

Considering they play in the best hitters' park in baseball, Rockies catchers have been downright awful. Henry Blanco, Kirt Manwaring, and Jeff Reed (before he was shipped to the Cubs) split time behind the plate with distinctly less-than-stellar results (.264 BA, .354 OBA, .407 SA, 14 HR, 62 RBI). None of the three hit for much power, and only Manwaring hit for a decent average (.299). Top prospect Ben Petrick should be the answer for the future. Even if he's not as good as expected, he certainly should be better than Manwaring et al.

ENOUGH ALREADY

As second-year franchise Arizona pulled away and Colorado slumped into the NL West basement in the second half, speculation mounted that Bob Gebhard, the only GM the team had ever had, would be fired. Gebhard was sure to leave after the season ended, and he certainly deserved to take responsibility for the team's failures, but the media frenzy rose to such a peak that Gebhard was forced to resign on August 20, while the team was in Chicago. The only real difference between sharks and members of the media when they smell some blood in the water is that sharks have bigger and sharper teeth.

Rockies' pitchers allowed an NL-record 237 home runs and 737 walks. Colorado's staff was shelled for a 6.01 ERA, highest in the NL since 1930.

Colorado will start this season with a new GM, Dan O'Dowd, and a new manager, Buddy Bell, both intent on retooling their team. The second era in Colorado baseball officially began on September 20, when O'Dowd received a five-year contract.

Less than a month after the end of the season, fan favorite Dante Bichette, who had been a fixture in each of the Rockies' seven seasons, was traded to Cincinnati for Jeffrey Hammonds and Stan Belinda.

The revamping of the team continued with a seven-player deal with St. Louis that sent washout starter Darryl Kile and surprising closer Dave Veres packing in return for Manny Aybar, Rick Croushore, Jose Jimenez, and infield prospect Brent Butler. Long-swirling rumors turned into reality in mid-December when slugger Vinny Castilla was shipped to Tampa Bay in a four-team trade.

Bell talked about dramatically increasing team speed by acquiring some new top-of-the-order hitters, and signed fleet-footed center fielder Tom Goodwin in December. O'Dowd talked about upgrading the team's underproductive farm system and making a big commitment to scout and sign talent from the Pacific Rim. The team snared highly regarded 18-year-old Taiwanese pitcher Tsao Chin-hui, with a $2 million bonus.

Despite all the positive activity, repairing the Rockies' extensive problems will likely take at least two years. Producing more talent from within the organization, as hard as that will be, represents only the first step.

Figuring out how to properly use that talent in the high-stress environment of Coors Field will be even more difficult.

BEST CASE

The Rockies will begin the new millennium with a new club, which isn't a bad way to go following a 72–90 season. Easily the best move the club made before Christmas was stealing Jeff Cirillo from Milwaukee. Cirillo, obviously undervalued by the Brewers, is much like Larry Walker—a truly excellent player who has already established himself as a hitter outside of the thin Denver air. Cirillo and Walker should team with Todd Helton to provide a solid top three. Pedro Astacio is blossoming into a number-one starter, and if Colorado can find a couple more arms to go with him, the club could wipe the slate clean and make a run at .500.

WORST CASE

Unloading Dante Bichette was a good move, but newly acquired outfielders Jeffrey Hammonds and Tom Goodwin won't win any pennants. Hammonds may put up big numbers in Colorado, but he doesn't do anything well enough to be above average. Goodwin is speedy and will improve the defense but hasn't demonstrated the necessary plate discipline to be a good leadoff man. Brent Mayne is a slight upgrade behind the plate, but will his presence hamper the development of top catching prospect Ben Petrick? The Rocks are at least a couple of years away from being truly competitive, and the organization will be in complete disarray if their winter moves don't pan out.

UNDER THE MICROSCOPE

BEN PETRICK: Petrick earned HOWE SPORTSDATA All-Prospect Team honors when he set career highs with a .311 average, 23 homers, and 86 RBIs in 350 at-bats between Double and Triple A last season. But his throwing ability raised concerns for the second straight year. Petrick threw out just 17 percent of base stealers for the second straight season in '99.

EDGARD CLEMENTE: A highly touted prospect for the past four years, Clemente was given an everyday audition in September when Darryl Hamilton and Brian McRae were traded away. He can do everything except steal bases, but his indifferent attitude and lack of plate discipline will have the Rockies looking around.

JOSH KALINOWSKI: The Rockies hope Kalinowski, who has fanned close to 400 batters over the past two years at Class A, will be a contributor in the future. Kalinowski, who throws a deceptive curveball and improving change-up that sets up his 89-91 mph fastball, is still a few years away.

BRENT BUTLER: It was no secret that Butler, a shortstop since being drafted in 1996, would move to second or third base because of questionable range and a bevy of talented shortstops in the Cardinals system. But the organization thought this highly regarded hitter would bat more than .269 with 35 extra-base hits and 26 walks in Double-A. Still,

COLORADO

TOP PROSPECTS

Since making the playoffs in 1995, the Rockies have fallen on hard times. The major-league club suffered its fourth straight losing season in 1999, even though player payroll has increased tenfold since 1993. In addition, the organization finished 27th out of 30 in minor league winning percentage, and hasn't finished higher than 23rd in the past four years—a gloomy realization that the system has not produced enough talent. Class A Salem, so frustrated with the poor clubs the Rockies have provided them over the years, is looking to affiliate with another organization.

These factors have caused ownership to clean house throughout the entire organization. New general manager Dan O'Dowd has brought in many of his former mates from the Indians' front office in an attempt to turn around the franchise.

Since their inception, the Rockies have concentrated on drafting and developing pitchers but have not had much success. Other than RHP **DAVID LEE** and LHP **JOSH KALINOWSKI**, the Rockies didn't see much progress from many of their pitchers in 1999.

Lee, who throws 90-plus with a deceptive delivery, had 13 saves and a 0.78 ERA at Double and Triple-A before getting the call and throwing 49 effective innings for Colorado. Kalinowski—who was two wins shy of a Class A Triple Crown—had his second straight outstanding season.

Many upper-level hopefuls struggled (Mark Brownson, Scott Randall, Lariel Gonzalez, Steve Shoemaker, Mike Saipe, Heath Bost, and Mike Vavrek) and many lower-level prospects did not perform up to expectations (Shawn Chacon, Aaron Cook, Jermaine Van Nuren, and Enemencio Pacheco). Injuries shut down LHP **MIKE KUSIEWICZ** and RHP **MATT RONEY**.

The Rockies have a few position players who could step in this season. Despite defensive shortcomings, the Rockies will hand over the catching job to **BEN PETRICK**. Much-maligned OF **EDGARD CLEMENTE** will get a long look in center field. It was hoped that he and OF **DERRICK GIBSON** would be mainstays in the Colorado outfield by now, but neither has come close. SS **JUAN SOSA**, a poor man's Neifi Perez, is the only other upper-level position player who could find a spot in the near future, but it would be in a reserve role.

Farther down, OFs **JODY GERUT** and **CHOO FREEMAN** have emerged as the top young players in the organization. Colorado also has hopes for 2Bs **JAVIER COLINA** and **BELVANI MARTINEZ** (acquired from the Diamondbacks for Lenny Harris), and SS **JUAN URIBE**, but with 66 walks among them, none has exhibited the plate discipline necessary to produce at higher levels. 3B **MATT HOLLIDAY** has made decent progress and should become a solid hitter.

▶ THE INSIDER 2000

LF
JEFFREY HAMMONDS 29
? Derrick Gibson ML 25 93/13H
? *Juan Pierre A- 22 98/13C

CF
***TOM GOODWIN 31**
#JEFF BARRY 31
○ Edgard Clemente ML 24 93/10C
#Chris Latham ML 27 91/11H
↑ Choo Freeman A- 20 98/1H

RF
***LARRY WALKER 33**
ANGEL ECHEVARRIA 29
○ *Jody Gerut A+ 22 98/2C

SS
#NEIFI PEREZ 25
ARRON LEDESMA 29
○ Juan Sosa ML 24 92/ND
? #Chone Figgins A+ 22 97/4H
? Juan Uribe A- 20 97/ND

2B
MARK LANSING 32
↑ Brent Butler 2A 22 96/3H
? #Elvis Pena 3A 23 93/ND
? Belvani Martinez A+ 21 96/ND
? #Jerome Alviso A+ 24 97/17C
? Javier Colina A- 21 97/ND

3B
JEFF CIRILLO 30
↑ Matt Holliday A- 20 98/7H

1B
***TODD HELTON 26**
? *Todd Sears A+ 24 97/3C
? #Rene Reyes A- 22 96/ND

SP/RP

RELIEVERS
JERRY DIPOTO 32
STAN BELINDA 33
MIKE MYERS 31
MANNY AYBAR 25
JULIAN TAVAREZ 27
RICK CROUSHORE 29
Lariel Gonzalez 3A 24 93/ND

C
***BRENT MAYNE 32**
↑ Ben Petrick ML 23 95/2H
? Rogelio Arias A+ 24 93/ND
○ Jeff Winchester A- 20 98/1H

STARTERS
PEDRO ASTACIO 30
*BRIAN BOHANON 31
*SCOTT KARL 28
ROLANDO ARROJO 31
JOHN THOMPSON 26
JOSE JIMINEZ 26
? Chandler Martin 2A 26 95/6C
↓ Shawn Chacon A+ 22 96/3H
? Ryan Price A+ 22 96/40C
? Mark Difelice A+ 23 98/15C
? Jermaine Van Buren A- 19 98/2H
? Enemencio Pacheco A- 21 97/ND
↓ Jason Jennings A- 21 99/1C
↑ *Josh Kalinowski A+ 23 96/33C
↓ *Mike Kusiewicz A- 23 94/8H

MAJOR-LEAGUERS IN ALL CAPS
minor-leaguers in upper-and-lower case

BEFORE A PLAYER'S NAME:
* left-handed hitter/pitcher
# switch-hitter
=prospect status (see explanation)

AFTER A PLAYER'S NAME:
level at which he spent most of 1999 season; age as of July 1, 2000; year he was drafted; round drafted (ND= non-drafted amateur free agent); drafted out of high school (H) or college (C)

EXPLANATION OF PROSPECT RATINGS

★ Potential big-league star

↑ Projected regular player in majors (for pitchers: rotation starter or closer)

○ Projected platoon or utility player in majors (pitcher: setup or middle relief)

? Possible big-league reserve or long reliever

↓ High draft pick or "tools" player who hasn't performed to expectations

COLORADO

LOS ANGELES DODGERS

MANAGEMENT
Manager	Davey Johnson	
G.M.	Kevin Malone	
President/CEO	20th Century Fox	

CAREER RECORD
1062–812 / .567
77–85 / .475
160–164 / .494

1999 RECORD

Won–Lost	Pct.	Finish/G.B. (Division)	Finish/G.B. (Wild Card)
77-85	.475	3/-26 (E)	5/19.5

PRESEASON CONSENSUS PROJECTION
1 (1.30)

1ST HALF	2ND HALF	HOME	ROAD	INTRADIVISION	INTERLEAGUE
34–41	43–44	37–44	40–41	21–23	8–7

COMEBACKS	BLOWOUTS	NAIL-BITERS	GRASS	TURF	SEPT.–OCT.
7–11	31–24	30–41	63–72	14–13	15–15

NUMBERS DON'T LIE

	TEAM (RANK)	OPPONENTS (RANK)	LEAGUE AVG.
Runs/Game	4.90 (11)	4.86 (8)	5.00
Batting Avg.	.266 (10)	.258 (5)	.268
On-Base Avg.	.339 (10)	.334 (7)	.342
Slugging Avg.	.420 (12)	.420 (8)	.429
Strikeouts	1030 (6)	1077 (8)	1072
Home Runs	187 (8)	192 (10)	181
Stolen Bases	167 (2)	156 (13)	122
ERA	4.45 (7)		4.57
Errors	137 (13)		120

▶ THE INSIDER 2000

OUT-FOXED

"Losing is unacceptable. It just won't be an option." With those definitive statements, cocky new Los Angeles general manager Kevin Malone set the tone in January for the 1999 season. In Kevin's orderly world, his Los Angeles Dodgers had a trip to the 1999 World Series wrapped up before spring training even started. After signing Kevin Brown to the richest contract in baseball history, and after trading for slugging catcher Todd Hundley, the Dodgers' GM figured playing 162 games would be a piece of cake.

It sure didn't turn out the way Malone planned, much to the delight of other baseball executives and fans. Malone's in-your-face arrogance made the Dodgers the team to hate in 1999, much like the swaggering Yankees of old. But at least those Yankees had a reason to swagger.

The Dodgers were a team full of name players, led by a name manager, all put together by a GM who was convinced before the first pitch was thrown that he'd built a world champion. Instead of a title, the Dodgers finished third in the NL West, 23 games behind Arizona, and wound up with the same record as the low-budget Philadelphia Phillies.

"I don't see where we can get a whole lot better. We are comparable on paper to any team in baseball."—GM K.M.

Trading Mike Piazza, the heart of the soulless Fox-owned Dodgers, proved to be a huge mistake in 1998. Malone can't be blamed for that one, but the trade that he should regret was the one he made trying to make up for the Piazza debacle. Explaining the trade for Hundley, Malone said, "We wanted him because he is a warrior."

Having a team full of warriors is all well and good, but a warrior doesn't do his team any good if he's physically unable to play. The Black Knight in Monty Python's Holy Grail movie was also a warrior, but, like Hundley, he wasn't much good after he lost his arm.

Malone made the trade believing Hundley was fully recovered from the reconstructive elbow surgery that caused him to miss most of 1998. Malone should have been more skeptical, because Hundley hadn't shown any signs of being 100 percent: Todd hit .161 with three homers in 124 at-bats for the Mets in '98, spending most of his time misplaying fly balls in left field. If he wasn't healthy enough to catch in September '98, there was no guarantee that another six months of rest would fix everything.

MOMENT OF TRUTH

The nightmare season began before Opening Day. The Dodgers traded for Todd Hundley in December 1998, and immediately began fooling themselves into thinking he was going to be able to handle the catching duties. Hundley, recovering from elbow surgery, still couldn't catch while with the Mets late in the '98 season, and he struggled through spring training, not catching a game until the last week. Hundley wasn't close to being ready to play, but the Dodgers put him in the lineup anyway. The results were disastrous, as base runners ran wild. Depending on Hundley when he obviously wasn't ready was yet another sign of how far the once-proud organization has fallen.

BIGGEST SURPRISE

Mark Grudzielanek improved a bit offensively in 1999, but one of the biggest reasons the Dodgers were happy with his performance was his much-improved defense. He committed only 13 errors in 1999, easily his lowest total since becoming a full-time shortstop in '96, though his range was below average in '99. Offensively he hit for the highest average of his professional career and boosted his power somewhat, although it wasn't as high as in his best seasons in Montreal.

BIGGEST DISAPPOINTMENT

For decades the backbone of the organization, the Dodgers' starting pitchers now struggle to be average. Kevin Brown had a decent season, though not that an established star who makes half his starts in the best pitchers' park in baseball. Darren Dreifort and Ismael Valdes both had awful starts mixed in with the good ones. Chan Ho Park was off all year, and Carlos Perez was sent back to the minors. All five of these pitchers have talent, but it's going to take a dramatic turnaround by before the Dodgers can hope to contend.

As bad as Hundley was at the plate (.207 BA, .105 against lefties; .295 OBA), he was even worse behind it. He threw out only 18 percent of runners trying to steal, made 16 errors, and finished dead last among major-league regular catchers in fielding percentage. Nobody can blame the stolen bases on the pitching staff, either, since reserve receiver Paul LoDuca threw out 29 percent of base stealers while Angel Pena threw out 26 percent.

Again, Hundley wasn't the entire problem. He just contributed to a poor defense, which was especially poor up the middle. Shortstop Mark Grudzielanek and center fielder Devon White both had below-average range, and second baseman Eric Young was only average.

JOHNSON'S PEDIGREE

Malone's biography in the Dodgers' 1999 media guide touts the acquisitions of Hundley, Brown, and Devon White thusly: "After only five months in Los Angeles, Malone has retooled the Dodgers to contend for the World Championship in 1999." Heady stuff, and the PR scribes went even further: "Most importantly, Malone also signed Davey Johnson . . . to manage the Dodgers for the next three seasons."

Johnson arrived in La-La Land with a great pedigree. He had the highest winning percentage of any active manager at .575, he had won the Manager of the Year award in the AL in 1997, and he had won a World Championship in 1986. In his 10 full seasons as manager, Johnson's teams had finished either first or second every year. But had Johnson ever had a bad team, or one in such complete disarray as the current Dodgers? Have his former teams gotten better or worse after he left town?

The Mets finished last in 1982, then lost 94 games and had the worst record in the National League in 1983. They won 90 games and finished second in 1984, Johnson's rookie season as a manager. New York finished second in 1985, first from 1986 through 1988, and second in 1989. Of course, Davey's Mets won one of the most memorable World Series in recent times in '86.

The Mets were 20–22 in 1990 when Johnson was fired; they finished 20 1/2 games out in 1991. Johnson was both very good and very lucky in New York, as his tenure coincided with the Mets' resurgence and it ended before their collapse.

The Reds finished second in 1992 under Lou Piniella, but Piniella then left for Seattle. Big Red Machine legend Tony Perez was named manager, but he lasted only 44 games before he was fired and Johnson was back in the dugout. The Reds suffered numerous injuries to key players, but Davey kept the team near .500 until September.

The next year, the Reds were in first place with the third-best record in the NL when the strike ended the season. In 1995 they won the NL Central and beat Los Angeles in the Division Series, but they were swept by the eventual world champion Braves in the NLCS. Johnson and the Reds parted company after that season, and the Reds chose to replace Johnson with Johnson's friend and former player Ray Knight. The Reds slumped to .500 and finished third in 1996, indicating that Davey did a pretty creditable job in the Queen City.

Johnson inherited a good team in Baltimore in 1996, riding it to a wild-card berth. The Birds beat the Indians in the Division Series but lost to the eventual world champion Yankees in five games in the ALCS. Davey's Orioles won the division the year afterward, defeating the Mariners in the Division Series before falling in six games to the Indians in the ALCS. Cleveland lost the 1997 World Series in seven games. Johnson departed Camden Yards after the '97 season because he refused to kowtow to Orioles' owner Peter Angelos. The O's finished 35 games back in '98 with essentially the same team.

GREEN WITH ENVY OVER BROWN?

*E*veryone *else is jealous of the Dodgers."* —You-know-who. Kevin Brown was good in 1999, but was he $15 million worth of good? Yes and no. Brown was one of the best pitchers in the NL, which might make him worthy of being one of the highest-paid hurlers, but he wasn't the best pitcher in the league, he wasn't close to being the best player in baseball, and he didn't make everyone else jealous of the Dodgers. In fact, Brown wasn't quite as good as he was in 1998, when he made only $4.8 million.

Brown finished 1999 tied for fourth in wins in the NL. He was also second in innings pitched and strikeouts, and fourth in ERA and complete games. Overall, he was 18–9 in 35 starts with a 3.00 ERA, 1.56 runs below the league average. Opposing batters hit .222 against him, 45 points worse than against the league. In '98 with San Diego, however, Brown was 18–7 in 35 starts with a 2.38 ERA, 1.85 runs better than league average. Opponents hit .235 against him, compared to .262 for the league.

In his career, Brown was a four-time All-Star, but he had never won a Cy Young. He had led his league in games started

SECRET WEAPON

Adrian Beltre is a decent offensive player who should continue to improve, but much of his value now comes from his defense. He has good hands and a strong arm, making it difficult for opposing hitters to bunt for hits down the third-base line. Beltre needs to get stronger, as he tired significantly at the end of the season (no homers in 102 at-bats after August), and he's not selective enough at the plate; but those are things he should be able to correct. The Dodgers feel it's only a matter of time before he becomes one of the best players in the game.

ACHILLES HEEL

Aside from the black hole at catcher, the Dodgers suffered from a weak top of the order. The composite on-base average of the L.A. lead-off hitters (primarily Eric Young) was .348, a point below league average. The OBA of their No. 2 hitters (primarily Grudzielanek and Vizcaino) was .320, 22 points below average. Thus the Dodgers' lead-off hitters scored only 103 runs combined (NL average was 117); the Dodgers' No. 2 hitters scored only 95 runs (the NL average was 108).

ENOUGH ALREADY

At the beginning of 1999, Dodgers' general manager Kevin Malone publicly said that Los Angeles was the team to beat in the NL West. Who knows if Malone actually believed that, or if he was just trying to create fan interest? It should have been fairly obvious that the Dodgers weren't going to win in 1999—other than Kevin Brown, L.A. essentially was the same team that finished poorly in '98, and it's hard for one pitcher to turn things completely around. Malone both overestimated the impact Brown and new manager Davey Johnson would make and ignored the multitude of other problems the team faced.

three times, in innings once, in wins once, and in ERA once. He was a very durable pitcher and, undoubtedly, a good pitcher. That didn't make him anywhere near the best pitcher in the game, nor did it instantly make the Dodgers a championship-caliber team.

LAYING OUT GREEN FOR GREEN

The Dodgers think they got a steal by acquiring right fielder Shawn Green from Toronto in a trade for Raul Mondesi. Straight up, the deal makes sense. Nonetheless, if Brown didn't deserve to become the highest-paid pitcher in the game, Green certainly didn't deserve to become the highest-paid hitter.

To be sure, Green was very good in 1998–99, hitting a combined .293 with 79 homers, 240 runs, and 223 RBI. Mondesi hit .266 in 1998–99 with 66 homers, 183 runs, and 189 RBI. However, SkyDome is a better hitters' park than Dodger Stadium, so the difference is smaller than it seems. Both have plus range in the field.

The big difference between the two is that Green is 27 and still in the prime of his career. Mondesi is 29 and entering career middle age, a time when he is less likely to perform at his best and more likely to suffer from injury. Adding Green's left-handed bat to a lineup overloaded with righties is another plus.

Mondesi's profane tirades against management last year had made his departure inevitable, so Malone made a good deal under pressure. That shouldn't be confused with making a deal that will, by itself, turn the team around. Green is no more a savior than Brown was, and the Dodgers' brain trust has yet to address their huge problems at catcher and with up-the-middle defense. If Hundley can't return to a semblance of his previous form, and if the rotation behind Brown doesn't improve, Los Angeles won't see the bright lights of October in 2000, either.

BEST CASE

A lot of things have to happen right for Los Angeles to improve. First of all, Todd Hundley has to be able to catch every day and hit the ball with some consistency. Then Kevin Brown needs to have a monster year to make up for other deficiencies on the starting staff. Gary Sheffield, Shawn Green, and Eric Karros have to stay healthy, and the infield defense simply has to be better. While all these things could happen, that's a lot of "ifs." Even if all goes right, it's not likely the Dodgers will make a run at first place.

WORST CASE

This is a team waiting to implode. Shawn Green, while a very good player, isn't its salvation, and the club hasn't upgraded significantly at any other position. There are glaring holes behind the plate and at second base. Other than Kevin Brown, the pitching staff is suspect; Davey Johnson wants Darren Dreifort to relieve, but Dreifort wants to start. Chan Ho Park has been frightfully inconsistent, and with Ismael Valdes gone and Carlos Perez coming off a 2–10 season, rotation spots must be filled. The Dodgers go into spring training with essentially the same team that finished poorly the year before. All in all, that doesn't leave much cause for optimism.

UNDER THE MICROSCOPE

ANGEL PENA: Pena was considered a "can't miss" prospect heading into 1999. Because of injuries to Todd Hundley and Paul LoDuca, Pena got an early opportunity to play. He did not hit or field well and was chastised for his lack of effort. An injured forearm put an end to his dismal season. With Hundley's future in question, the Dodgers need Pena to become the All-Star player he was projected to be.

CHIN-FENG CHEN: Chen is the first Taiwanese player in the minor-leagues since 1975. He was easily the top prospect in the Class A California League and is rapidly on his way to becoming his country's first major-league player, though he's still a few years away. The right-handed hitter has shown the electric bat speed and power potential.

ERIC GAGNE: Two years removed from Tommy John surgery on his right elbow, Gagne has regained the zip on his fastball and emerged as the top pitching prospect in the organization. Equipped with three solid pitches he can throw for strikes, a willingness to throw inside, and a fierce attitude, Gagne fanned 10 or more batters in his last five Double-A starts before going 1–1, 2.10 ERA in five outings for Los Angeles.

MIKE JUDD: After an outstanding 1997 season, Judd had a subpar '98 season, partially due to illness, and another poor season last year. Judd posted a 6.67 ERA at Triple-A and a 5.46 ERA in 28 major-league innings. He is not overpowering but has solid command of three pitches.

LOS ANGELES DODGERS

TOP PROSPECTS

1999 was an on-field disaster for the Los Angeles Dodgers and filled with mixed reviews down on the farm. 3B **ADRIAN BELTRE** held his own and showed the makings of a future star. RHP **ERIC GAGNE** and OF **CHIN-FENG CHEN** emerged as two of the best prospects in the minor-leagues, and LHP **RANDEY DORAME** emerged as a legitimate prospect, but the rest of the system fell on tough times.

Only three organizations had a lower winning percentage than the Dodgers' minor-league affiliates, the fourth straight season the system had played under .500. C **ANGEL PENA**, considered one of the best prospects in the game, played with such indifference that he got shipped back to the minor-leagues and was eventually suspended at Triple-A. OF **KEVIN GIBBS** missed virtually his second straight season with a right shoulder injury, and OF **JORGE PIEDRA**, coming off a .383 average in the rookie-level Pioneer League, went down with a back injury 89 at-bats into his season. OF **TONY MOTA** had a breakthrough season interrupted by shoulder problems, then a broken thumb. OF **BUBBA CROSBY**, a '98 first-round pick, hit just one home run after slamming 25 in his final year at Rice; OF **OMAR MORENO**, signed for just under $1 million a few years ago, failed to hit .200 in short-season ball.

On the mound, RHP **MIKE JUDD** got pounded at Triple-A for the second straight season, and RHP **LUKE PROKOPEC**, who emerged as a top prospect in '98, got pounded in Double-A. 1998 second-round pick RHP **MARK FISCHER** went down early with arm problems. The organization also received a black mark when 1B **JUAN DIAZ** and OF **JOSUE PEREZ** were declared free agents because the Dodgers had signed them out of Cuba illegally.

With all the bad news in the organization, the Dodgers did get great results from Gagne, Chen, and Dorame. Gagne had an outstanding season at Double-A, then pitched very well in 21 September innings for the Dodgers. Chen became the first 30-30 player in California League history and joined Gagne on the HOWE SPORTSDATA All-Prospect Team. Dorame won 14 games and was named California League Pitcher of the Year.

The Dodgers still have high hopes for Pena and 2B **HIRAM BOCACHICA**, a former Montreal first-round pick who has offensive talent but has been shifted among shortstop, center field, and now second base. SS **ERIC RIGGS** emerged as a fairly good all-around player last season, and 3B **LUKE ALLEN** is a solid hitter who needs to find a position.

Besides Dorame, the Dodgers have a pair of hard-throwing southpaws they like in **STEVE COLYER** and **LANCE CARACCIOLI**, though both need better command. RHP **MARCOS CASTILLO**, coming off a 14-win season and a perfect game in advanced Class A, has a shot.

LF
GARY SHEFFIELD 31
TRENIDAD HUBBARD 34
? #Glenn Davis 2A 24 97/1C
★ Chin-Feng Chen A+ 22 98/ND

CF
#DEVON WHITE 37
*TODD HOLLANDSWORTH 27
? *Bubba Crosby A+ 23 98/1C
↓ *Jorge Piedra A+ 21 97/NDH

RF
***SHAWN GREEN 27**
○ #Tony Mota 2A 22 95/17H

SS
MARK GRUDZIELANEK 30
#JOSE VIZCAINO 32
? *Alex Cora ML 24 96/3C
? #Mike Metcalfe 2A 27 94/3C
○ #Eric Riggs A+ 23 98/4C

2B
? Adam Riggs 3A 27 94/22C
○ Hiram Bocachica 2A 24 94/1H
? Ricky Bell A+ 21 97/3H
○ Jorge Nunez A- 22 95/ND

3B
ADRIAN BELTRE 22
KEVIN ORIE 27
? *Luke Allen 2A 21 96/NDH
? Jimy Gonzalez A+ 21 96/ND
? Damian Rolls A+ 22 96/1H

1B
ERIC KARROS 32
*DAVE HANSEN 31
? Robb Gorr A+ 23 98/14C

SP/RP

RELIEVERS
JEFF SHAW 33
ANTONIO OSUNA 27
TERRY ADAMS 27
*ONAN MASAOKA 22
ALAN MILLS 33
JAMIE ARNOLD 26
DAN NAUTLY 30
? Apostol Garcia 2A 23 92/ND
? Chad Ricketts 2A 25 95/9C

C
***TODD HUNDLEY 31**
PAUL LODUCA 28
↑ Angel Pena ML 25 92/ND

STARTERS
KEVIN BROWN 35
CHAN HO PARK 27
DARREN DREIFORT 28
*JEFF WILLIAMS 28
↑ Eric Gagne ML 24 95/NDH
? Mike Judd ML 25 95/9C
? Luke Prokopec 2A 22 94/ND
↓ Mike Fischer A+ 23 98/2C
? Marcos Castillo A+ 21 95/ND
? *Allen Davis 2A 24 98/24C
○ *Steve Colyer A+ 21 97/2C
↑ *Randey Dorame A+ 21 97/ND
○ *Lance Caraccioli A+ 22 98/10C

MAJOR LEAGUERS IN ALL CAPS
minor leaguers in upper-and-lower case

BEFORE A PLAYER'S NAME:
* left-handed hitter/pitcher
# switch-hitter
?=prospect status (see explanation)

AFTER A PLAYER'S NAME:
Level at which he spent most of 1999 season; age as of July 1, 2000; year he was drafted; round drafted (ND= non-drafted amateur free agent); drafted out of high school (H) or college (C)

EXPLANATION OF PROSPECT RATINGS

★ Potential big-league star

↑ Projected regular player in majors (for pitchers: rotation starter or closer)

○ Projected platoon or utility player in majors (pitcher: setup or middle relief)

? Possible big-league reserve or long reliever

↓ High draft pick or "tools" player who hasn't performed to expectations

LOS ANGELES

SAN DIEGO PADRES

Management
Manager	Bruce Bochy
G.M.	Kevin Towers
President/CEO	John Moores

Career Record
409–383 / .516
339–309 / .523
409–383 / .516

1999 Record

Won–Lost	Pct.	Finish/G.B. (Division)	Finish/G.B. (Wild Card)
74–88	.457	4/26 (W)	9/22.5

Preseason Consensus Projection
5 (4.60)

1st Half	2nd Half	Home	Road	Intradivision	Interleague
37–39	37–49	46–35	28–53	16–22	11–4

Comebacks	Blowouts	Nail-biters	Grass	Turf	Sept.–Oct.
10–8	20–19	28–42	68–72	6–16	13–16

NUMBERS DON'T LIE

	Team (Rank)	Opponents (Rank)	League Avg.
Runs/Game	4.38 (15)	4.82 (6)	5.00
Batting Avg.	.252 (16)	.266 (8)	.268
On-Base Avg.	.332 (13)	.332 (6)	.342
Slugging Avg.	.393 (16)	.429 (11)	.429
Strikeouts	1169 (13)	1078 (7)	1072
Home Runs	153 (15)	193 (11)	181
Stolen Bases	174 (1)	114 (8)	122
ERA	4.47 (8)		4.57
Errors	129 (11)		120

▶ THE INSIDER 2000

PADRE, CAN YOU SPARE A DIME?

The San Diego Padres are going to get their new ballpark the same way most other teams have in the past decade—because residents approved a tax increase to fund it. The decisive vote came soon after the team had finished its magical run to the World Series in 1998, when the fans' emotions were at their highest. That timing was partly by design and partly fortuitous, as the team had been pressing local politicians for years, and several other proposals had been floated and discarded.

Soon after the levy was approved, the Padres' pennant-winning team was dismantled. Most of San Diego's stars left because the Padres didn't want to pay the market rate to resign their own free agents. After the free-agent exodus, management traded away two more high-salaried veterans, Greg Vaughn and Joey Hamilton, in effect conceding that they weren't going to be competitive in '99.

Did San Diego management betray fans by dismantling the club after getting the public subsidy they needed? Was their one-year championship wonder merely the cold reality for even the best-run small-market clubs?

It's not entirely fair to put all the blame on San Diego's executives. Kevin Brown, like Billy Joe and Bobbie Sue, took the money and ran—and no other team besides the Dodgers thought he was worth anywhere near the seven-year, $105 million contract he got. Oft-injured fan hero Ken Caminiti, 35, wanted to go back to Houston so much that he turned down far more money from Detroit. Steve Finley, 33, was coming off a very poor season. Vaughn was eligible for free agency after 1999, and Hamilton was looking for a lucrative long-term deal, since he would be only a year away from free agency after '99.

Was that the right strategy for the franchise? Yes, if one takes a long-term view—which the fans almost never do. The Padres could have kept Vaughn and saved some public relations headaches, but Vaughn wouldn't have made a 26-game difference in the standings. Actually, Vaughn wasn't much better than the player he was traded for during most of the season: Vaughn had 29 homers and 81 RBIs through the end of August, but was hitting .230. Reggie Sanders had 23 homers and 63 RBI at that point in the season and was hitting .299. Vaughn's end-of-the-year hot streak, while crucial to Cincinnati, wouldn't have changed the way the season turned out in San Diego.

The trade also allowed the Padres to upgrade at shortstop with Damian Jackson, who had a fine season defensively and at

MOMENT OF TRUTH

After the Padres' dismal performance in the 1998 World Series, center fielder Steve Finley and third baseman Ken Caminiti accepted better offers from other teams. And with the Padres expending so much energy in the Kevin Brown sweepstakes—only to lose out to the stupendous contract offered by the Dodgers—they missed their chance to sign any big-name free agents. The Padres, realizing they would not be able to re-sign outfielder Greg Vaughn after 1999 if he repeated his 50-homer performance, traded him to the Reds in February. Since this trio represented 44 percent of the 1998 team's home runs, the Padres went from a power-hitting club to a club forced to rely on speed.

BIGGEST SURPRISE

With starting catcher Carlos Hernandez going down with a season-ending injury during spring training, Phil Nevin, who had come to the majors as a third baseman but was forced to learn to catch to keep a job, was acquired from the Anaheim Angels on March 29. The whole thinking behind the trade was to use Nevin off the bench in the infield and as the third-string catcher behind Ben Davis and Jim Leyritz. However, with a third of the season remaining, Nevin surprisingly became the Padres' regular third baseman. At about the same time Nevin took over at the hot corner, the Padres brought up Triple-A catcher Wiki Gonzalez to replace Leyritz, who had been traded to the Yankees two weeks earlier. This gave San Diego a promising tandem behind the plate in Davis and Gonzalez.

BIGGEST DISAPPOINTMENT

The Padres had high hopes for Ruben Rivera, touting him as the center fielder of the future. But, Rivera played the whole season as if he weren't even in the game. He never overcame his struggles at the plate, striking out 143 times in 411 at-bats.

age 26 should get better offensively. If that happens, and if the five high draft picks (first round or between the first and second rounds) that the Padres received as compensation for losing their free agents develop, then the club's strategy will have paid off. If many of those young players flop, moreover, it still wasn't the wrong choice—even if the timing left the fans feeling like they were misled.

HOW BAD CAN A FIVE-TOOL PLAYER BE?

Just how bad was Ruben Rivera in 1999, the first full season the five-tool prospect played in the majors? Really, really bad. "Wretched" might be the best word to describe Rivera's season. It's hard to remember when such a highly touted prospect, who already had seen action in the big leagues in parts of four different seasons, hit so badly in so many at-bats.

The Yankees signed the Panamanian native in 1990 shortly after his 17th birthday. Ruben first began to turn heads in 1994, when he was one of the best players at any Class A level. The Yankees didn't want to part with him, especially after he hit .284 in 46 games in the Bronx in '96, but they reluctantly sent him to the Padres in May 1997 for Hideki Irabu, believed to be a future ace.

Rivera had 281 major-league at-bats going into last season, but he performed as if he hadn't ever played above Class A. He hit .195 while striking out more than a third of the time; though he displayed good power as well as good range in the field, it was little consolation. He was easily the worst outfielder in the big leagues with that many at-bats.

Once one of the best prospects in all of baseball, Rivera is now 26 and at the very bottom of a pile of young, talented NL outfielders. In 1999, Vladimir Guerrero (who'll be only 24 in 2000) hit .316 with 42 homers and 131 RBIs for the Expos; Bobby Abreu (26) hit .335 with a .446 on-base average for the Phillies; Roger Cedeno (25) hit .313 with a .396 on-base average and stole 66 bases for the Mets; Dmitri Young (26) hit .300 and slugged .504 for the Reds; Geoff Jenkins (25) hit .313 and slugged .564 for the Brewers; and Preston Wilson (25) hit .280 with 26 homers for the Marlins.

Even other NL youngsters who were considered disappointments had much better seasons. J. D. Drew (24) hit .242 for the Cardinals last season with a .340 OBA, and Andruw Jones (23) hit .275 with 26 homers and 84 RBIs.

Rivera has fallen about as far as a hot prospect can without leaving the game or being banished to the minors. He will have to rebound quickly in the first months of the 2000 season if he wants to keep his job. The Padres understandably have run out of patience, and even a rebuilding franchise can't afford that kind of black hole in the lineup forever.

There is certainly hope for Rivera's future, since his biggest problems appear to be correctable if he would apply himself and listen to his coaches. Many other young players with less talent than Rivera have turned things around after bitterly disappointing years. One recent example is Mike Cameron. The White Sox were so disappointed with his performance in 1998 (.210, .285 OBA, 8 homers, 101 strikeouts in 396 at-bats) that they traded him to the Reds for another disappointment, Paul Konerko. Cameron bounced back with a decent year in '99 at age 26, hitting .256 with a .357 OBA, 21 homers, and 38 stolen bases.

PUTTING A LEGEND IN PERSPECTIVE

A respected national baseball columnist called Tony Gwynn "the greatest hitter of our generation" last winter. It's a popular misconception, brought about because of Gwynn's high career batting average (.339) and his immense popularity among fans, writers, and broadcasters. Despite popular opinion, though, Gwynn clearly hasn't been the best hitter of the past 20 years, nor even the best hitter in his division—that would be Barry Bonds.

In 18 seasons, Gwynn has 3,067 hits, 133 homers, 771 walks, an on-base average of .389, and a slugging average of .459. Bonds, who has played four fewer seasons, has only 2,010 hits, but he has 445 homers, 1,430 walks, a .288 BA, a .409 OBA, and a .559 SA. Bonds won three MVP awards (and deserved a fourth) because he was a much better hitter than Gwynn.

Comparing Bonds' and Gwynn's production, and adjusting them for park and league differences, *Total Baseball* says Bonds has been 65 percent better than the average hitter in his career, and he has been ranked much higher than that in the 1990s. Gwynn, on the other hand, has been 34 percent better than the average player in his career. That's still an excellent mark and it makes him one of the better hitters in the game, but not the best hitter of his generation.

Other top active hitters (minimum 10 years in the majors),

SECRET WEAPON

San Diego's team speed and stolen bases surprised many in 1999. Prior to the season, no one thought the Padres would top the NL with 174 stolen bases, or have four players (Reggie Sanders, Damian Jackson, Eric Owens, and Quilvio Veras) with 30 or more steals. Even better, the Flyin' Friars were caught only 67 times, for an excellent 72 percent success rate. Of course, all that running couldn't make up for a lack of power that saw San Diego finish next to last in the NL in homers.

ACHILLES HEEL

Age equals frequent injuries. Youth equals inexperience. With injuries to key players such as Tony Gwynn and Wally Joyner (seemingly a yearly occurrence) combining with injuries to Chris Gomez and Quilvio Veras, the Padres had ended up with a combination of over-the-hill veterans such as Carlos Baerga and Dave Magadan and ready-or-not young players. Inexperience plus injuries equaled a fourth-place finish for the drastically revamped defending NL champions.

ENOUGH ALREADY

Jim Leyrtiz's parting shots about Tony Gwynn could have been blown all out of proportion after it was learned that the local newspaper in San Diego sat on the story for a week, until Leyritz was traded to the Yankees. In the article, Leyritz supposedly claimed Gwynn was not a team player and that Leyritz felt Gwynn's main concern was to get his 3,000 hits—and that, in turn, hurt the team. Leyritz also claimed Tony kept to himself not only on the bench but also after the game. Those comments never swayed the fans, who thoroughly enjoyed watching Gwynn reach the 3,000-hit plateau.

who might reasonably be considered when making up a list of the greatest hitters of our generation, include: Rickey Henderson, 32 percent above average; Jose Canseco and Rafael Palmeiro, both 34 percent; Juan Gonzalez, 36 percent; Larry Walker, 37 percent; Gary Sheffield, 41 percent; Albert Belle and Ken Griffey, both 48 percent; Edgar Martinez, 50 percent; Jeff Bagwell, 62 percent; Mark McGwire, 66 percent; and Frank Thomas, 72 percent. Remember that this evaluation includes only batting, not base-running or fielding value, and that it is adjusted for league, ballpark, and seasonal differences. League averages also do not include pitcher batting.

Gwynn has been a better hitter compared to the other recent members of the 3,000-hit club. He's better than Wade Boggs—30 percent above average—partly because Boggs was below average the past four years while Gwynn has dipped below the mean. Eddie Murray and Dave Winfield, with their hundreds of homers, were both 30 percent above the norm during their careers. Paul Molitor was 22 percent better and Robin Yount was only 15 percent above par, as is Cal Ripken now.

At 39 in '99, Gwynn continued to be a superior hitter late into his career. His production has been consistent the past five years, while Boggs's dropped dramatically. Boggs was a below-average player during the past four years while he chased 3,000 hits.

The only way one could call Tony Gwynn the greatest hitter would be to ignore power and walks. Gwynn is a great hitter, a great player, and a great guy, but the spell of the 3,000-hit chase led to some overzealous accolades.

BEST CASE

Nothing is expected from the Padres in 2000, so losing fewer than 90 games will make for a successful season. What will it take for that to happen? For starters, the team needs to get something out of Ruben Rivera. His struggles are well documented, and he has been a huge disappointment. Even a super year from him, however, wouldn't necessarily avoid a last-place finish. Young pitchers Matt Clement and Buddy Carlyle are promising but need to continue their development. Lefty-hitting vets Wally Joyner and Tony Gwynn must remain healthy for the entire season. San Diego isn't going to contend, but good performances from these players will keep the club from being the doormat of the NL West.

WORST CASE

The Padres continued their trend of trading for younger players when the club dumped Andy Ashby, the club's lone remaining experienced starter, to Philadelphia. Worse yet for San Diego fans was news out of the winter meetings that executives were thinking about trading Reggie Sanders and Quilvio Veras. While neither player is a superstar, they're about the best the team has. If they get marching orders, it will make what already promises to be a long year even longer.

UNDER THE MICROSCOPE

BEN DAVIS: Known strictly for his defensive achievements early in his career, Davis has improved his offense steadily over the past few seasons, making him complete. The 23-year-old, who hit safely in 23 straight games before getting the call to the big leagues, will likely split time with Carlos Hernandez in 2000.

SEAN BURROUGHS: Burroughs, the son of former MVP Jeff, had an outstanding debut season. The 20-year-old reached base safely in each of his final 54 regular-season games and in all five postseason affairs. While he has yet to be tested in the higher levels of the minors, the Padres' need for a third baseman will push him through the system quickly.

BUDDY CARLYLE: The 22-year-old Carlyle made an immediate name for himself by holding the Brewers hitless for $5^{2}/_{3}$ innings in his major-league debut. While none of his pitches is much better than average, Carlyle has an advanced knowledge of how to pitch and is not afraid to pound hitters inside. Carlyle's projected velocity is in the low-to-mid-90s, and he will need every bit of that to have more consistent success in the majors.

WASCAR SERRANO: After a very strong '98 in which he ranked third in the Padres' system in strikeouts (143) and fifth in ERA (3.22) while pitching in lower-level Class A, Serrano posted almost identical numbers at the next level before getting seven Double-A starts in '99. The 21-year-old has a great arm, a low-90s fastball that has potential to improve, and a decent curveball.

TOP PROSPECTS

After a trip to the World Series in '98, the Padres cut costs and suffered through a losing season. The club parted with such big-name talents as Greg Vaughn, Kevin Brown, Steve Finley, and Ken Caminiti and replaced them with rookies and unproven players. While it will take some time before the club rebounds from these changes, the Padres did receive boosts from first-year players RHP **MATT CLEMENT**, C **BEN DAVIS**, RHP **BUDDY CARLYLE**, and C **WIKI GONZALEZ**, in addition to six of the first 51 picks of the '99 draft.

Clement, who had a great August and September, looks to be a fixture in the rotation for years to come while the emergence of Davis and Gonzalez will give the club numbers behind the plate when '98 starter Carlos Hernandez returns. Carlyle doesn't have any one dominant pitch but earned consideration for a spot in the rotation with his September showing.

Following behind Carlyle, 21-year-old righthanders **JUNIOR HERNDON** and **WASCAR SERRANO** have a chance to make the majors within the next couple of seasons. Herndon has an exceptional moving fastball, great control, and a full season of Double-A under his belt. Serrano struck out a career-high 158 batters in time split between advanced Class A and Double-A. RHP **RODRIGO LOPEZ**, who spent parts of three seasons in the Mexican League, is not overpowering but has good command. The organization's Pitcher of the Year, RHP **RICK GUTTORMSON**, led the organization with 14 victories while issuing just 36 walks in 174 innings. RHP **GERALDO PADUA**, acquired from the Yankees at midseason, made headlines for winning 20 straight decisions between 1997 and '99. He pitched eight innings of a combined no-hitter early in '99 and finished the season second in the minors with 196 strikeouts. RHP **ISABEL GIRON** struggled after coming over in a trade from the Blue Jays in July, but is still highly regarded.

3B **SEAN BURROUGHS**, the Padres' first-round pick in the 1998 draft, had a tremendous debut season in '99, earning the honor as the organization's player of the year and a spot on both HOWE SPORTSDATA's All-Prospect team and its All-Teen team. Besides him, however, the Padres are weak around the infield. SS **KEVIN NICHOLSON**, a first-round pick in '97, rebounded to have a strong repeat season at Double-A, but-despite a strong arm is suspect defensively.

In the outfield, **GARY MATTHEWS** and **MIKE DARR** are closest to the majors but have not shown enough consistency with the bat to be everyday candidates just yet. OF **PETE TUCCI**, acquired from the Blue Jays last off-season, suffered through a disappointing '99 after a breakthrough '98 campaign.

The Padres made the most of their draft picks, adding a number of quality prospects to the organization. Four of the picks were pitchers (RHP **GERIK BAXTER**, RHP **OMAR ORTIZ**, RHP **CASEY BURNS**, and LHP **MIKE BYNUM**). Bynum began his professional career with 28 scoreless innings, and Baxter won his first five decisions. RHP **JACOB PEAVY**, selected in the 15th round, won the pitching Triple Crown in the rookie-level Arizona League. OF **VINCE FAISON**, who has tremendous speed, was taken 20th overall.

CF
ERIC OWENS 29
RUBEN RIVERA 26
○ #Gary Matthews CF ML 25 93/13C
○ Jeremy Owens CF A+ 23 98/8C
○ *Kory DeHaan 2A 23 97/7C
↓ *Vince Faison CF A- 19 99/1H

LF
JOHN VANDER WAL 34
? *Shea Morenz LF 2A 26 95/1C

RF
***TONY GWYNN 40**
↑ *Mike Darr RF ML 24 94/2H
○ Peter Tucci RF 2A 24 96/1C
? Josh Loggins RF A- 23 98/11C

SS
DAMIAN JACKSON 26
CHRIS GOMEZ 29
↑ #Kevin Nicholson, SS 2A 24 97/1C
? Matt Halloran SS A+ 22 96/1H

2B
BRET BOONE 31
? *David Newhan 2B ML 26 95/17C
? #Jake Thrower 2B 3A 24 97/ND

3B
PHIL NEVIN 29
? #Ryan Balfe 3B 2A 24 94/8H
? Kevin Eberwein 3B 2A 23 98/5C
★ *Sean Burroughs 3B A+ 19 98/1H

1B
***RYAN KLESKO 29**
*DAVE MAGADAN 37

SP/RP

RELIEVERS
TREVOR HOFFMAN 32
*RANDY MYERS 37
DONNE WALL 32
BRIAN BOEHRINGER 30
STEVE MONTGOMERY 29
*DAN SERAFINI 26
*MATT WHISENANT 29
CARLOS ALMANZAR 26
○ Domingo Guzman ML 25 93/ND
○ Will Cunnane ML 26 92/NDH
? James Sak 3A 26 95/10C
? Brandon Kolb 3A 26 95/4C

C
#BEN DAVIS 23
CARLOS HERNANDEZ 33
? Wiklenman Gonzalez ML 26 92/ND
○ Wilbert Nieves A+ 22 95/47H
? *Tim DeCinces 3A 26 96/17C

STARTERS
*STERLING HITCHCOCK 29
WOODY WILLIAMS 33
MATT CLEMENT 25
CARLTON LOEWER 26
BRIAN MEADOWS 24
↑ Buddy Carlyle ML 22 96/2H
↑ Adam Eaton 3A 22 96/1H
↑ Isabel Giron 2A 22 94/ND
↑ Harry Herndon 2A 21 97/9H
↓ Jason Middlebrook 2A 25 96/9C
↑ Wascar Serrano 2A 21 95/NDH
? Rodrigo Lopez 2A 24 95/ND
? Rick Guttormson A+ 23 97/22C
○ Geraldo Padua A+ 23 94/ND
? Brian Lawrence A+ 24 98/17C
? Ben Howard A- 21 97/2H
? Doug Dent A- 23 97/13
↓ Gerik Baxter A- 20 99/1H
↑ *Mike Bynum A+ 22 99/1C

MAJOR LEAGUERS IN ALL CAPS
Minor leaguers in upper-and-lower case

BEFORE A PLAYER'S NAME:
* left-handed hitter/pitcher
# switch-hitter
?=prospect status (see explanation)

AFTER A PLAYER'S NAME:
Level at which he spent most of 1999 season; age as of July 1, 2000; year he was drafted; round drafted (ND= non-drafted amateur free agent); drafted out of high school (H) or college (C)

EXPLANATION OF PROSPECT RATINGS

★ Potential big-league star

↑ Projected regular player in majors (for pitchers: rotation starter or closer)

○ Projected platoon or utility player in majors (pitcher: setup or middle relief)

? Possible big-league reserve or long reliever

↓ High draft pick or "tools" player who hasn't performed to expectations

SAN DIEGO

SAN FRANCISCO GIANTS

Management
		Career Record
Manager	Dusty Baker	558–512 / .521
G.M.	Brian Sabean	265–222 / .544
President/CEO	Peter Magowan	558–512 / .521

1999 Record
Won–Lost	Pct.	Finish/G.B. (Division)	Finish/G.B. (Wild Card)
86–76	.531	2/14 (W)	3/10.5

Preseason Consensus Projection
2 (2.90)

1st Half	2nd Half	Home	Road	Intradivision	Interleague
43–35	43–41	49–32	37–44	19–18	7–8

Comebacks	Blowouts	Nail-biters	Grass	Turf	Sept.–Oct.
5–13	21–24	38–28	71–63	15–13	15–15

NUMBERS DON'T LIE

	Team (Rank)		Opponents (Rank)		League Avg.
Runs/Game	5.38	(3)	5.13	(9)	5.00
Batting Avg.	.271	(7)	.265	(7)	.268
On-Base Avg.	.356	(2)	.345	(10)	.342
Slugging Avg.	.434	(6)	.423	(9)	.429
Strikeouts	1028	(5)	1076	(9)	1072
Home Runs	188	(7)	194	(12)	181
Stolen Bases	109	(11)	129	(10)	122
ERA	4.71	(10)			4.57
Errors	105	(4)			120

▶ THE INSIDER 2000

THE BAKER, IN THE CANDLESTICK DUGOUT, WITH THE BONDS

San Francisco has been scraping by for years now, competitive but not really good, on the strength of the all-around excellence of Barry Bonds and the managerial acumen of Dusty Baker. With a gorgeous new ballpark making its long-awaited debut this year, will that kind of overachieving underdog performance be good enough to satisfy the expectations of the fans paying top dollar at PacBell Park?

Despite a lamentable neglect of his brilliant career by the media, combined with a curious level of fan apathy toward him personally, Bonds has by now demonstrated that he is inarguably the second-greatest left fielder in baseball history. If Barry can remain productive in the twilight of his great career, avoiding the kind of injuries that limited him to 102 games last year, he actually has a chance to be as good as the legendary Teddy Ballgame.

As a three-time MVP winner in the 1990s (1990 and '91 with the Pirates, and '93 in his first year with the Giants), Bonds is in very select, Hall of Fame company. Only seven other players have ever won three MVPs: Jimmy Foxx, Joe DiMaggio, Stan Musial, Roy Campanella, Yogi Berra, Mickey Mantle, and Mike Schmidt.

Fittingly, Bonds was named Player of the Decade for the 1990s by *The Sporting News* last year, joining an elite group of baseball immortals to have won that award. By winning, Bonds joined the only other legitimate candidates for the greatest left fielder of all time: Stan Musial and Ted Williams. Musial was *TSN*'s Player of the Decade in the 1940s; Williams in the 1950s. Willie Mays won the honor for the 1960s, Pete Rose for the 1970s, and Mike Schmidt for the 1980s.

One indirect measure of Bonds' greatness is the frequency with which enemy pitchers have given him intentional free passes. When Bonds was walked deliberately by Chan Ho Park time on June 27, he surpassed Hank Aaron's major league record with 293. Barry finished the year with 298 career intentional walks. Of course, one of the reasons that Bonds has been waved down to first so often is the relative lack of support he has had in the San Fran lineup.

MOMENT OF TRUTH

The Giants led the NL West early in the season despite Barry Bonds being on the disabled list for most of the first two months. Bonds returned to action on June 9, with the team only two games out of first, but the return of San Francisco's best player didn't have the expected effect. The Giants played only .500 ball for the next month and finally fell out of contention shortly after the All-Star break. Bonds returned to form and started carrying the club too late in the year—the Giants lost 10 games in the standings to the Diamondbacks from mid-July to mid-August before Bonds finally got hot.

SAN FRANCISCO GIANTS

BIGGEST SURPRISE

Armando Rios completed his climb from non-drafted free agent to big-league ballplayer in 1999. Rios was shipped to Triple-A after a bad spring, but he got a second chance when Barry Bonds went on the DL and made great strides before tearing a rotator cuff diving for a ball in right field. Rios played good defense, using his powerful and accurate arm, and became a much more disciplined hitter by midseason. He may not become a star, but he might be a useful regular in the immediate future.

BIGGEST DISAPPOINTMENT

The failure of starter Mark Gardner and closer Robb Nen to realize how badly they were injured hurt the club more than their actual ailments. Both tried to pitch through their injuries and ended up hurting the club. Gardner (5–11, 6.47 ERA) tried rest and cortisone injections for his aching shoulder, but eventually required surgery. Nen lost eight games and blew nine saves while not admitting how seriously he was hurt. He had elbow surgery the last week of the season.

CLINES' INFLUENCE

The Giants had legitimately the second-best offense in the NL in 1999, scoring more runs than everyone except Arizona and Colorado. (The latter's 34 more runs are, of course, far less important than the huge advantage bestowed by Denver's altitude.) Five Giants' hitters slugged 20 or more homers last season: Bonds (34 in only 355 at-bats), Kent (23), J.T. Snow (24), Rich Aurilia (22, more than double his previous career high), and Ellis Burks (31 round-trippers in only 390 at-bats).

The key ingredient in the team's robust attack was excellent plate discipline, as San Francisco led the NL in on-base average with a .356 mark. Nothing is guaranteed in baseball, but such an offense is much more likely to resist serious slumps than an offense based primarily on aggressive, high-average hitters who don't take many pitches. Batters with good strike-zone judgment can compensate somewhat when they're slumping by not swinging at bad pitches and getting themselves out in an attempt to make something positive happen. And, while a walk isn't as good as a hit in most circumstances, getting on base and giving the next guy in the lineup a chance to drive you in is far preferable to the alternative.

This kind of rigorous approach to hitting is a credit to Baker and his hitting coach, Gene Clines. Clines, who was hired in 1997, took over a team that was slightly below league average in production (after adjusting for ballpark effects) in 1994-96. Since 1997, the Giants have been substantially above the league norm in adjusted production, while finishing sixth in 1997 and second in '98 in the NL in OBA. Overall, the team's offense now resembles their manager's hitting profile when he played from 1969 through 1986: Baker hit for a decent average with good power and good on-base during his big-league career. In contrast, Clines was not a good hitter during his much briefer career in the majors (1970-79), mostly due to a complete lack of power—he hit only five career homers in 2328 at-bats. Like many astute benchwarmers, though, Clines obviously learned how to teach others to do what he didn't have the skills to do himself.

THE SUPPORTING CAST

Like all great performers, Bonds needs some help from his supporting cast. Aside from ample power, San Francisco's lineup was a mixture of pluses and minuses. At first, Snow compensates for subpar hitting at a power position with his brilliant defense, winning his fifth consecutive Gold Glove in '99. J. T. has committed only 36 errors in his eight major league seasons and ranks sixth in career fielding percentage at first base (minimum 600 games). Snow signed a four-year contract extension at midseason, so he will be a fixture in the team's lineup for the immediate future.

At the keystone position, Kent has been one of the most overrated players in the game since he arrived in Baghdad by the Bay in 1997. Jeff piles up RBI mostly because he bats behind Bonds, but he's hardly a great hitter and he's a liability defensively. His career year in 1998 was quite impressive but it was the only season in his career that he was anywhere near that good. At age 32, he's not likely to achieve that again.

On the left side of the infield, Aurilia and Mueller each have one strength that covers for their other weaknesses. Aurilia's newfound power put him well above most other shortstops with the bat, but his glove is a negative. Mueller's adequate defensively and can fill in at second base if needed; his .388 OBA makes him an asset when batting ahead of the boppers in the lineup. However, his weakness against lefties and his lack of power limit his value.

Across the outfield, the team is solid defensively with Bonds, Benard, and Burks. As a leadoff hitter, Benards surprising power last season would be a lot more impressive if he got on base more often (.359 OBA) and ran more effectively (27 steals in 41 attempts). Burks' biggest problem is remaining in the lineup with his knee problems; Ellis has managed to play 150 games in only two of his 13 seasons in the Show.

With the '99 platoon of Brent Mayne and Scott Servais departing, the Giants will be looking for prospects Bobby Estalella, Giuseppe Chiaramonte, or possibly Yorvit Torrealba to step up and contribute behind the plate. Estalella has big power but is suspect defensively and has been an all-or-nothing hitter in the majors. Otherwise, the team will be forced to rely on 29-year-old minor league veteran Doug Mirabelli.

Warts and all, the Giants' offense is far more dependable than their pitching. After young right-hander Russ Ortiz, the staff is full of question marks. Rookie righty Joe Nathan showed definite promise but has only 14 major league starts under his belt. Veteran righty Livan Hernandez needs to demonstrate that he can become a consistent winner; his 227 hits and 23 homers allowed in 199.2 innings isn't going to cut it. Southpaws Kirk Rueter and Shawn Estes need to improve if the Giants are going to make a run at Arizona in the NL West.

SECRET WEAPON

Center fielder Marvin Benard emerged as one of San Francisco's key offensive players by adding decent power to his game. Sometimes forgotten playing alongside bigger names, such as Barry Bonds and Jeff Kent, Benard scored 100 runs and drove in 67 while hitting a career-high 16 homers as a leadoff hitter. He also provided a constant presence in the lineup when other players were shuffling in and out with injuries, and he showed an ability to adapt during a midseason slump, when he frequently bunted for hits.

ACHILLES HEEL

San Francisco's starting staff never provided any rest for an overworked bullpen. The Giants had an entire staff of six-inning pitchers. Russ Ortiz and Shawn Estes both had problems throwing strikes while consistently running high pitch counts early in games, Kirk Rueter pitched well in the early innings but seemed to always hit a wall in the sixth. Mark Gardner rarely pitched well enough to make it even that far. All of this strained a bullpen that wasn't so good to begin with.

ENOUGH ALREADY

It should have been obvious early in 1999 that something was wrong with Mark Gardner. A valuable starter for three seasons, Gardner looked nothing like the pitcher who won 37 games the previous three years. He went on the disabled list only two weeks into the season and was awful when he returned to the active roster, losing his first 10 decisions. Yet team officials and broadcasters spent most of the season saying things like, "Gardy's won a lot of big ball games for us" and "He hasn't found his rhythm" instead of admitting to themselves and the fans that Mark was hurt. Realizing that Gardner needed shoulder surgery earlier wouldn't have won the pennant for the Giants, but it certainly would have put the club in much better position to contend with the Diamondbacks.

In the bullpen, the big Q is the status of closer Robb Nen's elbow. If Nen can return to his previous dominance, holdovers Alan Embree, John Johnstone, Felix Rodriguez, and Miguel del Toro could well form the core of a reliable bullpen. There is some pitching talent in the threadbare farm system, but most of it spent 1999 at Double- or Single-A. If Nen struggles in 2000, the whole relief staff could easily unravel.

TEN QUESTIONS: FAREWELL TO CANDLESTICK EDITION

1) Who scored the most runs at 3Com/Candlestick Park? Answer: Mays crossed home plate 598 times. McCovey was second with 540; Bobby Bonds was third with 406; Barry Bonds was fourth with 401.

2) Who hit the most home runs? A: McCovey bashed 236 through the swirling gusts at Candlestick Point. Mays was second with 203; Barry Bonds is third with 140.

3) Who had the highest batting average (minimum 100 at-bats)? A: Jeff Bagwell, .389. Rondell White was next at .368.

4) Which San Francisco batter posted the highest batting average (minimum 100 at-bats) at Candlestick? A: Shawon Dunston, .336, followed by Donell Nixon at .333.

5) Who played the most games? A: McCovey was the only player to see 1000 games at the Stick, playing in 1085. The rest of the top 10: Mays (886), Robby Thompson (657), Jim Davenport (612), Will Clark (598), Chris Speier (594), Darrell Evans (587), Matt Williams (573), Jack Clark (557), and Hal Lanier (549).

6) Who stole the most bases? A: Bobby Bonds swiped 141; Barry swiped 114. Brett Butler was third with 87.

7) Who pitched in the most games? A: Durable southpaw reliever Gary Lavelle, 317. Greg Minton was a distant second with 253, followed by Randy Moffitt with 234. Rod Beck and Marichal tied for fourth with 223.

8) Who hurled the most innings? A: Marichal, 1,708.2. Runner-up was Perry, who expectorated his way through 1,255.2 innings.

9) Which San Francisco pitcher compiled the lowest ERA (minimum 75 IP)? A: Robb Nen, 1.83. Bill Swift was next with 2.33. Frank Linzy rounded out the top three at 2.35.

10) Who suffered the most losses at Candlestick? A: Fernando Valenzuela, star of the hated Dodgers, took the "L" 16 times. Steve Carlton and Larry Jackson tied for second with 14. Don Drysdale, another feared and hated Dodger, was next with 12.

BEST CASE

The Giants had a good team in 1999 but still finished 14 games behind Arizona in the NL West and 10½ back of the Mets. San Francisco didn't make any moves before the end of the winter meetings, which means club executives think the Giants—moving into a new park—are capable of overtaking at least one defending playoff team with its current roster. The Giants will need some combination of a healthy Mark Gardner, a consistent Shawn Estes, and an improved Livan Hernandez if they want to make up those games in the standings. The Giants were third in the league in runs in '99 despite having Barry Bonds miss a third of the season because of elbow surgery; it's up to the pitching staff to provide the lift.

WORST CASE

The Giants can't win if Bonds isn't around most of the way. The new ballpark at China Basin was virtually built for him and his power swing. When healthy, Bonds is still the best player in the game and is one of the few players who can literally carry a team. Bonds's hot streaks are legendary, but San Francisco simply doesn't have the pitching, or enough other quality hitters, to make up for an extended absence.

UNDER THE MICROSCOPE

JOE NATHAN: Splitting the '99 season between Triple-A and the major-leagues, Nathan pitched seven innings of shutout ball in his big-league debut, displaying an explosive fastball that hit 97 mph and a knee-buckling curve. The Giants need Nathan to earn a starting spot this spring.

JAKE ESTEVES: Often compared to Russ Ortiz, Esteves took the biggest jump in the organization last season. The one-time reliever made the full-time switch to the starting rotation and went 14-3, 2.92 ERA at two levels. The LSU product has the best combination of stuff and command in the organization. Combining a 93-94 mph sinking fastball with a slider and newly developed change and curve.

GIUSEPPE CHIARAMONTE: The Giants had hoped Chiaramonte, an outstanding power hitter, would develop into an everyday player, but he hit too many fly balls and refused to hit the other way. He also threw out just 14 percent of base stealers. San Francisco could use an upgrade behind the plate, but Chiaramonte will have to improve significantly to get back into the picture.

TONY TORCATO: Torcato batted .291 with just four homers in the Class A California League. He was bothered by shoulder and ankle problems all season and was one of the youngest players in the league. His home-run production should increase as he matures. He has a firm grasp of the strike zone, but he needs some work on the finer points of his position.

SAN FRANCISCO G A

TOP PROSPECTS

For the third year in a row, the Giants traded away top prospects to acquire pennant help for the stretch drive. In 1999, RHPs **JASON GRILLI** and **NATE BUMP**, the Giants' most recent first-round picks, were dealt to the Marlins for Livan Hernandez. In the previous two years, the organization dealt away Keith Foulke, Bobby Howry, Lorenzo Barcelo, Joe Fontenot, Mike Caruso, and Jacob Cruz, among others. The system has been so ravaged that the most recent first-round pick left in the organization is RHP **STEVE SODERSTROM**, who was selected in 1993.

After drafting Will Clark, Matt Williams, Mike Remlinger, and Royce Clayton in the first round of consecutive drafts from 1985 to 1998, only first-round picks Calvin Murray, Dante Powell, and Soderstrom—who was dropped from the 40-man roster this winter—have appeared in the majors for the Giants.

Despite the departures of Grilli and Bump, pitching is still the strength of the organization. RHP **RUSS ORTIZ** established himself as a front-line major-league pitcher in 1999, and RHP **JOE NATHAN** displayed winning stuff. RHP **JAKE ESTEVES** has taken over the mantle of top prospect; but RHP **RYAN VOGELSONG** made solid progress, RHP **RYAN JENSEN** jumped successfully from Class A to Triple-A, and '99 first-round pick RHP **KURT AINSWORTH** had a strong debut, posting a 1.61 ERA and 64 strikeouts in 45 innings. Twenty-five-year-old LHP **MIKE RILEY** had a breakthrough season, posting a 2.11 ERA and a strikeout per inning at Double-A. RHP **SCOTT LINEBRINK**, a highly regarded second-round pick in '97, missed most of the season after undergoing shoulder surgery.

OF **ARMANDO RIOS**, 2B-SS **RAMON MARTINEZ**, and SS **WILSON DELGADO** proved capable reserves at the big-league level, but there isn't an everyday player in the two upper levels of the system. The Giants consider 3B **TONY TORCATO** their best prospect; he posted mediocre numbers as one of the youngest players in the California League. OF **DOUG CLARK**, a collegiate football player at the University of Massachusetts, opened eyes with his .315 average and Larry Walker-like swing in his first full season. The organization also likes OFs **MIKE BYAS**, **CHRIS MAGRUDER**, and **ARTURO MCDOWELL**, but each looks like a fringe prospect for now.

San Francisco has catching depth, but **GIUSEPPE CHIARAMONTE** did not prove he could hit or play defense consistently enough at -. **SAMMY SERRANO**, the 1998 NCAA batting champion, is farther along with the bat than behind the plate. 2B **JAY CANIZARO**, one of the Giants' top prospects three years ago, clubbed 26 homers at Triple-A and impressed in a September call-up, but he's 26 and a backup at best. Speedy but light-hitting SS **NELSON CASTRO** was acquired on waivers from the Angels this winter to add depth in the infield, which includes Class A SS **CODY RANSOM**, an athletic but raw player.

LF
*BARRY BONDS 35
- ? Mike Glendenning 2A 23 96/10C
- ? #Chris Magruder 2A 23 98/2C
- ○ *Doug Clark 2A 24 98/7C

CF
*MARVIN BENARD 30
- ○ #Mike Byas 3A 24 97/15C
- ↓ *Arturo McDowell A+ 20 98/1H

RF
ELLIS BURKS 35
- CALVIN MURRAY 28
- ? *Armando Rios ML 28 94/NDC
- ? Jeff Allen A+ 24 98/15C

SS
RICH AURILIA 28
- ○ Ramon Martinez ML 27 93/NDC
- ○ #Wilson Delgado ML 24 92/ND
- ? #Carlos Mendoza 2A 20 96/NDC
- ○ Cody Ransom 2A 24 98/9C
- ○ Nelson Castro A+ 24 94/ND

2B
JEFF KENT 32
- ? Jay Canizaro ML 26 93/4C
- ? Travis Young 3A 25 97/11C

3B
#BILL MUELLER 29
- ? *Edwards Guzman ML 23 95/50C
- ? Pedro Felix 3B 2A 23 94/ND
- ↑ *Tony Torcato A+ 20 98/1H

1B
*J.T. SNOW 32
- ? *Damon Minor 2A 26 96/12C

SP/RP

RELIEVERS
- ROBB NEN 30
- ALAN EMBREE 30
- JOHN JOHNSTONE 31
- FELIX RODRIGUEZ 27
- MIGUEL DEL TORO 28
- ? Steve Soderstrom 3A 28 93/1C
- ○ Robbie Crabtree 3A 27 96/21C
- ? Bill Malloy 2A 25 96/6C
- ○ Benji Miller A+ 24 98/21C
- ○ Randy Goodrich A+ 23 98/12C
- ? *Aaron Fultz 3A 26 92/6C
- *Jason Davis 2A 25 96/30C
- ○ *Mike Riley 2A 25 96/16C
- ↓ *Jeff Andra A+ 24 97/3C

C
DOUG MIRABELLI 29
- ○ Bobby Estalella ML 25 92/23C
- ? Yorvit Torrealba 3A 21 94/ND
- ○ Giuseppe Chiaramonte 2A 24 97/5C
- ○ Sammy Serrano A+ 23 98/2C
- ○ Mike Dean A+ 22 98/3C

STARTERS
- RUSS ORTIZ 26
- LIVAN HERNANDEZ 25
- *SHAWN ESTES 27
- *KIRK RUETER 29
- JOE NATHAN 25
- MARK GARDNER 38
- ? Ryan Jensen 3A 24 96/8C
- ↓ Scott Linebrink 2A 23 97/2C
- ○ Ryan Vogelsong 2A 22 98/5C
- ↑ Jake Esteves 2A 24 98/6C
- ↓ Kurt Ainsworth A- 21 99/1C
- ↓ Jerome Williams A- 18 99/1H
- ○ *Jeff Urban 2A 23 98/1C
- ○ *Chris Jones A+ 20 98/2H

MAJOR LEAGUERS IN ALL CAPS
Minor leaguers in upper-and-lower case

BEFORE A PLAYER'S NAME:
* left-handed hitter/pitcher
# switch-hitter
=prospect status (see explanation)

AFTER A PLAYER'S NAME:
level at which he spent most of 1999 season: age as of July 1, 2000; year he was drafted; round drafted (ND= non-drafted amateur free agent); drafted out of high school (H) or college (C)

EXPLANATION OF PROSPECT RATINGS

★ Potential big-league star

↑ Projected regular player in majors (for pitchers: rotation starter or closer)

○ Projected platoon or utility player in majors (pitcher: setup or middle relief)

? Possible big-league reserve or long reliever

↓ High draft pick or "tools" player who hasn't performed to expectations

SAN FRANCISCO

2000 PROJECTIONS

AMERICAN LEAGUE

Anaheim Angels

BATTERS

PLAYER	BA	G	AB	R	H	2B	3B	HR	RBI	BB	SO	SB	CS	Sa	OBA
Abbott, Chuck	.241	16	58	9	14	2	0	1	6	6	22	1	0	.328	.241
Anderson, Garret	.301	144	571	73	172	34	3	16	75	30	73	5	3	.455	.334
Barnes, Larry	.244	33	127	16	31	5	2	4	22	11	30	2	0	.409	.244
Christian, Eddie	.257	20	74	11	19	3	0	2	9	7	16	3	0	.378	.257
Colangelo, Michael	.289	42	166	23	48	11	3	1	14	18	37	3	0	.410	.289
DaVanon, Jeff	.254	46	173	32	44	9	4	5	21	19	40	7	0	.439	.254
Decker, Steve	.250	21	48	6	12	2	0	0	5	8	8	0	0	.292	.351
Decker, Steve	.200	31	110	17	22	6	1	5	17	15	22	0	0	.409	.200
DiSarcina, Gary	.276	70	243	31	67	13	1	1	26	11	25	4	3	.350	.314
Durrington, Trent	.258	38	132	24	34	7	0	1	9	15	29	11	0	.333	.258
Edmonds, Jim	.281	58	221	39	62	16	1	8	31	25	42	3	3	.471	.355
Erstad, Darin	.275	119	484	75	133	25	4	13	56	40	80	14	6	.424	.331
Foster, Jim	.250	22	76	7	19	5	0	1	10	6	13	1	0	.355	.250
Glaus, Troy	.240	150	533	81	128	29	0	25	77	67	144	5	1	.435	.240
Greene, Todd	.258	102	329	38	85	21	0	15	45	13	70	1	4	.459	.291
Guiel, Jeff	.229	34	105	18	24	5	2	3	12	17	24	1	0	.400	.229
Hemphill, Bret	.248	38	117	12	29	6	0	3	12	13	33	1	0	.376	.248
Herrick, Jason	.241	27	87	10	21	7	1	2	9	6	32	1	0	.414	.241
Huson, Jeff	.267	87	187	20	50	6	1	0	16	14	24	8	1	.310	.315
Hutchins, Norm	.266	23	94	15	25	5	1	1	10	8	27	3	0	.372	.266
Kieschnick, Brooks	.235	41	153	20	36	8	1	8	26	8	37	0	0	.458	.235
Luuloa, Keith	.264	35	121	15	32	6	0	1	13	12	19	2	0	.339	.264
Molina, Ben	.263	50	175	17	46	10	0	4	25	10	14	1	0	.389	.263
Murphy, Nate	.220	36	123	13	27	5	2	4	16	15	35	1	0	.390	.220
Palmeiro, Orlando	.287	117	307	47	88	12	2	1	26	39	28	6	5	.349	.374
Perez, Tomas	.254	19	67	7	17	4	0	1	9	4	12	1	0	.358	.254
Pritchett, Chris	.252	33	107	16	27	4	0	3	12	11	26	1	0	.374	.252
Salmon, Tim	.274	100	354	59	97	21	1	18	68	62	79	3	2	.492	.380
Sheets, Andy	.234	83	218	28	51	9	1	5	30	17	65	3	2	.353	.285
Silvestri, Dave	.269	21	78	11	21	4	0	1	9	4	12	1	0	.359	.269
Simonton, Benji	.255	17	51	4	13	3	0	0	6	8	19	1	0	.314	.255
Tolentino, Juan	.259	23	81	10	21	3	1	2	10	8	23	5	0	.395	.259
Vaughn, Mo	.293	122	468	65	137	20	0	29	89	50	112	0	0	.521	.369
Walbeck, Matt	.261	99	280	31	73	10	1	4	29	27	51	2	3	.346	.328
Wooten, Shawn	.248	27	101	11	25	4	0	3	14	8	24	1	0	.376	.248

PITCHERS

PLAYER	W	L	SV	ERA	G	GS	IP	H	HR	BB	SO
Alvarez, Juan	4	3	1	3.92	59	0	62	61	7	22	43
Beaumont, Matt	2	3	0	4.50	13	5	44	39	5	24	26
Belcher, Tim	6	6	0	5.35	19	19	106	122	19	35	51
Brow, Scott	1	1	1	4.50	19	0	24	24	2	9	12
Cooper, Brian	4	4	0	4.26	11	3	74	74	1	21	54
Edsell, Geoff	2	2	0	4.07	28	1	42	44	3	18	27
Etherton, Seth	4	4	0	4.14	11	2	74	76	3	21	56
Finley, Chuck	10	9	0	4.25	28	28	180	170	19	83	170

PLAYER	W	L	SV	ERA	G	GS	IP	H	HR	BB	SO
Hasegawa, Shigetoshi	4	4	2	4.25	59	1	72	72	11	29	47
Hawblitzel, Ryan	2	2	0	4.37	13	4	35	40	4	12	17
Hill, Ken	6	9	0	4.79	25	21	124	130	12	67	71
Holtz, Mike	3	4	0	5.57	53	0	42	46	4	22	36
Levine, Alan	1	1	0	4.06	48	1	82	83	12	29	35
Lomon, Kevin	2	2	0	4.26	7	5	38	46	6	9	23
Magnante, Mike	5	4	0	3.78	52	0	69	69	2	29	47
McDowell, Jack	2	4	0	5.67	10	10	46	60	8	13	30
Montoya, Norm	1	2	0	4.66	16	1	29	37	2	7	11
Morse, Paul	3	3	0	4.76	9	8	51	52	7	31	24
Ortiz, Ramon	5	5	0	4.02	15	15	94	85	12	39	75
Percival, Troy	4	6	32	3.90	63	0	60	42	8	27	70
Petkovsek, Mark	7	4	1	4.33	61	0	79	90	7	24	41
Pote, Lou	4	3	0	4.06	15	8	62	67	7	18	40
Salter, Cody	2	4	0	5.24	29	3	55	77	2	17	14
Schoeneweis, Scott	1	1	0	5.54	42	0	52	63	5	19	30
Shields, Scot	4	4	0	3.86	9	9	70	62	11	28	64
Sparks, Steve	6	8	0	5.08	25	23	131	141	18	68	69
Troutman, Keith	3	3	1	4.24	28	2	51	59	3	14	38
Washburn, Jarrod	4	5	0	4.34	18	14	83	73	9	28	50
Williams, Shad	2	3	0	4.81	13	6	43	49	5	13	18
Wise, Matthew	3	3	0	4.34	9	9	58	65	6	15	36

Baltimore Orioles

BATTERS

PLAYER	BA	G	AB	R	H	2B	3B	HR	RBI	BB	SO	SB	CS	Sa	OBA
Almonte, Wady	.265	38	147	19	39	7	1	5	23	9	27	2	0	.429	.265
Amaral, Rich	.287	60	101	17	29	5	0	0	8	10	17	7	4	.337	.354
Anderson, Brady	.265	134	502	91	133	27	4	19	65	80	88	26	7	.448	.383
Belle, Albert	.289	153	581	97	168	37	1	36	115	80	78	11	3	.542	.376
Bordick, Mike	.274	148	537	76	147	30	4	10	63	45	84	9	4	.400	.333
Casimiro, Carlos	.227	23	88	12	20	4	0	3	11	7	20	1	0	.375	.227
Clark, Howie	.255	47	161	17	41	9	1	3	14	15	17	1	0	.379	.255
Clark, Will	.300	68	237	38	71	16	0	9	34	32	39	1	1	.481	.383
Coffie, Ivanon	.212	15	52	6	11	3	1	1	7	6	15	1	0	.365	.212
Conine, Jeff	.277	129	404	47	112	27	1	12	65	33	56	1	2	.438	.332
Davis, Tommy	.258	33	120	14	31	5	0	3	16	7	23	0	0	.375	.258
DeShields, Delino	.281	91	324	51	91	13	5	6	34	38	48	18	8	.407	.356
Decinces, Tim	.218	43	133	16	29	7	0	5	16	19	33	0	0	.383	.218
Dent, Darrell	.250	25	60	12	15	2	1	1	6	10	17	4	0	.367	.250
Devarez, Cesar	.259	17	58	7	15	3	0	1	8	4	8	1	0	.362	.259
Garcia, Jesse	.263	37	118	15	31	5	1	2	12	6	14	3	0	.373	.263
Hairston, Jerry	.270	76	278	42	75	16	3	5	29	18	42	10	0	.403	.270
Isom, Johnny	.277	33	112	17	31	8	0	2	11	10	29	1	0	.402	.277
Johnson, Charles	.247	130	425	52	105	20	1	17	57	53	114	0	1	.419	.333
Kingsale, Eugene	.280	44	157	26	44	7	1	2	15	16	29	5	0	.376	.280
Matos, Luis	.260	23	100	16	26	4	0	3	14	6	16	4	0	.390	.260
May, Derrick	.271	54	155	17	42	8	1	4	21	11	21	1	0	.413	.271
Minor, Ryan	.224	63	210	27	47	12	0	9	29	17	80	1	0	.410	.224
Ojeda, Augie	.240	30	104	15	25	4	1	2	13	12	13	1	0	.356	.240
Otero, Ricky	.252	33	123	11	31	7	3	3	14	11	17	2	0	.431	.252
Paz, Richard	.254	37	126	16	32	5	1	1	8	21	19	4	0	.333	.254
Pickering, Calvin	.248	69	222	34	55	10	0	9	34	35	73	1	0	.414	.248
Reboulet, Jeff	.212	70	118	19	25	4	0	1	7	23	26	1	0	.271	.350
Ripken, Cal	.297	78	296	39	88	18	0	11	41	20	31	0	1	.470	.344

2000 PROJECTIONS

PLAYER	BA	G	AB	R	H	2B	3B	HR	RBI	BB	SO	SB	CS	Sa	OBA
Short, Rick	.254	39	138	17	35	5	0	4	17	12	20	2	0	.377	.254
Surhoff, B.J.	.295	151	589	88	174	33	1	23	94	43	71	5	3	.472	.341
Vinas, Julio	.264	57	220	26	58	12	1	8	32	10	40	1	0	.436	.264

PITCHERS

PLAYER	W	L	SV	ERA	G	GS	IP	H	HR	BB	SO
Bell, Mike	2	2	0	4.63	11	3	35	36	4	13	18
Bones, Ricky	1	3	0	5.19	36	2	52	64	7	22	31
Burrows, Terry	2	2	0	4.22	6	6	32	26	3	14	22
Corsi, Jim	2	3	0	3.78	49	0	50	51	6	22	33
Delahoya, Javier	2	2	0	4.24	6	5	34	33	6	10	23
Dykhoff, Radhames	3	3	0	4.09	32	0	55	47	7	21	32
Eibey, Scott	3	4	0	4.35	33	4	62	76	3	39	29
Erickson, Scott	12	9	0	4.52	27	27	185	201	19	68	104
Evans, Dave	1	1	0	4.15	11	0	13	11	2	4	10
Falkenborg, Brian	4	4	0	3.96	16	15	75	71	10	34	57
Fetters, Mike	1	3	0	4.79	41	0	47	50	5	26	36
Hamilton, Jimmy	3	3	0	4.04	46	0	49	35	3	43	39
Heredia, Maximo	3	3	0	4.18	37	0	56	59	9	24	34
Johns, Doug	4	4	0	4.79	29	4	77	82	9	26	39
Johnson, Jason	7	7	0	5.22	21	20	112	118	16	51	69
Kamieniecki, Scott	2	4	2	4.98	43	3	56	57	5	26	35
Kohlmeier, Ryan	4	3	6	3.65	61	2	69	52	12	34	72
Maduro, Calvin	3	3	0	4.27	10	10	59	65	8	22	43
McCommon, Jason	2	2	0	4.75	8	5	36	41	6	14	16
McDougal, Mike	3	3	2	4.14	39	0	50	57	8	25	32
Medina, Carlos	3	3	0	4.30	9	9	46	45	3	19	34
Molina, Gabe	4	4	4	3.82	59	0	73	59	6	34	55
Mussina, Mike	15	8	0	3.68	30	30	198	198	18	49	172
Orosco, Jesse	2	2	1	4.11	94	0	46	38	6	27	46
Parrish, John	3	4	0	4.35	14	11	62	57	5	50	39
Ponson, Sidney	11	11	0	4.84	28	28	186	204	30	68	103
Reyes, Alberto	4	3	0	4.43	52	0	65	54	9	38	66
Rhodes, Arthur	4	3	3	4.42	45	0	55	46	7	33	61
Riley, Matthew	5	5	0	4.04	15	15	89	90	12	38	75
Ryan, B.J.	2	0	0	3.35	30	0	43	28	0	28	61
Snyder, Matt	3	3	0	4.13	27	2	48	49	7	15	28
Timlin, Mike	3	6	26	3.52	63	0	64	59	7	20	48
Towers, Joshua	4	5	0	4.74	11	11	74	89	11	11	35

Boston Red Sox

BATTERS

PLAYER	BA	G	AB	R	H	2B	3B	HR	RBI	BB	SO	SB	CS	Sa	OBA
Abad, Andy	.257	47	175	24	45	8	2	6	26	20	28	2	0	.429	.257
Alcantara, Israel	.218	52	193	24	42	11	0	11	32	14	66	1	0	.446	.218
Buford, Damon	.258	96	291	42	75	16	2	8	42	24	71	10	4	.409	.316
Chamblee, James	.233	48	176	27	41	7	1	8	28	14	57	1	0	.420	.233
Chevalier, Virgil	.250	33	128	18	32	6	1	3	16	11	22	2	0	.383	.250
Coleman, Michael	.232	47	190	33	44	10	1	11	26	18	63	4	0	.468	.232
Daubach, Brian	.284	119	402	61	114	34	3	21	75	37	95	0	1	.540	.350
Depastino, Joe	.222	40	135	17	30	6	0	6	24	13	25	1	0	.400	.222
Eckstein, David	.262	40	149	28	39	6	1	2	13	23	18	7	0	.356	.262
Epperson, Chad	.218	16	55	8	12	3	0	1	5	10	16	0	0	.327	.218
Everett, Adam	.246	35	122	19	30	4	0	3	15	14	28	5	0	.352	.246
Fonville, Chad	.295	13	44	6	13	1	0	0	3	4	6	1	0	.318	.295
Frye, Jeff	.301	35	113	16	34	7	0	1	13	11	13	4	2	.389	.365

THE INSIDER 2000

PLAYER	BA	G	AB	R	H	2B	3B	HR	RBI	BB	SO	SB	CS	Sa	OBA
Garciaparra, Nomar	.323	150	617	111	199	42	6	30	111	45	54	15	5	.556	.373
Gibralter, David	.256	45	164	24	42	7	0	8	30	10	30	1	0	.445	.256
Gonzalez, Raul	.270	44	174	22	47	9	1	5	29	14	29	3	0	.420	.270
Hatteberg, Scott	.278	38	115	15	32	7	0	3	14	16	20	0	0	.417	.368
Hillenbrand, Shea	.250	23	92	13	23	5	0	2	12	5	11	1	0	.370	.250
Huskey, Butch	.277	123	401	58	111	18	0	20	74	31	69	5	3	.471	.326
Ingram, Garey	.235	24	85	14	20	4	1	2	11	5	18	2	0	.376	.235
Jackson, Gavin	.214	10	28	5	6	1	0	0	2	7	7	1	0	.250	.214
Jefferson, Reggie	.294	71	204	25	60	14	1	6	23	16	47	0	0	.461	.350
Lewis, Darren	.264	115	386	58	102	14	4	3	38	42	54	17	9	.345	.342
Merloni, Lou	.261	67	203	31	53	12	0	4	27	19	40	1	0	.379	.261
Mitchell, Keith	.240	38	125	18	30	8	1	3	14	21	24	2	0	.392	.240
Nixon, Trot	.267	135	409	71	109	23	5	15	53	55	79	3	1	.457	.352
Nunnally, Jon	.234	50	158	26	37	7	1	6	21	25	41	5	0	.405	.234
O'Leary, Troy	.278	145	547	78	152	33	5	23	87	44	86	1	2	.483	.333
Offerman, Jose	.296	144	564	96	167	32	11	7	62	84	80	24	11	.429	.387
Sadler, Donnie	.277	80	173	31	48	8	3	2	12	9	37	4	1	.393	.319
Stanley, Mike	.268	126	399	57	107	21	0	19	65	64	90	1	0	.464	.376
Stenson, Dernell	.246	53	191	25	47	11	1	7	33	22	62	1	0	.424	.246
Tebbs, Nate	.267	22	75	10	20	3	0	1	7	6	16	3	0	.347	.267
Valentin, John	.263	104	410	64	108	28	1	13	59	43	59	2	2	.432	.336
Varitek, Jason	.268	154	489	71	131	38	2	19	76	45	89	2	2	.470	.327
Veras, Wilton	.270	55	215	27	58	10	1	5	31	10	30	2	0	.395	.270

PITCHERS

PLAYER	W	L	SV	ERA	G	GS	IP	H	HR	BB	SO
Adams, Willie	2	2	0	4.89	7	6	35	44	4	5	17
Beale, Chuck	2	2	0	4.50	16	1	32	33	3	17	19
Beck, Rod	3	4	12	4.50	51	0	52	57	6	16	40
Betancourt, Rafael	3	3	3	3.76	40	0	55	52	7	10	48
Bullinger, Kirk	3	3	4	3.98	53	0	52	59	5	20	31
Cho, Jin	4	5	0	4.45	15	14	85	87	12	20	47
Cormier, Rheal	2	2	0	4.14	60	0	63	65	5	18	39
Crawford, Pack	4	4	0	4.57	12	12	69	67	5	26	39
Cumberland, Chris	3	3	0	4.12	36	1	59	53	3	34	31
Farrell, Jim	3	3	0	4.22	15	7	49	52	6	18	36
Fernandez, Jared	2	3	0	4.94	10	6	51	58	7	14	20
Florie, Bryce	4	3	0	4.74	38	5	76	84	8	34	58
Garces, Rich	5	2	3	2.48	43	0	58	42	4	30	46
Gordon, Tom	2	2	23	4.00	45	0	36	30	2	16	36
Gross, Kip	0	2	0	4.66	25	2	29	32	4	14	20
Harikkala, Tim	2	3	0	6.10	17	0	31	33	1	13	15
Hazlett, Andy	3	3	0	4.50	9	9	56	55	5	14	35
Kim, Sun	3	3	0	4.26	10	10	57	58	6	16	41
Lowe, Derek	4	5	14	3.63	71	0	104	95	7	30	73
Martinez, Pedro	21	6	0	2.56	35	33	239	190	16	56	316
Martinez, Ramon	4	2	0	3.29	10	10	52	42	5	23	45
Mercker, Kent	8	7	0	4.79	29	22	126	145	13	55	70
Mix, Greg	3	3	0	3.94	26	2	48	52	5	23	37
Ohka, Tomokazu	2	5	0	6.10	19	5	31	50	5	14	19
Pena, Juan	3	2	0	2.71	6	6	38	28	0	9	44
Portugal, Mark	7	8	0	5.02	27	23	129	150	22	32	72
Rapp, Pat	7	8	0	4.66	37	26	145	154	15	75	94
Rose, Brian	7	8	0	5.13	26	21	114	129	23	35	59
Saberhagen, Bret	10	6	0	3.71	24	24	131	139	14	18	83
Sekany, Jason	3	4	0	4.50	11	9	64	66	4	30	38
Smetana, Steve	2	2	0	4.30	20	2	44	48	4	14	26
Tweedlie, Brad	2	2	0	4.36	26	0	33	38	2	14	15

2000 PROJECTIONS

PLAYER	W	L	SV	ERA	G	GS	IP	H	HR	BB	SO
Wakefield, Tim	6	6	10	4.78	34	12	98	98	13	44	70
Wasdin, John	6	3	2	4.56	44	0	73	73	12	20	51
Wolcott, Bob	3	4	0	4.35	14	8	62	63	9	16	29

Chicago White Sox

BATTERS

PLAYER	BA	G	AB	R	H	2B	3B	HR	RBI	BB	SO	SB	CS	Sa	OBA
Abbott, Jeff	.261	53	180	23	47	11	1	7	24	9	25	1	0	.450	.261
Beamon, Trey	.267	21	60	9	16	4	0	1	5	7	14	2	0	.383	.267
Beltre, Esteban	.255	15	51	8	13	3	0	0	5	3	11	1	0	.314	.255
Bravo, Danny	.259	32	108	17	28	5	0	1	14	15	20	2	0	.333	.259
Brito, Tilson	.253	42	154	18	39	9	2	3	18	10	30	2	0	.396	.253
Caruso, Mike	.288	125	486	66	140	13	5	3	41	18	36	15	11	.354	.318
Christensen, McKay	.278	43	144	26	40	4	2	2	14	14	26	6	0	.375	.278
Christopherson, Eric	.250	38	112	17	28	8	0	1	13	14	28	2	0	.348	.250
Crede, Joe	.257	26	101	13	26	5	0	1	15	8	20	1	0	.337	.257
Dellaero, Jason	.238	38	126	16	30	5	1	4	18	6	44	2	0	.389	.238
Durham, Ray	.289	140	564	103	163	28	7	13	55	65	94	31	10	.433	.365
Eddie, Steve	.255	14	47	6	12	2	0	1	4	4	10	0	0	.362	.255
Fordyce, Brook	.288	117	347	34	100	25	1	9	47	23	54	2	0	.444	.334
Gomez, Ramon	.284	37	102	18	29	4	2	0	10	12	36	7	0	.363	.284
Inglin, Jeff	.252	44	159	21	40	8	1	5	21	18	29	5	0	.409	.252
Jackson, Darrin	.276	51	105	14	29	6	1	3	13	3	17	2	1	.438	.294
Johnson, Mark	.229	86	245	33	56	13	1	5	19	43	73	4	3	.351	.346
Konerko, Paul	.279	150	517	67	144	27	3	23	79	44	73	1	0	.476	.336
Lee, Carlos	.294	128	497	67	146	32	2	16	85	13	73	4	2	.463	.313
Liefer, Jeff	.253	60	150	11	38	10	1	0	19	11	38	3	0	.333	.302
Magdaleno, Ricky	.266	22	79	9	21	4	0	0	7	7	18	0	0	.316	.266
Moore, Brandon	.246	18	61	8	15	3	1	0	8	5	11	1	0	.328	.246
Mottola, Chad	.259	44	162	25	42	8	1	5	24	16	32	4	0	.414	.259
Newstrom, Doug	.262	27	84	9	22	3	0	1	7	9	17	1	0	.333	.262
Norton, Greg	.253	141	442	62	112	26	1	15	51	62	100	4	4	.419	.346
Ordonez, Magglio	.293	155	600	90	176	31	3	25	100	40	61	12	7	.480	.339
Paul, Josh	.254	36	122	17	31	7	1	1	15	10	31	2	0	.352	.254
Rodriguez, Liu	.266	54	177	25	47	7	2	2	25	17	29	2	0	.362	.266
Simmons, Brian	.249	59	185	29	46	7	1	7	28	19	48	4	0	.411	.249
Simons, Mitch	.253	20	79	13	20	5	0	1	8	7	13	2	0	.354	.253
Singleton, Chris	.299	132	491	71	147	31	6	17	71	22	44	20	5	.491	.327
Thomas, Frank	.287	126	457	75	131	30	0	18	79	82	63	3	2	.470	.397
Toth, Dave	.233	13	43	6	10	2	0	1	5	4	8	0	0	.349	.233
Valdez, Mario	.227	52	172	27	39	6	1	9	27	27	47	1	0	.430	.227
Wilson, Craig	.267	92	243	32	65	10	1	5	28	23	23	1	1	.379	.330

PITCHERS

PLAYER	W	L	SV	ERA	G	GS	IP	H	HR	BB	SO
Andujar, Luis	3	3	3	3.86	48	0	56	65	3	13	42
Baldwin, James	11	10	0	5.09	30	28	168	181	24	67	108
Beirne, Kevin	3	3	0	4.50	10	10	54	59	6	16	25
Bradford, Chad	4	4	1	4.08	55	0	75	81	2	22	39
Castillo, Carlos	4	4	0	4.27	26	7	78	73	14	20	45
Chantres, Carlos	4	4	0	4.36	13	9	66	64	7	32	41
Daneker, Pat	4	4	0	4.56	12	11	73	80	7	23	39
Davenport, Joe	3	4	2	4.58	48	0	59	62	3	24	25
Eyre, Scott	3	3	0	4.09	18	8	55	56	8	25	35
Fogg, Joshua	2	2	0	4.63	6	6	35	37	5	10	21
Fordham, Tom	2	2	0	4.50	14	6	38	36	6	20	25

PLAYER	W	L	SV	ERA	G	GS	IP	H	HR	BB	SO
Foulke, Keith	3	4	9	3.32	66	0	103	82	12	25	110
Hasselhoff, Derek	3	3	1	4.02	32	0	47	50	4	15	36
Heathcott, Mike	2	2	0	4.65	7	5	31	37	3	14	15
Howry, Bob	4	3	28	3.73	71	0	70	58	8	36	78
Iglesias, Mario	2	2	0	4.34	14	2	29	26	5	12	18
Lowe, Sean	3	3	0	4.30	60	0	90	91	10	45	57
Lundquist, David	2	2	0	7.24	32	0	41	48	6	21	34
Myette, Aaron	4	5	0	4.33	14	13	79	71	10	42	53
Navarro, Jaime	6	10	0	5.63	26	22	131	161	22	54	63
Olsen, Jason	3	3	0	4.21	15	7	47	49	6	16	31
Parque, Jim	9	12	0	5.08	28	27	156	188	20	70	102
Pena, Jesus	0	0	0	5.14	54	0	42	43	6	47	41
Rizzo, Todd	2	2	1	4.17	34	0	41	41	2	19	22
Roberts, Mark	3	4	0	4.43	17	9	63	63	6	24	36
Schmack, Brian	3	3	1	3.96	34	1	50	51	3	15	37
Secoda, Jason	3	3	0	4.34	10	8	56	57	6	18	37
Simas, Bill	5	3	2	4.00	70	0	72	71	8	31	48
Sirotka, Mike	11	13	0	4.43	30	30	195	228	24	50	118
Snyder, John	9	8	0	5.79	22	22	112	135	22	38	61
Sturtze, Tanyon	2	2	0	4.07	13	6	42	33	3	16	36
VanRyn, Ben	2	2	1	4.20	26	3	30	31	3	13	19
Ward, Bryan	0	2	0	5.94	51	0	50	70	11	13	41
Wells, Kip	9	2	0	4.11	16	16	81	76	5	34	65
Whitley, Curtis	2	2	0	4.89	25	0	35	40	3	17	14

Cleveland Indians

BATTERS

PLAYER	BA	G	AB	R	H	2B	3B	HR	RBI	BB	SO	SB	CS	Sa	OBA
Alomar, Roberto	.301	159	584	116	176	38	2	20	96	82	84	29	5	.476	.386
Alomar, Sandy	.279	43	154	20	43	12	0	5	23	6	20	0	1	.455	.309
Bady, Edward	.254	21	71	13	18	4	1	1	10	10	25	4	0	.380	.254
Baerga, Carlos	.273	47	165	18	45	8	0	3	17	9	21	1	0	.376	.273
Baines, Harold	.301	124	386	52	116	18	1	18	81	46	45	1	1	.492	.373
Betances, Junior	.267	31	105	13	28	4	2	1	9	10	22	2	0	.371	.267
Betts, Todd	.222	42	153	19	34	8	0	6	22	20	32	1	0	.392	.222
Branyan, Russell	.196	53	189	22	37	5	0	13	30	22	108	2	0	.429	.196
Budzinski, Mark	.250	41	132	22	33	7	2	2	17	19	36	3	0	.379	.250
Cabrera, Jolbert	.271	45	140	24	38	7	2	0	13	13	27	7	0	.350	.271
Cordero, Wil	.285	70	260	43	74	16	1	10	38	17	52	2	1	.469	.335
Cruz, Jake	.272	71	232	32	63	9	2	8	36	20	52	2	0	.431	.272
Diaz, Einar	.287	120	390	46	112	21	1	4	36	24	41	11	4	.377	.336
Fryman, Travis	.271	83	317	45	86	17	2	13	52	25	63	5	2	.461	.326
Hayes, Heath	.240	27	96	10	23	3	0	3	14	8	30	1	0	.365	.240
Houston, Tyler	.248	116	294	31	73	11	1	10	36	27	77	2	1	.395	.311
Justice, David	.281	126	430	72	121	23	1	20	80	77	80	3	3	.479	.387
Lofton, Kenny	.295	115	448	91	132	24	5	7	41	69	72	29	8	.417	.390
McDonald, John	.289	35	121	15	35	6	0	0	12	7	16	2	0	.339	.289
McKinley, Daniel	.284	21	88	15	25	4	1	1	8	5	20	1	0	.386	.284
Miller, David	.270	36	115	15	31	8	1	1	15	13	24	3	0	.383	.270
Miller, Orlando	.250	33	112	12	28	8	0	3	15	6	30	2	0	.402	.250
Morgan, Scott	.229	47	179	30	41	10	1	10	29	16	56	2	0	.464	.229
Ortiz, Nicky	.250	27	84	10	21	6	1	1	5	7	20	0	0	.381	.250
Peoples, Danny	.238	34	130	19	31	6	1	5	20	14	45	1	0	.415	.238
Perry, Chan	.255	40	149	22	38	10	0	5	28	10	25	2	0	.423	.255
PLAYER	BA	G	AB	R	H	2B	3B	HR	RBI	BB	SO	SB	CS	Sa	OBA
Ramirez, Alex	.279	81	265	37	74	16	2	9	41	12	63	3	0	.457	.279

2000 PROJECTIONS

PLAYER	BA	G	AB	R	H	2B	3B	HR	RBI	BB	SO	SB	CS	Sa	OBA
Ramirez, Manny	.303	162	591	123	179	36	2	43	153	90	130	3	4	.589	.399
Roberts, David	.276	52	196	38	54	9	4	1	21	22	32	14	0	.378	.276
Robinson, Adam	.248	34	121	17	30	5	2	2	14	9	30	1	0	.372	.248
Scutaro, Marcos	.255	44	157	24	40	8	1	3	16	19	28	5	0	.376	.255
Selby, Bill	.237	51	186	25	44	11	2	7	28	19	32	1	0	.430	.237
Sexson, Richie	.262	132	469	71	123	20	6	30	109	30	114	3	3	.522	.308
Thome, Jim	.270	151	519	101	140	30	2	34	104	119	164	0	0	.532	.406
Turner, Chris	.240	41	125	17	30	4	0	4	15	16	33	1	0	.368	.240
Vizquel, Omar	.310	142	554	98	172	31	5	4	57	61	53	39	10	.406	.377
Wilson, Enrique	.281	122	356	47	100	24	1	3	29	26	44	6	6	.379	.326

PITCHERS

PLAYER	W	L	SV	ERA	G	GS	IP	H	HR	BB	SO
Assenmacher, Paul	3	2	0	5.40	75	0	45	56	6	19	42
Atkins, Ross	1	2	0	4.82	11	2	28	26	3	14	12
Bacsik, Mike	3	4	0	4.80	10	10	60	67	10	19	28
Brammer, John	2	2	1	4.09	28	0	44	29	3	32	34
Brower, Jim	3	4	0	4.57	12	10	61	62	10	22	26
Brown, Jamie	3	4	0	4.57	10	10	61	63	5	17	36
Burba, Dave	13	9	0	4.38	30	30	191	191	27	80	144
Candiotti, Tom	5	7	0	5.34	22	16	86	95	14	30	47
Colon, Bartolo	15	7	0	4.14	31	31	198	192	21	77	153
DePaula, Sean	0	0	0	4.50	28	0	30	20	0	8	45
Deschenes, Marc	3	3	1	3.81	34	0	52	49	4	27	43
Driskill, Travis	2	2	0	4.62	9	5	37	40	6	9	21
Gooden, Dwight	5	4	0	5.19	23	20	104	110	14	52	73
Haney, Chris	2	3	0	4.70	14	6	44	45	5	15	21
Jackson, Mike	2	3	36	3.55	70	0	66	55	8	23	56
Karsay, Steve	7	4	1	4.11	51	3	81	84	8	30	63
Langston, Mark	2	3	0	5.28	23	5	58	68	8	28	39
Martinez, William	4	4	0	4.56	12	12	73	84	10	23	37
Matthews, Mike	1	1	0	4.74	11	3	19	18	3	11	9
Nagy, Charles	13	9	0	4.90	28	27	169	198	23	52	104
Poole, Jim	2	2	1	5.12	76	0	51	68	5	22	31
Rakers, Jason	3	3	0	4.41	9	7	49	52	6	12	26
Reed, Steve	3	3	0	3.98	63	0	61	58	9	21	48
Rigdon, Paul	4	4	0	4.63	13	12	72	74	7	21	33
Rincon, Ricardo	2	4	0	4.00	73	0	54	48	6	27	47
Riske, David	5	4	5	3.60	77	0	85	59	5	39	79
Sanders, Frankie	3	3	0	4.75	14	6	53	60	6	23	26
Shuey, Paul	8	5	6	3.87	71	0	79	71	8	41	97
Telgheder, Dave	1	1	0	4.74	6	2	19	21	2	4	8
Watson, Mark	2	3	0	4.98	8	7	47	65	4	17	20
Wright, Jaret	8	7	0	5.24	24	24	122	127	15	61	85

Detroit Tigers

BATTERS

PLAYER	BA	G	AB	R	H	2B	3B	HR	RBI	BB	SO	SB	CS	Sa	OBA
Alvarez, Gabe	.239	66	230	29	55	12	0	9	32	25	64	1	0	.409	.239
Ausmus, Brad	.274	128	441	60	121	21	5	8	51	50	70	12	7	.399	.359
Bartee, Kimera	.263	61	179	29	47	6	4	5	19	16	48	7	0	.425	.263
Cardona, Javier	.234	51	197	30	46	11	0	9	33	16	39	1	0	.426	.234
Catalanotto, Frank	.279	118	319	43	89	21	1	11	39	17	56	4	4	.455	.328
Clark, Tony	.276	135	508	72	140	28	0	28	91	60	118	2	2	.496	.355
Cradle, Rickey	.241	47	145	24	35	11	1	4	22	18	43	4	0	.414	.241
Cruz, Deivi	.284	157	517	63	147	33	1	10	57	14	62	2	5	.410	.305

► THE INSIDER 2000

PLAYER	BA	G	AB	R	H	2B	3B	HR	RBI	BB	SO	SB	CS	Sa	OBA
Easley, Damion	.266	134	496	76	132	29	1	20	67	44	104	13	4	.450	.343
Encarnacion, Juan	.269	126	487	64	131	29	7	19	71	15	109	31	12	.474	.300
Freire, Alejandro	.252	42	155	25	39	11	0	5	24	13	34	1	0	.419	.252
Garcia, Karim	.241	109	323	43	78	11	5	14	40	22	80	3	4	.437	.288
Garcia, Luis	.281	37	121	12	34	8	0	1	14	2	20	1	0	.372	.281
Gillespie, Eric	.258	45	182	26	47	9	2	6	28	17	41	4	0	.429	.258
Haselman, Bill	.278	49	144	14	40	9	0	5	17	9	27	1	0	.444	.318
Higginson, Bobby	.264	102	375	55	99	20	1	14	52	52	63	4	4	.435	.356
Jefferies, Gregg	.267	42	146	19	39	7	1	3	15	10	9	3	2	.390	.314
Jones, Ryan	.246	29	114	15	28	5	1	4	16	11	32	0	0	.412	.246
Kapler, Gabe	.248	133	427	62	106	22	5	18	50	43	77	12	5	.450	.317
Lemonis, Chris	.260	29	104	13	27	6	0	2	14	7	21	0	0	.375	.260
Lindstrom, David	.231	40	130	16	30	9	1	4	18	13	26	1	0	.408	.231
Macias, Jose	.258	35	132	15	34	6	3	1	12	11	22	2	0	.371	.258
Maxwell, Jason	.224	40	134	19	30	5	1	5	19	16	34	1	0	.388	.224
McCarty, Dave	.229	52	179	27	41	7	1	10	25	23	51	2	0	.447	.229
McKeel, Walt	.234	39	124	12	29	5	1	4	21	14	22	1	0	.387	.234
Mitchell, Derek	.239	27	92	12	22	4	0	2	11	12	30	1	0	.348	.239
Palmer, Dean	.262	140	526	80	138	24	2	32	96	48	134	4	2	.498	.329
Polonia, Luis	.303	93	314	44	95	17	6	7	27	18	33	15	8	.462	.342
Santana, Pedro	.258	30	128	21	33	8	1	1	11	8	29	6	0	.359	.258
Siddall, Joe	.204	20	54	6	11	3	0	2	7	8	21	1	0	.370	.204
Swann, Pedro	.261	42	134	21	35	6	1	4	15	15	33	1	0	.410	.261
Wakeland, Christopher	.238	55	214	32	51	12	2	10	27	26	64	4	0	.453	.238
Wood, Jason	.241	49	141	23	34	7	0	4	17	14	41	0	0	.376	.241

PITCHERS

PLAYER	W	L	SV	ERA	G	GS	IP	H	HR	BB	SO
Anderson, Matt	4	1	0	4.75	51	0	53	46	8	45	47
Blair, Willie	4	8	0	5.50	32	13	108	123	20	34	62
Blanco, Alberto	3	3	0	4.03	30	3	58	48	8	31	42
Borkowski, Dave	6	6	0	4.46	19	16	107	108	14	44	63
Brocail, Doug	4	4	2	2.96	70	0	82	66	7	28	75
Brunson, Will	2	1	0	5.59	41	0	29	40	6	14	20
Cordero, Francisco	6	5	7	3.62	92	0	97	102	9	75	88
Corey, Bryan	3	4	0	4.50	42	0	60	67	7	35	25
Darwin, David	3	3	0	4.75	8	8	53	64	6	19	24
Drews, Matt	1	1	0	5.32	5	4	22	22	3	12	9
Goldsmith, Gary	1	2	0	5.06	12	3	32	38	4	11	12
Graterol, Beiker	2	3	0	4.71	9	8	42	41	6	19	21
Hiljus, Erik	3	3	1	3.63	30	0	52	37	5	16	52
Jones, Todd	3	4	30	4.23	65	0	66	64	6	36	63
Keagle, Greg	2	2	0	4.63	7	6	35	43	3	15	17
Kida, Masao	1	0	1	6.00	45	0	60	66	6	27	46
Lira, Felipe	2	2	0	4.50	9	4	30	36	6	8	17
Martinez, Romulo	2	3	0	4.50	34	0	46	51	3	15	24
Miles, Chad	1	1	0	4.20	12	0	15	17	2	6	11
Mlicki, Dave	10	10	0	4.58	29	27	175	189	22	64	112
Moehler, Brian	9	12	0	4.69	27	27	167	187	20	49	92
Nitkowski, C. J.	4	5	0	4.56	65	7	79	66	9	43	62
Pettyjohn, Adam	3	3	0	4.58	9	9	57	59	6	16	35
Reed, Brandon	3	3	0	4.42	26	3	53	60	4	16	29
Roberts, Willis	2	3	0	4.50	15	6	44	46	4	24	21
Runyan, Sean	0	2	0	3.67	31	0	27	25	4	13	19
Santos, Victor	4	4	0	4.24	11	11	68	65	7	25	48
Thompson, Justin	8	9	0	4.47	23	23	135	139	17	51	86
Villafuerte, Brandon	4	4	1	3.97	20	7	68	70	7	32	48
Weaver, Jeff	8	11	0	5.42	27	26	146	155	24	49	102

2000 PROJECTIONS

PLAYER	W	L	SV	ERA	G	GS	IP	H	HR	BB	SO
Webb, Alan	3	4	0	4.71	12	10	65	63	8	29	34

Kansas City Royals

BATTERS

PLAYER	BA	G	AB	R	H	2B	3B	HR	RBI	BB	SO	SB	CS	Sa	OBA
Amado, Jose	.242	34	132	17	32	7	0	3	23	13	13	1	0	.364	.242
Beltran, Carlos	.292	143	607	104	177	26	7	19	98	42	113	25	7	.451	.337
Brown, Dermal	.257	65	210	39	54	9	2	8	36	24	47	6	0	.433	.257
Byington, Jimmie	.240	10	25	4	6	1	0	0	3	3	6	0	0	.280	.240
Carr, Jeremy	.264	23	87	15	23	4	0	1	8	13	22	4	0	.345	.264
Damon, Johnny	.291	145	567	94	165	31	9	14	67	59	60	29	8	.451	.359
Dodson, Jeremy	.241	39	133	17	32	5	0	6	16	14	34	2	0	.414	.241
Dye, Jermaine	.280	158	597	87	167	38	6	24	103	52	117	3	3	.484	.335
Escamilla, Roman	.262	13	42	5	11	3	0	0	6	3	12	1	0	.333	.262
Escandon, Emiliano	.219	37	105	16	23	5	1	2	15	19	17	1	0	.343	.219
Fasano, Sal	.223	70	211	32	47	9	0	11	32	20	65	1	0	.422	.223
Febles, Carlos	.263	127	460	73	121	22	10	10	54	49	94	21	4	.420	.344
Giambi, Jeremy	.281	99	317	37	89	15	1	4	38	46	72	0	0	.372	.372
Gibralter, Steve	.236	39	148	24	35	7	0	9	24	8	41	2	0	.466	.236
Hallmark, Pat	.253	26	83	11	21	2	1	2	7	7	25	4	0	.373	.253
Hansen, Jed	.216	71	171	30	37	5	3	6	16	24	85	4	0	.386	.216
Holbert, Ray	.268	53	123	18	33	4	0	0	7	11	29	8	4	.301	.324
King, Jeff	.250	15	56	9	14	2	0	3	11	7	9	1	0	.446	.338
Kreuter, Chad	.246	97	281	29	69	13	1	4	33	33	61	0	0	.342	.332
Lopez, Mendy	.264	52	163	21	43	6	1	4	20	10	38	2	0	.387	.264
Martinez, Felix	.245	29	94	14	23	6	1	1	9	9	18	4	0	.362	.245
McNally, Sean	.199	46	156	24	31	6	1	9	27	23	56	2	0	.423	.199
Medrano, Tony	.270	41	141	19	38	7	1	2	17	10	17	1	0	.376	.270
Mendez, Carlos	.267	38	131	16	35	11	0	4	16	3	17	1	0	.443	.267
Mercedes, Henry	.220	21	59	8	13	2	0	2	9	8	23	1	0	.356	.220
Moore, Kenderick	.258	10	31	5	8	2	0	0	4	3	9	2	0	.323	.258
Norman, Les	.255	27	102	15	26	6	1	4	11	4	16	2	0	.451	.255
Pellow, Kit	.222	50	180	26	40	8	1	10	29	6	53	2	0	.444	.222
Phillips, Paul	.264	25	91	13	24	5	0	1	13	6	11	1	0	.352	.264
Pose, Scott	.279	83	136	27	38	3	0	0	11	19	21	6	2	.301	.365
Prieto, Alejandro	.250	38	120	16	30	7	1	2	12	10	19	3	0	.375	.250
Quinn, Mark	.274	70	274	33	75	13	0	13	44	14	54	3	0	.464	.274
Randa, Joe	.298	152	574	79	171	31	7	13	73	48	77	6	5	.444	.354
Roberge, J.P.	.271	37	140	21	38	9	1	4	18	7	23	4	0	.436	.271
Sanchez, Rey	.300	134	437	61	131	19	4	2	49	21	52	8	4	.375	.335
Scarsone, Steve	.235	26	51	3	12	3	0	0	5	6	19	1	0	.294	.316
Spehr, Tim	.204	61	152	24	31	7	0	8	23	23	46	1	0	.408	.328
Sutton, Larry	.254	44	114	13	29	6	0	2	17	13	19	1	1	.360	.331
Sweeney, Mike	.298	162	580	91	173	40	1	20	93	52	55	6	2	.474	.363
Tomlinson, Goefrey	.267	31	116	23	31	7	1	1	11	17	24	4	0	.371	.267
Vitiello, Joe	.242	52	186	22	45	10	0	9	31	21	43	1	0	.441	.242

PITCHERS

PLAYER	W	L	SV	ERA	G	GS	IP	H	HR	BB	SO
Barber, Brian	3	3	0	4.35	12	10	60	61	10	15	29
Bluma, Jaime	2	2	1	4.50	27	0	34	34	8	11	19
Brewer, Ryan	1	2	0	4.80	19	0	30	35	4	7	13
Byrdak, Tim	0	4	2	5.40	59	0	45	52	10	30	31
Calero, Kiko	3	3	0	4.50	11	10	56	65	6	26	33
Carter, Lance	6	4	2	3.48	59	0	88	111	6	64	79
Chapman, Jake	3	3	1	4.20	34	0	45	55	2	18	29

▶ THE INSIDER 2000

PLAYER	W	L	SV	ERA	G	GS	IP	H	HR	BB	SO
Durbin, Chad	4	4	0	4.22	12	11	64	59	8	19	42
Fussell, Chris	5	5	0	4.25	21	14	89	80	11	39	63
Gooding, Jason	2	3	0	4.98	8	8	47	61	6	13	18
Krivda, Rick	1	2	0	4.85	8	3	26	30	4	10	13
Lineweaver, Aaron	1	2	0	5.10	6	5	30	32	3	11	12
Mathews, Terry	2	2	1	4.76	32	1	51	58	7	24	27
Montgomery, Jeff	1	4	12	5.47	49	0	51	60	7	19	35
Morman, Alvin	2	4	1	4.50	53	0	58	71	7	27	37
Mullen, Scott	3	3	0	4.50	9	9	54	57	8	21	31
Murray, Daniel	3	3	0	4.17	12	9	54	51	8	24	30
Prihoda, Steve	2	2	0	4.39	26	0	41	49	4	8	22
Ray, Ken	3	3	3	4.40	34	0	47	47	7	15	28
Reichert, Dan	4	4	0	4.15	13	13	78	67	5	39	63
Rigby, Brad	3	6	0	4.85	45	0	78	93	11	26	33
Rios, Danny	2	2	0	4.63	19	2	35	39	5	14	15
Rosado, Jose	9	13	0	4.30	32	32	201	200	25	70	140
Saier, Matt	2	3	0	4.60	7	7	43	51	6	10	23
Santiago, Jose	3	5	2	3.66	42	0	59	60	8	18	19
Service, Scott	4	4	7	5.18	60	0	66	70	9	33	66
Smith, Toby	2	3	0	4.69	13	8	48	66	5	14	20
Stein, Blake	5	5	0	4.19	16	15	86	72	11	42	59
Suppan, Jeff	8	11	0	4.84	29	29	188	206	26	56	99
Suzuki, Mac	2	4	0	6.04	28	10	82	88	12	45	52
Wengert, Don	1	3	0	6.00	19	2	42	54	8	13	23
Wilson, Kris	2	3	0	4.81	13	6	43	49	7	7	22
Witasick, Jay	8	11	0	5.44	28	25	139	166	22	72	95

Minnesota Twins

BATTERS

PLAYER	BA	G	AB	R	H	2B	3B	HR	RBI	BB	SO	SB	CS	Sa	OBA
Allen, Chad	.281	133	467	68	131	21	3	10	45	36	87	14	7	.403	.333
Barnes, John	.258	37	128	17	33	6	0	4	16	14	14	2	0	.398	.258
Buchanan, Brian	.271	23	85	13	23	5	0	2	12	5	22	2	0	.400	.271
Cey, Dan	.255	30	102	14	26	4	1	2	12	7	20	2	0	.373	.255
Coomer, Ron	.280	113	421	48	118	22	1	14	62	23	64	2	1	.437	.316
Cordova, Marty	.272	118	416	56	113	24	3	13	66	45	96	9	4	.438	.349
Cummings, Midre	.255	57	165	26	42	9	1	5	28	16	32	3	0	.412	.255
Davidson, Cleatus	.250	25	92	17	23	3	2	0	8	10	24	5	0	.326	.250
Ferguson, Jeff	.250	14	44	6	11	2	0	1	7	4	7	1	0	.364	.250
Gates, Brent	.265	108	306	38	81	14	1	3	40	35	53	2	3	.346	.339
Guzman, Cristian	.241	131	419	50	101	13	3	1	28	23	96	10	7	.294	.283
Hacker, Steve	.243	46	177	22	43	11	0	9	30	13	49	0	0	.458	.243
Hocking, Dennis	.268	152	380	51	102	18	3	7	40	25	65	9	6	.387	.313
Hunter, Torii	.265	137	388	53	103	18	2	9	37	28	77	10	7	.392	.321
Jones, Jacque	.282	93	330	52	93	23	2	8	43	16	76	5	0	.436	.282
Koskie, Corey	.298	130	379	45	113	22	0	12	62	43	80	4	4	.451	.374
Latham, Chris	.244	37	131	25	32	6	2	4	14	15	46	4	0	.412	.244
Lawton, Matt	.264	110	383	58	101	21	2	10	51	57	45	17	4	.407	.367
Lewis, Marc	.257	29	109	11	28	8	0	3	15	11	27	1	0	.413	.257
Mientkiewicz, Doug	.239	118	327	35	78	22	3	2	33	45	53	2	2	.343	.336
Moeller, Chad	.245	33	94	11	23	4	1	2	9	8	20	0	0	.372	.245
Moriarty, Mike	.227	25	75	11	17	4	1	1	9	10	15	1	0	.347	.227
Moss, Rick	.260	36	100	11	26	5	0	2	11	9	18	0	0	.370	.260
Mucker, Kelcey	.293	27	92	7	27	4	0	0	7	9	17	0	0	.337	.293
Nicholas, Darrell	.271	29	96	14	26	5	1	1	11	9	25	3	0	.375	.271
Ortiz, David	.239	53	180	25	43	10	1	7	30	23	53	1	0	.422	.239

PLAYER	BA	G	AB	R	H	2B	3B	HR	RBI	BB	SO	SB	CS	Sa	OBA
Peterman, Tommy	.244	33	127	15	31	6	0	4	19	14	24	0	0	.386	.244
Pierzynski, A.J.	.272	26	81	11	22	4	0	0	10	6	13	0	0	.321	.272
Rivas, Luis	.250	32	128	19	32	7	2	2	12	10	27	5	0	.383	.250
Rupp, Chad	.202	30	104	17	21	5	0	6	15	15	42	2	0	.423	.202
Smith, Jeff	.244	27	90	9	22	5	0	2	10	7	16	0	0	.367	.244
Steinbach, Terry	.269	89	305	34	82	17	2	7	39	31	59	2	1	.407	.338
Valentin, Javier	.246	92	260	25	64	14	1	6	34	25	50	0	0	.377	.309
Walker, Todd	.291	138	505	66	147	36	4	8	49	48	75	18	8	.426	.352
Williams, Eddie	.253	23	75	9	19	4	0	3	10	6	18	0	0	.427	.253

PITCHERS

PLAYER	W	L	SV	ERA	G	GS	IP	H	HR	BB	SO
Baptist, Travis	2	2	0	4.30	19	4	44	47	6	17	22
Bell, Jason	3	3	0	4.33	11	9	52	54	6	17	37
Bowers, Shane	2	2	0	4.17	10	6	41	43	7	16	29
Carrasco, Hector	2	3	1	4.75	44	0	55	57	4	24	42
Cressend, Jack	3	3	0	4.33	9	9	54	56	4	19	38
Espinal, Jose	3	4	0	4.66	13	7	58	65	4	17	33
Fiore, Tony	2	2	3	4.05	32	1	40	42	1	24	26
Gandarillas, Gus	1	2	0	4.33	17	0	27	27	3	10	18
Guardado, Eddie	2	4	2	4.58	73	0	55	49	8	26	54
Haigler, Phil	1	1	0	5.21	7	2	19	25	2	7	5
Harris, Jeff	3	3	0	4.42	46	0	57	63	5	31	22
Hawkins, La Troy	7	10	0	5.70	25	25	131	165	21	44	76
Hooten, David	4	3	0	3.98	31	3	61	59	6	31	44
Kinney, Matt	1	1	0	4.50	5	4	20	18	2	10	14
Lincoln, Mike	4	5	0	4.94	16	15	82	92	11	23	33
Lohse, Kyle	2	3	0	4.89	7	7	46	52	5	14	22
Mahaffey, Alan	3	3	0	4.24	17	7	51	58	7	21	36
Mays, Joe	6	11	0	4.47	48	20	167	177	23	66	112
Miller, Travis	2	4	0	3.90	63	0	60	70	4	23	47
Milton, Eric	7	12	0	4.86	31	31	187	184	26	63	139
Ohme, Kevin	3	3	0	4.33	32	2	52	63	5	21	25
Perkins, Dan	1	6	0	6.12	25	10	75	97	12	36	38
Radke, Brad	12	13	0	4.07	31	31	208	230	25	43	128
Radlosky, Rob	4	4	0	4.22	17	12	64	63	11	23	34
Rath, Fred	3	4	0	4.65	41	0	62	73	7	20	23
Rath, Gary	3	3	0	4.25	14	9	53	57	6	14	30
Redman, Mark	4	4	0	4.03	13	11	67	62	6	23	48
Romero, J.C.	5	4	2	3.81	53	1	78	83	7	48	61
Ryan, Jason	5	5	0	4.30	15	15	88	86	11	38	56
Sampson, Benj	3	1	0	6.20	26	3	61	78	13	26	49
Stentz, Brent	3	2	3	3.80	44	0	45	38	5	19	45
Trombley, Mike	3	6	22	4.28	69	0	80	82	13	29	74
Wells, Bob	6	3	1	4.56	71	0	81	81	10	26	45
Yeskie, Nate	2	2	0	4.50	7	6	36	40	4	12	24

New York Yankees

BATTERS

PLAYER	BA	G	AB	R	H	2B	3B	HR	RBI	BB	SO	SB	CS	Sa	OBA
Ashby, Chris	.248	49	157	27	39	9	1	6	23	15	35	3	0	.433	.248
Bierek, Kurt	.251	49	195	28	49	14	1	8	31	16	44	1	0	.456	.251
Brosius, Scott	.261	116	414	60	108	24	1	14	64	36	73	8	4	.425	.325
Brown, Richard	.262	35	130	16	34	6	3	2	18	12	33	1	0	.400	.262
Brown, Vick	.247	23	85	15	21	3	0	1	8	14	21	7	0	.318	.247
Carpenter, Bubba	.222	62	198	38	44	10	1	11	39	36	50	3	0	.449	.222

▶ THE INSIDER 2000

PLAYER	BA	G	AB	R	H	2B	3B	HR	RBI	BB	SO	SB	CS	Sa	OBA
Coolbaugh, Mike	.237	50	173	25	41	12	1	6	25	14	60	2	0	.422	.237
Curtis, Chad	.257	82	210	38	54	9	0	6	27	38	37	9	3	.386	.374
Davis, Chili	.270	124	404	51	109	21	1	17	65	62	82	3	1	.453	.366
Dennis, Les	.254	20	67	10	17	4	0	0	5	10	23	0	0	.313	.254
Girardi, Joe	.268	50	164	19	44	11	1	1	22	9	23	2	1	.366	.309
Glass, Chip	.257	31	105	17	27	4	2	2	16	14	26	2	0	.390	.257
Jeter, Derek	.322	162	656	130	211	33	8	21	93	79	118	23	8	.492	.400
Jimenez, D'Angelo	.268	63	257	39	69	13	2	6	36	24	45	9	0	.405	.268
Johnson, Nick	.258	73	233	48	60	14	2	6	36	51	59	3	0	.412	.258
Knoblauch, Chuck	.281	138	552	107	155	28	4	15	59	73	58	30	9	.428	.380
Ledee, Ricky	.272	108	287	51	78	15	6	9	46	31	87	5	3	.460	.341
Leon, Donny	.245	50	192	23	47	12	1	7	34	12	51	0	0	.427	.245
Leyritz, Jim	.256	69	176	23	45	8	0	7	26	26	45	0	0	.420	.361
Manto, Jeff	.202	85	223	36	45	7	0	15	30	46	73	2	0	.435	.202
Martinez, Tino	.268	132	492	80	132	25	1	26	98	57	71	2	2	.482	.344
McDonald, Donzell	.264	31	121	21	32	4	2	1	7	20	30	9	0	.355	.264
Molina, Izzy	.259	26	85	12	22	4	0	1	14	5	14	1	0	.341	.259
Morris, Jeremy	.267	24	86	12	23	4	0	2	12	7	24	1	0	.384	.267
O'Neill, Paul	.294	130	507	67	149	33	2	17	95	54	79	10	5	.467	.357
Ottavinia, Paul	.257	43	140	17	36	7	2	5	20	9	35	2	0	.443	.257
Posada, Jorge	.255	116	384	54	98	21	1	14	60	54	93	1	1	.424	.348
Powell, Alonzo	.254	50	181	30	46	7	0	7	28	26	51	0	0	.409	.254
Sojo, Luis	.276	39	105	16	29	4	0	1	13	4	13	1	0	.343	.303
Spencer, Shane	.258	74	209	30	54	10	0	11	30	18	51	0	4	.464	.322
Tarasco, Tony	.248	66	214	39	53	13	0	9	32	26	31	4	0	.435	.248
Thames, Marcus	.245	28	98	15	24	4	1	2	15	13	26	0	0	.367	.245
Valencia, Victor	.207	40	135	18	28	6	0	7	23	14	58	0	0	.407	.207
Waszgis, B.J.	.239	45	138	23	33	8	0	4	19	17	48	2	0	.384	.239
Williams, Bernie	.323	155	591	112	191	30	6	25	109	90	90	12	10	.521	.410

PITCHERS

PLAYER	W	L	SV	ERA	G	GS	IP	H	HR	BB	SO
Beverlin, Jason	3	3	0	4.25	9	8	53	50	5	27	38
Bradley, Ryan	2	2	0	4.40	9	7	43	40	7	19	30
Buddie, Mike	3	3	0	4.02	29	2	47	51	3	14	29
Clemens, Roger	12	7	0	3.78	26	26	162	145	12	68	163
Cone, David	13	8	0	3.61	30	30	187	166	19	79	182
De La Cruz, Francisco	2	2	0	4.50	8	5	38	40	3	21	22
De Los Santos, Luis	3	4	0	4.50	11	11	60	72	10	21	34
Dingman, Craig	5	4	2	3.51	57	0	77	87	3	19	78
Erdos, Todd	2	2	0	4.22	16	4	32	30	5	11	22
Ford, Ben	3	3	1	4.33	41	0	54	50	4	25	25
Grimsley, Jason	5	3	1	5.11	54	0	74	74	8	42	48
Hernandez, Orlando	15	7	0	4.01	28	28	184	160	19	74	144
Irabu, Hideki	11	7	0	4.73	29	25	154	156	25	51	120
Johnson, Mark	3	3	0	4.58	10	10	57	63	5	28	28
Juden, Jeff	2	2	0	4.00	6	6	36	30	4	14	26
Kaufman, Brad	2	2	0	3.92	19	2	39	35	3	18	32
Lisio, Joe	2	2	6	4.14	39	0	37	38	3	18	27
Maeda, Kats	1	2	0	4.50	9	2	26	29	2	14	14
Mairena, Oswaldo	4	4	0	3.97	58	0	68	70	4	39	47
Mendoza, Ramiro	7	5	2	4.19	43	5	101	114	10	23	59
Naulty, Dan	1	1	0	4.58	38	0	57	49	9	24	31
Nelson, Jeff	4	3	2	3.94	63	0	48	44	3	30	51
Pettitte, Andy	12	9	0	4.40	28	28	172	188	15	72	113
Rivera, Mariano	4	3	46	2.07	71	0	74	56	3	21	55
Robbins, Jake	2	3	0	4.93	8	0	42	42	0	22	20
Spence, Cam	1	2	0	4.67	6	5	27	31	2	8	15

2000 PROJECTIONS

PLAYER	W	L	SV	ERA	G	GS	IP	H	HR	BB	SO
Stanton, Mike	3	1	0	4.50	73	1	62	63	6	21	58
Tessmer, Jay	3	3	5	4.02	42	0	47	46	4	13	28
Watson, Allen	5	4	1	4.68	38	4	77	84	13	31	58
Williams, Matt	2	2	0	3.92	27	1	39	32	3	25	42
Yarnall, Ed	4	4	0	4.04	13	12	78	79	3	35	64
Zancanaro, Dave	2	2	0	4.38	7	6	39	44	4	18	22

Oakland Athletics

BATTERS

PLAYER	BA	G	AB	R	H	2B	3B	HR	RBI	BB	SO	SB	CS	Sa	OBA
Ardoin, Danny	.239	46	142	21	34	5	1	3	19	20	40	1	0	.352	.239
Ball, Jeff	.262	41	149	18	39	8	1	3	18	13	29	2	0	.389	.262
Becker, Rich	.247	137	292	43	72	10	2	7	29	58	93	9	2	.366	.375
Bowles, Justin	.244	32	119	15	29	6	2	4	15	9	36	2	0	.429	.244
Castro, Jose	.235	22	68	12	16	3	1	1	7	7	20	3	0	.353	.235
Chavez, Eric	.253	130	399	53	101	24	3	14	56	51	62	2	2	.434	.338
Christenson, Ryan	.241	105	290	47	70	15	1	4	30	38	75	6	5	.341	.327
Encarnacion, Mario	.256	44	164	25	42	8	1	6	25	15	52	4	0	.427	.256
Espada, Josue	.276	32	123	19	34	3	0	1	11	14	18	4	0	.325	.276
Freeman, Ricky	.250	29	96	14	24	7	0	2	13	10	22	0	0	.385	.250
Garland, Tim	.271	12	48	8	13	2	1	1	5	3	7	2	0	.417	.271
Giambi, Jason	.295	158	576	100	170	34	1	29	111	90	101	1	1	.509	.391
Grieve, Ben	.271	143	494	79	134	26	1	23	83	66	107	3	1	.468	.366
Hernandez, Ramon	.246	70	256	28	63	10	2	9	42	23	35	1	0	.406	.246
Hinch, A.J.	.240	76	208	26	50	5	1	7	25	16	51	5	1	.375	.297
Jaha, John	.254	137	437	79	111	19	0	29	95	92	120	2	1	.497	.392
Lesher, Brian	.257	48	171	26	44	12	1	5	25	16	39	2	0	.427	.257
Macfarlane, Mike	.253	66	186	23	47	13	0	5	28	12	40	0	0	.403	.300
Marcinczyk, T.R.	.233	35	133	20	31	9	0	5	26	14	36	1	0	.414	.233
Martins, Eric	.243	34	107	14	26	5	2	1	12	11	20	1	0	.355	.243
McDonald, Jason	.243	80	173	27	42	5	1	2	11	26	42	8	4	.318	.350
McKay, Cody	.253	27	95	14	24	5	0	1	11	9	14	0	0	.337	.253
Menechino, Frankie	.250	51	188	31	47	9	3	4	26	22	45	1	0	.394	.250
Morales, Willie	.226	25	84	9	19	5	0	3	14	5	16	1	0	.393	.226
Neill, Mike	.260	41	154	23	40	9	1	4	22	21	49	3	0	.409	.260
Ortiz, Santos	.260	55	192	31	50	13	1	4	21	13	31	5	0	.401	.260
Phillips, Tony	.251	89	338	60	85	21	2	10	38	61	76	8	3	.414	.369
Piatt, Adam	.219	61	224	38	49	14	1	11	40	29	56	2	0	.438	.219
Raines, Tim	.272	29	81	14	22	4	0	2	11	14	11	2	1	.395	.375
Saenz, Olmedo	.269	102	268	43	72	18	0	11	41	22	51	1	1	.459	.354
Sheff, Chris	.264	45	159	21	42	8	0	5	24	16	39	2	0	.409	.264
Spiezio, Scott	.255	86	274	35	70	19	1	8	36	30	40	1	1	.420	.331
Stairs, Matt	.265	147	510	86	135	27	2	33	98	74	105	4	5	.520	.360
Tejada, Miguel	.251	155	570	89	143	32	4	20	79	52	104	8	7	.426	.322
Vaz, Roberto	.261	48	161	22	42	8	2	3	19	23	37	2	0	.391	.261
Velarde, Randy	.305	136	545	88	166	23	6	13	66	64	88	20	7	.440	.383

PITCHERS

PLAYER	W	L	SV	ERA	G	GS	IP	H	HR	BB	SO
Anderson, Jason	2	2	0	4.89	7	7	35	39	4	12	19
Appier, Kevin	11	11	0	4.88	27	27	168	179	21	64	112
Baez, Benito	3	3	1	4.17	36	0	54	58	5	15	44
Chavez, Anthony	2	2	2	3.92	31	0	39	37	4	21	34
D'Amico, Jeffrey	2	2	1	4.28	30	0	40	44	3	17	26
Dubose, Eric	3	3	0	4.33	15	11	54	55	6	27	40
Gorrell, Chris	1	1	0	4.71	11	0	21	26	2	7	13

▶ THE INSIDER 2000

PLAYER	W	L	SV	ERA	G	GS	IP	H	HR	BB	SO
Gregg, Kevin	4	4	0	4.38	14	14	78	71	6	29	47
Groom, Buddy	3	2	0	4.75	87	0	53	57	3	20	36
Harville, Chad	0	5	0	6.35	35	0	34	41	5	23	35
Haynes, Jimmy	6	8	0	5.29	25	21	119	129	16	60	81
Heredia, Gil	11	8	0	4.71	28	28	170	193	19	28	100
Hudson, Tim	8	7	0	3.97	21	21	136	135	8	69	118
Isringhausen, Jason	2	4	9	4.98	33	5	65	69	7	33	48
Jarvis, Kevin	2	2	0	4.50	6	6	36	43	6	10	19
Jones, Doug	4	5	8	3.84	60	0	89	94	10	19	63
Kimball, Andrew	2	2	0	4.09	23	0	44	47	6	17	36
King, Bill	3	3	0	4.33	25	4	54	65	7	14	28
Laxton, Brett	3	4	0	4.50	10	10	64	70	4	23	38
Leyva, Julian	3	3	0	4.76	10	8	51	62	7	9	27
Mahay, Ron	3	3	0	4.33	24	6	54	57	6	24	30
Manwiller, Tim	3	3	0	4.67	11	9	52	62	6	14	28
Mathews, T. J.	8	5	3	4.06	52	0	62	55	8	23	47
McMichael, Greg	3	3	0	4.41	53	0	49	52	7	25	38
Niles, Randy	2	3	0	5.05	11	7	41	55	3	20	18
Nina, Elvin	3	3	0	4.50	11	8	52	54	2	32	30
Olivares, Omar	11	10	0	4.35	29	29	186	199	18	81	91
Oquist, Mike	7	8	0	5.26	25	21	125	138	17	49	80
Perez, Juan	2	2	0	4.34	19	0	29	30	2	11	19
Vasquez, Leo	3	3	0	3.88	32	0	51	47	5	34	43
Vizcaino, Luis	3	3	0	4.34	16	9	58	59	8	25	39
Worrell, Tim	2	3	0	4.84	52	0	67	70	8	28	57

Seattle Mariners

BATTERS

PLAYER	BA	G	AB	R	H	2B	3B	HR	RBI	BB	SO	SB	CS	Sa	OBA
Bass, Jayson	.226	39	137	21	31	6	1	6	18	20	61	8	0	.416	.226
Bell, David	.271	155	549	78	149	31	2	17	69	49	85	5	4	.428	.330
Bournigal, Rafael	.272	42	92	13	25	5	0	1	11	6	6	1	0	.359	.320
Brown, Randy	.224	27	98	12	22	4	2	3	13	8	31	1	0	.398	.224
Buhner, Jay	.229	79	253	38	58	9	0	15	42	56	85	0	0	.443	.373
Chavez, Raul	.262	31	107	12	28	6	0	1	12	8	23	0	0	.346	.262
Davis, Russ	.258	116	407	54	105	21	1	19	61	29	107	3	3	.455	.311
Gipson, Charles	.271	60	129	23	35	5	2	0	14	12	23	7	0	.341	.271
Griffey, Ken	.276	154	590	113	163	27	3	47	128	78	104	20	6	.571	.365
Harrison, Adonis	.274	22	84	10	23	3	0	0	9	7	17	3	0	.310	.274
Hills, Rich	.250	20	68	7	17	3	0	1	7	9	13	0	0	.338	.250
Horner, Jim	.256	21	78	8	20	4	0	2	13	4	17	0	0	.385	.256
Hunter, Brian	.263	109	434	66	114	16	4	3	30	33	79	39	9	.339	.315
Ibanez, Raul	.263	93	228	26	60	9	1	9	30	17	39	4	1	.430	.313
Jackson, Ryan	.280	61	182	21	51	11	1	3	25	15	46	3	0	.401	.280
Kingman, Brendan	.266	20	79	9	21	3	0	1	8	4	13	0	0	.342	.266
Lampkin, Tom	.270	81	200	26	54	10	1	7	29	17	30	2	2	.435	.341
Mabry, John	.264	85	250	31	66	14	0	7	31	21	56	1	1	.404	.322
Martinez, Edgar	.314	137	488	78	153	34	1	23	83	91	85	4	2	.529	.423
Mathis, Joe	.271	24	85	10	23	5	2	1	10	6	21	2	0	.412	.271
Matos, Francisco	.283	32	127	13	36	7	1	1	10	5	16	1	0	.378	.283
Monahan, Shane	.281	36	121	15	34	6	1	2	13	6	32	1	0	.397	.281
Murphy, Mike	.262	33	107	18	28	4	2	1	14	15	37	4	0	.364	.262
Radmanovich, Ryan	.253	47	170	24	43	9	1	6	29	18	45	3	0	.424	.253
Rodriguez, Alex	.286	141	570	110	163	29	2	38	108	50	108	28	8	.544	.347
Sealy, Scot	.226	18	53	7	12	1	0	2	8	6	18	0	0	.358	.226
Seitzer, Brad	.247	40	146	21	36	9	0	2	17	23	32	0	0	.349	.247

2000 PROJECTIONS

PLAYER	BA	G	AB	R	H	2B	3B	HR	RBI	BB	SO	SB	CS	Sa	OBA
Thomas, Juan	.218	27	101	16	22	4	0	5	17	5	42	0	0	.406	.218
Timmons, Ozzie	.219	51	183	28	40	11	0	10	33	26	60	0	0	.443	.219
Vazquez, Ramon	.243	30	103	13	25	6	1	1	10	14	22	1	0	.350	.243
Wathan, Dusty	.259	24	85	9	22	4	0	1	9	6	18	1	0	.341	.259
Weber, Jake	.248	29	105	14	26	5	0	2	13	14	19	1	0	.352	.248
Wilson, Dan	.271	115	391	47	106	23	2	9	45	29	74	4	1	.409	.324

PITCHERS

PLAYER	W	L	SV	ERA	G	GS	IP	H	HR	BB	SO
Abbott, Paul	6	2	0	3.53	25	7	74	56	9	34	66
Adamson, Joel	1	2	0	5.19	11	4	26	30	3	8	9
Anderson, Ryan	4	4	0	3.95	13	13	73	67	5	44	74
Brosnan, Jason	2	2	1	3.97	19	1	34	28	4	13	25
Bunch, Mel	3	3	0	4.08	9	8	53	54	5	19	41
Carmona, Rafael	2	1	0	4.82	22	0	28	32	5	17	14
Cloude, Ken	4	3	1	6.10	27	5	62	74	10	33	39
Davey, Tom	2	1	1	4.71	45	0	65	62	5	40	59
Fitzgerald, Brian	3	3	1	4.15	28	1	52	59	2	18	30
Flener, Huck	1	1	0	4.70	8	2	23	23	2	8	14
Franklin, Ryan	3	3	0	4.34	13	7	56	55	7	15	32
Fuentes, Brian	2	2	0	4.09	11	10	44	35	3	31	40
Garcia, Freddy	16	8	0	4.22	32	32	194	201	17	88	164
Gryboski, Kevin	3	3	2	4.18	42	0	56	73	5	22	31
Halama, John	10	9	0	4.50	37	23	172	189	18	56	102
Henry, Butch	4	1	0	4.42	17	9	59	67	4	19	36
Hinchliffe, Brett	4	4	0	4.22	13	10	64	61	9	22	40
Hodges, Kevin	3	4	0	4.81	10	8	58	69	4	22	24
Holdridge, David	2	2	1	3.94	21	0	32	30	1	11	27
Marte, Damaso	3	3	0	4.24	22	7	51	51	9	25	32
McCarthy, Greg	2	2	0	4.22	30	0	32	25	4	21	20
Meche, Gil	6	7	0	4.31	22	21	119	111	11	69	72
Mesa, Jose	4	5	31	4.43	64	0	65	73	8	32	44
Montane, Ivan	4	3	2	3.54	46	0	61	51	3	30	66
Moyer, Jamie	12	7	0	3.92	27	27	193	201	20	40	120
Paniagua, Jose	6	10	3	4.32	58	0	77	75	6	49	69
Pineiro, Joel	3	4	0	4.57	11	10	67	75	7	21	39
Ramsay, Robert	3	4	0	4.29	12	10	63	58	10	22	40
Rodriguez, Frank	2	4	3	5.43	26	5	68	81	8	28	45
Scheffer, Aaron	5	4	2	3.65	45	1	74	73	9	34	69
Sinclair, Steve	0	3	0	5.54	43	0	39	41	7	24	32
Smith, Cam	2	2	0	3.82	25	0	33	22	2	32	30
Stark, Dennis	3	3	0	4.24	10	9	51	52	4	21	30
Steenstra, Kennie	2	2	0	4.65	11	4	31	36	3	7	14
Sweeney, Brian	2	3	0	4.50	10	7	44	50	8	11	27

Tampa Bay Devil Rays

BATTERS

PLAYER	BA	G	AB	R	H	2B	3B	HR	RBI	BB	SO	SB	CS	Sa	OBA
Becker, Brian	.250	30	112	15	28	5	0	4	17	10	25	0	0	.402	.250
Boggs, Wade	.295	70	237	32	70	12	1	3	25	29	24	1	0	.392	.369
Butler, Rich	.258	55	186	26	48	10	2	6	27	19	44	1	0	.430	.258
Cairo, Miguel	.294	124	456	57	134	18	5	4	38	24	45	20	7	.382	.336
Canseco, Jose	.254	109	413	68	105	18	0	31	83	51	121	10	4	.523	.340
Carr, Dustin	.262	35	130	19	34	5	1	1	15	17	21	1	0	.338	.262
Clyburn, Danny	.257	50	171	24	44	7	0	6	19	13	53	1	0	.404	.257
Colina, Roberto	.256	26	82	11	21	5	0	1	13	9	15	0	0	.354	.256

▶ THE INSIDER 2000

PLAYER	BA	G	AB	R	H	2B	3B	HR	RBI	BB	SO	SB	CS	Sa	OBA
Cox, Steve	.266	64	252	38	67	18	1	9	46	24	42	1	0	.452	.266
De Los Santos, Eddy	.274	34	117	14	32	6	1	1	13	7	22	1	0	.368	.274
Difelice, Mike	.277	67	213	20	59	12	1	5	27	12	39	0	0	.413	.323
Flaherty, John	.274	112	409	44	112	18	0	11	57	23	62	1	3	.399	.314
Graffanino, Tony	.256	77	254	37	65	15	3	5	31	22	54	5	0	.398	.256
Guillen, Jose	.272	93	324	42	88	19	1	6	44	17	62	1	1	.392	.318
Hawkins, Kraig	.296	23	71	10	21	2	0	0	6	9	13	3	0	.324	.296
Holbert, Aaron	.260	51	177	33	46	8	2	5	24	11	34	5	0	.412	.260
Huff, Aubrey	.237	50	186	25	44	12	1	6	23	19	35	1	0	.409	.237
Lamb, David	.236	77	174	26	41	7	1	1	19	15	26	0	1	.305	.296
Ledesma, Aaron	.300	98	300	36	90	16	1	0	32	15	42	4	3	.360	.339
Lowery, Terrell	.258	93	275	48	71	18	3	8	37	32	85	4	0	.433	.258
Martin, Chris	.252	32	107	16	27	5	0	2	13	12	20	3	0	.355	.252
Martinez, Dave	.283	124	438	64	124	19	4	6	50	51	67	11	6	.386	.360
McClain, Scott	.221	48	181	32	40	10	0	8	30	22	64	1	0	.409	.221
McCracken, Quinton	.289	43	149	22	43	8	1	1	16	13	26	6	4	.376	.348
McGriff, Fred	.289	133	491	66	142	26	1	24	85	71	97	3	0	.493	.377
Mendoza, Carlos	.292	37	130	28	38	4	1	0	12	16	22	3	0	.338	.292
Mosquera, Julio	.275	28	91	11	25	4	0	1	12	5	17	0	0	.352	.275
Perry, Herb	.266	62	192	27	51	11	1	5	29	15	38	1	1	.411	.339
Pomierski, Joe	.229	43	131	19	30	6	2	6	20	13	37	1	0	.443	.229
Sanchez, Alexis	.294	17	68	11	20	2	1	0	5	4	14	5	0	.353	.294
Smith, Bobby	.250	83	272	36	68	11	2	9	38	24	96	5	0	.404	.250
Sorrento, Paul	.240	89	271	34	65	14	0	12	40	39	86	1	1	.424	.341
Stocker, Kevin	.272	85	272	36	74	11	2	3	25	26	53	7	5	.360	.343
Trammell, Bubba	.254	97	343	47	87	22	0	15	48	34	73	0	0	.449	.254
Wilcox, Luke	.231	51	186	29	43	11	2	9	31	18	34	1	0	.457	.231
Wilson, Tom	.207	50	164	20	34	8	0	9	25	25	58	0	0	.421	.207
Winn, Randy	.296	89	321	51	95	17	6	2	27	24	72	12	1	.405	.296

PITCHERS

PLAYER	W	L	SV	ERA	G	GS	IP	H	HR	BB	SO
Alvarez, Wilson	8	11	0	4.36	28	28	157	151	20	76	125
Arrojo, Rolando	7	10	0	4.57	22	22	130	141	18	50	99
Barnett, Marty	3	3	1	4.34	35	3	56	55	3	29	30
Belitz, Todd	2	2	0	4.62	6	6	37	35	5	13	23
Bowers, Cedrick	3	3	0	4.13	10	10	48	40	6	24	44
Callaway, Michael	3	4	0	4.64	13	13	66	77	5	26	37
Charlton, Norm	2	3	0	5.17	45	0	54	57	5	38	49
Daniels, John	4	3	2	4.08	43	0	64	59	3	20	40
Duvall, Mike	1	1	0	4.25	55	0	55	64	7	37	24
Eiland, Dave	3	3	0	4.42	12	10	55	60	6	14	32
Enders, Trevor	3	3	0	4.27	37	0	59	60	3	23	33
Gaillard, Eddie	3	2	4	3.67	46	0	49	57	7	21	41
Harper, Travis	2	2	0	4.40	8	8	43	39	5	14	34
Hernandez, Roberto	3	4	41	3.50	71	0	72	65	3	36	65
Hernandez, Santos	2	2	1	4.50	17	3	30	28	5	10	20
Lopez, Albie	4	3	1	4.50	51	0	64	67	7	26	44
Manon, Julio	2	2	0	4.20	13	2	30	33	4	9	20
Mecir, Jim	2	2	0	3.43	35	0	42	36	2	20	35
Munoz, Bobby	2	1	1	3.86	20	2	28	26	3	13	20
Newman, Alan	5	4	0	6.35	40	0	34	47	4	19	44
Nunez, Maximo	2	2	2	4.09	36	0	44	35	3	33	32
Ortega, Pablo	3	3	0	4.50	10	10	58	69	6	21	28
Pujals, Denis	2	3	0	4.50	27	0	46	57	4	13	21
Rekar, Bryan	6	7	0	5.26	30	13	106	126	17	39	63
Rupe, Ryan	8	9	0	4.66	24	24	143	138	17	58	98
Santana, Julio	2	3	0	5.50	22	5	54	60	8	26	28

2000 PROJECTIONS

PLAYER	W	L	SV	ERA	G	GS	IP	H	HR	BB	SO
Saunders, Tony	3	6	0	4.78	17	17	81	85	8	49	69
Small, Aaron	1	2	0	5.09	9	2	23	25	3	7	10
Sparks, Jeff	0	0	3	5.19	20	0	26	15	3	30	43
Tatis, Ramon	2	3	0	4.71	13	7	42	44	5	20	21
Wheeler, Daniel	5	5	0	4.23	14	14	83	91	14	22	58
White, Rick	4	4	0	4.26	54	1	93	111	8	33	64
Witt, Bobby	7	11	0	5.49	25	25	141	165	20	67	89
Yan, Esteban	3	3	0	5.10	49	1	60	67	8	30	48
Zambrano, Victor	2	2	0	3.86	20	2	42	44	2	18	35

Texas Rangers

BATTERS

PLAYER	BA	G	AB	R	H	2B	3B	HR	RBI	BB	SO	SB	CS	Sa	OBA
Alicea, Luis	.239	53	138	26	33	8	1	3	15	23	25	3	2	.377	.354
Barkett, Andy	.273	42	154	20	42	9	1	3	22	12	27	2	0	.403	.273
Bautista, Juan	.257	19	70	9	18	2	0	1	7	4	20	2	0	.329	.257
Bridges, Kary	.267	36	116	14	31	5	0	3	15	8	8	2	0	.388	.267
Brumbaugh, Cliff	.225	40	151	22	34	8	1	6	21	16	31	4	0	.411	.225
Clayton, Royce	.278	128	464	71	129	25	4	11	50	40	91	15	7	.420	.337
Cuyler, Milt	.269	17	52	9	14	2	1	0	5	5	13	2	0	.346	.269
Demetral, Chris	.237	28	80	12	19	3	0	2	7	11	18	1	0	.350	.237
Dransfeldt, Kelly	.234	35	124	18	29	7	1	3	15	8	43	1	0	.379	.234
Evans, Tom	.236	47	157	25	37	11	1	4	20	20	43	1	0	.395	.236
Forbes, P.J.	.283	15	53	8	15	2	0	0	3	4	8	1	0	.321	.283
Gallagher, Shawn	.257	36	148	18	38	9	1	5	23	8	33	0	0	.432	.257
Gonzalez, Juan	.305	146	574	105	175	37	2	40	131	45	107	2	2	.585	.353
Goodwin, Tom	.278	100	363	63	101	12	4	2	28	41	59	33	12	.350	.351
Green, Bertrum	.265	24	83	17	22	4	1	1	7	8	24	4	0	.373	.265
Greer, Rusty	.295	142	542	99	160	35	3	18	92	82	71	3	3	.470	.389
Hubbard, Mike	.262	27	84	9	22	4	0	2	10	5	20	1	0	.381	.262
Ibarra, Jesse	.222	15	54	6	12	2	0	2	8	8	18	0	0	.370	.222
Kelly, Roberto	.300	79	267	41	80	14	2	10	39	16	50	4	2	.479	.346
King, Cesar	.220	32	109	13	24	6	1	4	15	10	29	1	0	.404	.220
Lamb, Michael	.246	49	191	26	47	14	1	6	27	14	27	1	0	.424	.246
Lane, Ryan	.225	43	142	16	32	9	2	4	20	12	31	2	0	.401	.225
Mateo, Ruben	.263	73	293	47	77	14	1	16	54	12	60	5	0	.481	.263
McLemore, Mark	.271	123	473	85	128	17	4	5	42	75	68	13	6	.355	.369
Myers, Adrian	.259	16	58	11	15	2	1	0	5	8	12	4	0	.328	.259
Palmeiro, Rafael	.291	151	557	87	162	28	1	40	122	79	73	4	4	.560	.379
Piniella, Juan	.262	34	126	19	33	6	1	2	12	17	40	3	0	.373	.262
Rodriguez, Ivan	.319	149	609	106	194	33	2	29	102	28	74	18	7	.522	.349
Rosario, Mel	.227	26	88	11	20	6	0	4	14	4	26	1	0	.432	.227
Sagmoen, Marc	.242	37	120	17	29	4	1	5	17	10	31	1	0	.417	.242
Sasser, Rob	.246	39	142	18	35	11	0	2	17	16	40	2	0	.366	.246
Sergio, Thomas	.246	35	138	20	34	9	1	2	16	13	19	4	0	.370	.246
Shave, Jon	.286	38	70	10	20	4	0	0	9	4	17	1	1	.343	.333
Sheldon, Scott	.223	44	157	23	35	9	1	7	24	14	47	3	0	.427	.223
Stevens, Lee	.278	141	467	68	130	26	2	23	75	43	116	1	3	.490	.336
Valdes, Pedro	.259	59	197	26	51	11	1	8	27	21	36	1	0	.447	.259
Zaun, Greg	.237	47	118	12	28	5	1	2	14	15	17	2	0	.347	.321
Zeile, Todd	.280	141	521	73	146	31	1	21	85	57	85	3	3	.464	.352
Zywica, Michael	.270	30	111	18	30	7	1	2	18	7	32	1	0	.405	.270

PITCHERS

PLAYER	W	L	SV	ERA	G	GS	IP	H	HR	BB	SO
Buckles, Brandall	3	3	0	4.50	24	3	48	52	7	25	22

▶ THE INSIDER 2000

PLAYER	W	L	SV	ERA	G	GS	IP	H	HR	BB	SO
Burkett, John	7	7	0	5.31	26	22	127	154	14	33	86
Clark, Mark	4	6	0	5.48	18	18	87	100	13	27	58
Cobb, Trevor	2	2	0	4.65	14	1	31	30	5	13	15
Cook, Derrick	2	2	0	4.86	7	7	37	41	4	13	19
Crabtree, Tim	5	1	0	4.03	70	0	67	76	4	23	51
Davis, Douglas	4	4	0	3.77	13	11	74	79	8	29	62
Dickey, Robert	2	3	1	4.69	17	1	48	53	0	19	26
Fassero, Jeff	5	8	0	5.30	27	19	112	127	20	46	86
Glynn, Ryan	4	5	0	4.50	16	15	82	83	9	39	44
Helling, Rick	12	9	0	4.70	29	29	182	182	30	72	120
Johnson, Jonathan	2	2	0	4.72	12	5	40	48	5	12	20
Karp, Ryan	2	2	0	4.50	6	5	32	34	3	11	20
Knight, Brandon	3	4	0	4.58	10	9	59	60	8	16	29
Kolb, Danny	4	4	0	4.50	20	8	74	85	4	35	33
Lee, Corey	3	3	0	4.00	9	1	54	53	1	18	43
Loaiza, Esteban	8	6	0	4.61	30	15	121	133	13	38	77
Martinez, Jose	2	2	0	4.38	12	3	37	38	5	12	22
Miller, Matt	3	2	1	3.38	25	0	40	31	1	20	50
Moody, Eric	3	3	1	4.50	28	1	52	63	4	11	18
Morgan, Mike	8	7	0	5.29	28	20	114	137	18	37	55
Munoz, Mike	2	2	1	4.42	60	0	57	62	5	20	30
Patterson, Danny	3	2	0	4.88	52	0	59	69	6	19	42
Perisho, Matt	4	4	0	3.93	14	12	71	66	6	32	58
Pickett, Ricky	1	1	0	4.09	6	1	11	11	2	6	9
Poland, Trey	2	3	0	4.70	8	8	46	52	4	21	26
Raggio, Brady	3	3	0	4.50	10	7	50	55	4	13	28
Sele, Aaron	15	9	0	4.76	28	28	176	205	17	66	149
Silva, Ted	3	3	0	4.50	9	8	50	47	7	10	28
Sollecito, Gabe	4	3	1	3.90	33	0	60	67	5	23	42
Venafro, Mike	3	2	0	3.55	68	0	71	68	4	24	39
Wetteland, John	4	3	41	3.27	62	0	66	62	8	19	65
Zimmerman, Jeff	9	3	3	2.60	67	0	90	54	9	25	69

Toronto Blue Jays

BATTERS

PLAYER	BA	G	AB	R	H	2B	3B	HR	RBI	BB	SO	SB	CS	Sa	OBA
Abernathy, Brent	.253	34	146	24	37	9	0	3	14	12	14	6	0	.377	.253
Batista, Tony	.271	159	536	79	145	30	1	31	94	38	97	4	1	.504	.322
Blake, Casey	.216	51	176	27	38	7	1	8	27	23	44	2	0	.403	.216
Borders, Pat	.256	14	43	4	11	2	0	1	4	3	10	0	0	.372	.256
Brown, Kevin	.244	55	160	20	39	10	1	5	24	11	53	0	0	.412	.244
Brumfield, Jacob	.247	58	154	24	38	8	2	3	20	15	34	3	2	.383	.314
Bush, Homer	.325	139	477	71	155	25	4	5	53	21	84	32	9	.426	.358
Butler, Rob	.291	26	103	16	30	4	2	1	12	7	10	1	0	.398	.291
Cruz, Jose	.245	112	379	64	93	19	3	16	50	62	103	13	4	.438	.350
Delgado, Carlos	.266	149	552	99	147	39	1	39	118	76	134	1	1	.553	.364
Fernandez, Tony	.312	137	471	68	147	36	1	7	68	58	56	8	7	.437	.395
Fletcher, Darrin	.287	115	397	44	114	24	0	15	69	24	43	0	0	.461	.333
Giles, Tim	.268	40	153	20	41	6	1	5	30	15	34	0	0	.418	.268
Gomez, Rudy	.222	39	135	19	30	7	1	4	23	19	24	2	0	.378	.222
Gonzalez, Alex	.264	63	231	30	61	14	0	5	20	17	47	8	3	.390	.321
Goodwin, Curtis	.258	83	151	19	39	6	1	0	8	14	39	5	4	.311	.319
Grebeck, Craig	.303	42	122	16	37	7	0	1	10	14	15	0	1	.385	.381
Green, Shawn	.289	160	623	117	180	39	2	37	109	58	124	24	8	.536	.355
Greene, Willie	.236	72	212	27	50	9	0	10	36	29	51	2	1	.420	.329
Hollins, Dave	.234	44	154	25	36	8	0	4	16	17	36	2	0	.364	.234

2000 PROJECTIONS

PLAYER	BA	G	AB	R	H	2B	3B	HR	RBI	BB	SO	SB	CS	Sa	OBA
Jones, Chris	.250	14	40	7	10	2	0	1	6	3	13	1	0	.375	.250
Kelly, Pat	.250	46	128	19	32	7	0	5	17	12	33	3	1	.422	.315
Lawrence, Joseph	.221	38	136	24	30	7	1	3	11	25	31	3	0	.353	.221
Lennon, Patrick	.235	54	200	29	47	9	0	11	33	21	64	1	0	.445	.235
Lopez, Luis	.301	40	156	21	47	10	1	1	19	11	20	0	0	.397	.301
Loyd, Brian	.243	30	107	13	26	5	0	3	16	12	20	2	0	.374	.243
Martin, Norberto	.276	24	76	10	21	2	0	1	7	3	11	2	0	.342	.276
Matheny, Mike	.247	54	154	15	38	7	0	3	16	9	36	0	0	.351	.299
McRae, Brian	.240	110	358	48	86	19	3	11	44	50	68	7	7	.402	.341
Melhuse, Adam	.221	44	154	24	34	8	0	5	22	31	40	1	0	.370	.221
Mummau, Rob	.244	22	78	10	19	5	1	1	11	5	13	0	0	.372	.244
Otanez, Willis	.248	77	222	31	55	12	0	8	27	17	52	0	0	.410	.306
Sanders, Anthony	.243	34	136	19	33	6	1	5	16	12	37	4	0	.412	.243
Segui, David	.297	110	401	56	119	24	2	14	54	38	56	1	1	.471	.355
Solano, Fausto	.239	40	134	19	32	5	0	4	18	17	24	3	0	.366	.239
Stewart, Shannon	.295	138	549	92	162	28	3	10	60	59	77	39	14	.412	.372
Stromsborg, Ryan	.263	20	76	11	20	4	1	2	9	6	22	1	0	.421	.263
Thompson, Andy	.208	47	178	28	37	10	1	9	28	16	44	3	0	.427	.208
Wells, Vernon	.281	61	235	31	66	13	2	5	31	17	48	6	0	.417	.281
Witt, Kevin	.235	64	221	31	52	10	1	10	32	28	69	0	0	.425	.235
Woodward, Chri	.262	43	149	21	39	9	1	0	10	18	32	1	0	.336	.262

PITCHERS

PLAYER	W	L	SV	ERA	G	GS	IP	H	HR	BB	SO
Andrews, Clayton	4	4	0	4.50	14	14	72	76	9	41	42
Bale, John	3	3	0	3.67	25	5	54	49	5	17	55
Bleazard, David	3	4	0	4.65	10	10	60	67	3	28	28
Bogott, Kurtiss	2	2	0	4.07	23	2	42	37	5	20	31
Bovee, Mike	3	2	2	3.91	30	2	46	47	5	16	36
Bradford, Josh	2	2	0	4.64	11	4	33	32	3	15	21
Carpenter, Chris	9	8	0	4.53	24	24	151	174	16	52	110
Delgado, Ernie	2	2	0	4.40	25	2	43	43	2	21	22
Escobar, Kelvim	12	9	0	5.13	28	26	149	164	15	69	117
Frascatore, John	5	4	1	3.99	59	0	70	73	9	25	39
Glover, Gary	4	4	0	4.15	11	11	65	63	6	25	45
Halladay, Roy	8	7	1	4.04	38	19	158	166	20	83	89
Hamilton, Joey	7	6	0	5.13	23	18	100	109	10	43	63
Harris, D.J.	1	1	0	4.85	6	1	13	13	2	6	6
Hendrickso, Mark	1	1	0	4.76	4	3	17	19	1	5	10
Hentgen, Pat	10	10	0	4.74	29	29	171	191	26	57	99
Hudek, John	2	4	0	5.31	37	0	39	41	6	29	39
Koch, Billy	0	5	32	3.57	59	0	68	60	5	33	60
Lloyd, Graeme	5	2	3	3.55	73	0	71	68	10	22	44
Lowe, Benny	2	2	0	4.00	31	0	36	32	4	19	31
Ludwick, Eric	3	2	2	3.80	30	3	45	47	5	23	36
Lukasiewicz, Mark	2	2	0	4.09	17	4	44	43	8	16	29
Mann, Jim	3	3	1	3.70	40	0	56	42	8	28	52
Munro, Peter	5	5	0	3.98	34	9	86	93	8	37	61
Quantrill, Paul	3	3	0	3.00	48	0	57	66	5	17	37
Rivette, Scott	3	3	2	4.06	37	0	51	57	1	19	40
Rodriguez, Nerio	3	3	0	4.06	11	8	51	47	5	17	33
Romano, Mike	3	3	0	4.33	10	8	54	51	7	27	27
Schaffer, Trevor	1	2	0	5.10	21	0	30	36	5	20	11
Smith, Brian	2	2	3	3.98	31	0	43	45	6	16	32
Spoljaric, Paul	2	4	0	5.40	37	4	65	67	9	35	66
Stevenson, Jason	2	2	0	4.76	7	7	34	34	3	18	19
Wells, David	14	7	0	4.48	27	27	181	188	24	41	133
Yennaco, Jay	2	2	0	4.85	7	7	39	43	5	16	20

▶ THE INSIDER 2000

2000 PROJECTIONS

NATIONAL LEAGUE

Arizona Diamondbacks

BATTERS

PLAYER	BA	G	AB	R	H	2B	3B	HR	RBI	BB	SO	SB	CS	Sa	OBA
Barajas, Rod	.258	32	128	16	33	8	0	3	19	5	22	1	0	.391	.258
Bell, Jay	.272	152	573	108	156	30	5	30	94	78	123	6	4	.499	.360
Clark, Kevin	.257	21	74	7	19	4	1	1	11	4	18	0	0	.378	.257
Colbrunn, Greg	.303	83	175	22	53	9	2	5	27	12	31	2	2	.463	.358
Conti, Jason	.269	31	119	21	32	5	2	2	12	12	25	4	0	.395	.269
Dellucci, Dave	.303	83	208	32	63	11	4	2	26	18	49	2	2	.423	.367
Diaz, Edwin	.262	29	107	16	28	6	0	2	11	4	24	1	0	.374	.262
Durazo, Erubiel	.311	85	254	48	79	6	3	17	46	40	67	2	2	.559	.402
Finley, Steve	.259	138	528	87	137	30	7	24	81	49	86	9	3	.479	.324
Fox, Andy	.268	94	287	39	77	12	3	6	30	31	61	6	3	.394	.358
Frias, Hanley	.266	102	214	39	57	4	3	2	22	38	28	5	4	.341	.377
Gann, Jamie	.257	17	70	11	18	4	1	1	9	5	27	1	0	.386	.257
Gilkey, Bernard	.261	79	218	30	57	13	1	6	32	29	47	3	3	.413	.350
Gonzalez, Luis	.299	154	588	97	176	39	4	22	91	63	62	10	6	.491	.370
Harris, Lenny	.294	84	160	17	47	10	0	2	17	8	9	3	2	.394	.329
Huckaby, Ken	.263	11	38	4	10	2	0	0	4	1	4	0	0	.316	.263
Johnson, Keith	.231	23	78	12	18	4	0	2	9	5	19	0	0	.359	.231
Klassen, Danny	.240	26	96	13	23	5	1	2	11	7	27	1	0	.375	.240
Lee, Travis	.255	112	381	55	97	15	2	12	51	54	66	12	2	.399	.346
Maddox, Garry	.255	27	106	15	27	6	2	3	14	6	27	4	0	.434	.255
Matos, Julius	.271	13	48	6	13	2	1	1	4	1	5	1	0	.417	.271
Miller, Damian	.276	93	304	35	84	20	1	10	45	19	80	0	0	.447	.320
Patterson, Jarrod	.256	44	160	24	41	11	1	4	21	19	30	2	0	.412	.256
Powell, Dante	.258	45	120	16	31	8	1	4	14	9	29	10	0	.442	.258
Rexrode, Jackie	.254	36	122	19	31	4	2	1	11	17	19	5	0	.344	.254
Ryan, Robert	.234	44	141	20	33	8	1	5	24	15	30	1	0	.411	.234
Sell, Chip	.272	24	81	11	22	4	1	2	9	4	19	3	0	.420	.272
Spivey, Junior	.233	31	116	22	27	6	2	2	11	20	23	7	0	.371	.233
Stinnett, Kelly	.246	94	285	37	70	14	0	13	38	29	83	1	1	.432	.324
Ward, Turner	.272	43	92	10	25	4	1	3	14	10	12	2	1	.435	.343
Williams, Matt	.285	143	568	85	162	32	2	29	111	39	93	4	1	.502	.331
Wolff, Mike	.231	16	52	6	12	3	0	1	6	8	15	1	0	.346	.231
Womack, Tony	.287	125	526	86	151	22	8	3	37	40	70	57	9	.376	.336
Young, Ernie	.227	36	119	15	27	5	0	6	19	12	39	1	0	.420	.227

PITCHERS

PLAYER	W	L	SV	ERA	G	GS	IP	H	HR	BB	SO
Anderson, Brian	8	5	1	4.57	31	19	132	145	21	23	69
Andrews, Jeff	2	2	1	4.50	20	5	42	47	3	13	19
Benes, Andy	11	10	0	4.47	28	27	169	175	23	64	126
Bierbrodt, Nick	4	4	0	4.37	14	14	68	68	6	34	47
Carlson, Dan	2	2	0	3.86	11	5	35	33	5	12	29
Chouinard, Bobby	4	4	0	3.96	37	5	75	79	9	19	49

PLAYER	W	L	SV	ERA	G	GS	IP	H	HR	BB	SO
Clemons, Chris	2	2	0	3.73	27	2	41	37	5	21	38
Crews, Jason	2	2	0	4.78	20	3	32	38	4	12	15
Daal, Omar	13	11	0	3.81	31	31	208	193	19	76	150
Dace, Derek	3	3	0	4.31	37	3	48	49	3	19	26
Figueroa, Nelson	4	4	0	4.16	13	11	67	69	9	22	46
Holmes, Darren	4	3	0	4.18	51	0	56	62	5	24	39
Johnson, Randy	17	9	0	2.92	33	33	253	205	26	78	341
Kim, Byung-Hyun	2	4	2	4.68	46	0	50	37	4	37	56
Knott, Eric	3	3	0	4.83	9	8	54	68	4	14	23
Mantei, Matt	2	4	33	3.17	70	0	71	50	4	46	99
Mayo, Blake	1	1	0	4.76	13	0	17	21	1	7	9
Michalak, Chris	3	3	0	4.41	25	3	49	49	5	21	30
Norris, Ben	4	4	0	4.44	12	9	71	81	8	32	43
Olson, Gregg	6	4	14	3.92	62	0	62	57	7	26	46
Padilla, Vicente	5	5	0	4.23	24	11	83	100	7	25	44
Patterson, John	4	4	0	4.04	13	11	69	65	9	28	65
Penny, Brad	4	4	0	4.00	14	12	72	75	7	21	66
Plesac, Dan	3	4	1	4.86	73	0	50	51	7	18	59
Randolph, Stephen	3	3	0	4.34	13	12	58	56	5	36	36
Reynoso, Armando	10	6	0	4.41	29	25	157	166	17	64	78
Ruebel, Matt	2	2	0	4.50	8	4	30	30	5	11	18
Sabel, Erik	4	4	1	4.37	27	7	68	83	5	26	31
Sanchez, Martin	4	4	1	4.07	32	8	73	73	8	32	46
Schroeffel, Scott	1	1	0	4.13	15	1	24	23	3	10	16
Stottlemyre, Todd	7	5	0	4.06	19	19	113	114	13	44	95
Swindell, Greg	4	2	1	3.27	65	0	66	62	8	21	48
Tuttle, Dave	1	2	0	4.50	11	3	26	25	2	12	14

Atlanta Braves

BATTERS

PLAYER	BA	G	AB	R	H	2B	3B	HR	RBI	BB	SO	SB	CS	Sa	OBA
Boone, Bret	.260	134	511	78	133	33	1	18	63	43	99	10	6	.434	.321
Fabregas, Jorge	.235	82	221	20	52	9	1	3	26	22	32	0	0	.326	.305
Garcia, Freddy	.245	61	155	22	38	8	0	9	27	10	48	0	1	.471	.293
Glavine, Mike	.220	29	82	10	18	5	0	4	11	11	21	0	0	.427	.220
Goodell, Steve	.231	33	108	17	25	6	1	4	15	14	23	2	0	.417	.231
Guillen, Ozzie	.271	67	188	22	51	12	1	1	18	14	15	2	2	.362	.319
Hernandez, Jose	.266	153	485	77	129	21	4	20	65	46	139	8	4	.449	.333
Hunter, Brian	.245	108	188	26	46	13	1	6	29	25	41	0	1	.420	.342
Jones, Andruw	.267	162	569	90	152	32	5	26	84	63	111	24	10	.478	.346
Jones, Chipper	.299	162	596	113	178	37	2	38	107	108	91	21	4	.559	.404
Jordan, Brian	.288	137	510	87	147	26	4	20	92	41	67	13	6	.473	.347
Klesko, Ryan	.278	136	428	61	119	28	2	21	78	53	77	5	3	.500	.358
Lackey, Steve	.255	13	51	7	13	3	0	1	5	3	11	1	0	.373	.255
Lockhart, Keith	.274	67	135	19	37	5	1	3	17	14	16	1	1	.393	.342
Lombard, George	.226	51	146	18	33	7	2	5	19	23	72	10	0	.404	.226
Lopez, Javy	.292	79	291	40	85	17	1	16	55	22	50	1	2	.522	.346
Matos, Pascual	.273	17	55	5	15	2	0	1	7	2	14	1	0	.364	.273
Myers, Greg	.264	82	197	21	52	8	0	5	25	24	34	0	0	.381	.342
Nixon, Otis	.275	27	80	14	22	2	1	0	5	10	10	10	2	.325	.352
Norris, Dax	.227	20	66	8	15	4	0	2	9	6	12	0	0	.379	.227
Pendergrass, Tyrone	.250	14	48	8	12	2	0	1	4	5	10	2	0	.354	.250
Perez, Eddie	.247	85	263	29	65	15	0	8	36	19	58	2	0	.395	.247
Simon, Randall	.310	113	268	32	83	19	0	6	32	20	30	2	2	.448	.357
Smith, Demond	.259	26	81	12	21	3	1	1	10	9	17	4	0	.358	.259
Weiss, Walt	.259	82	239	37	62	12	3	1	23	36	40	5	2	.347	.357

PLAYER	BA	G	AB	R	H	2B	3B	HR	RBI	BB	SO	SB	CS	Sa	OBA
Williams, Gerald	.279	138	391	66	109	23	1	14	57	26	64	17	9	.450	.330

PITCHERS

PLAYER	W	L	SV	ERA	G	GS	IP	H	HR	BB	SO
Beasley, Raymond	4	3	1	3.92	38	4	62	59	6	18	45
Bergman, Sean	6	6	0	4.75	26	17	110	132	11	31	57
Carlyle, Ken	1	2	0	4.97	7	4	29	33	4	16	11
Cather, Mike	1	1	0	4.15	10	0	13	11	1	5	9
Chen, Bruce	6	5	0	3.99	22	16	97	83	15	38	82
Dishman, Richard	4	4	0	4.15	14	10	65	67	9	27	51
Ebert, Derrin	4	4	0	4.44	14	11	73	85	7	23	33
Glavine, Tom	13	8	0	3.70	30	30	202	209	15	71	126
Maddux, Greg	16	8	0	3.20	31	31	205	218	13	34	144
Manzano, Adrian	5	4	1	4.00	56	4	81	89	9	32	56
Marquis, Jason	4	4	0	4.50	16	14	72	68	9	38	38
McGlinchy, Kevin	7	3	0	3.12	69	0	75	74	6	34	72
Millwood, Kevin	19	9	0	3.31	34	34	234	199	24	68	212
Mulholland, Terry	8	8	1	4.21	39	22	156	175	18	45	82
Perez, Odaliz	4	7	0	5.55	21	20	107	111	14	58	92
Remlinger, Mike	7	5	1	3.90	73	0	83	75	10	41	80
Rocker, John	4	6	39	2.69	79	0	77	52	6	43	106
Seanez, Rudy	6	2	3	3.81	62	0	59	53	4	25	54
Shumate, Jacob	3	3	0	4.27	14	10	59	42	6	60	41
Smoltz, John	13	7	0	3.36	30	30	190	177	14	46	172
Speier, Justin	0	2	0	5.63	32	0	48	48	14	23	38
Springer, Russ	3	2	1	4.02	58	0	56	45	5	29	62
Winkelsas, Joe	3	3	3	4.25	50	1	55	68	5	28	28
Yankosky, Leonard	3	4	0	4.71	12	9	63	74	3	26	30

Chicago Cubs

BATTERS

PLAYER	BA	G	AB	R	H	2B	3B	HR	RBI	BB	SO	SB	CS	Sa	OBA
Alexander, Manny	.269	83	186	23	50	10	2	2	18	12	45	5	0	.376	.315
Almanzar, Richard	.261	34	111	17	29	4	1	1	9	10	14	6	0	.342	.261
Andrews, Shane	.221	111	344	39	76	16	0	17	51	47	106	1	2	.416	.312
Blauser, Jeff	.250	76	192	33	48	7	2	6	21	28	47	2	1	.401	.360
Brock, Tarrik	.236	31	106	18	25	5	1	2	8	19	40	3	0	.358	.236
Brown, Roosevelt	.255	80	259	31	66	19	1	12	45	16	66	4	0	.475	.255
Cline, Pat	.235	34	102	10	24	7	0	2	15	9	31	0	0	.363	.235
Encarnacion, Angelo	.250	11	40	4	10	3	0	0	6	2	7	1	0	.325	.250
Gaetti, Gary	.246	70	203	23	50	11	1	8	33	17	35	1	1	.429	.310
Gazarek, Marty	.264	47	159	15	42	11	1	6	23	5	15	1	0	.459	.264
Grace, Mark	.303	137	509	84	154	34	4	13	75	73	40	3	4	.462	.387
Hill, Glenallen	.291	91	258	40	75	13	1	15	46	19	56	3	1	.523	.339
Jennings, Robin	.251	45	175	26	44	10	2	6	27	14	28	3	0	.434	.251
Johnson, Lance	.284	81	289	44	82	10	5	2	21	31	20	12	5	.374	.352
King, Brad	.250	24	60	8	15	3	0	0	7	11	11	1	0	.300	.250
King, Brett	.203	23	69	11	14	3	0	2	6	15	24	2	0	.333	.203
Liniak, Cole	.241	49	174	24	42	11	0	5	19	17	34	0	0	.391	.241
Meyers, Chad	.268	58	213	35	57	14	1	1	17	22	40	12	0	.357	.268
Molina, Jose	.258	32	97	10	25	5	0	1	11	8	29	0	0	.340	.258
Morandini, Mickey	.274	113	387	57	106	17	3	4	33	45	56	7	4	.364	.356
Nelson, Bry	.243	38	140	18	34	6	1	4	21	11	19	2	0	.386	.243
Nieves, Jose	.256	62	223	27	57	13	2	5	29	12	42	3	0	.399	.256
Polanco, Enohel	.256	28	86	11	22	5	1	1	8	5	26	2	0	.372	.256
Porter, Bo	.235	56	183	30	43	8	1	9	22	23	67	4	0	.437	.235

2000 PROJECTIONS

PLAYER	BA	G	AB	R	H	2B	3B	HR	RBI	BB	SO	SB	CS	Sa	OBA
Quinlan, Tom	.236	25	89	11	21	5	0	3	10	7	36	0	0	.393	.236
Reed, Jeff	.272	92	228	31	62	14	1	6	30	36	51	1	1	.421	.373
Rennhack, Mike	.245	36	106	12	26	6	0	2	10	17	33	1	0	.358	.245
Rodriguez, Henry	.275	131	447	64	123	26	1	27	85	53	117	2	4	.519	.351
Santiago, Benito	.260	101	323	28	84	17	2	8	36	28	70	1	1	.399	.321
Sosa, Sammy	.276	158	619	109	171	22	2	56	134	67	161	11	8	.590	.346
Speed, Dorian	.239	41	142	21	34	6	2	4	17	8	43	5	0	.394	.239
Stahoviak, Scott	.213	34	108	18	23	6	0	5	15	15	42	1	0	.407	.213
Vieira, Scott	.258	44	159	19	41	14	1	3	18	16	53	2	0	.415	.258
Walker, Ronald	.210	36	105	14	22	7	0	3	14	13	36	1	0	.362	.210
White, Derrick	.240	30	104	14	25	6	0	3	15	9	25	1	0	.385	.240
Wilson, Brandon	.248	28	109	17	27	6	1	2	10	7	21	5	0	.376	.248
Zuleta, Julio	.258	51	186	25	48	12	1	7	33	12	57	1	0	.446	.258

PITCHERS

PLAYER	W	L	SV	ERA	G	GS	IP	H	HR	BB	SO
Adams, Terry	6	5	13	4.30	53	0	67	67	7	33	61
Aguilera, Rick	7	5	14	3.57	61	0	68	61	8	14	50
Ayala, Bobby	2	7	0	4.61	64	0	80	81	10	35	76
Barker, Richie	3	3	1	4.32	38	1	50	48	4	21	29
Bowie, Micah	4	4	0	4.13	16	13	72	71	6	23	60
Cole, Victor	1	1	0	3.96	14	0	25	23	2	16	17
Downs, Scott	4	4	0	3.77	14	11	74	77	6	33	77
Farnsworth, Kyle	5	9	0	4.98	27	21	130	139	28	52	70
Gajkowski, Steve	2	2	1	4.05	30	0	40	42	5	13	25
Gissell, Christopher	2	3	0	5.05	8	8	41	46	4	24	20
Guthrie, Mark	1	2	2	4.98	55	0	56	57	8	24	43
Heredia, Felix	4	2	1	4.81	77	0	58	60	5	31	55
Hernandez, Elvin	3	3	0	4.67	10	9	54	61	6	17	29
Juelsgaard, Jarod	1	1	0	4.76	5	2	17	17	2	5	9
Karchner, Matt	3	2	0	4.15	34	0	39	37	5	20	26
King, Ray	0	0	0	5.46	26	0	28	28	5	25	13
Lacy, Kerry	2	2	0	4.14	20	2	37	37	2	16	23
Lieber, Jon	9	12	0	4.29	29	29	189	209	26	45	166
Lorraine, Andrew	4	5	0	4.44	14	12	81	89	10	24	44
Manning, David	2	2	0	4.39	9	6	41	39	3	19	22
McNichol, Brian	3	3	0	4.12	11	10	59	61	7	18	38
Myers, Rodney	3	1	0	4.78	46	0	64	74	10	25	42
Negrette, Richard	2	2	0	4.50	23	0	32	28	2	27	19
Newman, Eric	2	2	1	3.95	28	0	41	33	3	26	37
Norton, Phillip	4	4	0	4.24	12	11	68	68	10	30	49
Quevedo, Ruben	4	4	0	4.09	14	12	77	69	13	26	64
Rain, Steve	4	4	6	3.84	63	0	68	71	5	29	62
Ricketts, Chad	4	3	2	3.63	53	0	62	55	8	21	62
Sanders, Scott	4	6	2	5.57	54	5	84	92	16	38	72
Schutz, Carl	2	1	0	4.00	21	0	27	27	2	15	20
Serafini, Dan	4	2	1	5.90	39	4	58	73	8	26	24
Tapani, Kevin	8	8	0	4.78	22	22	128	141	14	34	74
Trachsel, Steve	8	11	0	5.06	27	27	160	171	24	55	118
Watkins, Scott	1	1	0	4.15	19	1	26	24	4	11	19
Woodall, Brad	1	2	0	4.50	7	4	26	26	4	9	14
Yoder, Jeff	4	4	0	4.18	15	12	71	71	6	43	48
Young, Danny	2	2	0	3.83	18	5	40	34	1	27	37

Cincinnati Reds

BATTERS

PLAYER	BA	G	AB	R	H	2B	3B	HR	RBI	BB	SO	SB	CS	Sa	OBA
Boone, Aaron	.282	138	461	56	130	27	5	12	71	31	80	16	5	.440	.336
Branson, Jeff	.250	31	88	11	22	4	1	1	11	8	21	0	0	.352	.250
Burress, Andy	.269	26	108	17	29	5	0	3	12	7	21	4	0	.398	.269
Cameron, Mike	.246	153	520	85	128	29	8	18	63	70	139	36	11	.437	.340
Casey, Sean	.309	156	582	94	180	40	3	22	94	62	84	0	2	.502	.381
Clark, Brady	.257	42	152	24	39	9	1	4	18	21	21	5	0	.408	.257
Cromer, D. T.	.256	57	223	29	57	13	1	10	37	15	49	1	0	.457	.256
Frank, Mike	.275	62	218	35	60	17	3	4	28	17	34	3	0	.436	.275
Hammonds, Jeffrey	.273	115	286	50	78	15	1	15	43	31	64	6	5	.490	.346
Hardtke, Jason	.267	57	210	30	56	15	1	5	25	15	28	2	0	.419	.267
Hiatt, Phil	.224	36	143	20	32	5	0	8	23	13	57	0	0	.427	.224
Hollins, Damon	.268	52	157	28	42	9	0	4	21	15	26	4	0	.401	.268
Ingram, Darron	.219	31	96	15	21	4	1	4	14	10	41	1	0	.406	.219
Johnson, Brian	.250	42	124	14	31	5	0	5	17	10	28	0	0	.411	.309
Larkin, Barry	.294	147	531	93	156	29	6	12	66	83	56	27	6	.439	.389
Larkin, Stephen	.272	36	92	11	25	5	1	1	13	10	19	2	0	.380	.272
Larue, Jason	.235	68	226	34	53	12	1	9	29	16	65	2	0	.416	.235
Lewis, Mark	.264	65	178	20	47	11	1	5	23	13	34	1	1	.421	.314
Monds, Wonder	.258	22	93	14	24	4	1	3	9	5	18	3	0	.419	.258
Morris, Hal	.298	33	84	9	25	6	0	0	9	6	12	0	0	.369	.341
Nevers, Tom	.237	28	97	13	23	5	0	4	14	3	23	1	0	.412	.237
Owens, J.	.203	19	59	8	12	2	0	3	8	9	22	1	0	.390	.203
Presto, Nick	.257	23	70	10	18	2	0	1	8	11	13	1	0	.329	.257
Reese, Pokey	.282	150	536	79	151	31	4	8	49	36	85	34	7	.399	.330
Robinson, Kerry	.301	38	143	25	43	6	3	0	15	5	21	10	0	.385	.301
Salzano, Jerry	.262	36	126	17	33	7	0	2	15	15	24	5	0	.365	.262
Saunders, Chris	.245	29	106	12	26	5	0	3	13	13	25	0	0	.377	.245
Snopek, Chris	.248	45	145	22	36	8	1	3	19	15	28	4	0	.379	.248
Stynes, Chris	.275	60	138	22	38	3	0	3	15	13	15	7	1	.362	.340
Sweeney, Mark	.269	102	223	34	60	11	2	6	28	34	43	1	0	.417	.269
Taubensee, Eddie	.295	132	427	57	126	24	1	17	79	37	78	0	1	.475	.348
Tucker, Michael	.258	115	310	51	80	14	4	10	40	36	83	9	4	.426	.338
Vaughn, Greg	.245	141	498	92	122	19	2	39	101	73	118	12	3	.526	.343
Whitmore, Darrell	.254	60	173	26	44	11	1	7	27	16	56	1	0	.451	.254
Williams, Jason	.264	47	182	27	48	13	1	3	18	17	29	2	0	.396	.264
Young, Dmitri	.296	125	399	62	118	31	2	12	58	34	73	3	2	.474	.351

PITCHERS

PLAYER	W	L	SV	ERA	G	GS	IP	H	HR	BB	SO
Atchley, Justin	3	3	0	4.59	9	9	51	71	6	11	27
Avery, Steve	8	7	0	5.17	21	21	108	100	13	72	55
Barrios, Manny	2	2	0	4.09	24	4	44	41	4	16	29
Belinda, Stan	3	3	2	4.33	36	0	52	46	9	22	51
Bell, Rob	4	4	0	4.03	13	13	76	90	8	20	60
Crowell, Jim	2	3	0	4.83	7	7	41	47	3	23	18
Donaldson, Bo	4	3	2	3.54	42	0	56	36	2	19	61
Etler, Todd	3	3	0	3.88	33	0	51	44	3	28	43
Flury, Pat	3	2	3	3.75	42	0	48	38	4	31	47
Glauber, Keith	2	3	0	4.60	8	6	43	48	3	10	23
Graves, Danny	6	5	24	3.50	70	0	103	93	9	46	61
Greene, Rick	2	3	1	4.79	35	0	47	53	3	23	20
Guzman, Juan	10	13	0	4.17	31	31	190	183	25	86	149
Harnisch, Pete	14	9	0	3.81	32	32	189	181	23	59	124
Harriger, Denny	2	2	0	4.63	6	6	35	40	3	9	18

2000 PROJECTIONS

PLAYER	W	L	SV	ERA	G	GS	IP	H	HR	BB	SO
Janzen, Marty	2	2	0	4.26	21	5	38	35	3	19	22
Klingenbeck, Scott	2	2	0	4.63	6	6	35	39	5	11	20
LeBlanc, Eric	2	2	0	4.85	10	4	39	41	4	13	19
MacRae, Scott	3	3	0	4.68	15	7	50	56	7	20	26
Mallard, Randi	1	2	0	4.97	6	6	29	32	2	15	15
Neagle, Denny	9	5	0	3.97	21	20	118	108	17	36	87
Parris, Steve	10	5	0	3.88	23	22	137	135	16	54	97
Priest, Eddie	3	3	0	4.58	11	8	53	67	6	12	28
Reyes, Dennys	2	3	2	4.23	69	1	66	60	5	42	73
Riedling, John	4	4	1	4.03	56	0	67	65	3	41	46
Sullivan, Scott	5	4	3	3.84	72	0	103	88	11	41	79
Therneau, David	2	2	0	4.89	6	6	35	40	6	12	17
Tolar, Kevin	2	2	0	3.82	27	1	33	31	1	24	32
Tomko, Brett	7	8	0	4.67	30	24	158	155	23	53	121
Villone, Ron	8	6	2	4.44	29	22	144	122	9	80	97
White, Gabe	2	3	0	4.35	51	0	62	63	12	15	56
Williamson, Scott	12	8	19	2.65	64	0	95	58	8	46	110

Colorado Rockies

BATTERS

PLAYER	BA	G	AB	R	H	2B	3B	HR	RBI	BB	SO	SB	CS	Sa	OBA
Abbott, Kurt	.276	104	294	42	81	19	2	8	41	17	76	3	2	.435	.315
Bair, Rod	.274	45	168	22	46	11	2	4	26	9	33	4	0	.435	.274
Barry, Jeff	.250	77	196	26	49	14	0	6	24	17	43	2	0	.413	.250
Barthol, Blake	.248	37	125	14	31	6	1	3	9	11	29	0	0	.384	.248
Berry, Mike	.227	26	88	10	20	4	1	2	11	7	21	0	0	.364	.227
Bichette, Dante	.303	137	541	86	164	35	2	26	111	38	72	7	5	.519	.347
Blanco, Henry	.244	94	279	33	68	13	3	7	31	37	42	1	1	.387	.332
Castilla, Vinny	.288	140	546	79	157	22	2	32	99	41	72	2	4	.511	.338
Clemente, Edgard	.245	73	229	30	56	15	2	10	37	12	66	2	0	.459	.245
Cotton, John	.240	35	125	19	30	7	0	6	17	6	42	1	0	.440	.240
Echevarria, Angel	.292	127	233	35	68	10	0	12	43	20	40	1	3	.489	.358
Feuerstein, Dave	.283	16	46	5	13	2	1	0	4	4	8	1	0	.370	.283
Gibson, Derrick	.248	37	125	19	31	5	2	5	19	8	32	2	0	.440	.248
Hajek, Dave	.255	11	47	6	12	3	0	1	4	2	4	1	0	.383	.255
Hatcher, Chris	.255	47	153	21	39	8	1	7	23	8	51	4	0	.458	.255
Helton, Todd	.304	162	576	100	175	37	4	31	105	62	68	5	5	.543	.375
Kelly, Mike	.247	28	85	13	21	5	1	2	10	9	26	2	0	.400	.247
Kirgan, Chris	.232	28	99	12	23	6	0	3	18	13	29	0	0	.384	.232
Lansing, Mike	.289	42	166	24	48	11	0	4	19	11	26	3	1	.428	.335
Light, Tal	.213	15	47	5	10	4	0	2	6	3	26	0	0	.426	.213
Manwaring, Kirt	.270	48	137	14	37	6	1	1	13	15	26	0	1	.350	.353
Pena, Elvis	.263	42	137	19	36	8	2	1	10	16	29	6	0	.372	.263
Perez, Neifi	.288	144	608	92	175	25	10	10	62	30	57	10	5	.411	.320
Petersen, Chris	.256	12	39	6	10	2	0	1	3	3	11	0	0	.385	.256
Petrick, Ben	.226	70	234	36	53	10	2	11	40	26	59	5	0	.427	.226
Phillips, J. R.	.217	53	166	21	36	6	0	10	24	13	62	1	0	.434	.217
Shumpert, Terry	.325	104	277	56	90	25	3	10	37	31	43	13	0	.545	.390
Sosa, Juan	.268	33	123	17	33	5	1	2	10	7	19	7	0	.374	.268
Tatum, Jim	.262	21	65	8	17	3	0	2	10	4	18	0	0	.400	.262
Walker, Larry	.344	137	479	110	165	33	4	33	99	59	58	14	4	.637	.424
Watkins, Pat	.282	51	131	14	37	9	1	1	15	9	27	1	0	.389	.282

PITCHERS

PLAYER	W	L	SV	ERA	G	GS	IP	H	HR	BB	SO
Astacio, Pedro	13	10	0	5.14	27	27	182	200	30	59	158

PLAYER	W	L	SV	ERA	G	GS	IP	H	HR	BB	SO
Bailey, Roger	1	1	0	4.91	3	2	11	11	1	5	6
Beltran, Rigo	1	1	0	4.42	42	0	53	59	7	23	58
Bevel, Bobby	2	2	1	4.14	27	1	37	37	4	14	27
Bohanon, Brian	8	9	0	5.06	24	24	144	155	19	62	93
Bost, Heath	3	3	0	4.09	24	4	55	66	5	7	36
Brester, Jason	3	3	0	4.35	10	7	60	64	6	19	40
Brownson, Mark	4	4	0	4.50	12	12	68	69	13	13	43
DeJean, Mike	2	2	0	5.77	49	0	53	63	8	23	25
DeWitt, Scott	3	3	0	3.94	33	1	48	61	1	15	39
Dipoto, Jerry	4	4	1	4.28	58	0	80	83	8	36	61
Farmer, Michael	1	1	0	4.85	3	2	13	15	2	4	7
Hackman, Luther	3	4	0	4.36	11	10	64	65	6	30	44
Holzemer, Mark	2	2	0	4.03	24	0	29	34	4	10	19
Jacobs, Ryan	2	2	0	4.63	9	6	35	34	3	19	23
Jones, Bobby	6	8	0	5.60	28	19	106	118	17	62	73
Kile, Darryl	7	8	0	5.31	23	23	134	145	19	65	90
Lee, David	3	2	0	3.88	43	0	58	52	5	35	45
Leskanic, Curtis	6	2	0	4.97	56	0	76	77	7	42	65
Martin, Chandler	3	3	0	4.32	8	7	50	50	5	21	33
Porzio, Mike	0	0	0	6.62	36	0	34	42	11	20	23
Randall, Scott	3	3	0	4.35	11	9	60	66	4	23	45
Rawitzer, Kevin	2	2	0	4.14	17	3	37	42	3	15	24
Rossiter, Mike	4	3	1	3.86	43	0	63	56	4	34	50
Saipe, Mike	3	3	0	4.25	11	11	53	60	11	14	28
Shoemaker, Stephen	2	2	0	4.50	8	8	42	45	4	21	20
Stoops, Jim	3	3	0	4.31	30	3	48	47	6	28	25
Thomson, John	3	8	0	5.56	20	19	89	103	12	34	55
Veres, Dave	3	5	28	4.37	66	0	70	75	10	31	64
Wainhouse, Dave	1	0	0	5.87	31	0	46	55	8	24	28
Walker, Pete	2	2	1	3.97	26	0	34	33	5	14	26
Walls, Doug	3	3	0	4.18	10	9	56	63	6	18	44
Wright, Jamey	5	6	0	4.69	16	15	96	104	10	41	42

Florida Marlins

BATTERS

PLAYER	BA	G	AB	R	H	2B	3B	HR	RBI	BB	SO	SB	CS	Sa	OBA
Aven, Bruce	.284	144	391	59	111	19	2	12	70	44	84	3	0	.435	.364
Bates, Fletcher	.250	20	76	10	19	4	1	1	8	6	18	2	0	.368	.250
Bautista, Danny	.284	91	218	33	62	12	1	5	26	7	35	3	0	.417	.307
Berg, Dave	.295	116	308	40	91	19	1	3	28	31	65	3	2	.393	.363
Castillo, Luis	.289	132	492	74	142	21	4	0	28	67	91	44	16	.348	.373
Castro, Ramon	.226	39	133	14	30	8	0	5	19	10	30	0	0	.398	.226
Clapinski, Chris	.241	51	141	19	34	7	3	3	13	13	34	2	0	.397	.241
Dunwoody, Todd	.266	62	218	29	58	13	5	4	22	11	63	3	0	.427	.266
Erickson, Matt	.258	19	66	7	17	3	0	0	6	9	14	0	0	.303	.258
Floyd, Cliff	.284	82	296	43	84	22	1	12	50	30	56	10	7	.486	.352
Funaro, Joe	.274	32	117	14	32	6	0	1	13	10	12	2	0	.350	.274
Garcia, Amaury	.237	39	152	23	36	8	2	4	12	11	33	4	0	.395	.237
Garcia, Guillermo	.250	52	180	22	45	7	2	7	20	13	45	1	0	.428	.250
Gil, Benji	.231	22	78	12	18	5	0	3	10	4	23	2	0	.410	.231
Gonzalez, Alex	.276	135	548	81	151	27	8	15	59	18	120	3	5	.436	.312
Gulan, Mike	.222	21	72	8	16	5	0	3	10	2	25	1	0	.417	.222
Hastings, Lionel	.244	14	41	5	10	1	0	1	3	6	11	1	0	.341	.244
Hyers, Tim	.214	73	103	10	22	5	1	2	14	18	16	0	0	.340	.328
Jones, Jaime	.247	26	89	12	22	5	0	2	9	13	31	1	0	.371	.247
Kleinz, Larry	.231	27	78	8	18	5	0	1	11	10	17	1	0	.333	.231

PLAYER	BA	G	AB	R	H	2B	3B	HR	RBI	BB	SO	SB	CS	Sa	OBA
Kotsay, Mark	.281	136	473	58	133	22	8	8	52	29	50	8	5	.412	.319
Kuilan, Robles	.265	15	49	5	13	2	0	0	7	2	10	0	0	.306	.265
Lee, Derrek	.241	69	232	32	56	13	1	9	38	21	77	2	0	.422	.241
Lobaton, Jose	.255	18	47	7	12	3	0	0	4	4	16	1	0	.319	.255
Lowell, Mike	.260	107	334	35	87	16	0	13	51	28	75	0	0	.425	.323
Millar, Kevin	.284	106	352	48	100	17	4	9	67	40	64	1	0	.432	.361
Norton, Chris	.208	43	144	19	30	6	0	10	25	18	53	0	0	.458	.208
Orie, Kevin	.255	79	255	30	65	17	1	6	30	24	44	1	1	.400	.325
Ozuna, Pablo	.271	25	107	13	29	5	1	1	9	3	13	5	0	.364	.271
Ramirez, Julio	.257	28	109	16	28	6	2	2	12	7	35	8	0	.404	.257
Redmond, Mike	.311	90	264	24	82	12	0	2	29	25	37	0	0	.379	.381
Robertson, Ryan	.250	19	56	5	14	3	0	0	5	8	10	0	0	.304	.250
Rolison, Nate	.252	40	143	20	36	6	0	5	19	19	44	0	0	.399	.252
Roskos, John	.238	44	147	18	35	10	0	5	19	11	41	1	0	.408	.238
Wilson, Preston	.272	154	489	67	133	21	4	25	69	47	159	11	4	.485	.343

PITCHERS

PLAYER	W	L	SV	ERA	G	GS	IP	H	HR	BB	SO
Alberro, Jose	1	1	0	4.32	11	2	25	27	3	7	16
Alfonseca, Antonio	4	6	21	3.76	74	0	79	85	6	33	49
Almanza, Armando	0	2	0	1.95	33	0	37	20	2	22	47
Almonte, Hector	0	5	0	4.37	35	0	35	48	2	14	19
Arroyo, Luis	3	2	0	4.00	32	0	45	44	5	20	31
Benz, Jake	2	2	0	4.07	27	2	42	44	5	26	32
Billingsley, Brent	4	3	0	4.14	15	11	63	60	7	24	35
Burgus, Travis	3	3	1	3.94	36	5	48	50	5	20	38
Burnett, A. J.	4	5	0	4.22	17	13	81	77	8	44	65
Cames, Aaron	2	3	0	4.60	10	7	43	45	7	19	25
Corbin, Archie	1	1	0	5.18	32	0	40	41	3	30	46
Cornelius, Reid	2	3	0	4.68	13	5	50	51	5	19	30
Cornelius, Reid	3	3	0	4.31	8	8	48	50	2	19	31
Darensbourg, Vic	0	3	0	5.74	77	0	47	49	4	23	35
Dempster, Ryan	6	9	0	5.02	25	25	147	152	20	94	121
Drumright, Mike	2	2	0	4.50	8	5	34	30	4	14	18
Duncan, Geoff	4	4	1	3.88	46	6	72	68	9	39	51
Edmondson, Brian	4	6	1	5.18	58	0	80	86	10	37	47
Fernandez, Alex	9	8	0	3.65	25	25	148	141	14	45	109
Gonzalez, Gabe	3	3	0	4.13	38	1	48	49	3	13	34
Henderson, Scott	4	4	1	3.80	38	4	71	63	4	25	58
Knotts, Gary	4	4	0	4.25	11	10	72	75	11	31	47
Leese, Brandon	2	3	0	4.70	11	5	46	56	4	10	25
Looper, Braden	3	3	0	3.95	71	0	82	97	7	31	50
Meadows, Brian	10	12	0	5.27	26	26	152	183	24	45	66
Medina, Rafael	2	3	0	5.52	38	0	44	44	5	35	32
Menhart, Paul	1	2	0	4.50	7	5	26	31	2	10	14
Mercedes, Jose	3	3	0	4.67	10	9	52	66	5	14	21
Nunez, Vladimir	6	9	1	4.22	39	11	96	85	9	48	75
Ojala, Kirt	1	1	0	4.24	5	2	17	18	2	8	9
Pageler, Mick	3	3	0	4.09	33	2	55	70	4	13	40
Rodgers, Bobby	2	2	0	4.30	9	7	44	47	4	22	33
Sanchez, Jesus	4	5	0	5.14	54	9	70	73	11	45	56
Springer, Dennis	5	13	1	4.99	32	25	166	186	23	61	68
Stanifer, Robby	3	3	1	4.04	39	3	49	50	7	19	31
Tejera, Michael	5	4	0	3.83	14	12	80	83	8	27	65
Villano, Mike	2	2	0	4.03	18	1	29	36	7	8	20

▶ THE INSIDER 2000

Houston Astros

BATTERS

PLAYER	BA	G	AB	R	H	2B	3B	HR	RBI	BB	SO	SB	CS	Sa	OBA
Alexander, Chad	.260	41	150	16	39	10	1	4	17	13	35	2	0	.420	.260
Bagwell, Jeff	.285	160	565	127	161	34	1	38	118	129	111	26	9	.550	.423
Bako, Paul	.274	80	241	19	66	14	1	2	22	26	67	1	1	.365	.341
Bell, Derek	.272	108	427	61	116	23	1	12	63	39	99	13	4	.415	.335
Berkman, Lance	.261	77	249	35	65	15	0	8	44	35	64	7	0	.418	.261
Betzsold, Jim	.224	33	107	19	24	7	0	4	15	12	39	2	0	.402	.224
Biggio, Craig	.297	141	562	108	167	45	1	15	67	69	93	32	10	.461	.386
Bogar, Tim	.240	111	292	40	70	15	2	4	29	34	56	3	4	.346	.324
Burns, Kevin	.252	45	139	20	35	7	1	4	21	15	35	2	0	.403	.252
Caminiti, Ken	.268	73	254	45	68	13	0	14	48	41	57	5	1	.484	.368
Dallimore, Brian	.253	24	87	13	22	4	0	2	6	5	18	3	0	.368	.253
Eusebio, Tony	.277	104	314	29	87	13	0	3	39	38	63	0	0	.347	.356
Everett, Carl	.299	136	489	80	146	33	3	21	94	47	100	23	9	.507	.365
Gutierrez, Ricky	.269	87	283	34	76	11	4	1	28	34	49	5	4	.346	.351
Hernandez, Carlos	.293	37	123	20	36	5	0	0	15	9	26	6	0	.333	.293
Hidalgo, Richard	.246	119	402	53	99	27	2	15	60	53	77	8	5	.435	.335
Javier, Stan	.290	112	341	53	99	14	3	3	34	41	54	16	5	.375	.365
Johnson, A. J.	.266	21	64	7	17	3	0	2	7	3	17	1	0	.406	.266
Johnson, J. J.	.233	35	116	14	27	7	0	4	17	12	38	2	0	.397	.233
Johnson, Ric	.279	13	43	4	12	3	0	0	4	2	7	1	0	.349	.279
Johnson, Russ	.279	112	215	32	60	13	0	7	31	27	45	3	4	.437	.356
Knorr, Randy	.253	52	174	16	44	11	1	5	21	9	35	0	0	.414	.253
Lugo, Julio	.263	41	156	22	41	7	1	3	12	13	22	6	0	.378	.263
Mieske, Matt	.291	92	175	28	51	8	0	7	27	12	35	0	0	.457	.333
Miller, Ryan	.283	17	46	5	13	2	0	0	6	2	9	1	0	.326	.283
Neal, Mike	.218	30	78	12	17	4	0	2	10	10	24	1	0	.346	.218
Perez, Jhonny	.250	30	108	14	27	6	2	2	10	7	21	2	0	.398	.250
Sanchez, Victor	.227	30	97	13	22	4	0	4	15	9	26	2	0	.392	.227
Saylor, Jamie	.240	34	100	12	24	5	2	1	12	11	30	2	0	.360	.240
Spiers, Bill	.286	126	374	58	107	22	5	4	41	48	49	10	4	.404	.369
Truby, Chris	.231	42	156	21	36	6	1	8	24	10	35	5	0	.436	.231
Villalobos, Carlos	.257	41	152	23	39	9	0	3	14	15	37	2	0	.375	.257
Ward, Daryle	.247	111	340	45	84	14	1	24	63	22	79	1	0	.506	.247

PITCHERS

PLAYER	W	L	SV	ERA	G	GS	IP	H	HR	BB	SO
Braswell, Bryan	3	3	0	4.42	9	7	53	55	8	17	34
Cabrera, Jose	4	4	1	3.89	52	3	74	63	6	22	51
Creek, Ryan	2	2	0	4.38	7	4	39	41	4	22	23
Diorio, Mike	2	2	0	4.62	28	0	39	41	5	15	15
Elarton, Scott	7	4	1	3.72	37	13	109	97	7	39	106
Ellis, Robert	2	2	0	4.65	5	5	31	32	4	9	18
Franklin, Wayne	4	4	5	3.91	70	5	76	73	7	38	51
Hampton, Mike	18	6	0	3.40	34	34	241	234	15	101	169
Henry, Doug	4	3	3	4.24	45	0	51	50	8	29	45
Holt, Chris	5	11	1	4.35	30	25	155	175	12	52	94
Huisman, Rick	2	2	0	3.71	23	0	34	27	4	10	37
Kester, Tim	2	2	0	4.38	21	4	37	48	5	10	21
Lima, Jose	17	10	0	3.91	32	32	228	240	29	39	172
McKnight, Tony	5	5	0	4.29	13	8	84	88	10	29	52
Meacham, Rusty	1	1	0	3.86	6	1	14	15	2	4	10
Miller, Trever	3	2	1	4.58	53	0	57	66	6	29	38
Miller, Wade	4	4	0	4.08	14	12	75	70	8	28	52
Mounce, Tony	3	3	0	3.79	32	4	57	56	5	32	54

2000 PROJECTIONS

PLAYER	W	L	SV	ERA	G	GS	IP	H	HR	BB	SO
O'Malley, Paul	1	1	0	4.09	11	4	22	20	3	13	17
Powell, Jay	6	5	4	4.07	66	0	73	75	4	38	70
Reynolds, Shane	14	11	0	3.94	31	31	201	223	21	39	174
Robertson, Jeromie	4	5	0	4.39	12	10	82	94	11	23	48
Root, Derek	3	3	0	4.33	9	7	52	54	5	25	36
Scanlan, Bob	0	1	0	5.40	3	1	10	12	1	4	4
Sikorski, Brian	3	3	0	4.34	10	10	56	56	8	19	36
Slusarski, Joe	1	1	0	4.50	11	1	18	22	2	4	9
Wagner, Billy	5	3	40	2.28	71	0	79	49	6	30	131
Wallace, Kent	2	2	1	4.05	27	1	40	41	6	11	27
Williams, Brian	2	2	0	4.91	49	0	66	69	6	39	47

Los Angeles Dodgers

BATTERS

PLAYER	BA	G	AB	R	H	2B	3B	HR	RBI	BB	SO	SB	CS	Sa	OBA
Allen, Lucas	.257	54	210	33	54	6	4	5	30	16	48	4	0	.395	.257
Beltre, Adrian	.268	162	541	80	145	27	4	16	67	58	106	17	6	.421	.343
Bocachica, Hiram	.253	51	198	30	50	8	4	4	22	22	35	9	0	.394	.253
Castro, Juan	.256	25	78	10	20	4	0	1	8	6	16	0	0	.346	.256
Chamberlain, Wes	.258	29	97	11	25	4	1	4	17	5	20	1	0	.443	.258
Cookson, Brent	.225	57	187	27	42	8	0	13	33	18	45	4	0	.476	.225
Cora, Alex	.269	39	119	17	32	4	3	1	13	4	19	2	0	.378	.269
Counsell, Craig	.252	57	143	20	36	7	1	1	14	17	20	1	0	.336	.333
Davis, Glenn	.257	47	171	25	44	11	1	3	22	24	54	2	0	.386	.257
Diaz, Juan	.270	60	230	34	62	17	1	7	42	21	83	0	0	.443	.270
Dubose, Brian	.241	31	83	10	20	5	1	1	12	11	23	2	0	.361	.241
Gil, Geronimo	.238	66	214	25	51	14	1	8	31	26	44	1	0	.425	.238
Gilbert, Shawn	.237	23	80	13	19	5	0	1	8	9	19	4	0	.338	.237
Grijak, Kevin	.268	41	138	17	37	8	0	5	23	5	21	1	0	.435	.268
Grudzielanek, Mark	.305	125	492	65	150	25	3	7	47	26	64	11	6	.411	.350
Hansen, Dave	.267	107	135	16	36	8	1	2	19	28	26	0	1	.385	.398
Hollandsworth, Todd	.279	102	294	43	82	14	3	8	35	23	69	6	3	.429	.332
Hubbard, Trenidad	.304	57	92	17	28	4	0	2	9	10	21	4	2	.413	.375
Hundley, Todd	.219	116	360	49	79	14	0	22	56	49	115	3	1	.442	.317
Karros, Eric	.289	141	529	65	153	30	0	28	95	48	102	8	4	.505	.347
LoDuca, Paul	.244	48	127	16	31	2	0	4	15	13	12	1	3	.354	.322
Metcalfe, Mike	.272	43	158	25	43	8	1	1	18	20	20	14	0	.354	.272
Mondesi, Raul	.266	144	552	86	147	28	5	29	87	51	114	27	9	.493	.330
Moreta, Juan	.316	45	152	22	48	5	1	1	17	7	30	7	0	.382	.316
Mota, Tony	.264	72	254	39	67	19	1	9	45	25	49	7	0	.453	.264
Newson, Warren	.232	19	56	7	13	4	0	1	7	8	16	0	0	.357	.232
Ortiz, Hector	.255	17	51	5	13	2	0	1	6	3	9	0	0	.353	.255
Pena, Angel	.223	65	179	22	40	9	0	6	32	18	41	0	2	.374	.290
Riggs, Adam	.250	31	120	17	30	6	1	3	16	11	32	4	0	.392	.250
Saitta, Rich	.290	52	145	14	42	6	2	1	19	4	30	3	0	.379	.290
Sanford, Chance	.220	33	91	13	20	5	1	3	11	10	26	1	0	.396	.220
Sheffield, Gary	.283	149	523	92	148	22	1	29	92	102	61	14	6	.495	.402
Stovall, DaRond	.226	56	133	22	30	8	0	6	17	15	58	4	0	.421	.226
Vizcaino, Jose	.274	79	252	31	69	9	1	2	29	21	32	4	2	.341	.330
Warner, Mike	.259	54	166	24	43	11	3	2	17	23	30	7	0	.398	.259
White, Devon	.272	108	393	54	107	19	1	13	58	33	75	16	5	.425	.339
Young, Eric	.285	109	421	70	120	23	2	4	40	53	28	42	16	.378	.369

PITCHERS

PLAYER	W	L	SV	ERA	G	GS	IP	H	HR	BB	SO
Alvarez, Victor	3	4	0	4.58	9	8	59	67	6	12	38

▶ THE INSIDER 2000

PLAYER	W	L	SV	ERA	G	GS	IP	H	HR	BB	SO
Arnold, Jamie	2	4	1	5.37	35	3	67	77	6	32	25
Beckett, Robbie	1	1	0	3.86	5	3	21	16	2	13	18
Bochtler, Doug	0	1	0	5.52	28	0	31	29	6	19	20
Borbon, Pedro	4	3	1	3.86	78	0	56	45	4	28	42
Boskie, Shawn	1	1	0	4.50	3	2	14	16	2	5	8
Brown, Kevin	16	8	0	3.05	33	33	239	213	14	57	218
Checo, Robinson	3	2	0	3.72	12	9	46	38	8	21	43
Davis, Allen	2	3	0	4.60	10	7	47	53	5	17	26
Dreifort, Darren	10	11	0	4.56	27	26	162	158	15	65	137
Foster, Kris	3	2	1	3.80	29	0	45	39	3	23	38
Gagne, Eric	5	5	0	3.91	14	14	92	81	12	46	84
Garcia, Apostol	3	4	0	4.86	21	7	63	81	4	34	25
Garrett, Hal	3	3	0	4.24	23	4	51	40	5	31	34
Herges, Matt	3	3	0	4.15	13	4	52	51	7	18	30
Judd, Mike	4	3	0	4.08	15	8	64	59	10	22	57
Kubenka, Jeffrey	4	4	2	3.84	51	0	68	65	6	29	51
Maddux, Mike	2	2	0	4.05	53	0	60	63	5	21	42
Masaoka, Onan	2	4	1	4.43	56	0	69	57	8	49	63
Mills, Alan	3	4	0	4.06	67	0	71	65	9	46	50
Mitchell, Dean	2	2	0	4.09	23	5	44	46	5	20	33
Montgomery, Matthew	4	4	7	4.11	74	3	70	104	2	27	41
Osteen, Gavin	2	2	0	4.65	10	4	31	36	3	9	16
Park, Chan Ho	11	8	0	4.58	28	28	165	163	21	78	145
Pearsall, J. J.	1	2	0	4.33	21	0	27	23	3	15	20
Perez, Carlos	4	7	0	4.98	18	17	94	104	14	30	48
Ruffin, Johnny	3	3	2	3.60	47	0	55	45	8	28	56
Shaw, Jeff	2	5	33	2.70	66	0	70	66	6	15	46
Stone, Ricky	3	4	0	4.35	10	10	62	68	8	23	41
Valdes, Ismael	9	13	0	3.99	31	31	194	200	25	60	137
Weber, Neil	1	1	0	4.50	8	3	22	24	2	9	12
Williams, Jeffrey	3	3	0	4.42	19	7	59	64	6	22	32
Zamora, Peter	1	1	0	4.71	12	1	21	23	1	9	11

Milwaukee Brewers

BATTERS

PLAYER	BA	G	AB	R	H	2B	3B	HR	RBI	BB	SO	SB	CS	Sa	OBA
Alfano, Jeff	.240	32	96	7	23	6	0	2	11	13	30	1	0	.365	.240
Andreopoulos, Alex	.245	36	102	9	25	4	0	2	15	12	13	1	0	.343	.245
Azuaje, Jesus	.236	34	110	15	26	5	0	2	14	17	9	7	0	.336	.236
Banks, Brian	.252	101	202	32	51	7	1	5	22	24	57	5	1	.371	.329
Barker, Kevin	.250	72	252	41	63	12	2	10	44	27	61	1	0	.433	.250
Battle, Howard	.238	50	189	28	45	10	0	8	26	12	33	1	0	.418	.238
Belliard, Ronnie	.293	134	481	63	141	30	4	8	60	66	61	4	5	.422	.376
Benitez, Yamil	.230	35	100	13	23	6	1	4	16	9	33	2	0	.430	.230
Berry, Sean	.265	81	215	27	57	12	1	5	27	18	40	1	1	.400	.329
Burnitz, Jeromy	.260	135	484	81	126	29	2	31	98	76	121	8	4	.521	.369
Cancel, Robinson	.255	49	157	23	40	7	0	4	24	14	38	4	0	.376	.255
Cirillo, Jeff	.312	149	573	88	179	33	1	13	76	69	77	7	4	.442	.389
Collier, Lou	.258	82	190	22	49	10	2	2	25	19	44	3	2	.363	.327
Cromer, Brandon	.189	46	132	16	25	4	0	9	22	14	49	2	0	.424	.189
Elliott, Dave	.228	24	79	13	18	4	0	2	11	11	26	2	0	.354	.228
Green, Chad	.244	25	90	12	22	5	1	2	10	10	28	4	0	.389	.244
Grissom, Marquis	.276	130	504	71	139	24	2	14	66	37	87	18	7	.415	.324
Hughes, Bobby	.254	55	126	15	32	3	1	5	14	8	35	0	1	.413	.299
Iapoce, Anthony	.265	12	34	4	9	2	0	0	1	4	10	1	0	.324	.265
Jenkins, Geoff	.289	148	485	71	140	40	3	21	79	37	96	5	2	.513	.347

2000 PROJECTIONS

PLAYER	BA	G	AB	R	H	2B	3B	HR	RBI	BB	SO	SB	CS	Sa	OBA
Johnson, Adam	.260	28	104	12	27	6	0	3	16	7	23	1	0	.404	.260
Klimek, Joshua	.226	24	84	9	19	5	0	3	13	6	18	1	0	.393	.226
Kominek, Toby	.247	24	85	11	21	4	1	2	11	10	26	1	0	.388	.247
Krause, Scott	.269	47	175	19	47	9	2	5	30	11	44	2	0	.429	.269
Lopez, Mickey	.246	37	138	22	34	7	2	2	16	18	24	8	0	.370	.246
Loretta, Mark	.298	152	541	81	161	32	4	6	63	51	58	6	3	.405	.363
Macalutas, Jonathan	.260	29	96	15	25	6	0	2	14	12	12	1	0	.385	.260
Malloy, Marty	.260	43	150	19	39	8	0	3	12	17	22	5	0	.373	.260
Martinez, Greg	.272	29	103	20	28	3	1	1	7	14	15	8	0	.350	.272
Mouton, Lyle	.254	61	201	31	51	15	1	8	33	15	50	6	0	.458	.254
Nilsson, Dave	.286	123	381	55	109	20	1	19	64	50	64	1	2	.493	.368
Ochoa, Alex	.279	134	319	50	89	18	3	7	40	38	47	7	4	.420	.361
Ortiz, Luis	.257	32	101	12	26	4	0	4	11	8	16	0	0	.416	.257
Perez, Santiago	.244	36	135	18	33	7	2	2	12	10	37	5	0	.370	.244
Roberts, Lonell	.286	26	98	16	28	5	1	1	10	8	25	3	0	.388	.286
Rumfield, Toby	.257	44	152	21	39	9	0	6	23	11	27	0	0	.434	.257
Schall, Gene	.263	49	175	22	46	11	0	5	24	16	50	0	0	.411	.263
Sisco, Steve	.253	45	174	23	44	10	1	5	22	11	31	3	0	.408	.253
Sollmann, Scott	.280	34	118	19	33	2	3	1	5	19	23	8	0	.373	.280
Tyler, Brad	.239	48	163	24	39	7	1	7	26	23	47	5	0	.423	.239
Valentin, Jose	.236	92	275	43	65	13	2	10	36	42	62	6	4	.407	.337
Vina, Fernando	.296	39	159	22	47	9	1	2	13	13	10	5	3	.403	.365
Whatley, Gabe	.232	47	142	17	33	7	1	4	17	19	44	3	0	.380	.232
Williamson, Antone	.255	38	106	12	27	5	0	2	12	17	20	1	0	.358	.255
Zosky, Eddie	.259	31	112	14	29	5	1	3	11	5	22	1	0	.402	.259

PITCHERS

PLAYER	W	L	SV	ERA	G	GS	IP	H	HR	BB	SO
Abbott, Jim	4	8	0	5.97	23	17	95	114	15	45	42
Akin, Jay	3	3	0	4.22	27	5	49	54	5	18	30
Beck, Greg	2	2	0	4.38	7	5	39	40	6	12	20
Bere, Jason	7	3	0	5.47	25	20	97	105	13	64	66
Borowski, Joe	2	2	0	4.11	23	0	35	32	2	15	23
Brooks, Antone	3	3	0	4.15	40	0	52	55	2	20	30
Butler, Adam	2	2	1	4.25	29	2	36	43	4	11	23
Converse, Jim	2	2	1	4.09	18	2	33	32	4	15	21
Coppinger, Rocky	4	4	0	5.25	41	2	60	60	13	41	57
Dale, Carl	2	2	1	4.40	29	0	43	39	3	20	24
Eldred, Cal	3	7	0	5.70	22	17	90	101	15	43	61
Estrada, Horacio	3	3	0	4.09	12	10	55	46	8	23	39
Granger, Jeff	2	2	1	4.03	36	1	38	43	5	15	27
Harris, Reggie	0	1	0	4.66	19	0	29	26	2	19	24
Harrison, Tommy	1	1	0	4.50	3	1	10	10	1	5	5
Hawkins, Alsharik	3	3	0	4.82	11	8	56	68	5	16	26
Henderson, Rod	1	2	0	4.80	7	5	30	26	5	13	16
Huntsman, Scott	2	2	1	4.62	25	4	37	44	5	15	14
Johnston, Doug	3	4	0	4.57	11	9	61	63	8	21	34
Karl, Scott	9	10	0	4.68	29	29	173	208	19	60	78
Lee, Derek	3	3	0	4.66	10	8	56	63	7	23	26
Levrault, Allen	3	4	0	4.36	12	10	64	57	9	22	46
Minor, Blas	1	1	0	4.09	2	2	11	12	1	3	7
Myers, Mike	2	2	0	4.67	90	0	52	55	8	20	45
Nelson, Joe	3	3	2	3.86	33	7	56	48	4	27	50
Nomo, Hideo	10	9	0	4.59	25	25	157	147	22	76	155
Paredes, Roberto	3	3	0	4.20	24	2	45	43	4	26	25
Passini, Brian	3	3	0	4.75	12	9	53	52	5	28	25
Peterson, Kyle	6	6	0	4.37	20	16	107	107	10	41	62
Pittsley, Jim	1	3	0	5.60	25	6	53	62	8	28	28

PLAYER	W	L	SV	ERA	G	GS	IP	H	HR	BB	SO
Plunk, Eric	4	4	0	4.76	62	0	68	67	12	36	62
Pulsipher, Bill	5	6	0	5.24	22	19	103	114	17	41	59
Ratliff, Jon	1	2	0	4.33	5	5	27	26	4	7	18
Roque, Rafael	2	5	1	5.09	39	8	76	81	14	38	58
Seelbach, Chris	2	2	0	4.19	9	6	43	35	4	22	35
Stull, Everett	2	2	0	4.14	8	6	37	32	4	19	28
Theodile, Robert	1	1	0	4.29	11	1	21	24	2	11	11
Villegas, Ismael	3	3	0	4.13	29	1	61	60	5	25	34
Weathers, Dave	6	4	2	4.88	56	0	83	95	10	33	67
Wickman, Bob	4	8	36	3.65	71	0	74	76	6	37	61
Woodard, Steve	10	9	0	4.55	29	27	174	200	21	34	122
Wunsch, Kelly	3	3	0	4.24	21	2	51	59	3	24	26

Montreal Expos

BATTERS

PLAYER	BA	G	AB	R	H	2B	3B	HR	RBI	BB	SO	SB	CS	Sa	OBA
Adolfo, Carlos	.231	35	104	15	24	6	0	4	17	10	28	1	0	.404	.231
Barrett, Michael	.295	134	458	56	135	34	3	9	55	35	43	0	2	.441	.349
Bergeron, Peter	.272	58	202	34	55	12	2	3	17	25	45	8	0	.396	.272
Blum, Geoffrey	.224	67	219	31	49	10	1	9	26	26	42	3	0	.402	.224
Bradley, Milton	.268	42	168	24	45	9	2	5	20	13	36	5	0	.435	.268
Cabrera, Orlando	.270	114	400	57	108	25	6	8	41	22	42	4	3	.423	.311
Camilli, Jason	.233	23	60	9	14	3	0	1	6	8	14	1	0	.333	.233
Carroll, Jamey	.260	24	96	12	25	5	1	1	10	7	12	2	0	.365	.260
Carvajal, Jhonny	.262	19	65	6	17	4	1	0	7	4	15	1	0	.354	.262
De La Rosa, Tomas	.253	25	87	13	22	4	1	1	8	8	14	4	0	.356	.253
Fernandez, Jose	.252	41	151	21	38	9	1	4	20	9	53	3	0	.404	.252
Fullmer, Brad	.278	106	371	42	103	35	2	10	52	26	44	3	4	.464	.327
Guerrero, Vladimir	.305	162	620	99	189	36	5	38	116	48	71	12	7	.563	.360
Guerrero, Wilton	.299	125	348	46	104	15	8	2	31	13	49	7	5	.405	.325
Hunter, Scott	.248	28	101	9	25	5	0	3	17	8	28	1	0	.386	.248
Jones, Terry	.280	25	93	14	26	4	1	0	7	8	23	5	0	.344	.280
Martinez, Manny	.263	130	316	46	83	14	7	4	30	17	60	16	6	.389	.300
McGuire, Ryan	.245	83	163	20	40	8	1	2	19	32	46	1	0	.344	.245
Merced, Orlando	.269	79	197	24	53	12	1	7	28	24	29	2	2	.447	.350
Morales, Francisco	.240	22	75	10	18	2	0	2	10	7	24	0	0	.347	.240
Mordecai, Mike	.240	107	204	26	49	9	2	5	22	19	32	2	4	.377	.305
Mouton, James	.250	96	132	19	33	6	1	2	15	18	30	7	4	.356	.346
Nunnari, Talmadge	.263	35	133	20	35	8	0	3	13	17	31	3	0	.391	.263
Post, Dave	.248	35	121	15	30	5	1	3	11	10	21	2	0	.380	.248
Schneider, Brian	.235	28	98	10	23	4	0	4	14	7	16	1	0	.398	.235
Seguignol, Fernando	.237	81	270	37	64	15	2	15	44	24	102	1	0	.474	.237
Stowers, Chris	.266	26	94	15	25	4	1	1	9	9	24	4	0	.362	.266
Tracy, Andrew	.215	37	135	21	29	6	0	8	28	15	46	1	0	.437	.215
Tucker, Jon	.237	41	131	18	31	7	1	4	18	17	37	1	0	.397	.237
Vidro, Jose	.289	155	501	66	145	43	2	10	57	36	57	1	4	.443	.341
Ware, Jeremy	.256	24	82	12	21	5	0	2	12	8	20	2	0	.390	.256
White, Rondell	.297	136	526	78	156	26	5	22	68	33	84	13	7	.490	.347
Widger, Chris	.258	124	391	41	101	23	1	14	56	29	87	3	3	.430	.315

PITCHERS

PLAYER	W	L	SV	ERA	G	GS	IP	H	HR	BB	SO
Agamennone, Brandon	4	4	1	4.03	28	5	67	64	7	20	44
Armas, Tony	5	5	0	4.35	15	15	93	97	7	42	54
Batista, Miguel	6	7	1	4.67	38	17	131	141	11	60	92
Bennett, Shayne	2	2	1	4.28	22	2	40	39	4	15	23

2000 PROJECTIONS

PLAYER	W	L	SV	ERA	G	GS	IP	H	HR	BB	SO
Blank, Matt	3	4	0	4.85	11	11	65	80	12	22	27
DeSilva, John	2	2	0	4.14	9	6	37	36	2	20	26
Durocher, Jayson	4	4	1	4.04	37	2	69	60	7	44	39
Evans, Keith	3	4	0	4.50	12	10	64	74	9	12	34
Forster, Scott	2	2	0	4.50	33	0	34	30	2	27	16
Hermanson, Dustin	10	12	0	4.04	31	31	196	196	19	65	144
Johnson, Mike	3	3	0	4.05	12	11	60	62	9	22	40
Kline, Steve	6	5	0	3.86	83	0	70	63	7	36	69
Lilly, Ted	5	4	0	3.92	17	13	78	70	12	20	61
Marquez, Robert	2	2	0	4.19	30	0	43	49	5	17	26
Mattes, Troy	2	3	0	4.80	9	9	45	50	5	17	22
Mitchell, Scott	2	3	0	4.80	12	5	45	50	6	15	18
Mota, Guillermo	2	5	0	3.19	57	0	62	63	6	29	30
Parker, Christian	3	4	0	4.50	27	4	62	64	7	29	26
Pavano, Carl	6	8	0	5.03	20	19	111	117	11	36	72
Phelps, Tommy	2	2	0	4.97	8	7	38	42	7	14	18
Powell, Jeremy	6	7	0	4.50	22	20	118	127	14	52	60
Rojas, Mel	1	1	0	5.90	27	0	29	29	6	13	24
Saylor, Ryan	4	3	2	3.92	29	3	62	54	8	26	48
Small, Mark	1	1	0	4.50	8	0	12	14	1	5	7
Smart, J. D.	0	1	0	5.05	32	0	57	61	4	19	23
Stevenson, Rodney	3	3	1	4.24	40	0	51	50	9	20	28
Strickland, Scott	6	4	2	3.54	60	1	89	87	6	44	93
Telford, Anthony	4	5	2	3.98	71	0	86	94	5	35	60
Thurman, Mike	8	11	0	4.35	30	28	151	144	18	55	85
Tucker, Thomas	4	4	0	4.44	12	12	75	73	8	25	46
Urbina, Ugueth	6	6	40	3.27	72	0	77	57	6	38	102
Vazquez, Javier	7	9	0	5.23	25	25	148	152	22	52	112
Westbrook, Jake	4	5	0	4.80	12	12	75	85	7	30	32

New York Mets

BATTERS

PLAYER	BA	G	AB	R	H	2B	3B	HR	RBI	BB	SO	SB	CS	Sa	OBA
Agbayani, Benny	.276	113	301	44	83	19	3	15	44	34	65	6	5	.508	.352
Alfonzo, Edgardo	.293	159	617	112	181	36	1	22	96	78	80	9	3	.462	.372
Allensworth, Jermaine	.265	70	196	31	52	12	2	4	17	21	46	5	0	.408	.265
Bonilla, Bobby	.241	28	79	10	19	4	0	3	12	11	13	0	1	.405	.330
Buccheri, Jim	.286	20	63	7	18	3	0	0	6	5	12	2	0	.333	.286
Cedeno, Roger	.296	162	443	82	131	22	4	4	35	57	99	52	13	.391	.378
Darden, Tony	.259	38	112	13	29	4	0	2	12	12	23	3	0	.348	.259
Dunston, Shawon	.299	89	224	34	67	11	3	6	32	3	35	11	4	.455	.318
Franco, Matt	.256	124	156	21	40	6	1	4	21	27	25	0	0	.385	.364
Gainey, Bryon	.221	28	104	13	23	5	1	5	15	8	46	0	0	.433	.221
Halter, Shane	.257	35	109	15	28	5	0	1	8	12	25	2	0	.330	.257
Hamilton, Darryl	.305	124	446	73	136	19	3	7	40	56	44	8	7	.408	.384
Haney, Todd	.256	36	129	20	33	6	1	1	12	18	15	1	0	.341	.256
Henderson, Rickey	.275	106	378	74	104	19	0	10	36	76	73	37	10	.405	.399
Huff, Brent	.246	19	69	8	17	3	0	2	10	6	18	2	0	.377	.246
Kinkade, Mike	.265	65	204	29	54	11	2	5	28	12	27	3	0	.412	.265
Long, Terrence	.281	50	192	23	54	10	2	4	27	13	36	7	0	.417	.281
Lopez, Luis	.254	63	122	16	31	6	1	1	13	11	34	1	1	.344	.328
Mora, Melvin	.269	77	175	30	47	8	1	4	18	22	38	8	0	.394	.269
Neubart, Garrett	.271	23	70	10	19	3	1	1	5	7	13	4	0	.386	.271
Olerud, John	.301	150	528	90	159	34	1	18	86	100	61	2	1	.472	.416
Ordonez, Rey	.274	144	475	49	130	21	2	1	54	39	59	7	5	.333	.326
Piazza, Mike	.305	144	541	92	165	28	0	36	114	53	70	2	1	.556	.364

PLAYER	BA	G	AB	R	H	2B	3B	HR	RBI	BB	SO	SB	CS	Sa	OBA
Pratt, Todd	.292	78	154	20	45	8	0	3	27	15	38	2	0	.403	.362
Rodriguez, Sammy	.226	19	53	4	12	3	0	1	7	6	15	1	0	.340	.226
Romero, Mandy	.242	22	62	5	15	4	0	1	8	7	14	0	0	.355	.242
Tomberlin, Andy	.253	60	174	28	44	9	0	7	30	17	56	1	0	.425	.253
Tyner, Jason	.297	25	101	17	30	3	1	0	6	11	12	7	0	.347	.297
Valera, Yohanny	.222	32	108	13	24	6	1	4	16	7	35	1	0	.407	.222
Ventura, Robin	.281	153	558	80	157	33	1	26	101	72	100	1	1	.484	.363
Zamora, Junior	.227	20	75	8	17	5	0	3	9	3	22	1	0	.413	.227

PITCHERS

PLAYER	W	L	SV	ERA	G	GS	IP	H	HR	BB	SO
Benitez, Armando	5	5	22	2.71	82	0	83	51	7	48	127
Brittan, Corey	4	4	1	4.19	44	2	73	83	6	23	41
Cammack, Eric	5	3	5	3.36	63	6	75	47	4	52	98
Cook, Dennis	8	4	3	3.63	70	0	62	54	8	27	68
Corey, Mark	2	2	0	4.50	8	6	42	44	5	16	25
Della Ratta, Peter	4	4	0	3.93	36	3	71	87	5	15	49
Dotel, Octavio	6	5	0	3.88	21	16	102	73	13	50	96
Franco, John	1	4	24	3.23	60	0	53	53	2	24	50
Guerra, Mark	3	3	0	4.06	36	1	51	61	3	26	33
Henriquez, Oscar	3	3	5	3.76	51	0	55	50	7	31	52
Herbison, Brett	2	4	0	5.26	10	8	53	54	7	27	18
Hershiser, Orel	10	9	0	4.59	28	28	155	155	15	65	84
Isringhausen, Jason	4	3	0	3.92	15	9	62	52	6	32	52
Jones, Bobby	5	5	0	4.50	19	14	94	98	9	25	55
Leiter, Al	13	10	0	3.95	28	28	187	176	14	84	152
Lopez, Johann	3	3	0	4.27	20	5	59	57	7	26	40
Lyons, Mike	4	3	1	3.90	40	3	60	60	5	29	46
Mahomes, Pat	7	1	0	4.50	40	0	66	55	9	40	49
Manzanillo, Josias	0	1	0	5.21	25	0	38	39	8	17	42
McCrary, Scott	2	3	0	4.80	14	5	45	60	7	18	21
McElroy, Chuck	3	2	0	4.58	57	0	55	59	6	28	46
Pontes, Dan	1	1	0	4.00	11	1	18	16	3	7	14
Pumphrey, Ken	3	4	0	4.58	11	9	59	64	4	31	32
Reed, Rick	10	6	0	4.11	24	24	140	146	20	32	95
Roberts, Grant	3	4	0	4.43	11	10	65	65	4	23	42
Rogers, Kenny	10	5	0	4.19	28	28	176	182	15	61	108
Rusch, Glendon	3	3	0	4.03	11	9	58	63	6	16	35
Stewart, Scott	3	3	0	4.05	21	9	60	63	5	20	43
Tam, Jeff	1	1	0	5.46	25	0	28	21	6	9	18
Taylor, Billy	2	6	25	4.42	60	0	55	61	5	22	48
Walker, Tyler	2	2	0	4.50	8	6	40	39	5	16	29
Wallace, Derek	3	3	1	4.20	29	2	45	47	5	22	26
Welch, Mike	1	2	0	4.85	14	2	26	27	4	9	11
Wendell, Turk	5	3	3	3.43	78	0	84	77	7	40	71
Yoshii, Masato	9	8	0	4.39	29	27	160	158	22	53	101

Philadelphia Phillies

BATTERS

PLAYER	BA	G	AB	R	H	2B	3B	HR	RBI	BB	SO	SB	CS	Sa	OBA
Abreu, Bob	.309	162	563	101	174	33	9	19	87	100	122	25	9	.501	.413
Anderson, Marlon	.270	126	434	48	117	27	4	5	54	24	62	14	2	.385	.310
Arias, Alex	.299	129	344	43	103	19	1	4	46	36	34	2	2	.395	.370
Bennett, Gary	.289	47	121	11	35	5	0	1	27	8	18	0	0	.355	.326
Brogna, Rico	.274	137	526	74	144	29	3	20	89	44	114	7	5	.454	.328
Burnham, Gary	.246	37	114	15	28	6	0	4	15	13	19	2	0	.404	.246

2000 PROJECTIONS

PLAYER	BA	G	AB	R	H	2B	3B	HR	RBI	BB	SO	SB	CS	Sa	OBA
Burrell, Patrick	.227	64	229	32	52	10	2	11	34	30	68	1	0	.432	.227
Burton, Darren	.249	49	169	24	42	12	1	5	25	17	48	2	0	.420	.249
Carver, Steve	.230	43	126	14	29	8	0	5	16	15	53	1	0	.413	.230
Cedeno, Domingo	.242	39	95	11	23	6	1	2	12	8	25	1	1	.389	.308
Doster, David	.236	84	106	12	25	5	0	3	11	12	26	1	0	.368	.311
Ducey, Rob	.256	101	195	29	50	13	2	7	27	30	56	3	2	.451	.362
Estalella, Bobby	.219	52	178	24	39	9	1	7	26	23	59	1	0	.399	.219
Finn, John	.222	12	36	5	8	1	0	1	3	5	5	1	0	.333	.222
Flores, Jose	.263	33	118	19	31	3	1	0	10	20	27	5	0	.305	.263
Francia, David	.270	35	111	13	30	7	2	1	14	7	22	3	0	.396	.270
Frazier, Lou	.230	23	74	12	17	4	2	1	7	11	24	4	0	.378	.230
Gant, Ron	.251	128	459	85	115	22	4	19	69	69	109	11	2	.440	.348
Glanville, Doug	.308	141	577	92	178	31	6	9	57	40	73	27	4	.430	.356
Guiliano, Matthew	.227	14	44	5	10	4	0	0	6	4	15	1	0	.318	.227
Harris, Brian	.231	20	65	8	15	2	1	1	7	8	12	1	0	.338	.231
Horne, Tyrone	.259	33	108	15	28	5	1	2	15	17	32	4	0	.380	.259
Huff, Larry	.245	29	98	16	24	6	1	1	11	14	19	4	0	.357	.245
Jordan, Kevin	.288	127	333	35	96	17	2	4	48	19	37	0	0	.387	.333
Lieberthal, Mike	.279	153	538	80	150	32	2	27	94	43	86	1	1	.496	.340
Lovullo, Torey	.232	46	164	23	38	9	1	6	27	20	35	1	0	.409	.232
Lucca, Lou	.262	31	122	14	32	7	0	3	16	5	26	1	0	.393	.262
Magee, Wendell	.264	53	201	31	53	12	1	7	27	18	51	2	0	.438	.264
McMillon, Billy	.259	57	201	36	52	14	1	6	31	24	41	4	0	.428	.259
Pierce, Kirk	.229	34	105	13	24	4	0	3	15	15	28	1	0	.352	.229
Relaford, Desi	.255	70	235	29	60	13	2	2	26	20	42	5	3	.353	.322
Rolen, Scott	.271	124	462	82	125	31	2	24	81	69	114	12	4	.502	.368
Rollins, Jimmy	.248	35	141	20	35	5	2	3	14	13	15	5	0	.376	.248
Royster, Aaron	.259	33	112	17	29	5	1	3	15	15	39	3	0	.402	.259
Sefcik, Kevin	.284	126	229	31	65	14	3	2	16	30	30	8	4	.397	.374
Stewart, Andy	.239	38	134	13	32	11	0	4	23	9	15	0	0	.410	.239
Taylor, Reggie	.265	32	132	19	35	4	3	4	15	5	24	7	0	.432	.265
Zuber, Jon	.259	55	158	25	41	9	1	3	20	30	25	2	0	.386	.259

PITCHERS

PLAYER	W	L	SV	ERA	G	GS	IP	H	HR	BB	SO
Aldred, Scott	3	3	1	4.88	68	0	59	64	5	27	38
Bennett, Joel	2	2	0	4.28	7	6	40	40	5	14	32
Bolton, Rod	2	2	0	4.76	5	5	34	39	2	13	16
Brewer, Billy	2	2	0	3.97	21	2	34	29	3	14	25
Byrd, Paul	13	10	0	4.55	28	28	176	177	28	64	99
Dodd, Robert	3	3	1	4.03	26	2	58	59	1	17	45
Eaton, Adam	4	4	0	4.22	12	10	79	74	10	33	52
Fesh, Sean	3	2	0	4.00	38	0	45	41	4	25	27
Gomes, Wayne	6	5	19	4.44	72	0	73	73	6	45	60
Grace, Mike	2	4	0	5.88	26	5	52	67	5	22	27
Grahe, Joe	3	5	0	4.76	20	8	51	65	4	24	25
Green, Tyler	1	1	0	4.50	3	2	14	13	2	6	8
Herbert, Russ	2	2	0	4.50	12	4	38	40	3	14	21
Jacquez, Thomas	2	2	0	4.61	13	6	41	47	6	10	20
Johnson, Barry	1	1	0	4.50	5	3	24	27	2	8	13
Kershner, Jason	2	2	1	4.03	24	3	38	35	5	14	30
Loewer, Carlton	4	7	0	5.28	24	16	109	125	13	32	55
Montgomery, Steve	1	5	3	4.03	55	0	67	61	12	37	54
Nye, Ryan	2	2	0	4.19	10	7	43	41	5	11	36
Ogea, Chad	7	10	0	5.35	31	24	143	158	27	51	72
Perez, Yorkis	2	2	0	4.14	54	0	50	45	5	24	40
Person, Robert	9	7	2	5.01	40	21	142	137	24	79	128
Politte, Cliff	4	3	0	3.98	22	10	61	61	7	23	42

PLAYER	W	L	SV	ERA	G	GS	IP	H	HR	BB	SO
Ryan, Ken	1	2	0	5.56	33	0	34	34	4	24	21
Schilling, Curt	12	8	0	3.57	24	24	179	161	20	44	180
Schrenk, Steve	1	3	1	4.34	36	2	56	46	7	16	40
Scott, Darryl	2	1	1	4.00	15	1	27	25	3	12	20
Shumaker, Anthony	4	4	0	4.15	12	10	65	70	8	23	40
Telemaco, Amaury	3	2	0	4.82	52	0	56	57	8	21	37
Thomas, Evan	4	3	0	4.06	18	6	62	67	4	27	52
Wolf, Randy	7	7	0	4.17	21	20	121	112	16	54	95

Pittsburgh Pirates

BATTERS

PLAYER	BA	G	AB	R	H	2B	3B	HR	RBI	BB	SO	SB	CS	Sa	OBA
Benjamin, Mike	.270	106	330	42	89	24	4	2	36	18	82	7	1	.385	.311
Brinkley, Darryl	.259	47	158	23	41	12	1	5	26	11	30	2	0	.443	.259
Brown, Adrian	.272	115	261	38	71	7	2	3	18	33	42	7	3	.349	.357
Brown, Brant	.254	126	339	51	86	19	4	15	54	24	106	3	0	.466	.306
Brown, Emil	.267	48	180	33	48	7	2	6	21	12	42	4	0	.428	.267
Cruz, Ivan	.234	52	192	29	45	10	0	12	42	11	52	0	0	.474	.234
DeHaan, Kory	.277	37	148	21	41	10	2	2	19	9	43	8	0	.412	.277
Figueroa, Luis	.257	35	113	16	29	4	1	1	13	14	14	2	0	.336	.257
Giles, Brian	.285	161	555	102	158	31	3	34	110	99	87	9	3	.535	.391
Haverbusch, Kevin	.257	59	210	32	54	12	1	8	34	7	46	3	0	.438	.257
Hermansen, Chad	.226	59	230	33	52	11	2	12	35	15	68	6	0	.439	.226
Hernandez, Alexander	.253	43	162	25	41	9	1	5	21	18	45	2	0	.414	.253
Howard, Matt	.273	16	55	5	15	2	0	0	6	3	4	1	0	.309	.273
Hyzdu, Adam	.242	59	215	30	52	11	1	12	39	19	52	3	0	.470	.242
Kendall, Jason	.313	93	332	61	104	23	3	8	44	36	34	19	3	.473	.404
Laker, Tim	.248	39	129	13	32	8	1	3	17	8	26	1	0	.395	.248
Long, Garrett	.226	54	177	28	40	6	2	8	26	29	60	2	0	.418	.226
Mackowiak, Rob	.269	42	156	17	42	12	2	2	22	7	33	0	0	.410	.269
Martin, Al	.270	134	496	81	134	28	6	19	58	44	106	20	4	.466	.331
Meares, Pat	.286	31	112	14	32	6	1	2	14	6	21	1	1	.411	.331
Montgomery, Ray	.255	64	184	30	47	12	1	8	26	12	39	2	0	.462	.255
Morris, Warren	.287	146	508	64	146	20	3	15	72	59	87	3	7	.427	.361
Nunez, Abraham	.238	102	281	30	67	10	1	1	20	36	67	12	2	.292	.327
Oliver, Joe	.246	42	138	13	34	9	0	3	21	8	37	1	0	.377	.246
Osik, Keith	.233	49	120	11	28	4	1	1	11	12	25	0	1	.308	.306
Patzke, Jeff	.248	36	121	16	30	5	1	1	12	20	29	1	0	.331	.248
Polcovich, Kevin	.255	17	47	7	12	3	0	0	5	4	11	1	0	.319	.255
Ramirez, Aramis	.251	72	251	33	63	13	1	8	30	28	54	1	0	.406	.251
Redman, Tike	.277	40	155	25	43	6	4	1	18	16	18	6	0	.387	.277
Robertson, Mike	.252	45	139	19	35	8	0	5	17	10	25	1	0	.417	.252
Secrist, Reed	.229	20	48	5	11	3	0	1	6	5	13	0	0	.354	.229
Sprague, Ed	.252	128	457	63	115	25	2	19	66	41	89	2	4	.440	.329
Wehner, John	.245	32	49	6	12	2	0	0	3	5	9	1	0	.286	.315
Wilson, Craig	.229	66	214	29	49	11	2	10	35	20	74	1	0	.439	.229
Young, Kevin	.283	147	544	89	154	36	4	24	99	56	116	18	8	.496	.357

PITCHERS

PLAYER	W	L	SV	ERA	G	GS	IP	H	HR	BB	SO
Ah Yat, Paul	3	3	0	4.26	10	8	57	59	6	20	39
Anderson, Jimmy	5	5	0	4.24	18	11	87	100	4	32	47
Arroyo, Bronson	3	4	0	4.64	11	11	64	76	6	27	36
Baron, Jim	3	3	0	4.85	10	7	52	56	5	17	22
Benson, Kris	10	14	0	4.24	30	30	189	180	15	81	133
Castillo, Frank	2	2	0	4.34	6	5	29	31	3	8	18

2000 PROJECTIONS

PLAYER	W	L	SV	ERA	G	GS	IP	H	HR	BB	SO
Christiansen, Jason	3	3	4	3.57	55	0	53	42	2	28	54
Clontz, Brad	3	3	2	3.60	67	0	60	60	7	29	47
Cordova, Francisco	8	10	0	4.10	26	26	156	158	15	54	102
Daniels, David	3	3	1	3.86	46	3	56	55	6	19	44
Davis, Kane	2	3	0	4.89	9	8	46	52	4	19	22
Dougherty, Jim	1	1	1	4.26	17	0	19	19	2	8	13
Duff, Matt	4	3	3	3.72	45	1	58	50	6	41	50
Dunbar, Matt	1	1	0	4.00	19	1	18	16	1	9	12
France, Aaron	3	3	0	4.31	17	5	48	43	4	26	29
Giard, Ken	4	3	1	3.63	56	2	62	65	3	47	61
Hansell, Greg	2	3	0	4.58	45	0	55	59	8	17	43
Loiselle, Rich	2	4	0	3.97	30	0	34	37	3	19	31
McConnell, Sam	1	1	0	4.85	3	2	13	15	1	6	7
O'Connor, Brian	3	3	0	4.58	10	9	53	53	4	32	31
Peters, Chris	6	6	0	4.97	26	15	96	111	16	37	64
Ritchie, Todd	13	9	0	3.89	29	27	178	185	18	59	113
Robertson, Rich	1	1	0	4.24	6	2	17	19	1	7	13
Ryan, Matt	3	3	1	4.40	29	4	47	51	4	21	26
Sauerbeck, Scott	4	1	2	2.22	70	0	73	60	6	43	59
Sauveur, Rich	1	1	0	3.75	20	1	24	32	3	8	19
Schmidt, Jason	11	11	0	4.32	30	30	196	206	21	76	139
Schourek, Pete	5	8	0	4.98	30	17	112	120	19	48	89
Silva, Jose	3	6	3	5.16	29	10	82	89	8	30	61
Van Poppel, Todd	2	2	0	4.19	9	7	43	42	5	15	31
Wallace, Jeff	1	0	0	3.60	58	0	55	38	2	54	59
Wilkins, Marc	3	3	0	4.26	51	0	57	54	4	29	47
Williams, Mike	3	4	23	4.34	58	0	58	59	7	32	72

St. Louis Cardinals

BATTERS

PLAYER	BA	G	AB	R	H	2B	3B	HR	RBI	BB	SO	SB	CS	Sa	OBA
Ametller, Jesus	.271	39	133	16	36	8	1	3	16	1	8	1	0	.414	.271
Bieser, Steve	.250	24	72	10	18	4	1	2	8	8	17	1	0	.417	.250
Bragg, Darren	.267	91	281	37	75	16	1	6	32	38	67	4	1	.395	.359
Butler, Brent	.262	34	130	16	34	5	0	3	13	6	14	0	0	.369	.262
Castillo, Alberto	.266	99	256	24	68	9	0	4	31	27	52	0	1	.348	.336
Clapp, Stubby	.221	32	113	18	25	6	0	3	15	13	33	1	0	.354	.221
Davis, Eric	.288	48	163	26	47	9	1	7	28	19	40	4	2	.485	.362
Dishington, Nate	.210	41	119	21	25	6	0	6	21	14	70	1	0	.412	.210
Drew, J. D.	.249	111	386	76	96	17	6	15	45	52	82	19	3	.440	.345
Farley, Cordell	.265	24	83	9	22	3	2	2	8	4	23	4	0	.422	.265
Haas, Chris	.202	36	124	18	25	5	1	5	20	18	58	1	0	.379	.202
Hogan, Todd	.255	15	47	7	12	1	1	1	4	4	14	1	0	.383	.255
Howard, David	.250	39	72	7	18	3	0	1	7	7	21	0	1	.333	.325
Howard, Thomas	.275	89	178	16	49	10	0	5	22	15	28	1	1	.416	.337
Hulse, David	.287	35	94	15	27	5	1	2	12	4	22	1	0	.426	.287
Jensen, Marcus	.227	51	154	19	35	11	2	4	20	16	49	0	0	.403	.227
Kennedy, Adam	.261	56	211	31	55	12	2	4	30	12	24	7	0	.393	.261
Kleiner, Stacy	.254	24	67	7	17	3	1	1	5	8	21	1	0	.373	.254
Lankford, Ray	.290	116	403	71	117	29	1	18	68	56	105	16	4	.501	.377
Lariviere, Jason	.267	28	105	18	28	7	1	2	9	9	16	3	0	.410	.267
Leon, Jose	.218	41	124	13	27	6	0	6	19	9	51	1	0	.411	.218
Little, Mark	.273	31	110	20	30	6	3	2	11	6	34	5	0	.436	.273
Marrero, Eli	.232	110	314	36	73	17	1	7	35	25	62	12	2	.360	.289
McDonald, Keith	.250	41	128	16	32	7	0	3	16	14	33	1	0	.375	.250
McEwing, Joe	.279	144	481	63	134	27	4	8	42	39	83	7	4	.401	.337

PLAYER	BA	G	AB	R	H	2B	3B	HR	RBI	BB	SO	SB	CS	Sa	OBA
McGee, Willie	.280	88	189	19	53	7	1	1	20	13	42	5	2	.344	.324
McGwire, Mark	.263	151	510	107	134	20	1	60	131	125	134	1	0	.659	.408
Ordaz, Luis	.272	34	103	9	28	6	1	0	11	8	14	1	0	.350	.272
Paquette, Craig	.242	68	248	30	60	13	1	12	43	8	59	2	0	.448	.242
Polanco, Placido	.285	101	253	28	72	10	4	1	23	17	27	2	3	.368	.327
Renteria, Edgar	.284	147	567	90	161	29	2	8	53	51	86	38	13	.384	.343
Richard, Chris	.239	55	184	26	44	9	1	10	32	14	37	2	0	.462	.239
Saturria, Luis	.248	35	121	17	30	8	1	4	15	9	40	3	0	.430	.248
Stefanski, Mike	.257	22	70	8	18	4	0	1	7	5	12	1	0	.357	.257
Tatis, Fernando	.282	162	582	97	164	33	3	28	95	69	132	19	8	.493	.369
Warner, Ron	.244	33	90	11	22	4	0	3	10	10	31	2	0	.389	.244
Woolf, Jay	.245	38	143	19	35	7	2	3	6	11	46	4	0	.385	.245

PITCHERS

PLAYER	W	L	SV	ERA	G	GS	IP	H	HR	BB	SO
Acevedo, Juan	5	5	3	4.83	40	10	82	86	11	34	44
Ambrose, John	2	2	1	4.50	13	6	42	42	4	26	26
Ankiel, Richard	7	6	0	3.58	23	17	118	102	9	63	135
Aybar, Manuel	4	5	3	5.31	56	1	83	88	10	34	61
Barnes, Brian	1	1	0	3.68	9	2	22	21	3	7	18
Bottalico, Ricky	2	7	19	4.96	64	0	69	77	8	44	62
Bottenfield, Kent	13	7	0	4.23	29	29	181	187	20	84	124
Busby, Mike	2	2	0	4.50	19	3	36	39	4	14	20
Croushore, Rich	2	6	3	4.44	58	0	71	65	9	42	80
Detmers, Kris	3	3	0	4.58	10	10	55	56	7	18	33
Dewitt, Matt	3	4	0	4.50	11	10	62	64	9	25	37
Eversgerd, Bryan	3	3	0	4.11	43	0	46	45	7	12	27
Heiserman, Rick	3	3	4	4.04	41	0	49	49	6	16	38
Hutchinson, Chad	4	3	0	4.06	11	9	62	50	5	36	56
Jimenez, Jose	5	11	0	5.44	25	24	139	144	13	59	96
Karnuth, Jason	2	3	0	5.25	8	7	48	52	5	16	18
Lovingier, Kevin	3	2	0	4.00	29	0	45	34	4	21	32
Mlicki, Doug	2	2	0	5.03	19	0	34	37	7	12	11
Mohler, Mike	1	3	1	4.91	54	0	55	59	5	26	36
Nussbeck, Mark	2	2	0	4.20	10	5	30	31	5	9	21
Oliver, Darren	9	10	0	4.67	28	28	181	196	18	71	105
Osborne, Donovan	3	5	0	4.77	14	14	66	70	9	19	46
Painter, Lance	4	4	1	4.72	55	4	61	59	6	28	53
Radinsky, Scott	4	3	5	3.83	74	0	47	47	3	22	32
Reed, Steve	2	2	0	4.62	16	5	37	37	6	12	17
Slocumb, Heathcliff	2	4	2	4.57	50	0	63	67	5	40	56
Sodowsky, Clint	2	3	0	4.50	18	5	44	44	5	18	21
Stephenson, Garrett	7	5	0	4.54	24	16	111	117	13	43	78
Thompson, Mark	3	4	0	4.58	12	11	59	62	7	30	28
Weibl, Clint	3	3	0	4.41	14	5	49	52	5	20	29

San Diego Padres

BATTERS

PLAYER	BA	G	AB	R	H	2B	3B	HR	RBI	BB	SO	SB	CS	Sa	OBA
Allen, Dusty	.229	33	118	15	27	7	1	4	20	17	44	1	0	.407	.229
Arias, George	.251	66	183	23	46	9	1	8	23	8	64	0	0	.443	.286
Balfe, Ryan	.238	40	143	21	34	9	1	3	21	15	41	0	0	.378	.238
Charles, Frank	.256	13	43	4	11	3	0	0	5	2	12	0	0	.326	.256
Curl, John	.234	41	145	20	34	8	1	6	19	20	50	2	0	.428	.234
Darr, Mike	.259	50	174	22	45	12	0	4	23	19	59	4	0	.397	.259
Davis, Ben	.247	83	287	31	71	18	1	7	42	28	82	2	0	.390	.247

2000 PROJECTIONS

PLAYER	BA	G	AB	R	H	2B	3B	HR	RBI	BB	SO	SB	CS	Sa	OBA
Faggett, Ethan	.259	21	85	14	22	3	2	1	7	9	25	7	0	.376	.259
Giovanola, Ed	.228	47	57	9	13	1	1	0	4	10	9	1	0	.281	.343
Gomez, Chris	.267	77	243	27	65	12	1	2	21	28	52	1	2	.350	.347
Gonzalez, Jimmy	.239	37	109	13	26	6	1	3	14	11	33	0	0	.394	.239
Gonzalez, Wiklenman	.247	65	223	26	55	11	1	9	33	16	31	0	0	.426	.247
Guiel, Aaron	.209	38	115	18	24	10	1	5	15	17	46	2	0	.443	.209
Gwynn, Tony	.331	97	362	52	120	25	0	10	56	26	13	5	2	.483	.373
Jackson, Damian	.237	136	392	59	93	22	2	9	42	56	107	35	10	.372	.335
Jorgensen, Randy	.272	36	125	17	34	6	0	3	22	15	27	1	0	.392	.272
Joyner, Wally	.278	90	281	33	78	15	1	6	44	41	38	1	1	.402	.368
Kent, Robbie	.237	37	114	14	27	5	1	2	17	13	29	1	0	.351	.237
Lidle, Kevin	.215	27	79	10	17	4	0	3	10	11	22	0	0	.380	.215
Luzinski, Ryan	.244	27	82	9	20	6	0	1	9	11	24	0	0	.354	.244
Magadan, Dave	.284	98	218	21	62	11	1	2	26	38	31	1	2	.372	.383
Matthews, Gary	.252	37	119	16	30	6	1	2	15	17	35	4	0	.370	.252
Nevin, Phil	.255	137	411	53	105	25	1	22	78	48	96	1	0	.482	.334
Newhan, David	.238	39	126	15	30	7	0	4	14	8	34	5	0	.389	.238
Nicholson, Kevin	.246	37	142	21	35	9	1	3	20	11	32	4	0	.387	.246
Owens, Eric	.270	151	415	54	112	21	3	9	58	36	51	31	7	.400	.331
Paciorek, Pete	.235	31	85	15	20	4	1	2	7	15	27	1	0	.376	.235
Prieto, Chris	.235	21	68	13	16	3	1	1	6	9	12	3	0	.353	.235
Prieto, Rick	.265	33	102	16	27	4	1	2	11	15	19	6	0	.382	.265
Rivera, Ruben	.205	155	391	65	80	16	2	21	51	56	138	17	6	.417	.309
Rossy, Rico	.222	14	36	5	8	2	0	1	3	5	5	1	0	.361	.222
Sanders, Reggie	.271	129	465	84	126	22	6	22	66	58	114	28	11	.486	.358
Thrower, Jake	.245	30	110	13	27	6	1	2	13	11	26	1	0	.373	.245
Tucci, Pete	.252	29	111	16	28	5	0	4	13	9	35	3	0	.405	.252
Vander Wal, John	.267	145	236	27	63	18	0	6	38	36	59	2	1	.419	.364
Veras, Quilvio	.277	123	452	81	125	23	2	5	39	66	78	26	13	.369	.371

PITCHERS

PLAYER	W	L	SV	ERA	G	GS	IP	H	HR	BB	SO
Agosto, Stevenson	2	2	0	4.50	16	2	32	28	4	20	19
Almanzar, Carlos	1	1	0	5.82	38	0	51	58	8	17	39
Ashby, Andy	13	9	0	3.92	29	29	193	198	22	51	128
Boehringer, Brian	6	4	0	3.74	31	10	89	92	10	42	69
Carlyle, Buddy	5	5	0	4.31	15	13	94	94	14	26	66
Clement, Matt	10	11	0	4.58	29	29	171	182	16	82	129
Cunnane, Will	3	2	0	5.22	38	0	50	56	10	22	38
Doughty, Brian	2	3	0	5.02	11	4	43	51	6	9	18
Drumheller, Al	2	2	0	4.28	10	5	40	45	4	15	26
Guzman, Domingo	2	2	1	4.35	27	2	31	32	1	12	19
Herndon, Harry	3	4	0	4.85	10	9	65	70	10	21	29
Hitchcock, Sterling	11	12	0	4.36	31	31	190	191	28	66	171
Hite, Kevin	2	2	3	4.09	39	5	44	52	4	12	33
Hoffman, Trevor	3	3	40	2.28	68	0	71	50	5	19	82
Kolb, Brandon	4	3	1	3.81	40	0	59	68	3	28	53
Lopez, Rodrigo	3	4	0	4.43	10	8	61	67	5	21	42
Maurer, David	3	3	1	4.03	44	7	58	50	6	22	40
Miceli, Dan	5	4	2	4.24	65	0	68	65	7	32	61
Reyes, Carlos	2	4	1	4.20	64	0	75	78	10	24	53
Ricken, Ray	2	2	0	4.50	6	5	32	33	4	15	16
Sak, Jim	4	3	2	3.51	46	0	59	47	8	41	64
Skrmetta, Matt	2	2	0	3.86	24	2	35	29	3	16	31
Smith, Pete	1	1	0	4.26	6	3	19	21	2	6	12
Spencer, Stan	2	2	0	4.09	7	6	33	33	5	7	26
Sullivan, Brendan	2	2	0	4.38	27	0	39	39	3	17	25
Vosberg, Ed	1	1	0	4.85	44	0	26	34	2	10	18

PLAYER	W	L	SV	ERA	G	GS	IP	H	HR	BB	SO
Wall, Donne	6	5	0	3.42	56	0	71	62	10	27	54
Whisenant, Matt	3	3	1	5.05	69	0	57	53	3	35	40
Whiteside, Matt	1	1	0	4.20	9	1	15	15	2	4	12
Williams, Woody	10	10	0	4.50	29	29	182	184	30	66	122
Wolff, Bryan	3	3	0	4.11	9	9	57	60	7	17	41

San Francisco Giants

BATTERS

PLAYER	BA	G	AB	R	H	2B	3B	HR	RBI	BB	SO	SB	CS	Sa	OBA
Aurilia, Rich	.279	152	537	68	150	26	1	19	75	41	72	3	3	.438	.333
Benard, Marvin	.292	162	517	87	151	33	4	12	60	53	87	23	11	.441	.363
Bonds, Barry	.267	99	345	78	92	21	3	27	72	74	55	16	4	.580	.399
Burks, Ellis	.277	115	390	67	108	19	2	25	78	55	81	7	5	.528	.369
Byas, Michael	.298	25	94	16	28	2	0	0	8	14	18	4	0	.319	.298
Canizaro, Jay	.211	41	142	22	30	6	1	8	23	14	37	4	0	.437	.211
Chiaramonte, Giuseppe	.222	39	135	16	30	6	1	6	23	12	36	1	0	.415	.222
Crespo, Felipe	.245	65	188	31	46	10	2	7	28	27	44	5	0	.431	.245
Delgado, Wilson	.271	48	140	16	38	6	2	0	17	11	27	2	0	.343	.271
Dilone, Juan	.247	32	97	14	24	5	2	1	12	13	30	2	0	.371	.247
Feliz, Pedro	.248	34	129	13	32	6	2	3	20	5	28	1	0	.395	.248
Guzman, Edwards	.269	26	93	12	25	3	0	2	12	4	16	1	0	.366	.269
Hayes, Charlie	.247	80	235	29	58	8	0	7	44	28	41	2	1	.370	.327
Kent, Jeff	.280	134	503	83	141	36	2	24	104	52	107	11	5	.503	.351
Leach, Jalal	.252	35	111	15	28	5	1	4	19	7	24	2	0	.423	.252
Magruder, Christopher	.256	33	117	19	30	5	1	1	15	17	25	3	0	.342	.256
Martinez, Ramon	.273	84	183	28	50	8	0	6	23	19	22	1	2	.415	.340
Marval, Raul	.255	34	98	13	25	4	0	2	14	5	20	1	0	.357	.255
Mashore, Damon	.231	31	91	14	21	5	0	4	15	9	30	1	0	.418	.231
Mayne, Brent	.291	117	330	37	96	27	0	3	38	42	61	2	2	.400	.375
Mendoza, Carlos	.225	27	80	10	18	4	1	1	9	10	19	0	0	.338	.225
Minor, Damon	.232	45	155	21	36	9	1	6	23	22	45	0	0	.419	.232
Mirabelli, Doug	.233	50	163	23	38	10	0	5	20	18	40	2	0	.387	.233
Mueller, Bill	.290	117	414	64	120	23	0	4	41	62	59	3	2	.374	.383
Murray, Calvin	.266	40	158	27	42	7	2	5	17	11	31	8	0	.430	.266
Rios, Armando	.317	112	221	46	70	12	0	11	42	35	49	10	5	.520	.411
Santangelo, F. P.	.243	98	251	43	61	15	2	3	22	42	52	8	3	.355	.379
Servais, Scott	.262	67	195	21	51	10	0	4	22	14	31	0	0	.374	.319
Snow, J. T.	.267	145	495	78	132	26	1	21	87	74	103	1	3	.451	.362
Torrealba, Yorvit	.258	28	97	12	25	4	0	2	10	5	19	0	0	.361	.258
Tyler, Joshua	.257	22	70	9	18	4	0	1	8	6	13	2	0	.357	.257
Williams, Keith	.239	35	117	16	28	8	1	4	17	11	24	1	0	.427	.239
Woods, Ken	.290	25	93	14	27	4	1	1	13	6	11	3	0	.387	.290
Young, Travis	.250	24	92	15	23	5	1	1	9	7	21	2	0	.359	.250

PITCHERS

PLAYER	W	L	SV	ERA	G	GS	IP	H	HR	BB	SO
Brock, Chris	5	7	0	5.15	19	19	110	125	17	42	77
Bump, Nathan	3	4	0	4.50	11	10	62	68	6	21	35
Connelly, Steve	3	3	0	4.26	42	0	57	70	5	24	30
Corps, Edwin	2	2	0	4.75	11	0	36	43	0	13	15
Crabtree, Robbie	3	3	0	3.67	32	2	54	50	2	16	49
Davis, Jason	4	4	3	3.93	58	0	71	82	2	43	50
Del Toro, Miguel	4	3	0	3.92	35	0	62	62	10	25	49
Embree, Alan	4	2	0	3.71	72	0	63	52	6	28	55
Estes, Shawn	10	10	0	4.73	28	28	175	174	17	95	145
Esteves, Jacob	3	4	0	4.66	10	9	58	55	5	17	28

2000 PROJECTIONS

PLAYER	W	L	SV	ERA	G	GS	IP	H	HR	BB	SO
Estrella, Luis	3	3	1	4.17	25	3	54	53	3	21	35
Fultz, Aaron	3	3	0	4.00	15	8	54	50	11	18	50
Gardner, Mark	6	6	0	5.18	24	17	113	111	19	40	76
Hernandez, Livan	8	10	0	4.60	26	26	174	194	22	70	124
Jensen, Ryan	4	3	0	4.08	11	11	64	59	6	25	51
Johnstone, John	4	5	3	3.04	64	0	68	55	8	26	61
Knoll, Brian	3	3	0	4.50	13	7	52	53	7	16	31
McMullen, Mike	3	3	0	3.88	36	0	58	43	4	34	41
Nathan, Joe	6	6	0	4.23	20	16	100	91	16	51	69
Nen, Robb	4	7	35	3.42	71	0	71	69	6	27	80
Oropesa, Eddie	2	3	0	4.60	9	8	43	46	6	20	21
Ortiz, Russ	16	9	0	4.14	32	32	202	191	24	121	161
Patrick, Bronswell	2	2	0	4.09	12	6	44	46	7	12	29
Riley, Michael	5	4	0	3.92	21	9	78	77	6	51	63
Rodriguez, Felix	1	3	0	4.50	48	0	68	70	6	35	55
Rodriguez, Rich	3	0	0	4.50	61	0	56	59	7	23	39
Rueter, Kirk	12	8	0	4.82	28	28	155	173	22	46	82
Soderstrom, Steve	2	2	0	4.38	12	7	39	40	7	15	27
Spradlin, Jerry	3	2	0	4.50	62	0	60	59	6	24	53
Tavarez, Julian	3	1	0	4.82	49	0	56	64	5	24	32
Urban, Jeffrey	2	2	0	4.50	8	7	40	51	4	10	26
Verdugo, Jason	4	3	1	3.94	38	2	64	63	4	17	49